EARLY FAMILIES of STANDISH, MAINE

Albert J. Sears

HERITAGE BOOKS
2010

HERITAGE BOOKS
AN IMPRINT OF HERITAGE BOOKS, INC.

Books, CDs, and more—Worldwide

For our listing of thousands of titles see our website at
www.HeritageBooks.com

Published 2010 by
HERITAGE BOOKS, INC.
Publishing Division
100 Railroad Ave. #104
Westminster, Maryland 21157

Copyright © 1991 Standish Historical Society

Other Heritage Books by Albert J. Sears:
The Founding of Pearsontown (Standish), Maine

All rights reserved. No part of this book may be reproduced or transmitted in any form or by any means, electronic or mechanical, including photocopying, recording or by any information storage and retrieval system without written permission from the author, except for the inclusion of brief quotations in a review.

International Standard Book Numbers
Paperbound: 978-1-55613-501-9
Clothbound: 978-0-7884-8480-3

TABLE OF CONTENTS

Proprietors' Map of Pearsontown (Standish), Maine   *frontispiece*
Foreword   v

Families

Ayer	1	Dunham	76	Larrabee	126
Batchelder	10	Eastman	76	Libby	127
Beaman	11	Eaton	77	Linnell	129
Bean	12	Edgecomb	78	Lombard	132
Benson	15	Edmunds	79	Low	133
Berry	16	Elwell	80	Lowell	134
Black	19	Emery	80	McDonald	141
Blake	22	Fogg	81	McGill	143
Bolter	22	Foss	81	March	146
Bootman	32	Freeman	84	Marean	148
Boynton	33	Gilman	89	Marrett	151
Bradbury	33	Gould	90	Martin	153
Burbank	34	Gray	91	Mayo	155
Burnell	35	Green	92	Merrow	157
Burnham	37	Hall	93	Meserve	159
Butler	40	Hamlin	96	Miller	163
Butterfield	41	Harding	97	Mitchell	163
Candage	43	Harmon	98	Moody	166
Cannell	44	Haskell	102	Moor	168
Chase	46	Hasty	103	Morton	171
Clark	48	Heath	106	Moses	173
Colomy	49	Higgins	108	Moulton	174
Cookson	50	Hinckley	114	Murch	177
Cram	56	Hind	114	Mussey	178
Crocker	58	Hobbs	115	Newcomb	179
Crockett	59	Hodgdon	116	Nichols	180
Croxford	60	Hoit	117	Noble	180
Cummings	61	Hopkins	118	Ordway	182
Davis	63	How	119	Paine	183
Dean	68	Howe	120	Parker	191
Decker	69	Irish	121	Partridge	196
Dennett	71	Jones	121	Pearson	196
Dorsett	72	Kneeland	123	Philbrick	198
Dow	73	Knowles	124	Phinney	201
Dresser	75	Lampson	125	Pierce	202

Plaisted	204	Spring	249	Waterhouse	294
Rackliff	205	Starbird	253	Weeks	297
Rand	209	Stevens	253	Weeman	295
Rich	210	Strout	255	Wescott	298
Richardson	212	Stuart	258	West	299
Roberts	218	Swett	260	Whetcomb	303
Robinson	219	Tenny	262	White	303
Rowe	221	Thomes	264	Whitmore	305
Sanborn	223	Thompson	266	Whitney	308
Sargent	229	Thorne	269	Wiley	312
Sawyer	230	Titcomb	263	Wood	313
Segar	234	Tompson	286	Woodman	316
Shaw	234	Topping	288	Woods	317
Simpson	244	Tucker	290	Wooster	319
Small	245	Walker	291	Yates	320
Smith	245	Ward	292	York	322
Snow	246	Warren	293	Young	334
Sparrow	247				

Index   335

FOREWORD

The interest of the writer, a native of Standish, was aroused several years ago when he found among the acquisitions of the Maine Historical Society rough manuscript notes of Dr. Albion K. P. Meserve relating to the early history and families of Standish, Maine.

Dr. Meserve, the only child of Benjamin and Hannah (Anderson) Meserve, was born in Limington, Maine, on June 8, 1833. He was educated in the common schools and Standish Academy and graduated from the Maine Medical School in 1859. Following his graduation he practiced medicine in Standish for a while, but soon moved to Buxton where he lived until 1881 when he moved to Portland, which was afterwards his home and where he died suddenly on September 15, 1904. He did much research on Standish, as well as Buxton history, and on October 31, 1885, read a paper at the quarterly meeting of the Maine Genealogical Society on the early settlement and settlers of Standish. The notes of this address are now in the possession of the Maine Historical Society.

Dr. Meserve's address included mention of many actions taken by the Proprietors of Pearsontown (as Standish was first known) from its very beginning, so he had access to their records. The original Proprietors' records have been located and are at the office of the town clerk. According to the obituary notice at the time of his death, Dr. Meserve had compiled a manuscript history of Standish, but it is not known what became of it or whether the reference was to the notes now in the files of the Maine Historical Society.

Using Dr. Meserve's notes as a basis on which to start, and collecting names of early settlers of the town from tax valuations lists in possession of the society, as well as from United States census records and from other sources, I have compiled what information has been available concerning the families of those persons who lived in Standish from 1755 (about the time the original permanent settlement started) until about 1805, a period covering the first fifty years of the history of the town. An attempt has been made to determine the place in which a settler lived before taking up residence in Standish and, if he did not remain here permanently, to what location he moved. Research of deeds records at the Cumberland County Registry has been particularly successful in securing such information, as well as in determining in many cases what the trade or occupation of the individual settler was.

While at the start, the project was approached from a genealogical viewpoint, discovery of much information relating to the general history of the town has led to an attempt to compile such data of the very earliest days of its existence. No attempt has been made, however, to extend this much beyond the year 1800.

In compiling the family histories, reference is made to 1790 census records by using three figures separated by hyphens, such as 1-3-5. The first figure represents the number of males over 16 years of age, including the head of family; the second figure denotes the number of males under 16 years old; and the third indicates a family consisting of a man and his wife, three sons under 16 years of age, and four daughters. When reference is made in the family histories to deeds, two figures separated by a virgule or slanted line are used to indicate where the recorded deed may be found. Thus 23/175 indicates that the deed may be found recorded in Book 23, Page 175 at the Cumberland County Registry of Deeds. If the reference is to the registry of other than Cumberland County, specific mention is made of the fact.

In the case of many of the families included in the genealogical section, good family histories have been available for reference. In such cases a minimum of information in such genealogies has been used together with any additional information discovered. However, in the cases of those families about which little or no printed information has been available, more detailed records have been made of the data discovered.

Albert J. Sears

Additional Information

Albert J. Sears, the compiler and author of this work, was born June 8, 1896, in Standish and died August 12, 1983, in Portland, Maine. The sources of this genealogical study and his work on the early history of Standish can be found by consulting his original papers deposited at the Maine Historical Society.

Robert Taylor made a typescript of Mr. Sears' genealogy work and placed in additions.

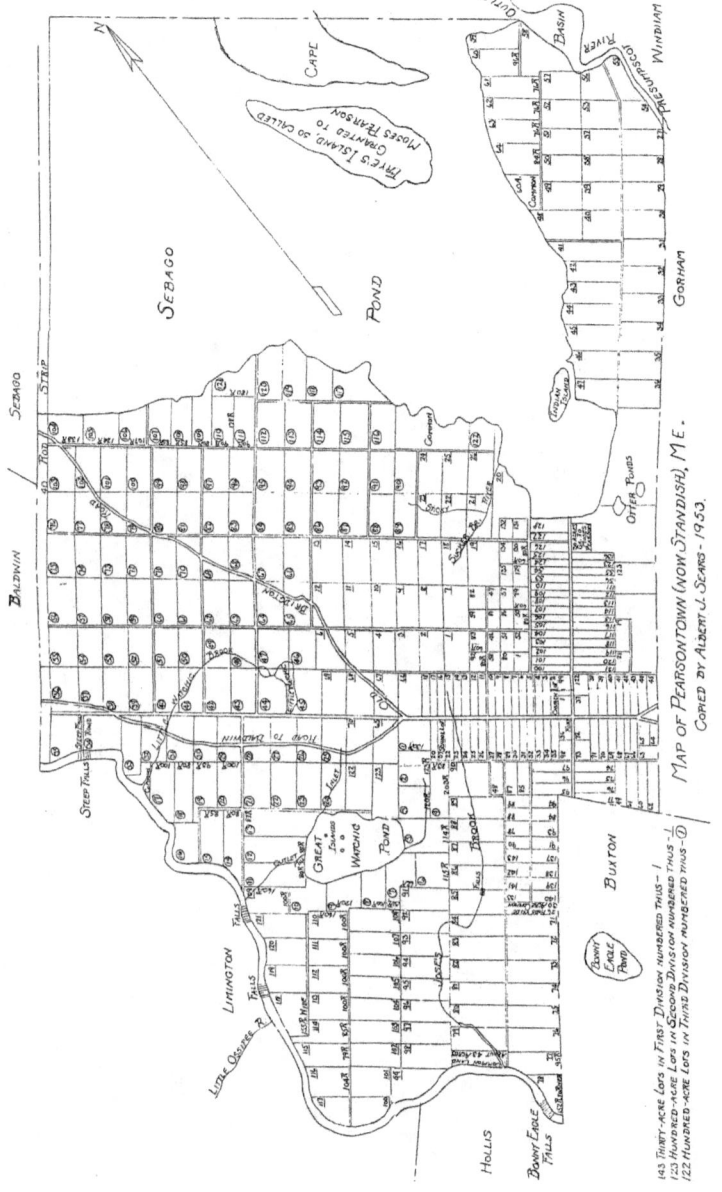

AYER

The Ayer family was represented among the inhabitants of Pearsontown from its earliest days. Although the majority of its members settled in Buxton, they lived in that part of Buxton which was annexed to Standish in 1824, so that they really can properly be included among this town's early settlers.

Lt. Ebenezer[4] Ayer (Samuel,[3] Peter,[2] John[1]) born Feb. 18, 1704-5, in Haverhill, Mass., son of Capt. Samuel and Elizabeth (Tuttle) Ayer settled in Methuen, Massachusetts. Upon the establishment of the Province line between Massachusetts and New Hampshire in 1741, his homestead became a part of Salem, New Hampshire. On March 29, 1726, he married Susannah Kimball of Bradford, Mass., who was born May 25, 1707, and died Sept. 26, 1749. After her death he married Elizabeth ____, who died Jan. 2, 1786, age 71 years. He died in Salem, N.H., March 3, 1763. It was from this Ebenezer Ayer that the settlers by that name in Buxton and Standish descended.

Although one account states that Ebenezer Ayer was the father of ten children by his first wife and five by his second, vital records consulted indicate that there were eleven children by his first wife and four by his second. The same account gives his son John as being a son of his second wife. Records, however, show a son bearing that name by the first wife, but none by the second. Children of Ebenezer and Susannah (Kimball) Ayer were as follows:

i. EBENEZER, born March 22, 1727, in Haverhill, Mass., settled in Pepperellborough (Saco), Maine, where he married on July 4, 1754, Mrs. Hannah (Plaisted) Scammon, widow of James Scammon. He was in the ill-fated excursion of Benedict Arnold through the wilds of Maine during the winter of 1775-6. At the close of the war he took up residence in in Buxton, Maine, where he afterward lived and where he died in 1786. His widow, Hannah, died in Saco on March 24, 1801. Ebenezer and Hannah (Plaisted) Ayer were the parents of the following children:

1. ELISHA, bapt. May 18, 1755, Biddeford, married Mary McLellan, bapt. Nov. 23, 1753, in Biddeford, daughter of James and Mary (Patterson) McLellan of Saco. About 1790 they moved to Newfield, Maine, where he died in 1807 and she on May 17, 1824. They were the parents of seven children who were baptized at Saco.

   (1) HANNAH, bapt. July 30, 1775, married Josiah Towle of Newfield. She died in Newfield on July 28, 1806, age 32.

- (2) ELISHA, bapt. July 13, 1777, married Sarah (Sally) Pease. They were living in Newfield from 1799 to 1815 and in Limerick from 1816 to 1832. He died Apr. 21, 1851, age 73, and she on May 21, 1866, age 77 yrs., 9 mos., both in Limerick.
- (3) JAMES, born July 23, 1778, married July 24, 1803, Nancy Robinson, daughter of Caleb and Mary (Waterhouse) Robinson. He was a merchant in Newfield and served as a captain in the War of 1812. He died Nov. 2, 1829, and his widow on July 6, 1866.
- (4) POLLY, bapt. May 13, 1781, married June 28, 1798, James Libby who was born in 1767 and died Oct. 29 or Nov. 29, 1836. They lived in Newfield after their marriage but later moved to Limerick and were the parents of 13 children.
- (5) JENNY (JANE) bapt. July 13, 1783, married Nov. 7, 1802, Hosea Lord of Parsonsfield who died in 1804; married second in 1806 Winborn Adams Drew of Newfield. She died Sept. 24, 1812, age 29 yrs.
- (6) SALLY, bapt. May 5, 1786, married Sept. 20, 1804, Chesley Drew.
- (7) MARTHA McLELLAN, born 1789, bapt. Mar. 21, 1790, married July 1, 1813, Winborn Adams Drew, widower of her sister Jane, and died Apr. 16, 1875, at the age of 85 yrs., 8 mos., 8 days.

2. MOSES, born in Biddeford Mar. 17, 1757, bapt. July 7, 1757, married Aug. 2, 1781, Mary Tyler who was born Aug. 10, 1759. They lived in Saco, where he died on July 12, 1815, and his widow, Mary, died Aug. 7, 1854, age 97 yrs., in Saco. They were the parents of the following children:
- (1) ELIZABETH, born May 27, 1782, bapt. Aug. 18, 1782, married Dec. 30, 1801, in Saco, Abraham Clark of Biddeford.
- (2) JOHN, born Sept. 27, 1783, died in Saco Nov. 1805, age 23 (*Eastern Argus*, issue of Nov. 30, 1805).
- (3) AN INFANT, who died Apr. 5, 1785, age 3 weeks.
- (4) SARAH, born Oct. 23, 1786, married 1804 Samuel Lowell of Saco. She died May 3, 1859.
- (5) AN INFANT, who died Mar. 16, 1789, age 1 week.
- (6) HANNAH, born Oct. 13, 1791, married (int. Sept. 29, 1823) Capt. Luther Walker of Limerick. She died Dec. 23, 1840, age 49 yrs., 2 mos., in Limerick.
- (7) ABIGAIL, born June 13, 1793, married 1812 Valentine Clark and died in Newfield in Sept. 1879.
- (8) ANDREW, born Mar. 18, 1795, married Nancy Kelly, daughter of Dr. Isaac Kelly. He was a clothier and moved to Newfield by 1820 where he died Oct. 1, 1882.
- (9) MOSES, born Feb. 9, 1797, married Sept. 6, 1821, in Limerick, Jane Moore. He moved to Newfield by 1820 where he was a farmer. He died May 21, 1860.

(10) TRISTRAM, born Feb. 19, 1799, married Aug. 13, 1820, Frances Moses of Buxton. He died Dec. 21, 1850, age 52 yrs., in Biddeford, formerly of Newfield. Buried at Saco.
3. JOHN, bapt. Feb. 25, 1759, married Jan. 23, 1780, Patience Jellison of Saco and had a daughter, Nancy Patten, bapt. there Feb. 24, 1782. John Ayer apparently died soon after because widow Patience Ayer of Saco married June 17, 1787, Solomon Burnham of Scarboro.
4. SUSANNAH, bapt. Dec. 25, 1763, in Saco, married on Sept. 3, 1778, Robert Cleaves of Saco. She died there Feb. 23, 1833, (Jan. 15, 1831?) and he on Dec. 3, 1828, age 74.
5. SARAH, bapt. July 12, 1767, married David Warren and second as his third wife Richard Libby on Dec. 3, 1813. Her second husband died in about a year and she returned to Saco.
6. WILLIAM, bapt. Apr. 2, 1769, in Saco and died Sept. 12, 1770, age 18 mos.

ii. ELIZABETH, born Jan. 25, 1727-8, apparently died young.
iii. SARAH, born Oct. 27, 1730, died Nov. 1, 1730.
iv. PHILIP, born Feb. 28, 1731-2, died Nov. 2, 1756; was perhaps the Philip Ayer who served as a corporal in Capt. John Lane's company in 1756.
v. TUTTLE, born Apr. 1734, died in infancy.
vi. TUTTLE, born May 17, 1735, evidently died young.
vii. PETER, born May 12, 1737, Methuen, Mass., and settled in Buxton about 1776 in that section that became Standish in 1824. He served in the Revolutionary War. He married first, prior to coming to Buxton, Rebecca Wheeler, daughter of Benjamin Wheeler, she was baptized in 1737 in Rowley, Mass., and mother of all his children. She died in Buxton Oct. 28, 1795, age 58 yrs. On Jan. 19, 1796, he married second Sarah Jenkins, widow of Paul Jenkins and daughter of Rishworth Jordan of Pepperellboro (Saco). In the 1790 census of Buxton he is listed with a family of 3-1-3. In a real estate inventory of Buxton taken in 1798 he is listed as owning and living on lot #3 in range H of third division. He died Mar. 23, 1805, and his wife, Sarah Ayer, died Apr. 9, 1828, age 80 yrs., in Gorham, formerly of Saco.

Children of Peter and Rebecca (Wheeler) Ayer were:
1. BENJAMIN, bapt. Dec. 9, 1759, at Salem, N.H., died young.
2. JONATHAN, bapt. Nov. 8, 1761, at Salem, N.H. A Jonathan Ayers of Buxton served in the Revolutionary War and was a return of men enlisted into the Continental army from Capt. Caleb L. Low's (2nd) company dated Feb. 14, 1778. He enlisted for the town of Danvers, Mass., and joined Capt. Lunt's company of Col. Hanley's regt. for a period of three years.
3. BENJAMIN, born in Salem, N.H., Nov. 23, 1763, married Apr. 25, 1785, Rachel Sanborn, born in Hampton Falls, N.H., July 19, 1762, daughter of John and Lucy (Sanborn) Sanborn of Pearsontown. At the time of the 1790 census he was living in Buxton with a family of 2-1-4, but in 1800 was living in Standish with a family consisting of him and his wife, three boys and one girl under 10 yrs. of age, and one boy and two girls between 10 and 16 yrs. old. He was living in Standish on Mar.

11, 1803, when he sold to Daniel Thomes and James Smith of Standish 50 acres of lot #109, 20 acres of lot #92, and all of lot #83, all in the third division of lots in Standish (58/60 and 58/61). However, he was living in Unity, Maine, on Oct. 4, 1808, when he sold to Nathaniel Chase the 100-acre lot #67 in the third division in Standish.

Benjamin Ayer served in the Continental army as a corporal from Buxton during the last half of 1780, enlisting when he was only 16 yrs. old. Besides being being a farmer he was an itinerant Methodist preacher and lived in numerous towns, including Freedom, Maine, in addition to those towns previously mentioned. His wife died on Mar. 2, 1832, at the home of her son Peter in Freedom, Maine. He died July 28, 1844. Children of Benjamin, and Rachel (Sanborn) Ayer were as follows:

   (1)   ANNIS MOORE, born Feb. 3, 1786, married May 9, 1805, Nathan W. Chase, son of Joseph and Olive (Woodman) Chase of Standish. She died June 17, 1867, and he Nov. 19, 1868, both in Bangor.

   (2)   LYDIA SANBORN, born Feb. 5, 1788, married (int. Dec. 19, 1806) William Richardson of Standish. They married in Unity.

   (3)   PETER WELLS, born Jan. 22, 1790.

   (4)   BENJAMIN JR., born May 18, 1792.

   (5)   RACHEL, JR. born Nov. 2, 1794, died Dec. 5, 1794.

   (6)   JOHN SANBORN, born Oct. 29, 1795.

   (7)   RACHEL SANBORN, born May 20, 1798.

   (8)   THOMAS BURNHAM, born June 3, 1800.

4. SARAH, born 1768, married Nov. 27, 1788, Thomas Lowell of Standish. She died Dec. 22, 1832, age 64 yrs., in Dixmont. He married second in 1833 at the age of 70 in Dixmont, Lucinda Corliss. For list of children see Lowell family.

5. EBENEZER, born Apr. 1766, married Jan. 22, 1789, in Buxton, Elizabeth Moore, born in Londonderry, N.H., Aug. 6, 1769, daughter of Capt. Hugh and Margaret (Nesmith) Moore, who settled in Buxton. They lived in that part of Buxton now Standish on lot H-3 in the third division on land adjoining that of Hugh Moore. At the time of the 1790 census he had a family of 1-1-1. He died in Buxton (now Standish) on Feb. 18, 1812, age 45 yrs., 10 mos. His widow married second Mar. 14, 1820, True Woodman of Minot and she died there Jan. 12, 1854, age 86 yrs., 6 mos.

   (1)   DR. ELI, born Oct. 26, 1789, married Feb. 9, 1814, Temperance G. Files, born June 20, 1791, and died Feb. 19, 1815, age 23, following the birth of a daughter on the sixth of that month. He married second in Jan. 1818 Sarah Eastman. He died May 28, 1857, in Palermo, Maine.

   (2)   REBECCA, born May 8, 1791, married May 22, 1811, William Spear, who died May 7, 1860, age 71 yrs., 17 days. She died Mar. 13, 1857, age 65 yrs., 10 mos.

- (3) MARGARET, born Dec. 24, 1792, married Feb. 26, 1815, Samuel Moore of Leeds, Maine.
- (4) ELIZABETH, born Apr. 17, 1795, married in 1821 Walter Boothby, born in 1798 son of Isaac and Hannah (Foss) Boothby of Leeds, Maine. He died in Leeds June 20, 1827.
- (5) SARAH, born Mar. 25, 1797, never married.
- (6) JANE, born Apr. 17, 1799, married Feb. 24, 1818, Amos Thomes Jr., born Aug. 26, 1792, son of Amos and Mehitable (Burnell) Thomes of Standish.
- (7) LUCY JENKINS, born Apr. 2, 1801, married June 24 (28?), 1822, Richard Hopkins Bacon of Gorham, she of Buxton. She died Apr. 13, 1880, Buxton.
- (8) MARY, born Apr. 27, 1803, died May 9, 1805.
- (9) MARY BOYNTON, born May 23, 1805, married Nov. 17, 1831, Isaiah Woodman, born in Minot, Maine, son of John and Hannah (Bates) Woodman. She died in Auburn on Mar. 2, 1882.
- (10) PETER, born Sept. 30, 1807, died Oct. 12, 1809.
- (11) EBENEZER HOWE, born Aug. 6, 1809, died Feb. 18, 1812.
6. ELIZABETH, born May 3, 1771, married Nov. 24, 1791, in Buxton, Josiah Paine, son of Richard and Thankful (Harding) Paine of Gorham. They lived in Buxton. He died Sept. 22, 1832, age 66, and she on Sept. 6, 1852, age 81.
7. PHILIP, born Nov. 11, 1778, married Jan. 27, 1803, in Buxton, Lucy Richardson born Oct. 8, 1782, daughter of David and Hannah (Mills) Richardson of Standish. She died Mar. 23, 1804, age 21 yrs., in Standish. He married second Sept. 13, 1809, Mary Moody, daughter of Rev. Gilman Moody; Mary Moody was born Jan. 22, 1783, died Aug. 6, 1850. He died Mar. 4, 1857. He was the father of nine children, only one of whom was by his first wife. He was a Methodist minister and lived in Monmouth, Maine.
viii. TIMOTHY, born July 16, 1740, in Salem, N.H., settled in Buxton, Maine, about 1776. He married July 20, 1770, in Haverhill, Mass., Elizabeth White, born May 31, 1746, daughter of Nicholas and Hannah (Ayer) White. He probably came to Pearsontown to live with his brother John before settling in Buxton, for his first two children are said to have been born in the former town. He is listed in the 1790 census of Buxton with a family of 2-3-6, and in a real estate inventory of that town taken about 1798 he is listed as owning and living in lot #2 on H range in the third division of lots. He may have died before 1800 since his name is not found in the census taken that year. On Apr. 23, 1798, he married as a second wife Elizabeth (Scammon) Moody of Saco, widow of William Pepperell Moody who died in 1787. She was born July 29, 1749, and died Oct. 29, 1833, age 86 yrs., in Saco. Children of Timothy and Elizabeth (White) Ayer were as follows:

1. ABIGAIL, born in 1770 in Pearsontown, married Oct. 20, 1791, Ephraim Sands 3rd of Buxton. She died Oct. 7, 1824, and he on July 8, 1827, in his 98th year. They were the parents of nine children.
2. ISAIAH, born in 1772 in Pearsontown, nothing further known.
3. DANIEL, born in 1775, married Oct. 26, 1797, in Buxton, Mary Boothby of Limington, born Oct. 18, 1778, daughter of Jonathan Boothby. They lived in Buxton and had three childern recorded there. Dominicus Mitchell of Standish kept a diary and mentions that he went to Daniel Ayer's funeral, Oct. 8, 1812.
4. SUSANNAH, born in 1778, married Jan. 19, 1797, Theophilus Waterhouse of Buxton.
5. HANNAH, born in 1780, married in May 1799 as his second wife Theophilus Waterhouse.
6. TIMOTHY, born Feb. 10, 1782, married on Apr. 9, 1807, Hannah Merrill, born Apr. 19, 1787, daughter of Humphrey and Elizabeth (McLucas) Merrill of Buxton. They moved to Newfield, Maine, about 1817-18 where he lived until between 1823 and 1830 when he moved to Otisfield. His wife died Dec. 1, 1828, age 42, and he married second Oct. 14, 1830, Susanna Johnson of Gorham, who died Feb. 15, 1867, in Naples. He died Feb. 5, 1868, age 86 yrs., in Naples and was buried in the Village Cemetery there. Children by first marriage were as follows:
    (1) BETSEY or ELIZABETH, born May 1, 1808, in Buxton, married Mark Carsley, died Mar. 18, 1831, age 22 yrs., 11 mos. in Harrison.
    (2) HUMPHREY MERRILL, born Mar. 7 or 17, 1810, in Buxton.
    (3) REV. AARON, born Apr. 3, 1812, in Buxton, married Mary C. Cleaves. He died Oct. 8, 1876, age 64 yrs., 5 mos.
    (4) DANIEL, born Sept. 1, 1816, in Buxton, died May 20, 1834.
    (5) MARY, born Jan. 11, 1819, in Newfield, married Oct. 17, 1837, in Naples, Samuel G. Scribner, both of Naples.
    (6) SAMUEL, born Apr. 8, 1821, in Newfield.
    (7) SALLY, born Aug. 19, 1823, in Newfield.
7. AARON, born in 1786, married Jan. 19, 1806, Ruth Merrill, born Apr. 25, 1784, daughter of Abel and Elizabeth (Page) Merrill of Buxton. He was a physician, and after his death she was a widow for seven years, then married Feb. 19, 1820, John Woodman of Minot, she of Buxton. She died Jan. 14, 1864, in Minot, Maine.
    Children were:
    (1) ALVAN BROWN, born Dec. 18, 1809.
    (2) ABEL MERRILL, born July 7, 1812.
    (3) NANCY, born June 15, 1817.
8. MARY, born Feb. 2, 1788, married Thomas Richardson, born in Standish Apr. 27, 1781, son of David and Hannah (Mills)

Richardson. She died in Nov. 21, 1818, in Monmouth where they moved to. He married second Mary Dearborn of Monmouth.
9. **ELIZABETH**, born Feb. 2, 1788, twin of Mary, married Dec. 1, 1808, in Buxton, Robert Cleaves Jr. of Saco. She died Mar. 10, 1814, and he married Nov. 30, 1815, Mrs. Patience Bryant of Saco.
10. **EBENEZER**, born ____, married Huldah Rich, May 6, 1788, in Gorham, she of Standish, he of Buxton. He was living in Durham, Maine, with a family of 1-2-2 at the time of the 1790 census. He was first taxed in that town in 1799. Dominicus Mitchell in his diary gives Ebenezer Ayer of Buxton funeral as being Feb. 12, 1832. Children of Ebenezer and Huldah (Rich) Ayer were as follows:
    (1) **RICHARD**, born Nov. 28, 1788.
    (2) **JOHN**, born Aug. 18, 1790.
    (3) **ISAIAH**, born Apr. 28, 1792.
    (4) **ELIZABETH**, born Aug. 5, 1794.
    (5) **HANNAH**, born Sept. 3, 1796.

ix. **JOHN**, born Apr. 2, 1744, in Methuen, Mass., was of Pepperrellborough (Saco) when he married Elizabeth Pike of Salisbury, Mass., on Nov. 18, 1767, according to the vital records of Salisbury. She was born Oct. 2, 1748, daughter of John and Mary (Hook) Pike of Salisbury, Mass. However, John Ayer, joiner, was given of Pearsontown when he bought land here of Timothy Crocker on Aug. 15, 1767, (5/429) which was several months before the date of the marriage. The land that he bought at this time is given as "Five acre lot #3, thirty acre lot #7, and thirty-five acres of the one hundred acre lot #42, lately laid out, and half the common and undivided land-belonging to right #42, all being equal to half a right." On July 11, 1771, he bought of Ephraim Batchelder of Pearsontown the 30-acre lot #68 (8/199). On Nov. 7, 1777, he sold some of this land to Joab Black of Gorham (12/492) and on Mar. 14, 1782, some more of it to James Moody, blacksmith, of Pearsontown (11/574). He is listed as being of Pearsontown on Sept. 25, 1782, when he sold the farm on which he then dwelt to Seth Spring of Conway, N.H. (12/332). Elizabeth (Pike) Ayer, his wife, was born Oct. 2, 1748, and living Nov. 26, 1781.

From Vol. I of *Eastern Deeds ... of Massachusetts*, it appears that in 1791 Nathaniel Wells deeded to John Ayer and Joseph Bean "settlers within Cutler's grant, so called, in the County of York, husbandmen, who settled in Cutler's grant and made separate improvements thereon the first day of January 1784" the land upon which they had settled. Cutler's grant was located in what is now the town of Hiram, Maine. Here then is evidence that John Ayer moved from Pearsontown into Hiram late in 1782 or early in 1783. He is said to have built the first mill in that town on "Thirteen Mile Brook" and with Capt. Charles Wadsworth to have built the first bridge across the Saco River in 1805. It is said that he was the leader of the earliest public religious services held in that town. John Ayer with a family of 2-3-5 was living in Hiram at the time of the 1790 census.

In 1797 John Ayer conveyed his property in Hiram to his son Humphrey, but perhaps did not move to Cornish for several years. However, two persons over 45 yrs. of age were living in the family of Humphrey Ayer in Cornish at the time of the 1800 census, so it seems likely that they were John Ayer and his wife since his name appears on Cornish tax lists for poll tax only in 1801, 1802, 1803, 1810, and 1811. The death dates of John and his wife have not been discovered, but it seems likely that he may have died about 1812. It is said that they were buried in an old graveyard on Towle's Hill, so called, in Cornish, but there is nothing now left to mark their resting place. Dominicus Mitchell of Standish has in his diary "went to Mr. Ayer's funeral Mar. 25, 1816," but it is not sure that this was John's funeral date.

John and Elizabeth (Pike) Ayer were the parents of the following Children:

1. **SARAH (SALLY)**, born in Pearsontown in 1768, bapt. there May 11, 1777, married in Parsonsfield June 22, 1789, Thomas Barker, both of Hiram. He born in 1766 in Stratham, N.H., and died July 25, 1819, age 53 yrs., in Portland. She died there Jan. 27, 1825, age 56 yrs. Both are buried in the Eastern Cemetery there. They were the parents of thirteen children.

2. **TIMOTHY**, probably born about 1770 in Pearsontown, baptized there May 11, 1777, moved with his parents to Hiram, Maine, about 1782. He was of Hiram on Oct. 10, 1795, when he sold land there to Francis McKusick of Cornish, but was living in Cornish on Oct. 21, 1795, when he bought from Thomas Barker of Cornish, probably his brother-in-law, lot #8 on range E in that town. From 1796 to 1816 he was taxed for this land in Cornish and also paid poll tax there, indicating he was a resident of the town.

   He, a resident of Cornish, sold part of the land on Jan. 4, 1817, and, as a resident of Coventry, N.H., on Oct. 28, 1817, sold the rest of it. His name appears on a check list of voters of Coventry in 1818 and he served as a surveyor of highways for that town in 1819 and 1824. He was a legal voter of that town in 1835, so his death must have occurred after that year.

   Timothy Ayer married in Parsonsfield Mar. 14, 1795, Betsey Burnham, both of Hiram. Children of this couple as compiled from the *History of Coventry, N.H.* were as follows:

   (1) **BETSY**, married on Dec. 2, 1819, Daniel Davis of Coventry.
   (2) **ALVAH**, on list of voters in 1835 and surveyor of highways in 1836 and 1843.
   (3) **JOHN P.**, on list of voters in 1835 and surveyor of lumber in 1836.
   (4) **STENETH (ASENATH?)**, married Milton Southard of Coventry on Feb. 5, 1814.
   (5) **JUDITH**, born 1814, died Jan. 13, 1834, age 19 yrs., 7 mos.

3. **ELIZABETH**, born about 1774 in Pearsontown, bapt. there May 11, 1777, married in Parsonsfield May 23, 1793, Joseph Chadbourne, son of Joshua and Susanna (Spinney) Chadbourne

of Cornish, she of Hiram. He died Dec. 24, 1844, age 80, and she died Apr. 3, 1812, age 38 yrs.
4. HUMPHREY, born about 1775 in Pearsontown, bapt. there May 11, 1777, settled in Cornish, Maine, where died Aug. 6, 1828, age 53 yrs. He married Sept. 25, 1799, in Berwick, Patience Chadbourne, daughter of Francis Chadbourne of Berwick, Maine, who died on Jan. 6, 1864, age 86 yrs., 10 mos., in Cornish.
5. JACOB, bapt. in Pearsontown Mar. 8, 1778, died young.
6. MARY, bapt. July 30, 1780, Standish, died young.
7. ANNE, born Dec. 8, 1783, in Hiram, married David Morrill of Berwick and died Sept. 9, 1855, in Cornish.
8. SUSAN, born May 22, 1785, married Feb. 17, 1806, Thaddeus Morrill of Berwick, she of Cornish. She died June 7, 1874, in North Berwick.
9. JOHN PIKE, born Jan. 1786, died July 6, 1866, age 80 yrs., 6 mos., Portland. Married June 10, 1810, Abigail Dinsdale, who died Nov. 11, 1862, age 70 yrs. They lived in Portland.
10. HANNAH, married at Cornish 9/23/1813, Nathan Hilton of Denmark. She died 9/30/1884, age 89 yrs., 2 mos., Bridgton.
11. LYDIA, married at Cornish Jatson (Jackson?) Smith of Eaton, N.H., on Dec. 3, 1816.
12. NANCY, never married.

x. JOSEPH, born May 22, 1746, in Methuen, Mass., later Salem, N.H., was living in Pearsontown when he married on Oct. 3, 1775, Eunice Clark, born Aug. 12, 1749, daughter of James Clark of Little Falls (Hollis), Maine. They settled in Buxton where most of their children were born, but they were living in Brownfield, Maine, at the time of the 1790 census with six children, four boys and two girls, in their family. On June 20, 1793, Joseph Ayer, blacksmith, of Brownfield, bought from Benjamin Coffin of Conway, N.H., land in Sudbury-Canada (Bethel), Maine. (29/491). He settled in that town at Bean's Corner and, although he purchased lot #7 in the seventh range there from Josiah Bean on July 19, 1796, he was living in Brownfield at the time of the 1800 census with a family consisting of him and his wife, one son between 10 and 16, and three sons and two daughters between 16 and 25. Joseph Ayer died on Aug. 19, 1814, and his wife, Eunice (Clark) Ayer, died in Newfield Apr. 5, 1822, age 73 yrs., formerly of Bethel (*Eastern Argus*, May 7, 1822). They were the parents of the following children:
1. MARY, born in Buxton, Nov. 5, 1776.
2. SAMUEL, born in Buxton Nov. 5, 1778, married Alice, daughter of John Kilgore of Bethel, and had eight children. They lived at Bean's Corner where she died in 1855 and he in 1863.
3. JONATHAN, married Mary Marston, born Jan. 25, 1787, daughter of David and Mary (Page) Marston of Parsonsfield. They lived in Bethel until about 1813, at which time they were the parents of three children.
4. JAMES, born in Buxton Sept. 26, 1781, married Nov. 7, 1805, Thirza Mason, born in Dublin, N.H., July 3, 1781, daughter of Moses Jr. and Eunice (Ayer) Mason. He was a physician in

Newfield, Maine, where he died Jan. 23, 1834. She died Oct. 17, 1864.
5. SARAH, probably died young.
6. HUGH MOORE, studied medicine with his brother James Ayer in Newfield and settled in North Carolina. He undoubtedly was the Hugh Moore Ayer taxed for one poll and a horse in Cornish, Maine, in 1809. He married Mar. 28, 1810, Susannah Burnham of Cornish, he of Newfield.
xi. ISAIAH, born Sept. 19, 1749, married Hannah ____. He died Sept. 25, 1772, age 23 yrs. Buried in Salem Center, N.H.
xii. WILLIAM, born May 23, 1752, married Dec. 30, 1778, Mary Messer of Methuen, Mass. They lived in Salem, N.H. He died there June 11, 1829.
xiii. ELIZABETH, born Sept. 28, 1753, married Phineas Carlton.
xiv. SAMUEL, born Sept. 1, 1754, married Anna Currier Jan. 17, 1782, and had daughter, Mary, born Dec. 9, 1782, in Salem, N.H.
xv. PHILIP, born Nov. 3, 1758.
xvi. JOHN, born Oct. 2, 1760, married in Haverhill, June 9, 1785, Rachel Morse.

BATCHELDER OR BACHELOR

While his name does not appear on any list used in compiling names of early inhabitants of Pearsontown, Ephraim Batchelder was apparently living in this town early, as Ephraim[7] Batchelder (Nathaniel,[6] Nathaniel,[5] Nathaniel,[4] Nathaniel,[3] Nathaniel,[2] Stephen,[1]) was born May 15, 1749, perhaps in Kensington, N.H., son of Nathaniel and Margaret (Tilton) Batchelder. He married first Apphia Lowell, born Apr. 14, 1742, died Nov. 2, 1807, and second Mrs. Lydia (Hall) Richardson, born in 1743, died Nov. 12, 1823, age 80, on May 13 (29?), 1808. His second wife was the widow of Moses Richardson of Standish and mother of Abigail and Anna Richardson who married sons of Ephraim Batchelder.

Ephraim Batchelder was a tailor, according to deeds, and was living in Pearsontown on July 11, 1771, when he sold land here to John Ayer (8/199) and on Aug. 16, 1771, when he bought other land here of Peter Moulton (11/468). He is given as a resident of Pearsontown when enlisted as a private in Capt. Wentworth Stuart's company on May 16, 1775, at the beginning of the Revolutionary War. His brother Samuel Batchelder, born Apr. 21, 1760, is also listed as being of Pearsontown at the time of the service in Capt. Whitmore's company in a return dated Dec. 25, 1777. Ephraim Batchelder and his wife, Apphia, of Pearsontown sold to Sylvanous Lowell of Newbury, mariner, lot #103 in first division in Pearsonstown, it being the lot where their dwelling house stood, on the road running from the meeting house to Sebago Pond on Nov. 18, 1782 (12/291). He was given as a resident of Flintstown (Baldwin) on Nov. 1, 1783, when he bought a 100-acre lot in that town from David Brown of Concord, Massachusetts. It is evident that he moved from one town to the other sometime between the dates of the two deeds. It is interesting to note that the Batchelder Genealogy gives no indication of his ever having lived in Pearsontown, but states that he moved directly from New Hampshire to Baldwin.

Ephraim Batchelder was among the earliest settlers in Baldwin and was a constable at the first town meeting held there in 1802. His farm was in the Pigeon Brook District of the town. He died there on June 15, 1815, age 66. Children of Ephraim and Apphia (Lowell) Batchelder were as follows:

i. SAMUEL, born Apr. 21, 1765, married on Dec. 11, 1783, Anna Richardson, born June 5, 1765, daughter of Moses and Lydia (Hall) Richardson of Pearsontown. He was a tailor by trade and moved to Danville, Vt., where he followed farming and reared his family. About 1810 with his wife and son Levi he migrated to New York State and died in Niagara County on Oct. 8, 1819. His wife died Sept. 22, 1849.
ii. TIMOTHY, born ____, married and went to Troy, N.Y.
iii. JOSIAH, nothing further known.
iv. EDWARD, born ____, died July 20, 1787.
v. JOHN, born Feb. 27, 1774, married (int. June 10, 1796) in Standish, Elizabeth Lowell of Biddeford.
vi. EPHRAIM, JR., born Oct. 5, 1775, was a blacksmith and lived in Baldwin and North Yarmouth, Maine.
vii. SYLVANUS, born Oct. 30, 1777, married Mar. 3, 1803, Abigail Richardson, born June 21, 1782, daughter of Moses and Lydia (Hall) Richardson of Standish, who died May 11, 1849, age 67. He married second on Nov. 31, 1853, Mrs. Nancy Bishop of Buxton, who died childless on May 2, 1864, age 80. He was a carpenter, stonemason and farmer and died in Baldwin on Feb. 3, 1868, age 90. He and first wife were the parents of ten children.
viii. SARAH, born June 4, 1779, married in Baldwin Sept. 11, 1803, Samuel Hardy. She died Oct. 31, 1804.
ix. MARGARET, born May 26, 1781.
x. THOMAS, born May 27, 1784.

BEAMAN OR BEEMAN

Noah Beaman, whose name is found in the 1790 census of Standish with a family of 1-1-5, was very likely the Noah Beaman Jr., born in Marlborough, Mass., Apr. 7, 1759, son of Noah and Lydia (Howe) Beaman of that town, and who on Nov. 9, 1780, married Elizabeth Jewell of Stow, Massachusetts. In a census of Bridgton, Maine, taken by Enoch Perley of that town on Dec. 31, 1787, Noah Beaman, age 28, with a family consisting of three males, age 25, 5, and 3 years and three females age 30, 4 and 1 years, is found. The male aged 25 years was probably his brother Aaron, born Nov. 25, 1762, who settled in Bridgton. Another brother, Samuel, born Oct. 29, 1766, also settled in Bridgton, but died July 3, 1791. On Mar. 24, 1793, Noah Beaman Sr. of Marlborough, Mass., yeoman, quitclaimed to Ezra Gibbs of Bridgton all rights in a house his son Samuel, lately deceased, had built on a certain lot in the latter town (30/106).

Nothing has been found as to how long Noah Beaman Jr. lived in Standish and no record of his owning land or paying taxes here has been discovered. Sometime before 1800 he moved to Portland where in the census of that year his family consisted of him and his wife, two males and one female under 10, one male and two females between 10 and 16, and one male and one female between 16 and 26 years of age. On June 23, 1803, Noah Beaman of Portland, trader, sold to Daniel Brigham and Aaron Beaman of Bridgton land in that town granted to him by the Proprietors (41/73). Daniel Brigham was his brother-in-law, being husband of his sister Anna. Noah's wife, Elizabeth (Jewell) Beeman, was born on Mar. 4, 1757, Stow, Mass., and was reported in newspaper notice as the widow of Noah, died Feb. 21, 1807, age 49 years, in Portland.

It is possible that Noah Beaman Jr., was the Noah Beaman of Marlborough who was a sergeant in Capt. William Brigham's company, Col. Jonathan Ward's regiment, in the Revolutionary War. Because he evidently resided in Standish for so short a time, no attempt has been made to find a record of his family.

BEAN

Members of the Bean family were among the settlers in Pearsontown prior to the Revolutionary War, but all of the males had left town before the 1790 census was taken. Jonathan Bean, according to an article in the *Oxford County Advertiser*, issue of May 26, 1893, was born about 1718 in Kingston, N.H., and was a great-grandson of John Bean, an emigrant from Scotland, who settled early in Exeter, New Hampshire. Jonathan Bean lived in Kingston, Brentwood, and Chester, N.H., where he married Sept. 14, 1745, Abigail Gordon. In 1759 Jonathan deeded land to David Bean in Chester on the Lamprey River (now Candia) and moved to Hampton, New Hampshire. After living there two or three years, he then in company with Ebenezer Shaw in 1762-3 moved with his family to Pearsontown and settled on the 30-acre lot #7, deed of which from Daniel Dole of Falmouth was not passed until Sept. 14, 1779 (12/2). He continued to live on Pudding Hill in Standish until he sold on Mar. 29, 1800, to Aaron Richardson of Newton, Mass. (11/242), and moved with his sons to Sudbury-Canada (Bethel) in the fall of 1781. He finally became deranged and committed suicide in Bethel by drowning or hanging Sept. 5, 1799, age 81. His widow, Abigail, died in 1821, age 96 years. She had 9 children, 66 grandchildren, 160 great-grandchildren, 5 great-great-grandchildren, making 239 in all, born during her lifetime. It was estimated that at the time of her death at least four-fifths of them were living, with all but two of the families residing in the state of Maine. Jonathan and Abigail (Gordon) Bean were the parents of the following children:

i.   **DANIEL**, bapt. June 8, 1746, Kingston, N.H., died young.
ii.   **ABIGAIL**, bapt. July 1, 1748, married Col. John York of Pearsontown and Bethel. For children see York family.

iii. JOSIAH, bapt. Oct. 17, 1748, Kingston, N.H., came to Pearsontown with his father and purchased from Moses Pearson the 30-acre lot #8 adjoining his father's land on July 17, 1772 (7/353). He also bought on July 15, 1772, the 30-acre lot #5 from Josiah Noyes of Falmouth (9/436) and on Dec. 19, 1774, the 30-acre lot #32 from Jonathan Moulton of Hampton, N.H. (8/463). He lived on lot #5 which he sold together with lot #32 on Oct. 25, 1779, to Jonathan Lowell of Pearsontown (17/549). He is given as living in Pearsontown on Nov. 3, 1780, when he bought land in Sudbury-Canada (Bethel) from Aaron Richardson of Newton, Mass. (12/93), but was living in Bethel on Oct. 16, 1781, when he bought other land there of Amos Powers of the same town (20/177).

Josiah Bean married Mary or Molly Crocker, daughter of Timothy and Hannah (Meserve) Crocker of Pearsontown and Bristol, Maine. He died by his own hand in 1832. Children were as follows:
1. DOLLY, born May 14, 1773, married Francis Keyes of Rumford.
2. TIMOTHY, born June 8, 1775, married Hannah Kimball, daughter of Asa Kimball.
3. AMOS, born Apr. 15, 1778, married Huldah Kimball, daughter of Samuel Kimball.
4. LUTHER, born Apr. 23, 1781, married Lydia Kimball, daughter of Samuel Kimball.
5. EDMUND, born Aug. 12, 1786, married Emma Kimball, born Jan. 4, 1795, and daughter of Asa Kimball. They lived in Rumford. He died Feb. 16, 1875, age 91.
6. JOSHUA, born Apr. 27, 1789, married Betsy Bartlett. He died May 19, 1871, age 83 yrs.
7. MARY OR MOLLY, born Jan. 27, 1792, married Moses F. Kimball of Rumford, son of Asa Kimball.
8. HANNAH, born June 29, 1794, married Israel Colby of Gray and second Capt. Timothy Hastings. She died Feb. 19, 1884, age 90, in Bethel.
9. ABIGAIL, born Dec. 1, 1797, married Phineas, son of Thomas Frost. They moved to Anoka, Minn.

iv. ANNE, born Mar. 19, 1753, bapt. June 4, 1775, married (int. July 17, 1779, in Gorham) as his second wife, Ithiel Smith. See Smith family.

v. JONATHAN, JR., born about 1754, served in the Revolutionary War. He married (int. Oct. 22, 1774, in Gorham) Abigail York, born daughter of John and Sarah (Strout) York of Pearsontown. They moved to Sudbury-Canada (Bethel) about 1781, where he died Nov. 19, 1826. They were the parents of the following children:
1. JONATHAN, born 1775 in Pearsontown, married Mar. 21, 1797, Anne McGill, born Apr. 17, 1776, daughter of John and Rebecca (York) McGill of Standish. He was killed by an Indian in the Shadagee fight in the War of 1812. He was about 21 years old at the time of his marriage and about 73 when he died. His wife died in Bethel several years later.

2. JOHN, born 1777-8 in Pearsontown, married Hannah McGill born Feb. 2, 1782, daughter of John and Rebecca (York) McGill of Pearsontown. They lived in the lower part of Bethel.
3. BENJAMIN, born 1780 in Pearsontown, married Priscilla Peabody. They lived in Shelbourne, N.H.
4. HANNAH, born Mar. 14, 1782, in Bethel, died Dec. 28, 1782.
5. LUCY, born Apr. 21, 1784, married Josiah Smith.
6. LOIS, born Oct. 24, 1786.
7. JOB, born Mar. 13, 1788, died Mar. 24, 1812.
8. ABIATHAR, born May 8, 1789, died Nov. 18, 1789.
9. NATHANIEL, born Apr. 10, 1791; married Nov. 25, 1816, Betsy York, born Sept. 25, 1792, daughter of Isaac L. and Elizabeth (Thompson) York of Bethel, his cousin. They lived at Magalloway.
10. ABIATHAR, born June 20, 1793, married Persis (Mercy) Fogg, daughter of Joseph Fogg. They moved to Berlin and Success, N.H.
11. EBENEZER, born Apr. 24, 1797, married Clarissa Newton and died Jan. 5, 1861.
12. EUNICE, born Feb. 7, 1799, married Samuel Wilson of Topsham.
13. SARAH, born May 6, 1800.

vi. DANIEL, born Mar. 16, 1757, served in the Revolutionary War. He was of Pearsontown on June 9, 1781, when he bought from Aaron Richardson of Newton, Mass., land in Sudbury-Canada (Bethel) (12/1). He moved there that fall along with his brothers. He married (int. Dec. 30, 1780, in Gorham) Margaret Shaw, born Jan. 7, 1758, daughter of Ebenezer and Anna (Philbrick) Shaw of Pearsontown. He died at West Bethel on Mar. 16, 1833, at the home of his son-in-law George W. Grover. They were the parents of the following children:
1. EBENEZER, SHAW, born in Pearsontown Mar. 25, 1781, married first Eunice Kendall, second Mary Holt.
2. SUSANNAH, born in Bethel Mar. 30, 1783, married William Burke.
3. ANNA, born Jan. 5, 1785, married Bezaleel Kendall.
4. SARGENT, born Nov. 14, 1787, died Jan. 15, 1792.
5. JUSTUS, born Nov. 8, 1790, married Sally Rumney.
6. ABIAH, born Dec. 31, 1792, married Cyrus Mills, died Aug. 14, 1896?
7. A CHILD, born Oct. 14, 1794, died Oct. 30, 1794.
8. HADASSAH, born Oct. 1, 1795, married Elijah Grover and lived in Machias.
9. DANIEL, born Dec. 8, 1796, married May 17, 1821, Betsy, daughter of Ithiel Smith, and moved to Upton, Maine. He died Feb. 14, 1882.
10. SARGENT, born May 30, 1799, married Anna Smith.
11. MARY, born Aug. 17, 1802, married first William Hall of Temple, second ____ Temple.
12. DOLLY, born Jan 25, 1804, married George W. Grover of Bethel. She died Apr. 16, 1864.

13. STEPHEN, born Jan. 7, 1806, married Hannah Townsend of Solon and lived in Grafton until 1862 when he moved to Iowa and died there.
vii. DOLLY, over 45 yrs. old in 1800, so born before 1755, married first Luther Topping of Falmouth and Pearsontown. He died Feb. 6, 1804, age 58, while on the way home from Portland. She married second on Aug. 10, 1806, Samuel Mountfort of Falmouth. She is said to have had no children.
viii. LOIS, over 45 yrs. old in 1800, so born before 1755, married (int. Nov. 10, 1781, in Gorham) John Marean of Pearsontown. They lived in Standish, where he died Feb. 17, 1804, and she in July 1843. For children see Marean family.
ix. EUNICE, born in 1763, married (int. May 12, 1780, in Gorham) Joseph Shaw of Pearsontown. They lived in Standish where he died Aug. 24, 1830, and she on Aug. 17, 1832. For children see Shaw family.

BENSON

Although the name of James Benson is found on the 1808 tax list of Standish, it is doubtful if he lived in town very long, but his wife was a native of Standish. He was a weaver and was born in Devonshire, England, on Feb. 20, 1772. He arrived in this country on Nov. 16, 1800, and taught school at one time in the Mosher District in Gorham. On Nov. 12, 1809, he married Abigail Dow, born in Standish Mar. 5, 1784, daughter of Abner and Martha (Sawyer) (Hinckley) Dow. He died May 16, 1832, in East Limington and she in Gorham on June 9, 1852, age 68 years. They lived in East Limington near Parker Rips on the Saco River for some years, where the record of the births of five of their children were filed. Children were as follows:
i. MARTHA, born May 15, 1810, in Gray, married Dec. 19, 1824, Henry S. Lewis of Waterboro, she of Limington. She died June 3, 1850 in Waterboro.
ii. MARY HASTY, born Nov. 11, 1811, never married, but lived in Gorham at her brother Arthur's for many years and there died Oct. 21, 1882.
iii. SUSANNA, born Jan. 25, 1814, married as his third wife on Sept. 12, 1843, Dominicus Frost of Gorham, Standish, and Thorndike, Maine. He died in Gorham Dec. 6, 1862, age 69, and she on Feb. 6, 1897, age 83, in Gorham.
iv. JOSEPH, born Mar. 2, 1815, married Maria Adams. He died Dec. 1, 1866, age 49 yrs., 10 mos., in Augusta, formerly of Bangor.
v. JAMES HARDING, born Feb. 2, 1819.
vi. ARTHUR McARTHUR, born Sept. 21, 1821, moved to Gorham in 1839. He married Dec. 1, 1844, Elizabeth Lowell, daughter of Stephen and Wealthy (Sawyer) Lowell of Standish and Gorham. He died Jan. 2, 1905, in Gorham.
vii. ELIZABETH, born Jan. 1824, married _____ Nickerson. She died Sept. 28, 1898, age 74 yrs., 8 mos., Bangor.

BERRY

There were two men by the name of Berry who settled in Standish shortly before 1800. They moved into town from Hollis and were the sons of James and Abigail (Philbrook) Berry who lived on the River Road in Hardscrable section of Limington just west of the Hollis line.

Walter Philbrook Berry was baptized in the First Church of Pepperellborough (Saco), Maine, on Mar. 6, 1768. He was living in Little Falls Plantation (Hollis) on Mar. 20, 1794, when he bought from Isaac York of Standish 79 acres of lot #103 in the second division of lots in that town (63/38), but was living in Standish on Sept. 6, 1794, when intentions of marriage to Polly Dearborn of Scarboro were filed in Standish. The other 21 acres of this lot he secured by tax deed from the town on June 18, 1795 (63/36). It was on this lot, located in South Standish almost directly across the Saco River from his father's farm in Hollis, that he evidently lived and made his home. Walter Berry Sr. died Mar. 11, 1837, age 69 years, in Standish, and his wife, Mary, died May 19, 1852, age 82 years, 6 months. Both are buried in the so-called Moses Cemetery on the River Road in the Boulter Neighborhood at South Standish.

They were the parents of seven children, six sons and one daughter, as follows:

i. **ROBERT JUSTIN (TUFTON?)** born Aug. 15, 1795, bapt. Sept. 7, 1797, married Nov. 2, 1817, Jane West, born Aug. 6, 1796, daughter of Joseph and Nancy (Cannell) West of Standish. They lived in Baldwin where he died Dec. 30, 1845, age 50 yrs., 4 mos., 15 days. She died Mar. 1875, South Bridgton. Children of Robert T. and Jane (West) Berry, all born in Baldwin except one, were:
   1. **JOSEPH TRISTRAM**, born in Standish Mar. 17, 1819, died in New Gloucester Aug. 15, 1879, married July 4, 1850, Mary Libby Tyler of Sebago, he of Baldwin.
   2. **WALTER**, born Feb. 21, 1821, Baldwin, died Feb. 19, 1821.
   3. **WALTER SCOTT**, born Oct. 5, 1823, Standish, died Aug. 15, 1879, New Gloucester, Maine. He married July 28, 1850, Mary L. Tyler of Sebago.
   4. **A SON**, born Mar. 8, 1825, Baldwin, died Mar. 11, 1825.
   5. **ROBERT ALMON**, born Apr. 16, 1826, Baldwin,
   6. **JOHN COLBY**, born Sept. 27, 1828, Baldwin, died July 10, 1903, South Bridgton.
   7. **LEONARD R.**, born Aug. 10, 1831, Baldwin, died Aug. 12, 1832, Baldwin.
   8. **LEONARD CHANDLER**, born Sept. 9, 1833, Baldwin, died June 29, 1907, New Gloucester.
   9. **SUSAN JANE**, born July 13, 1839, Baldwin.

ii. **RICHARD JR.**, bapt. July 18, 1799, died Jan. 5, 1843, age 43 yrs., 9 mos., in Standish. He was first burried in a family graveyard on his farm on the Milt Brown Road in South Standish, but later reburied in the Tory Hill Cemetery in Buxton. He married (int. Nov. 19, 1823) Lucinda B. Towle, born Apr. 22, 1803, daughter of Amos and Susan (Moulton) Towle of Effingham, N.H. She married Apr.

18, 1847, in Standish, John McKenney 3rd of Saco. She died Jan. 9, 1885, age 82 yrs., in No. Saco. Children of Richard and Lucinda (Towle) Berry were:
1. SUSAN T., born Dec. 2, 1823, married June 11, 1848, David McKenney, both of Saco, and died there Apr. 7, 1900. He died Aug. 24, 1894, age 74 yrs.
2. GEORGE, born about 1832, living in 1850 with his mother in Saco.
3. URIAH A., born 1833, died Apr. 15, 1914, age 80 yrs., in Buxton.
4. JASON and RICHARD W., mentioned in their father's deed in 1842.
5. ALMEDA, born about 1836, died Sept. 10, 1842, age 6 yrs.
6. WILLIAM L., born about 1839, died Dec. 15, 1842, age 3 yrs.
7. ALMEDA L., born Aug. 28, 1841, died Sept. 10, 1842, in Standish.
8. LUCRETIA, born about 1842, kept a store in Saco and died unmarried.

iii. WALTER, JR., bapt. Aug. 30, 1801, in Standish Church. He died Feb. 7, 1879, age 77 yrs., 7 mos., Biddeford. He married Jan. 24, 1828, Hannah Bacon of Gorham. She died Feb. 9, 1861, age 61 yrs.
iv. JOEL.
v. GEORGE, married Oct. 21, 1823, Hannah Burnham both of Standish. He is said to have died at sea. His widow married Nov. 19, 1837, Solomon Haskell of Standish. Their only son was Joel Berry, who died Feb. 15, 1886, age 62 yrs., 2 mos., in Standish.
vi. ELEANOR, born Aug. 12, 1806, married Nov. 19, 1837, Randall M. Foss, both of Standish. He was born Nov. 4, 1814, in Standish and died Apr. 7, 1895; she died on Oct. 27, 1887, age 81 yrs., 2 mos., 15 days, in Standish.
vii. JOHN HENRY, born Aug. 4, 1810, married Oct. 16, 1836, Mary Foss, daughter of Job and Hannah (York) Foss of Standish. He died Sept. 17, 1875, in Limington and she Nov. 11, 1885, in Salem, Mass.

Richard Berry was baptized in Saco on Mar. 22, 1778, son of James and Abigail (Philbrick) Berry. Richard Berry married July 14, 1800, Experience Higgins, both of Standish. Richard and his wife became members of the First Congregational Church of Standish on Sept. 25, 1803, and had several of their children baptized there.

On Apr. 16, 1802, James Warren of Gorham and Walter Berry of Standish, yeoman, purchased for $100 from Samuel Freeman of Portland the 100-acre lot #79 in the second division of lots in Standish (36/283). Josie's Brook runs diagonally across about the center of this lot, and Samuel Warren, James' son, settled on the lower half (50 acres) of it, while the upper half became the homestead of Richard Berry. On Mar. 23, 1835, Simon Berry, Richard's son, sold for $625 to Jonathan Nason of Buxton the farm formerly owned by his father, located on the River Road at South Standish near J. (John) and A. (Amos) Boulter's land, it being the same land that his father had purchased in 1802 (142/384). He died

Feb. 25, 1820, age 42, and she passed away Apr. 21, 1851, age 74 years, in Standish. She married second (int. July 30, 1836, in Standish) Ephraim Higgins, whose first wife, Rebecca (Higgins) Higgins, had died in 1834 at the age of 60. Ephraim Higgins survived his second wife until 1865.

In a family burial plot on the old James Berry farm on the River Road in Hardscrable section of Limington are gravestones bearing the following inscriptions:

Mr. Richard Berry, died Feb. 25. 1820, age 42 years.
Experience Higgins, wife of Richard Berry and second wife of Ephraim Higgins, died Apr. 20, 1851, age 74 years in Standish.

In the old cemetery at Dow's Corner in Standish are stones bearing these inscriptions:

In memory of Rebecca, wife of Ephraim Higgins, who died Mar. 27, 1834, age 60.

Ephraim Higgins, died Mar. 25, 1865, age 90 years, 5 months

The children of Richard and Experience (Higgins) Berry, all born in Standish were:

i. ELIZABETH D., born June 15, 1801, married in 1818 Caleb Sellea of Saco and married second (int. July 9, 1837, in Saco Maj. James Small, formerly of Limington). She died Mar. 14, 1887, in Saco.
ii. MARCY, born Mar. 15, 1803, died May 28, 1867, Dixmont; married Mar. 21, 1822, Moses Nason of Standish, she of Limington. He died Nov. 23, 1855, age 58 yrs., in Dixmont.
iii. SIMON, born June 3, 1807, died Sept. 14, 1841, married Sept. 26, 1835, Mrs. Lucy (Anderson) Nason of Standish, born Oct. 3, 1806, in Windham, daughter of Capt. Edward and Olive (Waterhouse) Anderson of Standish. She married second (int. Aug. 2, 1846, Stephen Estes of Limington).
iv. LOUISA, born Oct. 8, 1809, married (int. Sept. 29, 1833, in Standish) William Warren of Jackson, she of Standish.
v. MARY, born Sept. 5, 1812.

BERRY

The name of Timothy Berry is found on the 1789, 1790, 1795, and 1796 tax lists of Standish, in the 1800 census with a family consisting of him and his wife, two boys and three girls under 10 years of age, and one boy and two girls between 10 and 16 years old. He was the son of Timothy and Mary (Burnham) Berry of Scarboro, who were married there May 2, 1754, and is said to have been born in what is now Westbrook, Maine, in 1757, although pensions records indicate his date of birth about 1753. However, since his age in the 1800 census is given as under 45, it seems likely that the later date is correct. He served for three years in the Revolutionary War from Scarboro and later received a pension for his services.

On June 20, 1782, he married Susannah Waterhouse, born May 13, 1760, daughter of Joseph and Rachel (Norman) Waterhouse of Scarboro. Soon after their marriage they came to live on Standish Neck, where her brother Joseph Waterhouse Jr. had previously settled. He bought the northeast half of lot #34 in the second division located on Standish Neck on Apr. 10, 1801, (59/390) and sold it to John Plaisted and Elliot Harmon on Jan. 14, 1805, (59/391). He is given as living in Standish when he sold his land in Jan. 1805 but is listed as the owner of 50 acres of land in Cornish together with three cows and two horses in a tax inventory of that town for 1805. Therefore it is clear that he moved from Standish to Cornish during that year. Here he hereafter lived and died in 1841. His wife must have died sometime after 1800 since the intentions of marriage of Timothy Berry of Standish to Mrs. Sarah Sawyer of Scarboro on May 12, 1804, are found in the Standish records. She was Sarah (Chute) Sawyer, the widow of David Sawyer of Scarboro, and was listed as 65 years of age in 1820 when Timothy filed his Revolutionary War pension. No record of the family of Timothy and Susannah (Waterhouse) Berry has been discovered, but it is likely that the following were his children:

i. DANIEL, born 1788, died Apr. 27, 1861, age 73 yrs., 4 mos., married at Westbrook Dec. 29, 1811, Rebecca Pride, born 1791, died 1862.
ii. MARGARET, married Nov. 7, 1819, in Gorham, Christopher Strout of Cape Elizabeth. She married second about 1833 John Allen of Cornish.
iii. REBECCA, born about 1798, married Apr. 22, 1821, Daniel Strout of Cape Elizabeth, she of Gorham. She died Mar. 13, 1867, age 67 yrs.
iv. JOHN, of Cornish.

BLACK

Josiah and Joab Black were inhabitants of Pearsontown prior to 1780. They were brothers and both had served in the Revolutionary War from Gorham. Josiah Black, blacksmith, was living in Pearsontown on Apr. 21, 1778, when he bought from John Dean and Jonathan Philbrick 50 acres of the 100-acre lot #113 in the second division (12/492). This lot was located in the general vicinity of the Boulter Neighborhood in South Standish and later became the property of William Whitney. Josiah was still living in town on Mar 19, 1781, when he sold the same land to John Marean of Standish, also a blacksmith (12/498). It was probably about this time that he moved to Little Ossipee (Limington) where he afterwards lived and died. He was born Dec. 3, 1750, in York, probably the son of Josiah and Mary (Black) Black, who were married Mar. 4, 1733, in York, Maine, and who later settled in Sedgwick, Maine. Josiah was a resident of Gorham, Maine, on Nov. 6, 1773, when his intention of marriage to Mary Cookson of Pearsontown was published in that town. Her name is found variously as Mary, Mercy (Marcy), and Martha in different records but Mercy seems to occur most often. Her parentage has not been determined definitely but it is more than likely that she was the daughter of a John Cookson who was living in Pearsontown as early as 1767; she was born Aug. 15, 1751, and died in Limington on May 25, 1816. Josiah married second on Oct. 10, 1816, Olive (Woodman) Chase, baptized Feb. 1, 1756, daughter of Nathan and Olive (Gray) Woodman of Newbury, Mass., and Buxton, Maine, and widow of Joseph Chase of Standish. She died in Limington on Apr. 9, 1840. Josiah Black died there June 4, 1843, at the age of 93 years, 7 months. He is buried in a small graveyard on the Pine Hill Road in East Limington near Hamblen Brook, back of Elton Black's place.

Josiah and Mercy (Cookson) Black were the parents of the following children, the first three of whom were probably born in Gorham or Standish and the remainder in Limington:

i. MARY (POLLY), born May 10, 1775, married on Jan. 2, 1794, Jacob Small, son of Capt. Jacob and Sarah (Mayo) of Cape Elizabeth and Limington, who died between Mar. and Sept. 1815.
ii. JOHN, born Aug. 31, 1777, married Apr. 27, 1801, Abigail Small, born Jan. 2, 1777, daughter of Henry and Elizabeth (Dam) Small of Scarboro and Limington. He died Apr. 20, 1847, and she Apr. 22, 1866, both in Limington.
iii. JOAB, born Nov. 4, 1780, married Apr. 20, 1802, Hannah Hamblen, born Nov. 4, 1775, daughter of Gershom and Deborah (Jenkins) Hamblen of Gorham and Limington. He died Oct. 29, 1821, in Limington and she Oct. 8, 1836, in Portland.
iv. JOSIAH, JR. born Aug. 31, 1784, married (int. Apr. 30, 1808) Mary Ingerson Libby, born May 11, 1783, died Sept. 23, 1854. He died July 9, 1864, both of Newry, Maine.
v. MERCY, born Jan. 8, 1789, married Jan. 21, 1818, Amos Libby, born in Saco Jan. 28, 1781, son of Zebulon and Lydia (Andrews) Libby of Saco. He died during the War of 1812 and she Apr. 2, 1813, in Saco.
vi. AARON, born Sept. 13, 1791, married Oct. 16, 1817, Lydia Libby, born Sept. 23, 1795, daughter of Zebulon and Lydia (Andrews) Libby of Saco. He died Aug. 31, 1865, and she July 24, 1868, both in Limington.
vii. BETSEY, born Feb. 22, 1798, married Apr. 18, 1821, David Fogg, born Aug. 27, 1797, son of Charles and Anna (Small) Fogg of Scarboro and Limington. He died Apr. 22, 1871, in Brownfield and she died Feb. 29, 1892, in Brownfield.

Joab Black, born Sept. 10, 1752, in York, Maine, brother of Josiah, was living in Gorham on Nov. 7, 1777, when he bought from John Ayer 35 acres of the 100-acre lot #111 in the second division in Pearsontown (12/492) and was given as being a yeoman of Pearsontown when he sold the same land to John Marean on July 13, 1781 (12/493). He moved from town and settled in that part of North Yarmouth that is now Cumberland before Mar. 15, 1788, when he and his wife, Lydia, were mentioned in a deed as two of the heirs of her father, Abel Merrill of North Yarmouth (47/56). He married first July 25, 1785, Lydia Merrill of North Yarmouth, he of Nasheag (name of Sedgwick). She was born July 13, 1766, in North Yarmouth and died Sept. 19, 1806, in Cumberland. He married second Jan. 10, 1810, in North Yarmouth, Priscilla Titcomb, both of North

Yarmouth. She died Jan. 10, 1851, age 85 years, in Cumberland and he on Aug. 10, 1822, at the age of 69 years, 11 months, also in Cumberland. Children of Joab and Lydia (Merrill) Black as found in church records were as follows:

i. ABEL, bapt. in First Church of North Yarmouth on Nov. 1, 1792, married Feb. 5, 1810, in North Yarmouth, Abigail Winch, both of North Yarmouth. He married second Dec. 3, 1818, Rachel Field, both of North Yarmouth. She was a daughter of Zachariah and Tabitha (Lunt) Field of North Yarmouth and a sister to Hannah, wife of Joab Black. One daughter was Rachel (Black) Tibbetts who died Dec. 2, 1903, age 82 yrs., 18 days, in Corinth. Abel Black died Aug. 10, 1865, in Corinth, Maine.

ii. EUNICE, bapt. Nov. 1, 1792, married Nov. 30, 1809, in North Yarmouth, Ebenezer Buxton.

iii. HANNAH, born Oct. 18, 1788, married (int. May 25, 1813) Isaac Merrill, both of North Yarmouth. She died Sept. 17, 1880, Cumberland.

iv. JANE, born about 1792, living in 1850 in Gray, age 58 yrs. Married (int. Mar. 5, 1813) in Gray, John M. Doughty of Gray, she of North Yarmouth. They had a son, Enoch M. Doughty.

v. JOSIAH, born 1794, married (int. June 13, 1813) Jane Allen, both of North Yarmouth. He died May 26, 1881, age .87 yrs., in Cumberland. She died Sept. 2, 1872, age 82 yrs. They are buried in Methodist Church Yard, located near Allen's Corner in Cumberland. They lived in Limington once and are listed there in 1824 school poll.

vi. ABIGAIL, born Feb. 26, 1796, died Aug. 31, 1866. Married Jan. 18, 1816, Timothy Wentworth.

vii. ENOCH MERRILL, born Apr. 10, 1800, died July 1, 1868, in Chesterville, Maine. Married Pamela Wheeler. Children were: Augustus H., born Sept. 8, 1828; Lyman, born Feb. 2, 1829, died Aug. 3, 1892; Charles, born Mar. 13, 1830, died May 2, 1892; Amanda Melvina, born Sept. 18, 1831; Martha Ann, born Dec. 2, 1840; Mary Augusta, born Aug. 19, 1843.

viii. LYDIA, born June 1, 1802, North Yarmouth, married June 6, 1824, Enoch Nason of Limington, she of Gray. Died Nov. 7, 1880, age 78 yrs., 5 mos., 6 days, East Limington.

ix. JOAB, born Sept. 1804, died Mar. 28, 1888, age 83 yrs., 6 mos., in Cumberland, Maine, and was buried there with his father. Married Hannah Field of North Yarmouth, sister to Rachel (Field) Black. She died Mar. 26, 1895, age 59 yrs., 4 mos., Cumberland. One child, Josiah.

x. EDMUND, born Nov. 20, 1807, died Dec. 24, 1889, Yarmouth. There was one Edmund who died Mar. 26, 1882, age 77 yrs., in Augusta, and was born Nov. 8, 1804.

xi. OLIVE, bapt. in Second Church of North Yarmouth (Cumberland) on July 14, 1798. Married Oct. 20, 1829, Edward Skillings, both of Gray. Their daughter Olive married Joseph Hawkes and died Feb. 27, 1906, age 73 yrs., Gorham. Her mother was born in Cumberland.

BLAKE

A Joseph Blake was an inhabitant of Pearsontown in the 1780s. He was from Gorham and was probably born in Scarboro, the son of Benjamin and Elizabeth (Boulter) Blake. He married (int. Jan. 6, 1781, in Gorham) Hannah Hopkins of Pearsontown, the daughter of Theodore Hopkins who had settled there about two years before.

Joseph Blake was living in Gorham on May 15, 1781, when he bought from Nathan Knight of Falmouth the 100-acre lot #95 in the second division in in Pearsontown (11/522), and it is likely that he moved into town soon after for he is listed as living in Standish on Mar. 24, 1788, when he bought from Benjamin Boulter of Standish land in Gorham, probably at West Gorham where he later lived (18/155). His name is found on a 1788 valuation list of Standish taken in May of that year. He was living in Gorham on Nov. 10, 1791, when he sold to Mary Boulter of Standish 50 acres from the northwest end of the 100-acre lot #95, which he had purchased in 1781 (86/322). He was a soldier in the Revolutionary War and received a pension for his services. He died on Jan. 28, 1840, age 83, and his wife died on Jan. 27, 1842, age 78. They were the parents of the following children, the first four of whom were probably born in Standish:

i. ADRIEL, born Apr. 5, 1782.
ii. PHEBE, born Dec. 7, 1783, married on Sept. 26, 1804, Samuel Boynton, born Dec. 7, 1780. They lived in Brownfield, Maine. He is said to have died in the army.
iii. HANNAH, born Sept. 8, 1787, married Joseph Sturgis.
iv. EUNICE, born Sept. 8, 1787, married on Dec. 19, 1813, Richard Paine of Gorham.
v. LYDIA, born Aug. 21, 1790, married Thomas Paine of Gorham on Dec. 1, 1808.
vi. LUCY, born May 9, 1793, married (int. Aug. 26, 1815) Nathaniel Phinney, Jr.
vii. CHARLES, born Nov. 6, 1800 (bapt. June 18, 1801), married Rebecca Moody of Limington (int. Dec. 27, 1823). He died May 19, 1870, age 69 yrs., 6 mos., in Portland.
viii. JOSEPH JR., born Apr. 15, 1803, married Elizabeth Moody of Limington (int. Aug. 6, 1825). He died July 13, 1835.

BOLTER OR BOULTER

In the census of Standish appear the names of Nathaniel Bolter (2-1-2), Nathaniel Bolter Jr. (1-0-2), and Benjamin Bolter (1-0-1). All of these names as well as that of Lemuel Bolter are found on the 1789 and 1790 tax lists of the town. Research discloses that Nathaniel Bolter Sr. was the father and the others were his sons.

Capt. Nathaniel[4] Boulter (Nathaniel,[3] John,[2] Nathaniel[1]) was living in Scarboro, Maine, when he is said to have sold a coasting vessel together with other property in that town and to have moved to Standish, where he settled on a valuable tract of land bordering the Saco River in the southwestern section of the town, since known as the Boulter Neighborhood. The exact date on which he moved to Standish has not been discovered, but the latest date on which he is given as a resident of Scarboro in deeds is July 16, 1784, when he sold land in that town to William Vaughan of Falmouth (14/1). It seems likely therefore that it was about this time or soon after, that he moved from one town to the other.

Nathaniel Boulter Sr. was born in Scarboro in 1737, being baptized there Sept. 24, 1737, son of Nathaniel and Grace (Blye) Boulter, who had moved to that town from Hampton, N.H., shortly before 1730. He married on Dec. 2, 1756, Ruth Sprague of Scarboro, born July 17, 1739. He died in Standish on May 21, 1825, age 88 years, and she on Oct. 3, 1829, age 90 years. Both are buried in a graveyard located on the family homestead a short distance from the back of the Saco River. A list of the children of Nathaniel and Ruth (Sprague) Boulter is given as a footnote to the ancestry of Eliza (Boulter) Haskell in an account of the descendants of William Haskell of Gloucester, Mass., found in volume 32 of the Essex Institute Historical Collection. The only person not placed in this family is Grace Boulter who married Sept. 6, 1801, Nathaniel Townsend Jr., of Hollis. A list of ten children is given in this order:

i. JOHN, is named as the eldest child, but since his name is not found in Standish records, he may have died young.

ii. LEMUEL, born about 1758, married Mary Davis of Little Ossipee (Limington) on Sept. 18, 1788, as found in the Buxton Church records. She was probably the daughter of Ezra and Sarah (Edgecomb) Davis, and was baptized in Biddeford on Apr. 30, 1758. He apparently died about 1790 since his name is found on the 1789 and 1790 tax list but not on the 1790 census. A Mary Boulter, married woman of Standish, undoubtedly his widow, bought from Joseph Blake of Gorham 50 acres of the 100-acre lot #95 in the second division in Standish, it being the northwest end of the lot, on Nov. 10, 1791 (86/322). A Mary Boulter is found on the 1795 and 1796 tax lists of Standish. She married second on Nov. 16, 1797, William Meserve, born in 1761 son of John and Mary (Yeaton) Meserve of Standish. The child of Lemuel and Mary (Davis) Boulter was:

1. RUTH, born ____, was of Limington when she married Sept. 29, 1809, Robert Mayall of that town. He belonged to an English family of clothiers who had mills and carding machines in various Maine towns. On Nov. 6, 1819, according to deed (86/323) William Meserve of Standish and Mary, his wife, Robert Mayall of Lisbon (Maine) and Ruth, his wife, sold Samuel F. Boulter of Standish one-third part of 50 acres of the 100-acre lot #95 in second division in Standish, it being part of the 50 acres Mary bought from Joseph Blake on Nov. 10, 1791. Robert Mayall and his wife moved to Ohio where he died Sept. 18, 1826, age 49 yrs. His obituary is given in the Oct. 3, 1826, issue of *Maine Baptist Herald*. He was born June 24, 1776, Saddleworth, England.

iii. **BENJAMIN**, born about 1760, married by John Dean, Esq. on Jan. 22, 1789, to Sarah Brown, born June 19, 1772, daughter of Joseph Jr. and Hannah (Whitney) Brown of Gorham. He being of Standish sold Joseph Blake of Standish 45 acres in Gorham on Mar. 24, 1788, (8/155) and 50 acres of the 100-acre lot #95 in second division in Standish to Joseph C. Rackleff of Scarboro on Mar. 24, 1789 (16/282). While his name is found in the 1790 census of Standish with a family of 1-0-1, he was living in Buxton on Oct. 12, 1795, when he and his wife, Sarah, sold to Peter Thacher of Gorham land in that town from the estate of her father, Joseph Brown (25/178). He was living in Biddeford about the time of the 1830 census in a family consisting of him and his wife. The following were probably his children:
1. **SUSAN**, born about 1792, married May 13, 1810, Jacob York Jr., born in 1787 son of Jacob and Edie (Moody) York of Standish. They moved to Baldwin where she died on Nov. 14, 1868, age 76 yrs., 8 mos., and he in 1869, age 82.
2. **JOSEPH**, born about 1794 (age 56 in 1850), married Dec. 25, 1818, Mary Ladd of Biddeford. She died July 21, 1838, age 39 in Biddeford. He married second (int. Mar. 2, 1839) Belinda T. Colley, both of Saco. She died May 26, 1858, age 54 yrs., in Saco. Joseph married third Hannah Pulfrey Sept. 12, 1860, both of Saco, and he died there, June 6, 1862, age 69 yrs.(*Christian Mirror*, June 24,1862).
3. **SARAH**, married May 10, 1829, Isaac Hutchins of Kennebunkport.

iv. **MARY (MOLLIE)**, born Sept. 1760, married in Scarboro Nov. 17, 1783, Capt. William Smith of Buxton, who died Mar. 12, 1838, age 80 yrs., in Buxton. She died Apr. 23, 1842, age 81 yrs., 7 mos., in Buxton. They were the parents of the following children: (Smith)
1. **JOHN**, born Oct. 25, 1784, died Apr. 19, 1862, Buxton.
2. **NATHANIEL**, born Dec. 11, 1786.
3. **GEORGE**, born Dec. 11, 1786, twin to Nathaniel.
4. **JANE**, born Apr. 24, 1788, married Feb. 9, 1806, Nathaniel Durgin.
5. **MARY**, born Jan. 12, 1790, married Oct. 1, 1808, Enoch Coffin.
6. **WILLIAM**, born Jan. 29, 1792, died Aug. 11, 1863, New Vineyard, Maine.
7. **MARTHA**, born June 18, 1795.
8. **RUTH**, born May 1, 1798, married (int. June 7, 1816) Elijah Owen.
9. **SAMUEL**, born Jan. 21, 1799, died Sept. 1822, Standish.
10. **ELIZA**, born July 7, 1801, died Dec. 19, 1847, Buxton.

v. **NATHANIEL, JR.**, born in Scarboro in 1761, was married by John Dean Esq. of Standish on Apr. 8, 1790, to Martha Higgins. She was born in 1760 daughter of Ebenezer and Martha (Burgess) Higgins of Eastham, Mass. She was a sister of Elizabeth (Higgins) Martin, wife of Bryan Martin, and of Ebenezer Jr., Elkanah, and Seth Higgins, all of whom settled in Standish. Although she did not die until Oct. 14, 1813, age 53 yrs., 3 mos., Nathaniel Boulter Jr. married second on Feb. 20, 1794, Rev. Jonathan Gould officiating,

Eliza Linnell, born in Eastham, Mass., on Jan. 11, 1765, daughter of Elisha and Martha (Higgins) Linnell and sister to Martha (Linnell) Higgins, wife of Elisha Higgins. She died in Standish on Feb. 8, 1840, age 75 yrs., and he on Nov. 2, 1840, at the age of 79 yrs. Both are buried in the family graveyard in the Boulter Neighborhood. The list of children of Nathaniel Boulter Jr. as given in the Haskell Genealogy, before mentioned were: By first wife, Martha (Higgins) Boulter:

1. HANNAH, born in July 1791, married (int. Mar. 6, 1816, in Standish) Mar. 7, 1816, Thomas Smith, son of Thomas and Rhoda (Rounds) Smith of Buxton. He died Feb. 26, 1855, age 65 yrs., 3 mos., and she on Apr. 26, 1860, age 68 yrs., 9 mos., and 19 days, both in Standish. They are buried in the Boulter Cemetery at South Standish. Children were as follows: (Smith)
    (1) MARTHA, born July 28, 1816, married (int. Sept 1837) her cousin, John Boulter Jr., son of Samuel F. and Charity (Merrow) of Standish. She died Mar. 18, 1893, age 67 yrs., and he on Nov. 12, 1870, age 63 yrs., 9 mos.
    (2) RHODA E., born Dec. 4, 1817, died Nov. 3, 1838, age 21 yrs., of a fever.
    (3) ELIZABETH L., born Mar. 21, 1820, died Jan. 7, 1839, of a fever.
    (4) MARY ANN, born Mar. 21, 1822, married Nov. 22, 1847, Joseph W. McKenney of Limington, she of Standish. They moved to Anoka, Minn., where she died Oct. 29, 1895, age 52 yrs.
    (5) ROYAL, born Jan. 2, 1825, died June 15, 1826.
    (6) RUTH SPRAGUE, b. Apr. 26, 1827, married Dec. 1, 1850, Thomas Gannett Moses of Standish. In 1850 she was living with her parents in Standish.
    (7) ELBRIDGE G., born about 1832, died Feb. 9, 1836, age 4 yrs.
    (8) ANDREW J., born about 1830, living with his parents in 1850 census of Standish. He married twice and lived in Minn.
    (9) MARK MARQUIS, born July, 12, 1834, married (int. Nov. 16, 1860) Elizabeth Kelley of Limington, he of Standish.
    (10) EMELINE H., born July 12, 1834, a twin, married (int. Apr. 5, 1852) Israel Boothby of Limington, she of Standish. He died Feb. 3, 1880, age 53 yrs., in Augusta. She married second to John Bell and lived in Deering, Maine.
2. ROYAL, born about 1793, died in the army at Plattsburg, Lake Champlain. (His pension papers can be found in the Arthur McArthur Papers, in Special Collections at Bowdoin College.)

By second wife, Eliza (Linnell) Boulter:
3. JOHN, born Sept. 16, 1794, was known as Deacon Boulter. He married first on Nov. 28, 1816, Mary Whitney, born Apr. 27, 1798. She was a daughter of William and Hannah (Bangs) Whitney who lived on the outskirts of the Boulter Neighbor-

hood. She died Jan. 22, 1835, age 36 yrs., 8 mos., and 25 days, in Standish, and he married second Aug. 20, 1835, Eunice Merrill of Limington. She was born July 20, 1800, in Alfred and died Sept. 12, 1874, age 74 yrs., 1 mo., and 23 days, in Standish. He died May 23, 1863, age 68 yrs., 8 mos., 7 days. Children as in family register were:
- (1) ROYAL, born June 26, 1817, Standish, went to Georgia, at the age of twenty years, married Clara Scott and died in Florida in 1882.
- (2) WILLIAM, born Sept. 22, 1818, died July 14, 1895, age 76 yrs., 7 mos., 22 days; married (int. June 15, 1847) Sarah S. Merrill of Cornish, who died Jan. 23, 1899, age 74 yrs., 11 mos., and 14 days. They had a son, Charles F. Boulter, born about 1848, who married Feb. 17, 1874, Orianna Moses, born Aug. 25, 1856, daughter of Alonzo and Hannah E. (Burnham) Moses of Standish.
- (3) MARY ANN, born May 2, 1829, Standish, married May 25, 1854, Loronzo Mellon Sawyer of Limington, she of Standish. His wife, Mary A. Sawyer, was listed in the 1860 census of Standish with their two children, Alma J., age 3 yrs., and Chestina Emma, age 1 yr. He lived 14 yrs. in Minneapolis, Minn., where she died. He died Feb. 13, 1904, age 72 yrs., 9 mos., and 5 days, in Standish.
- (4) JOHN FRANKLIN, called Frank, born Apr. 4, 1831, Standish, married Sarah Woods Luflin, born Jan. 6, 1837, Yarmouth, Maine, of Minnesota when she died in Jan. 31, 1879, in Sauk Rapids, Minn. He married second Emeline Bennett and lived in St. Cloud, Minn. He died July 28, 1906, in Keefers, British Columbia.

4. NATHANIEL 3rd, born Apr. 13, 1798, married Sept. 11, 1823, Martha Foss of Standish, who died Oct. 14, 1853, age 53 yrs., 3 mos. He died July 28, 1875, age 77 yrs., 3 mos. She is buried in the Boulter Cemetery and he in cemetery on hillside on Route 107 in Bridgton. They left no issue. In 1850 census he and his wife, Martha, are listed in the family of James Boulter.
5. MARTHA, died young.
6. ALICE, born about 1803, age 47 yrs. in 1850 census of Limington, married May 9, 1824, Edmund Thomes, son of Thomas and Apphia (Blake) Thomes of Buxton. He born Feb. 28, 1803, in Buxton and died in Buxton. She married second Mar. 17, 1844, James Young, born May 19, 1786, son of David and Elizabeth (Small) Young of Limington, as his second wife. He died Dec. 24, 1852, in Limington and she died in Sebago. She had by her first husband a son Thomas of Boston and a daughter Martha Young, wife of Albert, who resided at Dedham, Mass., and is buried in Milan, N.H.
7. ELIZA, born June 5, 1806, married Apr. 3, 1828, Ephraim Chick Haskell, son of John and Eunice (Chick) Haskell of Scarboro. He died in Conway, N.H., on Sept. 11, 1858, age 52 yrs., 3 mos., and she on Mar. 25, 1883, age 76 yrs., 9 mos., 20 days, in Lowell, Mass. Children as follows (Haskell):

(1) REBECCA LINNELL, married Albert Abbott.
(2) MEHITABLE B., married Ira Jack. She died Oct. 31, 1858, age 28 yrs., 1 mo., 25 days.
(3) MARY ELIZABETH, married Henry Eaton.
(4) JOHN, died Apr. 12, 1857, age 17 yrs., 4 days.
(5) NATHANIEL BOULTER, died Oct. 23, 1894, age 58 Beverly, Mass.
(6) MARTHA ANN, married Henry Farrington.
(7) WILLIAM GOULD.
(8) EUGENE M.
(9) JAMES EDWIN, died Sept. 13, 1862, age 14 yrs., 10 mos., 1 day.
(10) JOHN FRANKLIN, born in 1853.

8. JAMES, born 1804, married first Feb. 16, 1830, in Hiram, Ruth H. Hancock, of Hiram, daughter of John Lane and Hannah (Prescott) who died in Jan. 1835, age 26 yrs., 3 mos. He married second (int. Oct. 1838) Abigail Merrill of Cornish, born about 1810. At the time of the 1880 census she was living in Sebago in the family of her son-in-law Samuel H. Weeman. James Boulter died Nov. 2, 1872, age 68 yrs., 2 mos. He was living in Sebago in 1870. Children were:

By first marriage:
(1) MARTHA, died Dec. 27, 1849, age 19 yrs., 1 mo., 7 days, Standish.
(2) ALMEDA, died Aug. 22, 1834, age 2 yrs.

By second marriage:
(3) JAMES G., died Oct. 14, 1840, age 3 yrs., 25 days.
(4) RUTH H., born in Aug. 1841, died unmarried June 15, 1883, age 41 yrs., 10 mos., in Sebago. She was living there in 1880 by census report.
(5) ALMEDA C., age 7 yrs., in 1850 census, age 37 in 1880 census and living in Sebago.
(6) ALBANUS K. M., died Apr. 22, 1845, age 8 mos.
(7) ALMIRA F., age 1 in 1850 census, married Samuel H. Weeman and was living as his wife, age 31 yrs., in Sebago in 1880.
(8) JENNIE MARTHA, born about 1854, married a Moran and lived in Lowell, Mass.

9. MEHITABLE L., born about 1810, was living in Sebago, Maine, in 1880 with her sister-in-law Abigail (Merrill) Boulter, widow of her brother James Boulter. She died unmarried about 1888, Bridgton.

vi. WILLIAM, born in 1768, married June 7, 1793, Mary Bradbury, both of Buxton, and settled in that town on the high land about half a mile from West Buxton Village. He died Jan. 1, 1852, age 83 yrs., 9 mos., and she on Aug. 24, 1856, age 88 yrs., 2 mos., both in Buxton. They had no children of their own but adopted two whose original name was Townsend, as follows:
1. WILLIAM T., born about 1803, was a Boulter when he married Aug. 17, 1829, in Hollis, Mary Berry, both of Buxton. She was born Feb. 7, 1809, daughter of James and Betty Berry of

Buxton. He died Oct. 29, 1860, age 57 yrs., 6 mos., 17 days. She died June 10, 1887, age 79 yrs., W. Buxton.
2. **ELINOR**, born ____, died a Townsend June 19, 1822, in Buxton.

vii. **RUTH**, born Apr. 11, 1771, in Scarboro, married Sept. 9, 1793, Nicholas Heath of Brownfield. They lived in that town and in Standish. She died on Oct. 1849 in Saco. See Heath family.

viii. **SAMUEL FOWLER**, born July 31, 1775, in Scarboro, lived on his father's homestead at South Standish. He married (int. Jan. 11, 1800, in Hollis) Charity Merrow, born Mar. 17, 1777, in Ossipee, N.H., daughter of William and Margaret (Haley) Merrow of Hollis and Standish. He died July 31, 1857, age 82 yrs., 7 mos., and she died July 17, 1869, age 92 yrs., 4 mos. Their children given in Haskell Genealogy, before mentioned, were:

1. **WADSWORTH**, born 1801 (Jan. 1823, age 21 by Masonic petition to Lodge at Limington), married Dec. 31, 1826, in Buxton, Rebecca M. Lane, born Nov. 20, 1803, daughter of Jabez and Mary Elizabeth (Knowlton) Lane of Buxton. They lived in Standish in 1830, but he must have died before 1850 when his widow, Rebecca, age 45, was living in Saco. A son Charles W. Boulter died in Boston on May 7, 1869, age 37 yrs., and is buried in Saco.
2. **ISAAC**, died young.
3. **ISAAC**, born about 1803, married Mar. 30, 1830 (int. Jan. 30, 1831), Hannah Rackleff, bapt. Mar. 19, 1812, daughter of George and Mary (Martin) (Nudd) Rackleff of Standish. He died June 13, 1833, age 30, and she married second (int. Nov. 19, 1837) John Green Eaton, born Aug. 10, 1802, son of John and Keziah (Dearborn) Eaton of Buxton. He had married previously on Apr. 7, 1833, Tamson Woodman, who died May 27, 1833. They lived in New Gloucester where he died Mar. 31, 1853, John G. Eaton and Hannah (Rackleff) (Boulter) Eaton were the parents of two children: (Eaton)
   (1) MARY, born June 17, 1843.
   (2) JOSIAH G.
4. **GRACE**, born about 1806, married (int. Feb. 11, 1839, in Buxton) Eli Thomes, born Apr. 11, 1808, son of Thomas and Apphia (Blake) Thomes. She died May 3, 1854, age 47 yrs. At the time of 1850 census, Eli Thomes, age 42, was living in Standish with his wife, Grace, age 44. Children: Alfred, born Mar. 5, 1840, Mary Elizabeth, born Sept. 8, 1841, and Charity M., age 4.
5. **JOHN**, born Feb. 1807, married (Oct. 5, 1837) Martha H. Smith of Standish, daughter of William and Mary (Boulter) Smith. She died Mar. 15, 1893, age 76 yrs. He died Nov. 12, 1870, age 63 yrs., 9 mos., in Standish. Children as follows:
   (1) ISAAC A., born Jan. 29, 1838, died July 5, 1907, age 69 yrs., 5 mos., 16 days, in Standish. Married Mary T. Johnson, born Apr. 29, 1848, daughter of Isaac and Hannah (Whitney) Johnson of Standish. They lived in Standish where she died Apr. 24, 1925.

(2) **RHODA E.**, age 10 in 1850.
(3) **JULIA A.**, born Sept. 17, 1842, married Sylvanus Bean Estes, born July 10, 1842, lived in South Standish. He died Dec. 20, 1917, and she died Apr. 3, 1925.
(4) **JANE D.**, died Oct. 25, 1848, age 1 yr.
(5) **MARTHA E.**, died Aug. 3, 1852, age 3 yrs., 8 mos.
(6) **JOHN C.** died at the age of 2 yrs., 3 mos., and 12 days.

6. JANE, born about 1809, married Sept. 10, 1829 (int. July 20, 1829), he being of Boston, Mass., at the time, William A. Dresser born July 5, 1805, son of Mark and Sally (Holbrook) Dresser of Buxton. She died in Bangor on Sept. 6, 1847, age 38, and he married her sister Charity Ann Boulter on Sept. 15, 1848.

7. AMOS, born Aug. 1811, married first on Jan. 5, 1852, Emily C. Usher, born Feb. 22, 1824, daughter of Col. Abijah and Susan (Nason) Usher of Buxton. She died Mar. 19, 1852, age 28 yrs., in Standish, and he married second on Feb. 24, 1867, Mary Davis of Standish. They were the parents of a son, Amos W., who died May 16, 1878, age 5 yrs. They adopted a son Charles Davis who was 8 yrs. old in 1880. At the time of the 1870 census Amos Boulter, age 57, was living in Standish with Mary, his wife, age 37; his brother Nathaniel, age 50, and Annis C. Thomes, age 24. Amos Boulter died May 16, 1896, age 84 yrs., 9 mos., and his wife, Mary, died Nov. 23, 1903, age 72 yrs., 2 mos., 8 days, in Standish.

8. SAMUEL, JR., born about 1817, was living in Standish, age 33 in 1850, with his wife, Rosilla, age 26, and Annis C. Boulter, age 13, Hadassah Boulter, age 2, and Lavinia Chase, age 19. At the time of the 1870 census, he was age 53; his wife, Rosilla F., age 45 and born in Solon, Maine; daughter Annis L., age 14 (she as Alice L. died Jan 10, 1871, age 14 yrs., 21 days, in Gorham). Mrs. Rosilla Boulter died Dec. 10, 1872, age 48 yrs., in Gorham.

9. NATHANIEL, JR., born June 14, 1819, living in the family of his father in 1850, age 26, and in the family of his brother Amos in 1880, age 59. He died Dec. 8, 1888, and was buried in the family burying ground. As far as known he was never married. His death was caused by an accident when he was driving an ox team. He was knocked down by one of his oxen, and the heavy cart passed over his body, injuring him internally. He managed to get back to the house, but died from his injuries.

10. MARY M., born about 1820, was living in Biddeford at the time of the 1850 (age 30) and 1860 census, married June 11, 1846, Lorenzo Dow Staples of Biddeford, son of William S. and Susannah K. (Small) Staples of Limington. He died Jan. 6, 1894, age 71 yrs., in Biddeford.

11. CHARITY ANN, born Jan. 17, 1822, married as his second wife on Sept. 15, 1848, William A. Dresser. She died Dec. 18, 1897, age 75 yrs., 11 mos., and 1 day, in Buxton. William A. Dresser died Jan. 6, 1880, age 72 yrs., Portland, of West

Buxton. They lived in Bangor and finally in Buxton where they are buried.

ix. DANIEL, born in 1778, according to an obituary notice, age 72 yrs. in 1850 census record, 76 yrs. in 1855 pension record, but born in 1781 according to cemetery stone in Unity, Maine, which seems to be in error. Married Sept. 5, 1799, Lettice Harding, born Mar. 21, 1781, daughter of Amaziah and Hannah (Warren) Harding of Chatham, Mass., and Standish and Unity, Maine. They moved to Unity about 1816 but were back in Standish by time of the 1850 census. He married second Dec. 30, 1849, Olive (Dennett) Dresser, born Nov. 3, 1799, in Buxton and who divorced her former husband, Joseph Dresser, about 1843. She married first June 14, 1830, in Hollis, Joseph Dresser, born Apr. 10, 1790, in Buxton, a veteran of the War of 1812. In 1857 Olive Dresser acting as his widow applied for his pension, the children were listed and living with her in 1850: William D. Dresser, age 17; Daniel R. Dresser, age 15 (born June 6, 1834); and Angelina, age 12 (born June 4, 1837). Daniel died in Unity in Apr. 1872, age 94, but by newspaper obituary it was in 1870 that he died. Daniel and Lettice (Harding) Boulter were the parents of the following children, the first eight born in Standish.

1. SEWALL, born Dec. 25, 1799, in Standish.
2. WILLIAM, and later added Dana as a middle name, born Aug. 24, 1801, in Standish, married (int. Nov. 30, 1829) Phebe Came, born Oct. 6, 1803, in Buxton. He died Sept. 29, 1879, age 77 yrs., and she on Apr. 11, 1883, age 79 yrs., 6 mos., in Saco. They are buried in the Laurel Hill Cemetery in Saco. At the time of the 1850 census he, a lumberman, was living in Limington, but later moved to Saco. There were at least the following children:
    (1) RUSSELL S., born July 9, 1830, and died Aug. 18, 1902, in Saco. Russell married Sarah Whittlemore who died Jan. 1909, age 83 yrs., 7 mos., in Saco. He was the veteran harness manufacturer of Saco.
    (2) BETSEY A., born in Standish Mar. 4, 1832, married May 20, 1853, John Lowell Berry, born in Buxton Apr. 17, 1832, son of Silas and Joanna (Lowell) Berry. He was a tanner and lived in Saco and Amesbury, Mass., and Woodfords, Cornish, and Windham, Maine. He and his wife died in Windham, she on Mar. 21, 1913, and he on Oct. 29, 1914.
    (3) NANCY L., born 1834 in Limington, died May 8, 1860, age 26 yrs., 4 mos., in Saco.
    (4) ROYAL BREWSTER, born Feb. 14, 1837, died May 27, 1904, age 67 yrs., 3 mos., and 13 days, in Saco.
    (5) ANNIS C., born about 1839 Limington, married June 25, 1859, Gilbert A. Sawyer, both of Saco. She died Aug. 3, 1915, in Plymouth, Mass.
    (6) CLARY C., born about 1842, Limington.
    (7) MARY F., born Dec. 18, 1845, Limington, died Feb. 26, 1926, in Saco.

3. SIMEON H., born Sept. 22, 1803, married Huldah S. Hutchins of Knox, Maine. He settled in Knox prior to 1830. He died in Knox Aug. 3, 1872, age 69 yrs., 11 mos., and she on Jan. 16, 1873, age 66 yrs., 7 mos. Their children were:
   (1) CHARLES H., born about 1828, living in 1850, age 22 yrs., in Knox. He was living in 1872.
   (2) LETICE MELINE, born about 1830, married May 3, 1853, Isaac E. Morse, both of Knox.
   (3) MARTHA J., born about 1832, married Feb. 22, 1856, John K. Brown, both of Knox. She died Sept. 16, 1905, in Knox.
   (4) MARY A., born about 1834, married Emery Worton Bradbury. She was living in 1880, aged 46 yrs., in Knox.
   (5) JOSEPH HAWKINS, born July 28, 1836, died Sept. 1, 1915, in Knox, Maine.
   (6) ALPHEUS, born about 1837, died Sept. 1862, age 25 yrs., in last battle of Bull Run.
   (7) ALMEDA, born about 1839.
   (8) HENRY HUTCKINS, born about 1844.
4. MARY, born Oct. 1, 1805, married Joseph Hockey of Freedom, Maine, on Sept. 11, 1825. They moved to Boston or vicinity.
5. GEORGE, born Dec. 13, 1807.
6. STEPHEN, born Feb. 17, 1809, married Rebecca P. Collamore, second Elizabeth H. Beck of Natick, Mass. He died June 22, 1845. Another source says he was born Feb. 16, 1810, and died Dec. 8, 1856.
7. DANIEL, JR., born Dec. 23, 1811, married (int. Feb. 1835, in Standish) Adeline Higgins, born Mar. 11, 1808, daughter of Robert and Sarah (Whitney) Higgins of Standish. He died in 1883 and she in 1881, both buried at Saco. Their children were:
   (1) MELISSA, born about 1835.
   (2) ELLEN, born about 1837, married Mar. 17, 1860, George Littlefield, both of Saco.
   (3) AUGUSTA, born about 1839 in Freedom, Maine, married Almon Hanson. She died May 9, 1898, age 58 yrs., 10 mos., 2 days, Kennebunk.
   (4) BIANCA, born about 1841.
   (5) MARTHA, born 1843, died 1866. Buried at Saco.
   (6) ADELINE LOANTHA, born 1848 in Thorndike, married John E. Webster. She died May 24, 1910, age 61 yrs., at Old Orchard.
   (7) MARY, born about 1847.
   (8) LEWIS, went west.
8. ROYAL, born Sept. 17, 1813, according to Standish records, Sept. 24, 1815, according to family register. Whether this is the same or two persons, the first dying, is not known. But the second Royal married Caroline M. Fairbanks on Apr. 26, 1836, in Freedom, Maine. She was born at Bristol, Maine, on June 14, 1814, and died in Unity, Maine, Apr. 11, 1892. He died there on Jan. 3, 1895, age 79 yrs., 3 mos., and 11 days. They were the parents of the following children, all born in Unity:

(1) LLEWELYN, born June 6, 1837.
   (2) EUGENE, born June 16, 1838.
   (3) WILLIAM F., born Mar. 1, 1842, died Aug. 31, 1870.
   (4) LAROY S., born Feb. 26, 1844.
   (5) FLAURIS B., born Feb. 3, 1846, died July 9, 1848.
   (6) JUNIUS B., born Dec. 26, 1849, died Mar. 26, 1861.
9. AMAZIAH HARDING, born in 1818 in Unity, died in 1901, married first Lydia Boothby; second Esther Johnson, born in 1817, daughter of Elisha Johnson, died in 1846; third Mary F. Jones, born in 1836, died in 1882; fourth Mrs. Eunice (Lampson) Gove; fifth Mary Patterson.
10. RUTH, born ____, married Fletcher Johnson of Unity.
x. GRACE, born ____, married Sept. 16, 1801, Nathaniel Townsend Jr. of Hollis.
xi. BETSEY, born about 1782, living in 1850 age 68, and 1860 age 78 in Sebago with her daughter. She married Apr. 2, 1806, Abraham York, born about 1783 son of Isaac and Betsey (Meserve) York of Standish. They were living in Sebago in 1830. For children see York family.

BOOTMAN OR BUTMAN

A Broadstreet (Bradsteet?) Bootman is found on the 1789 and 1790 tax lists of Standish, but by the time the 1790 census was taken he was living in Portland with a family of 1-2-3. It seems likely that this was the same Broadstreet Bootman who with his mother Mary Bootman was ordered to leave the town of New Gloucester or to bring sufficient bonds to the selectmen on behalf of the town on Oct. 22, 1774, as found in a document recorded in Book 8, page 14 at the Cumberland County Registry of Deeds. A Bradstreet Bootman served in the Revolutionary War from the town of New Boston (Gray), Maine.

Bradstreet Bootman and Susanna Riggs, both of Falmouth, entered their names and purpose of marriage on Feb. 16, 1777, and were married on the twenty-seventh of the same month. She was the widow of Lt. John Riggs who was killed at the Battle of Lake Champlain on Oct. 11, 1776. Broadstreet Bootman married second Dec. 25, 1794, Thankful (Parker) Sawyer, widow of Barnabas Sawyer who died in the Revolution, she then of Cape Elizabeth. She died Aug. 21, 1834, age 83 years, and was buried in the Eastern Cemetery in Portland.

It has not been determined how long he was an inhabitant of Standish, nor has the record of ownership of any land in the town been found.

Because of the comparatively short length of his stay in town, no attempt has been made to uncover data concerning his family.

BOYNTON

Daniel Boynton and his wife, Mary, were admitted to the Congregational Church of Standish on Jan. 26, 1794, probably about the same time that their son Hugh Moor Boynton was baptized there. It is likely that they were inhabitants of Buxton, but perhaps were living in that part of the town which in 1824 was annexed to Standish, as did his wife's parents.

Daniel Boynton was born Mar. 12, 1771, son of William and Mary (McLucas) Boynton of Buxton and was known as junior to distinguish him from his Uncle Daniel. On Dec. 6, 1792, he married Mary Moor, born Aug. 9, 1774, daughter of Hugh and Margaret (Nesmith) Moor of Buxton. About 1808 he and his brother Moses Boynton moved with their families to Monmouth, Maine, and settled on the Moses Waterhouse place in that town. Here he died in 1837. He was a mason. Among children of Daniel and Mary (Moor) Boynton were the following:

i. HUGH MOOR, born in Mar. 1793, married first Mary, daughter of Daniel Prescott of Monmouth; second Mrs. Harriet Batchelder of Belmont, Maine.
ii. MARY M., born Aug. 8, 1795, married Cyrus Stebbins Hillman, son of Rev. Samuel Hillman.
iii. EBENEZER A., born Aug. 8, 1797, married his cousin Ann M. Heath, daughter of Rev. Asa and Sarah (Moor) Heath. He died Mar. 6, 1869.
iv. MARGARET M., born Nov. 10, 1800, married her cousin Dr. Asa Heath, son of of Rev. Asa and Sarah (Moor) Heath.
v. DANIEL, born Feb. 5 1805, married Eliza, daughter of Benjamin Kimball Jr. of Monmouth. He died in July 1852 while on his way to California.
vi. JAMES COCKRANE, born Apr. 1, 1808, married Harriet Warren. He was a physician and lived in Richmond, Maine. He died July 27, 1875, and she died in 1884.

BRADBURY

Thomas Bradbury was one of those who fled from Falmouth (Portland) to Pearsontown after the burning of that place by the British in Oct. 1775. His name is found on a list of the inhabitants of Pearsontown dated July 15, 1776, signed to an agreement relating to lands granted by the Proprietors for support of a school. It is likely that his stay in town was not very long, probably lasting only until return to Falmouth was considered safe and living guarters for his family had been rebuilt.

Thomas Bradbury (Wymond,[4] Wymond,[3] Wymond,[2] Thomas[1]), born May 8, 1736, son of Wymond and Mary (Donnell) Bradbury, married Sept. 18, 1764, Hannah Freeman, born about 1745 daughter of Joshua and Patience (Rogers) Freeman of Falmouth. Since his father-in-law, Joshua Freeman, was one of the active Proprietors of Pearsontown and his brother-in-law George Freeman was one of the earliest permanent residents of the town, while another brother-in-law, Reuben Freeman, lived in town for a number of years during its earliest history, it is clear why he happened to retire to this town after the burning of Falmouth. He was a housewright or carpenter and owned the 30-acre lot #6 which he sold to John Marean on Dec. 18, 1798 (36/242 and 36/243). His wife died in Aug. 1829 and he died in Sept. 1812, age 76 years, in Portland (*Eastern Argus*, Oct. 1, 1812). Thomas and Hannah (Freeman) Bradbury were parents of the following family:

i. MARY, born Aug. 11, 1765, married first Pettingill, second Joseph Plummer.
ii. HANNAH, born Mar. 21, 1767, married William Moulton.
iii. JABEZ, born Jan. 1, 1769, died Mar. 1778.
iv. DANIEL, born May 17, 1771, married Rhoda Plummer.
v. THOMAS JR., born Mar. 4, 1775, married Dorcas Mitchell.
vi. CHARLES, born Oct. 20, 1777, bapt. Oct. 26, 1777, married Jane Brackett.
vii. WILLIAM, born Apr. 18, 1781, bapt. Apr. 29, 1781, married Mary Brackett.
viii. ALMIRA, born Dec. 14, 1784, married first Joseph Hale, second James P. Stetson.
ix. HENRY, born Aug. 19, 1787, died unmarried.

BURBANK

John Burbank was another of those men who lived in Standish for a few years at the beginning of the nineteenth century. His name is found on the 1808 and 1814 tax lists of the town and in 1810 census with a family consisting of him and his wife, both between 26 and 45 years of age, one male and one female between 10 and 16 years old, and five females under 10 years of age. He was born in Kennebunkport on Aug. 19, 1776, son of Asa[5] (John,[4] Caleb,[3] Caleb,[2] John,[1]) and Eunice (Hutchins) Burbank and married first on Feb. 1, 1798, Susan (Stowell) Burbank, widow of his brother of his brother David. She died in Saco in 1805, age 35, and he married second (int. Dec. 6, 1805) Sarah, daughter of Abijah and Lydia (Clark) Felch of Limerick, Maine. In his early life he was a cabinet maker and lived in Saco. About 1805, probably soon after his second marriage, he moved to Standish where he continued to live at least until after the War of 1812, in which he served as a lieutenant colonel from Standish in command of a regiment of militia that saw service from Sept. 7 to Sept. 20, 1814. By 1822 he was living in Bridgton where he sold a farm located at North Bridgton that year. He died Oct. 29, 1842, age 66 years, and his wife died Sept. 9, 1845, age 67 years, both in Bridgton. John Burbank was the father of at least the following children:

i. DAVID, born in 1799, was living in Portland when he married Sept. 16, 1823, Sophia Andrews of Bridgton.
ii. TAMAR, born June 26, 1800, married Capt. Hezekiah Adams and died in Warrenton (?), Maine, in 1876.
iii. JOHN, born July 7, 1802, died young.

iv. SUSANNA, born July 5, 1804, married Samuel McLellan of Upper Stillwater, Maine.

By his second wife:

v. SARAH PHIPS, born Jan. 4, 1807, in Standish, died 1854, married Feb. 28, 1828, Timothy Sedgley of Limington, Maine, at which time she was a resident of Bridgton, and lived in New Portland, Maine.
vi. SOPHRONIA, born Mar. 28, 1808, in Standish, married Capt. Samuel Andrews of Bridgton, Maine.
vii. NANCY EMERY, born Aug. 10, 1809, in Standish, married Elias Berry of Bridgton and died June 23, 1893, age 83 yrs., 10 mos., 13 days, in West Boylston, Mass.
viii. JOHN F., born Dec. 4, 1811, in Standish, died Nov. 15, 1853, married (int. Feb. 20, 1841) Lucy Ann Loring of Portland. She died in 1847, age 34 yrs. He was a Baptist minister.
ix. DANIEL EDWIN, born Dec. 22, 1813, in Standish, died in Oct. 24, 1840, at the age of 27. He married May 1837 Catherine Stevens of Guilford. He was a Baptist preacher in Winthrop, Maine.
x. LYDIA C., born about 1816, married in 1837 Mial Jordan Merrill of Bridgton.
xi. HARRIET RIPLEY, born Oct. 17, 1817, married John Felch, born Jan. 1, 1795, Limerick and died May 20, 1870, Livonia, Minn. She married second Mar. 28, 1871, in LeRoy, Minn., Hiram Hall Bither, who was born Aug. 9, 1836, in Linneus, Maine, and died June 7, 1920. She died Apr. 10, 1895, in LeRoy, Minn.
xii. ABIJAH FELCH, born about 1820, died June 19, 1888, age 68 yrs., Worcester, Mass., formerly of Bridgton. He was a jeweler.
xiii. ASA L., born about 1821, died Mar. 18, 1899, age 77 yrs., 8 mos., 9 days, in Worcester, Mass.
xiv. CHARLES W., born 1824, died 1851, married Eliza J. Phillips of Worcester, Mass.

BURNELL

A John Burnell was one of those who were living in Pearsontown prior to 1760. He was one of the men serving as a guard for the new fort here in 1755. His residence was given as Pearsontown at the time of filing of his intention of marriage to Elizabeth Freeman of Falmouth on Sept. 6, 1756, to whom he was married on Nov. 18, 1756, by the Rev. Ephraim Clark of Cape Elizabeth. He was sergeant of the Pearsontown garrison to 1757 and was given as a resident of the town when he served from May to September in 1759 in Capt. William Gerrish's company in His Majesty's Service. His name is also among those of men from Pearsontown who were paid for work on Gorham roads for the years 1760 and 1761. He was granted the 5-acre lot #2 in Pearsontown by right of settlement.

Since his name is found on a tax list of Gorham for 1763, it is likely that he moved to that town before that date. He is given as living in Gorham on Feb. 20, 1767, when he sold the 5-acre lot to Ebenezer Shaw of Pearsontown. He also was living in Gorham on Apr. 14, 1766, when he bought from Isaac Illesley Jr. of Falmouth the 30-acre lot #39 in Pearsontown and on Mar. 26, 1767, when he sold the same lot to Daniel Cram of Pearsontown (5/60, 5/62, and 5/64). After living for a number of years in Gorham, where all of his children are said to have been born, he moved about 1780 to Flintstown (Baldwin) where he afterward lived and where he died in 1804, his wife, Elizabeth, surviving him until 1827.

Although nothing definite has been discovered about his parentage, he may have been the John Burnell, born about Apr. 1717 son of John and Mehitable (Edmonds) Burnell according to Lynn, Mass., records. If so, he must have been about 40 at the time of his marriage, but the fact that he was sergeant of the guard at the Pearsontown Fort may indicate that he was an older man.

John and Elizabeth (Freeman) Burnell were parents of the following children:

i. MARY, born Dec. 17, 1763, married (int. Nov. 24, 1781) Thomas Skillings, born May 8, 1748, son of Benjamin and Mary (Pride) Skillings of Falmouth and Gorham. They lived in Gorham where he died May 12, 1810, age 61, and she on Aug. 5, 1846, age 82. They were parents of the following children: (Skillings)
   1. BENJAMIN, born Oct. 12, 1782, married Mar. 14, 1804, Anna Hamblen, born Jan. 16, 1783, daughter of Timothy and Anna (Harding) Hamblen. They lived in Gorham and Westbrook.
   2. JOHN H., born Aug. 2, 1784, married (int. Apr. 6, 1822) Mary Cobb, born in Mar. 1803 daughter of Elisha Jr., and Molly (Murch) Cobb of Gorham. They moved to Strong, Maine.
   3. ISAAC, born May 24, 1786, married June 8, 1810, Elizabeth Thomes, born Sept. 26, 1784, daughter of Amos and Mehitable (Burnell) Thomes of Standish. She died Nov. 9, 1861, age 77 yrs. They lived in Standish where the following children were born to them: (Skillings)
      (1) EUNICE T., born Apr. 9, 1811.
      (2) THOMAS, born June 25, 1814.
      (3) AMOS T., born Nov. 9, 1816, married Margaret Cotton.
      (4) CALEB C., born July 27, 1820.
      (5) MARY M., born June 7, 1824.
   4. THOMAS, born Apr. 12, 1788, died unmarried Nov. 19, 1850.
   5. MEHITABLE, born June 19, 1791, married Dec. 19, 1813, John Thomes, born Nov. 16, 1790, son of Amos and Mehitable (Burnell) Thomes of Standish. They lived in Standish.
   6. BETSEY, born Nov. 15, 1793, died unmarried Nov. 26, 1850.
   7. POLLY, born Sept. 20, 1796, died unmarried Dec. 14, 1850.
   8. CALEB, born Dec. 3, 1798, married Nov. 21, 1833, Esther Irish, born in 1806 daughter of Benjamin and Jenny (Libby) Irish of Gorham.
   9. DANIEL, born Dec. 15, 1802, died in Aug. 1847.
   10. MARTHA, born ____.

ii. JOHN, born Feb. 14, 1766, married Jane Holbrook Jan. 25, 1787, and settled in Baldwin with his father.

iii. BENJAMIN, born Feb. 27, 1768, married Dorcas Carsley Dec. 28, 1788, she born Aug. 5, 1768, daughter of Ebenezer and Patience (Phinney) Carsley of Gorham. He died June 17, 1851, age 83, and she on July 19, 1842, age 73 yrs., 11 mos.

iv. SAMUEL, born July 17, 1770, married Sept. 18, 1791, Amy Irish, born Apr. 3, 1770, daughter of Thomas and Deliverance (Skillings) Irish of Gorham. They lived in Baldwin where she died Jan. 26, 1861, age 90 yrs. He died Aug. 27, 1860, age 90. Children as follows:
1. MARY, born Jan. 9, 1792.
2. SUSAN, born May 10, 1794, died Aug. 22, 1828.
3. REBECCA, born Feb. 28, 1795, died Mar. 17, 1874.
4. THOMAS, born Apr. 5, 1796, married Dec. 12, 1819, Lydia Butterfield, daughter of John and Elizabeth (Lord) Butterfield. She died Nov. 30, 1867, age 68 yrs., 9 mos., and he on Nov. 22, 1877, in West Baldwin, age 81 yrs., 6 mos.
5. DELILAH, born Nov. 4, 1797.
6. JONATHAN, born Jan. 4, 1799, died June 6, 1888, W. Baldwin.
7. SALLY, born Feb. 28, 1800.
8. BENJAMIN, born Sept. 14, 1802, died in May 1866.
9. RUTH, born Feb, 23, 1804.
10. AMOS, born Oct. 5, 1806, according to Bible, 1805 according to gravestone, died Nov. 9, 1855, in Baldwin.
11. ELEAZER, born Apr. 25, 1808, died Aug. 11, 1883.
v. ELIZABETH, born Sept. 21, 1772, married Sept. 8, 1791, William Nason, born Feb. 1, 1770, son of Uriah and Abigail (Knight) Nason of Gorham. They settled in Sebago where he died by drowning.
vi. STEPHEN, born Apr. 22, 1775, married Nov. 28, 1799, Polly Sanborn, born Aug. 11, 1779, daughter of Jonathan and Rachel (Fifield) Sanborn. They lived in Baldwin where she died July 23, 1847, age 67 yrs., 11 mos. Children as follows: (Burnell)
1. MARY, born Mar. 1, 1801.
2. ELIAS, born Feb. 5, 1803.
3. ELIZA, born Sept. 25, 1804.
4. RACHEL, born May 25, 1807.
5. STEPHEN, born Sept. 30, 1810, died July 13, 1885.
6. ALFRED, born Apr. 10, 1813.
7. CYRUS FREEMAN, born July 27, 1819, died June 17, 1913.
vii. JONATHAN, born Aug. 14, 1778, married Mar. 8, 1802, Eliza Richardson of Baldwin.
viii. NABBY (ABIGAIL), born June 11, 1781, married (int. Feb. 1, 1802) David Lowell of Baldwin.
ix. SALLY, born Oct. 1784 or 1786, married Joseph Harden and lived in Denmark where they both died, she in 1856.

BURNHAM

In the records of the Congregational Church of Standish is found the admittance of Reuben Burnham to full communion on Sept. 19, 1779. Research discloses that he was from Ipswich and Boxford, Massachusetts. On March 10, 1756, he married Elizabeth (Smith) Smith of Ipswich. They lived in Ipswich, Winchendon, Lunenburg, and Boxford,

Mass., until about 1774 when they settled on lot #6, range 12 in Bridgton, Maine. At that time there was no organized church in Bridgton and the breaking out of the Revolutionary War making Indian raids upon the infant settlement likely, some of the settlers including (probably) Reuben Burnham moved their families to Pearsontown for safety. This is the likely reason he became a member of the Pearsontown Church and why his son Jeremiah is given as enlisting in the Revolutionary army from Pearsontown. He returned to his settlement in Bridgton as soon as it was deemed safe to do so and was killed in the woods in 1785 by the falling of a tree. When the Bridgton Church was organized he became its first deacon.

His first wife apparently died not long after their removal to Bridgton, for in the Boxford, Mass., records under the date of Oct. 23, 1777, is found the marriage of Reuben Burnam of Bridgton and widow Hannah Foster.

Reuben and Elizabeth (Smith) Burnham were the parents of the following children:

i. PHEBE, born at Lunenburg, Mass., Apr. 6, 1757.
ii. JEREMIAH, born at Ipswich, Mass., July 18, 1759.
iii. SALOME, born at Ipswich, Mass., Sept. 1, 1761, died between 1763 and 1766.
iv. EUNICE, born at Ipswich, Mass., Sept. 17, 1763.
v. ABRAHAM SMITH, born at Winchendon, Mass., Dec. 30, 1765.
vi. TIMOTHY DORMAN, born at Ipswich, Mass., Feb. 2, 1768.
vii. NATHANIEL, born at Boxford, Mass., Dec. 22, 1769.

BURNHAM

While he did not become a resident of Standish until 1820 or after, Joel[5] (David,[4] Moses,[3] Moses,[2] Thomas[1]) Burnham became a prominent citizen of the western part of the town. He was born in Scarboro, on Jan. 17, 1781, son of David and Olive (Berry) Burnham, and married there on Nov. 27, 1799, Anna Foss, according to the records of the Second Congregational Church. Her name by family register is given as Anna but appears as Nancy on her gravestone inscription. They moved from Scarboro to Hollis where they lived near Hollis Center and where the births of their first six children were recorded. Later on, they moved to a farm on the bank of the Saco River in Standish near Limington Bridge on the River Road. He and his sons were operators of sawmills at Limington Falls on both sides of the river. Just when he came into town is not known but it probably was before 1825. He continued to live in Standish until his death on Feb. 3, 1866, at the age of 85 years and 18 days. His wife passed away on Sept. 2, 1860, age 77 years, 3 months, and 11 days. Both were buried in a family graveyard on their farm in Standish. They were the parents of thirteen children as follows:

i. JOHN, born Apr. 28, 1800 in Hollis, died Jan. 29, 1815, in Hollis.
ii. BENJAMIN, born Jan. 3, 1802, married Oct. 16, 1822, Sarah Phinney, born about 1800, daughter of Coleman and Margaret (Moor) Phinney of Standish. He died June 9, 1874 in Bristol, R.I.

iii. HANNAH, born Dec. 30, 1804, married George Berry of Standish and second Solomon Haskell, born in Standish in 1805 son of John Haskell and Eunice (Chick) Foss, widow of Job Foss. She died June 7, 1861.
iv. AMOS, born June 7, 1806, in Hollis, married Feb. 11, 1830, Sarah (Sally) M. Whitmore, born in 1812 daughter of William Jr., and Betsey (Heath) Whitmore. He died in Taunton, Mass., May 10, 1872, and she died in 1885. They lived in Taunton, Mass., over 30 years.
v. NICHOLAS STICKNEY, known as Stickney, born Sept. 28, 1808, married first on June 30, 1830, Elizabeth (Betsey) Chick, born June 24, 1810, daughter of Peter and Abigail (Haskell) Chick of Limington, and she died Aug. 12, 1833; second (int. Nov. 1834) Thankful H. Whitney, born Oct. 15, 1805, daughter of William and Hannah (Bangs) Whitney of Standish, and she died July 6, 1841; third on Nov. 27, 1841 Hannah Hutchinson, born July 5, 1813, daughter of Matthias and Nancy Hutchinson of Standish. He died Nov. 8, 1873, in Gorham. Children by Hannah (Whitney) Burnham were as follows:
1. HANNAH ELIZABETH, born Oct. 22, 1835, died July 28, 1911, married Nov. 30, 1854, Alonzo Moses, born Feb. 5, 1836, son of Cyrus and Eunice (Underwood) Moses of Standish, and he died Jan. 13, 1913. Both were buried in the Moses Cemetery on the River Road at South Standish. They lived in Standish.
2. WILLIAM W., born about 1839 (age 11 in 1850). He was living Taunton, Mass., in 1874. He died Feb. 16, 1907, age 67 yrs., Westbrook.
3. LEWIS NAPOLEAN ("POLE"), born Apr. 5, 1840, married Martha M. Pinkham, born in 1844 daughter of James E. and Martha T. (_____) Pinkham of Buxton.
4. AN INFANT, born in 1841, died at the age of six weeks, and was buried in the same grave as his mother in Moses Cemetery.
By Hannah (Hutchinson) Burnham:
5. LAURETTA, born about 1842 (age 8 in 1850).
6. MARY T., born 1843, died Feb. 27, 1896, age 52 yrs., 4 mos., Westbrook.
7. SARAH, born about 1846 (age 4 in 1850).
8. CHARLES E., born about 1849 (age 1 in 1850).
9. NANCY A., born in 1850 (age 2 mos. in 1850).
vi. PERLEY FOSTER (Foster in Hollis records), born July 25, 1810, married Mar. 15, 1832, Sophronia B. Hutchinson of Standish, who died Jan. 8, 1897, age 86 yrs., 10 mos. She was a sister of Nicholas S. Burnham's wife. He died Nov. 10, 1892, age 82 yrs. They lived in Standish and were buried in the family graveyard on the old Joel Burnham place.
vii. A DAUGHTER, born Feb. 15, 1813, died in infancy.
viii. OLIVE MARY, born Feb. 26, 1814, married Feb. 17, 1834 Benjamin Kennerson, son of Nathaniel and Lydia (Nason) Kennerson of Limington. She died May 10, 1890, at Barre, Mass.

ix. JOHN, born Mar. 30, 1817, married in Standish Aug. 15, 1843, Eliza York, born in Freedom, Maine, Dec. 16, 1815, daughter of David and Sally (Haselton) York of Alfred, Freedom, and Naples, Maine. They lived in Standish where she died Mar. 5, 1856, and he married second Sarah M. Libby, who died Sept. 11, 1896, age 71 yrs., 4 mos. Both were buried in the family graveyard on the Burnham farm, as well as his first wife, Eliza York. He died in Standish Aug. 18, 1883, age 60 yrs. and 4 mos.

x. ELIZA ANNE, born Apr. 30, 1819, married Nov. 29, 1839 Isaac Kennerson, born Mar. 16, 1818, son of Nathaniel and Lydia (Nason) Kennerson of Limington. After his death she married Sept. 13, 1866, Charles D. Capen, both of New Bedford, Mass.

xi. RUTH WADSWORTH, born May 17, 1822, married Joshua Gammon and died Feb. 5, 1886.

xii. EUNICE CLARK, born Apr. 26, 1825, married Nelson Leadbetter.

xiii. SARAH JANE, born Sept. 1, 1828, married William S. Hall.

BUTLER

The name of William Butler is found on the 1795, 1796, 1808, and 1814 tax lists of Standish and in the 1800 census with a family consisting of him and his wife, four males and one female under 10 years of age and one male between 16 and 25 years old. He was born in Berwick, Maine, May 5, 1771, son of Moses and Keziah (Nason) Butler, and married Abigail Cross of Portsmouth, New Hampshire. They evidently moved to Standish soon after their marriage, for all of their children were born there. He is given as a blacksmith in a deed passed June 26, 1807, when he bought one-quarter acre of the south corner of 30-acre lot #32 from William Lamson (54/490). William Butler and Abigail, his wife, of Standish sold two pieces of land in Standish to Nehemiah Cram of Sandwich, N.H., on Jan. 5, 1819. Dates and place of death of William Butler and his wife have not been found. They were parents of the following family:

i. WILLIAM E. born Aug. 5, 1793, married May 27, 1817, Hannah Paine, born Feb. 17, 1792, daughter of Myrick and Dorcas (Myrick) Paine of Standish. They moved to Thomaston, Maine, and were the parents of seven children. He died Dec. 13, 1880, age 88 yrs. Buried in Hillcrest Cemetery, Hollis.

ii. IVORY, born Dec. 3, 1794, married May 11, 1817, Sarah Shaw, born Mar. 21, 1794, daughter of Ebenezer Jr. and Salome (Green) Shaw of Standish. They lived in Standish, Lebanon, N.H., and other places until 1846 when he received a grant of land in Lawn Ridge, Ill., to which they moved and where he died in 1870. They were the parents of five children.

iii. THOMAS CASS, born Mar. 6, 1796, married and lived at Derby Line, Vt., where he was collector of customs. He was the father of one child.

iv. JOHN O., born Feb. 7, 1798, died Dec. 28, 1817.

v. **ABIGAIL C.**, born Oct. 19, 1800, married Samuel Butler of Moultonborough, N.H., on Mar. 1, 1825, had one child, and died Feb. 3, 1831.
vi. **SUSAN G.**, born Oct. 23, 1802, married Ebenezer Ricker of Lebanon, Maine, and had four children. She died Sept. 1877.
vii. **MOSES**, born June 30, 1805, married June 18, 1832, Grace B. Vittum, born in Sandwich, N.H., on Dec. 12, 1808. They had five children.
viii. **MARY ANN**, born Feb. 1, 1810, nothing further known.

BUTTERFIELD

Joseph Butterfield was an inhabitant of Pearsontown prior to the Revolutionary War, in which as far as is known he did not see service. His name is found in a list of those living in town in 1776, on the 1788, 1789, 1790, 1795, 1796, 1799 and later tax lists, in the 1790 census with a family of 1-6-5, and in the 1800 census when his family consisted of him and his wife, one male and three females between 16 and 25 years of age, and two males between 10 and 16 years old. He was of Pearsontown on Oct. 30, 1770, when he bought from Benjamin Titcomb of Falmouth the 100-acre lot #41 in the second division bordering Sebago Pond. This lot was located on Standish Neck, on which he is said to have been the first settler. A Joseph Butterfield was taxed for one poll on a tax list of Falmouth in 1776, and it seems likely that he was the same man as the Pearsontown settler. On Mar. 14, 1781, Joseph Butterfield bought from Benjamin Titcomb of Falmouth the 30-acre lot #107 (10/536); on May 25, 1779, the 30-acre lot #108 from Ebenezer Shaw, on which Shaw then lived (13/179); and on Dec. 21, 1790, the 30-acre lot #109 from Joshua Whitney (17/470). It appears that he moved from Standish Neck to these lots located on the road from Standish Corner to Sebago Lake Village. Joseph Butterfield (William,[4] Samuel,[3] Nathaniel,[2] Benjamin[1]) was born July 1, 1741, either in Chelmsford, Mass., or Londonderry, N.H., son of William and Rebecca (Parker) Butterfield. He married Nov. 25, 1773 (int. Sept. 2, 1773, in Gorham), Mary Harding, born in 1750 daughter of John and Thankful (Rich) Harding of Eastham, Mass., and Gorham, Maine. They were admitted to membership in the Pearsontown Church on Mar. 24, 1776. He died in Standish Sept. 12, 1819, age 78 years, and she died Sept. 30, 1830, age 80 years. They were the parents of the following children:

i. **MARY**, born May 16, 1774 (bapt. July 16, 1775), married Oct. 5, 1796, (int. July 30, 1796) Isaac B. Elwell, son of Jonathan and Abigail (Hilton) Elwell of Gorham. For children see Elwell family.
ii. **JOSEPH**, born Dec. 7, 1775 (bapt. Sept. 1, 1776), married Sarah Richardson, born Dec. 6, 1776, daughter of Moses and Lydia (Hall) Richardson of Standish, on Oct. 11, 1798. They were the parents of the following children:
1. **LYDIA**, born Feb. 16, 1799.
2. **JOSEPH**, born Dec. 7, 1800.

3. JESSE, born May 27, 1803, died Sept. 30, 1886, W. Baldwin.
4. EDMUND, born Aug. 14, 1805.

iii. JOHN, born May 24, 1777, bapt. July 20, 1777, married first Elizabeth Lord of Standish on Jan. 22, 1798, and second on Jan. 13, 1825, Catherine Colburn, widow of Abner Benson and daughter of Jerathnael Colburn Sr. He died in Paris Sept. 2, 1824. He was the father of eight children, four by second wife and four by first, one of whom was John, born Jan. 23, 1802, who married first Clarissa Andrews, born Dec. 1801 and died Mar. 24, 1824, at Sumner, Maine; second Elvecy Lurvey, born in Woodstock, Maine, daughter of Job and Betsey (Tobey) Lurvey; and third Martha ____, who died in 1883 at West Sumner.

iv. WILLIAM, born July 14, 1778 (bapt. Oct. 4, 1778), married Oct. 11 1801, Susanna Boothby, daughter of Brice Boothby of Buxton, where they resided. She died Dec. 18, 1837, age 55 yrs., and he on Feb. 12, 1840, 61 yrs., 6 mos. They were the parents of the following children:
1. BRICE, born June 29, 1802.
2. JOSEPH, born Mar. 7, 1804.
3. MIRIAM, born Mar. 6, 1806.
4. WILLIAM, born Aug. 6, 1808, died Aug. 4, 1875, age 68 yrs.
5. ENOCH, born Aug. 20, 1810.
6. SAMUEL, born July 15, 1812.
7. MARY ANN, born Oct. 20, 1814.
8. DANIEL, born May 19, 1817, died June 1818, age 15 mos., Standish.
9. JOHN, born Feb. 12, 1819.
10. SUSAN, born Sept. 27, 1821.
11. LUCINDA, born Apr. 15, 1824.
12. ABIGAIL BRADBURY, born May 5, 1826.
13. BENJAMIN.

v. LUCY, born Dec. 5, 1779 (bapt. Nov. 3, 1780), died July 2, 1861, unmarried. The marriage intentions of William Bangs of Gorham and Lucy Butterfield of Standish were filed in Standish on Feb. 27, 1806. He, born Jan. 17, 1781, was a sailor, and died unmarried of yellow fever in a foreign port.

vi. ANNA, born Nov. 5, 1781 (bapt. Aug. 15, 1794), married Dec. 20, 1801, Levi Cram, son of Daniel and Sarah (Green) Cram of Standish. They lived in Windham where he died Mar. 16, 1816, and she on Mar. 25, 1856. They were the parents of eight children.

vii. THANKFUL, born July 1, 1783 (bapt. Aug. 15, 1794), married on May 19, 1813, "after a comfortable courtship of 12 yrs" William Mussey, born about 1782 son of Daniel and Mary (Gilkey) Mussey of Portland. They lived in Standish where he died Oct. 7, 1863, age 81 yrs., 2 mos., and she on Mar. 30, 1851, age 67 yrs., 9 mos. For children see Mussey family.

viii. SAMUEL, born Apr. 27, 1785, married Jan. 19, 1809 (int. June 12, 1809), Mary Wood, born Feb. 28, 1789, daughter of Charles and Sarah (Davis) Wood of Gorham. They lived in Buxton where he died Nov. 9, 1810. They had a daughter, Eliza Ann, born Aug. 5, 1809.

ix. MOSES, born June 14, 1787 (bapt. Aug. 15, 1794), lived in Standish.

x. JESSE, born Apr. 17, 1789 (bapt. Aug. 15, 1794), married June 10, 1813, Mary (Polly) Morton, born in 1788 daughter of David and Mary (Sanger) Morton of Gorham. He died Aug. 11, 1863, age 74 yrs., in Gorham, formerly of Standish. She died on July 31, 1858, age 70 yrs., 4 mos. They both are buried on old Butterfield farm. They had at least the following children:
1. MARY, bapt. Sept. 29, 1816.
2. MOSES, bapt. Sept. 29, 1816, died Dec. 28, 1889, age 74 yrs., 3 mos.
3. MAJOR, bapt. Nov. 1, 1818, died Apr. 4, 1860, age 41 yrs., 6 mos., Standish.
4. ANNA, bapt. July 22, 1821.

CANDAGE OR CAVENDISH

Among the early settlers living in Pearsontown prior to 1760 was a man by the name of James Cavendish or Candage. Facts as to his parentage have not been discovered but it is thought that he may have been the son of Thomas Cavendish 3rd of Marblehead and born in that town about 1730. On Jan. 29, 1748-9 his intentions of marriage to Elizabeth Millett, born in Gloucester, Mass., Oct. 26, 1724, daughter of John and Bethiah (Bennett) Millett of Gloucester and Falmouth, Maine, were published in Falmouth. He served as a chairman with Joshua Small in Feb. 1753 in party of John Small surveying land in Gorham. His name is found on the roster of Capt. George Berry's company dated July 7, 1749, and he of Falmouth served with Clement Meserve Jr. of Gorham in the company of Captain Daniel Hill of Newbury during the same year.

He was among those men who served in the guard at the fort in Pearsontown and no doubt lived with his family within the walls of the fort. He was one of the men from Pearsontown who served in Lt. Charles Lessner's party scouting eastward from Broad Bay (Waldoboro) about 1759-60 and was also among the Pearsontown men working on Gorham roads in 1760, the name being spelled 'Cavendish'.

By 1763 or before, James Candage had moved to North Yarmouth, because he is given as living in that town on Sept. 7, 1763, when he bought of Benjamin Thrasher right No. 54 in Pearsontown (2/440). However, he was of Falmouth on Aug. 2, 1764, when he bought from Austin Alden of Gorham the 30-acre lot #66 in the first division of lots in Pearsontown (3/74) and was still living in Falmouth on Oct. 27, 1766, when he sold the lot to James Moody, blacksmith, of Falmouth (3/240).

No futher trace of James Candage has been found on the local scene, but it appears almost certain that he was the man by that name who settled in Blue Hill, Maine, in 1766, the same year in which he sold the last of his holdings in Pearsontown. The following account of this James Candage is taken from page 131 of volume 4 of the *Bangor Historical Magazine*:

James Candage settled in Blue Hill, upon the neck, in 1766. He was of the Massachusetts family of that name and went thither it is said from Beverly. At the time he settled at Blue Hill he had a family consisting of his wife, Elizabeth; three sons, James, Joseph, and John; and two daughters, Betty and Lydia. Another daughter, Lucy, was born after removal to Bluehill. Reverend Jonathan Fisher, the first settled minister of the town, says of him in his record, "his name was originally spelled Cavendish, but custom has changed it to Candage; he was one of the first settlers." The maiden name of his wife, Elizabeth, is not known to me; she lived to an advanced age and died in 1809. It is not known in what year James Candage and his wife were born or married. He died in 1788. The family descent so far as I am able to give it is as follows:

James Candage, died 1788; Elizabeth Candage, his wife, died 1809. Children:

i. JAMES, born May 9, 1753, married Hannah Roundy Apr. 13, 1775, died Jan. 12, 1819.
ii. JOSEPH, born Nov. 1754, married Abigail Carter Jan. 7, 1777, died Jan. 12, 1834.
iii. BETTY, born Feb. 1758, married James Day Dec. 2, 1776.
iv. JOHN, born May 10, 1759, married Charity Roundy July 3, 1790, died July 22, 1822. She died Dec. 15, 1848, age 94 yrs., 9 mos., in Bluehill, Maine.
v. LYDIA, born Aug. 1763, married Henry Carter Nov. 25, 1783.
vi. LUCY, born Aug. 19, 1767, at Blue Hill, married Thomas Carter.

CANNELL

The name of Philip Cannell is found on the 1789, 1790, 1795, 1796, 1808, and 1814 tax lists of Standish and in the 1790 census with a family of 4-2-5. He is said to have come from Isle of Man to Falmouth (Portland) before the Revolution and to have removed to Pearsontown about 1770. He was living in Pearsontown on Jan. 4, 1772, when he bought from Timothy Hamblen of Gorham the 30-acre lot #54 in Pearsontown (15/91). He is called a cooper on May 17, 1783, when he bought from Moses Parker of Newton, Mass., the 30-acre lot #53. On May 22, 1784, he bought from Jonathan Sanborn of Pearsontown the 30-acre lot #123 (15/92). He died June 6, 1824, age 81 years, and his obituary mentions that he was a native of Isle of Man, in the June 11, 1824, issue of *Christian Mirror*. His wife, Jane, maiden name unknown, died in 1826, age 81 years. They were the parents of the following children:
i. NANCY, born on Isle of Man Oct. 16, 1766, married Aug. 16, 1789 (int. July 30, 1789), Joseph West, then of Raymond. She died in Standish Feb. 7, 1835, age 78 years. For children see West family.

ii. THOMAS, born about 1768, married (published June 30, 1797, in Gorham) Margaret Nason, daughter of Uriah and Abigail (Knight) Nason of Gorham. Shortly after his marriage he moved to Gorham, where he afterwards lived in the Nason District. He died there Mar. 12, 1854, age 86, and his wife on Dec. 28, 1855, age 77 yrs., 5 mos. They are buried at North Gorham. They were the parents of the following children:
 1. HANNAH, born Mar. 28, 1798, married Ebenezer Gilman Jr. (published July 22, 1820).
 2. WILLIAM, born June 2, 1799, married Ann Plaisted of Standish Nov. 1, 1832. In 1850 they were of Gorham.
 3. JOSEPH, born Mar. 28, 1801, married Temperance Sturgis Apr. 29, 1821. He died Oct. 22, 1873, she on Dec. 26 1887, age 89 yrs., 5 mos. Buried in cemetery at North Gorham.
 4. WYER, born Feb. 23, 1803, married Francis Plaisted in 1831, who died Jan. 30, 1841, age 27 yrs., 9 mos. He married second Sarah Harmon of Scarboro. He died Mar. 8, 1848, age 45 yrs. Buried in cemetery at North Gorham.
 5. LOT, born Feb. 13, 1805, went to Bangor when young, died in Calif.
 6. JANE, born Oct. 23, 1806, married Daniel Nason of Sebago Sept. 21, 1828.
 7. MARGARET, born Aug. 1, 1808, married John Bennett of New York, died May 13, 1882, age 73 yrs., 9 mos.
 8. HULDAH, born Jan. 27, 1811, died June 10, 1821.
 9. ESTHER, born Jan. 27, 1813, married John Rhodes (or Rowe).
 10. CLARK, born Jan. 28, 1815, married first Mar. 15, 1840, Sarah A. Harmon; married second Dorcas M. Plaisted in 1846; married third Elsie Wood. He died in Feb. 1900.
 11. BARNABAS, born Nov. 28, 1816, married Lorana Manchester, May 16, 1847, died in Mar. 1900.
 12. HEMAN, born Mar. 5, 1821, married Lucy A. Gilman. He died in 1895 and she in 1868.

iii. PHILIP, JR., born Aug. 18, 1771, married Feb. 10, 1802, Rebecca Green, born May 26, 1782, daughter of John and Mary (Stuart) Green of Gorham. They lived in Standish where he died Mar. 18, 1849, age 77 yrs., 8 mos. They were the parents of the following children:
 1. JOHN GREEN, born Dec. 8, 1802, died Nov. 3, 1883, in Naples. He married Sept. 8, 1833, in Biddeford, Susannah Tarbox.
 2. JANE, born, Feb. 13, 1805, married (int. Feb. 20, 1830) William Libby of Gorham.
 3. JOSEPH, born Mar. 3, 1808, died Jan. 27, 1861, Malden, Mass.
 4. ELIZA (ELIZABETH), born July 8, 1810.
 5. ESTHER, born July 3, 1812.
 6. ALMIRA, born Nov. 11, 1814.
 7. MARINDA, born Aug. 24, 1818.
 8. JOSHUA, born Jan. 6, 1821.

iv. JANE, born about 1775, died unmarried on Aug. 30, 1855, age 80.
v. JOSEPH, born ____, went to sea and died abroad.

vi. ELLEN (ELEANOR), born ____, married Feb. 12, 1821, Daniel Ridlon, who settled in Porter and raised a family of thirteen children. She died before July 5, 1835.

CHASE

The names of Isaac Chase and Joseph Chase are found on the 1789 and 1790 tax lists of Standish and in the 1790 census with families of 1-2-2 and 1-4-3 respectively. They were second cousins and of the Aquila Chase family. Isaac^5 Chase (Eleazar,^{4} Moses,^{3} Ens. Moses,^{2} Aquila^1) was born in Windham, Maine, Dec. 15, 1757 (1758 on gravestone), son of Eleazar and Jane (Elder) Chase of that town. He served in the Revolutionary War from Gorham in 1779 and in his later years received a pension for his services. He is listed as living in Pearsontown on Sept. 13, 1783, when his intentions of marriage to Lois Smith of Gorham were filed in that town. On June 12, 1787, he being of Standish bought from Richard Codman of Portland the northeast half of the 100-acre lot #72 in the second division in Standish (25/181). This became his homestead farm. Isaac was said to have been a tall and comely man, while his wife was not the handsomest woman in the world. His father, Eleazar, came from Newburyport to hunt Indians when Massachusetts was offering a bounty for Indian scalps. After pursuing his game awhile, he settled in Windham where he raised a family.

Family tradition states that Isaac married an Indian maiden, Lois Smith. The father of Lois was the captain of an East India vessel; he sailed from Salem and was never heard from again. He left an Indian wife and daughter on Cape Cod, and after the mother died from a broken heart, a neighbor took the little girl and brought her to Standish. This story is taken from the Isaac Chase Jr. family that settled in Turner (see the Aug. 24, 1905, issue of the *Lewiston Journal*). Isaac was living with his son Isaac on June 1, 1840, and died Nov. 12, 1840. His wife, Lois, born July 26, 1760, died Dec. 26, 1845. They are buried in the small cemetery located on the Dow Road at Dow's Corner. Isaac and Lois (Smith) Chase were the parents of the following children, all born in Standish:

i. GIDEON, born May 16, 1784, married (int. June 25, 1809, in Otisfield) Salome Lombard of Otisfield, he of Standish. She was born about 1792 and died July 25, 1870. He died Aug. 25, 1856. They lived in Hiram and perhaps elsewhere, and were the parents of thirteen children.

ii. ELEAZAR, born May 27, 1786, married May 26, 1812, Sarah Davis, born in Buxton June 17, 1790. They lived in Buxton and were the parents of nine children. Eleazer died Mar. 17, 1846, in his 60th year in Gray on his way to Turner.

iii. ABIGAIL, born Dec. 1, 1788, died unmarried in Standish on Mar. 3, 1866.

iv. ISAAC JR., born Mar. 20, 1791, married in 1822 his cousin, Eunice Chase, daughter of Rev. Nathaniel and Rhoda (Elliot) Chase of Buckfield, Maine; second Hannah Brigham. They lived in Turner, Maine, where he died May 17, 1864. He was the father of seven children.
v. DAVID, born Apr. 15, 1793, married Mar. 14, 1821, Hannah Moor Phinney born in Gorham Feb. 15, 1805, daughter of Coleman and Margaret (Moor) Phinney of that town. He was a house carpenter and lived in Standish where he died Mar. 26, 1866. She died Oct. 23, 1887, age 82 yrs., 8 mos. They were parents of thirteen children.
vi. JANE, born Oct. 28, 1795, married Ebenezer Harmon.
vii. MARY F., born Nov. 18, 1797, married Thomas Eames, born Sept. 23, 1797, and died Aug. 30, 1871. She died Mar. 27, 1879.
viii. JAMES, born Feb. 20, 1800, died Apr. 22, 1873, unmarried.
ix. ZENAS S., born Aug. 15, 1802, died unmarried Nov. 25, 1829, Standish.

Joseph[5] Chase (Dea. Amos,[4] Samuel,[3] Ens. Moses,[2] Aquila[1]) born in Saco, Maine, Oct. 10, 1754, son of Amos and Sarah (Cole) Chase, died Mar. 1, 1811, of cancer, age 56 years, in Standish. His obituary is given in Apr. 18, 1811, issue of *Eastern Argus*. He is buried in Burnham Cemetery located on bank of the Saco River in Standish near East Limington Bridge and his crude gravestone gives Mar. 1, 1812, as his death date which is an apparent error. He was of Saco when he married in Buxton Maine, Sept. 5, 1776, Olive Woodman, baptized in Newbury, Mass., Feb. 1, 1756, daughter of Nathan and Olive (Gray) Woodman, who later settled in Buxton. They were members of the Buxton Church into which they were admitted Dec. 28, 1777. They lived in Buxton and Little Ossipee (Limington) before they settled in Standish. Joseph Chase was of Standish on Apr. 20, 1789, when he bought from Samuel Chase of Pepperrellborough (Saco) the 100-acre lot #118 in second division in Standish (16/393). His widow married Oct. 10, 1816, as his second wife Josiah Black of Limington, where she died in Apr. 9, 1841, age 87 years. Children of Joseph and Olive (Woodman) Chase were as follows:

i. MARY, born Apr. 1777, bapt. in Buxton Church Dec. 28, 1777, married Oct. 8, 1795, Benjamin Small Jr. of Limington and died on May 9, 1859, age 82 yrs., 1 mo., Limington.
ii. DANIEL, born June 1779, died unmarried at sea.
iii. AMOS, born in Jan. 1781, died in Oct. 1829, married in Feb. 1805 Hannah Chase, born in York, Maine, Feb. 25, 1782, daughter of Col. Josiah and Hannah (Grow) Chase. She died Apr. 17, 1859, age 77. They lived in Standish and New Hampshire.
iv. NATHAN WOODMAN, born in Aug. 1783 in Standish, married May 9, 1805, Anna Ayer, daughter of Benjamin and Rachel (Sanborn) Ayer of Standish. He died in Bangor Nov. 6, 1868, age 85 yrs., and she June 17, 1867, age 82 yrs.
v. OLIVE GRAY, born Apr. 27, 1786, married Jan. 5, 1804, Abner Libby of Limington, born May 29, 1781. She died Jan. 30, 1851, in Limerick.

vi. **JOSEPH**, born Dec. 23, 1788, died in Upton, Maine, May 14, 1866, married July 1, 1809, Sabra L. Wheeler, who died in Wisconsin in 1869. He married second Affia (Bartlett) Jackson and lived in Bridgton until 1830 when he moved to Upton.
vii. **JOHN**, born May 25, 1790, died at sea on a voyage to New Orleans in 1814.
viii. **SARAH C.**, born Aug. 31, 1793, married (int. June 19, 1814) Stephen Libby of Limington. She died Mar. 18, 1875, age 80 yrs., in Limerick.

CLARK

A John Clark and his family were living in Pearsontown in the very early days of the township. He was one of the two men by the name of John Clark who drew rights #12 and #114 to land in the town at the drawing of lots in 1752. It may have been that they were father and son.

It is said that John Clark lived with several other families on the shore of Sebago Lake. He was living in Pearsontown with his wife and three children on March 13, 1757, when he is said to have shot and killed James Wooster (born Sept. 15, 1712, son of Francis and Mary [Chaney] Wooster of Bradford, Mass.) who married Feb. 26, 1740, a widow, Patience Low, the daughter of James Mills. Patience Wooster, a resident of Pearsontown after the death of her husband married on April 1, 1761, Dennis Lary of Gorham. Parson Smith of the First Parish Church of Falmouth (Portland) wrote in his diary under the date of March 13, 1757: "One Clark of Sebago Town killed Worcestor and wounded Gray and Sands."

John Clark testified on March 16, 1757, that "he was born in Leith in the North of Scotland about the year 1707, about 16 years since he came from Scotland to Boston and that he lived at Nutfield divers years after his arrival at New England, that about 20 months ago he moved into the Eastern Country, that he has lived with his family at a place called Pearson Town about twelve months and has a wife and four children."

The following records copied from the Massachusetts Archives best give what little is known concerning this unhappy event:

> John Clark, late of a place called Pearsontown, labourer, being indicted for the murder of one James Wooster at Pearsontown on the 13th of March 1757 and Jane and Mary Clark for being present and aiding and abetting, returned their verdict that the said Mary and Jane Clark is not quilty. As to the said John that on the 9th day of March Elizabeth Clark [widow of Eleazer Clark of Wells] having certain goods stolen from her, she made complaint to John Storer, Esq., and the 11th day of March made a warrent which Alexander Gray, a Deputy Sheriff, suspected Clark although Elizabeth did not inform him. He went to the dwelling house of John to search for them and asked that said John to let him come in but did not show the Warrent. John denied him entrance and took down his gun and threatened to shoot him if he did not go

off. He then said Alexander with aids attempted by force to enter and said John shot and killed James Wooster. If said Alexander might enter lawfully without reading, they find him guilty of manslaughter. Continued to be argued at the next Boston Court--York, June 27, 1757.

FALMOUTH PETITION, JUNE 6, 1757

The Petition of the Selectmen of the Town of Falmouth in the County of York Humbly Sheweth:

That whereas John Clark of a place called Hobbs and Pearson Town, without the boundaries of any town but within said County for about three months past has been confined in York Jail for supposed murder and his wife and daughter for the same space of time in the jail in this town for supposed accessorys in said crime; by means whereof two young children of said Cleark have ever since been supported by the said town of Falmouth: Upon which your Petitioners requested the Court of General Sessions of the Peace at April Term last to relieve them in that case. Whereupon the Court of Sessions appointed three Gent overseers of the same according to Law; And the said Gentlemen having done their [best?] to bind out sd children Apprentice, Could not find any person that would take them by reason of their being so young, and therefore left them on the hands of your Petitioners, And as they do not belong to this town Any more than any town in said County your Petitioners think it not equal that said Town of Falmouth should bear the Burthen of their support alone: And therefore humbly pray your Honours they may be relieved In that case and that the Charge of supporting said young children may be on the Province in general or at least the Whole County of York and your Petitioners as In Duty Bound Will Ever Pray.

It was not until March of the following year that the county of York was ordered to care for the children until parents could take care of them. Nothing further has been discovered concerning the disposition of the case against John Clark nor as to what became of his family, but as far as known they never again appeared in Pearsontown.

COLOMY

David Colomy (Collomy) was born before 1765 by census report, probably in New Durham, N.H., where he married Aug. 12, 1796, Polly Nason, they both of New Durham. He is listed in the census of Standish with a family of three males under 10 years of age, and one female between 26 and 45 years old. No Colomy was listed as head of a family in Limington in 1810 nor does the name appear in the Standish tax list for 1808. About 1813 David Colomy moved to Limington and was there when on Apr. 15, 1819, he purchased by quitclaim deed from David Nason a certain piece of land lying in Saco River and known as Nason's Island and located opposite land then owned by Clement Gould (81/405). He was probably the "Old Colomy" and "your father" (John's) named in Frost's account in Limington in 1813.

David Colomy's wife, Polly, died 1820 in Limington and he married second June 23, 1822, in Limington, Martha (Nason) Horn, widow of William Horn who died in 1821 in Limington. David Colomy died Dec. 1827 in a section of North Limington known as Colomy's Corner, located on the Whaleback Road. His widow, Martha Colomy, died July 21, 1830, in Limington.

In 1827 the town of Limington was to assist David Collome; widow Collome and child were struck off to Robert Boody of Limington Dec. 31, 1827. One child of David and Martha (Horn) Colomy recorded in Limington was Eliza Ann, born Nov. 3, 1822, published to John Small in 1853. Children of David and Polly (Nason) Colomy were as follows:

i. SAMUEL, born Dec. 14, 1796, New Durham, N.H., and died Aug. 16, 1872, at Parsonsfield. He was a private in War of 1812 and in 1818 gave power of attorney to Wingate Frost of Limington to sell his bounty land in Illinois. He married in Limington Mar. 28, 1824, Mary Cobb. He bought land in Parsonfield the same year and was living there in 1833.

ii. JOHN, surely an adult in 1813.

iii. DAVID, named in a newspaper notice placed in *Morning Star* issue of Feb. 10, 1832, by his brother Samuel Colomy of Parsonsfield, who was seeking his brother's whereabouts. Samuel mentions in his article that he has two brothers, Ivory and David, from whom he has not heard from for several years. He states that David "left New Durham, N.H., about nine years since to go to Boston, and nothing since been heard of him. But as he had formerly lived in New Haven, Conn., it is thought probable that he may now be somewhere in that vicinity."

iv. IVORY, according to his brother Samuel's notice placed in 1832 newspaper, "Ivory left this part of the county about fifteen years ago [1817] and has not been heard from since."

v. POLLY, born about 1797 and died Feb. 5, 1887, age about 90 yrs., in Limington. She was published to Robert Boynton in 1824 and to James Davis in 1827 but never married. She was eccentric and remained a town charge for many years.

vi. GEORGE, was in Limington in 1850, then age 40 yrs. and idiotic, living then with Edmund Bragdon as a town charge.

COOKSON

There were two families of Cooksons living in Pearsontown prior to Revolutionary War. Since it has been impossible so far to trace the exact line of descent of these Pearsontown families, it may be of interest to investigate the early history of the Cookson family in this country.

As early as 1700 there was living in Boston, Mass., a John Cookson who was a gunsmith by trade. On June 1, 1701, by vote of the selectmen of the town he was given "the liberty and benefit of sweeping chimneys," which apparently was a nice monopoly. In 1714 he was authorized to prosecute those who swept chimneys contrary to town bylaws. He employed Negroes to do the work and was in business as late as 1723. He held several minor town offices, being constable in 1705 and tithingman in 1706, 1715, and 1718. He was master of the artillery company and its clerk in 1726. Apparently he was a rather prosperous merchant and owned several valuable pieces of property in the city of Boston, as well as land in the Georgetown section of Maine. He built a tomb in the Copp's Hill Burying Ground in Boston where presumably many of his family were buried.

John Cookson married on Nov. 2, 1704, the Rev. Cotton Mather officiating, Rachel Proctor of Boston. He and his wife joined the Second Church of Boston on Nov. 12, 1727. In Boyle's *Journal of Occurrences in Boston* under the date of Oct. 21, 1762, is found the following: "Died in the 89th year of his age Mr. John Cookson, a noted whitesmith." Nothing has been discovered as to his ancestry, but due to his occupation of gunsmith, it is possible that he may have been a descendant of the John Cookson, a gunsmith in London, England, who in 1586 developed a magazine, breech-loading flintlock gun with a smooth bore and having a capacity of ten shots. John and Rachel (Proctor) Cookson were the parents of the following children, all born in Boston:

i. JOHN, born July 2, 1706, attended Harvard College, from which he graduated in 1727. At college he was quiet and ate in the commons for three years. He and his sister Rachel joined the Second Church of Boston on Nov. 12, 1727. He was a small merchant in Boston, but was acquainted with the District of Maine, as is evidenced by the fact that on June 17, 1731, he was witness to a deed transferring land in Biddeford, Maine, from Ensign Pendleton Fletcher to Capt. Samuel Jordan, both of Biddeford, and again on July 17, 1731, he was witness to a deed transferring land in Falmouth, Maine, from Moses Gould to Rev. Thomas Smith, both of Falmouth. On Dec. 21, 1741, he married Mary Beaker or Baker of Eastham, Mass. Although the account concerning him in *Sibley's Harvard Graduates* states that he died before the printing of the memorial catalog early in 1742, I rather doubt this and am inclined to believe that he was the John Cookson whose poll tax was taken from those to be collected in 1760 by Constable Smith of Eastham, due no doubt to the fact that he was living in Wellfleet, a newly established town including what was formerly the North Precinct of Eastham. I also believe that he was the John Cookson who was married on June 4, 1761, by Samuel Smith, justice of peace, to Abigail Cavender, both of Eastham. If so, she was his second wife. No proof to absolutely establish such identity has been found.

John Cookson of Pearsontown was living in Pearsontown as early as 1767, for Ephraim Jones of Falmouth records in account with Pearsontown Proprietors under date of Mar. 27, 1767, that payment was made to John Cookson for three days' work on roads in Pearsontown. He was also recorded as being in 1774 the nearest southerly neighbor to Benjamin Ingalls, the first settler of Hiram.

In the deed in which on Mar. 20, 1776, Moses Pearson sold to John Cookson of Pearsontown the 30-acre lot #11 here he is given as an "armourer." Again on June 25, 1787, when he sold to John Cookson Jr. armourer, his son, "my farm in said Standish containing thirty acres lying on the Northwest Road, being the orginal thirty-acre lot numbered eleven as by the Proprietor's May of said town will appear, together with the buildings, stock and wearing apparell and tools of every kind and all my estate in Bonds Notes and otherwise that is mine, etc." he designated himself as armourer (15/406). This designation of his occupation clearly connects him with the Cookson family of Boston. He continued to live on his farm until his death in 1790, which occurred while the body of his son John was being carried from the house for burial. Thomas Shaw, the Standish poet, refers to this sad event in one of his many poems and indicates that John Cookson was a very old man.

The fact that John Cookson of Pearsontown was an aged man at the time of his death, that Reuben Cookson, who also lived in Pearsontown, was born in Wellfleet, Mass., according to pension records, that John Cookson Jr. was born in 1761 and could have been the son of John and Abigail (Cavender) Cookson of Eastham--all are strong indications that he was the John Cookson (born 1706) of Boston who married Mary Beaker of Eastham and doubtless went there to live. All of the following were probably children of John Cookson of Pearsontown:

1. REUBEN, born in Wellfleet, Mass., about 1745, was living in Pearsontown prior to 1771 because he was listed as a resident of the town at the time of his marriage on Feb. 1, 1769, to Mary York, also a resident of Pearsontown and the probable daughter of Abram and Lydia (Jordon) York. It is likely that they lived on part of the 100-acre lot #114 in the second division, which bordered on the Saco River and which they sold on Jan. 8, 1802, to their son-in-law Daniel Smith of Standish (36/78). It was probably about this time that they moved to Unity, Maine, where they afterward lived and where he bought land the same year.

    The name of Reuben Cookson is found on the 1789, 1790, 1795, and 1796 tax lists of Standish, in the 1790 census with a family of 2-3-7, and in the 1800 census where his family consisted of him and his wife, both over 45 years of age, one male under 10, one male and two females between 10 and 16, and one male and two females between 16 and 26. Reuben Cookson served in the Revolutionary War and according to pension records died Feb 14, 1829, age 84 yrs. Children of Reuben and Mary (York) Cookson were as follows:

    (1). REUBEN, bapt. in Pearsontown on Sept. 8, 1771, died young.

    (2) JOSEPH, bapt. July 12, 1772, settled in Unity, Maine. Marriage intentions of Joseph Cookson of Buxton to Jenny Lagben of Gorham on Jan. 7, 1797, are found in the Buxton Church records. In the records of Hampden, Maine, is also found the marriage on July 26, 1798, of

Joseph Cookson of Standish and Polly Rawlins of Hampden. It seems likely that all of these records refer to the same Joseph Cookson and that he was twice married. At the time of 1800 census he was living in Standish with a family consisting of him and his wife, each between 16 and 26 years of age, and one male child under 10 years old. About 1803 they moved to Unity, Maine, where at the time of 1810 census his family consisted of himself and wife, three sons (two under 10 and one between 10 and 16), and a daughter. He moved to North Belmont, Maine, between 1813 and 1820, but before 1830 moved to Greenfield in Penobscot County, Maine. He died in Greenfield June 28, 1849, age 76 yrs., 2 mos., 8 days. Both are buried in the Greenfield Cemetery. Children probably included the following:
   (i) REUBEN, born about 1799, drowned in 1818, age 18 yrs.
   (ii) ABRAM, born about 1804, moved to Greenfield, Maine. He married Sybil Witham, daughter of Peter and Joanna (Whitney) Witham of New Sharon, Maine. He was a farmer living in Etna, Maine, in 1870. His wife wife died there Apr. 14, 1885, age 74 yrs., 11 mos., 24 days.
   (iii) BENJAMIN, married Jane _____ about 1808, died Aug. 27, 1882, age 73 yrs., 8 mos., 13 days. He is buried in Greenfield Cemetery in same lot as Joseph.
   (iv) EDWARD, born in Etna, Maine, in 1850, age 33.
   (v) JOSEPH, born about 1818, died in Greenfield. In 1870 he was living in Etna, age 52.
   (vi) HANNAH, died in Enfield, Maine, married Arthur Lamb who died in Costigan, Maine.
   (vii) BETSEY, died in Greenfield, a Civil War veteran.

(3) MARY, bapt. June 5, 1774, married Sept. 30, 1798, Charles Meserve, born about 1774 son of John and Sarah (Strout) Meserve of Standish. At the time of the 1800 census he was living in Standish with a family consisting of him and his wife and one male and two females under 10 yrs. old. They moved from Hollis to North Belmont, Maine, about 1813-1814. He served in the War of 1812. He died at Morrill, Maine, in Jan. 1861, and his wife died at North Belmont on July 17, 1840, age 70. At the time of the 1850 census he was living in the family of Samuel York in Standish at the age of 76. For children see Meserve Family.

(4) JONATHAN OR JOHN, bapt. May 19, 1776, in Standish, married Apr. 13, 1796, Jemima Hall, born Mar. 13, 1773, daughter of John and Noami (York) Hall of Standish. They were living in Standish in 1800 with one son and one daughter. They had children Jenny, John, and Jemima baptized in the Standish Church on Sept. 10, 1801. They probably moved to Unity, Maine, about 1805

53

and between 1813 and 1820 to North Belmont, Maine, but before 1830 he ran away, leaving his wife and children. As far as known these were his children as follows:
(i) JENNY, bapt. Sept. 10, 1801.
(ii) JOHN JR., bapt. Sept. 10, 1801, was mentally deranged.
(iii) JEMIMA, bapt. Sept. 10, 1810.
(iv) EBENEZER, born about 1806, died at Fairfield, Jan. 27, 1885, age 79 yrs. In 1850 he was living in Belmont, age 43.

(5) ABIGAIL, bapt. June 14, 1778, married June 10, 1798, Edward Smith, son of Daniel and Susannah (Haley) Smith of Hollis, Maine. She married second as his third wife Sept. 18, 1817, Nicholas Davis of Limington.

(6) MERCY, bapt. Sept. 23, 1778, as daughter of Reuben and Mary Cookson at "Ossabee" (Limington) by Rev. Chadwich, pastor of the Second Church of Scarboro as found in the records of that church. Nothing further known.

(7) REUBEN, born in Oct. 1780, bapt. May 22, 1782, in Standish, moved to Unity, Maine. He married first Polly McDaniel. He was living in Unity, age 69, at the time of the 1850 census.
Children:
(i) ABRAHAM, born in 1805, died Dec. 25, 1878, age 73 yrs., and was buried in South Unity Cemetery. He married first Eliza Johnson of Freedom, Maine, and second in 1840 Elsie Cross, born about 1812 daughter of William W. and Lois (Smith) Cross. He settled in North Belmont between 1820 and 1830, but by 1840 had moved to South Unity. In 1850 he was living in Freedom, Maine.
(ii) SAMUEL, born 1807, married May 23, 1828, Lois or Louise Noyes of Belmont. At the time of the 1850 census he was living in Freedom, Maine, with a family consisting of himself, age 43, and his wife, Louise, age 44, and children.

(8) LUCY, born 1783, married Nov. 27, 1800 (int. Nov. 15, 1800, in Hollis), Daniel Smith, son of Daniel and Susannah (Haley) Smith of Hollis. He died July 12, 1860, and she on Apr. 21, 1861, both of Hollis.

(9) ABRAHAM Y. (YORK?) born _____, probably moved to Unity, Maine.

2. MERCY, born Aug. 15, 1751, was living in Pearsontown on Nov. 15, 1773, when intentions of marriage to Josiah Black were filed in Gorham. They settled in Limington where she died May 25, 1816. For further particulars see Black family.

By second wife:

3. JOHN, born in Sept. 1761, doubtless came into town with his father prior to 1767. His intentions of marriage to Elizabeth Beal of Newton, Mass., are found in the Gorham records under the date of July 30, 1785. They were married Aug. 21, 1785. She was born Aug. 21, 1764, in Newton, daughter of Thomas

and Elizabeth (Hall) Beal and died May 3, 1852, at Battle Creek, Michigan. He died in June 1790 and on Aug. 31, 1791, she married second at Standish, Gideon Lowell, born Sept. 12, 1761, son of Moses and Miriam (Knowlton) Lowell. About 1800 he with his family moved with his father and his brother David to Grove, Allegheny County, New York. In 1832 they moved to Michigan, he dying at Battle Creek on Sept. 20, 1845. Gideon and Elizabeth (Hall) (Cookson) Lowell were the parents of seven children. The family of John Jr. and Elizabeth (Hall) Cookson was as follows:
(1) SAMUEL, born June 30, 1786, married Anne Messenger, and died Feb. 20, 1876.
(2) JOHN JR., born Oct. 19, 1788, married Lydia Nash, who died Mar. 23, 1828. He died Mar. 28, 1842.

ii. RACHEL, born Sept. 10, 1707, married about 1732 Hensley Hobby of Boston.
iii. ELIZABETH, born Oct. 10, 1708.
iv. OBEDIAH, born Feb. 1, 1709, married Apr., 26, 1737, Margaret Smith, daughter of Thomas Smith of Boston, and she died Jan. 19, 1742. He married second June 22, 1742, Faith Waldo, born Jan. 1, 1713-14, daughter of Cornelius and Faith (Savage) Waldo, and she died Nov. 8 or 9, 1784, in Boston. He died before Jan. 1, 1771. Children as follows:
By first wife:
1. JOHN, born Apr. 10, 1738, married Dec. 3, 1767, Margaret Freeman, named in grandfather Cookson's will, died Feb. 23, 1800.
2. MARGARET, born Mar. 29, 1740, married Sept. 27, 1759, Samuel Webb, named in her grandfather Cookson's will.
By second wife:
3. SAMUEL, born 1744, married first Dec. 25, 1769, Mary Church, born June 18, 1743, daughter of Benjamin Church of Boston; second Mrs. Susannah Osborne of Boston on Oct. 3, 1793. He was named in his grandfather Cookson's will and received all his smith's tools. He was living in Boston with a family of 2-1-1 at the time of the 1790 census. He died Mar. 7, 1806, age 63 yrs.
4. ELIZABETH, bapt. July 28, 1745, probably never married.
5. LYDIA, bapt. July 30, 1749, probably never married.
v. REUBEN, born May 10, 1711.
vi. MARY, born Feb. 26, 1712.
vii. SAMUEL, born Jan. 29, 1716.

There was living in Boston at the same time that John Cookson dwelt there a Reuben Cookson, who according to Christ Church records was buried Jan. 22, 1766, age 92 years. Nothing further has been found concerning him, but because of his age and the fact that John Cookson named a son Reuben it appears probable that he was a brother to John.

CRAM

Daniel[4] Cram (Thomas,[3] Thomas,[2] John[1]) was one of those men who came from from New Hampshire to settle in Pearsontown around 1762. On Sept. 6, 1762, Daniel Cram, yeoman of Hampton, N.H., bought from Isaac Illesley of Falmouth the 30-acre lot #40 in Pearsontown (5/65). He was of Pearsontown on Mar. 26, 1767, when he bought from John Burnell of Gorham the 30-acre lot #39 together with so much of the undivided lands and after divisions in Pearsontown as shall make one-half right or single share (5/65). The name of Daniel Cram is found on the 1789, 1790, and 1796 tax lists of Standish and in the 1790 census with a family of 4-0-2.

He was born in Hampton in Hampton Falls, N.H., on Mar. 28, 1724, son of Thomas and Mary (Brown) Cram. He married Sarah Green of Hampton Falls sometime before he moved to Pearsontown. He and his wife, Sarah, were admitted to the Pearsontown Church on July 16, 1775. His wife died in Standish in Aug. 1807 and he died here Mar. 3, 1815. They were parents of the following children:

i. MARY, born _____, bapt. July 22, 1770, in Standish, died unmarried.

ii. STEPHEN, born 1766, bapt. July 22, 1770, married Mar. 20, 1822, Betsey Plaisted, born Dec. 20, 1787, daughter of Andrew and Molly (Libby) Plaisted of Gorham. He lived on his father's farm consisting of 30-acre lots #39 and #40, receiving a deed thereof on Mar. 26, 1806. He died Dec. 1838, age 72 yrs., 2 mos., and was buried in Village Cemetery. They were the parents of the following children:
1. HARRIET, born Jan. 7, 1824, married William Perry and lived on the old homestead. Harriet died Sept. 25, 1909, age 82 yrs., 8 mos., 18 days, Standish.
2. CLARISSA, an epileptic, died unmarried.

iii. THOMAS, born Dec. 31, 1768, bapt. July 22, 1770, married Mar. 27, 1798, Sarah Hasty, born Apr. 5, 1774, daughter of Daniel and Martha (McLaughin) Hasty of Standish. On Oct. 30, 1795, he bought from Joseph Dow of Standish the 30-acre lot #93 and on this lot lived and reared his family. He also bought the 30-acre lot #137 on the same day from John McGill, who was living on the lot at the time (49/408). He died May 23, 1843, age 74 yrs. He and his wife, Sarah, were parents of the following children:
1. SALLY, born Jan. 7, 1799, died Jan. 14, 1799.
2. SALLY, born Dec. 14, 1799, bapt. June 8, 1800, died Oct. 12, 1846, age 47 yrs., and was buried with her brother Daniel in Bridgton.
3. ASHBEL, born Dec. 9, 1801, bapt. Apr. 25, 1801, married Mary M. Perley of Bridgton where he lived and died on Jan. 8, 1840, in Albion, Maine. They were parents of two children, both of whom died while young.
4. MARSHALL, born Jan. 16, 1804, married Sept. 24, 1827, in Bridgton, Sarah A. Perley of Bridgton and lived in Brunswick. He died Jan. 13, 1888, age 84, in Brunswick.

5. OCTAVO, born Mar. 25, 1806, bapt. July 6, 1806, died unmarried on Jan. 15, 1845.
6. GARDINER, born Aug. 29, 1808, bapt Jan. 30, 1809, died unmarried on Aug. 17, 1834.
7. DANIEL HASTY, born Apr. 27, 1811, bapt. July 21, 1811, died June 15, 1864, age 53 yrs.
8. RENSELEAR, born Nov. 25, 1813, bapt. Nov. 25, 1813, married Mary M.P. Cram, widow of his brother Ashbel. He died Dec. 28, 1872, age 59 yrs., and was buried in Bridgton. Had children Ashbel H. and Mary Ellen.
9. LEVI, born Aug. 14, 1816, bapt. Nov. 3, 1816, married Janette P. Beaman of Bridgton where he lived and died without issue on Apr. 1, 1865. His widow lived in Woburn, Mass.

iv. DANIEL, JR.. born ____, bapt. July 22, 1770, married (int. Aug. 26, 1780, in Gorham) Chloe Stevens of Bridgton. They were admitted to the Standish Church May 3, 1795. His name is found on the 1789, 1790, 1795, 1796, and 1808 tax lists of Standish and in the 1790 census with a family of 2-5-2. He evidently came to Pearsontown with his father about 1762. On Apr. 2, 1776, he bought from the Pearsontown Committee the 30-acre lot #143 (10/487) and on May 21, 1779, from Joseph Ingraham of Falmouth the 30-acre lot #91 (10/365). These lots located on the Buxton Road, being nearly opposite each other, adjoined those which were later purchased by his brother Thomas. Daniel died Mar. 5, 1815, in Standish and is buried in the Old Cemetery at Standish Corner.

Daniel and Chloe (Stevens) Cram were parents of the following family:
1. GREEN, born Nov. 21, 1781, bapt. Nov. 13, 1785, married (int. Feb. 20, 1808) Abigail Lowell, who died Dec. 1842, age 56 yrs., Standish. She was daughter of Jonathan and Rachel (Morton) Lowell of Hiram. Green and Abigail (Lowell) Cram had children as follows:
    (1) MARY, born Aug. 29, 1808, married on Oct. 5, 1828, John Atkinson of Saco. They were living in 1850 in Standish.
    (2) HENRY LAURENS, born Oct. 6, 1809.
    (3) MARCELLA born 1803, married June 2, 1835, Arza Mayo of Standish. She died Feb. 10, 1894, age 81 yrs., 19 days, in South Limington, at the home of her daughter, Mrs. William Anderson.
    (4) ANGELIA, born 1820, married Charles H. Thorn or Thorpe of Woodfords Corner. She died June 19, 1894, age 74 yrs., 3 mos., in Deering, Maine.
    (5) CASSANDRA.
    (6) OTIS.
    (7) CAROLINE.
    (8) ARRIETTA.
2. WYER or WEAR, born Sept. 14, 1783, bapt. Nov. 13, 1785, married Jan. 14, 1810, Mercy Sanborn, probably daughter of John Jr. and Abigail (Jones) Sanborn of Standish. They lived on Oak Hill and both are buried in the cemetery there. He died

Mar. 21, 1861, age 77 yrs., 6 mos., 21 days, and she on May 22, 1855, age 68 yrs., 2 mos., and 24 days. They were parents of the following children:
- (1) BRADLEY, born Mar. 2, 1810.
- (2) HARRIS, born Mar. 27, 1812.
- (3) ERASTUS, born Oct. 27, 1813.
- (4) ANGELINA, born Aug. 7, 1815.
- (5) ABIGAIL SANBORN, born May 31, 1817.
- (6) DANIEL, born Apr. 13, 1819.
- (7) JOHN SANBORN, born July 17, 1821, died in Baldwin.
- (8) MIRANDA, born June 27, 1823, died unmarried Apr. 20, 1855, age 31 yrs., 9 mos., 24 days.
- (9) ALVIN, born Aug. 18, 1826, living in 1860 in Standish.
- (10) CASSANDRA, born Feb. 23, 1830, married William H. Dresser.

3. AARON, born June 29, 1785, bapt. Oct. 16, 1785, married Apr. 15, 1835, Hannah Robinson of Buxton. He died Feb. 21, 1848, age 63 yrs., and she died Apr. 16, 1871, age 82, in Standish.
4. MESHACK, born Apr. 6, 1787, bapt. June 17, 1787, died unmarried Apr. 8, 1867, Standish.
5. ASAHEL, born Feb. 27, 1789, bapt. Aug. 23, 1789.
6. DANIEL, born Oct. 9, 1791, died in infancy.
7. DANIEL, born Apr. 9, 1793, bapt. July 21, 1793, died unmarried in 1820.
8. THOMAS, born Aug. 3, 1797, bapt. Sept. 3, 1797, married Susan Sanborn, born Jan. 29, 1822.
9. LEVI, born Aug. 3, 1797, bapt. Sept. 3, 1797, and twin of Thomas, died in infancy.

v. SARAH, born ____, bapt. July 9, 1775.
vi. LEVI, born in 1776, bapt. June 6, 1776, married Dec. 20, 1801, Anna Butterfield, born Nov. 5, 1781, daughter of Joseph and Mary (Harding) Butterfield of Standish. They lived in Windham where he died Mar. 16, 1816, and she on Mar. 25, 1856. They were the parents of eight children.

CROCKER

Timothy Crocker was one of the early inhabitants of Pearsontown; he was recorded as living here prior to 1760. He probably moved into town from Gorham where his marriage to Hannah Meserve, daughter of Clement Sr. and Sarah (Decker) Meserve, is recorded under date of Dec. 1754. He was one of the eight men who served as a guard at the fort in Pearsontown in 1755 and it is likely that these men had their families with them at that time. The name of Timothy Crocker is found on a muster roll of a company in His Majesty's Service under the command of Capt. Joseph Woodman bearing the date of Nov. 23, 1757, indicating the length of his service as being from May 3 to Sept. 28 of that year and his place of residence as Pearsontown. He is also listed as being from Pearsontown on a muster roll of the company commanded by Capt. William

Gerrish of Berwick with service from May to September in 1759 and one of those who served in the party of Lt. Charles Lessner scouting eastward from Broad Bay (Waldoboro) in 1760. His name is among those of men from Pearsontown who worked on Gorham roads in 1760 and 1761.

Timothy Crocker was granted by right of settlement the 5-acre lot #3 on which he lived and the 30-acre lot #71 adjoining it. This land he sold to John Ayer on Aug. 15, 1767 (5/429). About 1771 he moved to Bristol, Maine, along with his father-in-law, Clement Meserve Jr.

The parentage of Timothy Crocker has not been definitely established, but in view of the fact that he is known to have had a brother John who also settled in Bristol, he may have been that Timothy Crocker born Aug. 23, 1728, in Barnstable, Mass., son of Deacon John and Mary (Hinckley) Crocker, who had a brother John whose date of birth was Apr. 1, 1722. John Crocker moved from Bristol to Machias, Maine, in 1768, several years before Timothy moved from Pearsontown to Bristol. Timothy later also moved to Machias, but probably not until after 1790 since it is likely that he was the Timothy Crocker (1-2-2) listed as living in Cushing Town in the census of that year.

Timothy and Hannah (Meserve) Crocker were parents of the following children:

i. PAUL, born married Aug. 23, 1783, in Bristol, Nancy Marston and had eight children.
ii. JAMES, born ____, married Peggy Cook and had five children.
iii. MARY OR MOLLY, born ____, married Josiah Bean, son of Jonathan and Abigail (Gordon) Bean of Pearsontown and Bethel, Maine. They were the parents of nine children, for list of whom see Bean family.
iv. SARAH OR SALLY, bapt. July 28, 1771, at Pearsontown, married Oct. 9, 1785, at Bristol, William Clark and had nine children.
v. ABIGAIL OR NABBY, bapt. July 28, 1771, at Pearsontown, married (int. Aug. 23, 1789) at Bristol William Martin.
vi. ELIZA, bapt. July 28, 1771, at Pearsontown, nothing further known.
vii. MARGARET, born married Abraham Fletcher and had six children.
viii. SUSAN, born ____, married Eben Foster and had three children.
ix. HANNAH, born ____, married at Bristol Oct.17, 1785, William Richards.

CROCKETT

The name of Ephraim Crockett is found on the 1795, 1796, 1808, and 1814 tax lists of Standish as well as in the 1800 census of the town. He was born Jan. 13, 1766, son of Andrew and Rebecca (Hunt) Crockett of Gorham. On Jan. 5, 1792, he married Martha Gray, born about 1765, perhaps daughter of Taylor and Tabitha (Murch) Gray of Gorham. He was living in Gorham on May 4, 1792, when he bought from Andrew and Mary Titcomb of Falmouth the 100-acre lot #38 in the second division located on Standish Neck (19/62). This was evidently the site of his homestead farm, part of which he sold to his son Henry Crockett of Standish on Nov. 28, 1842, the deed indicating that he was living there at the time

(180/184). He was still living in Standish on Aug. 8, 1846, when he and his wife, Martha, sold for $900 to James M. Gray of Acton, Mass., the farm in Standish on which they then resided (199/117). On May 24, 1847, he deeded to Leonard Shaw of Standish 40 acres of land there with buildings, on condition that Shaw should maintain and support Ephraim; Martha, his wife; and Andrew and Joanna, their children, during the life of Ephraim and Martha (203/414). Martha Crockett, age 85, Joanna Crockett, age 52, and Andrew, age 50, were living in the family of Leonard Shaw at the time of the 1850 census. Ephraim Crockett died Mar. 1, 1850, evidently previous to the time the records were taken. He was a veteran of the War of 1812 and received a pension for his services. Children of Ephraim and Martha (Gray) Crockett were as follows:

i. HENRY, born May 13, 1793, married (int. Apr. 4, 1818, in Standish) Ruhama Newbegin, who died Nov. 4, 1863. She was the widow of John Newbegin who died Dec. 17, 1872.

ii. JOANNA, born about 1798. She was age 63 yrs. in the 1860 Standish census.

iii. ANDREW, born about 1800. He was age 50 yrs. in the 1850 Standish census.

CROXFORD

John Croxford was another one of those whose connection with the town was of short duration. His name is found on the 1789 and 1790 tax lists and on the 1790 census with a family of 1-2-2. At the time of the 1800 census he was living in Limerick with a family consisting of him and his wife, three boys and one girl under 10 years of age and one girl between 10 and 16 years old.

He is given as being of Scarboro on Sept. 18, 1782, when he bought from Nathaniel Knight of Falmouth lot #79 in the second division in Pearsontown. He married Oct. 12, 1783, in Scarboro, Wilmot Foster, daughter of Isaiah and Lydia (Fogg) Foster of Limerick. He moved into town soon after his marriage since his residence is given as Pearsontown in an order for wages due him for service in the Revolutionary War, which is dated Sept. 9, 1785. He was living in town on Nov. 17, 1789, when he sold the northeast half of lot #79 to James Berry of Ossipee (Limington) (15/507). However he was of Limerick, Maine, on Feb. 9, 1792, when he mortaged to John Meserve of Standish the half of this lot which he still owned (25/159). It is therefore that he moved to Limerick not long after 1790.

John Croxford served in the Revolutionary War and in an enlistment record dated July 1, 1781, it is stated that he was 24 years old, five feet five inches tall, of light complexion with brown hair, born in N.H., by occupation a seaman, and a resident of Scarboro. According to pension records he was living in Newburgh, Maine, when he died in Newburgh, Maine, on Dec. 26, 1820, at the age of 68 years. Limited research has failed to disclose his parentage.

He moved to Limerick about 1792 and thence to Newburgh sometime in May 1808. By his obituary notice he died Dec. 6, 1820, age 68 years, and his widow died Oct. 9, 1838, age 79 years, 2 months, at the home of her son Ezekiel in Newburgh. According to her obituary given in the Apr. 10, 1839, issue of the *Morning Star*, she was the mother of eleven children, five still living at the time of her death. She had at the time eighty-eight grandchildren, and one of the fifth generation. All the children of John and Wilmot (Foster) Croxford are not known, but they were the parents of the following:

i. KEZIAH, known as Dolly, born about 1785, married Jan. 1801 John Fenderson Jr. of Parsonsfield, she of Limerick. He was born Oct. 14, 1777, and died in 1848 in Old Town, Maine, and his widow died June 19, 1854, age 69 yrs., in Owego, N.Y., and is buried next to her son John who died there on Apr. 12, 1877.

ii. EZEKIEL, born July 22, 1787, married June 20, 1808, in Hampden, Nancy Goodridge both of Hampden. He died Aug. 22, 1849, age 61 yrs., 1 mo., in Newburgh, Maine.

iii. ISAIAH, born about 1789, died Aug. 8, 1826, age 37 yrs., in Newburgh. He was crushed to death beneath a cartwheel and died at the residence of his brother Ezekiel.

iv. JOHN, born Apr. 25, 1791, married (int. Jan. 20, 1817) Wilmot Fogg, born Aug. 8, 1792, she of Buxton, he of Jackson. He died Nov. 16, 1864, age 73 yrs., 6 mos., and she Jan. 28, 1877, both in Jackson.

v. DANIEL F., born June 21, 1793, died Jan. 8, 1833, age about 41 yrs., in Newburgh, Maine. He married May 23, 1823, Sophronia Stanley in Belfast.

vi. THIAH (or THESIS), born June 18, 1799, married Aug. 25, 1816, Portius Johnson of Limerick, she of Newburgh.

vii. CHILD, died in 1796 in Limerick.

CUMMINGS

The names of William, Thomas, and John Cummings are found on the 1789, 1790, 1795, 1796, and 1808 tax lists of Standish and in the census of 1790 and that of 1800. They were the sons of Thomas Cummings born Mar. 22, 1722, in Falmouth, Maine, and his wife Mehitabel Rackleff, who he married in Scarboro on Jan. 1, 1747. This Mehitabel Rackleff has erroreously been thought to have been the Mehitabel (Chandler) (Davis) Rackleff, the widow of John Rackleff of Scarboro and the mother of Benjamin and Joseph Chandler Rackleff of Pearsontown, but that Mehitabel died June 3, 1764, age 66 years, and her husband John outlived her, dying on Mar. 3, 1773.

William Cummings, born about 1750, was of Pearsontown about 1780 when he bought the 100-acre lot #45 in second division (10/548). On Dec. 15, 1774, he married Ann Jackson, daughter of Francis Jackson of Cape Elizabeth. In the 1790 census he is listed as head of a family of 1-2-4. At the time of the 1800 census his family consisted of him and his wife, one male between 16 and 26, one between 26 and 45, one female between 10 and 16, one between 16 and 26, and one between 26 and 45. It is likely that his son William Jr. and his wife were included in this list. William died Aug. 6, 1823, age 73 years, in Standish, and his wife Sept. 17, 1822, age 75 years. William and Ann (Jackson) Cummings were the parents of the following children:

i. WILLIAM, born at Cape Elizabeth June 20, 1777, married first Mar. 27, 1800, Anna Libby, born in Scarboro Jan. 7, 1779, daughter of Daniel and Elizabeth (Harmon) Libby. He moved to Cape Elizabeth in 1801 and there died Apr. 23, 1846, age 69 yrs., and his wife Sept. 10, 1811. He married second Sarah Moses, born July 11, 1788, daughter of Josiah and Elizabeth (Harmon) (Libby) Moses, half-sister of his first wife. She died Apr. 14, 1858, age 70 yrs., Cape Elizabeth. They lived in Cape Elizabeth on his grandfather's homestead where they were first buried, but later the bodies were taken up and reburied in Brown's Hill Cemetery at South Portland. Children were as follows:
  1. ELIZABETH, born Sept. 13, 1800, at Standish, married May 15, 1819, John Brooks of Scarboro.
  2. DANIEL, born Dec. 19, 1801, at Cape Elizabeth, died in Haynesville, Maine, Jan. 25, 1882.
  3. FRANCIS JACKSON, born Sept. 19, 1803.
  4. GEORGE WASHINGTON, born Aug. 13, 1805.
  5. MARY ANN, born Sept. 7, 1807.
  6. WILLIAM LIBBY, born Aug. 24, 1810.
  7. ANN LIBBY, born Sept. 10, 1811.
  By second wife:
  8. ESTHER, born Jan. 25, 1815, died Mar. 15, 1815.
  9. ESTHER, born July 8, 1816.
  10. CATHERINE SKILLIN, born Dec. 6, 1819.
  11. SIMON, born Apr. 19, 1822.
  12. LUCY MORTON, born Oct. 7, 1825.
  13. MOSES, born Dec. 25, 1829, died Feb. 21, 1830.
ii. ANN, born June 2, 1780.
iii. SIMON, born May 10, 1783, served in the War of 1812, married (int. Feb. 5. 1812) Abigail Libby Brown of Raymond.
iv. LUCY, born Aug. 31, 1786, married (int. Mar. 2, 1811) Thomas Morton of Standish, son of Ebenezer and Susannah (Irish) Morton of Standish.
v. MEHITABLE L., born about 1787, married June 29, 1831, George Robinson, born Apr. 3, 1783, son of John and Deborah (Cummings) Robinson of Limington. He died Jan. 29, 1875, age 91 yrs., in Limington, and she died Apr. 14, 1860, age 73 yrs.

Thomas Cummings, born about 1755, was living in Cape Elizabeth on Dec. 20, 1780, when he bought from Samuel Dean of Falmouth the southwest half of the 100-acre lot #44 in second division in Standish (11/423). It was probably about this time that he moved to Standish. He served in the Revolutionary War and received a pension for his services. On Dec. 30, 1779, the Rev. Ephraim Clark officiating, he married Rachel Jackson, sister of his brother William's wife. At the time of the 1790 census he is credited with a family of 1-1-4. The 1800 census lists his family as consisting of him and his wife, one son between 10 and 16

years of age, one daughter between 10 and 16, and one between 16 and 26 years old. He and his wife were members of the Standish Church. He died in Limington on June 15, 1837, at the age of 82 years, and is buried in West Baldwin Cemetery in West Baldwin. Children as far as known were as follows:
i. GEORGE, an only son, killed in 1803 while hauling a mast.
ii. RACHEL, born May 12, 1789, in Standish, married May 2, 1809, James Boothby, born Aug. 10, 1787, son of David Boothby of Limington. He died Mar. 12, 1863, and she on Sept. 30, 1873, both in Baldwin.
iii. MEHITABEL, married Jan. 13, 1808, Aaron Richardson, born Sept. 1, 1779, son of Moses and Lydia (Hall) Richardson of Standish.

Thomas Cummings married second July 1, 1810 (int. June 2, 1810), Susanna (Thomes) Gray, widow of John Gray of Standish.

John Cummings, born about 1758, married on Nov. 21, 1782, Lydia Jones of Cape Elizabeth. He was of that town on Nov. 15, 1782, when he bought from Samuel Dean of Falmouth the northeast half of 100-acre lot #44 in the second division in Standish (11/425). It is likely that he settled on this lot soon after his marriage. He was living in town with a family of 1-1-3 at the time of the 1790 census. In the 1800 census he is credited with a family consisting of him and his wife, one son between 10 and 16 years of age, one son between 16 and 26 years old, one daughter under 10 years of age, and two daughters between 16 and 26 years old. Both he and his wife were members of the Standish Church. He died in Dec. 1828, age 71, in Standish, and his obituary notice was given in Jan. 9, 1829, issue of the *Christian Mirror*. His widow, Lydia, born Jan. 27, 1757, was living in 1846, age 92 years, in Standish. Children of John and Lydia (Jones) Cummings were as far as known:
i. RHODA, married Nov. 13, 1806, William Proctor Jr. of New Gloucester, Maine. He died Oct. 14, 1857, age 70 yrs.
ii. JOHN, born about 1789, married first (int. Feb. 19, 1812) Lydia Libby of Scarboro and second Nancy Haskell. He served in the War of 1812 and died May 19, 1860. His first wife died Mar. 24, 1819, age 32.
iii. CHARLOTTE, bapt. Sept. 3, 1797, as daughter of John Cummings. She died Jan. 8, 1885, age 89 yrs., in Standish, and was never married.
iv. HIRAM, bapt. May 16, 1800, as son of John Cummings.

DAVIS

There were several Davis families living in Pearsontown after 1780. The name of James Davis is found on the 1788 and all later tax lists consulted. At the time of the 1790 census his family consisted of himself and six females. In the 1800 census he is listed with a family consisting of him and his wife, both between 26 and 45 years of age; two boys under 10 and one between 10 and 16; one girl under 10 and one between 10 and 16; one female between 16 and 26; and one female over 45 years of age. He was baptized May 2, 1762, son of Robert and Prudence (Long) Davis of Andover, Massachusetts. While no early deeds have been found of his owning land in Standish, his father, Robert, at that time of Andover, bought from Benjamin Mussey the 100-acre lot #66 in the second division in Standish on June 13, 1780 (15/276 & 277). It was on this lot, bordering on the northwest road at Oak Hill that James Davis settled. The father, Robert, was living in Pearsontown on May 14, 1785, when he sold township rights in Bridgton to Asahel Foster (15/397) and was living in Standish when on Feb. 22, 1787, he sold some 100-acre lots in Bridgton to Thomas Hopkins of Portland. According to an entry in an account book of his son James, Robert Davis died on May 26, 1787, and it seems likely that he was living in Standish at the time.

Robert Davis and his son James served in the Revolutionary War from Andover during 1780. In an account of his service, James Davis is described as being 18 years of age, 5 feet 9 inches in statue, and of light complexion. James Davis married in Andover, Mass., on Oct. 3, 1782, Chloe Wiley, born about 1761 daughter of James and Bethia (Frye) (Johnston) Davis of Andover, who later resided in Standish for a number of years. It seems likely that James Davis and his bride moved to Pearsontown soon after their marriage. Here they continued to live until their deaths, hers occurring on May 12, 1829, at the age of 67 years and his on Apr. 8, 1835, at the age of 73 years. Both are buried in the Oak Hill Cemetery located directly across the town road from the lot on which they lived. It seems likely that Prudence (Long) Davis, widow of Robert and mother of James, was one of the six females in James Davis's family in 1790 and the female over 45 living in his family at the time of the 1800 census.

James Davis was elected pound keeper at the first town meeting of Standish held on Mar. 27, 1786. He and his wife, Chloe, joined the First Parish Church of Standish in 1797 about the time that their children were baptized there. He along with Thomas Shaw and others protested against and tried to prevent the use of instrumental music in church services. Unsuccessful in their efforts, they later joined the Methodist Society of Gorham, Buxton, and Standish. It was probably because of this action that they were excommunicated from the Standish Church. James and Chloe (Wiley) Davis were the parents of the following children, all probably born in Standish:

i.   HANNAH, born Dec. 14, 1783, bapt. June 25, 1797, in the Standish Church, married Sept. 5, 1841, Daniel Moody of Standish as his second wife, died Feb. 25, 1878, age 94 yrs., 2 mos., 9 days.
ii.   SARAH (SALLY), born Mar. 31, 1785, bapt. June 25, 1797, married on July 3, 1808, William Binford Jr. of Baldwin, son of William and Dorcas (Richardson) Binford of that town. He died Sept. 28, 1845, age 61 yrs., and she July 21, 1855, age 70 yrs., 3 mos., 21 days, both in Baldwin.
iii.   NATHANIEL, born in May 1786, bapt. June 25, 1797, married Nov. 29, 1827, Nancy York, born about 1806 daughter of Isaac and Polly (Merrow) York of Standish. On Apr. 28, 1816, his father sold to him the northwesterly half (50 acres) of lot #66 (80/318), on which he

continued to live until his death on Dec. 29, 1843, at the age of 57 yrs. and 7 mos. At the time of his death Nathaniel was greatly in debt so that his wife, Nancy, had to sell the property at public auction. She moved moved to Biddeford, where she was living in 1850, and bought up her family. She died Nov. 17, 1885, age 79 yrs. in Biddeford. Their children were:
1. MARY S., born 1828 (on Addison Day) in Standish, married Joseph William Greenleaf. They resided in Boston twenty-four years, and in 1892, accompanied by her sister, Mrs. Chloe W. (Davis) Knight, widow of Dr. James Knight of Waterbury, Maine, moved to Los Angeles, Calif. Mary was living in Los Angeles on Sept. 25, 1903, when she furnished information told her by her mother about the York family to a man who was preparing an article about Abram York of Pearsontown.
2. CHLOE WILEY, born about 1831, (age 19 in 1850), married James Knight. She died May 29, 1900.

iv. JAMES WILEY, born Mar. 9, 1791, bapt. June 25, 1797, married Apr. 7, 1822, Mary Jane Jones, born Mar. 29, 1798, in Scarboro daughter of John and Lydia (Wescott) Jones of that town. He continued to live in Standish for some years and was living there as late as 1830 when his family consisted of him and his wife, both between 30 and 40; one male child under 5; and one female child between 5 and 10 yrs. of age. About 1815 his father sold to him the southwesterly half of lot #66, where he undoubtedly lived. He joined the First Parish Church of Standish on Apr. 29, 1830, and his wife was dismissed to the Standish Church from the First Congregational Church of Scarboro on June 9, 1833. A record of the births of his children is found in the Buxton records, so he must have moved to that town. He is also said to have lived in Westbrook at the time. He served in the War of 1812 from Newbury, Mass., and later received a land grant in Illinois for his services. He moved to Schuyler County in that state about 1850 and settled on a farm about six miles south of Richville. He died there on Oct. 1, 1857, and his wife, Mary Jane, Sept. 24, 1865, age 67 yrs., in Standish, she succumbing to typhoid fever. Both are buried on their homestead farm. James Wiley and Mary Jane (Jones) Davis were parents of the following family:
1. EDWIN AUGUSTUS, born Sept, 17, 1827, bapt. July 14, 1830, in the Standish Church, married Apr. 24, 1853, Melissa Ellen Dimock born in Rushville in 1834 daughter of Ebenezer and Marguerite (Philips) Dimock. They later moved to Missouri and from there about 1887-88 to California, where they homesteaded land in the San Joaquin Valley. He died in 1909 at Delano, Kern County, Calif., and she died there in 1920.
2. SUSAN JANE BLAKE, born Aug. 20 (21), 1823, bapt. in Standish Church July 14, 1830, died Aug. 20, 1847, unmarried.
3. JOHN JONES, born Feb. 13, 1832, died May 23, 1860, never married.
4. CHARLES WILLIAM, born Aug. 5, 1834, in Buxton, married Sarah Stubman; he died in Oct. 1918 in Rushville, Ill.

v. LYDIA, born about 1794, bapt. June 25, 1797, died July 13, 1869, age 75 yrs., in Standish. She never married and was living with her sister Sally (Davis) Binford in 1850 and may be buried in a grave marked only by a fieldstone alongside that of her brother Nathaniel in the Oak Hill Cemetery.
vi. WILEY, born ____, died in infancy.
vii. WILLIAM, bapt. Sept. 8, 1800, evidently died young.
viii. WILLIAM, born 1804, married Mary Ridlon, born 1807; they lived in Gorham. He died Aug. 9, 1879, age 75, and she on Mar. 18, 1898, age 91 yrs., 13 days. Both are buried in the Sapling Hill Cemetery on Route 237 in Gorham.

The name of Samuel Davis is found on the 1808 and 1814 tax lists of Standish. He was the Samuel Davis Jr. born July 4, 1762, in Barnstable, Mass., son of Samuel and Mary (Gorham) Davis who moved to Gorham before 1777. They lived on a farm above West Gorham. Samuel Davis Jr. served in the Revolutionary War in Capt. Whitmore's company. On Nov. 11, 1784, he married Mary Skillings, born Jan. 13, 1767, daughter of Isaac and Susannah (Watson) Skillings of Gorham. He died Jan. 22, 1856, age 93 years, 8 months, and she on Apr. 25, 1852, age 85 years, 3 months. He was the last of the Revolutionary soldiers in Standish. Both are buried in Standish Corner Cemetery. They had the following children born in Gorham:

i. ELIZABETH, born Aug. 5, 1785, died unmarried Apr. 4, 1876.
ii. SARAH, born Jan. 26, 1787, married first ____ Frost, second Parsons Pingree of Denmark. She died June 24, 1867, age 80, and is buried in the Standish Corner Cemetery.
iii. MARY C., born Sept. 8, 1788, died June 15, 1886, age 98, in Standish, unmarried.
iv. ISAAC, born Mar. 28, 1790, married Oct. 20, 1818, Hadassah Shaw, born May 18, 1793, daughter of Thomas and Anna (Wood) Shaw of Standish. She died May 26, 1824, age 31 yrs., in Standish and he married second Abigail (Whitney) Boucher. She died July 15, 1863, age 73 yrs., 4 days, in Standish and he died Sept. 5, 1867. Children of Isaac Davis and his first wife were:
1. AMOS S., born Apr. 30, 1818.
2. DANIEL, born May 10, 1820, died July 30, 1907, age 87 yrs., 2 mos., 20 days, in Standish.
3. LEVI S., born Oct. 11, 1822.
By second wife:
4. EMILY, born Dec. 21, 1830.
5. JOHN HENRY, born Oct. 21, 1833.
6. JOSHUA WHITNEY, born Aug. 18, 1835.
v. ZACHARIAH, born Sept. 24, 1791, married first Susan Ingalls, and second Nancy Ingalls. He lived in Bridgton and died Mar. 23, 1876.
vi. DANIEL, born Apr. 18, 1793, married Rebecca Plummer July 3, 1824. No children. He died at White Rock in Gorham on June 12, 1873 and she on Dec. 17, 1868.
vii. SUSANNA, born Feb. 3, 1795, married William Barker of Bridgton Feb. 17, 1820.

viii. SAMUEL, born July 13, 1796, went to South America and was never heard from again.
ix. JOHN, bapt. Apr. 15, 1798, married Nancy Whitten, lived in Naples, and died June 10, 1864.
x. JOANNA, born June 19, 1800, married June 23, 1842, Rev. John Buzzell of Parsonsfield and died in Gorham in Mar. 25, 1880.
xi. TABITHA, born Oct. 10, 1801, bapt. Nov. 21, 1816, died unmarried in 1831.

In Mar. 1803 Mr. Davis moved to Standish where the following children were born:

xii. MARK, born Apr. 23, 1803, married Lydia Staples, lived in Naples, and died in Mar. 12, 1842, age 38 yrs., 11 mos., Naples.
xiii. MARTHA, born Jan. 11, 1805, died unmarried Jan. 10, 1864, Standish.
xiv. HANNAH, born June 28, 1806, married Joseph Martin, lived in Naples, and died July 26, 1888.
xv. CAROLINE, born Jan. 25, 1808, married Francis Kimball of Naples. She died Oct. 9, 1881, Naples.
xvi. INFANT, born Oct. 20, 1809, died Nov. 4, 1809.

Joseph Davis, born in Gorham Aug. 10, 1776, son of Josiah and Thankful (Gorham) Davis, married Sept. 29, 1799, Abigail Whitney, born in Gorham Mar. 10, 1781, daughter of Asa and Patience (Weston) Whitney and probably settled in Standish soon after. They had one child:

i. NANCY, born Feb. 21, 1801, bapt. Nov. 21, 1805, married Jan. 7, 1819, James Frost, born Feb. 21, 1801, son of Wingate Frost of Limington. He died Jan. 31, 1865, and she Oct. 6, 1862, both in Limington.

His wife, Abigail, having died Jan. 28, 1802 (she is buried in Standish Corner Cemetery), he married second on Jan. 20, 1803, Sarah Mitchell, born May 6, 1786, daughter of Dominicus and Anna (Small) Mitchell of Standish. They had the following children, all but the last born in Standish.

ii. JAMES, born Apr. 13, 1804, bapt. Nov. 21, 1805, died in Brooks, Oct. 1, 1838.
iii. ABIGAIL, born Aug. 6, 1806, died Jan. 28, 1839.
iv. MARY ANN, born Aug. 25, 1808, died in Brooks Feb. 14, 1828.
v. ALLEN, born Dec. 31, 1810, died in Brooks Dec. 26, 1874.
vi. CAROLINE, born Apr. 5, 1813, died Oct. 9, 1857.
vii. MARSHALL, born Dec. 25, 1815, died in Brooks in Jan. 1885.
viii. WOODBURY, born July 25, 1818, died in Brooks Aug. 13, 1871.
ix. JOSEPH M., born in Brooks Dec. 6, 1821, died Aug. 3, 1825.

In the winter of 1820 Joseph Davis with his family moved to a farm in Brooks, Maine, where he resided until his death on Dec. 16, 1862. His wife died there Oct. 3, 1852.

There was another James Davis who lived in Standish for a brief period. He was born in Gorham Sept. 23, 1773, son of Josiah and Thankful (Gorham) Davis of Barnstable, Mass., and Gorham, Maine. He married Mar. 21, 1793, Thankful Paine, born in Gorham Nov. 26, 1773, daughter of William and Sarah (Mayo) Paine of Eastham, Mass., and Gorham, Maine. They moved to Standish and were parents of the following children:

i.   JOSIAH, born Dec. 5, 1793, married Oct. 19, 1821, Eunice Frost, born July 7, 1803, daughter of Wingate and Anna (Mitchell) Frost of Limington.
ii. PHEBE, born Jan. 31, 1795.
iii. MARTHA JONES, born Sept. 3, 1801, bapt. Oct. 11, 1803. married Jan. 24, 1827, Issacher Small of Limington.
iv. SAMUEL, died at sea.

James Davis died in Standish Aug. 25, 1801, age 29 years, and is buried in the cemetery at Standish Corner. His widow, Thankful, was found on the 1808 and 1814 tax lists of Standish and died in Standish in Sept. 1825, age 52 years (*Eastern Argus*, Oct. 14, 1825).

DEAN

John Dean Esq. was one of the most prominent of the early inhabitants of Pearsontown. His name is found on all the town tax lists consulted and in the 1790 census with a family of 2-1-4. At the time of the 1800 census his family consisted of him and his wife, one male under 10, one male and one female between 10 and 16, one male and one female between 16 and 26, and two females between 26 and 45 years of age. He was born at Dedham, Mass., June 11, 1743, son of Samuel and Mary (Avery) Dean, who later moved to Norton, Massachusetts. He was brother of the Rev. Samuel Dean, second pastor of the First Parish Church of Portland, who wrote in his diary under date of June 3, 1774, "Brother John and family arrived." Again under the date of June 7, 1774, he wrote as follows: "I accompanied brother John and family to Pearsontown; lodged at Mr. Tompson's." The Mr. Tompson referred to was without doubt the Rev. John Tompson, first pastor of the Pearsontown Church.

John Dean was living in Pearsontown on Mar. 27, 1776, when he purchased of Moses Pearson the 30-acre lots Nos. 63, 64, and 65 here (8/466).

He is said to have put up at Shaw's Tavern when he first moved into town and soon became active in town affairs, serving on the first board of selectmen elected in 1786. He was a justice of the peace for many years and as such officiated at the weddings of many of the young people of the town. On June 30, 1776, he was admitted into membership in the Pearsontown Church. When the tax of 1808 was assessed he was the heaviest taxpayer in town.

John Dean married at Norton, Mass., on June 16, 1766, Miriam Hodges, who was born about 1750. She died Aug. 25, 1791, in Standish, age 41, and he married second on May 18, 1793, Mary Jewett, sister of the Portland merchants, James and Joseph Jewett. She died Aug. 25, 1812, at the age of 62 years. He died in Standish at the age of 83 years on May 6, 1826. Children of John Dean, all by his first wife, were as follows:

i. RACHEL, born at Norton, Mass., Oct. 21, 1766, bapt. May 19, 1776, married (int. May 17, 1783, in Gorham) James Hasty of Pearsontown. They were the parents of eight children, for list of whom see Hasty family.
ii. JOHN JR., born at Norton, Mass., Sept. 29, 1769, bapt. May 19, 1776, was never married. He ran a wholesale grocery store in Portland on the south side of Middle Street near the junction with Free Street. He died suddenly in Boston, where he had gone on business, on Apr. 9, 1829, at the age of 59 yrs., and is buried in the Village Cemetery at Standish.
iii. NANCY, born at Norton, Mass., July 20, 1772, bapt. May 19, 1776, died unmarried at Standish on Apr. 21, 1832.
iv. LUCY, born about 1775, bapt. May 19, 1776, probably in Pearsontown, died unmarried in Standish on July 23, 1851, age 76 yrs.
v. MIRIAM, born in Pearsontown about 1778, bapt. Apr. 12, 1778, died in Standish Jan. 5, 1786, age 7 yrs.
vi. HENERETTA, born in Pearsontown in 1785, died in Standish Jan. 24, 1786, age 8 mos.
vii. MIRIAM, born in Standish about 1788, bapt. July 23, 1790, married Nov. 6 or 3, 1813, Enoch F. Higgins, born in Gorham July 13, 1789, son of Capt. Joseph and Mercy (Cook) Higgins of Eastham, Mass., and Gorham, Maine. He died Jan. 25, 1834, and she about 1885, age 96 yrs. Enoch and Miriam (Dean) Higgins were the parents of the following children:
1. HARRIET MARIA, born Aug. 19, 1814.
2. MARY, born May 26, 1818.
3. CAROLINE, born Apr. 7, 1820.
4. JOHN DEAN, born Jan. 23, 1826.

DECKER

A John Decker was living in Pearsontown for some time prior to the Revolutionary War. His name is found on the 1789, 1790, 1795, 1796, and later tax lists of Standish and in 1790 census with a family of 1-2-4. At the time of the 1800 census he was living in Standish with a family consisting of him and his wife, one male and two females under 10 years old, one male between 10 and 16, and two females between 16 and 26.

It seems without question that he was the John[4] Decker, son of David[5] and Eunice (Place) Decker, whose baptism on July 16, 1749, is found in the records of the North Church of Portsmouth, New Hampshire. He had a brother Joshua, baptized in the same church on Feb. 9, 1752, who settled in Buxton where the births of nine of his children are recorded. David and Eunice (Place) Decker moved to Boothbay, Maine, where they afterward lived and died. Several of their other children settled in that same general area.

The intentions of marriage of John Decker and Catherine Hall, daughter of Charles and Jemima (Dolliver) Hall, both of Pearsontown, are found in the vital records of Gorham, Maine, under the date of Sept. 14, 1771. Prior to that time John Decker had cleared five acres of land and built a house on 30-acre lot #125, since the Proprietors of Pearsontown on Feb. 2, 1771, had deeded that lot to him on fulfillment of conditions of settlement (7/223). Although he continued to live at this location for many years, the last years of his life were spent on a farm on Pudding Hill, where he died on Feb. 18, 1834. His wife died on Sept. 9, 1826, age 72 years, and both are buried in the cemetery at Standish Corner. John and Catherine (Hall) Decker were parents of the following children:

i. EUNICE, born ____, married Sept. 3, 1797 (int. Aug. 24, 1797), Benoni Woods of Standish and had children. After her death he married second on Apr. 4, 1807, Eleanor McDonald, born June 14, 1785, daughter of Peletiah McDonald of Standish. He ran away and left his family and, according to report, was never heard from again.

ii. CHARLES, born about 1778, bapt. Apr. 26, 1795, died in 1795 at the age of 17 yrs.

iii. JEMIMA, born about 1779, married Feb. 11, 1796, David Decker, a native of Boothbay, Maine, and probably her cousin. They lived for some years in Standish near Sticky River, but about 1810 moved to Raymond and settled on a farm in the part of that town which later became Casco. He was a successful farmer as well as being a minister of the Free Baptist Church. He died in 1843 at the age of 72 and his wife died in Casco on Jan. 26, 1842, at the age of 63. They were parents of the following children:
   1. MARY, married James Garling of Portland.
   2. DAVID JR., born Mar. 8, 1802, a farmer and lumberman, married Eliza Dunham of Otisfield.
   3. WILLIAM, a farmer, married Mary Whitney of Harrison.
   4. JOHN, a farmer, married Mary Furlong of Greenwood.
   5. EUNICE, married Ira Smith, a cooper of Standish.
   6. CHARLES, a farmer, married Mary Jackson of Casco.
   7. NATHAN, born in Casco Mar. 18, 1814, married Mrs. Hannah (Stewart) of Harrison.
   8. SPENCER, a merchant in Casco, married Rebecca Walker of that town.

iv. MOLLY, died Aug. 11, 1840, unmarried.

v. BETSEY, died unmarried.

vi. JOHN, was of West Gore Plantation on Nov. 9, 1806, when his intentions of marriage to Eliza Rowe of Standish were filed. They were married on Mar. 18, 1807. He married second on Sept. 18, 1809 (int. Jan. 25, 1809), Abigail Hall, his cousin. On Apr. 8, 1823, he married third Eunice Hall, born Nov. 4, 1793, sister of his second wife. He married fourth on Mar. 6, 1836, Abigail McLucus of Hiram. He died Sept. 19, 1844.

vii. HANNAH, born about 1791, married June 29, 1816 (int. Dec. 9. 1815), Abraham Tibbetts, born in 1792 son of Stephen and Hannah (Decker) Tibbetts. They lived for awhile near Pudding Hill in Standish, but later settled in Brownfield, Maine, where he died Sept. 4, 1875, age 83, and she on June 5, 1863, age 72.

viii. DORCAS, born about 1792, married first Jan. 9, 1817, Jonathan Lowell, born in Standish Sept. 17, 1787, son of Jonathan and Mary (Pierce) Lowell. They were the parents of three children when he was drowned in Sebago Lake by the upsetting of a boat on Nov. 2,

1826. She married second her cousin Oliver Hall, born Jan. 31, 1792, son of John and Emma (York) Hall of Standish. They lived on the David Decker place near Sticky River. She died May 28, 1854, age 62, and he about 1855.

ix. CHARLES, born 1804, married Feb. 8, 1822, his cousin Lydia Hall, born Apr. 28, 1805, daughter of Charles and Lydia (Noble) Hall. He died in 1886 and she died Nov. 16, 1880, age 76 yrs., Baldwin. The children of Charles and Lydia (Hall) Decker were:
1. LYDIA, born Jan. 9, 1823.
2. EDMUND, born May 13, 1827.
3. MARY ANN, born May 9, 1833.
4. CHARLES, born Sept. 11, 1834.
5. SARAH MARIA, born May 11, 1837.
6. LUCINDA, born Feb. 1, 1840.

DENNETT

The name of Samuel Dennett is found on the 1796 and later tax lists of Standish, in the church records, and in the 1800 census with a family consisting of him and his wife, one male and one female under 10 years old. He was born Dec. 10, 1770, son of Nicholas and Phebe (Fabyan) Dennett of Pepperellborough and baptized in the church there on Dec. 16, 1770. He was a tanner and as Samuel Dennett 3rd of Pepperellborough on July 10, 1793, bought from Ephraim Jones of Standish, 2.5 acres of lot #35 in first division in Standish, said tract of land being about 8 rods distant from the meeting house on the northwest road (24/399). On Apr. 20, 1801, Samuel and Polly Dennett of Standish sold Benjamin Swett and Peter Rowe of Standish 15 acres of lot #95 in first division (34/418).

On Apr. 23, 1797, Samuel Dennett married Mary (Polly) Lowell, born in Standish Apr. 8, 1779, daughter of Daniel and Mercy (Davis) Lowell. He died Feb. 22, 1844, age 74 years, 2 months, and she on Mar. 15, 1872, age 92 years, 11 months. They were the parents of the following children:

i. HANNAH, born Nov. 7, 1797, married Oct. 26, 1820, as his second wife, Capt. Benjamin Poland, born Dec. 26, 1784, son of Benjamin Poland of Falmouth. She died Feb. 28, 1824, age 26 yrs., in Standish and was buried in Dennett Tomb in Standish Village as is he. Capt. Poland married first Nov. 8, 1807, Sally Dinsdall, born Feb. 2, 1789, and died Aug. 18, 1818. He married third May 9, 1829, Lucy Sanborn, born Aug. 28, 1799, and after he died June 4, 1834, in Standish, she married July 18, 1837, Jacob S. Rollins.
ii. JOHN, born Nov. 4, 1799, died May 31, 1826.
iii. GEORGE, born Nov. 14, 1801, was insane and died Dec. 8, 1850, at Augusta, Maine.
iv. SALLY GRAY, born July 3, 1804, married Jonathan Moore of Standish, born Nov. 3, 1805, son of Jonathan S. and Hannah (Richardson) Moore. She died in Portland Jan. 4, 1869.

v. **MARY**, born Sept. 1, 1806, married June 17, 1832 Greenleaf Howe, born Apr. 5, 1807, son of Dr. Ebenezer and Catherine (Spring) Howe of Standish. They lived in Cambridgeport, Mass., where she died Mar. 15, 1872. He died in Somersville, Mass., in 1873.
vi. **EMELINE**, born Sept. 17, 1808, married Daniel Ruggles of Bridgton.
vii. **GARDINER**, born June 14, 1811, married Oct. 19, 1836, Eliza R. Howe in Dorchester, Mass. She died Mar. 11, 1854. Four children.
viii. **LOUISA**, born July 21, 1813, lived in Standish.
ix. **OLIVE**, born Sept. 24, 1815, married Rev. William McDonald and died Jan. 1, 1859. No issue.
x. **ABIGAIL**, born Mar. 12, 1820, died Mar. 24 or 31, 1854.

DORSETT

Peter Dorsett, a shoemaker, is given as a resident of Gorham when he bought land in Standish in 1799. He was born about 1773. Dr. Meserve says he was a Frenchman. On May 4, 1800, he married Joanna Rowe, born Apr. 4, 1777, daughter of Caleb and Priscilla (Perkins) Rowe of Standish. In 1800 census they were living in Standish with no children, each being between 26 and 45 years of age. Joanna (Rowe) Dorsett died on Apr. 10, 1807, age 29 years, in Standish, leaving three sons. He married second (int. Sept. 5, 1807, in Standish) Mary (Coss) Hinckley of Standish, widow of Stephen Hinckley, a sea captain who was lost at sea in a hurricane on Dec. 25, 1804. She was born in Portsmouth, N.H., on Jan. 4. 1778, and died in Standish on May 12, 1812, age 34. At the time of the 1810 census Peter Dorsett was living in Standish with a son between 10 and 16 years old, probably his wife's son Stephen Hinckley by her first marriage, they both being between 26 and 45 years of age. It would appear that Peter's children by his first marriage were not living with him but had been residing with some of their mother's relatives.

Peter Dorsett married third on July 9, 1815, Lucy Eaton of Standish who probably was the daughter of Israel Eaton. His name appears on 1808 and 1814 tax lists of Standish. In 1830 he, being between 50 and 60 years of age, was living alone in Brownfield and married fourth (int. Aug. 7, 1834) Mrs. Mary W. Lewis of Hiram, he being a resident of Standish at the time. He was a member of the Brownfield Congregational Church and listed in the church records as having died on Apr. 2, 1841. According to his obituary given in Apr. 15, 1841, issue of the *Christain Mirror*, he died in Brownfield Mar. 30, after a week's confinement, age 68 years. As far as has been discovered, Peter Dorsett was the father of the following children:

i. **THOMAS**, born Apr. 1, 1801, died Dec. 3, 1860.
ii. **SYLVANUS BATCHELDER**, born Jan. 7, 1802, married (int. May 30, 1825) Mary Gray of Denmark, he of Baldwin. He divorced her and she married Aug. 31, 1835, Albion Peter Strout, whose alias is Sally Strout of Limington and Buxton. He was of Bartlett, N.H.,

when his intention of marriage to Patience Strout of Standish was filed in Standish on Aug. 29, 1839. He was listed as a cooper living in Standish in 1850 census. His wife died in Limington on May 21, 1882, age 75 yrs., 3 mos., 29 days, and he died July 11, 1891, age 89 yrs., 1 mo., 4 days, Steep Falls.

iii. NANCY, born May 22, 1804.
iv. PETER STEELE, born Jan. 15, 1807, according to deeds in Woodstock, Conn., he died in Albany, Vt., on Oct. 16, 1850, married at Newark, Vt., Oct. 31, 1830, Tirzah Palmer, daughter of Charles. According to his granddaughter he was an orphan and raised by his grandparents.

By his third wife, Lucy Easton:
v. JOANNA, born July 29, 1815.
vi. AGNES MOULTON, born Sept. 21, 1816, died Oct. 6, 1836, age 21 yrs., North Limington, in the family of Benjamin Meserve.
vii. ASAHEL BURT, born Mar. 1, 1819.
viii. ALICE IRENE, born Dec. 29, 1822.

DOW

The names of Jabez Dow (1-0-2), Joseph Dow (1-3-2), and Abner Dow (2-2-4) are found in the 1790 census of Standish and on the 1789 and 1790 tax lists. Jabez Dow, the father of the other two, was born Aug. 12, 1727, son of Samuel and Sarah (Shepard) Dow of Salisbury, Massachusetts. He married (int. Aug. 11, 1750) Dorothy Wood, born Dec. 10, 1727, of Salisbury. After the birth of their first two children, they moved to Falmouth, Maine, where they bought a truck farm. He was living in Falmouth on Sept. 9, 1760, when he sold to John True of North Yarmouth land in that town which he purchased Nov. 10, 1749 (1/373). Jabez Dow and his wife, Dorothy, sold land in North Yarmouth to Abraham Sawyer of Falmouth on Apr. 14, 1762 (2/176). He was still living in Falmouth on July 26, 1763, when he bought #104 in Pearsontown from Ephraim Jones and Dec. 26, 1770, when he bought from John Wood the 30-acre lot #93 in Pearsontown (8/475). He continued to live in Falmouth until after the burning of the town in 1775, his name being found on a list of men from Falmouth who were living in Pearsontown in 1777. It is likely that he settled on 30-acre lot #93 when he came to Pearsontown to live. Here he continued to dwell until his death on Feb. 19, 1820, age 92 years, in Standish (*Eastern Argus*, Feb. 29, 1820). His wife died in Feb. 1808 in 81st year of her age (*Eastern Argus*, Feb. 25, 1808). According to her obituary she was taken into the church in Salisbury in the twenty-fourth year of her age. She was a pious, exemplary Christian, an affectionate and faithful wife and parent, an amiable and pleasant friend.

Jabez and Dorothy (Wood) Dow were the parents of the following children:

i. ABNER, born Aug. 28, 1751, in Salisbury, Mass., was a shoemaker in Falmouth, Maine, and one of the first ten to enlist May 12, 1775, in the company of Capt. David Bradish at the outbreak of the Revolutionary War. He served through 1781 and was living in

Pearsontown on July 27, 1782, when his intentions of marriage to Martha (Sawyer) Hinckley, widow of Stephen Hinckley, were filed in Gorham. On June 1, 1785, he bought from Ebenezer Higgins of Pearsontown two-thirds of the 30-acre lot #33 on which he evidently lived. He died in Standish in 1794. His widow died Apr. 16, 1816, age 64. They were parents of the following children:
1. SAMUEL, born Jan. 3, 1783, bapt. Nov. 13, 1785, evidently died young.
2. ABIGAIL OR NABBY, born Mar. 5, 1784, bapt. Nov. 13, 1785, married Nov. 12, 1809, James Benson of Gorham, Standish, and Limington. He died May 16, 1832, and she died in Gorham June 9, 1852, age 68. For children see Benson family.
3. MERCY OR MARCY, born Aug. 27, 1785, bapt. Nov. 13, 1785, married May 10, 1807, Luther Topping of Standish and Baldwin. She died Oct. 1869. For children see Topping family.
4. ELIZABETH (BETSEY), born Apr. 1, 1787, bapt. Elizabeth Knowlton Oct. 19, 1794.
5. SETH HINCKLEY, born Aug. 3 or 13, 1790, bapt. Oct. 19, 1794, married in Mar. 1815 Harriet (Martha?) Sanborn, born in Baldwin Dec. 9, 1794, and died at Turner, Maine, Aug. 23, 1884. He was a cooper and lived at West Baldwin where he died Mar. 25, 1841. They had eight children. She was daughter of Joseph and Abigail (McKenney) Sanborn.

ii. SAMUEL, born Apr. 22, 1753.
iii. SARAH, born Mar. 2, 1756, died young.
iv. JOSEPH, born Mar. 17, 1758, in Falmouth, served in the Revolutionary War. He was living in Pearsontown on Apr. 26, 1782, when his intentions of marriage to Lucy Sanborn, born Oct. 19, 1755, daughter of John and Lucy (Sanborn) Sanborn of Hampton Falls, N.H., and Pearsontown, were filed in Gorham. Capt. Joseph died in Standish on Oct. 31, 1805, age 48 yrs., and his wife on Sept. 1, 1836. They were parents of the following children:
1. SUSANNAH (SUKEY), born Nov. 26, 1782, married Apr. 11, 1805, Daniel Hasty Jr., born May 3, 1780, son of Daniel and Martha (McLaughlin) Hasty of Scarboro and Pearsontown. She died July 20, 1858, age 76, and he on May 18, 1863. For children see Hasty family.
2. JABEZ born Mar. 13, 1785, married Dec. 24, 1810, Lucy Sanborn, born in Standish Sept. 1, 1789. They lived in Standish, where he died Oct. 31, 1868, and she on Oct. 4, 1854. They were the parents of eight children among whom were Wilson, Susan, Almira, Lucy, Matilda, Benjamin A., and John J.
3. JOSEPH, born 1789, died Nov. 23, 1789, age 3 mos.
4. JOSEPH, born Oct. 22 or 23, 1790, married (int. Oct. 14, 1817) Catherine Rounds, born July 13, 1794, daughter of Joseph and Susanna (Mosher) Rounds of Buxton. She died Feb. 4, 1840, age 45. He served in the War of 1812 and died Apr. 24, 1875. He married second Lydia (Thompson) (Cole) Small. She was born Apr. 20, 1803, and died Nov. 24, 1878, in Standish. They lived in Standish. Children by first marriage: Harriet Rounds born Aug. 20, 181-; Emeline, born June 9, 1821; Rachael Ayer,

born Sept. 9, 1823; Eliza Irish, born Dec. 28, 1826; Mary Rounds, born Sept. 27, 1828; Benjamin Ayer, born Oct. 28, 1832; and Oliver, who died July 8, 1905, age 67 yrs., 7 mos., 5 days, in Standish.
5. ABNER, born Nov. 20, 1792, died Dec. 7, 1850, age 58 yrs. He married Apr. 6, 1817, Francis Thompson, born Mar. 17, 1795, daughter of Dr. Isaac Snow and Charlotte (Hay) Thompson of Standish. She died in Gorham Sept. 29, 1873. Children were: Franklin, Susan, Frances S., Deborah T., Benjamin L., Alfred A., and Leander Abner.

v. JABEZ JR., born July 17, 1760, lost at sea in navy at time of Revolutionary War.
vi. JONATHAN, born Nov. 20, 1762, died Dec. 24, 1773.
vii. SARAH, born Aug. 20, 1766, married Richard Pierce.
viii. MERCY, born July 5, 1771, died Nov. 19, 1773.

DRESSER

The name of Benjamin Dresser is found on the 1789 and 1790 tax lists of Standish but for a poll tax only. It appears likely that he was the Benjamin Dresser of Fryeburg, who was born in Andover, Mass., Jan. 6, 1768, son of Jonathan and Sarah (Foster) Dresser of that town. The Dresser family moved to Fryeburg about 1777. The eldest child of Jonathan and Sarah (Foster) Dresser, Sarah by name, born Sept. 17, 1750, married (int. Jan. 23, 1776, in Gorham) Job Eastman of Fryeburg. The Eastmans were inhabitants of Standish from 1789 to 1792 and it is possible that Mrs. Eastman's brother Benjamin was living with them during that period.

Jonathan Dresser[5] (Nathan,[4] John,[3] Lt. John,[2] John[1]) son of Nathan and Lydia (Foster) Dresser, was born in Rowley, Mass., in 1724. He married at Andover, Mass., Sarah Foster of that town on Nov. 24, 1748, he being of Boxford. He settled in Andover where all his children were born. He served in the French and Indian campaign of 1757 and about 1777 moved to Fryeburg, Maine, where he was living at the time of the 1790 census and died there in 1800. Children:

i. SARAH, born Sept. 17, 1750.
ii. ELIZABETH, born July 23, 1752.
iii. STEPHEN, born Oct. 25, 1754, living in Suncook Town, Maine, in 1790.
iv. JONATHAN, born Sept. 14, 1757.
v. SIMEON, born Feb. 21, 1759, served in Revolution from Andover, Mass.
vi. LEVI, born Feb. 24, 1761, served in Revolution from Fryeburg, Maine, was living in Suncook Town, Maine, in 1790.
vii. MARY, born Nov. 1, 1762.
viii. CHLOE, born Dec. 15, 1765.
ix. BENJAMIN, born Jan. 6, 1768 (Andover, Mass., vital records)

DUNHAM

An Elijah Dunham was among the very earliest of those who lived for awhile in Pearsontown. He was one of the men hired to guard the fort and, as was the case with most of those so employed, it is likely that he had his family with him there. He was a member of the guard in 1755 and was listed as a resident of Pearsontown when he served from May to September in Captain William Gerrish's company in His Majesty's Service in 1759. He was given as being 35 years old and a resident of Pearsontown, but originally coming from Middleton, Mass., when he enlisted on Mar. 3, 1760, in His Majesty's Service. Last record of his living in Pearsontown was in 1761 when his name is found on a list of Pearsontown men who worked on Gorham roads during that year.

Although no actual proof has been found to substantiate the fact, it appears probable that he was the Elijah Dunham who with sons Elijah Jr. and Joseph, is said to have settled in Deer Isle, Maine, in 1766. In the 1800 census of Deer Isle is found the name of an Elijah Dunham (whether this was Elijah Sr. or Jr. has not been discovered), who is listed as coming to that town from St. Georges, Maine. Therefore it seems likely that Elijah Dunham of Pearsontown left there about 1762 and moved to St. Georges, remaining there for a few years until his final settlement on Deer Isle in 1766. Date of his death has not been found, but it was probably after 1785 since his name is found on a list of inhabitants of Deer Isle on Aug. 23 of that year. He is said to have died at an advanced age.

Elijah Dunham Sr. was twice married but the maiden names of neither of his wives have been discovered. Children by first wife were:

i.   **ELIJAH JR.**, born about 1752, married first _____ Haskell, daughter of Capt. Mark Haskell, by whom he had one son and three daughters; second a widow Choate, mother of Mr. George G. Choate; third Polly Morey, daughter of Elias Morey.
ii. **JOSEPH**, was married, and died about 1830.
iii. **A DAUGHTER**, married Samuel Pickering.

By second wife:
iv. **ELISHA H.**, born _____, married first Abigail Gross, daughter of George Gross; second _____ (Staples) Emerson, daughter of Samuel Staples and widow of Joshua Emerson.
v.   **A DAUGHTER**.
vi. **A DAUGHTER**.

EASTMAN

The name of Job Eastman is found on the 1789 and 1790 tax lists and the 1790 census with a family of 1-1-2, but it is not likely that he lived in town for any great length of time. He held an innholder's license in Standish for the year 1788. He was born July 26, 1754, in Pembroke, N.H., son of Deacon Richard and Mary (Lovejoy) Eastman, and was of

Fryeburg, Maine, when his intentions of marriage to Sarah Dresser of that town were published on Jan. 23, 1776, in Gorham. She was born in Andover, Mass., Sept. 17, 1750, daughter of Jonathan and Sarah (Foster) Dresser of Fryeburg.

He was living in Standish on Feb. 19, 1789, when he got a tax deed for 68 acres of lot #2 in the third division in Standish (27/529). He was of Norway, Maine, on Aug. 15, 1798, when he sold the same land in Standish to Dr. Stephen Cummings of Waterford, Maine. He had settled in Norway in 1792, going to live in the house built for his nephew Jonathan Cummings Jr., son of his sister. He taught the first boys' school in Norway in 1793. When the town was incorporated in 1797 he was elected chairman of the selectmen and town treasurer. He was town clerk for about forty years and a justice of the peace for forty-seven years.

The date of death of his first wife has not been discovered, but on Jan. 1, 1827, Job Eastman and his wife, Jane G. Eastman, of Norway sold land in Poland, Maine, to Joseph Jackson of Poland, it being part of the farm willed to her by her former husband, the late Daniel Jackson of Poland (117/30). He died Feb. 28, 1845. His widow died after 1852. Both the *History of Norway* and an article in Vol. 9 of the *Maine Historical and Genealogical Recorder* state that he left no children, so apparently those that he would appear to have had at the time of the 1790 census must have died before him.

EATON

The name of Israel Eaton is found on the 1789, 1790, 1795, 1796, 1800, 1808, and 1814 tax lists of Standish and in the 1790 census lists. Since he paid only a poll tax in 1789 and 1790, it is evident that he did not own real estate in town until after that date. It was on Mar. 1, 1791, that he bought from James Randall of Limington the 30-acre lot #83 in first division in Standish (73/399). Here he established his homestead, which he sold on Dec. 23, 1815, to Dr. Ebenezer Howe of Standish (73/400), the deed being signed by Israel and Sarah Eaton, this giving a clue to the given name of his wife.

At the time of 1790 census Israel Eaton was credited with a family of 1-1-6 while in 1800 his family consisted of him and his wife, both over 45 years of age, one male child under 10, and two females between 10 and 16 years old. Positive identification of the parentage of Israel Eaton has not been established. However, an Israel Eaton, born in Reading, Mass., Sept. 2, 1750, son of Israel and Jemima (____) Eaton, married July 25, 1775, Sarah Muckintire of Reading and had daughter Sarah born there Sept. 7, 1777. The similarity of names makes it an interesting possibility that this Israel Eaton was the one who settled in Standish, especially since he disappears from the Reading records after the birth of his daughter Sarah.

Israel Eaton's death is given in the Mar. 4, 1825, issue of the *Christian Mirror*, age 71 years, in Windham, formerly of Standish. In the *Eastern Argus*, issue of Jan. 6, 1824, is given the death of Mrs. Sarah, wife of Israel Eaton, formerly of Standish, age 70 years, in Westbrook.

No definite information has been found as to the children of Israel and Sarah (_____) Eaton of Standish, but it is likely that some or perhaps all of the following were their offspring:
i. SUSANNA, married May 2, 1800, Zachariah Mitchell of Windham.
ii. JEMIMA, married Nov. 27, 1808, Moses Richardson of Standish.
iii. MARY, married (int. Dec. 16, 1809, in Windham), Reuben Mitchell of that town.
iv. LUCY, married July 9, 1815, Peter Dorsett of Standish.

EDGECOMB

The name of Gibbins Edgecomb appears in the 1810 census of Standish with a family consisting of him and his wife, each between 26 and 45 years of age, one male and one female under 10, two males and one female between 10 and 16, and one male and one female between 16 and 26 years old. It appears that he was the Gibbons Edgecomb born Apr. 13, 1770, son of Gibbins and Rhoda (Elwell) Edgecomb of Saco, Maine. On Feb. 7, 1790, he married Abigail Lane, born Mar. 28, 1761, daughter of Capt. John and Elizabeth (Hancock) Lane of Buxton. It is not known to this writer where he lived before his sojourn in Standish, which was probably of short duration, but he moved to Gardiner, Maine, where he is said to have raised his family and where his brothers Thomas and Eliphalet Edgecomb also settled. According to Gardiner vital records, Gibbins Edgecomb, husband of Abigail and late of Standish, died Jan. 7, 1814, age 46, in Plattsburgh, N.Y. (was this during service in the War of 1812?), and Abigail Edgecomb died Oct. 27, 1859. age 98 years, 7 months. A list of the children of this couple has not been found but undoubtedly some of those bearing the Edgecomb name found in the Gardiner vital records belonged to them.

It seems likely that John Lane Edgecomb, age 59 in 1850, who on Nov. 19, 1815, married Martha York, age 56 in 1850, daughter of Isaac and Betsey (Meserve) York of Standish, and settled in Standish on the westerly side of what is now Route 25 near its junction with Dow Road (now discontinued) was a son of Gibbins and Abigail (Lane) Edgecomb. Dates of their deaths have not been found as they were buried in a family graveyard on their farm located at the top of Deer Hill, and where several graves it contains are marked only by fieldstones. The graveyard is now lost in the woods. Said to have been buried there are John L. Edgecomb and his wife Martha (York) Edgecomb, Isaac L. Edgecomb and his wife, Mary A. (Edgecomb) Johnson and her husband Royal A. Johnson, and William G. Edgecomb.

John L. Edgecomb lived in Gardiner and Limington before finally settling in Standish and was the father of the following children:
i. GIBBINS, born May 3, 1816, died Jan. 29, 1857.
ii. ISAAC L., born July 6, 1818, married Elizabeth Bradbury of Hiram and settled on the northerly side of the Deer Hill Road in Standish near the top of the hill. He died July 6, 1890, age 71 yrs., in Standish. His wife, Elizabeth, was age 52 in 1870 census of Standish. They were parents of the following children:

1. **WILLIAM GARDNER**, born about 1848, lived on old Edgecomb place in Standish, never married. He was lame from an accident in which he was involved in Mass.
2. **ALPHONZO W.**, born about 1848, died Aug, 12, 1883, age 34 years in Boston, Mass.
3. **ELLEN M.**, born about 1850.
4. **JOHN L.**, born Apr. 27, 1855, married Eleanor E. Haskell, born in 1869, of Standish. She died in 1896 and he on June 13, 1930, and are buried in the Dow's Corner Cemetery.
5. **MARY ANN**, born Feb. 26, 1856, married Oct. 23, 1880, Royal A. Johnson, born Dec. 3, 1850, son of Isaac L. and Hannah B. (Whitney) Johnson of Standish. They lived in Standish, where she died June 7, 1897, and he in Apr. or May 1916.
6. **ABBY B.**, born about Mar. 1861, married James Stillman Chick of Standish.

iii. **ELIZABETH**, born Sept. 20, 1820, married Nov. 14, 1844, Isaac Marr Jr. of Limington. She died Oct. 10, 1849, age 29 yrs., in Limington.
iv. **FANNIE**, born Dec. 3, 1822, died Sept. 19, 1829, in Standish.
v. **JOHN YORK**, born Feb. 20, 1824, in Limington, died Feb. 5, 1897, age 78 yrs., 3 mos., 11 days, West Buxton.
vi. **WILLIAM**, born Mar. 19, 1826, in Hollis.
vii. **MARY ANN**, born Aug. 1, 1829, in Standish.
viii. **ABIGAIL JANE**, born Feb. 21, 1832, in Standish.
ix. **RHODA**, born Aug. 8, 1834, in Standish.

EDMUNDS

Asa Edmunds was another of those early inhabitants whose stay in Standish was of rather short duration. He was born in Dudley, Mass., Aug. 19, 1757, son of Joseph Jr. and Ruth (Putney) Edmunds. He married Eunice Hawley, who was born Dec. 17, 1756. He served in the Revolutionary War, being credited to the town of Winchendon, Mass., and is said to have been one of the picked men who under Maj. William Barton in July 1777 crossed over to R.I., and succeeded in capturing General Prescott of the British army.

On Sept. 21, 1786, he bought of James Frost of Falmouth two 30-acre lots of land in Little Ossipee Plantation, later Limington, as found in York deeds. He is listed in the 1790 census of that town with a family of 1-1-1. At the time of the incorporation of the town of Limington in 1792, he was elected the first town clerk, a post which he held for only one year. On Nov. 4, 1792, Asa Edmunds and Daniel Dyer sold 35 acres of lot #4 on Range C in Limington at the northwest corner of the lot as found recorded in Book 56, page 261 at the York County Registry of Deeds.

Just when he left Limington and moved to Standish has not been discovered, but he sold his property in Nov. 1792 and was living here on May 24, 1797, when he bought Standish land from Ephraim Jones (26/199). On May 2, 1800, he and his wife, Eunice, sold John Quinby and Jonathan Sparrow of Falmouth, merchants, the 100-acre lot #80 in third division of lots in Standish (32/400). Asa and Eunice Edmunds of Standish sold Daniel Lowell of this town land here on July 21, 1803.

About 1805 or before, Asa Edmunds and his wife, Eunice, moved to Belfast, Maine. He was by profession a schoolteacher, which he followed in Belfast and no doubt had practiced in Limington and Standish. He was Chairman of the Board of Selectmen of Belfast during the War of 1812 when that town was occupied by the British. A prominent member of the Masonic fraternity, he was the first treasurer of the Belfast Lodge, where his portrait adorns the lodge hall.

Asa Edmunds was a Revolutionary War pensioner, as was his widow, Eunice. He died in Belfast May 3, 1838, and she survived him until June 3, 1843. Their only child, as far as has been discovered, was a son Alvan Edmunds, born July 21, 1780. Alvan Edmunds' name is found in an account book of Thomas Shaw of Standish from Sept. 1802 through May 1803. He moved to Belfast by 1804 and built a house on Main Street where he had his saddler's shop in the second story. He married Nov. 6, 1806, Elizabeth Durham, born Apr. 8, 1785, daughter of John and Elizabeth (Brown) Durham of Belfast. He died June 6, 1843, and she on Nov. 8, 1846.

ELWELL

The name of Isaac Elwell is found on the 1795 and 1796 tax lists of Standish. He was baptized in the First Parish Church of Falmouth (Portland) on Feb. 20, 1774, as Isaac Battle Elwell, son of Jonathan and Abigail (Horton) Elwell, who soon after moved to Gorham to live. On Oct. 5, 1796, he married Mary Butterfield, born May 16, 1774, daughter of Joseph and Mary (Harding) Butterfield of Standish. They lived in Standish until about 1798 when they moved to Gorham. Children were:
i. **DAVID**, born in Standish May 9, 1797.
ii. **JOHN**, born in Gorham, Nov. 17, 1798.
iii. **SALLY ADAMS**, born in Gorham Aug. 28, 1802.

EMERY

The Joshua Emery whose name is found on the 1795 tax list of Standish was perhaps the Joshua[6] (James,[5] Thomas,[4] James,[3] James,[2] Anthony[1]) Emery who was born in Biddeford, Maine, Apr. 7, 1774, son of James and Mary (Scamman) Emery and who on Aug. 13, 1797, married the daughter of George and Martha (Thorn) Freeman of Standish. They lived in Portland where he died in 1858.

FOGG

Edmund Fogg was one of the early inhabitants of the town of Pearsontown who did not live here very many years. His name appears in a list of inhabitants of the town prior to the burning of Falmouth in 1775 and in the Standish Church records. He was the son of Samuel and Rachel (Mariner) Fogg of Scarboro, in which town he was born Mar. 28, 1748, and baptized Apr. 3, 1748. On Aug. 6, 1772, he married Sarah Warren of that town. It was on Jan. 8, 1770, that he being of Scarboro bought from Ephraim Jones of Falmouth the two 30-acre lots Nos. 109 and 110 in Pearsontown, the condition of sale being that he was to clear land, build a house, and settle a family thereon (5/275 and 8/507). On Mar. 11, 1779, he being of Pearsontown bought land in New Gloucester of Ebenezer Mayo of that town. It was on Jan. 28, 1780, that while still living in Pearsontown he sold his land here to Nathaniel Bacon of Gorham (13/15).

His father, Samuel Fogg of Scarboro, who settled in New Gloucester in 1776, states in a short family history that his son Edmund Fogg together with his family moved in Mar. 1780 from Pearsontown into the western room of his father's (Samuel) house in New Gloucester whence he moved in September of the same year into a house of his own in that town. Edmund Fogg died in New Gloucester on Apr. 25, 1801, and she Apr. 25, 1803. Children of Edmund and Sarah (Warren) Fogg were as follows:

i. MARY, born in Pearsontown June 11, 1773, bapt. there Aug. 23, 1773, married Jan. 3, 1795, Jacob Randall of Freeport.
ii. RACHEL, born Mar. 21, 1775, married Thomas Wharf of New Gloucester.
iii. EDMUND, born Mar. 31, 1777, in Pearsontown, bapt. there June 22, 1777, married Dec. 24, 1804, Hannah York of New Gloucester and lived in that town. Widow of Edmund Fogg died May 21, 1843.
iv. WALTER, born Feb. 15, 1779, in Pearsontown, bapt. there May 26, 1779, married in Mar. 1803 Dorothy McIntire of New Gloucester and about 1805 moved to Greene, Maine.
v. ANNA, born June 13, 1781, in New Gloucester, died young.
vi. SAMUEL, born Aug. 10, 1783, married Mary Cushman and moved to Guilford, Maine.
vii. SARAH, born Aug. 10, 1783 (twin), died in Feb. 180_.
viii. WILLIAM, born Apr. 23, 1785, married Esther Moody of New Gloucester and died there May 29, 1828.
ix. ELIZABETH, born Mar. 24, 1793.

FOSS

There were several Foss families that appeared in Standish in the early years of the nineteenth century. They descended from Job Foss of Falmouth, Maine, who lived in the Stroudwater section of that town and his wife, Eunice (Chick) Foss, married in Falmouth on Apr. 13, 1784.

Job Foss moved to Limington after his marriage, with his wife's brother, Ephraim Chick, and lived there until 1800, when by deed dated Apr. 10, 1800, they sold their property in Limington, returned to Stroudwater, and purchased land of Peter Chick. The year after returning to Stroudwater, Job Foss, while attempting to walk across a stringer of the bridge at Stroudwater, fell into the river and drowned. Parson Caleb Bradley, in his record of funerals, made the following entry: May 6, 1801, Mr. Foss drowned, aged 35 years.

His widow married (int. Aug.27, 1803) John Haskell of Standish, she of Falmouth, and moved to Standish taking her children with her. By her second husband she had four children, viz: Solomon, Ephraim, Francis and Mehitable.

Job and Eunice (Chick) Foss were the parents of five children, as follows:

i. EBENEZER, born Jan. 18, 1785, grew up in Standish after his father's death and on Nov. 11, 1811, married Hannah York, born Oct. 26, 1791, daughter of Ebenezer and Mehitable (Jones) York of Standish. They lived near the Saco River on York's Hill on the River Road near the Boulter Neighborhood at South Standish, where she died Dec. 28, 1825, age 31 yrs., 2 mos., and he on Aug. 20, 1855, age 69 yrs., 7 mos., and were buried in a small burying ground on their farm. They were parents of the following children: (Foss)

1. JOB, born Feb. 4, 1813, married Nov. 24, 1840, Lucinda Meeds, born Jan. 25, 1813, in Limington daughter of Artemas and Desire (Johnson) Meeds of Limington and Standish. They lived in Standish were she died Jan. 20, 1858, age 45 yrs., 9 mos., 26 days. He married second int. May 27, 1860, Betsey L. Haines of West Buxton and divorced. They divorced in Apr. 1861 and he filed marriage intentions Nov. 19, 1864, to Mrs. Jane Burbank. He then married third Oct. 20, 1867, in Gorham, Mrs. Dorcas (Moody) Fogg, both of Standish. She died Dec. 21, 1897, and he died Nov. 30, 1888, age 75 yrs., 9 mos., 26 days, in Standish. He and his first wife are buried in the Moses Cemetery on the River Road at South Standish.

2. MARY, born Oct. 26, 1815, married Oct. 16, 1836, John Henry Berry, born Aug. 10, 1810, son of Walter and Polly (Dearborn) Berry of Standish. He died Sept. 19, 1875, age 65 yrs., 1 mo., 15 days and she on Nov. 11, 1885, age 70 yrs., 17 days, in Salem, Mass.

3. MEHITABLE H., born Oct. 24, 1818, married in Lyman Jan. 29, 1854, Jotham Welch Roberts, born Nov. 10, 1807, in Lyman. She died Feb. 1, 1908, in Dayton and he Aug. 20, 1869, in Dayton.

4. EUNICE HASKELL, born Jan. 22, 1825, married Oct. 17, 1844, Daniel Twombley, born Jan. 27, 1821; he died Nov. 23, 1846, in Standish. She married second in Lyman Jan. 25, 1852, Robert Roberts, born Feb. 10, 1836, in Lyman. She died Oct. 20, 1912, and he May 14, 1883.

5. EBENEZER JR., born Jan. 22, 1821, died Jan. 25, 1841, in Limington, unmarried and was buried in the family graveyard with his parents.

ii. JOHN, born Sept. 1794, married July 3, 1814, Mary or Polly York, bapt. Sept. 7, 1794, daughter of Ebenezer and Mehitable (Jones) York, and so sister to his brother Ebenezer's wife. They lived in Standish and had one child. He married second Elizabeth (Higgins) Hancock, born Jan. 25, 1793, daughter of Elkanah and Jemima (Cole) Higgins of Standish. After his second marriage, he moved to Rome, Maine, and resided there with his family until his death on July 18, 1861, age 66 yrs., 9 mos. The children by his second marriage were Mary, Joshua, Elkanah, John, Harriet A., Ebenezer, Colby, Martha Jane, and Eunice.

Child of John and his wife, Mary (York) Foss:
1. RANDALL M., born Nov. 2, 1814, married Nov. 19, 1837, Eleanor Berry. They lived in Standish where he died on Apr. 7, 1895, age 80 yrs., 5 mos., and she on Oct. 27, 1887, age 81 yrs., 2 mos., 15 days, and were buried in the Moses Cemetery. They were parents of the following children:
   (1) MARY ELLEN, born Aug. 31, 1838, married Oct. 1860, Amos S. Moody, both of Standish. She died Jan. 20, 1920, age 81 yrs., 2 mos., 28 days, in Standish.
   (2) SUSAN MELISSA, born Feb. 20, 1840, married Darius Gustin, died June 6, 1894, age 56 yrs., in Bridgton, Maine.
   (3) MEHITABLE YORK, born Apr. 15, 1842, married Jonathan Haskell, born Apr. 29, 1839, son of Francis and Jemima (Nason) Haskell. He died May 6, 1888, and she on Mar. 20, 1925, both in Standish.
   (4) EBENEZER YORK, born Nov. 29, 1844, died Dec. 10, 1844.
   (5) JOHN RANDALL, born Nov. 29, 1844, died Aug. 29, 1920, in Standish, married July 4, 1862, Clara E. Brown daughter of James Madison and Sarah J. (York) Brown of Standish.
   (6) HARRIET FRANCES, born Aug. 1, 1847, married John Henry Nason of West Bridgton.
   (7) EBENEZER YORK, born July 4, 1849, died Sept. 15, 1850.

iii. HANNAH, born in Nov. 1795, married on June 11, 1818, as his second, Ebenezer Higgins, born July 20, 1795, son of Elkanah and Jemima (Cole) Higgins of Standish. She died on Feb. 5, 1859, age 63 yrs., 3 mos., from burns that she suffered from a fire that destroyed their dwelling. They lived near Higgins Four Corners on Route 25 where his son Ephraim later ran a tavern and stage stop. Ebenezer later died in Standish on May 18, 1883. His first wife was Mary (Thompson) Higgins, whom he married on Nov. 24, 1816; his second wife was Hannah (Foss) Higgins; and his third wife was Miriam (Strout) (Thorne) Higgins, born July 27, 1800, daughter of Elisha and Betsey (Adams) Strout, widow of Daniel Thorne. He was buried with his three wives in a small family graveyard just off the County Road from York's Corner to Higgins Four Corners near its intersection with Route 25.

iv. NICHOLAS, died young.

v. MARTHA, born July 18, 1800, married Sept. 11, 1823, Nathaniel Boulter, 3rd born in Apr. 1798, son of Nathaniel Jr. and Eliza (Linnell) Boulter of Standish. They lived in Standish where she died on Oct. 14, 1853, age 53 yrs., 3 mos., and he in Bridgton, Maine, on July 24, 1875, age 77 yrs., 3 mos.

FREEMAN

Capt. Joshua Freeman, born in May 1706 son of Col. Edmund and Phebe (Watson) Freeman of Harwich, Mass., married Sept. 17, 1728, Patience Rogers, daughter of Dr. Daniel and Sarah (Appleton) Rogers of Ipswich, Mass., at which time he was a resident of Plymouth, Massachusetts. Shortly before 1740 he moved from Barnstable, Mass., to Falmouth, Maine, purchasing in that year the lot at the corner of Exchange and Middle Streets, where he kept a store and tavern. Although not one of the original grantees of Pearsontown, he soon acquired land here, owning at one time or another the following lots: Nos. 13, 20, 27, 42, 47, 53, 55, and 112 in the first division; Nos. 32, 34, 37, 57, 58, 69, 77, 81 and 112 in the second division; and Nos. 53, 86, and 111 in the third division. For this reason he was an active Proprietor of the town, but as far as can be determined never established residence here, at least not for any length of time. However, two of his sons, George and Reuben, did live here and were among the active residents of the township. Capt. Joshua Freeman died in Falmouth on Sept. 30, 1770, following the death of his wife on Dec. 31, 1769. They were parents of the following children:

i. JOSHUA JR., born May 1731 and bapt. on the 23rd of that month in Harwich, Mass., married June 19, 1750, Lois Pearson, daughter of Moses and Sarah (Titcomb) Pearson. They lived in Portland where he died Nov. 11, 1796, and she on Mar. 21, 1813, age 79 yrs., Portland.
ii. MARY, born Apr. 7, 1735, in Harwich, Mass.
iii. GEORGE, born in 1739, was one of the early permanent settlers of Pearsontown. His name is found on all the tax lists consulted and the 1790 census with a family of 2-2-4. At the time of the 1800 census his family consisted of him and his wife, one girl between 10 and 16 yrs. of age, and one boy and one girl between 16 and 25 yrs. old. He served in the French and Indian War and is said to have been taken prisoner at Fort McHenry on Aug. 9, 1757. He is mentioned among those in captivity in 1758. Because of his father's holdings, it is likely that he was acquainted with Pearsontown in its earliest days, although he probably did not establish his residence here until after 1760. He is recorded as having been the enlisting officer for Elijah Dunham, James Low, George Tinny and Samuel Knowles, all residents of Pearsontown, at the time of their enlistment in His Majesty's Service in May 1760.

George Freeman was living in Pearsontown on Feb, 15, 1764, when his father deeded to him 30-acre lots Nos. 76, 96, and 97 here (2/471) and on June 30, 1767, when he bought 30-acre lot #75 from Austin Alden of Gorham (6/39). Dr. Samuel Deane, at that time associate minister of the First Parish Church of Falmouth (Portland), wrote in his diary under date of Feb. 3, 1767, as follows:

> I set out 20 minutes after 8 in company Capt. [Ephraim] Jones and wife [Mary, daughter of Moses Pearson] Mrs. Bradbury [Hannah Freeman, sister of George] and Mrs. T. Smith, Mr. [Benjamin] Titcomb and Mrs. Wise [Elizabeth Pearson, daughter of Moses]. Capt. Cox and wife and arrived at Shaw's [Ebenezer] in Pearsontown at half past 1 o'clock; we visited the pond in the afternoon, lodged at G. [George] Freeman's; had a lecture at R. [Reuben] Freeman's at 10 o'clock on Wednesday the 4th; dined there; set out at one o'clock, got home at 6.

George Freeman was active in the Standish Church and was one of its first deacons. The intentions of marriage of George Freeman and Martha Thorn, both of Falmouth, were published there on Jan. 26, 1760, and they were married on the fourteenth of the following month. Although both Thomas Shaw and Dr. Meserve state that Martha was the daughter of Joseph Thorn of Pearsontown, there is considerable evidence that this may not be true. A gravestone in the Standish Village Cemetery records that Martha, wife of Deacon George Freeman, died Sept. 11, 1807, age 69 yrs., which wife would make the date of birth about 1738. There is no record of the birth of a daughter to Joseph Thorn about this time, but his son Bartholomew is recorded as having been born on Jan. 14, 1738, with a daughter Mercy born prior to that on Apr. 14, 1736, and another daughter Jane born later on Mar. 15, 1740. Thus it appears doubtful that he could have had a child other than Bartholomew born between Apr. 14, 1736, and Mar. 15, 1740.

At this time there was living in Topsham, Maine, a William Thorne with a family of ten children. He had a daughter Martha, born Oct. 14, 1738, who had a twin sister, Sarah. Her age therefore would correspond very closely to that of the wife of George Freeman of Pearsontown. Since Reuben Freeman, brother of George, married Katherine Thorne, another daughter of William Thorne of Topsham and since Lucy Freeman, sister of George and Reuben, married William Thorne Jr. of Topsham, brother of Katherine, there is good reason to believe that Martha, the wife of George Freeman, was from the Topsham rather than from the Pearsontown family of Thorns. It is not likely that there was any connection between the two Thorn families since William Sr. of Topsham was the son of Thomas and Mary Thorn, who were among the Scotch-Irish settlers at Merrymeeting Bay between 1718 and 1722, while Joseph of Pearsontown is thought to have descended from the Thorn family of Hingham, Mass.

Deacon George Freeman died Mar. 1, 1829, age 90 yrs., in Standish, and as previously stated, his wife, Martha, died Sept. 11, 1807, age 69 yrs., Standish. As far as known they lived in Standish all of their married life and were parents of the following children:
1. PHEBE, born Jan. 13, 1761, married (int. Sept. 16, 1780, in Gorham) Richard Lamb of Buxton. She died June 16, 1825, age 64 yrs., in Buxton. Richard and Phebe (Freeman) Lamb were parents of the following children: (Lamb)
    (1) SAMUEL, born Dec. 30, 1783, died Nov. 11, 1800.
    (2) NANCY, born Mar. 3, 1785
    (3) ELIZABETH, born Aug. 7, 1786, married Mar. 17, 1808, David Paine, probably the one born May 30, 1784, son of Richard and Elizabeth (Patrick) Paine of Gorham.
    (4) EDMUND, born Aug. 17, 1788, died Jan. 1860.
    (5) CHARLOTTE, born Apr. 29, 1790.
    (6) MARTHA, born June 4, 1792.
    (7) PHEBE, born Oct. 4, 1794.
    (8) MARY, born June 24, 1796, married Oct. 18, 1821, Richard Greenlaw of Brownfield, Maine, born July 1797 son of John and Lucy (Whitney) Greenlaw. He died in Brownfield on Aug. 21, 1863, and she died there on Oct. 6, 1874.
    (9) EUNICE, born Oct. 17, 1798.
    (10) SAMUEL, born Nov. 28, 1800, died June 1802.
2. HANNAH, born Sept. 5, 1762, married (int. Sept. 16, 1780, in Gorham) William Farrington, then a resident of Pearsontown. They were living in Portland at the time of the 1790 census with a family of 1-0-4. On Nov. 27, 1795, William Farrington of Portland, housewright, bought land in Poland, Maine, from Davis Woodward (23/363). William and Hannah Farrington were of Poland on June 19, 1800, when they sold land there to William Davis of that town (36/559). He served in the Revolutionary War and died Aug. 11, 1832, age 72. His wife died in Mar. 1802, age 38 yrs., in Poland, as given in Mar. 29, 1802, issue of *Eastern Argus*.
3. WILLIAM, born July 10, 1764.
4. EDMUND, born May 1, 1766.
5. CHARLOTTE, born June 15, 1768, married Apr. 26, 1795 (int. Mar. 14, 1795) Charles Hill of Biddeford.
6. REUBEN, born May 6, 1770, bapt. May 6, 1770.
7. MARTHA, born July 12, 1772, bapt. Aug. 16, 1772, married on May 8, 1797, Joshua Emery of Pownalborough and lived in Portland.
8. NANCY, born Sept. 15, 1774.
9. GEORGE ROGERS, born July 19, 1776.
10. DANIEL, born Feb. 16, 1779, bapt. Mar. 14, 1779, married (int. Mar. 25, 1810, in Standish) Hannah Davis of Poland. He lived on the homestead of his father, the old gambrel-roofed house being on lot #96 and the barn across the road on lot #75. Daniel Freeman died Mar. 21, 1853, age 64. Both are buried in the Standish Village Cemetery. They were parents of the following children:

    (1)   GEORGE, born Sept. 5, 1813.
    (2)   MARTHA, born Oct. 10, 1815, married July 3, 1839, Eliphalet Davis of Wilton, Maine.
    (3)   WILLIAM DAVIS, born Sept. 26, 1817, married on Oct. 29, 1845, he being of Bridgwater Plantation, Mary Phinney, daughter of Samuel and Mary Phinney born Dec. 20, 1818. He succeeded his father on the family farm and died Feb. 4, 1872.
    (4)   LEANDER, born Dec. 19, 1819, died Sept. 1838 Standish.
    (5)   LUCY, born Dec. 8, 1821, married William Rich.
    (6)   LORENZO, born Dec. 3, 1823.
    (7)   ISAAC SOMES DAVIS, born July 28, 1826, died in army in Civil War.
    (8)   URSULA CUSHMAN, born Jan. 28, 1830, married Jan. 12, 1852, William C. Goodwin of Lowell, Mass.
    (9)   HESTER ANN ROGERS, born Nov. 27, 1832.
11. EUNICE, born Feb. 15, 1782, bapt. Sept. 26, 1784, married Dec. 21, 1806, Reuben Bradbury of Portland. She died Dec. 6, 1875, and he died Feb. 20, 1829, age 48 yrs., in Portland.

iv. REUBEN, born July 21, 1740, bapt. July 12, 1741, in Harwich, was an early settler in Pearsontown. On Aug. 10, 1763, Joshua Freeman of Falmouth deeded to Reuben Freeman, mariner, of Falmouth the right or share No. 122 in Pearsontown (4/381) and on June 26, 1766, Isaac Illesley Jr. sold Reuben Freeman, yeoman, of Pearsontown, the 30-acre lot #99 here (5/18). His father and he on Nov. 27, 1772, exchanged the 100-acre lot #104 for the 100-acre lot #67, both in the second division (7/450 and 7/451). Reuben Freeman was of Pearsontown on Apr. 12, 1773, when he sold to David Richardson of Newton, Mass., lot #122 containing 40-acres with house and barn thereon (this was the 30-acre lot #122 and 5-acre lots #11 and #12) and 30-acre lot #99 (7/528). However, he was living in Bristol, Maine, on Mar. 20, 1775, when he sold the 100-acre lot #67 in the second division in Pearsontown to Jonathan Morse Jr. of Falmouth (8/388).

    Reuben Freeman married Sept. 26, 1764, Katherine Thorne, born June 7, 1743, daughter of William and Martha Thorne of Topsham, Maine. He and his wife owned the covenant in the First Parish Church of Falmouth (Portland) on Oct. 17, 1765. It was about this time that they moved to Pearsontown where they continued to live until about 1773 when they moved to Bristol, Maine. In 1775 he bought from Samuel Milliken a lot of 100 acres at Pretty Marsh on Mount Desert Island, where he settled sometime before 1784. Here he was living with a family of 3-0-6 at the time of the 1790 census. He died at Pretty Marsh in 1812. He may have been the Reuben Freeman of Mount Desert who was united in marriage to Margaret Flatt of Portland by the Rev. Samuel Deane on Dec. 21, 1794. Children of Reuben and Katherine (Thorne) Freeman were as follows:
1. LUCY, born June 23, 1765, probably in Falmouth, married Daniel Keene of Hog's Island.
2. ELIZABETH, born Jan. 24, 1767, at Pearsontown, bapt. at Falmouth Feb. 4, 1767, married Silas Coolidge of Hancock.

3. **REUBEN**, born Apr. 11, 1771, bapt. at Pearsontown June 23, 1771, married first Sept. 16, 1794, Rhoda Richardson, daughter of James and Rachel (Gott) Richardson of Mount Desert. She died Mar. 1, 1813, age 39, and he married second Polly E. Lord, who died Nov. 20, 1829, age 47. He married third Margaret Bowen, who died Feb. 2, 1856, age 64 yrs. He died Aug. 19, 1850, age 79 yrs., 4 mos.
4. **GEORGE**, born Nov. 11, 1772, bapt. in Pearsontown Jan. 17, 1773, married Sept. 19, 1796, at Mount Desert Tamson Richardson, born about 1772 daughter of James and Rachel (Gott) Richardson. He died Apr. 18, 1844, and she on July 23, 1836.
5. **MARY**, born Apr. 26, 1769, bapt. at Pearsontown May 14, 1769.
6. **SARAH**, born Nov. 22, 1774, probably at Bristol, Maine, married Mar. 2, 1793, Isaac Reed of Sedgwick.
7. **JENNIE**, born Jan. 8, 1776.
8. **SUSIE (LOIS)**, born Jan. 20, 1778, married John Dorify of Sedgwick.
9. **MARTHA**, born Jan. 30, 1781, married Samuel Ober of Sedgwick.
10. **DANIEL**, born Dec. 2, 1783.
11. **NANCY**, born Nov. 6, 1786, married Humphrey Herrick, born Sept. 25, 1773, son of Samuel and Rachel Herrick.

v. **WILLIAM**, bapt. May 15, 1743.
vi. **LUCY**, born 1743 in Falmouth, married William Thorne Jr. of Topsham, Maine. She died Mar. 21, 1833, in Canton, Maine.
vii. **HANNAH**, bapt. in 1745 in Falmouth, married Thomas Bradbury.
viii. **MARY**, bapt. in 1746 in Falmouth.
ix. **ELIZABETH**, bapt. in 1752 in Falmouth. She died Nov. 1827, age 76 yrs., in Standish. (*Maine Baptist Herald*, Nov. 14, 1827).

A Jonathan Freeman is said to have been an inhabitant of Pearsontown. If this be true, it is likely that he was only one of the soldiers forming the guard at the fort and his stay in town was probably not of very lengthy duration. He was probably the Jonathan Freeman of Falmouth, born May 18, 1737, who married Nov. 28, 1759, Sarah Parker of that town and moved from Falmouth to Gorham in the latter part of 1762. He settled in the southern part of Gorham near Stroudwater River. He served in the Revolutionary War and was at the Battle of Bunker Hill.

Jonathan and Sarah (Parker) Freeman were the parents of nine children, one of whom, Benjamin by name, did live for a few years in Standish. He was born in Gorham on June 18, 1765, and married (int. Dec. 15, 1787, in Gorham) Eunice Seavey. On June 12, 1790, Jonathan and Benjamin Freeman of Gorham, yeomen, bought from Samuel and Enoch Freeman of Portland and Falmouth respectively the 100-acre lot #29 in the second division in Standish (30/219). This lot was located on Standish Neck adjoining the Gorham line and it is likely that Benjamin settled on it soon after its purchase, for his name is found on the 1795 and 1796 tax lists of Standish. He being of Standish quitclaimed the same lot to Jonathan Freeman on Feb. 27, 1801 (49/243). In Sept. 1804 Jonathan Freeman of Gorham deeded to Benjamin Freeman of Standish 20 acres of this lot (49/477) and on June 24, 1806, Benjamin and Eunice Freeman of

Standish deeded these 20 acres to Ebenezer Allen of Windham (50/22). It was probably about this time that he moved to Scarboro since his name is not found on the 1808 tax list of Standish.

GILMAN

Ebenezer Gilman was another one of those settled in Standish after 1790. His name is found on the 1795, 1796, 1799, 1808, and 1814 tax lists of the town. It is evident that he was from Falmouth and the son of Edward Gilman of that town, who was an original grantee of right No. 11 in Pearsontown. The family was originally from Exeter, N.H., his grandfather Edward Gilman having been born about 1703 son of Edward and Abigail (Folsom) Gilman of that place and having owned land along the Presumpscot River in Falmouth, Maine. It is likely that Ebenezer's father was the Edward, son of Phebe Gilman, who was baptized in the First Parish Church of Falmouth (now Portland) in 1745 and who was married to Agnes Stevens of Windham on May 1, 1766, by the Rev. Peter Smith. She was the daughter of John and Hannah (____) Stevens of Newburyport, Mass., and Windham, Maine.

On Mar. 31, 1792, Ebenezer Gilman of Standish, Zachariah Small and Mimar, his wife, and Phebe Gilman, the second of Falmouth, spinster, sold to Nathan Winslow of Falmouth their rights in the real estate of their honored father Edward Gilman, late of Falmouth deceased (19/175); and on Jan. 25, 1804, Ebenezer Gilman of Standish, John Gilman of Falmouth, Zachariah Small and Jemima, his wife, of Falmouth, Paul Leighton and Phebe, his wife, of Falmouth, and Edward Gilman of Bolton in Canada sold to Nathan Winslow their rights to land in Falmouth and Presumpscot River belonging to their grandfather Edward Gilman, late of Falmouth, which he purchased of Edward Gilman of Exeter, N.H., on Oct. 12, 1741 (45/415). These deeds are very good evidence as to the parentage of Ebenezer Gilman.

Ebenezer Gilman was born Jan. 26, 1767, probably in Falmouth, son of Edward and Phebe (Hall) Gilman, and married first ____ and second on Oct. 27, 1790, in Falmouth Lydia Bonney, born Nov. 22, 1764, daughter of Joel and Lydia (Kinney) Bonney. Evidence that he moved to Standish soon after his marriage is indicated by the tax lists and first deed previously quoted. He was given as being a resident of Standish on Dec. 1, 1801, when he bought from Jacob Ashton, et al. of Salem, Mass., the 100-acre lot #27 in the second division located on Standish Neck (36/413) and on Apr. 18, 1803, when he purchased from the estate of Benjamin Titcomb one quarter part of the adjoining 100-acre lot #28 (41/323). This farm, comprised of 120 acres, more or less, he sold to his son John of Standish on Oct. 14, 1813 (72/152). He died in Standish on Feb. 22, 1834, age 68, and his widow died there on Dec. 19, 1853, age 89. Both are buried in Harding Cemetery on Standish Neck.

Children of Ebenezer were as follows:
By his first wife: (name unknown)
i. KATHERINE, born Mar. 20, 1785, died Jan. 9, 1805.

ii. JOHN, born Jan. 26, 1790, died Dec. 8, 1867, age 76 yrs., 10 mos., 12 days; married at Standish Almira (Elmira) Shaw, born Apr. 18, 1799, daughter of Enoch and Delilah (Morton) Shaw, who died Dec. 10, 1882, age 83 yrs., 7 mos., 22 days. Both were buried in Harding Cemetery.

By second wife, Lydia Bonney:

iii. MARY, born Oct. 29, 1792, married Sept. 3, 1820, Peter Chick, born July 23, 1798, son of Peter and Abigail (Haskell) Chick of Limington. She died Jan. 27, 1875, and he on Oct. 13, 1848, of Limington.

iv. EBENEZER JR., born Aug. 27, 1795, died in Gorham in 1868, married (int. July 22, 1820) Hannah Cannell, born Mar. 28, 1798, daughter of Thomas and Margaret (Nason) Cannell of Gorham, who died in 1877. Both were buried in North Gorham Cemetery.

v. LYDIA, born June 13, 1796, died in Nasonville, Wisconsin, Apr. 1, 1872, age 75 yrs., 9 mos., but has a stone in her memory in Harding Cemetery; married in Standish May 3, 1818, Capt. Solomon Nason, born Mar. 31, 1794, died in Standish Feb. 24, 1868, age 74 and was buried in Harding Cemetery.

vi. FANNY, born Sept. 22, 1798, died at Standish Nov. 28, 1876, age 78; married Oct. 1, 1820, Capt. John Whitmore, born Nov. 4, 1796, son of John and Jane (Roberts) Whitmore of Gorham, who died in Standish Feb. 11, 1869, age 72 yrs., 3 mos. Both were buried in Harding Cemetery.

vii. DAVID, born 1800, died in 1883, Richfield, Minn., married (int. Mar. 16, 1822) Irene Whitmore, born 1801 daughter of John and Jane (Roberts) Whitmore of Gorham. She died 1868 in Richfield, Minn.

viii. SARAH, born Dec. 24, 1802, married as his second wife Solomon Anderson of Baldwin on Oct. 20, 1835. He died Mar. 14, 1874, age 74 yrs., in Limington.

ix. CATHERINE, born Apr. 1805, died Sept. 28, 1894, age 89, Westbrook, unmarried; was buried in Harding Cemetery.

x. EDWARD, born Nov. 1, 1807, died Dec. 1, 1828, age 20, and was buried in Harding Cemetery.

xi. WILLIAM, born Jan. 11, 1811, died in California in 1850, age 39, according to inscription on a stone in his memory in Harding Cemetery.

GOULD

Rev. Jonathan Gould, the second settled pastor of the First Church of Standish was born in New Braintree, Mass., in 1762, son of Deacon Jonathan and Abigail (Howe) Gould of that town. He was a graduate of Brown University in the class of 1786 and from sometime in 1789 until March 14, 1791, he was pastor of the Church of Boothby, Maine, on a temporary basis. At a meeting on the latter date this church voted not to settle him or to employ him any longer. Reason for his dismissal was given as doctrinal rather than for any moral fault. Since the majority of the church members were of the Presbyterian faith, it is likely that his Congregationalist views did not please them.

The church at Standish was without a settled minister from the time of the dismissal of the Rev. John Tompson in April 1783 until the ordination of the Rev. Jonthan Gould on Sept. 18, 1793. His period of service in this capacity was cut short by his sudden death from tuberculosis on July 26, 1795. On May 25, 1795, shortly prior to his death, he had purchased from Benjamin Titcomb his farm in Standish containing 100 acres, more or less, and comprising 5-acre lots Nos. 4, 5, 6, and 10; 3-acre lots Nos. 38 and 121, and ten acres of 30-acre lots Nos. 119 and 120 (22/452). On Nov. 15, 1796, Jonathan Gould of New Braintree, father of the late pastor, sold the 5-acre lots Nos. 4, 5, 6, and 10, along with one acre and 68 square rods of the 30-acre lot #38 of this property to the Rev. Daniel Marrett, new pastor of the Standish Church (25/291). This is the same property on which the Marrett homestead is now located. An inscription on the gravestone of the Rev. Jonathan Gould in the Standish Cemetery reads as follows:

> In memory of the Rev. Jonathan Gould late pastor of the Church in Standish son of Deacon Jonathan Gould of New Braintree and Abigail his wife, who departed this life July 26, 1795, in the 33rd year of his age and 2d of his ministry. He was a fervent and zealous preacher of the gospel, very exemplary in his life and conversation and bid fair to adorn the ministerial character with peculiar honor.

GRAY

The name of James Gray is found on the 1795 and 1796 tax lists and and the 1799 valuation list of Standish, while that of Susannah Gray is found on the 1808 tax list. James Gray was born in Gorham April 20, 1767, son of Taylor and Tabitha (Murch) Gray. On Jan. 2, 1791, he married Susanna Thomes, daughter of Thomas and Mary (Banfield) Thomes of Falmouth and Gorham and sister of Amos Thomes who settled in Standish. They probably moved to Standish soon after their marriage, for they are given as living here on Sept. 3, 1794, when they are mentioned among the heirs of Thomas Thomes in transfer of land in Gorham (45/492). On Nov. 20, 1799, James Gray of Standish bought of Isaac Lobdell of Falmouth 79 acres of the southwest part of the 100-acre lot #50 in the second division in Standish (57/21). This land was located on Standish Neck. At the time of the 1800 census his family consisted of him and his wife, three boys under 10 years of age, one female under 10, and one male and one female over 45 years old. He died July 26, 1806. His widow married second on July 1, 1810, as his second wife Thomas Cummings of Standish. Children of James and Susannah (Thomes) Gray, all named in land transfer, were as follows:

i. SAMUEL, born Feb. 29, 1791, married Martha Morton of Standish on April 10, 1817. He was living in 1855 in Buxton, a veteran of the War of 1812.
ii. CHARLES, born Jan. 29, 1793, drowned in July 1816, age 22 yrs., in Standish (*Eastern Argus*, July 10, 1816).
iii. GEORGE, born May 17, 1795, married Apr. 23, 1819, Eunice Shaw, born Jan. 1, 1799, daughter of Sargent and Ann (Thompson) Shaw of Standish. They lived in Standish, Windham, and Buxton, where she died Oct. 25, 1854, and he in 1866. They were the parents of six children.
iv. SARAH, born Sept. 17, 1798, married Oct. 21, 1819, Caleb Morton, son of Ebenezer and Susanna (Irish) Morton of Standish.
v. LYDIA, born Dec. 29, 1801, married May 12, 1825, Isaiah Rogers of Windham. She died Dec. 3, 1878, and was buried in Harding Cemetery.

GREEN

The name of John Green is found on the 1795 and 1796 tax lists of Standish and in the 1800 census with a family consisting of him and his wife, two females under 10 years of age, one male and one female between 10 and 16, and one male between 16 and 26 years old. He came from Gorham and was a brother-in-law of Wentworth Stuart Jr. He was perhaps the son of Joseph and Hannah (Conant) Green of Gorham, whose marriage at Cape Cod on Mar. 8, 1749, is found in Gorham records. On July 3, 1770, John Green married Mary Stuart, born Jan. 20, 1754, daughter of Wentworth and Susanna (Lombard) Stuart of Gorham. It is likely that all of their children were born in Gorham and it is certain that they did not move to Standish until after 1790. Dates of death of John Green and his wife, Mary, have not been discovered, but John was living as late as 1808 since his name is found on a tax list for that year.

Children of John and Mary (Stuart) Green were as follows:
i. SALOME, born Feb. 11, 1771, married as his second wife on Mar. 4, 1793, Ebenezer Shaw Jr., born Jan. 3, 1749, son of Ebenezer and Anna (Philbrick) Shaw of Standish. She was the mother of fourteen of his twenty-four children and died in Bangor, Maine, in 1847. He died in Standish Aug. 11, 1836, age 87 yrs. For children see Shaw family.
ii. STUART, born May 22, 1773, married Apr. 14, 1806, Patience Phinney, born May 2, 1782, daughter of Decker and Hannah (Hamblen) Phinney of Gorham. They lived on Fort Hill in Gorham. She died Oct. 22, 1814, age 32, after the births of three children, and he married second on Sept. 13, 1835, Susanna Thomes, born July 3, 1788, daughter of Charles and Anna (Gray) Thomes of Gorham. She died in Hiram.
iii. WYER (WEAR), born Apr. 30, 1775, married Apr. 20, 1802, Ruhamah Morton, born about 1783 daughter of Ebenezer and Susannah (Irish) Morton of Standish. They lived on Standish Neck where he died Oct. 12, 1825.

iv. JOHN JR., born June 12, 1777, married Mar. 13, 1800, Esther Shaw, born in 1782 daughter of Joseph and Eunice (Bean) Shaw of Standish. They lived on Raymond Cape where she died about 1806. He married a second time and moved east. There were four children by his second marriage.
v. MARY (MOLLY), born Dec. 15, 1779, married Dec. 11, 1800, Nathan C. Penfield of Gorham, who may have been a son of Benjamin and Joanna (Cook) Penfield of Wellfleet and Eastham, Mass. Widow Joanna C. Penfield married Bryan Martin of Standish about 1786. Nathan and Molly (Green) Penfield lived in Gorham where he died Oct. 14, 1850, age 74. They were the parents of ten children.
vi. REBECCA, born May 26, 1782, married Feb. 10, 1802, Philip Cannell Jr., born in July 1771 son of Philip and Jane (_____) Cannell of Standish. They lived in Standish where he died Mar. 18, 1849, age 77 yrs. She died in Canton, Maine, at about 92 yrs. of age. For children see Cannell family.
vii. JOSEPH, born Aug. 24, 1786, married on May 31, 1812, Eliza Marean, born Mar. 31, 1794, daughter of John and Lois (Bean) Marean of Standish. They lived in Standish where he died in Oct. 1836.
viii. ELIZABETH, born May 6, 1789, nothing further known.
ix. SARAH, born _____, bapt. July 21, 1806, married Aug. 15, 1818, Benjamin Morton, born Feb. 14, 1792, son of Thomas and Betty (Frost) Morton of Gorham. They lived in Standish. He died Nov. 1858 and she at about 90 yrs. of age.
x. SUSAN, born _____, married _____ Pierce. (A Susan Green of Standish married Hiram Varney of Windham.)

HALL

A Charles Hall was among the very early settlers in Pearsontown. His parentage has not been definitely determined but he may have been a son of Ebenezer and Jane (Bumpas) Hall of Mansfield and Middleboro, Mass., and Falmouth, Maine. He was living in Falmouth on June 14, 1741, when his intention of marriage to Jemima Dolever or Dolliver of that town was published. She probably was the daughter of the John Dolliver who was granted land by the town of Falmouth on Mar. 8, 1728.

Charles Hall, cooper, of Falmouth, on May 10, 1742, bought from William Elwell, yeoman, of Falmouth, five acres of land lying next to Elwell's dwelling house in Falmouth (York deeds 25/207). On Mar. 14, 1745, John Strout, fisherman, of Falmouth sold to Charles Hall, cooper, of Falmouth one-half of his 30-acre lot on Barren Hill in Falmouth (25/206 York deeds). This doubtless was the same John Strout who later was an early settler in Pearsontown. On Mar. 10, 1746, he, a cooper, sold the 5 acres of land in Second Parish in Falmouth which he purchased from Elwell in 1742, "it being my now dwelling house and land that I now live upon, to Archeleus Stone, shoemaker of Falmouth." The deed was signed by Charles and Jemima Hall, both by marks. On Jan.

12, 1749, Charles Hall, laborer, of Falmouth, sold to Elisha Parker of Falmouth, carpenter, the half of the 30-acre lot he purchased from John Strout in 1745 and where he then dwelt (York deeds 27/308). He was a resident of Gorham, however, on Feb. 8, 1754, when he purchased land in Gorham from Christopher Strout Esq. (4/138). He, a yeoman of Gorhamtown, sold this same land on Feb. 2, 1756, where he then lived, to Seth Harding, cooper (York deeds 36/5). By a study of these deeds one can get a good idea of the activities and places of residence of Charles Hall from the time of his marriage in 1741 until about 1756 when he came to Pearsontown.

Charles Hall was probably one of those living in the fort at Pearsontown from 1756 to 1760, since he was the original grantee of 5-acre lot #12, which he sold to Reuben Freeman prior to March 1768 when it was confirmed to Freeman by the Proprietors of the town. His name is found on a list of men from Pearsontown who about 1759-1760 served in Lt. Charles Lessner's party scouting eastward from Broad Bay (Waldoborough) and also on lists of Pearsontown men who worked on Gorham roads in 1760 and 1761. He was living in town on Mar. 15, 1765, when he sold land in Gorham to William McLellan of that town (4/129) and purchased on the same date from Hugh McLellan of Gorham 130 acres of land in Pearsontown lying on Sebago Pond, it being part of right No. 91. including the 30-acre lot #91 and 100 acres of the common and undivided lands of the township. The following month on Apr. 13, 1765, Simon Gookin of Falmouth deeded to him for six shillings and in consideration of his having made the settlement required by the general court in their original grant of the township the two 30-acre lots Nos. 119 and 120 (5/177). Charles Hall evidently died about 1771 since on August 1 of that year James Milk deeded to the heirs of Charles Hall, late of Pearsontown, the 30-acre lot of right No. 119 in Pearsontown. His widow, Jemima, evidently survived her husband to live an advanced age, for she was living with her unmarried children William and Betty in 1794 according to notes of Thomas Shaw, and was probably the female member over 45 in the family of William Hall at the time of the 1800 census. Children of Charles and Jemima (Dolliver) Hall as far as have been established were as follows:

i. SARAH, born ____, married Dec. 9, 1765, David Sanborn, bapt. in Hampton, N.H., May 23, 1742, son of Jonathan and Priscilla (Bryant) Sanborn. For children see Sanborn family.

ii. JOHN, born ____, (over 45 in 1800), was living in Pearsontown in its earliest days. He was one of the Pearsontown men who worked on Gorham roads in 1761, but his name is found on a county tax list of Gorham in 1763. In a mortgage deed dated Aug. 1, 1768, he, being of Pearsontown, was granted the 30-acre lot #136 by the Proprietors on the condition that before the first day of August 1770 he would have a good dwelling house 18 feet square and 7-foot stud built on this lot and would have at least 5 acres of the same lot cleared and brought to English grass or fit for plowing and mowing (6/211). He was living on this lot in 1771 when he exchanged 30-acre lot #132 and 30 acres more on the northeast side of the road to the pond beginning at the northerly corner of lot #136 with Moses Pearson for the two five-acre lots Nos. 13 and 14 which he apparently owned. On Jan. 17, 1777, he and his wife, Naoma, relinquished their rights in 30-acre lot #94 all belonging to the estate of his late father, Charles Hall (12/238). His name is found on the 1788, 1789, 1790, 1795, 1796, 1799 and later tax lists, in the 1790 census with a family of 1-5-4, and in the 1800 census with a family consisting of him and his wife, one boy and one girl under 10, two boys between 10 and 16, and one boy between 16 and 25 yrs. of age.

John Hall married Feb. 1, 1769, Naoma York, born in 1751 daughter of John and Sarah (Strout) York of Pearsontown. They lived on the hill back from the road near Sticky River where he died May 2, 1819. His widow died Feb. 23, 1840, age 88. They were parents of the following children:

1. ANNE, born Apr. 28, 1769, married (int. July 25, 1794) Enoch Bartlett of Bethel.
2. SARAH, born Apr. 2, 1771, married Feb. 3, 1794, Jonathan Ward of Gorham. They lived in Standish. For children see Ward family.
3. JEMIMA, born Mar. 13, 1773, married (int. Mar. 10, 1797, in Standish) John Cookson, son of Reuben and Mary (York) Cookson of Standish. For family see Cookson family.
4. WILLIAM, born Mar. 28, 1777, was probably the William Hall who married (int. July 14, 1800, in Gorham) Mary Ward, sister of Jonathan who married his sister Sarah. They both died in Gorham.
5. MARY, born Nov. 5, 1781, married Feb. 7, 1803, Abraham Horr of Waterford, Maine.
6. ISAAC, born Sept. 1, 1784.
7. EBENEZER, born Sept. 19, 1786, was living in family of his brother Oliver in 1850.
8. JOHN, born Nov. 17, 1788.
9. DANIEL, born Oct. 21, 1790.
10. OLIVER, born Jan. 31, 1792, married June 12, 1831, his cousin Dorcas (Decker) Lowell, born 1792 daughter of John and Catherine (Hall) Decker and widow of Jonathan Lowell Jr. of Standish. She died May 28, 1854, age 62 and he about 1855 or 1856. They were the parents of two children: Eliza Ann, born July 28, 1833, and Hannah Olive, born Sept. 8, 1835.
11. ELIZABETH, born July 27, 1794, married Aug. 11, 1817, James Jordan of Baldwin.

iii. WILLIAM, born ____, was of Pearsontown on July 12, 1768, when he secured by right of settlement from Pearsontown Committee the 30-acre lot #128 (6/220). He is mentioned in deeds dated Jan. 17, 1777 (12/239), May 9, 1783 (12/239), and Feb. 24, 1784 (12/408). He is listed in the 1790 census with a family of 1-0-2. Thomas Shaw states that he was living with his mother and sister in District No. 4 in 1794. He was the head of the same family at the time of the 1800 census. It seems likely that he was never married.

iv. CATHERINE, born ____, (over 45 in 1800), married (int. Sept. 14, 1771, in Gorham) John Decker of Pearsontown. She died Sept. 9, 1826. For children see Decker family.

v. **CHARLES**, born about 1755, probably came to Pearsontown in his father's family. His name is found on all the tax lists consulted, in the 1790 census with a family of 1-1-4 and in the 1800 census with a family consisting of him and his wife, five girls under 10, one boy and one girl between 10 and 16, and one girl between 16 and 25 yrs. of age. He served in the Revolutionary War and is given as a resident of Baldwin, age 85, on an 1840 pension list. On May 9, 1783, in return for a quitclaim deed of 20 acres of the 30-acre lots Nos. 119 and 120 on which he lived, he deeded the remaining 40 acres of these lots to his brother William; his mother, Jemima; and his sister Betty (12/239). He sold these 20 acres to Benjamin Titcomb of Falmouth on Feb. 24, 1784 (12/408). Previously on May 7, 1783, he had bought from Christopher Noble, his father-in-law, the 30-acre lot #124 and probably moved onto it.

Charles Hall married (int. July 28, 1781, in Gorham) Lydia Noble, baptized at Pearsontown May 19, 1776, daughter of Christopher and Martha (Rowe) Noble. They were parents of the following children:

1. **HANNAH**, born June 2, 1784, bapt. Aug. 15, 1794, married Dec. 6, 1801, Thomas Anderson of Windham. They had seven children.
2. **MOSES**, born June 4, 1786, bapt. Aug. 15, 1794, never married. At age 65 he was living in Standish, a pauper, in 1850.
3. **ESTHER**, born Mar. 1, 1789, bapt. Aug. 15, 1794, married (int. July 19, 1806, in Standish) John Wentworth of Gorham and had children.
4. **ABIGAIL**, born June 5, 1791, bapt. Aug. 15, 1794.
5. **EUNICE**, born Nov. 4, 1793, bapt. Aug. 15, 1794, died young.
6. **MARTHA**, born Aug. 1, 1795, bapt. Nov. 15, 1808.
7. **JOANNA**, born June 20, 1799, bapt. Nov. 15, 1808.
8. **MARY**, born June 4, 1801, bapt. Nov. 15, 1808.
9. **LYDIA**, born Apr. 28, 1805, bapt. Nov. 15, 1808, married on Feb. 8, 1822, her cousin Charles Decker. She died Nov. 16, 1880, age 76 yrs., W. Baldwin, and he, born in 1804, died in 1886.

vi. **REBECCA**, born ____ (under 45 in 1800), married (int. Mar. 31, 1778, in Gorham) Thomas Thompson of Pearsontown. For children see Thompson family.

vii. **BETTY**, born ____ (under 45 in 1800), mentioned in deed dated May 9, 1783 (12/239) and called spinster in deed dated Feb. 24, 1784 (12/408). Was living with her mother and brother William as late as 1800. Nothing further known.

HAMLIN

The name of Seth L. Hamlin is found on the 1795 and 1796 tax lists of Standish. He was born Seth Lewis Hamlin in Barnstable, Mass., Jan. 1, 1765, son of Samuel and Temperance (Lewis) Hamlin, who settled in Gorham about 1768. His intentions of marriage to Jerusha Sawyer of

Standish are found in the Gorham records under date of June 11, 1791. They were married Sept. 25, 1791. She was born in Falmouth Sept. 15, 1772, daughter of John and Lettice (Whitney) Sawyer, and was undoubtedly the Jerusha Sawyer, daughter of John, whose baptism on Nov. 1, 1772, is found the records of the First Parish Church of Portland. Seth Hamlin is given as living in Standish on Mar. 30, 1795, when bought from Isaac and Jacob York of Standish the westerly half of the 100-acre lot #115 in second division (41/500). He sold this same land on Aug. 23, 1801, to Joab Black of Limington, the deed also being signed by his wife, Jerusha (41/501).

He was a mason and bricklayer. At the time of the 1800 census he was living in Standish with a family consisting of him and his wife, and three boys and one girl under 10 years of age. In 1801, probably about the time he sold his land in Standish, he moved across the Saco River into Limington where he resided until about 1811 when he moved to Brownfield. In the latter town he lived in a small house located on the lot occupied by the Congregational Church in 1903. Later on he moved to Shenango in New York State with his son Lewis, near whose home there he was found dead on Nov. 10, 1834. His wife died at the home of her son Seth in Fryeburg on Apr. 18, 1851. Seth and Jerusha (Sawyer) Hamlin were the parents of the following children:

i. ISAAC, born in Standish Apr. 27, 1792, died near Shenango, N.Y., where he settled in early life. He was a mute.
ii. LEWIS, born June 16, 1794, died Mar. 12, 1825.
iii. THOMAS, born June 24, 1796, died June 25, 1798, in Standish.
iv. JAMES MOOR, born Apr. 23, 1798, died in Brownfield.
v. LETTICE, born Mar. 19, 1800, died Mar. 18, 1803, in Limington.
vi. BARBARA, born Apr. 5, 1802, in Limington, married Lewis Hamlin, her cousin in Paris, Maine, on Nov. 19, 1818.
vii. ELIJAH born Apr. 2, 1804, died in Saco, married Sally Huntress, Jan. 14, 1826.
viii. SELINA, born June 24, 1806, married Jan. 3, 1831, Levi Chick of Limington. She died there Jan. 30, 1892, age 86 yrs., 7 mos., 18 days. He was born Apr. 4, 1802, son of William and Selina (Sawyer) Chick of Limington, and thence he and his wife were first cousins.
ix. TEMPERANCE, born Sept. 25, 1808, died in Fryeburg.
x. SETH JR., born in Brownfield Sept. 25, 1811, died in Fryeburg Apr. 22, 1880, married July 30, 1832, Lucinda Kennison, who died Aug. 22, 1873.

HARDING

The name of Amaziah Harding or Harden is found on the 1796 tax list of Standish and in the 1800 census with a family consisting of him and his wife, one son under 10 years of age, two daughters under 10 and one daughter between 10 and 16 years old. His parentage has not been definitely established, but information available indicates that he was probably the son of Sylvanus and Keziah (Burge) Harding of Chatham,

Mass. He is known to have come to Standish about 1795 or 1796 from Chatham, his wife being a stepsister of Stephen Sparrow and half-sister to Jonathan Sparrow and Knowles Higgins, all of whom lived in Standish for periods of varying lengths.

Records in the family Bible indicate that he was born Apr. 7, 1759, and his wife, Hannah, was born Feb. 19, 1760. She was the daughter of John and Hannah (Knowles) Warren. After the death of John Warren, her mother married as his second wife on Mar. 12, 1766, Jonathan Sparrow Jr. of Eastham and following his death she married third on Dec. 3, 1772, as his second wife Zacheus Higgins of Eastham.

Amaziah Harding was living in Standish on May 3, 1796, when he bought from Josiah Hopkins the southwest part of the 100-acre lot #76 in the second division except 40 acres previously sold to John Meserve Jr. (39/164). On Jan. 1, 1803, he still being of Standish sold his homestead there, it being the same land which he purchased in 1796 (38/490). It was evidently about this time that he moved to Unity, Maine. He died in Wiscasset May 17, 1829, and his wife died on Dec. 10, 1835, age 85 years.

Amaziah and Hannah (Warren) Harding were the parents of the following children:

i. LETTICE (LETTIS), born Mar. 21, 1781, married Sept. 5, 1799 Daniel Boulter of Standish and Unity, Maine. She died in Nov. 1836. For children see Boulter family.
ii. SIMEON, born Oct. 27, 1782.
iii. MARY, born May 31, 1785.
iv. STEPHEN, born Apr. 25, 1788.
v. AMAZIAH, born Jan. 5, 1789, died Apr. 25, 1789.
vi. AMAZIAH, born July 16, 1792.
vii. HANNAH, born Mar. 22, 1795, died Dec. 11, 1819, age 24 yrs.
viii. KEZIAH, born May 5, 1798, bapt. July 8, 1798, in Standish, married George D. Bacon and was mother of nine children.
ix. JOHN WARREN, born Mar. 24, 1801, in Standish.

HARMON

The names of Daniel, William, and John Harmon are found in the 1789 and 1790 tax lists of Standish and in the 1790 census.

John[3] Harmon (Samuel,[2] John[1]) was born in Wells, Maine, in 1716. He lived in Scarborough as a yeoman or farmer until 1779 when he purchased from from John and Jane Stewart the 100-acre lot #46 in the second division in Standish located on the Neck. This same lot on which he was then living he sold to his son William Harmon Jr. of Pearsontown on Aug. 19, 1782 (11/582). At the time of the 1790 census he is recorded with a family of 1-1-2 and in the 1800 census with a family consisting of only him and his wife. He probably died soon after.

John Harmon married first on Dec. 2, 1742, Mary Hasty, daughter of Daniel Hasty of Scarborough. She died Dec. 10, 1753, and he married second on May 30, 1754, Abigail (Tibbetts) Foss, widow of Joseph Foss.

She died Dec. 24, 1759, and he married third Abigail (Hoyt) Harmon, widow of his cousin William Harmon. He had children by all three wives, as follows:

By first wife:
i. ABIGAIL, bapt. Jan. 8, 1744, died young.
ii. MARY, born ____, died Jan. 12, 1747.
iii. DANIEL, born Apr. 13, 1747, in Scarborough, married (int. Mar. 19, 1768) Sarah York, born in Scarborough in 1742 daughter of Samuel and Joanna (Skillings) York. He was living in Pearsontown on Aug. 14, 1772, when he bought from Ephraim Jones of Falmouth the 30-acre lot #56 in first division here (9/18). On Dec. 1, 1784, he bought from Winslow Warren of Lisbon in the kingdom of Portugal the adjoining 30-acre lot #55 (15/215). He served in the Revolutionary War. He and his wife, Sarah, were admitted to the Pearsontown Church on Feb. 4, 1775. He is credited with a family of 1-4-3 in the 1790 census. On Mar. 15, 1792, he sold his two lots in Standish to Thaddeus Richardson of Ossipee (Limington) (35/37). It was about this time that he moved to Durham, Maine, where he was living in 1794. He died there Aug. 22, 1806, and his wife on Oct. 28, 1832. They were parents of the following children:
1. MARY, born Sept. 7, 1769, bapt. Dec. 1, 1771, married (int. Feb. 6, 1787) Mar. 23, 1787, George Foss of Scarborough. They moved to Limington and then to Wales. She married second Samuel Robinson of Wales. She died Jan. 21, 1852, age 82 yrs.
2. FRANCIS, born in Standish June 1, 1772, bapt. June 14, 1772, married Oct. 15, 1797, Susannah Bagley.
3. SUSANNAH, born June 2, 1774, bapt. June 12, 1774, married Jan. 18, 1798, Moses Roberts.
4. DANIEL JR., born Feb. 9, 1778, bapt. Apr. 12, 1778, married Sept. 27, 1798, Mary True.
5. LYDIA, born Mar. 12, 1780, bapt. Apr. 3, 1780, married Mar. 18, 1801, Aaron Davis, second Feb. 3, 1806, Josiah S. Libby.
6. JOHN, born Mar. 14, 1782, bapt. June 8, 1785, married first Dec. 9, 1804, Eliza Riggs, second Mary Malan.
7. ROBERT, born Feb. 28, 1786, bapt. June 2, 1786, married in 1815 Eunice Gould.
8. SARAH, born Dec. 22, 1792, married John Robinson.
9. ZEBULON, born ____, bapt. July 23, 1790, married Mary King of Baltimore, Md.
10. HANNAH, born ____, married Sept. 4, 1814, Rufus Warren of Durham, Maine.
iv. JOHN S., born May 24, 1749, married July 12, 1792, Eleanor Roberts.
v. MARY, born May 24, 1751, married Nov. 15, 1773, Benjamin Foss of Saco.
vi. ABIGAIL, born Nov. 1, 1753, died Mar. 25, 1782, age 20 at her brother-in-law Benjamin Foss's house in Saco of consumption.

By second wife:

vii. **WILLIAM**, born in 1758, probably came to Pearsontown with his father and lived with him on Standish Neck, his father deeding the 100-acre lot #46 to him on Aug. 19, 1782 (11/582). He served in the Revolutionary War and married first (int. Aug. 17, 1782, in Gorham) Abigail Moulton, born Jan. 20, 1763, daughter of Peter and Joanna (Shaw) Moulton of Pearsontown. She died July 19, 1831, in Belfast, Maine, and he married second Mar. 1833 in Standish, Mehitable Brackett, born Oct. 14, 1785, in Gorham, daughter of James and Mehitable (Fabyan) Brackett. She died Mar. 1, 1865, age 80. Except for a period when he lived with his son-in-law Peter Rowe in Belfast, he spent most of his life in Standish, where he died Dec. 13, 1848. He is listed in the 1790 census with a family of 1-0-4, while in 1800 his family consisted of him and his wife, one male and three females under 10 and one female between 10 and 16. William and Abigail (Moulton) Harmon were parents of the following children:
1. JOANNA, born in 1783, married in Apr. 1809 Peter Rowe of Standish. They lived in Belfast, Maine, where he died Aug. 21, 1847. She died in Standish Aug. 11, 1857.
2. HANNAH, born in 1786, married May 31, 1812, Col. Levi Hall, born Jan. 28, 1787, son of Winslow and Mary (Hussey) Hall of Windham. They lived at North Gorham. She died July 25, 1813, age 27.
3. SARAH, born ____, married first Dec. 10, 1808, Theodore Libby, second Nov. 4, 1828, William Wescott.
4. MARGARET, born in 1792, married in 1815 Daniel Hall, born Aug. 17, 1789, son of Winslow and Mary (Hussey) Hall. They lived in Windham and Sebago, Maine, and were the parents of eleven children. He died Jan. 9, 1864, and she on July 31, 1860, age 68.
5. JAMES, born 1795, married May 27, 1821, in Belfast, Mary Campbell.
6. FANNY, born in 1798, married as his second wife Abraham Mayberry, born in Windham Jan. 4, 1785, son of William and Rose (Walden) Mayberry. He died Jan. 26, 1870. They lived in Standish.
7. MARY, born in 1802, married as his second wife Bryant Morton, born June 7, 1801, son of David and Mary (Sanger) Morton of Gorham. They lived in Bridgton, Maine.
8. ELI, born in 1808, married Mar. 18, 1832, Jane Whitney, and second Mary Woodman. He died Sept. 3, 1858, age 50 yrs., in Westbrook.

viii. **JOSIAH**, born Nov. 5, 1759, in Scarborough, probably came to Standish with his father. He married (int. Sept. 27, 1785, in Gorham) Anna Moulton, born Mar. 16, 1764, daughter of Peter and Joanna (Shaw) Moulton and sister to his brother William's wife. She died in Thorndike, Maine, on Dec. 18, 1836, age 72. He served in the Revolutionary War and is listed in the 1790 census of Buxton with a family of 1-2-2. At the time of the 1800 census he was living in Standish with a family consisting of him and his wife, three males and three females under 10, and one male and one female between 10 and 16. He purchased from Thomas Morton

of Standish one acre and 64 square rods of the 100-acre lot #36 in second division on July 3, 1815 (108/396). This land he sold to Josiah Harmon Jr. of Thorndike, Maine, blacksmith, on May 4, 1827 (108/397). He went to live with his son Luther in Corinna, Maine, and died there May 10, 1845. Josiah and Anna (Moulton) Harmon were parents of the following children:
1. PETER, born June 11, 1786, married Lydia Gordon of Thorndike.
2. LUTHER, born about 1791, married Sarah Philbrick.
3. DANIEL, born ____, died unmarried in Trinidad, West Indies, age 22 yrs.
4. BETSEY, born about 1790, married (int. July 14, 1810) Sept. 9, 1810, Samuel Thomes of Denmark, Maine. She died Apr. 25, 1865, age 75 yrs., and was buried in Denmark.
5. LYDIA, born about 1797, married Oct. 26, 1817, Daniel Jewett of Denmark, Maine. She died Dec. 29, 1873, age 76 and was buried in Denmark.
6. SARAH, born ____, died Nov. 1832, married Isaac Plummer, born in Gorham, Oct. 21, 1795. She was his first wife and the mother of four children. He married second Margaret Smith and had nine more children. They lived at White Rock in Gorham.
7. ANN, born in Standish Mar. 22, 1800, married Daniel Gordon of Thorndike in Aug. 1826 where he was a farmer.
8. JOSIAH JR. born in Standish Oct. 4, 1802, married Betsey Gordon of Thorndike, daughter of John and Betsey (Knowles) Gordon.
9. ABIGAIL, born ____, married Sept. 2, 1812, as his first wife Caleb Hodgdon, son of Israel and Lucy (Snow) Hodgdon. She died May 11, 1834

By third wife:
ix. BENJAMIN, born 1862, died unmarried in Standish.
x. RUFUS, born ____, married Mar. 14, 1798, Eunice Sawyer, born Feb. 19, 1775, daughter of Joel and Elizabeth (Stone) Sawyer of Gorham. He was a farmer and cooper and settled in Gorham just south of the Standish line. His wife died in Gorham at the home of her daughter Betsey on Nov. 20, 1850, age 74 yrs. 6 mos. He died in Harrison, Maine.
1. JONATHAN, bapt. Nov. 15, 1808, married Hannah Cranmore, lived and died in Bridgton.
2. BETSEY, bapt. Nov. 15, 1808, married first James Brown of Harrison on Mar. 20, 1830; second William J. Lewis, born July 7, 1801, son of Samuel and Phebe (Irish) Lewis of Gorham.
3. RUFUS JR., bapt. Nov. 15, 1808, married May 28, 1826, Lucy Higgins of Standish. Moved to Corinna, Maine, and died there.
4. WEALTHY S., bapt. Nov. 15, 1808, married Dec. 7, 1834, Isaac Moody, bapt. Oct. 5, 1806, son of William and Elizabeth (Sawyer) Moody of Standish.
5. REUBEN, married (int. Nov. 27, 1834) Axina Chase. Lived and died at Buxton. He died Feb. 6, 1873.

6. ANN, born Oot. 5, 1808, bapt. Nov. 15, 1808, in Standish, married Alvah Libby June 28, 1831.
7. EUNICE, born in 1813, married Hezekiah Crockett (int. Nov. 28, 1839).
8. MARY J., born June 10, 1814, in Standish, married Nov. 25, 1839, Peter Elder.

xi. ELLIOT, born Mar. 7, 1766.
xii. SAMUEL (?) of Livermore, Maine.
xiii. DODAVAH C., (of Livermore, Maine).
xiv. ANNE, born ____, married Feb. 7, 1805, John Haskell 3rd., born 1784 son of John and Mary (Paine) Haskell of Gorham.

HASKELL

The names of Benjamin and Jonathan Haskell are found on all the tax lists of Standish which were used in compiling a list of the early settlers of the town. Benjamin Haskell is found in the 1790 census with a family of 1-2-2 while Jonathan Haskell is listed with a family of 1-0-0. They were brothers and sons of John and Abigail (Libby) Haskell of Falmouth and Gorham.

Benjamin[5] Haskell (John,[4] Thomas,[3] Benjamin,[2] William[1]), born in Falmouth, Maine, Feb. 14, 1761, served as a substitute for his father in the Revolutionary War. His father moved to Gorham about 1765 and Benjamin was a resident of that town when he married (int. July 24, 1784, in Gorham) Sarah or Sally Berry of Falmouth, she born July 7, 1765, daughter of George and Sarah (Stickney) Berry of that town. Soon after their marriage they moved to Standish Neck where he was a farmer. At the time of the 1800 census his family including him and his wife consisted of two males between 26 and 45 years of age, two males between 10 and 16 years old, one female between 26 and 45, one female between 10 and 16, and two females under 10 years of age. He died May 3, 1827, age 66, and his wife died June 14, 1853, age 88 years.

Benjamin and Sarah (Berry) Haskell were parents of the following children:

i. REBECCA, born Apr. 6, 1785, married John Wescott, born Sept. 10, 1782, probably son of Eliakim Wescott who owned land adjoining the Haskell farm on Standish Neck. John Wescott died Oct. 23, 1866, age 84 yrs., 1 mo., 13 days. Rebecca (Haskell) Wescott died July 27, 1870, age 85 yrs., 3 mos., 21 days. They were parents of four children.

ii. BENJAMIN JR., born May 23, 1786, married (int. July 9, 1833) in August 1833 Nancy B. Pride who died July 20, 1842, age 46 yrs. and 1 mo. He married second Eleanor, who died Jan. 17, 1892, age 96 yrs., 5 mos. He died Oct. 28, 1859, age 73 yrs., 5 mos. They had children: Rachel; Sarah T.; Benjamin T.; and Rebecca P., who married Joseph Haggett.

iii. **LEVI QUIMBY**, born Sept. 1788, married Aug. 29, 1811, Abigail Waterhouse, born in Standish Aug. 16, 1790, daughter of Joseph and Lydia (Harmon) Waterhouse who also lived on Standish Neck. They lived in Limington where he died June 3, 1837. She died in Standish Jan. 30, 1855.
iv. **ABIGAIL**, born Jan. 1793, married Sept. 10, 1820, William Wescott, born in Jan. 1788 probably son of Eliakim Wescott. She died June 17, 1865, age 72 yrs., 5 mos., and he died Oct. 22, 1874, age 86 yrs., 9 mos. They were parents of seven children.
v. **SALLY**, born _____, married Israel True of Pownal on Jan. 28, 1819.
vi. **NANCY**, born in Mar. 1801, married John Cummings, born about 1789 son of John Cummings of Standish Neck. He died May 19, 1860. They were parents of two children. She died after Aug. 22, 1878.
vii. **POLLY**, born Dec. 4, 1802, married Nov. 1, 1832, Capt. Josiah Shaw, born May 12, 1805, son of Joseph and Eunice (Bean) Shaw of Standish Neck. He died suddenly at East Baldwin on Apr. 22, 1881, and she died Aug. 26, 1895. They were the parents of five sons.
viii. **RACHEL**, born in 1806, died Mar. 17, 1833.
ix. **CYRUS**, born Aug. 22, 1812, married Jan. 8, 1843, Mary Holt, born Aug. 22, 1812, died Aug. 31, 1858. He died Dec. 8, 1851. They had two children, Josiah and Sarah M.

Jonathan[5] Haskell (John,[4] Thomas,[3] Benjamin,[2] William[1]) born Mar. 24, 1765, in Falmouth son of John and Abigail (Libby) Haskell, married Sept. 19, 1793, Martha Phinney, born Apr. 24, 1764, daughter of John Jr. and Rebecca (Sawyer) Phinney of Gorham. Although in the 1800 census of Standish he was credited with a family consisting of one male and one female under 10 years of age and one male and one female between 10 and 16 years of age besides him and his wife, the only child of whom we have found a record was a daughter Abigail who married Ebenezer Moody (int. Mar. 1, 1823).

HASTY

Two brothers, Daniel and James Hasty, were settlers in Pearsontown prior to the Revolutionary War. They were born in Scarboro, sons of William and Hannah (Fogg) Hasty and their names are found on the 1789, 1790, 1796, 1796 and later tax lists of Standish.

Daniel[3] (William,[2] Daniel[1]) Hasty, born in Scarboro Mar. 18, 1749, married Martha McLaughlin of that town. On Apr. 11, 1770, while a resident of Scarboro, he bought from Clement and John Meserve the two 30-acre lots Nos. 3 and 4 in Pearsontown on which he made his home (5/295). On Dec. 31, 1776, he bought from Richard Codman of Gorham the two 30-acre lots Nos. 34 and 35 located across the road from his other land (8/549). He took an active part in town affairs, serving as selectman in 1786, 1790, 1801, and 1808, and collector in 1789, 1791 and 1806.

He and his wife were admitted to full communion with the Pearsontown Church on Dec. 8, 1771, and to membership therein on Oct. 25, 1772. At the time of the 1790 census he was credited with a family of 1-5-3, while at the time of the 1800 census his family consisted of him and his wife, two males between 10 and 16 years old, two males and two females between 16 and 26 years old, and one male between 26 and 45 years old. His wife died in Standish on Oct. 24, 1804, age 56, and he on June 1, 1818, age 69 years, in Standish. Daniel and Martha (McLaughlin) Hasty were parents of the following children:

- i. WILLIAM, born ____, bapt. Dec. 8, 1771, probably died young.
- ii. SARAH, born Apr. 5, 1774, bapt. June 5, 1774, married Mar. 27, 1798, Thomas Cram, born Dec. 31, 1768, in Pearsontown son of Daniel and Sarah (Green) Cram. She died Sept. 26, 1835, and he on May 23, 1843. For children see Cram family.
- iii. JAMES JR., born May 3, 1776, bapt. June 16, 1775, died unmarried June 16, 1812.
- iv. WILLIAM, born Mar. 3, 1778, bapt. Mar. 8, 1778, died in 1825.
- v. DANIEL JR., born May 3, 1780, bapt. May 6, 1780, married Apr. 11, 1805, Susannah Dow, born Nov. 26, 1782, in Pearsontown daughter of Joseph and Lucy (Sanborn) Dow. She died July 20, 1858, age 75 yrs., 7 mos. and he on May 18, 1863. age 83. They were the parents of the following children:
  1. JOSEPH DOW, born Nov. 11, 1805, died July 21, 1866, age 60 yrs., 2 mos. He was unmarried and died in insane hospital.
  2. MAHLON, born June 8, 1807, died Mar. 23, 1820.
  3. MARTHA, born May 25, 1809, married (int. Oct. 18, 1883) Josiah Moulton, born June 8, 1805, son of Simon and Abigail (Plaisted) Moulton of Standish. He died Sept. 25, 1894. They were parents of four children.
  4. LUCY, born Aug. 5, 1811, died Mar. 24, 1820.
  5. MARY W., born Sept. 19, 1815, married Daniel Dole of Windham.
  6. JOHN, born Jan. 19, 1818, married Emeline Dow, daughter of Joseph and Catherine (Rounds) Dow, born June 9, 1821.
  7. MAHLON, born Aug. 6, 1820, died 183_.
  8. LUCY ANN, born Mar. 11, 1822, married John Webb of Windham.
  9. LUCINDA, born Feb. 23, 1827, married Lendall B. Lowell and died in 1862. No children.
- vi. MARY, born Dec. 20, 1782, bapt. June 16, 1784, died unmarried.
- vii. SAMUEL, born Mar. 12, 1785, bapt. Sept. 8, 1785, died unmarried Oct. 6, 1818, age 34 yrs., in Standish.
- viii. HIRAM, born Sept. 11, 1789, bapt. July 23, 1790. Married July 6, 1820, Mary Moulton, born Nov. 19, 1796, in Standish, daughter of Simon and Abigail (Plaisted) Moulton. He died Feb. 15, 1866, age 76 yrs., 5 mos., in Standish. She died on July 2, 1872. He lived on homestead of his father. Children as follows:
  1. LUCY, born Aug. 5, 1821, married E. Cotton Hamlin, son of Charles Hamlin on Sept. 25, 1842.
  2. SARAH, born June 10, 1823, married Dec. 7, 1851, John Merrill or Morrell and lived in Iowa.
  3. JAMES LESTER, born Oct. 7, 1828, married Hannah Stone.

4. ANDREW, lived in Boston.
5. ABBY, born ____, married Cotton Hamblin as his second wife.

James[3] (William,[2] Daniel,[1]) Hasty born in Scarboro May 2, 1751, married (int. May 17, 1783, in Gorham) Rachel Dean, born in Norton, Mass., Oct. 21, 1766, daughter of John and Miriam (Hodges) Dean, later of Pearsontown. He was given as a resident of Pearsontown at the time the intentions of marriage were filed. He settled at Standish Corner on the Portland Road on land which later became the town farm. He also owned the 30-acre lot #31 near his brother's land, which he bought from Winslow Warren, merchant of Lisbon, Portugal, on Feb. 2, 1785 (13/224). He was a selectman in 1807 and collector in 1801. He died in Standish on July 8, 1835, age 85, and she July 9, 1842, age 76. Children of James and Rachel (Dean) Hasty, all born in Standish, were as follows:

i. JOHN DEAN, born Oct. 13, 1784, was a sea captain and lost at sea with his ship, unmarried. *Eastern Argus*, issue of Dec. 2, 1811, gives death of Maj. John D. Hasty, on Nov. 28, age 27 yrs., in Standish.

ii. JOSEPH, born Mar. 1, 1787, bapt. June 17, 1787, married (int. Feb. 21, 1818) Ruth McLaughlin, daughter of Robert and Martha (Johnson) McLaughlin of Scarboro. They lived on Standish Neck and raised a large family of children. He died Sept. 15, 1864, age 77, in Standish.

iii. WILLIAM, born June 18, 1789, bapt. Aug. 23, 1789, married Betsey or Elizabeth Fitch of Baldwin. He died Dec. 29, 1837, age 48 yrs., in Standish. Children as follows:
1. OLIVE S., born Feb. 13, 1823, married Richard T. Flint, then of Pekin, Ill.
2. JOHN D., born Apr. 15, 1825, a sea captain. He fell overboard and drowned while boarding a vessel to take him to his bride to get married.
3. SAMUEL C. born Mar. 14, 1826.
4. FRANCIS HENRY, died unmarried of fever in Kansas in 1857 (?)
5. ELLEN, born Dec. 9, 1833.
6. EMILY, twin to Ellen, born Dec. 9, 1833. Both were married and had children.

iv. JAMES, born July 24, 1791, bapt. Oct. 9. 1791, was a trader at Standish Corner for many years and town clerk for twelve years. He was a suicide by hanging in 1844.

v. MIRIAM, born Oct. 14, 1793, married Jan. 23, 1815, John Philbrick, born in Standish June 18, 1791, son of Jonathan and Sarah (Mussey) Philbrick. He died July 4, 1816, and she by suicide in an old well in 1841. They had one child, a son John H., born Oct. 26, 1815.

vi. AGNES, born Jan. 15, 1796, bapt. June 19, 1796, married Feb. 16, 1818, William McLaughlin of Scarboro. They were the parents of three sons, one of whom was the Hon. Charles McLaughlin of Portland. He died Apr. 11, 1837, and she on Jan, 12, 1884.

vii. CHARLES, born Jan. 16, 1799, bapt. Jan. 20, 1799, married Electa Goodenough Eaton, and lived on the old homestead until about 1840 when he went to Ohio and died there. She died Aug. 6, 1894.
viii. SAMUEL DEAN, born May 18, 1801, bapt. June 7, 1801, married on Nov. 28, 1833, Abigail Boucher, born Dec. 26, 1807, died, Nov. 24, 1887, in Lansing, Mich. He died there in 1863. Three sons.

HEATH

According to Standish vital records, Nicholas Heath of Brownfield and Ruth Boulter of Standish filed intentions of marriage on July 13, 1793, and were married on Sept. 9 of that year. While he was not a long-time resident of Standish, the fact that his wife came from an early Standish family and the unusual facts of his ancestry seem to make an account of his life and descendants pertinent to these annals. We are indebted for facts concerning his ancestry to a family record prepared by his grandson George Parker Anderson (1847-1927), who lived in the Limington section of Steep Falls.

This record states that Nicholas Heath was born in Portsmouth, N.H., in February 1769 son of Joshua and Molly (Cotton) Heath, died in Saco, Maine, in March 1849 at the age of eighty years, and was buried in a cemetery on the Ferry Road there. His parents, both natives of England, died at an early age, leaving him an orphan in Portsmouth. His father was believed to have been lost at sea while serving with the navy during the Revolutionary War and, according to the family record, his mother was shot in the street while fleeing from British soldiers. Nicholas stated that he could remember as a little boy lying down, looking under a gate, and seeing the red coats in the street. This event, if true, must have occurred elsewhere than Portsmouth because, as far as known, British soldiers were never in Portsmouth during the Revolution and, if a woman had been shot by them there, there would probably have been a record of such an occurrence.

At any rate, the young orphan boy was picked up by Capt. Henry Young Brown, a veteran of the Indian Wars and a land speculator, to whom the land that later became the town of Brownfield, Maine, which was named in his honor, was granted by the General Court (Legislature) of Massachusetts. It is said that Capt. Brown raised cattle for the market and drove them to Newburyport for sale. It was probably on one of these trips that he ran across the little orphan while passing through Portsmouth and took him back with him to his home in Brownfield. The trip was made with the little boy riding behind Squire Brown, as he was called, on the back of a horse. While on their way, Nicholas Heath, who was probably about 5 or 6 years old at the time, dropped off to sleep and fell from the horse unbeknown to the squire, who continued on his way quite a distance before missing him. Retracing his course, he found the lad beside the road picking flowers and gathering him up, he resumed the journey.

Nicholas Heath, who is said to have had a "square end" nose, grew up in the household of the Brown family and it was undoubtedly he who was listed as one "other free person" living in the family of Henry Brown of Brownfield township in the 1790 census. About the time Nicholas reached his majority, Capt. Brown deeded to him on June 28, 1791, fifty acres of land on the north side of Burnt Meadow Mountain above the Spring farm in Brownfield, a portion of which later became known as the Heath field, in consideration of 13 years, 8 months service as an apprentice and other considerations. In his younger days Nicholas used to work in the crews driving logs on the Saco River, and while on these drives, boarded at the home of Nathaniel Boulter Sr. on the River Road at South Standish. Here he became acquainted with Mr. Boulter's daughter Ruth and eventually married her as previously noted. They settled on the land in Brownfield given him by Capt. Brown, but at various times, particularly in his later years, lived in Standish. When he was about 45 years old, he contracted yellow fever from a sailor who was passing though the area and as a result of this sickness became a cripple for the rest of his life. His later years were spent in poverty, charges for his support being paid by Brownfield to the town of Standish where he evidently was living.

Nicholas and Ruth (Boulter) Heath were the parents of nine children, as follows:

i. ELIZABETH BOULTER, born Jan. 29, 1794, in Standish, married Apr. 26, 1812, William Whitmore Jr., born in Oct. 1791 son of William and Amy or Ruhama (Knight) Whitmore of Gorham, Limington, and Standish. He was a blacksmith at York's Corner in Standish and died in 1873, while she survived him until 1877. They were the parents of at least five children.

ii. SAMUEL, born Sept. 16, 1795, died at the age of 20 while serving in the War of 1812.

iii. DANIEL, born Oct. 22, 1797, in Brownfield, married (int. Apr. 24, 1812, in Standish) Mary Lane, born Feb. 7, 1796, daughter of Jabez and Mary Elizabth (Knowlton) Lane of Buxton. They lived in the Steep Falls area of Standish and he built mills there. He died Aug. 11, 1858, age 59 yrs., 1 mo., 11 days, in Saco. He is said to have died of consumption and was buried there.

iv. HENRY, born May 14, 1800, died Apr. 1, 1801.

v. HENRY, born Feb. 22, 1802, married Deborah Dyer, born about 1803, died in Mar. 1837, daughter of John and Mary (Dearborn) Dyer of the Coal Kiln Corner area of Scarboro. He died at South Standish in 1825.

vi. SALLY BROWN, born about 1805, married int. Nov. 27, 1828, John Pierce of Standish and lived at Steep Falls in Standish and Nashua, N.H. He died Mar. 10, 1860, in Nashua, N.H., and she died July 8, 1877, age 72 yrs., in Taunton, Mass.

vii. JOHN, born Feb. 15, 1807, never married but followed the sea and it was never known what became of him. Last known was that he left Portland for Havana when about 25 yrs. old.

viii. WILLIAM, born Feb. 13, 1809, married Feb. 6, 1842, Eliza Waterman, born Apr. 8, 1814, daughter of Gen. William and Betsey (Watts) Waterman of Buxton. They lived in Saco where he died Mar. 27, 1859, age 50 yrs. and was buried in the old Groveville Cemetery in Buxton.

ix.   ABRAM, born ____, ran away to sea when 16 yrs. old and was never heard from again.

HIGGINS

The Higgins family was another of those from Cape Cod that had a number of representatives among the early inhabitants of Pearsontown. The names of Ebenezer, Elkanah, Robert, Timothy, and William Higgins are found on the 1789, 1790, and later tax lists of Standish and in the 1790 census. They were all related to a lesser or greater extent.

Ebenezer[6] Higgins (Ebenezer,[5] Samuel,[4] Jonathan,[3] Jonathan,[2] Richard[1]), born Aug. 23, 1749, son of Ebenezer and Martha (Burgess) Higgins of Eastham, Mass., married Apr. 14, 1772, Rebecca Dyer of Truro, Mass., born ____, died Dec. 25, 1820, in Gorham, Maine. He lived in Truro and Provincetown and about 1780 moved to Pearsontown on Apr. 9, 1781, when he bought from Zebulon Knight of Falmouth the 30-acre lot #33 (11/294). He sold two-thirds of this lot to Abner Dow of Pearsontown on June 1, 1785 (15/186). He is listed with a family of 1-2-5 in the 1790 census, but had died prior to 1795 when his name is missing from the tax list of that year while, that of his widow, Rebecca, is found upon it. She married on Nov. 7, 1801, Col. Nathaniel Frost of Gorham as his third wife. Children of Ebenezer and Rebecca (Dyer) Higgins were as follows:

i.   EBENEZER JR., born July 4, 1775, at Truro, married Mrs. Joanna Atkins, was a sea captain who lived at Castine, Maine, and was lost at sea.

ii. REBECCA, born Apr. 11, 1780, in Provincetown, married Nov. 26, 1801, Nathaniel Blake of Gorham, born Oct. 1, 1780, son of Ithiel and Apphia (Higgins) Blake.

iii. HANNAH ATKINS, born in Pearsontown Aug. 20, 1782, married May 26, 1804, Jeremiah Frost of Gorham, born Aug. 31, 1780, son of Nathaniel and Mary (Berry) Frost. He died Feb. 7, 1845, age 64, and she Sept. 27, 1856, age 74; were the parents of eleven children.

iv. MARTHA, born June 21, 1784, bapt. Sept. 26, 1784, married Apr. 8, 1812, John Cressey of Gorham, born Aug. 22, 1785, son of Joseph and Hannah (Ashley) Cressey. She died Mar. 27, 1863, age 79, and he on Sept. 21, 1871, age 86. They were the parents of six children.

v.   DAVID, born Nov. 3, 1787, bapt. May 18, 1788, married Catherine Jordan of Otisfield and lived in Gorham on the Fort Hill Road. They had three children born in Gorham, but moved to Illinois where other children were born.

vi. SUSANNA, born Apr. 14, 1789, bapt. Aug. 23, 1789, married Nov. 29, 1810, Timothy Blake of Gorham, born May 26, 1789, son of Ithiel and Apphia (Higgins) Blake. She died Apr. 12, 1862, age 73, and he on Jan. 7, 1883, age 93. They were parents of six children.

vii. DESIRE PARKER, bapt. May 19, 1793, married Dec. 13, 1813, Ephraim Blake of Gorham, born June 26, 1789, son of Nathaniel and Mary (Fogg) Blake.

Elkanah[6] Higgins (Ebenezer,[5] Samuel,[4] Jonathan,[3] Richard[1]), born in Eastham, Mass., Nov. 18, 1764, son of Ebenezer and Hannah (Yates) Higgins and half brother to Ebenzer Higgins above, may have served in the Revolutionary War. He lived in Eastham and prior to 1789 moved to Pearsontown, where at the time of the 1790 census he was listed as the head of the family of 2-0-2. His family at the time of the 1800 census consisted of him and his wife, four males and one female under 10 years of age. He married (int. June 26, 1790) Jemima Cole of Limington. She was baptized in Standish Church July 30, 1797. He lived in Rome, Maine, with his daughter, Mrs. John Foss, and there he died Nov. 4, 1864. They were the parents of the following children:

i. SAMUEL, born Feb. 2, 1791, bapt. Sept. 7, 1797, married Dec. 19, 1811, Olive Chute and lived in Clinton, Maine.
ii. ELIZABETH, born Jan. 25, 1793, bapt. Sept. 7, 1797, married first on Jan. 9, 1813, Stephen Hancock, born Apr. 24, 1792, son of John Lane and Hannah (Prescott) Hancock of Buxton. She married second John Foss and died in Rome, Maine.
iii. EBENEZER, born July 20, 1795, bapt. Sept. 7, 1797, married first on Nov. 24, 1816, Mary Thompson, second Hannah Foss on June 11, 1818. She died Feb. 5, 1859, age 63 yrs., 3 mos. He married third Miriam (Strout) Thorne on Sept. 9, 1860, both of Standish. She was born July 27, 1800, in Limerick and was the widow of Daniel Thorne of Standish. She was living in 1870, age 70 yrs., in Standish. He died May 18, 1883, and is buried with his two wives in a family cemetery located off Route 25 at Higgins Corner.
iv. ABNER, born Nov. 25, 1797, bapt. Apr. 29, 1798, married Anna Shute, died in Belgrade, Apr. 15, 1879.
v. YATES, born June 11, 1799, bapt. July 18, 1799, married Almira Chandler on Oct. 13, 1825. He was a minister.
vi. JONATHAN, born Apr. 20, 1801, bapt. June 21, 1801, married Oct. 24, 1822 (int. Sept. 20, 1822) Martha Sanborn. They lived in Standish.
vii. ELKANAH JR., born Nov. 13, 1802.
viii. HEMAN, born Apr. 29, 1804, bapt. June 12, 1804, married Mary Gross Higgins of Orland, Maine. He lived in Orland and Sedgewick, Maine.
ix. RELIANCE, born Jan. 25, 1806, bapt. Aug. 28, 1806, married Dec. 20, 1824, Stephen B. Knight of Durham, Maine.
x. EXPERIENCE, born Feb. 11, 1808.
xi. CURTIS, born Aug. 19, 1810, married first Harriet Decker, second Mrs. Rose A. Hoxie; third a Mrs. Mack. He was a cooper and lived at Smithfield, Augusta, and Belgrade, Maine.

Seth[6] Higgins (Enbenezer,[5] Samuel,[4] Jonathan,[3] Jonathan,[2] Richard[1]), born May 14, 1744, at Eastham, Mass., son of Ebenezer and Martha (Burgess) Higgins, married Dec. 3, 1772, Martha Linnell, born Jan. 2, 1751, daughter of Elisha and Martha (Higgins) Linnell and sister of John and Samuel Linnell who settled in Standish, sister of Elizabeth Linnell who married Nathaniel Boulter Jr. of Standish, sister of Hannah Linnell who married Thomas Lombard of Gorham, and sister of Mary Linnell, who married James D. Tucker of Standish. They were married in Eastham at the time of the 1790 census and it is not certain just when they moved to Standish, but he is listed in the valuation list of Standish in 1799. He died before 1808 since Seth Higgins heirs are listed for that year. Children of Seth and Martha (Linnell) Higgins were as follows:

i. SELINA, born June 14, 1773, married Sept. 25, 1799, Prince Higgins, born Sept. 25, 1772, son of Timothy and Reliance (Yates) Higgins. She died in Standish Jan. 22, 1847. Seven children, for list of whom, see Prince Higgins.

ii. REBECCA, born Dec. 21, 1774, married Nov. 15, 1798, Ephraim Higgins, born Oct. 11, 1775, son of Timothy and Reliance (Yates) Higgins. She died in Standish Mar. 22, 1834. Their children were:
1. DANIEL, born June 7, 1799.
2. TIMOTHY, born Mar. 8, 1802.
3. STEPHEN, born Aug. 20, 1803.
4. LOUISA, born Mar. 3, 1806, died May 15, 1842.
5. MARTHA, born Mar. 31, 1808.
6. RELIANCE, born Feb. 9, 1811.
7. CATHERINE, born Sept. 13, 1813.
8. REBECCA, born Sept. 17, 1816.

iii. SETH, born Aug. 28, 1776, married July 10, 1803, Experience Higgins, born Sept. 20, 1777, daughter of Timothy and Reliance (Yates) Higgins. He was lost at sea on Dec. 25, 1804, and she married second, July 7, 1810, Daniel Lowell Jr. of Buxton. Widow Experience Higgins was baptized in the Standish Church on Sept. 16, 1810, and on June 30, 1811, John and Seth, sons of widow Experience Higgins, were baptized there.

iv. THANKFUL, born Dec. 28, 1779, married Nov. 13, 1805, Josiah Yates, born about 1782 son of John and Mercy (Hopkins) Yates of Standish, Baldwin, and Monroe, Maine. For children see Yates family.

v. MARTHA, born Dec. 31, 1781, married J. Cole.

vi. ELIZABETH, born Jan. 14, 1785, married Oct. 20, 1808, Capt. James Higgins.

vii. ELISHA, born Nov. 14, 1787, married Nov. 29, 1804, Rebecca Rich of Truro. They are said to have lived at Orrington, Maine.

viii. MARY, born Apr. 2, 1790.

ix. ABISHA, born Aug. 8, 1793, died from falling from a masthead, unmarried.

Timothy[5] Higgins (Freeman,[4] Benjamin,[3] Benjamin,[2] Richard[1]), born Mar. 28, 1748, at Eastham, Mass., son of Freeman and Martha (Cole) Higgins, married Mar. 9, 1771, Reliance Yates, born Jan. 18, 1751, daughter of John and Thankful (King) Yates of Harwich, Mass., and sister of John Yates, who settled in Standish. About 1787 he came from Eastham to Maine by water, landing at the Saco River and continuing overland from there. John Yates came with them. He probably served in the Revolutionary War. In the 1790 census he is listed with a family of 2-2-4 while at the time of the 1800 census his family consisted of him and his wife, one male under 10, and one male and two females between 10 and 16. His homestead farm was located on Oak Hill. Both he and his wife died in Standish, she Dec. 14, 1825, age 74 years, and he on Jan. 27, 1829. They were parents of the following children:

i. PRINCE, born Sept. 25, 1772, married first on Sept. 25, 1799, Selina Higgins, born June 14, 1773, daughter of Seth and Martha (Linnell) Higgins of Standish. She died in Standish Jan. 22, 1847, and he married second Mrs. Decker. He died in Standish in Jan. 1860. Children of Prince and Selina (Higgins) Higgins were as follows:
   1. MARY, born Aug. 12, 1800, bapt. Oct. 14, 1804.
   2. LEWIS, born July 18, 1803, bapt. Oct. 14, 1804, married Mar. 25, 1828, Susan Whitney. He died Mar. 11, 1888, age 85 yrs., 1 mo.
   3. MARTHA, born Jan. 31, 1805, bapt. May 19, 1805.
   4. ESTHER, born Sept. 18, 1806, bapt. Nov. 9, 1806.
   5. LUCINDA, born Sept. 15, 1808, bapt. Sept. 22, 1811.
   6. FREEMAN, born June 11, 1812, bapt. Aug. 16, 1812, died Mar. 1824, age 11 yrs., Standish.
   7. CHESLEY, born July 4, 1816, bapt. Oct. 13, 1816.
ii. EPHRAIM, born Oct. 11, 1775, married Nov. 15, 1798, Rebecca Higgins, born Dec. 21, 1774, daughter of Seth and Martha (Linnell) Higgins. She died in Standish Mar. 22, 1834, age 60, and he on Mar. 25, 1865.
iii. EXPERIENCE, born Sept. 20, 1777, married July 10, 1803, Seth Higgins Jr., born Aug. 28, 1776, son of Seth and Martha (Linnell) Higgins. He was lost at sea about 1804 and she married second Daniel Lowell of Buxton. She had two children by each marriage.
iv. THANKFUL, born Sept. 29, 1779, died unmarried at Standish on July 22, 1823. Buried Standish Corner Cemetery.
v.   AN INFANT.
vi. FREEMAN, born June 21, 1787, bapt. June 13, 1802, died Nov. 17, 1809, at Standish, unmarried, age 22 yrs., 4 mos., 27 days.
vii. TIMOTHY, born June 20, 1791, bapt. June 13, 1802, married first on Jan. 1, 1818, with Caleb Bradley officiating, Mary Ann Winslow of Westbrook (int. Nov. 28, 1817); second on Dec. 30, 1823, Rosanna (Stuart) Moody, born Sept. 27, 1797, daughter of Wentworth and Hannah (Shaw) Stuart and widow of James Moody of Standish. She died Dec. 14, 1858, and he on May 21, 1863, both in Standish. Two children.

William[5] Higgins (Joshua,[4] Richard,[3] Benjamin,[2] Richard[1]), born Sept. 5, 1734, at Eastham son of Joshua and Ruth (Twining) Higgins, married first on Apr. 1, 1756, Abigail Mayo; second on Aug. 6, 1761, Elizabeth Young. He served in the Revolutionary War. At the time of the 1790 census he was living in Standish with a family of 1-0-0. On May 15, 1779, he together with Zaccheus Higgins and Theodorus Hopkins, all of Eastham, Mass., bought the 100-acre lots Nos. 80 and 81 in the second division in Pearsontown (10/378). All three are given as living in Pearsontown on Oct. 1, 1779, when they divided this land among themselves (10/379). Date of his death has not been found, but it was sometime after Mar. 1, 1791, when he sold his rights in 100-acre lots Nos. 80, 81 and 73 in second division to his son Robert Higgins (20/79). Children were as follows:
i. EXPERIENCE, born Jan. 28, 1757.

ii.   ABIGAIL, born Sept. 20, 1758, married Dec. 7, 1778, Thomas Snow of Eastham. For children see Snow family.

By second wife:

iii. RUTH, born Sept. 9, 1762, married Dec. 15, 1781, John Foy of Gorham, Maine.

iv.   HANNAH, born Nov. 17, 1764.

v.   ROBERT, born Jan. 17, 1767, married Jan. 21, 1790, Sarah Whitney, born June 20, 1769, daughter of Abel and Thankful (Morton) Whitney of Gorham and Standish. They lived in Standish where he died in Apr. 1834 and she during the same year. They were parents of the following children:
   1. HANNAH, born Feb. 4, 1791, married Oct. 8, 1810, Gideon Swett, born in 1786 son of Benjamin and Apphia (Rowe) Swett of Baldwin and Standish. He died in 1839.
   2. THANKFUL, born Oct. 11, 1793, died young.
   3. WILLIAM, born Jan. 9, 1796, died young.
   4. SIMEON, born Apr. 25, 1798.
   5. JERUSHA MORTON, born July 24, 1800.
   6. SARAH, born July 9, 1803, bapt. Dec. 5, 1806, died Dec. 1821 in Standish.
   7. MERCY, born Oct. 9, 1805, married Jan. 1, 1825, Nathaniel Strout whose wife Mercy was 44 in 1850 census.
   8. ADELINE, born Mar. 11, 1808, bapt. Dec. 5, 1816, married (int. Feb. 1835) Daniel Boulter of Standish. She died in 1881.
   9. MARY, born Dec. 1, 1810, bapt. Dec. 5, 1816, died in Dec. 1822 in Standish.

vi.   WILLIAM, perhaps a son, who on Jan. 8, 1795, married Phebe Paine, born Sept. 24, 1773, daughter of Joseph and Phebe (Rich) Paine of Eastham, Mass., and Standish. She died Dec. 3, 1829, and he on Sept. 20, 1834. (There was a Dea. William Higgins who died Apr. 14, 1820, age 52 yrs., in Standish.)

They were parents of the following children:
   1. ELIZA, born Oct. 15, 1795, bapt. July 10, 1803, married Nov. 22, 1821, Joseph Moody, born Sept. 16, 1798, son of Daniel and Mary (Sawyer) Moody of Standish. She died May 1829, age 30, in Standish.
   2. PHEBE, born Apr. 13, 1797, bapt. July 10, 1803.
   3. HULDAH, born May 26, 1799, bapt. July 10, 1803, married Dec. 16, 1823, Daniel Moody Jr., born Apr. 9, 1801, son of Daniel and Mary (Sawyer) Moody of Standish.
   4. ABIGAIL, born June 8, 1801, bapt. July 10, 1803.
   5. LUCY, born May 23, 1803, bapt. July 10, 1803, married May 28, 1826, Rufus Harmon Jr., bapt. Nov. 15, 1808, son of Rufus and Eunice (Sawyer) Harmon of Standish. They settled in Corinna, Maine.
   6. JOSEPH, born July 2, 1805, bapt. Oct. 6, 1805, died Feb. 25, 1877, age 71 yrs., Standish.
   7. NANCY, born July 20, 1807, bapt. Oct. 4, 1807, Standish.
   8. WILLIAM JR. born Apr. 12, 1809, bapt. Oct. 22, 1809.
   9. ROBERT G., born Oct. 1, 1811, bapt. Aug. 2, 1812.
   10. ALMIRA, born Apr. 23, 1813, bapt. Oct. 31, 1813.
   11. ANSEL, born Nov. 6, 1815, bapt. July 21, 1816.

Zacheus[5] Higgins (Joshua,[4] Richard,[3] Benjamin,[2] Richard[1]), born Oct. 8, 1727, at Eastham, Mass., son of Joshua and Ruth (Twining) Higgins, married first Oct. 7, 1749, Mercy Crosby of Harwich, who died in 1772; second on Dec. 3, 1772, Mrs. Hannah (Knowles) (Warren) Sparrow, daughter of Paul Knowles of Truro, Mass., and widow of John Warren and of Jonathan Sparrow Jr. Zacheus Higgins and his son Zacheus Higgins Jr. both served as privates from Sept. 6-13, 1778, in Lt. Samuel Knowles company during the Revolutionary War. In 1779 he bought land in Pearsontown together with his brother William and Theodorus Hopkins and moved into town. On Mar. 8, 1788, he sold his third part of this land to his stepsons Stephen and Jonathan Sparrow and probably returned to Eastham, since a Zacheus Higgins with a family of 1-0-1 is found in the 1790 census of that town but not in the 1790 census of Standish. Date of his death and that of his wife have not been discovered but his estate was administered on Mar. 22, 1817. He was father of the following children:

i. JERUSHA, born Nov. 19, 1750, married Feb. 4, 1776, Gowel Chase of Chatham.
ii. MERCY, born June 7, 1752, married Sept. 18, 1777, Elisha Atwood of Harwich.
iii. RICHARD, born Aug. 31, 1754, perhaps married on Aug. 19, 1777, Molly Smith of Chatham.
iv. SETH, born June 1, 1756.
v. MARY, born Feb. 27, 1759.
vi. ZACHEUS, JR., born Apr. 1, 1761, married Hannah Twining, lived in Eastham and died Jan. 15, 1816, age 56. Eight children.
vii. TULLY, born Aug. 31, 1762.
viii. KNOWLES, born Sept. 25, 1773, married Mar. 26, 1795, at Standish, Mary Rand, born May 23, 1771, daughter of Jeremiah and Lydia (Blake) of Gorham. They lived in Standish where he died July 3, 1831, and she on Aug. 3, 1832. They were parents of the following children:
1. ZACHEUS, born Sept. 9, 1796, married (int. Apr. 10, 1822) Hannah Martin, born May 31, 1794, daughter of Jonathan and Widow Leah (Fogg) Martin of Buxton. He died Feb. 24, 1874, and she on May 11, 1875, age 80 yrs., 11 mos., 11 days. Buried at Sebago Lake. They were parents of the following children:
(1) MARY, born Feb. 4, 1823, died Feb. 4, 1884.
(2) JAMES LEWIS, born Apr. 7, 1826, died Apr. 22, 1894, Standish.
(3) ELIZA ANN, born Jan. 24, 1828, died Mar. 24, 1854.
(4) ARDELIA, born July 17, 1832, died Sept. 17, 1835.
(5) JOHN MARTIN, born 1834, died 1862.
2. HANNAH, born Jan. 9, 1799.
3. KNOWLES JR., born Sept. 1, 1807, married July 10, 1831, in Standish, Eliza Page of Buxton, born Feb. 21, 1811. They were the parents of eight children. He died Aug. 25, 1858, age 51, and she on May 6, 1870, age 59, both in Buxton.

HINCKLEY

The name of Stephen Hinckley is found on the 1795 tax list of Standish. He was baptized in Falmouth (Portland) Dec. 3, 1774, son of Seth and Martha (Sawyer) Hinckley. His father was one of the men from Falmouth who settled in Pearsontown following the burning of Falmouth by the British in October 1775. His father having died, his mother married (int. July 27, 1782, in Gorham) Abner Dow, born Aug. 28, 1751, in Salisbury, Mass., son of Jabez and Dorothy (Wood) Dow of Falmouth and Pearsontown. Both were given as residents of Pearsontown at time marriage intentions were filed. Stephen Hinckley evidently grew to manhood in Standish, but left town to follow to follow the sea, being a captain when he went down with his ship in a hurricane when only one night out from Portland following the start of a voyage on Dec. 25, 1804. On Nov. 5, 1797, he married Mary Coss, born in Portsmouth, N.H., Jan. 4, 1778, who died in Standish May 12, 1812. They were the parents of a son, Stephen, born in Standish May 5, 1799, who became a prominent citizen of Gorham.

HIND OR HINE

The name of Richard Hind is found in a list of inhabitants of Pearsontown who were settled here before the burning of Falmouth (Portland) by Mowattin October 1775. The name is also found spelled 'Hines' or 'Hinds'. He was born in Milford, Conn., April 6, 1747, son of William[3] (Samuel,[2] Thomas[1]) and Elizabeth (Hollingworth) Hine of that town. He married at Roxbury, Conn., on Jan. 15, 1770, Amy Hurd. She divorced him in Aug. 1778 for desertion on Mar 15, 1774. His father's will, probabted Sept. 5, 1781, gave him but 20 shillings.

During his lengthy service in the Revolutionary War at some times he is given as serving from Pearsontown and at others from Gorham. It is evident that his stay in Pearsontown was of short duration, perhaps only during the early period of the Revolutionary War. On Feb. 11, 1775, his intentions of marriage to Abiah Jenkins were published in Gorham, Maine. She was born in Barnstable, Mass., Jan. 21, 1754, daughter of Samuel and Mary (Chipman) Jenkins, who later settled in Gorham.

Richard Hine's name is found on a list of inhabitants of Flintstown (Baldwin) dated April 1786. On Sept. 20, 1788, he was granted land in that town by the proprietors (20/418). However, he is listed as living in Gorham, Maine, with a family of 1-2-4 at the time of the 1790 census, but he was living on June 20, 1794, in Buckfield, Maine, when he sold his land in Flintstown (21/440). He was living in Hartford, Maine, when he later bought land in that town from Actor Patten of Topsham, Maine (34/126). Other deeds indicate that he continued to live there as late as 1804. He is said to have died in Turner, Maine, on July 26, 1834. According to pension records, Abiah Hine, widow of Richard, died July 13, 1837. Children of Richard and Abiah (Jenkins) Hine were as follows:

i. **JOSIAH**, born Apr. 29, 1776. A Josiah Hine and wife, both under 45 were living in Standish at the time of the 1800 census.
ii. **PRUDENCE**, born Oct. 19, 1778.
iii. **HOLLINGSWORTH**, born Aug. 12, 1781.
iv. **ABBY**, born Apr. 27, 1784.
v. **MARY**, born Apr. 15, 1787.
vi. **CHIPMAN**, born Feb. 20, 1791.
vii. **THADDEUS**, died Nov. 5, 1857, age 63 yrs., 4 mos., and 20 days.

HOBBS

Capt. Humphrey Hobbs, commander of the company of veterans of King George's War who together with the men of Capt. Moses Pearson's company became grantees of the land now comprising the town of Standish, probably never saw any part of the land covered by the grant. While the town was known as Hobbs and Pearsontown in its earliest days, there is no record of Capt. Hobbs having taken any really active part in its settlement. At what was probably the first meeting of the Proprietors, he was chosen moderator. This meeting was held at the house of Edward Ingraham in York on June 17, 1752. At another meeting held in November of the same year at the house of Moses Pearson in Falmouth, Humphrey Hobbs was chosen as a treasurer to collect any monies due the Proprietors from persons living westward of the Piscataqua River. This is the last appearance of his name in the Proprietors' Records.

Besides the mention of his name in connection with the grant of the township on April 20, 1750, and its appearance on the list of grantees as owner of right No. 35, the only other record of him we have found in the Massachusetts records in connection with the affairs of the township is in connection with a petition dated May 1752 in which he and twenty-two other grantees asked for more time to comply with the terms of settlement on the land granted them, citing as a reason for their failure to do so up to that time the unsettled conditions caused by the Indian raids and forays throughout the eastern part of Province. An extension of two years' time beginning on the first of April following was granted them on Jan. 3, 1753.

Humphrey Hobbs was born in Topsfield, Mass., Feb. 18, 1711-12, son of William and Sarah (Knight) Hobbs and married Jan. 3, 1737, Anna Symonds, born Nov. 20, 1713, and died Sept. 9, 1791. He was one of the first members and a deacon of the church at Souhegan West (Amherst) N.H., to which he was dismissed from the church at Middleton, Mass., on Sept. 6, 1741. In 1744 he resigned as deacon when he went into military service against the French and Indians. He was a noted Indian fighter and won many battles against them, particularly around No. 4 (Charlestown), New Hampshire. His Indian enemies said about him "Souhegan deacon no very good, he fight Sabbath-Day." This probably referred to the fight on June 26, 1748, a Sunday, which he and his company of forty men had with a band of Indians led by Chief Sackett, in which the whites were outnumbered four to one, but which they won after a four-hour battle.

He was a captain in Winslow's expedition to build Fort Halifax on the Kennebec River in 1754 at which time he acted as a guide. He also was with the expedition to Nova Scotia in 1755 which resulted in the expulsion of the Acadians. Governor Shirley selected him as captain of one of the companies of rangers organized in 1756 to serve along the New York frontier. Two companies were organized and arrived for service at Albany in the middle of September of that year, Capt. Hobbs with thirty-two men leaving Boston on August 23. In October they were moved to Fort William Henry to form part of the winter garrision of that post and in January 1757 became a part of Rogers' Rangers. However, Hobbs did not live to see any service under Rogers' command for he contracted smallpox, of which he died at Fort William Henry on Febuary 22, 1757.

With his continuous activity in the military affairs of the Province, it can clearly be understood why he did not take a more active part in the affairs of Hobbs and Pearsontown. On June 29, 1754, Humphrey Hobbs of No. 2 in the Province of New Hampshire sold to Moses Pearson of Falmouth in the county of York, one right or share in the new township granted to himself and Pearson and others bounded on Narragansett No. 1 and No. 7, Presumpscot River, Saco River, and Province lands consisting of a 30-acre lot #64 with all the after divisions belonging to right (31/258). This right, orginally granted to Samuel Nutting, had probably been purchased by Hobbs from him. The 30-acre lot of this right was purchased from Moses Pearson by John Deane in 1776, right No. 35, which was the original grant to Humphrey Hobbs, was sold by the Proprietors to Richard Codman of Falmouth on Feb. 1, 1769. The 30-acre lot of this right was sold by Codman on Dec. 31, 1776, to Daniel Hasty.

Humphrey and Anna (Symonds) Hobbs were parents of the following children, all of the births recored in Middleton, Mass.

i. ANNA, born Mar. 28, 1739, married John Brown.
ii. JOSEPH, born Apr. 20, 1743.
iii. SUSANNAH, born Sept. 1, 1745, married May 4, 1769, Aaron Peabody. She died on Aug. 7, 1827, age 82, in Milford, N.H. They were the parents of seven children.
iv. SAMUEL, born Sept. 17, 1750, died in 1781.

HODGDON

The name of Joseph Hodgdon is found on the 1795 and 1796 tax lists of Standish. It is likely that he was the Joseph Hodgdon born Jan. 20, 1768, son of Jeremiah and Abigail (____) Hodgdon of Gorham. Joseph married Feb. 24, 1789, Mary Snow, born in Barnstable, Mass., daughter of Benjamin and Bathsheba (____) Snow of Gorham. She was a sister to the wife of Michael Philbrick Jr.

Joseph Hodgdon moved to Orrington, Maine, whence his wife's parents had moved in 1794. He was living in Gorham with a family of 1-0-1 at the time of the 1790 census and in a back settlement called Goshen (Vienna), Maine, when the 1800 census was taken. He died in Orrington, Maine.

HOIT (HOYT)

The name of Daniel Hoit is found on the 1789 tax list of Standish, but for a poll tax only. He undoubtedly was the Daniel Hoit of Falmouth, Maine, whose intention of marriage was published there in 1743 to Bethiah Millett, born in Gloucester, Mass., Dec. 13, 1722, daughter of John and Bethiah (Carter) Millett of Gloucester and Falmouth, Maine. He is said to have died in Falmouth about 1790 while his widow died about 1810, age about 84 years. His descendants say that he came from Amesbury, Mass., to Falmouth, but his parentage has not been determined. Daniel and Bethiah (Millett) Hoit were parents of the following children:

i. JOHN MILLETT, born Nov. 23, 1744, married first Abigail (Nabby) Teal, who died in childbed Jan. 25, 1785, at the age of 30. He married second on Apr. 26, 1785, Catherine Cox of Falmouth, who died in Gorham, Maine, Mar. 8, 1839, according to pension records. He served in the Revolutionary War and died in Standish Feb. 5, 1829, age 84 yrs., 2 mos., 12 days. He was buried in the Wood burial plot in the Village Cemetery at Standish Corner. Children were as follows:
By first wife:
1. MARY, bapt. Feb. 16, 1777, died Aug. 10, 1782
2. ELIZABETH.
3. JOHN TEAL, bapt. Apr. 27, 1783.
By second wife:
4. MARY, born Jan. 24, 1786.
5. JOSEPH, born Feb. 12, 1788.
6. THOMAS, born June 12, 1790.
7. FANNY, born Feb. 18, 1792.
8. HANNAH.
9. WILLIAM.
10. RHODA.
ii. DAVID, born ____, married Polly Plummer in Portland and died in Boston. He served in the Revolutionary War.
iii. HANNAH, born ____, married ____ Robinson. Jane Robinson of Portland who married Moses Wood of Standish on May 6, 1791, was perhaps a daughter.
iv. JOSEPH, died at sea, unmarried.
v. JANE, born about 1760, married Enoch Wiswell of Portland. He was a veteran of the Revolutionary War and died in Portland Feb. 22, 1811, and Jane, his wife, died in Feb. 1837. They had a daughter Abigail (Nabby) Wiswell who married in 1808 Edward Wood of Standish, brother of Moses Wood who married her cousin Jane Robinson.

HOPKINS

The name of Theodore Hopkins is found on the 1789, 1790, 1795, and 1796 tax lists of Standish and in the 1790 census with a family of 3-0-2. In the 1800 census there were two families listed under his name consisting of three male children under 10 years of age, one male between 26 and 45, one male over 45 (himself), one female child under 10 years old, one female between 26 and 45, and two females over 45.

Theodurus[5] Hopkins (Stephen,[4] Stephen,[3] Giles,[2] Stephen[1]), born Nov. 9, 1726, was son of Samuel and Lydia (Rich) Hopkins of East Brewster, Mass. He served during the French and Indian Wars in Capt. Jabez Snow's company during 1759 and 1760. He married Dec. 17, 1751, Hannah Hurd, who died prior to 1775. He married second (int. Oct. 30, 1775) Lydia Smalley, who died in Eastham in 1779.

On May 5, 1779, he is given as living in Eastham when together with Zacheus and William Higgins, also of Eastham, he bought the 100-acre lots Nos. 80 & 81 in second division in Pearsontown (10/378). All of them, however, are given as living in Pearsontown on Sept. 25, 1779, when they divided this land equally among them (10/379). He, of Pearsontown, mortaged 10 acres of land with buildings there to Mary Stone of Harwich on Mar. 3, 1784 (12/455), and sold to Joseph Chandler Rackleff of Standish 10 acres of land, probably the same as above, on Jan. 20, 1800 (33/618).

He was admitted to full communion in the Standish Church on Mar. 26, 1797, and was living as late as Apr. 13, 1801, when he sold 65 acres of lots Nos. 80 & 81 in second division to Joseph Cressey of Gorham (37/437). Nothing further has been found concerning him. Children of Theodore and Hannah (Hurd) Hopkins, all born in Eastham, Mass., were:

i. THEODORE, born in Eastham, Nov. 1, 1752. He was a Revolutionary War prisoner in England and lived there later.
ii. BENJAMIN, married July 7, 1789, Hannah Jordan and lived in Portland, where he died about 1803.
iii. PHEBE, born about 1760, married Thomas Harding, brother to Amaziah of Eastham. They moved to Unity, where she died Oct. 31, 1834, age 74.
iv. HANNAH, born about 1763, listed as of Pearsontown when her intentions of marriage to Joseph Blake were filed Jan. 6, 1781, in Gorham. They lived at West Gorham and were the parents of eight children. He died Jan. 28, 1840, age 83, and she on Jan. 27, 1842, age 78.
v. RICHARD, lived in New York City.
vi. REBECCA, (intentions Aug. 26, 1797, give Betty), married Sept. 28, 1797, Stephen Sparrow. They settled in Unity, Maine.
vii. LUCY, born about 1768, listed as living in Standish on Feb. 28, 1788, when intentions to marry Josiah Bacon were filed in Gorham. They were married Dec. 27, 1788, and lived in Gorham near the Buxton line. They were the parents of ten children. She died Mar. 1, 1836, age 68, and he married second Mrs. Hannah Hamblen of Standish. He died Dec. 24, 1845, age 80 yrs., 4 mos.

viii. **CHARLES**, married Mar. 7, 1793, Martha Bacon, born in Gorham May 15, 1769, daughter of Nathaniel and Apphia (___) Bacon of Gorham and sister to Josiah Bacon who married his sister Lucy.
ix. **JOSIAH**, born May 4, 1772, bapt. Nov. 1, 1772, in First Church of Orleans, Mass., married Nov. 23, 1790, Sarah Rackliff, born Feb. 17, 1770, daughter of Joseph Chandler and Mary (Welch) Rackliff of Scarboro and Standish. They were admitted to the Standish Church June 15, 1795, and about 1797 moved to Unity, Maine, where they were living at the time of the 1800 census. He died July 7, 1856, and his wife, Sarah, died June 25, 1850, both in Dexter, Maine. Their children were:
1. **THEODORE**, born Apr. 15, 1791, Standish, bapt. in Standish Church June 21, 1795.
2. **CHANDLER**, born Dec. 16, 1792, Standish, bapt. June 21, 1795, married Betsey (Libby) Johnson born June 22, 1803, daughter of Isaac and Rebecca (Crockett) Libby of Gorham and widow of Henry Johnson.
3. **RICHARD**, born Jan. 18, 1795, Standish, bapt. in Standish Church June 21, 1795.
4. **GEORGE**, born Jan. 29, 1797, bapt. in Standish Church Jan. 22, 1800.
5. **SALLY**, born July 19, 1799, Unity, Maine, bapt. in Standish Church Jan. 22, 1800.
6. **SEWALL**, born June 13, 1801, Unity, Maine.
7. **LEWIS**, born Aug. 30, 1803, Unity, Maine.
8. **CONY**, born Aug. 27, 1805, Unity, Maine.
9. **LAVINIA**, born Aug. 29, 1807, Unity, Maine.
10. **REBECCA**, born Mar. 7, 1810, Unity, Maine.
11. **BOWMAN**, born Oct. 13, 1814, Unity, Maine.

HOW

The name of Daniel How appears in the 1789, 1790, and 1795 tax lists of Standish as well as in the 1790 census with a family of 3-0-2. However, his name does not appear on the 1796 or later tax lists so he apparently left town between 1795 and 1796. Under date of Nov. 15, 1785, Daniel How of Methuen, Mass., bought of Rev. John Tompson of Berwick, Maine, part of ten acres of land in Pearsontown at the corner southward of the meeting house on the north west road (15/63). On July 25, 1801, Daniel How of Portland sold the same land to William Butler of Standish, which is described as one-half acre of land beginning at a stake 16 rods southeast form the south corner of the meeting house on the northwest road (35/345). He was a trader and probably kept a store at this location. Reference to the How Family Genealogy discloses that Daniel[6] Howe (Joseph,[5] James,[4] John,[3] James,[2] James[1]) was born June 8, 1762, in Methuen, Mass., son of Joseph and Hannah (Carlton) How. On Aug. 6, 1789, he married Abigail Mussey, baptized Dec. 11, 1768, in First Parish Church of Portland, daughter of Benjamin and Abigail (Weeks) Mussey of Falmouth and Pearsontown. He died in Portland

Sept. 16, 1819, and his widow died there Sept. 6, 1837. Daniel and Abigail (Mussey) How were parents of the following children:
i. JOSEPH, born in Standish May 31, 1791, married in Feb. 1816 Elizabeth Douglas of Portland. He died there Aug. 1, 1820, and his widow married Samuel Holbrook of Freeport. She died Oct. 8, 1863. One child, a daughter.
ii. JOHN, born in Standish Sept. 30, 1793, married Dec. 25, 1817, Susan Gates. They lived in Portland where he died June 26, 1859.
iii. DANIEL, born in Standish Oct. 5, 1795, married Jan. 29, 1818, Eliza Thrasher, born about 1793. They lived in Portland where he died in 1874. Five children.
iv. WILLIAM, born in Portland May 18, 1800.
v. CAROLINE MUSSEY, born Jan. 15, 1803, married Martin Gore.

Christopher How, whose name is found on the 1795 tax list of Standish, was a brother of Daniel How and was born in Methuen, Mass., Oct. 12, 1772. On Jan. 18, 1796, he married Elizabeth Philbrick, born Apr. 20, 1775, daughter of Deacon Jonathan and Sarah (Pike) Philbrick of Standish, he being then of Berwick, Maine. They lived in that town where they had two children born, both of whom died young. She died and he married second Mrs. Elizabeth Pike, a widow and daughter of John Rollins. He died in May 1841.

HOWE

Dr. Ebenezer[5] Howe (Ebenezer,[4] Ebenezer,[3] Samuel,[2] John[1]) born in Sturbridge, Mass., Apr. 21, 1773, son of Ebenezer and Sarah (Rice) Howe, was the second physician to settle in Standish. He came to town about 1800 and on Feb. 2, 1807, married Catherine Spring, born in Conway, N.H., Feb. 5, 1780, daughter of Jedediah and Elizabeth (Saltmarsh) Spring. He lived and practiced his profession in Standish for many years, dying here on June 4, 1841. His widow died April 1860, age 80, in Standish. Ebenezer and Catherine (Spring) Howe were parents of the following children:
i. ELIZA, born Sept. 24, 1802, married Feb. 5, 1829, Lewis Spring, born Dec. 5, 1805, son of John and Olive (Storer) Spring of Saco, her first cousin once removed. They were parents of two children.
ii. MARSHALL SPRING, born June 12, 1804, was an officer in the regular army for many years and died in Kentucky about 1878.
iii. SARAH RICE, born Jan. 8, 1806.
iv. GREENLEAF, born Apr. 5, 1807, married June 17, 1832, Mary Dennett, born in Standish Sept. 1, 1806, daughter of Samuel and Mary (Lowell) Dennett. They lived in Cambridge, Mass., where she died on Mar. 15, 1872. He died in Somerville, Mass., in 1873.
v. MARY ANN, born Jan. 11, 1811, married Dec. 28, 1835, Simeon G. Clement of West Gorham. Three children.
vi. ALBION PARIS, born Mar. 25, 1818, served in Union army during Civil War.
vii. LEANDER M., born July 18, 1815, died young.

IRISH

The name of Ebenezer Irish is found on the 1795 and 1796 tax lists of Standish, but it is likely that he did not live in town for any great length of time. He was born in Gorham Apr. 5, 1763, son of James Jr. and Mary (Phinney) Irish. On Jan. 1, 1785, he married Martha (Patty) Morton, born May 19, 1762, daughter of Ebenezer and Sarah (Whitney) Morton of Gorham. At the time of the 1790 census he was living in Little Ossipee Plantation (Limington) with a family of 1-1-3. He is also listed in the school district list in 1792 in that town.

On Jan. 11, 1793, he purchased from Joseph Holt Ingraham the 100-acre lot #120 in the second division in Standish located on Saco River. Here he probably settled soon after. However, he was back living in Limington on Mar. 30, 1798, when he bought from Samuel Dennett the 100-acre lot #109 in second division in Standish (29/496). There is no doubt but that he actually lived in Standish in 1795 and 1796 since he was charged for a poll tax both of those years. At the time of the 1800 census he was living in Limington with a family consisting of him and his wife, one male child under 10, three females under 10, two females between 10 and 16 years of age. They moved to Fryeburg in 1805. His wife died in Fryeburg Dec. 15, 1824, age 67 yrs., and he died there Jan. 22, 1851. They were parents of the following children:

i. SALLY, born 1786, died Feb. 21, 1820, age 33 yrs., Fryeburg.
ii. MARY, born Mar. 4, 1788, married Nov. 9, 1809 William Fessenden of Fryeburg. She died Mar. 22, 1875, in Fryeburg.
iii. STEPHEN, born July 1792, died Jan. 8, 1863, age 70 yrs., 6 mos., Stow, Maine; married Apr. 3, 1817, in Fryeburg, Hannah Abbot.
iv. NANCY, born 1794, married Dec. 3, 1817, Moses Abbott and died before 1830.
v. ELIZABETH, born Sept. 30, 1796, married Feb. 6, 1821, in Fryeburg, Isaac Abbott of Fryeburg, born Jan. 28, 1796. She died Mar. 16, 1869, age 73 yrs., in Fryeburg.
vi. MARTHA, born Mar. 14, 1800, married Jan. 23, 1834, in Stow, Maine, Abiel Frye Whiting. She died Apr. 22, 1877, in Topeka, Kans.
vii. DOROTHY, born Oct. 1803, married Dec. 3, 1822, in Fryeburg, Ebenezer Howe of Fryeburg. She died Apr. 29, 1887, age 84 yrs., 6 mos., in Fryeburg.
viii. MEHITABLE C., born Jan. 3, 1805, died Apr. 5, 1885, age 80 yrs., 3 mos., 2 days, married Apr. 11, 1832, James Guptill of Cornish, she of Fryeburg.

JONES

Ephraim Jones Esq. as a son-in-law of Moses Pearson was one of the active Proprietors of Pearsontown. He was born in the west precinct of Watertown, Mass. (later called Weston), on Dec, 10, 1712, son of

Capt. James and Sarah (Moore) Jones, where he grew to young manhood. He was dismissed from the Weston Church to the church in Falmouth, Maine, on May 8, 1743, but he was living in Falmouth several years prior to that date for his intentions of marriage were published there Feb. 18, 1739, to Mary Pearson, born Dec. 4, 1720, daughter of Moses and Sarah (Titcomb) Pearson. He was a mariner and lived in Falmouth on the east side of Exchange Street. After the bombardment of the town in 1775 by the British he retired to Pearsontown with his family, as did a number of other men living in Falmouth at that time, and settled on some of the land he owned in town. He was living in Pearsontown on May 15, 1779, when he sold to the heirs of Moses Pearson several different parcels of land in Pearsontown (10/336). His wife died Sept. 19, 1775, and he on Dec. 16, 1783, at the age of 71 years. Children of Ephraim and Mary (Pearson) Jones were as follows:

i. SARAH, born Jan. 7, 1740, married Aug. 26, 1762, Theophilus Bradbury of Falmouth.
ii. MARY, born Apr. 5, 1742, married Nov. 12, 1762, Daniel Illesley of Falmouth.
iii. ELIZABETH, born Feb. 10, 1744, married Oct. 18, 1774 (?) Timothy Pike of Windham.
iv. PEARSON, born July 16, 1747, married Nov. 26, 1771, Betty or Elizabeth Illesley. He died Jan. 9, 1781.
v. EPHRAIM JR., born May 27, 1749, settled in Pearsontown prior to the burning of Falmouth in 1775. He was a housewright or carpenter and lived on 30-acre lot #73 and the 5-acre lot #18 adjoining it. His name is found on the 1789, 1790, and later tax lists of Standish, in the 1790 census with a family of 2-1-5 and in the 1800 census when his family consisted of him and his wife, two male and two female children under 10 yrs. of age and one male and one female child between 10 and 16 yrs. old. He married (int. Jan. 31, 1780, in Gorham) Judith Philbrick, born Aug. 27, 1763, in Pearsontown daughter of Jonathan and Sarah (Pike) Philbrick. They moved to Lewiston about 1815 and there he died Mar. 31, 1833, age 83 yrs., 10 mos., and his wife died July 1, 1833, age 70 yrs., 10 mos. They were the parents of the following children:
1. SARAH, born Mar. 1, 1781, in Standish, bapt. Dec. 1, 1793, married Apr. 28, 1809, Thomas Pennell of Falmouth.
2. MARY, born Feb. 19, 1783, in Standish, bapt. Dec. 1, 1793.
3. JONATHAN PHILBRICK, born Dec. 26, 1784, in Portland, bapt. Dec. 1, 1793, died Aug. 16, 1805.
4. BETSEY, born Aug. 17, 1787, in Portland, bapt. Dec. 1, 1793.
5. HARRIET, born Mar. 9, 1790, in Standish, bapt. Dec. 1, 1793, married Rev. Josiah G. Morrill of Otisfield on Dec. 13, 1814.
6. ANNA, born Mar. 26, 1792, or Standish, bapt. Dec. 1, 1793.
7. DANIEL ILLESLEY, born Mar. 29, 1794, in Standish, bapt. Apr. 13, 1794.
8. SOPHIA, born Sept. 25, 1796, in Standish, bapt. June 25, 1797.
9. EPHRAIM, born Sept. 7, 1798, in Standish, bapt. Aug. 4, 1799, died Oct. 11, 1840.
10. EUNICE TITCOMB, born Jan. 6, 1801, in Standish, bapt. Aug. 9, 1803, and died June 23, 1841.

11. **WILLIAM**, born Apr. 20, 1803, in Standish, bapt. Aug. 28, 1803, died Jan. 15, 1848.
12. **ABIGAIL F.**, born May 20, 1805, in Standish, bapt. Sept. 7, 1806.

vi. WILLIAM, born June 17, 1751, went to sea in his early manhood, but finally settled in the 1789, 1790, and later tax lists and in the 1790 census with a family of 2-0-2. He died in Apr. 1823, age 71 yrs., in Standish (*Eastern Argus*, May 13, 1823).
vii. ABIGAIL, born Mar. 10, 1753, died May 4, 1759.
viii. EUNICE, born Dec. 25, 1754, married Joseph Titcomb on Apr. 2, 1783.
ix. ANNE, born June 17, 1757, married in 1772 Enoch Titcomb of Newburyport.
x. ABIGAIL, born June 11, 1759, married Nathaniel F. Fosdick in 1784. She died Apr. 5, 1851, age 91 yrs., 10 mos., in Portland. He graduated from Harvard College and died in 1819 in Salem, Mass.

KNEELAND

The name of David Kneeland is found on the 1789 and 1790 tax lists of Standish. According to the vital records of Otisfield, Maine, where he later settled he was born in Ipswich, Mass., Mar. 5, 1741. However, the Kneeland Genealogy states that he was born on Jan. 3, 1747, son of Philip and Mary (Potter) Kneeland of Topsfield, Massachusetts. This data in the family history appears to be in error as is the case in regard to other data in the sketch concerning him. It appears likely that he was the David Kneeland baptized in Topsfield Apr. 19, 1741, son of Philip and Elizabeth (Wooding) Kneeland of that town as found in the vital records of Topsfield.

In 1769 David Kneeland moved to Bridgton, Maine, and settled on lot #9, range 5 on which the first apples in Bridgton were raised. He cleared a farm from the wilderness and lived there until about 1785. It was at this time that he moved to Standish, for he was of Bridgton when on Aug. 30, 1785, he bought from Joshua Stone of Falmouth in the 30-acre lot #13 in first division and the 30-acre lot #14 adjoining with house barn and buildings thereon (14/437). He was living in Standish on July 30, 1787, when he sold Thomas Hopkins of Portland land in Bridgton (16/75) and on Mar. 13, 1790, when he sold Stephen Phinney of Gorham lots Nos. 13 and 14 in Standish (18/302). However, he was living in Otisfield, Maine, on Nov. 18, 1790, when he sold other land in Bridgton (18/81). Here then is a pretty accurate record of the time he lived in Standish.

David Kneeland was twice married. It seems likely that he was the David Neeland of Topsfield who married Sarah Smith of Ipswich on Jan. 1, 1761, as found in the Ipswich records. She evidently died sometime before 1776, for under date of May 18, 1776, is found in the Gorham records the marriage intentions of David Kneeland and Joanna (March) Murch, both of Bridgton. According to Otisfield records, Joanna or Johanna (Murch) Kneeland was born in Saco Dec. 25, 1752. He died in

Otisfield on Oct. 10, 1797, age 56 yrs., 7 mos., 5 days, but the date of death of his wife, Joanna, has not been discovered. Children were as follows:
By first wife Sarah (Smith) Kneeland:
i. BETTY, bapt. July 11, 1762.
ii. ABRAHAM, bapt. June 17, 1764, died in Bridgton.
iii. LOIS, bapt. May 4, 1766.
iv. SARAH, bapt. Jan. 24, 1768.
v. DAVID, bapt. Jan. 5, 1770, in Bridgton, married (int. June 18, 1791, in Standish) Dorcas Meserve, daughter of John and Sarah (Strout) Meserve of Standish. He settled in Bridgton but moved to Sweden, Maine, in 1803. His first wife died about 1815 and he married second Dec. 25, 1822, Hannah, widow of Jacob Gibson, who was born Sept. 3, 1766. He died in 1833. Children, all by first wife were as follows:
1. A BOY, burned to death in Bridgton.
2. A BOY, burned to death in Bridgton.
3. SARAH.
4. NANCY.
5. WILLIAM H., born Mar. 14, 1803, married Mary Giles.
6. ELIZA, born Oct. 9, 1818, married Dr. Alonzo Robbins.
7. ABIGAIL (twin), born Oct. 9, 1808, married June 21, 1827 William Nevens.
8. HANNIBAL H., born Apr. 14, 1810, married June 6, 1830, Lydia Stearns.
vi. ABRAHAM, born July 10, 1772.
By second wife Joanna (Murch) Kneeland:
vii. EPHRAIM, born Oct. 21, 1776, in Bridgton, married Lydia Piper.
viii. HANNAH, born Jan. 29, 1781, in Bridgton.
ix. ASA, born Apr. 16, 1783, in Bridgton, married Apr. 25, 1811, Almira Mayberry.
x. AARON, born July 10, 1787, in Standish, died July 10, 1797.
xi. MARY, born May 20, 1792, in Otisfield.
xii. MOSES, born Oct. 9, 1797. Moved to Ohio in 1817.

KNOWLES

Another of the early settlers in Pearsontown was Samuel Knowles, who was living here prior to 1760. He was born in 1733 posthumously to Elizabeth (Bacon) Knowles, whose husband, Nathaniel, had died in 1732. She later married as his third wife Beriah Smith of Provincetown. Sometime before 1743 Beriah Smith, his wife, Elizabeth, and children by both of their previous marriages moved to Cape Elizabeth, Maine, where his name is found on a tax list for that year.

The name of Samuel Knowles first appears in accessible records when his intention of marriage was recorded in Falmouth on Dec. 27, 1754, to Sarah Elwell, who may have been a sister or otherwise related to Bethiah Elwell, who married (int. May 9, 1759) George Tinney, another early inhabitant of Pearsontown. Beginning in January 1757 and continuing until Oct. 4, 1762, there are charges against Samuel Knowles of Pearsontown in an account book of Ephraim Jones of Falmouth. He is listed as a private in Capt. Loring Cushing's Cape Elizabeth training company on a return dated Apr. 29, 1757. Under date of July 20, 1757, a petition to the Massachusetts government from Pearsontown Plantation bears the three names of Thomas Stevens, Samuel Knowles, and John Walker. In 1759 he is listed in a return of Capt. William Gerrish's marching company for the protection of the frontier, he no doubt being one of the men stationed at the Pearsontown Fort. At the time of an enlistment in His Majesty's Forces on Mar. 8, 1760, his residence is given as Pearsontown, his birthplace Cape Cod, and his age 27. His name is also found in a list of Pearsontown men who worked on Gorham roads in 1761.

It is said that following his residence in Pearsontown he moved his family back to Cape Elizabeth. He was granted the 5-acre lot #10 in Pearsontown, which he later sold to Benjamin Titcomb of Falmouth (Portland) as is indicated in a deed by which Titcomb sold this lot along with others to Rev. Jonathan Gould, the second minister of Standish, on May 25, 1795 (22/452). Not long after leaving Pearsontown he evidently moved "down east" to Washington County, for in the grants of townships in far eastern Maine in 1764 his name is included among the grantees of No. 6, now Addison, and his signature is attached to an undated petition to Gov. Hutchinson from the inhabitants of Pleasant River (Addison) in 1770. His grant was confirmed to his son Freeman Knowles, as his heir, on June 4, 1794. He died about 1777, for in the census of Addison on Apr. 27, 1778, appears a "Widow Knowles" with four in her family. She probably survived him until at least 1799. Children of Samuel and Sarah (Elwell) Knowles, all born in Cumberland County, Maine, were as follows:

i. ELIZABETH, married William Ingersoll of Addison, who died at Columbia, Maine, in 1807. They were parents of nine children, five boys and four girls.
ii. FREEMAN, born Dec. 1754, died at Addison, Maine, Nov. 27, 1797, married Susanna (or Abigail) Nash, daughter of Joseph Nash, who survived him. Seven children, one boy and six girls.
iii. SAMUEL, born June 4, 1759, died at Sedgewick, Maine, Oct. 7, 1819, married Oct. 4, 1784, Jane Gray, born Jan. 1, 1764, died at Sedgewick, Maine, Dec. 29, 1836. He served in the Revolutionary War from Pleasant River, now Addison. Eight children, three boys and five girls.
iv. SARAH, born June 22, 1762, married Nov. 17, 1779, John McCaslin, born Apr. 3, 1757. Eleven children, six boys and four girls.

LAMPSON

The name of William Lampson is found on the 1789, 1790, 1795, 1796, 1808, and 1814 tax lists of Standish, assessment for the years 1789 and 1790 being for polls tax only. He was a hatter and was born at Haverhill, Mass., on Mar. 25, 1767. On Feb. 17, 1793, he married at

Fryeburg, Maine, Mercy (Marcy) Lowell, born at Epping, N.H., Dec. 10, 1771, daughter of Daniel and Mercy (Davis) Lowell of that town and Standish, Maine. In 1815 he moved his family to Conway, N.H., where he died on Mar. 6, 1836, and his wife at Bridgton, Maine, on Jan. 30, 1858. Children, all born in Standish, were:

i. DANIEL LOWELL, born Sept. 15, 1801, died at Bridgton Sept. 23, 1852, unmarried.

ii. LUCY LOWELL, born Dec. 19, 1803, married in 1836 William S. Jacobs, born June 4, 1799, son of Nathaniel and Nancy (Sears) Jacobs of Bridgton. She died June 12, 1864, and he Nov. 1, 1863. They were parents of Fannie P., Anne E., Eleanor F. R., Charles Nathaniel, and Lucretia Ann Jacobs.

iii. BETSEY A., born Dec. 11, 1805, married William Stone in 1837. They lived in Bridgton where she died Oct. 14, 1839.

iv. EWARD PREBLE, born Feb. 15, 1808, married Lois J. Farrington in 1832. They lived at Fryeburg, where he died Oct. 9, 1886, age 78 yrs., 7 mos., 23 days, Fryeburg.

v. LUCRETIA ANN, born Sept. 11, 1811, and when 24 yrs. old married Nathaniel Jacobs of Bridgton, who died in early manhood, and sometime after married his brother, Charles R. Jacobs, born May 31, 1811. He died Jan. 13, 1883, age 72, and she on Sept. 27, 1906, age 95.

LARRABEE

Isaac Larrabee, baptized in Scarboro May 18, 1755, son of Samuel and Sarah (Brown) Larrabee, married Apr. 19, 1781, Sarah Freeman, born May 9, 1761, daughter of Jonathan and Sarah (Parker) Freeman of Gorham. Previous to his marriage he lived in Scarboro for a number of years, but moved to Little Ossipee Plantation (Limington) by 1788 at least. He was living there at the time of the 1790 census with a family of 1-2-3. His name is also found on a 1792 school list of that town. However, about 1795 he moved to Standish, his name being found on 1795, 1808, and 1814 tax lists. His family in Standish at the time of the 1800 census consisted of him and his wife, one male and one female under 10, one male and two females between 10 and 16, and one female between 16 and 26. He lived in town until about 1815 when he moved to the town of Sebago in that part now forming the town of Naples, where he died at the home of his son Benjamin in the summer of 1843 at the age of 92. Among the children of Isaac and Sarah (Freeman) Larrabee were:

i. MARY, born Dec. 23, 1786, died Sept. 8, 1859, Portland, married Jan. 24, 1824, Ebenezer Cobb.

ii. BENJAMIN, born June 14, 1791, married Jan. 1, 1816, Hannah Martin, born Dec. 7, 1797, daughter of Robert Martin of Baldwin. He died in Naples Apr. 9, 1860, and she in Bridgton Apr. 15, 1869. They were the parents of the following children:
  1. ISABELLA, born about 1819, died in 1825 age 6 yrs.
  2. DANIEL P., born Oct. 13, 1821.
  3. WILLIAM H., born Aug. 30, 1823.

    4.   **HANNAH**, born Feb. 17, 1827.
    5.   **BENJAMIN F.**, born Dec. 23, 1828.
    6.   **ISAAC**, born 1830, died in 1843.
    7.   **STEPHEN**, born 1832, died in 1834.
    8.   **MEHITABLE**, died in 1835 age 7 mos.

iii.   **ISAAC**, born Apr. 12, 1796, married Sally Martin, sister of his brother's wife, on Sept. 17, 1818, and settled in Sebago. He died Mar. 19, 1873, age 76 yrs., 11 mos., 7 days.

LIBBY

    The name of Isaac Libby is found on the 1790, 1795 and 1796 tax lists of Standish and in the 1790 census with a family of 1-3-2 and the 1800 tax list with a family consisting of him and his wife, two boys and three girls under 10 years of age, and two boys and one girl between 10 and 16 years old. He was born in Scarboro in 1760 (baptized Oct. 12, 1760) son of Capt. David and Dorcas (Means) Libby of that town. On Dec. 11, 1783, he married Sarah Waterhouse, daughter of Joseph and Rachel (Norman) Waterhouse of Scarboro. They moved to Standish about 1788 and settled in Standish Neck where his wife's half-brother, Joseph Waterhouse, had settled several years previously and her sister, Susannah, wife of Timothy Berry, had settled about the same time.

    Isaac Libby and his family lived in Standish until 1800, when he moved to Freedom, Maine, where he afterward lived and died on Dec. 1, 1838. His widow died Apr. 15, 1839. He was a deacon of the Christian Church at Freedom for many years. Children of Isaac and Sarah (Waterhouse) Libby were at follows:

i.   **HANNAH**, bapt. Nov. 20, 1785, in Scarboro, married Abel Works of Unity.
ii.   **ISAAC**, bapt. June 29, 1787, in Scarboro, died young.
iii.   **JOSEPH**, born July 31, 1788, in Standish, married Lucy H. Grant. They were the parents of nine children and lived in Freedom, Albion and Exeter, Maine.
iv.   **DAVID**, born about 1789 in Standish, married first Mary Fowler; second Abigail Libby, born Sept. 4, 1797, daughter of Mark and Anna (Libby) Libby of Standish and Unity, Maine. He was the father of two children by his first wife and at least three by his second wife.
v.   **ROBERT**, born in Standish Sept. 6, 1790, married Oct. 8, 1815, Anna Clark Hasty. They were parents of three children.
vi.   **SALLY**, born 1792, died at the age of 22 yrs.
vii.   **BETSEY**, born in 1794, died in Freedom in 1865, unmarried.
viii.   **JOSIAH**, died at the age of 14 yrs.
ix.   **ISAAC**, born Apr. 21, 1797, married Oct. 10, 1826, Hannah Abbott. Lived and died in Freedom. They were parents of two children.
x.   **ABRAM**, born Apr. 2, 1801, in Freedom, married Sept. 13, 1840, Jane Bragdon. Two children died at birth.

The name of Jonathan Libby is found on the 1796 tax list of Standish and in the 1800 census with a family consisting of him and his wife and two boys and one girl under 10 years of age. He was born in Gorham Oct. 9, 1772, son of Joab and Susannah (Lombard) Libby, but was living in Standish when his intentions of marriage to Mary Stevens of Windham were filed on Aug. 18, 1792. Following her death he married second (int. Dec. 19, 1806) Abigail, daughter of Isaac Jordan of Raymond, was a farmer and was living on Standish Neck at the time of the 1800 census. He later moved to Gorham, but returned again to Standish, where he died in Jan. 1848. Children by first marriage were as follows:

i. JOAB, born Apr. 24, 1793, married first Jane Marwick, second Sarah Libby. Lived in Raymond and Naples and had eight children by both marriages.
ii. DANIEL, born Mar. 7, 1800, married Eunice Cook of Casco. Lived in Gorham and Windham. Two children.
iii. MARY, born about 1799, married June 4, 1820, Jacob Morton, born about 1796 son of Ebenezer and Susannah (Irish) Morton of Standish.
iv. RICHARD, died at the age of 4 yrs.

Children by second marriage, all born in Gorham, were as follows:
v. THOMAS, died in Casco, unmarried.
vi. SUSAN, married Bradley Cram of Gorham.
vii. MARGARET, married first James Cates, second David Frost.
viii. JANE, born July 4, 1816, married James Staples.
ix. ABIGAIL, born June 4, 1823, married Charles Dingley.
x. ANN REBECCA, born twin to Abigail, married Andrew R. Gay.

Jonathan Libby died Mar. 25, 1848, age 79, and Abigail, his wife, died Apr. 16, 1848, age 65. Stones in cemetery at White's Bridge in Standish.

Mark Libby was living in Standish with a family consisting of him and his wife, two boys and one girl under 10 years of age, and one boy and one girl between 10 and 16 years old at the time of the 1800 census. He was born in Scarboro Feb. 15, 1765, son of Allison and Mary (Libby) Libby and on May 24, 1785, married Anna Libby, born Apr. 24, 1767, daughter of Elisha and Abigail (Meserve) Libby of Scarboro. He was one of the early settlers of Unity, Maine, probably around 1800. He and his wife were members of the Methodist Church. Her brother Benjamin Libby married Phebe Rackliff, her sister Abigail married Joseph Stevens and John McDaniel. Mark Libby died June 22, 1838, and his widow died Sept. 12, 1858. They were the parents of the following children:

i. ANNA, born 1787, married 1806 John McDaniel. He married second her aunt, Lucy Libby.
ii. RUFUS, born 1789, died 1808.
iii. MARK, born 1791, died in 1814 at Plattsburgh, N.Y., in War of 1812.
iv. SAMUEL DEAN, born Mar. 24, 1793, married Betsey Libby.
v. ABIGAIL, born Sept. 4, 1797, bapt. Feb. 5, 1801.
vi. SALLY, born June 1, 1802.
vii. ELISHA, born Apr. 12, 1805, married Sarah Patterson.
viii. ALLISON, born Apr. 12, 1807, married Sarah J. Mitchell.
ix. RUFUS B., born Nov. 6, 1809, unmarried.

John Libby, born July 13, 1770, son of Joab and Susannah (Lombard) Libby of Gorham and thence brother of Jonathan Libby above, was living in Standish at the time of the 1800 census. He married (int. Nov. 4, 1797) Hannah Gray of Standish. He was a farmer and died about 1815 leaving no children. His widow married Gabriel Welch of Raymond.

LINNELL

The names of Enoch and Samuel Linnell are found on the 1789, 1790, 1795 and 1796 tax lists and in the 1790 census with families of 2-0-5 and 1-1-2 respectively. These two were undoubtedly brothers and sons of Elisha and Martha (Higgins) Linnell of Eastham, Massachusetts. Martha (Higgins) Linnell was born Oct. 2, 1723, in Eastham, Mass., and spent her last days in Standish where many of her children settled. The widow Linnell was admitted to the Standish Church in 1794 by letter from Eastham. She died in Jan. 1821 at the age of 97 years, according to her death notice placed in the Jan. 9, 1821, issue of the *Eastern Argus*. The following were the children of Elisha and Martha (Higgins) Linnell:

i. REBEKAH, born Nov. 17, 1745.

ii. JOHN, born June 25, 1747, in Eastham and was likely the John Linnell of Pearsontown who with Enoch Linnell of the same town bought from John Sawyer of Pearsontown the northeast half (or 50 acres) of the 100-acre lot #82 in the second division of lots in this town on Dec. 2, 1783 (12/356). Little has been discovered concerning him, but it is likely that he was unmarried and living with his brother Enoch at the time of the 1790 census. His name does not appear on any of the tax lists, but he is mentioned as being deceased on Sept. 15, 1799, when Enoch Linnell sold to James D. Tucker, his brother-in-law, the 50 acres he and John Linnell had purchased from John Sawyer in 1783 (220/405). He died Sept. 15, 1799.

iii. ENOCH, born Mar. 23, 1749, was living in Pearsontown prior to Dec. 2, 1783, when he and his brother John bought land here as indicated in the deed previously mentioned. It appears likely that he was married at the time of the 1790 census (2-0-5) and that the two males over 16 indicated therein were he and his brother John, while the five females may have been his mother and four of his sisters. He became active in town affairs and was a selectman in 1787, 1791, 1797, and 1798. On Dec. 26, 1791 (int. Nov. 19, 1791) he married Susanna Sanborn, born Aug. 13, 1753, daughter of John and Lucy (Sanborn) Sanborn of Hampton Falls, N.H., and Standish. He and his wife Susannah were admitted to membership in the Standish Church on Apr. 26, 1795, on which date he was baptized. He died sometime between Sept. 15, 1799, when he sold 50 acres of lot #82 to his brother-in-law James D. Tucker, as previously mentioned, and June 25, 1800, when his widow, Susannah, married as his second wife John Pierce of Standish. No record has been found of any children by either marriage.

- iv. MARTHA, born Jan. 2, 1751, married Dec. 3, 1772, Seth Higgins of Eastham, who settled in Standish after 1790. For children see Higgins family.
- v. MEHITABLE, born Sept. 23, 1753, died Mar. 1819, age 65 years in Standish (*Eastern Argus*, Apr. 6, 1819).
- vi. ELICE (ALICE?) born Sept. 2, 1755.
- vii. DESIER (DESIRE?) born Sept. 6, 1757, married Nathaniel Hopkins of Eastham Nov. 5, 1783, she also of Eastham. They moved to Hampden, Maine, where he died in 1810 and she in 1830.
- viii. ELISHA, born July 23, 1760.
- ix. SAMUEL, born Jan. 12, 1763, in Eastham and living in Pearsontown on June 15, 1782, when his intentions of marriage were filed in Gorham to Anna York, born in Aug. 1764, baptized as wife of Samuel Linnell on July 3, 1803, daughter of John and Sarah (Strout) York of Pearsontown. She died May 13, 1821, aged 56 yrs., 9 mos., and he married second (int. Apr. 26, 1823) Mrs. Susannah (March) Newcomb of Portland, widow of Joshua Newcomb of Buxton. On April 26 she was admitted by letter from the Chapel Congregational Church in Portland to the Standish Church. She died Mar. 10, 1854, age 91 yrs., in Standish. He served in the Revolutionary War and received a pension for his services. At the time of the 1800 census his family consisted of him and his wife, three males and one female under 10 years of age, and one male and one female between 10 and 16 yrs. old. He established his homestead farm on the 100-acre lot #87 in second division where he was evidently living at the time of his death on May 13, 1837. He and his wife were buried in the small cemetery on Dow Road, so called, at Dow's Corner. Children of Samuel and Anna (York) Linnell, all born in Standish, were as follows:
  1. ISRAEL, born Dec. 2, 1782, married his cousin Desire York, born Apr. 7, 1791, daughter of Job and Sarah (Jones) York of Standish and Bethel, Maine. He served in the U.S. Navy in the war with Tripoli in 1804. He moved from Bethel, Maine, about 1830 and settled in the Magalloway region near Upton, Maine, on a lot which his brother Luther Linnell had partially cleared but abandoned. He was living in Lincoln Plantation at the age of 75 yrs. on Dec. 14, 1857. He is said to have died in Manchester, N.H., in 1871 at the home of his youngest daughter at the age of 92 yrs. His wife died in Magalloway Apr. 22, 1858, and was buried at Wilson's Mills. Among the children of Israel and Desire (York) Linnell were the following:
     - (1) JONAS, born Sept. 9, 1812.
     - (2) ANNA YORK, born Oct. 6, 1814.
     - (3) MARTHA.
     - (4) LORENZO DOW, born Sept. 12, 1825, in Bethel, died in 1916.
     - (5) GEORGE W., killed May 27, 1863, at Port Huron during the Civil War.
     - (6) MARY JANE, married Jacob Jewell of Warren, N.H.
     - (7) ELIZABETH, married Albert Whitten of Manchester, N.H.

2. JOHN, born May 8, 1786, bapt. Aug. 5, 1803, lived in Otisfield where he was killed by lightning on June 13, 1868. He married Polly or Molly Files, born June 7, 1789, daughter of Ebenezer and Molly (Elder) Files of Gorham, who died May 28, 1860. They were the parents of nine children, as follows:
   (1) WILLIAM ELDER FILES, born Nov. 24, 1809, died May 1, 1865, married Oct. 3, 1839, Rhoda (Moors) Haskell, who died Mar. 14, 1886. They were the parents of twelve children.
   (2) MARY, born Nov. 18, 1811, died Aug. 17, 1868, married Aug. 25, 1834, Joseph G. A. Waterhouse of Poland, Maine.
   (3) ANNA, born Mar. 20, 1815, died Mar. 25, 1860, married Feb. 23, 1840, Allen Pulsifer of Poland, Maine. He was born in Poland Feb. 19, 1815, and died there Jan. 14, 1892. He was a carriage maker. Both he and his wife are buried in Maple Grove Cemetery in Poland.
   (4) JOHN ADAMS, born Feb. 2, 1817, died ____ unmarried.
   (5) ABIGAIL, born Dec. 24, 1818, died Oct. 20, 1890, married Apr. 28, 1839, Benjamin F. Woodsum of Harrison. Four children.
   (6) DESIRE, born Oct. 29, 1821, died Mar. 10, 1893, married Dec. 26, 1843, Moses True of New Gloucester, Maine.
   (7) JACOB TEWKSBURY, born May 4, 1823, died Jan. 8, 1874, Lewiston, married Sept. 19, 1847, Diana, daughter of John and Eliza (Raynes) Edwards, born July 17, 1823, died Aug. 10, 1900. At one time he ran a livery stable in Lewiston. Five children.
   (8) STEPHEN WATERHOUSE, born July 6, 1829, died Nov. 21, 1852, of consumption, Otisfield.
   (9) NEWELL H., born Mar. 19, 1832, died Jan. 22, 1914, married Oct. 6, 1855, Polly Frost of Norway, Maine.
3. ABIGAIL, born Apr. 14, 1788, bapt. Aug. 15, 1803, married as his first wife on Nov. 30, 1809, Joshua York, born 1788 son of Jacob and Edith (Moody) York of Standish and Baldwin. She died about 1820 and he married second in 1821 Martha Tibbetts of Buxton.
4. ELISHA, born Dec. 4, 1791, bapt. Aug. 5, 1803, moved to Bangor, Maine.
5. DESIRE, born Jan. 1, 1794, died unmarried 1877 in Standish. She was buried in Standish Corner Cemetery.
6. SAMUEL, born July 8, 1797, bapt. Aug. 5, 1803, and died Jan. 29, 1852, Veazie, Maine.
7. ENOCH, born Mar. 2, 1800, bapt. Aug. 5, 1803, married Mar. 19, 1820, Betsey Bryant, both of Gorham. He died Aug. 2, 1843, age 43 yrs., in Portland, formerly of Minot (*Christian Mirror*, Aug. 13, 1843).
8. LUTHER, born Jan. 26, 1803, bapt. Aug. 5, 1804, married Mar. 11, 1824, his cousin Desire Lombard, born in 1801 daughter of Thomas and Hannah (Linnell) Lombard of Otisfield. They lived in Otisfield and Oxford, Maine. She died Dec. 11, 1871, and he on Jan. 17, 1875, in East Rochester, N.H.

9. IRA, born Aug. 22, 1805, bapt. Nov. 21, 1805, died Sept. 1865, Ashland, Maine. He moved to Levant in 1829.
10. RUSSELL, born Feb. 10, 1808, married Elizabeth Thomes and was a merchant in Gorham. He died May 28, 1854, in Gorham.
x. ELIZABETH, born Jan. 11, 1765, married Nathaniel Boulter Jr. of Standish on Feb. 20, 1794, Rev. Jonathan Gould officiating.
xi. HANNAH, bapt. June 23, 1767, married Dec. 15, 1785, Thomas Lombard of Gorham and lived in Raymond and Otisfield, Maine. For children see Lombard family.
xii. MARY, born Jan. 30, 1770, married Sept. 16, 1792, James Davenport Tucker of Saco and Standish, Maine, John Dean Esq. officiating. For children see Tucker family.

LOMBARD

There were two Lombard families living in Standish at the time of the 1790 census. Thomas Lombard had a family of 1-1-1 and Jedediah Lombard one of 1-1-2.

Thomas Lombard was born Oct. 20, 1761, in Truro, Mass., and baptized there May 8, 1763, son of John and Sarah (Cole) Lombard. He came with his father to Gorham, probably after the Revolutionary War, and married (int. Oct. 15, 1785, in Gorham) Hannah Linnell, born June 23, 1767, in Eastham, Mass., daughter of Elisha and Martha (Higgins) Linnell, but given as a resident of Pearsontown at the time of her marriage. Sometime in the 1790s they moved to Otisfield Gore where he was first taxed in 1801. Thomas and Hannah (Linnell) Lombard were parents of the following children:

i. JOSHUA, born Apr. 1787, married Fanny Morton, daughter of Joseph, on Apr. 2, 1812, and settled in Magalloway, where he died in 1869.
ii. ENOCH, born about 1790, married Abiah, daughter of Joseph Morse.
iii. THOMAS JR., born about 1792, died in 1814, age 22 yrs.
iv. JOHN, born about 1793, married Elizabeth, daughter of Barnabas Sawyer on Nov. 29, 1820, and settled in Magalloway in 1828.
v. HENRY, born about 1795, married Melina Brown and went to Boston.
vi. DANIEL, born about 1796, went to Boston.
vii. ELISHA LINNELL, born Apr. 25, 1797, died Aug. 13, 1872.
viii. DESIRE, born in 1801, married on Mar. 11, 1824, her cousin, Luther Linnell, born Jan. 26, 1803, son of Samuel and Anna (York) Linnell of Standish and lived in Otisfield. She died Dec. 11, 1871, age 70, and he on Jan. 17, 1875. They were the parents of four children.
ix. NATHAN, born Mar. 1806, went to Boston.
x. RANDALL, born in 1808, married in Cape Elizabeth, Maine. Thomas Lombard died in Township No. 5, Oxford County, Maine, (probably Magalloway), on Jan. 1, 1837. His widow, Hannah, died Sept. 3, 1856, place unknown.

Jedediah Lombard, born about 1760 son of Jedediah and Susan (Dorsett) Lombard of Gorham, married July 12, 1785, Lydia Rand, daughter of Jeremiah and Lydia (Blake) Rand of Gorham. He served for several years in the Revolutionary army and again in the War of 1812. He lived in Gorham, but had moved to Standish by 1790. His name appears on the 1795 tax list and on the 1800 census with a family consisting of him and his wife, two boys and two girls under 10 years of age and one boy and one girl between 10 and 16 years old. He evidently lived in Standish Neck on the 100-acre lot #54, the northeast half of which he sold to Philip Cannell Jr. of Standish on Apr. 8, 1801 (35/462). He is given as living in Standish on this date. His wife died in Standish on Jan. 13, 1830, age 61, and he died here on Mar. 16, 1842, age 82. They were the parents of the following children:

i. MARCY, born in Gorham Apr. 27, 1786, married Jeremiah McLucas (int. July 8, 1809), died in 1874.
ii. NATHANIEL, born in Gorham June 24, 1788, married Elizabeth McLucas, who died Apr. 5, 1840, age 54 yrs., and he on Feb. 25, 1851, both on Raymond Cape.
iii. BETSEY, born in Gorham Aug. 13, 1798, married Ebenezer Meserve Dec. 29, 1824. Lived in Standish.
iv. JOHN, born _____, married Sally Welch or Witham. She died Feb. 15, 1880, age 83 yrs., 10 mos., in Raymond.
v. POLLY, married William Knight on Nov. 27, 1822 (int. Oct. 18, 1822) and died in Standish Neck.
vi. SARGENT, born in 1803 probably in Standish, married (int. July 28, 1817) Eunice West, born Mar. 12, 1799, daughter of Joseph and Nancy (Cannell) West of Standish. They lived in Standish near Sebago Lake. He died Nov. 11, 1876, and she in 1885. They were parents of the following children:
   1. SARAH, born May 4, 1829, married first _____ Robinson, second Thomas Bragdon.
   2. ANDREW JACKSON, born June 15, 1831.
   3. EMELINE, born July 30, 1833, married Elisha Whitney.
   4. CHARLES BEANE, born Apr. 15, 1835.
   5. MARY KNIGHT, born Feb. 20, 1839, married Lewis Smith of Windham Nov. 12, 1865.
   6. JOHN WEST, born Dec. 29, 1836.
vii. WILLIAM, born in 1806, married Sally Cole, lived at Richville in Standish and died in 1868.
viii. HEZEKIEL, born _____, married a Mrs. Witham.
ix. ESTHER, born _____, died unmarried.
x. SALLY, born _____, died unmarried.

LOW

James Low was for a short while an inhabitant of Pearsontown around 1760. He was 26 years old and listed as a resident of Pearsontown, originally coming from Scarboro when he enlisted in His Majesty's

Service on Mar. 3, 1760. He served with other Pearsontown men from May to Sept. 1759 in Captain William Gerrish's company of scouts. In Dec. 1761 he bought from Benjamin Stevens one-half of the 100-acre lot #115 in Gorham but is listed as being a laborer in Pearsontown when he sold the same land in Gorham to Wentworth Stuart on May 4, 1765 (3/44).

On Feb. 19, 1762, he married at Gorham Esther Linsket, their intentions being published in Falmouth on Jan. 20, 1762. It is likely that he was the James Low of Falmouth and Cape Elizabeth who served in the Revolutionary War from Mar. 16, 1776, until July 7, 1777, when he was reported killed in battle. An Esther Low with a family of 0-1-2 is listed in the 1790 census of Falmouth Town. On Jan. 20, 1851, Mary Chapman of Starks, Maine, applied for bounty land on basis of service of her father, James Low of Falmouth, who was killed while serving in the Revolutionary War.

It appears likely that there was some relationship between James Low and Patience (Mills) Low, widow of Daniel Low, who as Patience Wooster (widow of James Wooster) of Pearsontown married third on Apr. 1, 1761, Dennis Lary of Gorham.

LOWELL

Two brothers, Moses and Daniel Lowell, were settlers in Pearsontown during the first thirty years of its existence. They were sons of Moses and Frances (Colby) Lowell of Amesbury, Massachusetts.

Moses Lowell Jr. (Moses,^{5} Gideon,^{4} Percival,^{3} Richard,^{2} Percival^1) was born in Amesbury, Mass., Feb. 2, 1736, and married Miriam Knowlton. He was a shipwright and came to Pearsontown to settle about 1763. He was living in town on Mar. 30, 1764, since his name appears on a petition of that date for settlement of the location of roads, all petitioners being residents of the town at that time. On Sept. 24, 1767, Joshua Freeman of Falmouth deeded to him the 30-acre lot #102 in consideration of his compliance with terms of settlement (3/286). He mortaged this lot on which he was then living to his brother Daniel Lowell of Epping, N.H., on the same day (3/823), and on Dec. 12, 1770, he sold it together with his house and barn to Joseph McLellan of Falmouth (5/341). Just when he left Pearsontown has not been determined, but record has been found of his having been a resident of Flintstown (Baldwin) in Apr. 1786, and his name is found in the 1790 census of that town with a family of 2-1-3.

About 1800 Moses Lowell together with his sons Gideon and David and their wives moved to New York State and settled in the town of Grove, Allegheny County, New York. Dates of death of Moses Lowell and his wife have not been discovered. They were parents of the following family:

i. THOMAS, born about 1763, married first in Buxton, Maine, on Nov. 27, 1788, Sarah Ayer, probably daughter of Peter and Rebecca (Wheeler) Ayer of Buxton; second about 1833 at the age of 70 Lucinda Corliss. He lived in Bridgton, Freeport, Freedom and

Dixmont, Maine. He saw lengthy service in the Revolutionary War and received a pension for his services. He died June 10, 1843.
Children of Thomas and Sarah (Ayer) Lowell were as follows:
1. JONATHAN, born in Freedom, Maine, about 1790, married in 1812 Anna E. Gould. He died in 1823. Five children.
2. BENJAMIN, born in Freeport, Maine, Jan. 27, 1799, married June 19, 1822, Eliza H. Ferguson and died in Palmyra, Maine, Jan. 16, 1851. Nine children.
3. PETER, born in Freedom, Maine, Oct. 22, 1801, married first Feb. 8, 1828, in Freedom, Susan Briggs; second Betsey Towle. He died in Monticello, Maine, about 1881.
4. THOMAS.
5. RUFUS, born in Freedom, Maine, married Rachel Ayer, probably daughter of Benjamin and Rachel (Sanborn) Ayer, his cousin. He died in Palmyra, Maine, about 1850. Two children.
6. REUBEN, born about 1797 Freedom, Maine.
7. PHILIP, born about 1807 Freedom, Maine, died young.
8. REBECCA, born in Freedom, Maine, married Elisha Higgins. No issue.

Children of Thomas and Lucinda (Corliss) Lowell were as follows:
9. JOHN C., born May 24, 1841, Freedom, Maine, lived in Patten, Maine, and Oak Park, Sacramento County, Calif.
10. MARIAM KNOWLTON, born in Freedom, Maine, Dec. 28, 1835, married Dec. 11, 1851, Freeman M. Libby. They lived in Charleston, Maine. Thirteen children.
11. LUCINDA, born in Freedom, June 6, 1837, died July 10, 1850.
12. DAVID KNOWLTON, born in Freedom Apr. 23, 1839. One child.

ii. JONATHAN KNOWLTON, born in 1756, died in 1852, married Dec. 11, 1783, Rachel Morton, daughter of Thomas and Rachel (Elwell) Morton of Pearsontown and Gorham. He was living in Flintstown (Baldwin) at the time intentions of marriage were filed. He served in the Revolutionary War and is said to have been in the Battle of Bunker Hill. He lived in Baldwin, Denmark, and Hiram, Maine.
Children of Jonathan K. and Rachel (Morton) Lowell were as follows:
1. EBENEZER, settled in eastern Maine.
2. MOSES, born in 1787, died in Hiram, Maine, in 1847, married Rachel Newcomb, born 1786 daughter of Enos and Thankful (Morton) Newcomb, his cousin. Seven children.
3. ABIGAIL, born about 1786 and died Dec. 1842, age 56 yrs., Standish (Dec. 20, 1842 *Zion Advocate*), married Greenleaf Cram, born Nov. 2, 1781, son of Daniel and Chloe (Stevens) Cram of Standish. Eight children, for list of whom see Cram family.
4. REUBEN, born in Baldwin May 14, 1790, died in Hiram Sept. 17, 1871, married first Mar. 26, 1815, Rhoda Lord of Hiram; married second Feb. 1, 1838, Charlotte Jewell of Cornish. Nine children by first marriage.
5. THOMAS, born ____, died in Corrina, Maine, married Eliza Paine of Standish. Four or more children.

6. JONATHAN K., born ____, died about 1870, married Mary Howard of Hiram. Four children.
7. RACHEL, born ____, married (int. Feb. 2, 1816) William Storer of Hiram. She died Apr. 27, 1860, age 66 yrs., 2 mos.
8. DAVID, born about 1794, married Sept. 21, 1825, Mrs. Louisa (Brown) Merrifield of Hiram. He drowned in Penobscot River about 1847. Five children.
9. MIRIAM, born ____, married 1825 Rev. Aaron Cross of Hiram. Five or more children.
10. ELIZABETH (BETSEY), born about 1803, married about 1832 Charles Wilson who was drowned in Saco River in 1850; second George Dutch of Brownfield.

iii. GIDEON, born Sept. 12, 1761, died in Battle Creek, Mich., Sept. 20, 1845, married in Standish Aug. 31, 1791, Mrs. Elizabeth (Beal) Cookson, widow of John Cookson Jr. of Standish, born Aug. 20, 1764, daughter of Thomas and Elizabeth (Hall) Beal of Newton, Mass. She died in Battle Creek, Mich., May 3, 1852. About 1800 they moved to New York State with his brother and father and in 1832 to Michigan. They were parents of seven children.

iv. DANIEL, born in Standish June 12, 1765, died Dec. 28, 1849, married at Bridgton, Maine, Apr. 10, 1792, Lucy Foster, who died Aug. 23, 1857. They settled at East Denmark, Maine, and resided there until their deaths. Children:
1. DANIEL, born Sept. 1793, died same month.
2. MARY, born Nov. 24, 1794, died Feb. 29, 1884, married May 4, 1815, Theophilus Smith of Cornish.
3. GIDEON, born Sept. 14, 1796, died Oct. 13, 1825, in Denmark, unmarried.
4. ASAHEL F., born Aug. 25, 1798, died Nov. 19, 1869, married Mehitable Dodge, and lived at East Denmark. Five children.
5. JOANNA F., born Oct. 26, 1800, died Jan. 6, 1868, married in 1826 James B. Perkins of Bridgton, Five children.
6. EDMUND P., born Aug. 27, 1804, died June 12, 1881, age 76 yrs., 9 mos., Standish. Married Sept. 26, 1833, Elizabeth J. Ingalls and lived in Denmark.
7. MARGERY W., born Aug. 21, 1808, married William Stone of Bridgton, died Feb. 4, 1891. One child.
8. FRANCIS F., born Oct. 24, 1811, died Nov. 9, 1811.
9. SARAH S., born Feb. 25, 1816, died Aug. 2, 1889, married Dec. 26, 1839, Augustus Wilkins of Waterford, Maine. Five children.
10. DANIEL, born Nov. 9, 1818, died June 15, 1891, age 72 yrs., 7 mos., 6 days, E. Denmark. Married Jan. 23, 1846, Mary A. Smith, daughter of his sister, Mary. He lived in East Denmark, Maine. Four children.

v. JAMES, born Sept. 8, 1771, married Nov. 19, 1795, Mary (Mercy) Sanborn, born May 12, 1777, daughter of Jonathan and Rachel (Fifield) Sanborn of Standish and Baldwin. He died Dec. 18, 1834, and she died Dec. 18, 1855. They lived in Baldwin. Five children.

vi. DAVID, born May 14, 1780, died in Dalton, N.Y., Mar. 21, 1861. Married in Maine Mar. 11, 1802, Abigail Burnell. He moved to New York State with his father and brother Gideon about 1800. Ten children.
vii. MIRIAM, born ____, married Nov. 8, 1793, Daniel Sanborn, born May 29, 1766, son of Jonathan and Rachel (Fifield) Sanborn of Standish and Baldwin. They lived at East Baldwin.
viii. BETSEY, born about 1797, died Jan. 20, 1879, age 81 yrs., Baldwin. Marriage int. Apr. 29, 1821, Thomas Rowe, both of Baldwin.
ix. JANE.
x. EZRA, probably.
xi. LUCY, probably.

Daniel^6 Lowell (Moses,^{5} Gideon,^{4} Percival,^{3} Richard,^{2} Percival^1) was born in Amesbury, Mass., Feb. 20, 1744, and died Mar. 14, 1828, in Bridgton, but lived in Standish. On Aug. 7, 1764, Daniel Lowell of Amesbury, Mass., gave bond in the sum of 50 pounds to move into the township of Pearsontown by the last of October that year, to build a house, clear land, and pay taxes, etc., on the 30-acre lot #118. He evidently did not comply with the terms of this agreement since there is no record of his ever owning this lot, which was sold by Daniel Dole of Falmouth to Caleb Rowe of Pearsontown on Sept. 14, 1779. On Mar. 12, 1773, Robert Buffum Jr. and Joseph Buffum of Salem, Mass., sold Daniel Lowell of Epping, N.H., the 30-acre lot #60 (8/49) and on Oct. 20 of the same year Moses Pearson conveyed to him (still a resident of Epping, N.H.) the 30-acre lot #62. These lots contained much more than 30 acres each, the total acreage being nearer 90 acres. He, however, did not move into town until several years later.

Daniel Lowell served in the French and Indian Wars and was on an expedition to Canada in 1763. On Aug. 29, 1765, he married in Amesbury Mercy Davis of Newbury, who died in Standish Sept. 11, 1817, age 64. He was a cordwainer (cobbler) and as early as Jan. 9, 1767, bought land in Epping, N.H., which he sold in 1773, and bought in Brentwood, N.H., where he was living in 1777. It was not until the following year after the birth of his fifth child that he moved to Pearsontown. He was a man of much energy with a desire to own land. It was once said of him that he wanted to own all that adjoined him. He was somewhat intemperate in his habits and had an impediment in his speech so that he was nicknamed "Uncle Tut." His usual ending of the story (he had a large fund of stories) was "tut, tut, tut and sowrut, sowrut, sowrut." He built his house on the northerly corner of the 30-acre lot #60. His name is found on the 1789, 1790, 1795, 1796 and later lists, in the 1790 census with a family of 4-2-5, and in the 1800 census with a family consisting of him and his wife, two females between 10 and 16, one male between 16 and 25, and two males between 25 and 45. Children of Daniel and Mercy (Davis) Lowell were as follows:
i. SYLVANUS, born in Epping, N.H., Feb. 20, 1767, died in Standish Dec. 6, 1814. He married first (int. Dec. 4, 1790) Betty Fuller of Newton, Mass., second a Mrs. Jones. His name is found on all the tax lists of Standish consulted. He probably was living in the family of his father at the time of the 1790 census. Children as follows, by first wife:

1. CATY, born Mar. 8, 1791, died young.
2. SABINA, born between 1796 and 1800.
By second wife:
3. HANNAH, born Feb. 1800, died in July 12, 1877, age 67 yrs., in Conway, N.H., and formerly of Standish.
4. CHARLES, died in Saco, Maine, in 1860, married Theodate Lang of Saco.
5. NANCY, died in Hiram, Maine, in 1859, married Simeon Mansfield, proprietor of the Mt. Cutler House in Hiram.

ii. NATHANIEL, born in Epping, N.H., May 7, 1769, died July 20, 1858, married first (int. Feb. 23, 1788, in Standish) Dorcas Meserve; second July 29, 1797, Betsey Low, who died Sept. 20, 1846, age about 85, Steep Falls, Standish. No issue.

iii. MARCY (MERCY), born in Epping, N.H., Dec. 10, 1771, died Jan. 30, 1858, married at Fryeburg, Maine, Feb. 17, 1793, William Lamson. For children see Lamson family.

iv. JOHN, born in Brentwood, N.H., July 4, 1774, died at Standish Sept. 28, 1835. Married (int. Aug. 17, 1810, in York) Abigail M. Sewall, born Sept. 18, 1789, in York, died in Standish Apr. 25, 1873. They lived in Standish. Children as follows:
   1. HANNAH SEWALL, born Jan. 24, 1811, died in Gorham July 9, 1891, married Charles Paine of Gorham.
   2. LUCY MOULTON, born Feb. 13, 1812, died July 29, 1829, Standish.
   3. JOHN RANDOLPH, born June 13, 1814, died Apr. 20, 1829, Standish.
   4. WILLARD, born Apr. 18, 1816, died Apr. 12, 1841, unmarried.
   5. FREDERICK, born May 11, 1818, died Nov. 30, 1889, unmarried.
   6. SAMUEL, born Mar. 27, 1820, died Aug. 15, 1820.
   7. WILLIAM HENRY, born Nov. 24, 1821, died San Francisco, Calif., May 19, 1896.
   8. SAMUEL SEWALL, born Oct. 10, 1823, died in Nevada, Colo., Dec. 24, 1850.
   9. LENDALL BOYD, born Aug. 12, 1825, married Abigail Whitney Hunt Sept. 8, 1865. Lived in Westbrook and Standish. He died Aug. 8, 1907, age 81 yrs., 11 mos., 26 days, Standish.
   10. DANIEL DAVIS, born July 28, 1827, went to sea when about 21 yrs. old and is presumed to have died at sea.
   11. LUCY MOULTON, born Nov. 1, 1829, died in Standish Oct. 14, 1888, unmarried.
   12. ABBY MARIA, born Jan. 18, 1836, died Mar. 10, 1894, unmarried.

v. DANIEL, born in Brentwood, N.H., Aug. 5, 1776, died Mar. 30, 1828. Married first on Apr. 18, 1799, Mercy Higgins, born Aug. 6, 1778, daughter of Capt. Joseph and Mercy (Cook) Higgins of Gorham. She died Jan. 15, 1814. He lived in Buxton and following the death of his first wife married July 7, 1841, Experience (Higgins) Higgins, widow of Seth Higgins, born Sept. 20, 1777, daughter of Timothy and Reliance (Yates) Higgins of Standish. She died Sept. 8, 1865. He later settled in Bridgton and lived there until his death. Children of Daniel Lowell were as follows:

By first wife:
1. JOHN, born about 1800, died Aug. 17, 1830, age 30, in Bridgton.
2. JOANNA, born _____, married Silas Berry of Buxton.
3. SARAH, born _____, married Daniel Kimball of Buxton.
By second wife:
4. MERCY, born _____, bapt. July 14, 1816, married Joshua Paine of Standish.
5. ELIZA ANN, born in Sept. 1818, bapt. Sept. 6, 1818, married Joseph Paine of Standish.

vi. MARY (POLLY), born in Pearsontown Apr. 23, 1779, bapt.there Nov. 27, 1779. Married Apr. 23, 1797, Samuel Dennett, bapt. in Saco Dec. 16, 1770, son of Nicholas and Phebe Dennett of that town. They lived in Standish where he died Feb. 22, 1844, age 74 yrs., 2 mos., and she on Mar. 15, 1872, age 92 yrs., 11 mos., in Standish. For children see Dennett family.

vii. STEPHEN, born in Pearsontown Sept. 27, 1781, bapt. Oct. 16, 1785, married Oct. 19, 1809, Wealthy Sawyer, born in 1788 daughter of Joel and Eizabeth (Stone) Sawyer of Gorham. They lived in Standish until 1829 when they moved to Gorham where they afterwards lived and died, were parents of six children, as follows:
1. WILLIAM L., born Nov. 17, 1810, married Catherine Ramsey and moved to Mass.
2. AMOS, born Feb. 9, 1814, married Caroline Cutts about 1834. He was a sail maker and lived in Mass. Three children.
3. MARY, born May 2, 1816, died Apr. 7, 1879, married first _____ Anderson of Windham, Maine; second Henry Broad; third Stephen Brown of Limington.
4. ELIZABETH, born May 14, 1819, married Dec. 1, 1846, Arthur M. Benson, born Sept. 21, 1821, son of James and Abigail (Dow) Benson of Limington and Gorham. Three children.
5. GEORGE W., born Jan. 29, 1822, died Apr. 10, 1897. Married first Aug. 5, 1843, Lucy J. Landers of Buckfield, Maine; second Apr. 27, 1851, Sarah J. Lowell, daughter of Reuben and Rhoda (Lord) Lowell of Hiram.
6. FRANCIS, born Sept. 12, 1826, went whaling and was lost at sea.

viii. SARAH, born in Pearsontown Dec. 10, 1783, bapt. Oct. 16, 1785, married Sept. 11, 1803, Nicholas Dennett Jr., born in Saco, Maine, July 22, 1776, son of Nicholas and Phebe Dennett and brother to the husband of her sister Mary. They had one child who died in infancy. She died June 17, 1805, age 22.

ix. LUCY, born in Standish Aug. 18, 1786, married Jan. 7, 1816, Moody Foster of South Bridgton, Maine. She died Sept. 10, 1850. Five children.

x. ANDREW, son of Daniel Lowell, bapt. Oct. 16, 1785.

Jonathan Lowell settled in Pearsontown during the Revolutionary War. He was perhaps the Jonathan Lowell born about 1749 in Ipswich, Mass., son of Jonathan[5] (Gideon,[4] Percival,[3] Richard,[2] Percival[1]) Lowell and hence a cousin of Moses and Daniel Lowell, the other settlers by that name in Pearsontown. On Oct. 3, 1777, Jonathan Lowell of

Pearsontown bought from Joshua Noyes of Falmouth the 100-acre lot #81 in second division of lots in Pearsontown (10/68) and from Josiah Noyes of Falmouth the adjoining 100-acre lot #80 (10/70). He, still being of Pearsontown, sold these same two lots to Zacheus Higgins, William Higgins, and Theodoreus Hopkins, all of Eastham, Mass., on May 15, 1779 (10/378). He finally settled on Oak Hill where he carried on farming. His name is found on the 1789, 1790, 1795, 1796, and later tax lists of Standish, in the 1790 census with a family of 2-3-3, and in the 1800 census with a family consisting of him and his wife, both over 45 years of age, two males and two females under 10, two males between 10 and 16, and one male between 16 and 25.

Jonathan Lowell married (int. July 18, 1774, in Gorham) Mary (Molly) Pierce, born in Hampton, N.H., daughter of John and Elizabeth (Johnson) Pierce of that town and Pearsontown. He died Jan. 21, 1816, age 67 years, in Standish (*Eastern Argus*, Feb. 13, 1816). Children of Jonathan and Mary (Pierce) Lowell were as follows:

i. MARTHA, born in Pearsontown May 24, 1780, bapt. there June 11, 1780, married Samuel Higgins of North Yarmouth, Maine. No issue.

ii. ELIZABETH (BETSEY) born Sept. 29, 1781, bapt. May 14, 1784, married Oct. 12, 1805 (int. in Falmouth, Maine, Sept. 8, 1805) William or Samuel James. Two children.

iii. SAMUEL, born Feb. 9, 1784, bapt. May 14, 1784, moved "down east" sometime after 1808.

iv. GEORGE, born Sept. 19, 1785, bapt. Oct. 9, 1791, died in Standish Oct. 1824, age 38 yrs. (*Eastern Argus*, Nov. 9, 1824).

v. JONATHAN JR., born Sept. 17, 1787, bapt. Oct. 9, 1791, married in 1816 Dorcas Decker born about 1792 daughter of John and Catherine (Hall) Decker of Standish. He drowned in Sebago Lake on Nov. 2, 1826. By newspaper account the accident happened about 4 o'clock when a small boat that he was in capsized near a camping place about one-half mile from shore. He was ejected and drowned but Samuel Weeks, who was in the boat at the time, was saved. Jonathan's widow married second Oliver Hall, born Jan. 31, 1792, son of John and Naoma (York) Hall of Standish and had two children by that marriage. She died May 28, 1854, and her second husband in 1855 or 1856. Children of Jonathan and Dorcas (Decker) Lowell were as follows:

1. MARTHA, born Dec. 2, 1818, married Nov. 26, 1835, Moses Decker, born 1809, died 1882. They lived at Sebago Lake Village in Standish and were the parents of ten children.
2. IRA TOWLE, born in 1821, died 1827.
3. LORENZO DOW, born June 8, 1823, married Jan. 9, 1847, Hannah E. Ward of Sebago. He died May 29, 1904, age 80 yrs., 11 mos., 21 days, Standish. They lived in Standish and were the parents of seven children.
4. MARY, born Oct. 19, 1825, died unmarried.

vi. JOHN PIERCE, bapt. in Standish Apr. 26, 1793. He married (int. in Falmouth, Maine, Oct. 29, 1815) Mrs. Eda (Chase) Lunt of Wiscasset and Portland, Maine. He lived and died in Portland.

vii. MARY (POLLY), bapt. July 16, 1799, married _____ Jordan of Casco.

viii. RICHARD, born Jan. 25, 1797, bapt. July 16, 1799, died in Burlington, Maine, about 1888. He married in 1859 Mrs. Hannah (York) Varney of Burlington. He settled in Thorndike, Maine, but afterwards lived in Chester, Lowell, and Burlington, Maine.
ix. SARAH (SALLY), also mentioned by some as Mehitable, born Nov. 27, 1800, bapt. as a "child of Widow Mollie" Dec. 5, 1816. On Feb. 25, 1819, she married William McCorrison, probably born Nov. 13, 1792, son of Lemuel and Mehitable (Richardson) McCorrison. They lived in Burlington, Maine, where she died May 27, 1864.
x. JOSEPH, bapt. as a "child of Widow Mollie" Dec. 5, 1816, married Cordelia Llewellyn of North Yarmouth and settled in Thorndike, Maine.
xi. OLIVER, bapt. as a child of Widow Mollie Lowell on Dec. 5, 1816.

McDONALD

The name of Samuel Melcher McDonald is found on the 1795 & 1796 tax lists of Standish and in the 1800 census with a family consisting of him and his wife and a son and daughter, each under 10 years of age. He was born Jan. 28, 1771, son of Robert and Mary (Kendrick) McDonald of Gorham and is given as a resident of Standish when on Dec. 25, 1794, he married Anna Whitten of Gorham. He lived at Bonney Eagle where he and his brother Robert ran a sawmill located at a site on the Saco River there. Robert McDonald, born May 3, 1775, was drowned by falling from a stringer while attempting to cross the river with a heavey chain laid over his shoulders.

Samuel McDonald was living in Fryeburg on July 3, 1809, according to deed for land sold in Bridgton on that date (57/218). He moved to a wild tract of land in Chatham, N.H., where he engaged in his trade of millwright and while employed in Milan, N.H., near the Umbagog Lakes is said to have been stricken by a fatal illness. His body was interred in the forest until the following spring, when it was exhumed and moved for burial on the homestead. Samuel and Anna (Whitten) McDonald were parents of the following children, all of whom are said to have been born in Standish:
i. MARY, married about 1823, John Bryant of Chatham, N.H.
ii. FREDERICK S., born 1795, married Lucinda Usher, lived in Chatham, N.H. He died Aug. 2, 1846, age 51 yrs., 10 days.
iii. BETSEY, born about 1799, married (int. Apr. 8, 1822, in Fryeburg) James Osgood of Fryeburg. She died June 26, 1862, age 63 yrs., 3 mos., in Hiram, and was buried there.
iv. NOAH, born Apr. 1800, married Sept. 18, 1824, in Chatham, N.H., Abigail Durgin of Hiram. She died Apr. 21, 1861, age 59 yrs., 9 mos., in Porter. He died July 2, 1849, age 49 yrs., 3 mos., in Porter.
v. JOHN, born Nov. 1802, married Mar. 26, 1825, Patience Gray of Hiram. He died Sept. 29, 1882, age 79 yrs., 10 mos., Hiram.
vi. MARIA, died unmarried.

vii. ABNER, born July 6, 1808, married in Porter Nov. 2, 1828, Naomi Durgin, born in Hiram June 18, 1809. He died Sept. 29, 1898, in Porter, and she died Feb. 18, 1875, age 64 yrs., in Porter.

The name of Peletiah McDonald is found on the 1808 tax list of Standish and in the 1800 census of Gorham with a family consisting of him and his wife, one male and three females under 10, one male and two females between 10 and 16, and one male between 16 and 26. He was born May 2, 1754, according to gravestone and according to pension records in York, Maine, son of John and Susanna (Lombard?) McDonald and was an uncle to Samuel McDonald above. He served in the Revolutionary army from Gorham and is said to have married during his service a Virginia lady by the name of Elizabeth Pollard. Following her death he married on Aug. 6, 1787, Dorcas Stuart, born June 8, 1766, daughter of Wentworth and Susanna (Lombard) Stuart of Gorham. He was living in Gorham at the time of the 1790 census with a family of 1-3-2. Upon moving to Standish he settled at Bonney Eagle where he died in his sleep Aug. 31, 1841, his wife, Dorcas, surviving him until Mar. 3, 1847. Both are buried in Maplewood Cemetery in Standish. Children of Peletiah McDonald were as follows:

i. WILLIAM, born at Fort Putnam, N.Y., Apr. 3, 1779.
ii. ELINOR, born at Gorham June 14, 1785, married on Apr. 4, 1807, Benoni Wood of Standish. See Wood family.
iii. A DAUGHTER, who married _____ Dow and lived in Saco, Maine.

By second wife:

iv. RANDOLPH, died at sea about 1805.
v. EDMUND.
vi. CATHERINE, married Robert Nason of Hollis and died Sept. 16, 1875, age 81 yrs., 10 mos.
vii. GEORGE, born about 1790, married Betsey Palmer and lived at Bonney Eagle in Standish. He was living in 1851, age 61, in Bonney Eagle.
viii. JOANNA, born about 1797, married Dec. 26, 1826, William R. Sturgis of Gorham and Standish and died Jan. 24, 1878, age 80 yrs.
ix. MARTHA, married Sept. 10, 1809 (int. Aug. 10, 1809) Edward Rogers of Standish.
x. MARY STUART, born about 1800, died June 23, 1836, age 36 yrs.
xi. FRANCIS, born June 5, 1801.
xii. STUART, born May 28, 1803.
xiii. JOHN, born June 5, 1806.
xiv. ABNER, born Aug. 8, 1808, married (int. Feb. 1835) Eunice Shaw, born in 1800 daughter of Joseph and Eunice (Bean) Shaw of Standish. After her death he married Nov. 17, 1853, Esther McDonald, born Mar. 10, 1814, daughter of Joseph and Dolly (Shaw) McDonald and niece of his first wife. He died Dec. 19, 1887 age 79 yrs., 4 mos., 13 days.
xv. MAJOR.

McGILL

Arthur McGill was living in Pearsontown prior to 1760. He was living in the vicinity as early as 1749 when he served in the company of scouts led by Capt. Daniel Hill of Newbury which was doing guard duty along the frontier. Soon after, he must have settled in Gorham for he was living on 30-acre lot in that town on Aug. 21, 1754, when Governor William Shirley of Massachusetts deeded it to him for fulfillment of the conditions of settlement (York deeds 32/47). This same lot sold on Oct. 22, 1754, to Benjamin Stevens of Gorham, the deed being signed by marks by him and his wife, Mary (York deeds 30/251). It seems likely that he may have taken up residence in Pearsontown about this time and that his was one of the sixteen families living in the fort in 1757 because he was the grantee of the 5-acre lot #6, one of those given to men who remained in town during the last of the French and Indian Wars. His name is also found in a list of Pearsontown men who worked on Gorham roads in October of 1760. This 5-acre lot was taken from him in settlement of a judgment obtained against him by Ebenezer Mayo of Falmouth on Nov. 4, 1766 (Cumberland deeds 4/499). On Aug. 19, 1767, Moses Pearson deeded to him for fulfillment of the conditions of settlement the 30-acre lot No. 101 in Pearsontown (6/212). This lot he sold on Apr. 16, 1771, to Joseph McLellan of Falmouth (5/374). No later record of him has been found so it is not known whether or not he left town or died soon after this transaction.

Nothing has been discovered as to the parentage of Arthur McGill, but his name would indicate that he may have been a Scotch-Irish immigrant. The maiden name of his wife is not known but that her given name was Mary is evidenced by her signature by mark on deeds. No record of children of this couple has been found, but it is likely that some or perhaps all of the following were their offspring:

i. JOHN, born Sept. 6, 1744, living in town as early as 1761 when he was one of the Pearsontown men who worked on Gorham roads during that year. He was a hunter and is said to have lived in the Pearsontown Fort until it was torn down about the time the meeting house was erected around 1766. His name is found on a list of those living in town prior to the burning of Falmouth by Mowatt in October 1775. His name is also found on 1788, 1789, 1790, 1795, 1796, and 1799 tax lists of the town and in the 1800 census with a family consisting of him and his wife, both over 45 yrs. of age, three males under 10 yrs. old, two males between 10 and 16 yrs. of age, two females under 10 yrs. old, and one female between 26 and 45 yrs. of age. In 1810 his family consisted of him and his wife, both over 45, one male from 10 to 16 yrs. old and one female from 16 to 26 yrs. of age.

About 1771 or before, he married Rebecca York, born Feb. 20, 1754, daughter of John and Sarah (Strout) York of Pearsontown. On Oct. 30, 1795, John McGill, yeoman of Standish, sold Thomas Cram of Standish the 30-acre lot #137 in that town, it being the farm on which he (McGill) then lived (49/408). This deed was signed by John and his wife, Rebecca. On Mar. 16, 1796, he bought from David Richardson Jr. of Limington the 100-acre lot #88 in second division in Standish and established his home upon it (69/104). On Jan. 7, 1814, with him and his wife, Rebecca, signing the deed, he sold six acres of this lot to Asa Mayo of Standish (71/207). When William McGill as administrator of the estate of his father, John McGill, sold on Mar. 29, 1816, ninety-four acres of this lot to Nathaniel Davis of Standish, it was described as having been the homestead farm of John McGill (79/242).

John McGill died sometime during the year 1814 because, while he signed on Jan. 7 the deed referred to above, Rebecca McGill, widow, is listed in a Cumberland County tax list of the town for 1814. Date of death of his wife, Rebecca, has not been found, but it is clear that she survived him. John and Rebecca (York) McGill were parents of the following children:

1. **WILLIAM**, born Jan. 27, 1772, married Nov. 29, 1797, Mercy Jones, bapt. Feb. 19, 1769, daughter of John and Mary (Savage) Jones of Scarboro. She was a sister to Mehitable Jones who married Uncle Ebenezer York, to Sarah or Sally Jones who married his Uncle Job York, and to Hannah Jones who married Israel Thorne Jr., the half-brother of his mother and uncles. He is said to have been one of the tallest men in Standish. A great hunter like his father, he is reported to have shot the last wolf killed in the town. They lived on a farm near Pudding Hill in Standish, where he died on Sept. 14, 1841, age 69 yrs., 8 mos. His wife died on Feb. 18, 1850, age 81 yrs. Both are buried in the small cemetery located on the Dow Road near Dow's Corner. It is interesting to note that on Apr. 8, 1796, the intentions of marriage of William McGill of Standish and Anna McGill of North Yarmouth were filed in the latter town, while on the next day, Apr. 9, 1796, they were filed in Standish. There is no record of their marriage, which probably did not take place, since in 1797 he married Mercy Jones and on May 24, 1798, Anna McGill married Nehemiah Shaw according to the records of the Second Church of North Yarmouth. This Anna McGill may have been his first cousin and a daughter of William McGill of Falmouth and Brunswick, Maine. A descendant of John York through his son Ebenezer, Jotham B. Roberts of Dayton, Maine, in an account of the York family written in 1885, states that William and Mercy (Jones) McGill had no children. That this is true seems evident because in the 1800 and 1810 censuses they are listed as having no one in their family but themselves. William McGill died intestate and his heirs included his living brothers and sisters and the children of of those who died.
2. **MARY**, born Feb. 28, 1774, married Jan. 24, 1798, Samuel Gossum of Bethel, Maine. They lived on Swan's Hill in that town. Following his death she married second Edward Goad of Bethel. Children by first marriage were as follows: (Gossum)
    (1) BETSEY, born Dec. 19, 1798, married Joshua Philips.
    (2) REBECCA, born June 9, 1801, married Vier Bean.
    (3) MARBIE, born Feb. 6, 1803, married Nathan Hall.

  (4) JOHN DEAN, born May 6, 1803, married Rachel Shaw of Oxford.
  (5) IRA, born May 6, 1806.
  (6) HANNAN, born Mar. 15, 1808, died Nov. 27, 1814.
  (7) ELIJAH, born May 30, 1809.
  (8) SALLY, born Nov. 2, 1811.
  (9) JOSHUA, born Mar. 8, 1815.
  (10) ELIAS, born Feb. 15, 1820.
3. ANNA (ANNE), born Apr. 17, 1776, married Mar. 21, 1797, Jonathan Bean 3rd, born about 1775 in Pearsontown son of Jonathan Jr. and Abigail (York) Bean of Pearsontown and Bethel. They were first cousins. He was killed by an Indian in the Shadagee fight during the War of 1812, leaving his widow and three children.
4. REBECCA, born July 30, 1779.
5. HANNAH, born Feb. 2, 1782, married about 1799 in Pearsontown, John, brother of Jonathan Bean 3rd, who married her sister Anne. They were also first cousins. They lived in the lower part of Bethel and were the parents of thirteen children.
6. BENJAMIN, born Mar. 22, 1784, was living in Bath, Maine, in 1844 when he sold to Moses Sanborn, administrator of the estate of William McGill, all his interest in that estate (186/214).
7. JOHN, born Feb. 19, 1787, was of Buxton, Maine, when he married on Nov. 22, 1810, Thankful Paine, born Sept. 21, 1792, daughter of Josiah and Elizabeth (Ayer) Paine of Buxton. They became the parents of a daughter Margaret McGill born June 5, 1812, who was of Windham when she married (int. Apr. 27, 1833) William Haskell, son of Daniel and Mary (Bolton) Haskell of Gorham, who died without issue on Feb. 7, 1840. Sometime around 1830 John McGill died and his widow, Thankful (Paine) McGill, married second (int. Mar. 27, 1831) Simeon Bradbury of Buxton as his third wife. They had a son Josiah Paine Bradbury born Apr. 27, 1833.
8. JOSHUA, born May 14, 1791.
9. SARAH, born May 22, 1793, married Dec. 4, 1817, Thomas West of Baldwin and Standish. He was born Oct. 16, 1794, son of Joseph and Nancy (Cannell) West. For list of children see West family.
10. JOSEPH, born Apr. 14, 1796, married his first cousin Rebecca York, born Mar. 6, 1795, daughter of Job and Sally (Jones) York of Standish and Bethel. They were the parents of a son Sewall Emery McGill who was born on Feb. 6, 1819. Rebecca (York) McGill was struck and killed by lightning on July 11, 1819, in Bethel.

ii. WILLIAM, born about 1747, was probably the one who served in the Revolutionary War from Brunswick and may have been a son of Arthur McGill of Pearsontown. He probably was the William McGill who with a family of 1-1-3 was living in Falmouth at the time of the 1790 census and the one by that name who in 1800 was living in Brunswick with a wife, one male child under 10 yrs. old, and two females, one under 10 and the other between 10 and 16 yrs.

of age. He died Sept. 19, 1828, age 81 yrs. His wife, Martha, died Jan. 4, 1842, at the age of 85 yrs. They with their son Peter are buried in the Growstown Cemetery in Brunswick. Children of this couple were possibly as follows:
1. DORCAS, bapt. May 31, 1792, in Cumberland Church and in 1816 in Growstown Church.
2. HANNAH, bapt. in 1816 in Growstown Church.
3. PETER, bapt. Aug. 8, 1792, in Cumberland Church (Second Church of North Yarmouth), died Nov. 21, 1833, age 40 yrs.
4. ANNE, perhaps was of North Yarmouth when her intentions of marriage to William McGill of Standish were published on Apr. 8, 1796. She married Nehemiah Shaw on May 24, 1798.

iii. MARY, whose intentions of marriage to Brice McLellan of Falmouth are found in the Gorham records under date of June 5, 1773. It is possible, however, that this may have been the widow of Arthur McGill, who may have died before that date.

iv. ANNA, whose marriage to Joshua Bigford on Sept. 25, 1784, is found in the Falmouth records. A Joshua Bigford with family of 1-0-1 was living in Cape Elizabeth in 1790. The name of Joshua Bigford is also found on a county tax tist of Standish in 1814.

MARCH

The name of Samuel March is found on the 1795 tax list and 1796 tax of Standish; on a 1799 valuation list; in the 1800 census with family consisting of two males up to 10 years of age, one male male between 10 and 16 years old, and one female between 26 and 45 years old; in the 1810 census with a family consisting of three males up to 16 years of age, one male 10 to 16 years old, one male over 45 years of age, two females up to 10 years, and one female between 26 and 45 years of age. In addition, a Benjamin March is found on an 1814 tax list of the town but no Samuel appears. In a letter written by him to a descendant he wrote as follows:

> My mother died after birthing a child. Afterwards my father married a second time, and she raised us. Your sister is named after her. I had three brothers and three sisters. My younger brother Benjamin, who was married to our cousin, was the only one who stayed back at our old home.

Samuel March was born in Scarboro May 20, 1763, son of Col. Samuel and Anna (Libby) March. He had a twin brother, Benjamin, who died young. As a young boy he served in the Revolutionary War when only 16 years old. On Dec. 13, 1788, he married Lydia Chapman, daughter of Edward and Eleanor (Small) Chapman of Stroudwater. He may have been the Samuel March living in Falmouth at the time of the 1790 census with a family of 2-0-2. He lived in Gorham and sometime after 1790 and before 1795 moved to Standish. Just when he left Standish is not known but it must have been sometime after 1810 and before 1814 making his sojourn in Standish about twenty years up to that point. Pension record gives that he died in Nov. 1848 in Standish.

Samuel and Lydia (Chapman) March were the parents of several children; the names of six are known. These are as follows:

  i. JAMES, born Oct. 25, 1789, in Gorham, went west about 1818 and settled first at Mercer Co., Pa., where on May 25, 1818, he married Susan Potter, born July 31, 1799, at Canaan Township, Columbia Co., N.Y., daughter of Christopher and Phoebe (Elmore) Potter. They continued to live in Pennsylvania until 1834 when they moved to Jefferson, Ashtabula County, Ohio, where he died Sept. 26, 1859, and she on Mar. 7, 1885. They were the parents of ten children, the first eight of whom were born in Delaware Township, Mercer Co., Pa., and the other two in Jefferson, Ashtabula County, Ohio. Children were as follows:
1. DANIEL, born Nov. 13, 1819.
2. SALLY, born Apr. 1, 1822.
3. JOHN, born Apr. 21, 1824, married Nov. 22, 1847, Nancy Wigent.
4. CHRISTOPHER, born Nov. 21, 1827.
5. MARY ANN, born Nov. 1828, married Truman Shaw.
6. PHOEBE, born Oct. 24, 1829.
7. POLLY ANN, born Jan. 1832.
8. SUSAN JANE, born Feb. 15, 1835.
9. ELIZABETH MARCH, born June 23, 1838.
10. JAMES ELMORE, , born July 22, 1839.

  ii. BENJAMIN, born Nov. 18, 1791, in Gorham, married Nov. 30, 1815 (int. Sept. 25, 1815), his cousin, Jane Small, born Oct. 23, 1793, in Limington, daughter of William and Mary (March) Small of Limington. He was on the 1814 tax list of Standish and later lived at Windham. His wife died Dec. 29, 1887. They were the parents of the following children:
1. MARIA, born Nov. 11, 1816.
2. WILLIAM, born Apr. 19, 1819.
3. ALVIN, born Feb. 3, 1820.
4. LUCY JANE, born Apr. 26, 1826, died Oct. 12, 1841, Windham.
5. EDWARD CHAPMAN, born Feb. 6, 1829.
6. SUMNER CHARLES, born Mar. 18, 1831.

  iii. LYDIA, married John E. Merrill.

  iv. MOSES.

  v. SALLY, born about 1788, married Aug. 16, 1812, Joshua Hutchinson Jr., both of Buxton. She died Apr. 25, 1876, age 88, in Buxton. He died July 3, 1858, age 72 yrs., in Buxton.

  vi. SALOME, married (int. Feb. 20, 1825, in Westbrook) William Lowell. She removed to Brookville, Pa., after the death of her husband and was living there in 1855 (pension record of James March found in Zebulon K. Harmon papers at Maine Historical Society).

MAREAN

The name of John Marean is found on the 1788, 1789, 1790, 1795, 1796, and 1799 tax lists of Standish, in the 1790 census with a family of 2-3-1, and in the 1800 census with a family consisting of him and his wife, both over 45 years of age; one male and one female between 10 and 16, and one male between 16 and 26 years of age. His ancestry has not been determined, but since there were Marean families in Newton, Roxbury, and Eastham, Mass., it seems likely that he descended from one of them. He was a blacksmith and moved to Pearsontown about 1780 from Cape Elizabeth because he was a resident of the town prior to Nov. 10, 1781, when his intention of marriage was filed in Gorham to Lois Bean, born before 1755 daughter of Jonathan and Abigail (Gordan) Bean of Chester, N.H., and Pearsontown. They lived on the 30-acre lot #7 located on the Northwest (Oak Hill) Road where his father-in-law, Jonathan Bean, had resided before moving to Bethel, Maine. He died Feb. 17, 1804, age 45, in Standish. The details of his death were given in the Mar. 16, 1804, issue of the *Eastern Argus*, as follows: "John Marean came home drunk on a cold night and being cross, his wife shut him out of doors. He lay in the snow and became chilled, and death soon followed." His widow passed away in July 1843. They were parents of the following family:

i. AARON, born Sept. 16, 1782, married in 1815 Abigail Crocker of Bethel. He was blacksmith and in 1844 bought an acre of land in Rumford, Maine. He died Feb. 25, 1836, age 53 yrs., and his widow on Feb. 3, 1875, age 86 yrs. They had sons Moses, Aaron, and Paul C., who died Feb. 11, 1838, age 3 yrs., 5 mos., and was buried with his parents in the Village Cemetery at Standish Corner.

ii. ENOCH, born Jan. 29, 1785, married Apr. 14, 1808, Mary Shaw, born Sept. 15, 1785, daughter of Joseph and Eunice (Bean) Shaw, and thence his cousin, of Standish. He died on May 15, 1843, in Standish, and she in 1855. Children were as follows:
1. JOHN, known as John Jr., born Dec. 4, 1808, married first (int. Aug. 15, 1835) Paulina Davis, born 1814 daughter of Elisha and Susan (Larrabee) Davis of Limington. She died May 3, 1843, age 29, and was buried in the Village Cemetery at Standish Corner; he married second in 1848 Lucinda Emerson of Chatham, N.H., who was born in Chatham and died Dec. 1, 1880, age 68 yrs., 5 mos., in Standish. John Jr. was the father of at least the following children:
    (1) JOSIAH, born May 13, 1836, died in 1890, married Joanna F. Elwell, born Aug. 24, 1844, in Gorham, daughter of George and Nancy (Smith) Elwell. She married second Winthrop Dresser. Josiah and his wife are buried in the Dow's Corner Cemetery on Route 35 A.
    (2) LUCY ANN, born July 15, 1838, died June 14, 1865, age 26 yrs., 11 mos., and was buried in the Village Cemetery at Standish Corner.

      (3)   ARALINDA, born May 11, 1841, married (int. Oct. 20, 1865) Greenville Monroe Foss, both of Standish. She died Dec. 24, 1875, in Standish and he married second Lena Gove Marean, half-sister of his first wife.
      (4)   ENOCH PREBLE, born May 3, 1849, married May 5, 1877, Mary Eliza Libby, born Sept. 18, 1849, and died Sept. 4, 1922. He died Apr. 12, 1924, in Standish.
      (5)   DANIEL E., born Mar. 16, 1851, died Dec. 30, 1920, age 68 yrs., 3 mos., 16 days, Standish. He married Annie Elwell and married second Jan. 20, 1894, in Gorham, Cora Hanson of Buxton.
      (6)   PAULINE G. (or LENA GOVE), born about 1853, married Greenville Monroe Foss and died Dec. 8, 1883, age 30 yrs., 8 mos., 27 days, in Standish. He was born Aug. 1, 1841, son of Job and Lucinda (Meeds) Foss of Standish.
  2. ESTHER, born Jan. 6, 1812.

iii. JOHN, born Dec. 17, 1787, married Aug. 20, 1815, Anna Shaw, born July 8, 1792, daughter of Ebenezer and Sarah (Wood) Shaw of Standish. They lived in Standish where he died June 6, 1853, and she on June 6, 1860. She was buried in the Village Cemetery at Standish Corner. They were the parents of the following children:
1. AARON, born Jan. 15, 1816, died in infancy.
2. ABIGAIL, born Jan. 15, 1816, so Aaron's twin sister, married June 3, 1838, Chesley Higgins, born July 4, 1816, son of Prince and Selina (Higgins) Higgins of Standish. She died Oct. 4, 1855.
3. DOLLY, born Jan. 19, 1818, married on Mar. 31, 1842, Moses K. Marean, probably her cousin son of Aaron and Abigail (Crocker) Marean, and died in 1889.
4. LOIS, born Mar. 17, 1820, married July 23, 1855, William Metcalf of Gorham, she of Standish. She died Oct. 12, 1898.
5. CHARLES, born July 4, 1822, married (int. June 15, 1847) Louisa Marean of Standish. He died Apr. 1, 1898, and his wife died Oct. 12, 1898, also in Standish.
6. EUNICE, born Jan. 5, 1824, married on Oct. 25, 1848, William D. Mayo, born in 1826. They lived in Standish where she died on Mar. 13, 1896, and he on Nov. 5, 1903.
7. MARY, born about 1827 (age 23 in 1850), married on Aug. 31, 1851, Jeremiah Johnson of Lisbon, Maine.
8. WILLIAM, born Dec. 31, 1831, married (int. Feb. 24, 1855) Elizabeth Thorn, both of Standish. She was born July 7, 1834, daughter of Marrett and Elizabeth (Strout) Thorn. He died Dec. 25, 1911, and she on Dec. 29, 1918, in Standish.
9. ELIZA G., born Dec. 17, 1831, a twin, married Albert G. Thorn, born Jan. 14, 1828, son of Marrett and Elizabeth (Strout) Thorn. She died Aug. 3, 1896, age 64 yrs., 8 mos., in Standish.
10. ELLEN AUGUSTA, born Apr. 29, 1834, married (int. Sept. 28, 1856) Charles W. Guptill, both of Standish.

iv. JOSIAH, born July 15, 1791, was probably the Joshua H. Marean who married Mary B. Higgins on Aug. 7, 1817. In 1826 Joshua H. was of Westbrook, some years afterward moved to Cape

Elizabeth, where he died Aug. 23, 1861, age 68 yrs., 6 mos. (*Christian Mirror*, Oct. 29, 1861). His wife, Mary B., died Apr. 10, 1885, age 88 yrs., in Portland, she of Cape Elizabeth.

v. ELIZA, born Mar. 31, 1794, married May 31, 1812, Joseph Green, born Aug. 24, 1786, son of John and Mary (Stuart) Green of Standish. They lived in Standish where he died in Oct. 1836.

vi. AMOS, born July 13, 1797, married (int. Feb. 28, 1823) Elizabeth Knight of Standish, born June 27, 1799, daughter of Nathaniel and Susanna (Roberts) Knight. He died Mar. 7, 1858, and she May 3, 1864, both buried in Hasty Cemetery, Raymond. They were the parents of the following children:
1. AARON, born July 23, 1823, married Dec. 6, 1848, Mary Ann Thorn, born Jan. 28, 1826, daughter of Marrett Thorn.
2. LOUISE A., born Feb. 17, 1825, married June 15, 1847, Charles Marean and died Oct. 12, 1898, age 73 yrs., 7 mos., 26 days, in Standish.
3. WILLIAM, born Jan. 7, 1827 (int. May 19, 1864) married Elizabeth Mains, both of Standish. He died Mar. 2, 1906, age 79 yrs., 1 mo., in Casco and she on Sept. 7, 1900, age 61 yrs., 4 mos., 1 day, in Raymond.
4. CATHERINE, born Feb. 10, 1829.
5. STEPHEN R., born July 22, 1832, married Eliza C. Fickett, daughter of Daniel and Anna (Barton) Fickett. He died Feb. 25, 1902, age 69 yrs., 6 mos., in Casco.
6. ADELINE S., born Apr. 25, 1834.
7. NATHAN W., born July 30, 1837, died Feb. 10, 1864.

vii. GEORGE WASHINGTON, born Dec. 7, 1800, married May 12, 1839, Mary Davis, born Mar. 18, 1815, daughter of Noah and Sarah (Larrabee) Davis of Standish. He died in 1885 and she in 1888 and were buried in the Village Cemetery at Standish Corner. They lived in Scarboro in 1850.

viii. WILLIAM, born Jan. 2, 1804, married (int. Oct. 14, 1832) Charity Davis, daughter of Elisha and Susan (Larrabee) Davis of Limington. She died May 1, 1848, age 38 yrs., in Standish, and he married second on Feb. 3, 1851, Mrs. Louisa B. Warren, both of Standish (she age 62 in 1870). He died Aug. 18, 1879. Children were:
1. FRANCIS, born 1833 in Standish, died July 30, 1906, in Westbrook.
2. ELVIRA, born about 1835 (age 15 in 1850), married June 8, 1856, Ivory Page Higgins of Buxton, born Nov. 29, 1833, son of Knowles and Eliza (Page) Higgins.
3. LAURA E., born about 1837, married Aug. 25, 1860, Oren F. Carpenter of Hollis, she of Standish.
4. ALMON H., born July 23, 1840, married July 4, 1864, Gene A. Dolloff, both of Standish. She was born in 1845 and died in 1927. They are buried in the Oak Hill Cemetery in Standish.
5. ABBY E., born about 1842 and in 1860 was age 18 yrs. old.
6. EMERY, born about 1846, died Feb. 18, 1898, age 51 yrs., 11 mos., 20 days, Standish. Married Margaret Sawyer.
7. EDWIN, born about 1848 (age 2 in 1850).
8. CLARENCE, born about 1850 (age 20 in 1870).

MARRETT

The Rev. Daniel[6] Marrett (Amos,[5] Amos,[4] Edward,[3] John,[2] Thomas[1]) born July 18, 1767, in Lexington, Mass., son of Amos and Abigail (Tidd) Marrett, was installed as the third minister of the Standish Congregational Church on Sept. 21, 1796, and served until Dec. 23, 1829, when the pastoral relationship was dissolved, a period of more than twenty-three years. He married first on July 24, 1796, Mary Muzzy, born Jan. 2, 1770, daughter of William and Lydia (Reed) Muzzy of Lexington. She died in Standish Mar. 6, 1810, and he married second on Oct. 8, 1810, Dorcas Hastings, born June 27, 1785, daughter of Samuel and Lydia (Nelson) Hastings of Lexington. He died in Standish on Apr. 14, 1836, and she on Aug. 6, 1857.

He was a graduate of Harvard College in the class of 1790 and on Nov. 15, 1796, soon after assuming his clerical duties in Standish purchased from Jonathan Gould Sr. of New Braintree, Mass., "20 acres and 68 square rods of land in the Standish with the house and barn standing thereon," it being part of the farm which the Rev. Jonathan Gould Jr., deceased, and son of the conveyor of the property, "purchased of Deacon Benjamin Titcomb, that is to say the five-acre lots Nos. 4, 5, 6, and 10, which the said Benjamin Titcomb bought of John Wood, Clement Meservey, Sargent Shaw and Samuel Knowles respectively, and one acre and 68 square rods of thirty-acre lot #38 which said Benjamin bought of Bartholomew Thorne" (25/291). This property became the Marrett homestead, site of the Marrett House which is in existence today.

Daniel Marrett was a remarkable man. Besides being pastor of the Congregational Church, he was undertaker for the town and much interested in pomology, establishing a large apple orchard and becoming a pioneer of grafting in the state. He owned the first "horse cart" or chaise in town, was first to introduce the cooking stove in place of the spit, the crane and the old fashioned tin oven and also introduced the Franklin stove.

The Rev. Daniel Marrett was the father of fourteen children, as follows:

By his first wife, Mary Muzzy:
i. DANIEL, born July 15, 1797 (bapt. July 16, 1797), married on July 26, 1825 (int. Jan. 1, 1825), Abigail March, born July 5, 1803, daughter of Col. James March of Gorham. He was a merchant in Portland and died Dec. 3, 1875, age 78 yrs., 4 mos., 18 days. Both are buried in Westbrook. Daniel moved to Portland in 1831. He was the father of three children:
1. EDWIN AUGUSTUS, born Mar. 12, 1826, married Mary Louisa Nelson, daughter of Samuel Nelson. He was a merchant in Portland and died on Feb. 10, 1907, age 80 yrs., 10 mos., and 28 days.
2. JAMES SULLIVAN, born May 30, 1827, married Sarah J. Gorham, daughter of Hon. Jason Gorham of Barre, Mass. He was a merchant and carpet manufacturer in Portland and died Dec. 26, 1900, age 77 yrs., 6 mos., and 26 days. He was the father of two.

3. ORLANDO MELVILLE, born May 19, 1829, married Dec. 4, 1851, Louisa Small, daughter of Francis and Dorothy (Libby) Small of Windham. He was a merchant ship chandler in Portland and died Jan. 9, 1870. He had one child:
   (1) JAMES E., born Apr. 7, 1854, and lived in Portland. He died Feb. 8, 1922, age 67 yrs.

ii. JOHN M., born Feb. 1, 1799 (bapt. Feb. 3, 1799), died unmarried on May 3, 1821, age 22 yrs., 3 mos., and 2 days.

iii. AMOS, born Nov. 27, 1800, on Thanksgiving day (bapt. Nov. 30, 1800), married Apr. 12, 1826, Mary S. Strothers of Bridgton, Maine, and died there Sept. 8, 1826, age 25 yrs., 9 mos., and 1 day in Standish.

iv. CAROLINE, born July 3, 1802 (bapt. July 4, 1802), died Dec. 27, 1807, age 15 yrs., 5 mos., 24 days, of consumption.

v. WILLIAM, born Sept. 5, 1804, and bapt. the same day, graduated from Bowdoin Medical School in 1830 and established practice in Westbrook, Maine. On Dec. 6, 1832, he married Adeline Irish, born Sept. 26, 1810, daughter of Gen. James and Rebecca (Chadbourne) Irish. He died Oct. 3, 1859, in Westbrook and she on Feb. 14, 1901, age 90 yrs., 5 mos., 18 days. They were the parents of one child, a daughter Mary Muzzy Marrett, born Sept. 22, 1834, died Jan. 27, 1877, who on Aug. 29, 1863, married Fabius M. Ray, born in Windham, Maine, Mar. 30, 1837.

vi. MARY ANN, born Feb. 1, 1808 (bapt. Feb. 7, 1808), married June 2, 1833, Warren Duren, born in Billerica, Mass., Apr. 14, 1809, son of Abraham and Mary (Russell) Duren. She died Oct. 4, 1839, in Woburn, Mass., and he married second on Oct. 18, 1848, Mary Chandler, born May 22, 1819, died Aug. 1, 1892. They lived in Woburn, Mass., where he died Aug. 18, 1884. One child by his first wife: Caroline Augusta, born Oct. 23, 1835, died May 13, 1852, unmarried.

By second wife, Dorcas Hastings:

vii. LEANDER, born Mar. 18, 1811 (bapt. May 19, 1811), died July 13, 1814.

viii. LORENZO, born Mar. 18, 1816 (bapt. May 19, 1816), graduated from Bowdoin College in Sept. 1838. He settled as a lawyer in Cambridge, Mass. On Aug. 14, 1845, he married Eliza Anthony Winsor of Pawtucket, R.I., who died Feb. 25, 1876. He died Mar. 31, 1887, age 71 yrs., 13 days. No children.

ix. ISABELLA ANNETTE, born July 20, 1817 (bapt. Sept. 14, 1817), died Mar. 4, 1818, age 7 mos., 14 days.

x. AVERY WILLIAMS, born Jan. 19, 1819 (bapt. May 30, 1819), married Nov. 25, 1847, Elizabeth Bancroft Weston, born Jan. 5, 1820, in Augusta, Maine, daughter of Rev. James and Sarah (Chase) Weston. He was a farmer and lived on the homestead in Standish. He died Feb. 12, 1894, age 75 yrs., 24 days, and she on Mar. 27, 1905, age 85 yrs., 2 mos., and 22 days. They were the parents of seven children, as follows:
   1. HELEN MARIA, born Jan. 20, 1849, died unmarried on May 13, 1936, age 87 yrs. She was a teacher.
   2. WALTER HASTINGS, born Oct. 28, 1850, died Jan. 20, 1938, age 87 yrs.

3. MARY ELIZABETH, born Feb. 21, 1852, married on Sept. 14, 1892, the Rev. Myron S. Dudley. He died Nov. 17, 1905, age 68 yrs., 8 mos., 17 days. She died Oct. 26, 1933, age 81 yrs., 9 mos., 26 days.
4. CAROLINE LOUISE, born Dec. 26, 1855, died Feb. 6, 1941, age 85 yrs.
5. HENRY WESTON, born Apr. 19, 1857, married on Oct. 10, 1894, Frances Winston Barron who died Jan. 24, 1901. He died Jan. 11, 1921.
6. CHARLES NELSON, born Feb. 4, 1860, died July 12, 1872, age 12 yrs.
7. FRANCES SARAH, born Oct. 10, 1865, died July 8, 1944, age 78 yrs.

xi. DANE APPLETON, born Jan. 12, 1822 (bapt. July 7, 1822), married June 7, 1848, Eliza Ann Locke of Lancaster, Mass., and lived in Chelsea, Mass. They were the parents of three children, as follows:
1. SAMUEL HASTINGS, born Aug. 10, 1850, died July 17, 1870, age 19 yrs., 11 mos., 7 days.
2. DANE APPLETON JR., born July 1, 1855, died Oct. 4, 1877, age 22 yrs., 3 mos., 3 days.
3. AUGUSTUS, born May 14, 1859.

xii. SAMUEL HASTINGS, born Jan. 12, 1822, twin to Dane Appleton (bapt. July 7, 1822), married on June 7, 1848, Frances A. Locke, twin sister of his brother's wife, at a double wedding ceremony. He died May 22, 1850, and she married second William Dana and died Apr. 18, 1875, age 52 yrs. Samuel H. and Frances (Locke) Marrett were the parents of a daughter.
1. FRANCES HASTINGS, born Aug. 27, 1849, died Feb. 21, 1850.

xiii. HELEN MARIA, born July 3, 1823 (bapt. July 1823), died on Mar. 15, 1846, age 23 yrs., umarried.

xiv. FRANCIS GRENVILLE, born Sept. 8, 1826, died in Cambridge, Mass., May 16, 1859, age 34 yrs., 8 mos. and 8 days, unmarried. He was a builder in Detroit, Mich., and is buried in Standish.

MARTIN

Bryan Martin was another one of the settlers of Pearsontown who hailed from Cape Cod. His parentage has not been discovered, but he was living in Eastham, Mass., on Nov. 11, 1767, when he married Elizabeth Higgins, born Jan. 24, 1742-3, daughter of Ebenezer and Martha (Burgess) Higgins of Eastham and sister of Seth, Ebenezer, and Elkanah Higgins, who settled in Standish. He had been a member of the Eastham Church for many years according to Standish Church records when he was admitted by letter to the latter church on Apr. 30, 1818. His wife, Elizabeth, was admitted to the First Church of Orleans, Mass., formerly First Church of Eastham, on Jan. 23, 1779, and six of their children were baptized there on Feb. 28, 1779.

On Sept. 24, 1779, William Higgins and Bryan Martin "both late of

Eastham in the County of Barnstable, but now of Pearsontown, so called, yeomen" bought from Richard Codman of Falmouth, merchant, for 50 pounds the 100 acre lot #73 in the second division in Pearsontown (11/185). It was on the northeastly half of this lot that he settled and established his homestead. His name is found on the 1789, 1790, 1795, 1796, 1808, and 1814 tax lists of Standish and in the 1790 census with a family of 1-3-3. At the time of the 1800 census his family consisted of him and his wife, one male child between 10 and 16 years of age and two female children under 10 years old.

It appears that Bryan Martin had several wives. His first wife, Elizabeth, apparently died prior to Jan. 16, 1786, when his intentions to Joanna Penfield, both being of Pearsontown, were published in Gorham. It seems likely that she was the widow of Benjamin Penfield of Wellfleet, Mass., whose marriage to Joanna Cook of Eastham took place there on Dec. 24, 1767. It also seems probable that Sally Penfield, whose marriage to Ezra Fickett on Dec. 15, 1796, and Nathan Cook Penfield, whose intentions of marriage on Aug. 25, 1800, to Molly Green of Standish are found in the Gorham records were children of their first marriage. No records have been found of children by her second marriage.

On Feb. 8, 1798, a Bryan Martin married Anna Morton, born Mar. 30, 1781, daughter of James and Susan (Dyer) Morton of Gorham. They had a daughter Hannah born May 22, 1798, according to Gorham records. On May 10, 1808, Bryan Martin of Standish and Anna Carle of Limington, probably born Aug. 23, 1788, at Saco, daughter of Elias and Mary Carle. Whether these last two marriages were those of Bryan Sr. or Bryan Jr., we have not been able to definitely establish.

Bryan Martin Sr. died in Standish sometime between Apr. 30, 1818, when he was admitted to the Standish Church and June 29, 1827, when his son Abner sold part of lot #73 to Edward Tompson of Standish and makes reference to its having been conveyed to him by the last will and testament of his father Bryan Martin (115/405). Bryan Martin was the father of at least the following family:

i. JOHN, born in Eastham Dec. 9, 1768, bapt. there Feb. 28, 1779, may have been the John Martin whose marriage to Hannah (Hanscom) Swett, widow of Josiah Swett, born Mar. 12, 1761, daughter of George and Abigail (Fogg) Hanscom, took place on Nov. 5, 1794.

ii. ELEANOR, born in Eastham June 13, 1770, bapt. there Feb. 28, 1779, married Aug. 7, 1794, Joseph Paine, born Aug. 6, 1771, son of Joseph and Phebe (Rich) Paine of Standish. She died Aug. 28, 1848, age 78, and he died in Bridgton on Apr. 28, 1859. For children see Paine family.

iii. ZILPHA, bapt. in Eastham Feb. 28, 1779, married Mar. 16, 1794, Nathaniel Whitney, born in Gorham June 20, 1769, son of Abel and Thankful (Morton) Whitney. For children see Whitney family.

iv. JAMES, bapt. in Eastham Feb. 28, 1779, perhaps died young. Nothing further known.

v. BRYAN JR., bapt. in Eastham Feb. 28, 1779. Was it he or his father who married Anna Morton and Anna Carle? Nothing further known.

vi. EBENEZER, bapt. in Eastham Feb. 28, 1779, nothing further known. Perhaps died young.

vii. MARY, born Sept. 29, 1780, in Standish, bapt. June 16, 1784, married Feb. 22, 1798, Joseph Nudd of Standish. As widow Nudd she had the following children baptized in the Standish Church:
1. SARAH, born Nov. 23, 1800, bapt. Apr. 19, 1807, married Jan. 21, 1824, Daniel Paine, born Dec. 9, 1800, son of Uriah and Ruth (Adams) Paine of Standish.
2. JOSEPH, born Mar. 8, 1803, bapt. Nov. 9, 1806.
3. ELIZABETH, born Nov. 6, 1805, bapt. Nov. 9, 1806.
4. MARTIN N., born July 10, 1806, bapt. Nov. 9, 1806.

Mary (Martin) Nudd married second Jan. 25, 1807, as his second wife George Rackliff, born Sept. 30, 1773, son of Joseph C. and Mehitabel (Chandler) (Davis) Rackliff of Standish. For children by this marriage see Rackliff for family. She died Jan. 14, 1870, age 89 yrs., 3 mos., and 13 days. He died in Standish May 30, 1849, age 75 yrs. and 8 mos.

viii. ABNER, born Nov. 19, 1782, in Standish, bapt. June 16, 1784, married Feb. 15, 1807, Sarah Whitmore, born Jan. 18, 1789, daughter of William and Amy (Knight) Whitmore of Standish. He lived on the homestead of his father and sold it to his son Ebenezer on Dec. 21, 1830 (124/216). He died May 6, 1865, age 82 yrs., 5 mos., 17 days, and his wife on Oct. 10, 1873, age 84 yrs., and 10 mos., according to gravestones in Maplewood Cemetery at Bonney Eagle in Standish. They were parents of the following children:
1. EBENEZER, born July 30, 1809.
2. JAMES, born Apr. 30, 1812.
3. ABNER, born Jan. 22, 1815.
4. WILLIAM W., died July 17, 1861, age 35 yrs., 9 mos., 21 days according to stone in Maplewood Cemetery.

ix. ELIZABETH, bapt. in Standish Church Oct. 8, 1786, married May 9, 1809, Joseph Whitmore, born Mar. 14, 1779, son of William and Amy (Knight) Whitmore of Gorham and Standish, and brother of Abner's wife. According to Buxton records they had a son Joseph Jr. born May 15, 1812. Nothing further known.

MAYO

Two brothers by the names of Asa and Shubael Mayo were living in Standish prior to 1800. On June 14, 1799, James Wiley of Standish sold to them the westerly half of the 100-acre lot #87 in the second division (37/474), they being inhabitants of the town at that time. It appears likely they were the Asa and Shubael Mayo, who with brother Isaac and sisters Sarah and Ruth were baptized July 9, 1775, as children of Asa Mayo Jr., deceased, and widow Hannah Mayo according to the records of the First Church of Orleans, Massachusetts.

Asa Mayo, born in July 1772 according to gravestone, son of Asa Jr. and Hannah (Covell) Mayo, married Aug. 31, 1794, Hannah Higgins, born Oct. 15, 1767, daughter of Edmund and Esther (Higgins) Higgins of Eastham, Massachusetts. About 1799 they moved to Standish, where he and his wife were living at the time of the 1800 census with a family consisting of two male children under 10 years of age, two females under 10, and one female between 10 and 16 years old. His name is found on the 1808 and 1814 tax lists of Standish. He died in Standish on May 22, 1838, age 66 years, 10 months, and is buried in a small cemetery on the Dow Road, so called, at Dow's Corner. Children of Asa and Hannah (Higgins) Mayo were as follows:

i. EDMUND, born Apr. 3, 1795, at Orleans, Mass., married Dec. 25, 1825, Esther Thompson of Standish. He died Apr. 14, 1865, age 70 yrs., 11 days, and his wife died Mar. 1, 1859. Buried in Sandy Creek Cemetery. The children of Edmund and Esther (Thompson) Mayo were:
  (1) DELANAY COVIL, born Sept. 28, 1826.
  (2) EMILY JANE, born Jan. 8, 1828, she was Mrs. Jackson of Gorham in 1904. She married Sept. 3, 1848, James P. Skillings of Biddeford, she of Bridgton.
  (3) HANNAH FRANCES, born Dec. 6, 1829.
  (4) CHARLES AUGUSTUS, born Oct. 17, 1832.
  (5) GARDNER GREEN, born Oct. 8, 1834.
  (6) EDMUND FREEMAN, born Feb. 22, 1836, died Jan. 1904, Gorham.
  (7) ASA, born Jan. 23, 1838, died Apr. 14, 1854, age 16 yrs., 5 mos.
  (8) JOHN FRANKLIN, born June 1, 1840, in 1904 of Lynn, Mass.
  (9) ORLANDO M., died Apr. 7, 1852, age 5 yrs., 9 mos. He and his brother Asa and their parents are buried at Sandy Creek Cemetery in Bridgton, Maine.
ii. MERCY, born Sept. 6, 1796, at Orleans, Mass.
iii. LYDIA, born Apr. 28, 1798, at Orleans, Mass., died Oct. 27, 1804, at Standish.
iv. ASA, born Jan. 9, 1800, at Standish, died Oct. 31, 1804, age 4 yrs., 9 mos., and 21 days.
v. JOSIAH, born Oct. 15, 1801, married int. Mar. 17, 1828, Mary Nason of Buxton, he of Standish. She was born Aug. 6, 1805, in Limington, daughter of Edward and Susannah (Small) Nason. They lived in Westbrook and Naples. He was living in 1850, age 49 yrs., in Naples. They had five children.
vi. ESTHER, born Mar. 25, 1803, died Nov. 1804.
vii. ESTHER, born Nov. 19, 1804, died Nov. 19, 1845, aged 41 yrs.
viii. ASA, born Sept. 1, 1806, married (int. May 1, 1831) Eliza P. Warren, born Sept. 12, 1804, daughter of Samuel and Anna (Pinkerton) Warren of Standish. They had children: Helen M. died Aug. 11, 1844, age 7 yrs., 2 mos.; and Aramantha F. died Sept, 11, 1846, age 14 yrs., 11 mos.
ix. ARZA, born Oct. 13, 1808, married June 2, 1835, Marcella Cram. He died Oct. 30, 1894, age 81 yrs., 19 days. Both are buried in the Johnson Cemetery at South Limington. Children: Leonidas, born May 6, 1836; Maria Peabody, born Sept. 22, 1841; Esther Abby, born Mar. 3, 1849.

Shubael Mayo, baptized in Orleans Church July 9, 1775, son of Asa Jr. and Hannah (Covell) Mayo, married (int. Oct. 13, 1793) Thankful Higgins of Eastham, sold on Jan. 10, 1793, land in Harwich from the estate of his father to Thomas Arey of Harwich. He probably came to Standish a short time before his brother Asa, for his name is found on the 1799 valuation list taken in May of that year, while his brother's is not. At the time of the 1800 census his family consisted of him and his wife, one male child under 10 years of age, and three females under 10.

On Jan. 3, 1801, he sold to Samuel Linnell one acre of land at the south corner of Linnell's homestead, the deed being witnessed by Asa Mayo and John Linnell and signed by himself and his wife, Thankful (152572). On June 12, 1803, Thankful, wife of Shubael Mayo, was baptized in the Standish Church and on Aug. 5, 1803, Lois, Abigail, Isaac, and Patience, their children, were baptized. According to church records, Shubael and Thankful (Higgins) Mayo moved out of town, but it has not been discovered where they went.

MERROW OR MERRY

The names of William and Amos Merrow are found on the 1808 tax list of Standish and that of William Merrow only on an 1814 tax list of Cumberland County. In the 1810 census of Standish there were in William Merrow's family two males under 10 years of age, one male between 26 and 45 years old, one female under 10, and one female between 26 and 45 years of age. This would indicate a family consisting of William and his wife and three children less than ten years old.

The name of Merrow was also spelled 'Merrey' or 'Merry' in some records. William[4] (Samuel,[3] Samuel,[2] Henry[1]) was born 1754, son of Samuel Jr. and Abigail (____) Merry of Pepperrellborough (Saco), Maine, and Margaret Haley of Biddeford were married by the Rev. Moses Morrill. She was born Mar. 10, 1755, daughter of William and Rachel (Edgecomb) Haley of Biddeford. Her twin sister, Charity Haley, married July 23, 1777, Nicholas Davis, who settled in Limington.

William Merrow or Merry served in the Revolutionary War but his service was interrupted by periods of desertion. In 1775 an advertisement in the *Essex Gazette* of Salem, Mass., read as follows:

> Deserted from Capt. Theodore Bliss's Company of Col. Patterson's regiment in Charleston Camp William Merry of Biddeford in Saco, about 5'3" high of a thick stature, very large legs, had on fustian [cloth made of cotton and flax] coat, striped gingham waistcoat, and a pair of velvet breeches.

He was also listed as a deserter from Capt. Jabez Lane's company in a return dated Feb. 20, 1778.

At the time of the 1790 census William Merry was living in Little Falls Town (Hollis) with a family of 1-2-2. Soon after 1800 he moved to Standish where he afterwards lived. He was living in town on Oct. 25, 1806, when he bought from Nicholas Davis (his brother-in-law) of Limington 12 acres of 100-acre lot #80 and 50 acres of 100-acre lot #96 in Standish with adjoining mill privilege (78/252). On June 24, 1817, he mortgaged to Dr. Ebenezer Howe this same property, indicated as his homestead farm with buildings containing 60 acres and described as bordering on the northeast side by the County Road from Buxton through Standish, on the northwest by Joseph C. Rackliff, on the southwest by Daniel Bolter and Richard Berry and on the southeast by Joseph Cressey's land on which William Whitmore then lived (78/253). It was on Aug. 18, 1821, he and his son Joseph sold to Samuel F. Boulter (his son-in-law) the same property, noted in the deed as being "the same farm on which we have lived in Standish for 15 years" (94/108). According to state of Maine bounty records he died in Newfield on Mar. 12, 1836, 82 years, but his place of burial is not known. His date of death is also given in the *Christian Mirror* issue of Mar. 31, 1836. A gravestone in the Boulter Cemetery on the River Road at South Standish indicates the death of Mrs. Margaret, wife of William Merrow, on Feb. 13, 1841, at the age of 87 years. Children of William and Margaret (Haley) Merrow were as follows:

i. MARY (POLLY), born Nov. 1, 1776, perhaps in Hollis, married Oct. 20, 1803, Isaac York, born Aug. 15, 1758, son of Abraham and Lydia (Jordan) York of Standish, as his second wife. Both died in Standish, he on Nov. 25, 1846, and she on Nov. 22, 1861, and were buried in a small family graveyard on their farm off the River Road in the Boulter Neighbohood. For children see York family.

ii. CHARITY, born in Mar. 1777 perhaps in Hollis, married (int. Jan. 11, 1800, in Hollis) Samuel Fowler Boulter, born in 1775 son of Nathaniel and Ruth (Sprague) Boulter of Standish. They lived on the Boulter homestead on the River Road at South Standish where he died July 31, 1857, age 82 yrs., 7 mos., and she on July 31, 1857, age 92 yrs., 4 mos., and were buried in the Boulter Cemetery on the bank of the Saco River. For children see Boulter family.

iii. AMOS, born May 16, 1780, in Hollis, married Mar. 26, 1818, probably in Shapleigh, Maine, his first cousin Phebe Merrow, born May 23, 1782, daughter of Joseph and Mary (Dore) Merrow. They both were residents of Shapleigh at the time of their marriage, but later moved to West Newfield, Maine, sometime between 1823 and 1830. He was a shoemaker or cobbler. Both died at West Newfield, she on Dec. 8, 1865, age 83 yrs., 6 mos., and 15 days, and he on May 23, 1867, age 87 yrs., 7 days. They were parents of two children as follows:
1. MARY, born June 12, 1817 (or 1818). Married as his third wife Benjamin Murray of Newfield on Apr. 13, 1871. She died Nov. 15, 1890, age 75 yrs., 5 mos., 3 days.
2. WILLIAM, born Nov. 5, 1819, in Shapleigh (part that later was Acton), married Feb. 27, 1850, Eliza Ann Hodsdon, born Apr. 7, 1823, daughter of Israel and Zillah (Lord) Hodsdon of Somersworth, N.H. She died Feb. 7, 1900, age 76 yrs., 10 mos., and he on Feb. 10, 1900, age 83 yrs., 3 mos., 5 days.

iv. SARAH, born 1797, married Apr. 18, 1824, in Limington (int. Mar. 8, 1824) William Hanscom of Buxton, she of Limington. They lived in Newfield where she died in Oct. 16, 1870, age 73 yrs., 8 mos., 21 days.

v. ABIGAIL, born Sept. 20, 1791, married Jan. 13, 1814, Watson Dyer, born June 6, 1786, in Cape Elizabeth, son of Isaac and Mary (Watson) Dyer of Limington. They lived in Limington where he died on Apr. 22, 1879, age 92 yrs., 10 mos., and 16 days, and she on June 27, 1882, age 90 yrs., 9 mos., 7 days, and were buried on their farm there.

vi. OLIVE, born in 1794, married Jan. 13, 1813, White Dyer, brother of sister Abigail's husband, born in Oct. 1788. They lived in Limington and Baldwin where he died Aug. 15, 1873, age 84, and she Jan. 3, 1874, age 79 yrs., 10 mos., in Sebago.

MESERVE

One branch of the Meserve family was well represented in Pearsontown in its earliest days. The best representative was Clement Meserve Sr., who was born in Portsmouth or Newington, N.H., about 1703, son of Clement and Elizabeth (Jones) Meserve. He evidently followed his father to Scarboro, but is known to have been one of the dwellers in fort on Fort Hill in Gorham during the seven-year Indian War beginning in 1745. It is likely that along with the Thorn family he and several of his sons were among the earliest inhabitants of Pearsontown, perhaps as early as 1753.

On Dec. 28, 1768, Moses Pearson of Falmouth sold to Clement Meserve of Pearsontown "for five shillings and in consideration of said Clement's having performed settlement according to Act of General Court one whole right in Pearsontown," this is to say the 30-acre lot #4 in first division with the after divisions belonging to right No. 4, a 5-acre lot near the meeting house being already confirmed to said Clement, all according to the agreement made with said Clement Meserve Mar. 25, 1755 (5/200). It was on lot #4 near where the Congregational Church now stands that he settled, selling it together with #3 belonging to his son John to Daniel Hasty of Scarboro on Apr. 11, 1770 (5/295). The 5-acre lot that he owned, which was #8, was sold together with 5-acre lot #9 owned by his son John to Rev. John Tompson of Pearsontown on Apr. 9, 1770 (8/462). It was about this time that he moved to Bristol, Maine, in company with his sons John and Clement Jr., his son-in-law Timothy Crocker, and their families.

Clement Meserve Sr. married in Newington, N.H., on Oct. 13, 1726, Sarah Decker of that town, who probably died before his marriage on Aug. 14, 1738, to Mrs. Sarah Stone of Scarboro. Children were as follows:

By first wife, Sarah Decker:

i. JOHN, bapt. Oct. 13, 1728, moved to Gorham with his father and later followed him to Pearsontown. He as one of the men making up the guard at the fort in Pearsontown on Apr. 16, 1755, but was living in Gorham on Aug. 12, 1760, when he sold land and buildings in that town to Nathaniel Whitney. He is given as a resident of Pearsontown on Aug. 10, 1765, when he sold to David Gorham of Barnstable, Mass., 100 acres of land in Gorham (4/381), this probably being the same land he purchased from Gorham on Aug. 29, 1753. He secured by right of settlement the 30-acre lot #3 in Pearsontown, which James Lunt of Falmouth confirmed to him on Apr. 11, 1770, and the 5-acre lot #9 which he sold to the Rev. John

Tompson on Apr. 9, 1770 (8/462). He moved to Bristol, Maine, with his father about 1771 but later returned to Standish at least by 1792. He may have been the John Harvey listed as living in Standish at the time of the 1790 census with a family of 3-1-2 since the name of Meserve appears as 'Misharvey' or 'Harvey' in many of the early records. At the time of the 1800 census he was living in Standish with a family consisting of him and his wife, one male and one female between 26 and 45 and one female under 10 yrs. of age. He is also listed on the 1795, 1796, and 1799 tax lists of Standish.

John Meserve married first in Mar. 1757 Mary Yetty or Yeaton of Gorham, he being given as an inhabitant of Pearsontown in the intentions filed in Falmouth on Mar. 4, 1757. She evidently died a few years later, perhaps following the birth of their son William, for he married second on Jan. 28, 1762, Sarah Strout, both being listed as residents of Pearsontown. She may have been the daughter of John and Ruth (Mayo) Strout who were living in Pearsontown prior to 1760. He is said to have died at the home of a daughter in Bridgton, Maine. Children by both marriages were as follows:

By first marriage:
1. **ELIZABETH OR BETSEY**, born Apr. 14, 1760, died June 29, 1804, married (int. May 6, 1780) in Gorham, Isaac York of Pearsontown, Aug. 15, 1758, son of Abram and Lydia (Jordan) York of Pearsontown. They were the parents of nine children, list of whom may be found in the records of the York family. Following her death in 1804, he married second on Oct. 20, 1805, Polly Merrow, born Nov. 1, 1776, daughter of William and Margaret (Haley) Merrow of Standish, by whom he had five more children. He died Nov. 24, 1846, and she on Nov. 22, 1861.
2. **WILLIAM**, born in 1761, may have been married twice. A William Meserve married Polly Dustin of Bethel in 1788 with Simon Frye Esq. of Fryeburg officiating. If this was the William Meserve of Standish, his wife must have died, for on Nov. 16, 1797, he married Mary (Davis) Boulter, widow of Lemuel Boulter of Standish. They had daughters: Polly, born Mar. 22, 1799, bapt. July 18, 1799, and Eunice, born Sept. 2, 1802. At the time of the 1800 census he was living in Standish with a family consisting of him and his wife, one female under 10 yrs. of age and one between 10 and 16 yrs. old, the latter probably being Ruth Boulter, daughter of his wife by her first marriage. They are said to have moved to Illinois about 1823.

By second wife:
3. **JOSEPH**, nothing further known.
4. **CLEMENT**, lost at sea.
5. **JANE**, married Josiah Segar of Rumford on Mar. 6, 1788. They lived in Rumford, Standish, and Unity, Maine.
6. **DORCAS**, married Feb. 6, 1792, David Kneeland of Bridgton, born Jan. 5, 1770, son of David and Sarah (Smith) Kneeland. They lived in Bridgton and Sweden, Maine. She died about

1815; he married second Dec. 25, 1822, Hannah, widow of Jacob Gibson. He died in 1833. For children see Kneeland family.
7. SARAH, married Jan. 5, 1800, Caleb Dodge of Bridgton. They had a daughter Eleanor, born Aug. 18, 1800.
8. JOHN, born Aug. 11, 1775, married Apr. 26, 1797 (int. Mar. 14, 1797, in Standish) Mary (Polly) Blaban or Laban of Wells, Maine. Following her death he married second Dec. 1, 1816, in Albion, Eunice (Myrick) Bither, widow of Stephen. He died Apr. 24, 1865, age 90 yrs., in Monroe.
9. CHARLES, born about 1774, married Sept. 30, 1798, Mary Cookson, bapt. June 5, 1774, born about 1770 daughter of Reuben and Mary (York) Cookson of Standish. They moved to Unity, Maine, and about 1813-1814 settled in North Belmont, Maine. He was on a list of voters there in 1840 but at the time of the 1850 census was living in Standish in the family of Samuel York, age 76. He served in the War of 1812 from Belmont. He died in Morrill in Jan. 1861 and his wife died at North Belmont on July 17, 1840, age 70. They had the following children:
   (1) SARAH, born Jan. 2, 1800, married Mar. 13, 1823, Samuel York, born July 4, 1802, son of Isaac and Betsey (Meserve) York, her cousin. She died Jan. 24, 1863, and he June 14 or 28, 1883. For children see York family.
   (2) POLLY, died young.
   (3) CHARLES JR., born Aug. 14, 1806, died Aug. 21, 1876, married Sarah V. Smith, born June 20, 1812, daughter of Daniel and Lucy (Cookson) Smith of Hollis, Maine, his cousin. She died at Morrill, Maine, on July 6, 1901. They had six children born in North Belmont, Maine.

ii. ELIZABETH, born Sept. 2, 1730, bapt. Nov. 21, 1731, probably died young.
iii. ELIZABETH, bapt. Sept. 2, 1733, married about 1750 Col. Edmund Phinney of Gorham, born in Barnstable, Mass., July 27, 1723, son of John and Martha (Cookson) Phinney. They were the parents of nine children. She died on Aug. 6, 1795, age 65, and he married second on Nov. 21, 1796, Mrs. Sarah Stevens, widow of Benjamin Stevens. He died Dec. 15, 1808, age 85.
iv. CLEMENT JR., born Sept. 2, 1733, bapt. Nov. 11, 1733, lived in Gorham, as did his father, before settling in Pearsontown. He, together with his brothers John and Joseph, was among the eight men hired Apr. 15, 1755, for two months' service as a guard for the fort at Pearsontown. He secured title to the 5-acre lot #5 by right of settlement and sold it to Benjamin Titcomb of Falmouth on Mar. 28, 1771 (8/395). On Oct. 28, 1762, Isaac Illesley of Falmouth sold Clement Meserve Jr. of Pearsontown one whole right of land in Pearsontown including the 30-acre lot #69 in the first division, it being 1/23 of the township (5/395). Moses Pearson of Falmouth deeded to him by right of settlement the 30-acre lot #70 on Feb. 9, 1769 (6/311). These two lots he sold to William Hasty of Scarboro on Aug. 3, 1771, at which time he was still living in Pearsontown. However, it was soon after this time that he moved to Bristol, Maine, with his father and brothers.

Clement Meserve Jr. married on Sept. 19, 1757, Mary Wooster, both being given as inhabitants of Pearsontown when their intentions of marriage were filed on Feb. 25, 1757, in Falmouth. She probably was the daughter of James and Patience (Mills) (Low) Wooster of Falmouth. James Wooster was shot to death in Pearsontown on Mar. 13, 1757, by one John Clark. For details of this affair see Clark family. Mary (Wooster) Meserve died in June 1834, age 92 yrs., Palermo (*Christian Mirror*, issue of July 17, 1834). Clement Jr. and Mary (Wooster) Meserve were the parents of the following family:

1. PATIENCE, bapt. June 10, 1770, in Pearsontown.
2. LUCY, bapt. June 10, 1770, in Pearsontown, was perhaps the Lucy Meservy of Bristol who married (int. June 10, 1787) Richard Christy of that town.
3. SARAH, born Mar. 11, 1766, died Oct. 14, 1831, age 65, married Nov. 20, 1794, Richard Paine, born Sept. 24, 1773, son of Joseph and Phebe (Rich) Paine of Standish. For children see Paine family.

v. HANNAH, bapt. Mar. 7, 1736, married in Dec. 1754 Timothy Crocker. For children see Crocker family.

vi. JOSEPH, bapt. Dec. 3, 1738, was of Pearsontown on May 6, 1758, when his intentions of marriage to Mary Martin, born July 7, 1741, daughter of John and Margaret (____) Martin of Brunswick were recorded in Falmouth. He was one of eight men comprising the guard at the fort in Pearsontown on Apr. 16, 1755. He is said to have lived later on in Union, Maine, and to have had several children, but nothing further has been discovered concerning him.

By second wife Sarah (____) Stone:

vii. MARGARET, bapt. Aug. 23, 1741, is listed of Pearsontown at the time her intentions of marriage to William Wescott were filed on Sept. 22, 1756. Their marriage in Feb. 1757 was recorded in Gorham. They settled in Scarboro and raised a family of ten children.

viii. BENJAMIN, bapt. July 4, 1744, was married and had sons Joseph who married Letty Martin and George who moved to Ohio, but nothing further is known. He lived at Bristol, Maine.

ix. NATHANIEL, born Jan. 26, 1748, bapt. Jan. 20, 1749, in Windham and married Rebecca Martin and settled in Bristol, Maine, where he was living in 1790 with a family of 4-1-5. He and Rebecca were living in 1806 at Appleton, Maine, when they give their place to Charles and Nancy (Meserve) Bryant who left about 1814 and went west. He died in Oct. 1815. Children were as follows:

1. NATHANIEL JR., born Feb. 5. 1769, married Ruth Winslow (int. Nov. 24, 1794, at Bristol). He lived in Jefferson and Morrill, Maine, and had eight children among whom was Alden born about 1807. He died May 19, 1849, age 80, in Hope, now Appleton, Maine.
2. JOHN, born 1770, married at Bristol, Martha McLain on Jan. 9, 1794.
3. WILLIAM, born 1773, married Damaris Whitney.
4. SAMUEL.

5. ELIZABETH OR BETSEY, married Fergus McLain (int. Oct. 9, 1785, at Bristol).
6. SARAH, married Zedediah or Prince Pease (int. Oct. 12, 1790).
7. JENNIE, married ____ Meservey.
8. ANNE OR ANNIE, married ____ Butler.
9. NANCY, married Charles Bryant and about 1814 they went west.

MILLER

John Miller had children baptized in the Standish Congregational Church. He is given as residing in Flintstown on Feb. 25, 1794, when he married Molly or Polly (Sawyer) Wood, widow of John Wood Jr. of Standish and Buxton. He was born about 1753 according to pension records and was from the Cape Elizabeth group of Millers. They moved to Limington where he probably had relatives between May 1797 and Oct. 1799 and were living there at the time of the 1800 census with a family consisting of themselves, one male and three female children under 10 years of age and one female between 10 and 16. He took care of the Congregational Meeting House in Limington during 1808, 1809 and 1812. On July 18, 1820, he signed a pension affidavit that he had been a private in Capt. Richard Mayberry's company, Col. Tupper's regiment, during the Revolutionary War. He died in Limington Nov. 25, 1825, age 72 years, and his wife Aug. 20, 1826. Children of John and Mary (Sawyer) (Wood) Miller were as follows:

i. SARAH MOOR, bapt. May 21, 1797, in Standish, married (int. Sept. 13, 1823, John Davis of Limington. She died Jan. 1, 1889, age 92 yrs., 8 mos., and 27 days, Limington.
ii. JENNIE, bapt. May 21, 1797, in Standish.
iii. CATY OR KATHERINE, bapt. Oct. 27, 1799, in Limington, married Nov. 15, 1822, Oliver Chase of Limington.
iv. SUSAN, born about 1802, died Mar. 1821 in Limington. She was an invalid.
v. ANNA, born about 1805, died Jan. 2, 1830, in Limington. Non compos mentis.
vi. GEORGE, born 1806, died Sept. 16, 1823, age 16 yrs., 11 mos., 23 days, in Limington.
vii. EUNICE, married Nathaniel Norcross.
viii. JAMES, born before 1814.

MITCHELL

The name of Dominicus Mitchell is found on all of the tax lists consulted, in the 1790 census with a family of 2-3-5, and in the 1800 census with a family consisting of him and his wife, one female under

10 and 16, and two males and one female between 16 and 26. He was born in Cape Elizabeth Apr. 19, 1744, son of Robert and Miriam (Jordan) Mitchell and on Aug. 1, 1765, married Anna Small, born Aug. 12, 1744, in Scarboro daughter of Joshua and Susannah (Kennard) Small of that town and Little Ossipee Plantation (Limington). Dr. Meserve states that Dominicus Mitchell was living in Pearsontown in 1766, but this seems doubtful because he is given of Cape Elizabeth on Dec. 2, 1769, when he purchased from Moses Pearson of Falmouth the two 30-acre lots Nos. 88 and 89 in the first division in Pearsontown (6/382). He may have been led to settle in town by the fact that his wife's sister's husband, the Rev. John Tompson, was pastor of the Pearsontown Church, of which he later became a deacon. He was admitted to the church on June 9, 1771, and his wife, Anna, on July 24, 1774. He served in the Revolutionary War as lieutenant in Capt. Samuel Whitmore's Company of Col. Reuben Fogg's regiment of militia on Dec. 25, 1777. His wife died July 20, 1814, and he on Sept. 6, 1822, age 78 years, in Standish. They were buried in the old cemetery at Dow's Corner in Standish. Dominicus and Anna (Small) Mitchell were parents of the following children:

 i. ELIZABETH, born May 15, 1766, married as his first wife on July 8, 1790, Wingate Frost, born Sept. 3, 1768, son of James and Love (Wingate) Frost of Falmouth and Limington. She died May 4, 1799, and he Mar. 9, 1856, in Limington.

 ii. DANIEL, born June 23, 1768, married Anna Small, daughter of Benjamin and Phebe (Plummer) Small on June 23, 1791, and settled in Limington. He was dismissed from the Limington Church to the one in North Yarmouth on Sept. 20, 1807. She died Jan. 16, 1836, and he on Oct. 10, 1851. They lived in Chesterville, Maine. No children.

 iii. MARY, born Aug. 19, 1770, bapt. Aug. 26, 1770, married first on Oct. 20, 1791, Abraham Parker of Limington, second on June 11, 1815, Thomas Harmon of Buxton. She died Sept. 30, 1843, in Limington.

 iv. DOMINICUS JR., born Aug. 23, 1772, bapt. Aug. 23, 1772, married Feb. 12, 1795, Apphia Whitney, born Jan. 6, 1774. He died May 6, 1856, Meldola, LaSalle Co., Ill., formerly of Norridgewock, Ill. Children were:
  1. MARY, born Sept. 26, 1795.
  2. CROSBY, born Sept. 7, 1797.
  3. BETSEY, born Jan. 1, 1800.
  4. DANIEL, born Jan. 15, 1803, died Oct. 10, 1815.
  5. JOHN, born Nov. 25, 1804, died Apr. 6, 1873, Sterling, Nebr.
  6. OTIS, born Apr. 26, 1807.
  7. JOSHUA, born Mar. 24, 1807.
  8. ISAAC, born Oct. 28, 1815.
  9. OLIVER, born Nov. 11, 1818.

 v. JOSHUA, born Oct. 17, 1774, bapt. Nov. 27, 1774, married first Nov. 19, 1795, Hannah Myrick, born July 3, 1771, Eastham, Mass., sister to Mrs. Myrick Paine. She died Mar. 20, 1797; married June 2, 1798, Sarah Hamilton, born Apr. 22, 1774. He died Sept. 14, 1850, in Dover, Maine, and his widow died in 1864. Child by first wife:
  1. PHEBE, born Sept. 25, 1796, died Apr. 3, 1798.

Children by second wife:
2. DOMINICUS, born Apr. 14, 1799.
3. JOSHUA, born May 23, 1801.
4. JOHN, born Feb. 8, 1803, died Apr. 6, 1873, in Sterling, Nebr.
5. WILLIAM HAMILTON, born Nov. 23, 1804.
6. MARY ANN, born Aug. 3, 1806, died Jan. 1, 1807.
7. ISAAC SKILLING, born Apr. 2, 1808.
8. SARAH, born Jan. 25, 1810.
9. DANIEL, born Aug. 14, 1812.
10. SAMUEL, born Feb. 2, 1816.
11. MARY MASON, born Apr. 17, 1819.

vi. ROBERT, born July 22, 1776, bapt. July 28, 1776, married Sept. 17, 1804, Lydia Berry, born Oct. 31, 1779, daughter of Elisha and Jane (Libby) Berry of Scarboro. He died Sept. 12, 1821, and his widow married Myrick Paine, who died Apr. 4, 1858. She died July 8, 1853. Children:
1. DANIEL, born Sept. 7, 1802, bapt. Nov. 7, 1802, died Mar. 20, 1830, Standish.
2. SEWALL, born Oct. 19, 1804, bapt. Dec. 1, 1804, married Nov. 8, 1833, Celia Mitchell, born Dec. 18, 1811. He died May 21, 1879 in Bridgewater, Mass., he of Standish and she Nov. 4, 1878.
3. CYRUS, born Feb. 22, 1806, bapt. July 5, 1807, died Oct. 5, 1833, age 26, in Standish. He married Oct. 31, 1830, Tamson Robinson.
4. ANNA, born June 14, 1809, bapt. July 20, 1809. She died Mar. 20, 1836.
5. JANE, born Sept. 4, 1811, bapt. Oct. 27, 1811, married Nov. 24, 1830, Samuel Osborne Paine. She died Aug. 8, 1888, in Standish.
6. ABRAHAM PARKER, born Feb. 22, 1814, died Feb. 22, 1842, Standish. He married Nov. 5, 1840, Mary Ann Harmon.
7. HENRY ERASMUS, born May 17, 1817, bapt. July 11, 1817, died Dec. 12, 1822, Standish.
8. SALLY BERRY, born May 17, 1820, died June 17, 1820.

vii. ISAAC, born Jan. 18, 1779, died Feb. 4, 1779.
viii. ISAAC born Jan. 31, 1780, bapt. Mar. 12, 1780, married Nov. 26, 1801, Martha, daughter of Philemon and Martha (Small) Libby of Limington, born Aug. 28, 1783, and died Jan. 3, 1877. They lived in Limington where he died Jan. 26, 1863.
ix. ANNA, born Mar. 21, 1788, bapt. Mar. 22, 1782, married on Mar. 23, 1800, as his second wife Wingate Frost of Limington. She died June 6, 1848. He died Mar. 9, 1856, age 88.
x. SAMUEL, born Feb. 6, 1784, married first Sept. 6, 1809, Margaret Berry, born Dec. 14, 1784, in Scarboro, daughter of Elisha and Jane (Libby) Berry of Scarboro. She died Apr. 27, 1842. He married second on Feb. 1, 1844, Miriam Phinney, born Mar. 18, 1789, in Gorham. He was born, lived, and died on the Mitchell homestead in Standish on Apr. 5, 1860, age 76 yrs. Children, all by the first wife, were:
1. ELISHA BERRY, born Sept. 15, 1810, bapt. Sept. 29, 1816, died Dec. 14, 1875.

2. IRENE, born Jan. 22, 1812, bapt. Sept. 29, 1816.
3. ANN ELIZABETH, born Oct. 14, 1817, bapt. Mar. 22, 1818.
4. RUFUS BANKS, born Oct. 18, 1824.
xi. SARAH, born May 6, 1786, bapt. June 20, 1786, married as his second wife on Jan. 20, 1803, Joseph Davis, born Aug. 10, 1776, son of Josiah and Thankful (Gorham) Davis. They moved from Standish to Brooks, Maine, about 1820. She died Oct. 3, 1852, and he in Dec. 1862. Children may be found under Davis family.

MOODY

James^5 Moody (Joshua,^{4} Samuel,^{3} Joshua,^{2} William^1), born in 1750 son of Joshua and Tabitha Cocks (or Cox) of Falmouth, was living in Pearsontown before 1770. His name is found on the poll tax list of Falmouth in 1766. On Oct. 27, 1767, James Moody, blacksmith, of Falmouth bought from James Candage, yeoman, of Falmouth the 30-acre lot #66 in Pearsontown (3/240). He probably moved into town soon after this date for he married in 1769 (int. Sept. 2, 1769, in Gorham) Elizabeth Shaw, born Mar. 21, 1751, daughter of Ebenezer and Anna (Philbrick) Shaw of Pearsonfield. He later bought 30-acre lots Nos. 67 and 68, which together with lot #66 purchased in 1767 constituted his homestead farm, being bounded by a road on all sides. He was the first blacksmith to locate in the town and was elected warden at the first town meeting in 1786. His wife, Elizabeth, died May 27, 1816, age 67, and he on Jan. 4, 1818, age 67. They were parents of the following children:

i. ABIAH, bapt. Oct. 20, 1771, married July 31, 1794, Hezekiah Brown, born May 28, 1771, son of Sylvanus and Fear (____) Brown of Gorham. They were the parents of eight children. He died in Brownfield, Maine, and she died there Sept. 15, 1855.
ii. SAMUEL, bapt. Nov. 15, 1772, married Sarah Rogers of Cape Cod.
iii. DANIEL, bapt. May 28, 1775, married Dec. 3, 1797, Mary Sawyer, born May 22, 1778, daughter of Joel and Elizabeth (Stone) Sawyer of Gorham. They lived near Oak Hill in Standish. She died July 19, 1840. They were the parents of the following children:
 1. JOSEPH, born Sept. 16, 1798, married Nov. 22, 1821, Eliza Higgins, born Oct. 11, 1795, daughter of William and Phebe (Paine) Higgins. They had sons: William Higgins, born July 31, 1823, bapt. Aug. 23, 1823; Charles Henry, born May 7, 1826, bapt. Mar. 27, 1828.
 2. DANIEL JR., born Apr. 9, 1801, bapt. May 27, 1804, married Dec. 16, 1823, Hulda Higgins and had daughter, Caroline Augusta, bapt. July 20, 1825.
 3. ELIZA, born May 2, 1804, bapt. May 27, 1804.
 4. CALEB, born Jan. 6, 1806, bapt. July 20, 1806, married Jan. 6, 1828, Eunice Whitney of Standish.
 5. ARTEMAS, born Mar. 26, 1809, died Nov. 1811.
 6. MARY, born Aug. 7, 1811, bapt. Nov. 10, 1811.

7. NANCY, born Aug. 10, 1814, bapt. Nov. 13, 1814, married (int. Sept. 14, 1834) Rev. Mark B. Hopkins of Baldwin. She died Aug. 20, 1847, age 33.
8. ARTEMAS, born Aug. 13, 1817.
9. HARRIET NEWELL, born July 7, 1823, bapt. Oct. 29, 1820.
10. JAMES LORING, born May 27, 1823, bapt. Oct. 5, 1823.
11. CAROLINE AUGUSTA, bapt. July 10, 1825.

iv. RHODA, born about 1776, bapt. July 29, 1787, married Mar. 5, 1809, Friend Loring of Portland.
v. ANNA, born about 1778, bapt. July 29, 1787, married Oct. 14, 1804, Benjamin Rand of Standish. He died in 1829 and she on Feb. 23, 1827.
vi. WILLIAM, bapt. July 20, 1777, married Sept. 25, 1803, Elizabeth Sawyer, born July 23, 1783, daughter of Joel and Elizabeth (Stone) Sawyer of Gorham. He died Feb. 4, 1852, age 74 yrs., and she in 1871, age 88. Both are buried in Oak Hill Cemetery in Standish. Children as follows:
1. ISAAC, bapt. Oct. 5, 1806, married (int. Dec. 1834) Wealthy S. Harmon of Standish. He born 1805 and died Dec. 27, 1886, age 82, Standish.
2. WILLIAM, bapt. Oct. 5, 1806.
3. MARY ANN, bapt. Aug. 12, 1811.
4. DORCAS, bapt. Aug. 14, 1816.
5. JAMES, bapt. June 22, 1823.

vii. ENOCH, bapt. May 30, 1781, married first on Feb. 16, 1809, Dorcas Sawyer, born Mar. 29, 1786, daughter of Joel and Elizabeth (Stone) Sawyer of Gorham. She died in 1814 and he married second on Dec. 13, 1821, Damaris S. Whitney, born July 3, 1797, daughter of Daniel and Abigail (Stone) Whitney of Gorham. He married third on Feb. 7, 1830, Mary Whitney, born Dec. 31, 1792, sister of his second wife. He was a blacksmith and lived at Oak Hill. He died Feb. 22, 1856, age 75, and his third wife died Nov. 4, 1867, age 74 yrs. Both are buried in in the Oak Hill Cemetery. Children as follows:
By first wife:
1. AMOS, bapt. Sept. 15, 1811, evidently died young.
2. WILLIAM, bapt. Sept. 20, 1812, died Mar. 23, 1892, in Porter.
3. SAMUEL, bapt. Mar. 8, 1815.
By second wife:
4. AMOS, bapt. June 22, 1823 (born Sept. 10, 1822).
5. CALVIN, baptized Mar. 26, 1827 (born Mar. 11, 1825).

viii. BETSEY, born ____, married Daniel Smith.
ix. APPHIA, bapt. Aug. 23, 1799, died 1781.
x. EUNICE.
xi. JAMES, born ____, married Apr. 7, 1820, Rosannah F. Stuart, daughter of Wentworth and Hannah (Shaw) Stuart, her cousin.

Joshua Moody of Scarboro was the original grantee of right No. 118 in Pearsontown. On July 18, 1753, he sold all his title and interest in this right to Moses Pearson of Falmouth (7/57). As far as known he never lived in the town.

Another Joshua Moody, whose name is found on the 1789 and 1790 tax lists of Standish and in the 1790 census with a family of 1-1-1, was the son of Joshua[4] (Samuel,[3] Joshua,[2] William[1]) Moody and a brother of James Moody who settled in Standish. He is described in deeds as a cordwainer or shoemaker. His name is found on the poll tax list of Falmouth in 1766. He married (int. Dec. 13, 1769, in Gorham) Mary Carsley of Gorham, perhaps a sister of John and Ebenezer Carsley of that town. He probably moved to Gorham about the time of his marriage, for his name is found on the 1773 tax list of that town. He is given as living in Gorham on Oct. 20, 1773, when he sold the 30-acre lot #127 in Pearsontown to Stephen Sanborn (11/10). He enlisted in the Revolutionary army at Gorham.

His first wife evidently died fairly young, for on June 22, 1783, he married Zube Nicholson or Nickerson, both being indicated in the intentions of marriage filed in Gorham as residents of Pearsontown. He was living in Standish on May 24, 1786, when he and William Moody of Falmouth sold land in Falmouth to Hatevil Hall (15/176). His second wife apparently having died, he married third, ceremony performed by John Dean Esq. of Standish on Nov. 25, 1788, Rebecca Phinney, born Aug. 18, 1757, daughter of John and Rebecca (Sawyer) Phinney of Gorham. On Mar. 24, 1791, he and his brother James, both of Standish, sold to Samuel Mountfort of Falmouth land in Falmouth on the Presumpscot River laid out to their late father. He was still living in Standish on Mar. 13, 1793, when he sold to Nathaniel Whitney of Standish the 30-acre lot #17 here (28/112) and bought from Jonathan Elwell of Gorham and Abel Whitney of Standish land in Gorham on Apr. 5, 1793 (33/46). He probably moved back to Gorham about this time as he is given as living there in a deed dated Sept. 15, 1795, (38/238) and his name does not appear on the 1795 tax list of Standish. He later evidently moved to Baldwin since his name is found on a list of voters of that town for 1822. Revolutionary pension rolls indicate that he died in Baldwin on Dec. 28, 1828, age 82, which would make the date of his birth about 1746. His widow, Rebecca, is listed in the 1840 pension list, age 83, as living in Sebago.

Only known child of Joshua Moody was a son Daniel, born in 1773 and so a child of his first wife and probably the child indicated in the 1790 census. It seems likely that the John and Ebenezer Moody also found on the 1822 voter's list of Baldwin were his sons and, if so, must have been children of his third wife. An Ebenezer Moody married (int. Mar. 1, 1823) Abigail Haskell of Standish.

MOOR OR MOORE

While he never lived in Pearsontown, Hugh Moor resided in that section of Buxton (Cabbageyard area) which was annexed to Standish in 1824 and attended the Pearsontown Church in its early days. He is listed in the 1790 census of Buxton with a family of 4-2-6. In a tax list of that town taken about 1798, he is given as owning and living on lot H-4 in the third division of lots. At the time of the 1800 census his family consisted of him and his wife, both over 45 years old; one male under 10; one male and two females between 10 and 16; and two males and one female between 16 and 26. He was one of the prime movers in the organization of the Methodist Church in Buxton in 1798, the first meetings of which were held in his house, from which he had removed the partitions in order to provide open space for accommodation of the congregation.

Hugh Moor was born in Londonderry, N.H., in 1742, son of James and Elizabeth (Gregg) Moor, Scotch-Irish immigrants from Northern Ireland, where his father was born in 1706. James Moor died in Londonderry, N.H., on Sept. 30, 1755. Hugh Moore married Margaret Nesmith, born in Londonderry, N.H., Feb. 7, 1747/8 daughter of James and Mary (Dinsmoor) Nesmith, who also were immigrants from Northern Ireland. It is said that when Hugh Moore and his wife left Londonderry, N.H., it was his intention to to settle at Falmouth (now Portland), but arriving at that place the day after it was burned by the British (Oct. 20, 1775), he proposed to his wife that they proceed to Buxton (now Standish), where good land might be bought very cheap. Their guide for a part of the way was "blazed" trees. Their worldly possessions were carried on the backs of the horses they rode. His first habitation was a log house a short distance in back of the old house. A large granite post with the initials H M and the date 1775 carved in it, which at one time marked one corner of Hugh Moor's lot, has for some years had a prominent place in the front yard of one of his descendants for use as a hitching post. At any rate it is certain that he was there by 1776 because he had a daughter baptized in the Pearsontown Church on June 16 of that year. In 1780 he enlisted in the New Hampshire forces of the Continental army for a period of three years, being credited to the town of Windham, N.H., but little has been found as to details of his actual service. He died in Buxton on Mar. 2, 1814, age 72 years, and his widow survived him until July 25, 1823, when she passed away at the age of 75 years in Buxton. Both were buried in a family graveyard on their farm. Children of Hugh and Margaret (Nesmith) Moor were as follows:

i. ELIZABETH, born Aug. 6, 1769, Londonderry, N.H., married Jan. 22, 1789, Ebenezer Ayer, born in Buxton in Apr. 1776 son of Peter and Rebecca (Wheeler) Ayer. They lived in Buxton, now Standish, on lot #H-3 in the third division, which adjoined the property of her father, Hugh Moor. He died Feb. 18, 1812, age 45 yrs. and 10 mos. She married seond Mar. 14, 1820, True Woodman of Minot and died there Jan. 12, 1854.

ii. MARY, born Aug. 9, 1774, Londonderry, N.H., married Dec. 6, 1792, Daniel Boynton, born Mar. 12, 1771, son of William and Mary (McLucas) Boynton of Buxton. About 1808 they moved to Monmouth, Maine. He was a stone mason and died there July 21, 1823.

iii. MARGARET (PEGGY), born May 13, 1776, Buxton, bapt. in Pearsontown Church on June 16, 1776, married Sept. 18, 1793, Coleman Phinney of Gorham. He died in Portland on Aug. 25, 1856.

iv. JENNET (JANET OR JANE), born Jan. 25, 1779, Buxton, bapt. Mar. 14, 1779, in Pearsontown Church, married Mar. 26, 1801, Dr. James Cochrane, born in Windham, N.H., Oct. 23, 1777. He was a physician in Limington, Monmouth, and Rockland, Maine, where he died in Oct. 1860. She died in Mar. 1865.

v. SARAH, born Apr. 28, 1781, Buxton, married Mar. 26, 1801, the Rev. Asa Heath, born July 31, 1776, son of Bartholomew and Ann (Millard) Heath of Hillsdale Columbia County, N.Y. He was a Methodist minister and served in many towns throughout Maine including Monmouth. They both died in Standish, he on Sept. 1, 1860, age 84 yrs., 1 mo., and she on Apr. 1, 1862 (Mar. 31, 1862, age 80 yrs., 11 mos., according to gravestone). They are buried in the Moore family graveyard in Standish and were the parents of seven children.

vi. JONATHAN S., born Jan. 17, 1783, Buxton, married first on Apr. 18, 1804, Hannah Richardson, born Aug. 4, 1779, daughter of David and Hannah (Mills) Richardson of Standish and Monmouth, Maine. She died June 10, 1809, age 29, and was interred in the Moore family graveyard. He married second on Dec. 12, 1809, Sally Rich, born Apr. 19, 1788, daughter of Amos and Eunice (Woodman) Rich of Gorham, who died Sept. 16, 1858. He died Dec. 19, 1844, age 62, in Standish (*Christian Mirror*, Jan. 9, 1845).

Children by first marriage were:
1. JONATHAN JR., born Nov. 3, 1805, married (pub. June 4, 1838) Elmyra or Almira Kimball, born 1805 daughter of Daniel and Polly (Briant) Kimball of Buxton. She died Jan. 31, 1839, age 33 yrs., and was buried in the Moore family graveyard. He married second Sarah Dennett, born July 3, 1804, who died Jan. 4, 1869.
2. HANNAH RICHARDSON, born Dec. 5, 1807, married Dec. 26, 1825, Asa Berry of Standish. He was born 1803, died in 1889, and she died Mar. 1, 1898, in Standish, having outlived all her brothers and sisters. Both are buried in the Moore family graveyard.

By second marriage:
3. LOUISA RICH, born Mar. 31, 1811, married Nov. 21, 1830, Joslyn C. Robinson, born in 1806, probably at Chatham, N.H., son of Capt. Increase and Mary (Cox) Robinson. They lived in Standish where he died Sept. 13, 1885, and she on Apr. 2, 1881, age 70, Standish. A son Roscoe C. or G. Robinson, died Nov. 15, 1851, age 19 yrs., 10 mos., and was buried in the Moore family graveyard.
4. BETSEY AYER, born Oct. 12, 1812, married June 27, 1837, in Standish Nathaniel Gorham Sturgis. He was born June 27, 1811, died Feb. 1, 1880, in Auburn and she died there May 6, 1893.
5. LORENZO HUGH, born June 8, 1814, married Sept. 16, 1845, Sarah Cressey, born Apr. 18, 1820, daughter Noah and Hannah (Watts) Cressey of Gorham and Standish. Noah Cressey died Apr. 20, 1839, age 40 yrs., 10 mos., and was buried in the Moore family graveyard.
6. AMOS RICH, born May 22, 1816, married Elizabeth Hamlen, born Mar. 24, 1816. They lived in Standish on the Moore homestead. He died May 12, 1884, age 67 yrs., 1 mo., 20 days, in Standish, and she on May 1, 1904, age 88 yrs., 1 mo., 7 days. They were buried in the Moore family graveyard.
7. SALLY SOPHRONIA, born Mar. 9, 1818.

8. RUFUS WOODMAN, born Feb. 24, 1821, died Mar. 18, 1832, age 2 yrs., and was buried in Moore family graveyard.
9. MARY ANN, born Feb. 26, 1823, died unmarried on June 9, 1861, buried in Moore family graveyard.
10. SAMUEL CUSHMAN, born Apr. 16, 1826.

vii. HANNAH, bapt. in Pearsontown Church on Nov. 13, 1785, nothing further known.

MORTON

There were a number of families bearing the name of Morton living in Standish between 1750 and 1800. They were all descendants of Bryant and Thankful (Parker) Bryant of Yarmouth, Mass., who settled in Cape Elizabeth and Gorham. Thomas Morton, the first by that name in town was born about 1730 in Cape Elizabeth, a son of the above-mentioned couple. He probably moved to Gorham with his father about 1750 and married (int. May 9, 1751 in Gorham) Rachel Elwell of Cape Elizabeth, sister of Jonathan Elwell who settled in Gorham.

Thomas Morton must have served at the siege of Louisburg for he was the original grantee of right No. 58 in Pearsontown and was an early inhabitant of the town. The title of this right must have been lost by non-payment of taxes, for on Mar. 27, 1758, Thomas Morton, laborer, of Pearsontown bid in at a vendue held in Falmouth the right No. 58 in Pearsontown, which was confirmed to him by the Proprietors on Jan. 10, 1759 (2/329). He, being a yeoman of Pearsontown, sold all of this right except the 30-acre lot to Stephen Woodman of Falmouth on Apr. 2, 1762 (2/330). He also acquired the 30-acre lots Nos. 42 and 43, the first of which he sold to Ebenezer Shaw and the second to Josiah Shaw on Apr. 4, 1763 (2/331& 2/332). His residence is given as Pearsontown at the time of passing of these deeds, but he must have moved soon thereafter to Gorham since he was living in that town on Apr. 18, 1763, when he bought land there from Stephen Longfellow of Falmouth (2/299). It is evident that Thomas Morton lived in Pearsontown from 1757 or earlier until 1763. He was a member of the guard at the fort here prior to 1760 and his name is found among the men from the town who worked on Gorham roads in 1759 and 1760.

He was probably the Thomas Morton of Gorham who served in Capt. Samuel Whitmore's company in 1777 during the Revolutionary War. Dr. Meserve states that he died during his service in the army, but we have found nothing to corroborate this. Date of his death and that of his wife has not been discovered. Children of Thomas and Rachel (Elwell) Morton were as follows:

i. JAMES, born in June 1753, married Susan Dyer of Cape Elizabeth on July 12, 1777. He lived in the north part of Gorham and was a mason. He also served in the Revolutionary War. His wife died Oct. 8, 1816, age 62, and he on Apr. 10, 1840, age 87. They were the parents of eleven children.

ii. ELISHA, born in 1756, is said to have lived in Unity or Thorndike, Maine.

iii. **EBENEZER**, born 1758 and served in the Revolutionary army. On Dec. 7, 1780, he married Susanna Irish, born Oct. 22, 1760, daughter of Thomas and Deliverance (Skillings) Irish of Gorham. They lived in Gorham, where at the time of the 1790 census he is credited with a family of 1-2-5. Sometime after 1796 he moved to Standish where he was living in 1800 with a family consisting of him and his wife, two boys and two girls under 10 yrs. of age, two boys and two girls between 10 and 16 yrs. old, and two girls between 16 and 26 yrs. of age.

He is given as living in Standish on June 21, 1798, when he bought from Benjamin Titcomb of Portland the southerly half of the 100-acre lot #40 in second division located on Standish Neck (49/441). On Sept. 1 of the same year he sold Caleb Shaw of Gorham land in Gorham adjoining the Standish line (34/531). Thereafter he lived in Standish where he died sometime prior to May 20, 1826, when some of his children quitclaimed their rights in his estate to their brother James Morton (171/229). Children of Ebenezer and Susannah (Irish) Morton were as far as has been determined as follows:

1. **THOMAS**, born about about 1786, living in 1850, age 64, in Naples, married (int. Mar. 2. 1811) Lucy Cummings, both of Standish. He married second Nov. 16, 1833, in Otisfield, Mrs. Betsey Paul of Otisfield, who died Apr. 16, 1874, age 81 yrs., Naples.
2. **CALEB**, named in 1826 deed, married Oct. 21, 1819, Sarah Gray of Standish.
3. **JACOB**, born about 1796, named in 1826 deed, died in Standish Nov. 27, 1854, married at Raymond June 4, 1820, Mary Libby, born about 1799. He served in War of 1812.
4. **JAMES**, lived in Standish on his father's farm, born about 1788. He married Molly Shaw, daughter of Joseph and Eunice (Bean). He was living in 1855, age 66 yrs., in Standish.
5. **THANKFUL**, married Daniel Bolton of Windham, named in 1826 deed.
6. **RACHEL**, married July 1, 1804, Ephraim Hicks of Gorham and had six children. She married second Edward Harmon of Gray.
7. **DELILAH OR DELIVERANCE**, married June 20, 1806, Enoch Shaw of Standish, born Oct. 11, 1780, son of Joseph and Eunice (Bean) Shaw. They lived on Standish Neck and on Raymond Cape. Five children. He died Apr. 22, 1860.
8. **RUHAMAH**, born about 1783, married Apr. 20, 1802, Wyer Green and lived on Standish Neck. He died Oct. 12, 1785, and she was living in 1855, age 72 yrs., in Standish.
9. **ANNA**, born 1791, married Ebenezer Shaw, born Feb. 12, 1784, son of Joseph and Eunice (Bean) Shaw. She died Jan. 12, 1863, age 71 yrs., 5 mos., 23 days. They lived on Standish Neck and Chatham, N.H.
10. **BETSEY**, a single woman at time of 1826 deed, married _____ Burnham.

iv. DAVID, born June 22, 1761, married about 1783 Mary Sanger of Watertown, Mass. He died Jan. or June 22, 1827, on his 66th birthday and his wife on Jan. 20, 1841, age 74. They lived in Gorham and were the parents of twelve children, several of whom settled in Standish. He served in the Revolutionary War.
v. THANKFUL, born ____, married on Jan. 23, 1783, Enos Newcomb, Feb. 9. 1759, son of Samuel Newcomb of Cape Cod and Gorham. She died Apr. 29, 1796, after the birth of six children and he married second on Jan. 16, 1797, Mrs. Abigail (Myrick) Libby, by whom he had five more children. He died Apr. 10, 1843.
vi. THOMAS, born in 1765, married Aug. 23, 1787, Betty Frost, born Aug. 31, 1767, daughter of Benjamin and Susanna (Frost) Frost of Falmouth and Gorham. They lived in Gorham and Standish. He married second June 17, 1835, Lydia Cotton of Standish and died June 19, 1846, age 81.
vii. RACHEL, born ____, married Dec. 11, 1783, Jonathan K. Lowell of Standish, Baldwin, and Hiram. He was born in 1756 son of Moses and Miriam (Knowlton) Lowell of Pearsontown. They were the parents of ten children. He died in 1852.
viii. REUBEN, born married on Jan. 27, 1793, Mary (or Mercy) Dyer of Cape Elizabeth. He was a merchant in Portland in 1797.
ix. ABIGAIL, born ____, married Ephraim Riley of Baldwin on Nov. 6, 1791.

The name of Elisha Morton is found on the 1796 tax list of Standish. He was probably the Elisha Morton of Standish who on Feb. 18, 1796, married Bathshuah Lombard of Gorham. He was born Jan. 25, 1770, son of Ebenezer and Sarah (Whitney) Morton of Gorham and thence a cousin to Ebenezer Morton above. He about 1800 moved to Jackson, Maine, with his father and brother Ebenezer and were among the first settlers there. Both his father and brother were killed in 1809 by the falling of a tree on them. Elisha moved to Thorndike in 1810 and there his children are recorded in that town's records. Three years before his death, he removed to Plymouth, Maine, where he died on Apr. 1, 1834.

MOSES

The names of Daniel and Josiah Moses are found on the 1789 tax list of Standish and that of Josiah only on the lists for 1790, 1795, and 1796, and in the 1790 census with a family of 1-2-3. They were both living in Pearsontown on Oct. 9, 1786, when they bought from James Lunt of Falmouth the 100-acre lot #47 in the second division of lots, located on Standish Neck and on which they were then living. However, by the time of the 1790 census, Daniel Moses had left Standish and is recorded as living in the section listed as Gorham and Scarboro with a family of 1-0-5.

These two men were brothers and son of George and Frances (___) Moses of Scarboro. Daniel Moses served as a sergeant in the Revolutionary War, and on Jan. 23, 1777, married Lydia Coolbroth. They lived in Scarboro, Standish, and Windham, Maine.

Josiah Moses was baptized in Scarboro (Dunstan Church records) on June 27, 1756. He served in the Revolutionary War and on July 1, 1779, married first Sarah Ringe. After her death he married second on Oct. 4, 1787, Elizabeth (Harmon) Libby, born in 1759, widow of Daniel Libby of Scarboro, captain of a vessel which was lost with all aboard. She died in Dec. 18, 1834, age 76 (*Morning Star*, issue of Dec. 31, 1834). He married third on Sept. Sept. 12, 1837, Martha Atwick of Westbrook, age 77 in 1853, who survived him. He died in Standish May 19, 1839, age 83 yrs. Children of Josiah and Elizabeth (Harmon) (Libby) Moses were as follows:

i. SARAH, born July 11, 1788, bapt. Sept. 13, 1788, married as his second wife William Cummings of Standish and Cape Elizabeth. She died Apr. 4, 1858, in Cape Elizabeth. For children see Cummings family.
ii. DANIEL, born about 1793, died in Aug. 1828 following an explosion of the powder mill at Gambo Falls that year.
iii. JOSIAH JR. born in Aug. 1799, married (int. May 11, 1822) Lydia Parker. He died Feb. 22, 1860, age 60 yrs., 6 mos., and she on June 30, 1879, age 81 yrs., 8 mos. They are buried in a cemetery at North Gorham.
iv. WILLIAM, born about 1802 (in 1820 age 18 yrs., by father's pension record), died July 19, 1828, killed by same explosion which caused the death of his brother Daniel.
v. MEHITABLE, born about 1799 (in 1820 age 21) married May 22, 1823 (int. Mar. 14. 1823), Joseph Libby, born in 1795. She died May 9, 1861.

Children of Elizabeth (Harmon) (Libby) Moses by her first marriage, who probably were brought up in Standish, were: (Libby)
i. ANNA, born Jan. 7, 1779, married Mar. 27, 1800, William Cummings of Standish and Cape Elizabeth. She died Sept. 10, 1811, and he married second Sarah Moses, her half sister.
ii. WILLIAM, bapt. May 1781.
iii. JONATHAN, bapt. July 1782. With his brother William he followed the sea and both died in early manhood unmarried.

MOULTON

The names of Peter and Simon Moulton are found on the 1789, 1790, 1795, and 1796 tax lists of Standish, while that of Peter Moulton is found in the 1790 census with a family of 3-2-3. Simon was a son of Peter.

Peter[5] Moulton (Worthington,[4] Josiah,[3] Henry,[2] John[1]) was born in Hampton, N.H., in 1742, son of Worthington and Abigail (Garlard) Moulton. He was a cooper, and on July 7, 1762, married Joanna Shaw, born, Apr. 4, 1743, daughter of Ebenezer and Anna (Philbrick) Shaw of Hampton,

N.H., and Standish, Maine. He probably was induced to settle in Pearsontown about 1766 by his father-in-law who had preceded him to the town. On Aug. 23, 1771, Moses Pearson deeded to him the 30-acre lot #103 in consideration of his having complied with the terms of settlement (7/158). It was here that he settled and raised his family. His father, Worthington Moulton, came to Pearsontown with him and died here. He saw service in the Revolutionary War, and died in Standish on June 3, 1812, age 70 yrs., and his wife passed away on Jan. 16, 1834, at the age of 91, also in Standish. Her obituary is given in the Feb. 13, 1834, issue of the *Christian Mirror* states that she had 12 children, 8 then living, 76 grandchildren (62 living, and 123 great-grandchildren, of which 111 were living). Peter and Joanna (Shaw) Moulton were the parents of the following children, the first three born in Hampton, N.H., and the rest in Pearsontown:

i. ABIGAIL, born Jan. 20, 1763, married (int. Aug. 17, 1782 in Gorham) William Harmon of Pearsontown, born in Scarboro in 1758 son of John and Abigail (Tibbetts) Harmon. They lived in Standish and Bethel, Maine, where she died July 19, 1831. For children see Harmon family.

ii. ANNA, born Mar. 16, 1764, married (int. Sept. 27, 1785, in Gorham) Josiah Harmon of Pearsontown, born in Scarboro Nov. 5, 1759, son of John and Abigail (Tibbetts) Harmon. They lived in Standish and in Thorndike, Maine, where she died Dec. 18, 1836. For children see Harmon family.

iii. SIMON, born Apr. 15, 1766, in Hampton, N.H. was just a baby when his parents moved to Pearsontown. He married first on Nov. 3, 1791, Abigail Plaisted, born Nov. 4, 1768, daughter of Samuel and Elizabeth (Libby) Plaisted of Scarboro, who died June 14, 1844; and second Elizabeth Walker. They lived in Standish, where he died Feb. 13, 1854. Children, all born in Standish, were:

1. JOHN, born Apr. 29, 1792, died Sept. 13, 1821, unmarried, in Standish.
2. ELIZABETH, born Oct. 7, 1794, married as his second wife on Nov. 4, 1819, William E. Files, born Apr. 3, 1781, son of Ebenezer and Molly (Elder) Files of West Gorham. He died Dec. 24, 1843, and she on Feb. 24, 1857, age 62. Six children.
3. MARY, born Nov. 19, 1796, married Hiram Hasty, born Sept. 11, 1789, son of Daniel and Martha (McLaughlin) Hasty of Standish. He died in 1866 and she on July 2, 1872. For children see Hasty family.
4. SIMON, born Apr. 22, 1799, died in Brewer, Maine, unmarried on Feb. 13, 1854.
5. HANNAH, born Apr. 27, 1801, married Sept. 22, 1823, Gardner Libby of Standish. Nine children.
6. EBENEZER, born June 21, 1803, married Elizabeth D. Blake, born Apr. 27, 1809, daughter of Benjamin and Betsey (Moody) Blake of Limington on Feb. 17, 1831. They lived near Sebago Lake. He died Sept. 27, 1885. They had five children:
   (1) ELIZABETH, born Jan. 27, 1832.
   (2) JOHN PLAISTED, born Dec. 11, 1833.
   (3) SIMON MOODY, born Apr. 27, 1837.

(4) LYDIA P., born Sept. 24, 1847.
(5) LEWIS WILLARD, born Feb. 28, 1852.
7. JOSIAH, born June 8, 1805, married Martha Hasty, born May 25, 1809, daughter of Daniel Jr. and Susannah (Dow) Hasty of Standish. He died Sept. 25, 1894. They had four children:
(1) AMANDA, born Apr. 16, 1836.
(2) GILBERT, born May 29, 1838.
(3) LEANDER HUSSEY, born Aug. 22, 1840.
8. PETER, born May 7, 1807, died young.
9. ABIGAIL, born Nov. 18, 1811, married Apr. 15, 1845, her cousin Ebenezer Moulton of Gorham, son of Daniel and Anna (Shaw) Moulton. She was living in 1860 in Harrison.

iv. LYDIA, born Dec. 27, 1767, in Pearsontown, married Nov. 9, 1786, John Plaisted, born in Scarboro July 1, 1759, son of Samuel and Elizabeth (Libby) Plaisted. They lived in Standish where he died on Jan. 16, 1834, and she on Feb. 13, 1854. No children.

v. JONATHAN, born Jan. 2, 1770, bapt. Mar. 18, 1770; was a tanner and lived in Standish. He married first Aug. 5, 1793, Agnes Foss of Pepperellborough (Saco); second May 27, 1832, Ann Blake. He died in Standish Nov. 4, 1836. His first wife died here on Dec. 22, 1831, age 57 yrs. He was the father of the following family:
By first wife.
1. BENJAMIN, born Dec. 1, 1793, married Sept. 6, 1818, Hannah Harding, Mar. 23, 1798, daughter of Elkanah and Martha (Knight) Harding of Gorham. He died May 25, 1845, in Thorndike, Maine. Five children.
2. LYDIA, born Jan. 6, 1796, married Calvin Stevens on Oct. 7, 1818.
3. AGNES, born Feb. 28, 1798, married Feb. 25, 1818, William Harding, born Jan. 30, 1790, son of Elkanah and Martha (Knight) Harding of Gorham. They lived in Standish and Gorham, where he died Apr. 13, 1844, age 54 yrs. His widow married in 1846 as his second wife Joseph McDonald, born in 1788 son of Joseph and Sarah (Fowel) McDonald of Gorham. He died Nov. 4, 1854. She died Sept. 25, 1870, and was the mother of nine children by her first husband.
4. HORACE, born Apr. 14, 1800, married Mary Stuart and settled in Gorham, Maine.
5. EBENEZER, born Oct. 10, 1802, married in Dec. 12, 1822, Martha Philbrick of Standish. They lived in Wilmington, Ill. Five children.
6. THEODORE, born Oct. 20, 1806, lived in Freedom, Maine, and was twice married. He died Jan. 12, 1879, age 72 yrs., in Freedom, Maine.
By second wife:
7. LEVI, born July 31, 1831, married Mary Ann Corner and died Mar. 1, 1886. No children.

vi. EBENEZER, bapt. May 10, 1772, died young.
vii. EBENEZER, born Mar. 23, 1773, married on Oct. 25, 1795, Mary (Polly) Plaisted, daughter of Samuel and Elizabeth (Libby) Plaisted of Scarboro. They lived in Waterford, Maine, where three

children were born to them. He died Aug. 1, 1802, and she married second Josiah Willard of Waterford.
viii. JOSIAH, born May 28, 1775, bapt. July 9, 1775, married first Mary Lane of Standish on Mar. 23, 1797, who died on June 23, 1808, age 37 yrs., in Standish. He married second on June 19, 1809, Nancy Dearborn, daughter of Jacob Dearborn of Buxton. They moved to Thorndike, Maine, and settled there in 1811. He died there on Jan. 5, 1862. Nine children.
ix. SARAH, born May 25, 1777, bapt. July 20, 1777, married Sept. 14, 1797, Ephraim Rowe 3rd, born in Pearsontown in 1775 son of Ephraim and Mary (Philbrick) Rowe. They moved to Belfast, Maine, where she died Dec. 22, 1849, age 72, and he on Oct. 26, 1856, age 81 yrs., 5 mos.
x. PETER, bapt. Aug. 1, 1779, died young in 1781.
xi. DANIEL, born Apr. 1, 1781, bapt. Nov. 13, 1785, married on July 17, 1808, Anna Shaw, born June 6, 1788, daughter of Sargent and Ann (Thompson) Shaw of Standish. They lived in the northerly part of Gorham where she died Jan. 8, 1861, age 73. He died June 30, 1855, aged 73 yrs., 11 mos. They were the parents of nine children, as follows:
   1. JONATHAN, born Dec. 7, 1808, married Lucy A. Hanson (int. Oct. 21, 1849) and died Oct. 8, 1852, age 44 years.
   2. EBENEZER, born Nov. 5, 1810, married Abigail Moulton, his cousin, born Nov. 11, 1811, daughter of Simon and Abigail (Plaisted) Moulton of Standish. They lived in Harrison and were the parents of one child. He died Nov. 8, 1887, and she on Sept. 22, 1894.
   3. FANNY H., born May 8, 1815, died unmarried in Gorham Apr. 3, 1857, age 41 yrs., 11 mos.
   4. SARAH, born Aug. 26, 1817, married George Gould.
   5. MARY, born Aug. 26, 1817, twin to Sarah.
   6. DANIEL, born Feb. 2, 1820, died Feb. 28, 1820, age 26 days.
   7. DANIEL, born Feb. 4, 1822, married Mary A. Shaw.
   8. ABIGAIL, born Apr. 2, 1824, married Albion Rounds.
   9. HANNAH, born June 15, 1826, married Samuel M. Rand in 1850.
xii. JOANNA, born Oct. 20, 1783, bapt. Nov. 13, 1785, married Feb. 25, 1802, Tristram Coffin of Gorham. They lived in Thorndike, Maine, and were the parents of thirteen children. She died Apr. 13, 1849.

MURCH

The name of Stephen Murch is found on the 1808 tax list of Standish. He was probably the Stephen Murch, born in Buxton Apr. 12, 1770, son of Daniel and Mary (Simpson) Murch of that town, who married Sept. 19, 1793, Miriam Watson, born Dec. 24, 1776, daughter of John and Tabitha (Whitney) Watson of Gorham. He lived for some time at Gorham Village. His wife died in 1795, age 19, after the birth of a daughter Betsey in 1794. He died Aug. 25, 1867.

MUSSEY

Although Benjamin Mussey did not take up permanent residence in Pearsontown until Revolutionary War times, he was active in its affairs from very early in its history. Although not one of the original grantees of land in the township, he early purchased several rights and became one of the active proprietors. In 1758 he purchased right No. 116 from the Proprietors, the 30-acre lot of which became the site of his farm. According to the records he was moderator of a meeting held in the town in 1761 and his name appears in connection with nearly every subsequent meeting of the Proprietors for many years.

There is some question as to his ancestry, but one account states he was born May 22, 1722, in Kingston, N.H., son of John[3] (John,[2] John[1]) and Hannah (Dymond) Mussey who had moved from Salisbury, Mass., to Kingston, N.H., prior to 1720. He learned the hatter's trade and settled in Falmouth, now Portland, when a young man. In 1747 he married Abigail Weeks, born Mar. 31, 1730, daughter of William and Sarah (Tukey) Weeks of Falmouth. They lived on Middle Street, near Temple, until the burning of the town by the British in 1775, when he retired to his farm in Pearsontown where he spent the remainder of his days. He died here on Sept. 13, 1787, while his widow survived him until June 4, 1815. Benjamin and Abigail (Weeks) Mussey were the parents of ten children, all born in Falmouth:

i. SARAH, born Mar. 29, 1749, married Dec. 11, 1786, Deacon Jonathan Philbrick of Standish as his second wife. For children see Philbrick family.

ii. JOHN, born Feb. 15, 1751, married Nov. 14, 1789, Mary (Smith) Merrill, widow of Levi Merrill. She was born about 1757 and died Aug. 6, 1796, age 39. He died Aug. 7, 1823, age 49 yrs., in Standish. They lived in Portland and were the parents of seven children.

iii. ESTHER, born Mar. 29, 1753, died unmarried in Standish on May 18, 1845, age 92 yrs.

iv. DANIEL, born July 8, 1755, married Dec. 7, 1775, Mary Gilkey of Gorham. They lived in Portland where he died Aug. 31, 1828. They had a son, William Mussey, born in Falmouth (Portland) about 1782 (age 67 in 1850 census) who was brought up by his uncle and aunts in Standish. He married May 19, 1813, after a comfortable courtship of twelve years, Thankful Butterfield, born in Pearsontown July 1, 1783, daughter of Joseph and Mary (Harding) Butterfield. He lived in Standish after his marriage and settled on his grandfather's farm. His wife died in Standish Mar. 30, 1851, age 67 yrs., 9 mos., and he died here on Oct. 7, 1863, age 81 yrs., 2 mos. They had children: William Jr. who married (int. Nov. 11, 1832) Eunice Whitmore, both of Standish; Nancy, who died May 28, 1861, age 47 yrs.; Edmund; Mary; and a child who died young.

v. THEODORE, born Aug. 5, 1757, in Falmouth (Portland), moved to Pearsontown with his father following the burning of Falmouth in the Revolutionary War. He was active in the affairs of the town, being the first town clerk, an office which he held for various periods for a total of 16 years. He also served one or more terms as selectman, was town treasurer for two or more terms, served as a member of the Constitutional Convention of Maine in 1819, was the first representative of the town to serve in the state legislature, and also served for many years as justice of the peace.

On July 7, 1791, he married Dolly Sanborn, born in Hampton, N.H., May 30, 1757, daughter of Daniel and Jane (Moulton) Sanborn of Standish. He died in Conway, N.H., Sept. 5, 1825, age 68 yrs., and his widow died at North Bridgton Feb. 5, 1849, age 91 yrs., 3 mos. They were the parents of the following family:

1. MARY, born July 26, 1792, married (int. Sept. 22, 1815) Oct. 16, 1815, Andrew Bradbury. He died Feb. 24, 1827, age 42, and she on Sept. 26, 1867, age 75. They had three children.
2. NANCY, born May 4, 1797, married Sept. 16, 1817, Samuel Farnsworth Jr., son of Dr. Samuel and Betsy (Fitch) Farnsworth from Groton, Mass. They lived in Bridgton and were the parents of six children. He died Apr. 13, 1842, and his widow in Dec. 1882.

vi. BENJAMIN JR., born June 8, 1760, was lost at sea in September gale in 1779.
vii. EDMUND, born July 28, 1763, died unmarried in Standish on July 18, 1816, age 53 yrs., very suddenly. He was a father of a son, Edmund, by Olive, daughter of Michael Philbrick, born in June 1787, who lived in Unity, Maine, where he died in 1852, age 65.
viii. JOSEPH, born Nov. 26, 1765, married (int. Mar. 6, 1819) Mar. 31, 1819, Esther Morton. They lived in Portland where he died Aug. 16, 1842, and his widow, Esther, died May 20, 1855, age 66.
ix. ABIGAIL, born Dec. 4, 1768, married Aug. 6, 1789, Daniel How of Standish and Portland. They lived in Portland where he died Sept. 16, 1819, and she on Sept. 6, 1837. They were the parents of five children, for list of whom see How family.
x. MARY, born Apr. 21, 1775, bapt. Apr. 23, 1775, died unmarried in Standish Feb. 22, 1824, age 49 yrs., in Standish.

NEWCOMB

The name of Solomon Newcomb is found in the 1800 census of Standish with a family consisting of him and his wife, both between 26 and 45 years of age, and one male child under 10 years old. It is likely that he did not live long in town. He probably was the Solomon[7] (Solomon,[6] Joshua,[5] Andrew,[4] Simeon,[3] Andrew,[2] Andrew[1]) Newcomb born about 1769 in Wellfleet, Mass., and died about 1813, who married first Jan. 10, 1790, at Buxton, Hannah Jackson, both residents of Buxton; second Feb. 26, 1798, Sarah, daughter of Isaac and Mary (Crockett) Whitney, who died about 1810; third on Dec. 11, 1811, Abigail, daughter of Ephraim and Eleanor Nason. She married second on June 22, 1815, John Crockett, born Jan. 25, 1789, son of Peter and Polly (Warren) Crockett.

Solomon Newcomb made a carding machine from seeing one when it was first introduced and had a carding mill in the northern part of Gorham on what is known as the West Branch on land owned by Benjamin Irish. Here the neighboring farmers brought their wool to have it carded into rolls ready for spinning. This was kept in operation as long as he lived. Child by second wife, Sarah (Whitney) Newcomb, was:

i. ISAAC, born about 1810 in Gorham, died Feb. 5, 1858, married Dec. 14, 1834, at Gorham, Martha Paine, born Sept. 3, 1814, daughter of Richard and Eunice (Blake) Paine. No record of children.

NICHOLS

John Nichols was one of the men from Falmouth who moved to Pearsontown following Mowatt's bombardment and burning of Falmouth in Oct. 1775. He probably did not live very long in town, but certainly was an inhabitant on July 15, 1776, as his name is found in a list of those living in town on that date. His ancestry has not been discovered, but he married June 13, 1771, Lucy Milk, daughter of James Milk of Falmouth. He was a bricklayer and with Jonathan Bryant, also of Falmouth, bought from the Proprietors of Pearsontown on Aug. 12, 1771, all of right No. 43 except the 30-acre lot there (19/166). He sold his half of this land to Benjamin Titcomb of Falmouth on July 4, 1777 (9/522).

John Nichols was living in Portland with a family of 2-2-6 at the time of the 1790 census. John Nichols and Jonathan Bryant were the mason contractors who built Portland Head Light. Lucy (Milk) Nichols died in Jan. 1810, age 56 years, in Portland (*Eastern Argus*, Jan. 28, 1810).

John and Lucy (Milk) Nichols had the following children baptized in the First Parish Church of Falmouth (Portland):

i. SAMUEL, bapt. Mar. 22, 1772.
ii. POLLY, bapt. June 26, 1774.
iii. SALLY, bapt. Dec. 22, 1776.
iv. DORCAS, bapt. Nov. 11, 1781.
v. JOHN, bapt. Dec. 8, 1782, died in May 1819 in Portland.
vi. ABIGAIL INGRAHAM, bapt. Jan. 9, 1785.
vii. SAMUEL, bapt. July 22, 1787.

NOBLE

Christopher[3] Noble (Christopher,[2] Christopher[1]) was one of those early settlers in Pearsontown whose stay covered a period of only a few years. He was baptized in the South Church of Portsmouth, N.H., on Apr. 7, 1723, son of Christopher and Lydia (Jackson) Noble. He was of that place on Dec. 25, 1744, when he married (Rev. Samuel Parsons of Rye, N.H., officiating) Martha Rowe, also of Portsmouth. Facts as to her parentage have not been definitely established, but it is possible that she may have been a sister or otherwise related to Lazarus Rowe, an early settler of Baldwin.

Christopher Noble is said to have lived at various places during his early life, including York, Maine, and Dover, Allenstown, and Barrington, New Hampshire. He bought land at Allenstown on Aug. 18, 1750, and probably lived there until he moved to Barrington in 1763. He settled in Pearsontown about 1775, for the record of the baptism of a son Moses on Feb. 16, 1776, is found in the Standish Church records.

No record has been found of the purchase of land in Pearsontown by Christopher Noble. He is given as being of Pearsontown on May 7, 1783, when he sold to Charles Hall, his son-in-law, the 30-acre lot #124 on which he was then living. It was probably about this time that he took up residence in Flintstown on the 100-acre lot #5 in the second range west, it being bounded by the Saco River, Half Moon Pond, and the brook flowing from that pond into the Saco River. He mortaged portions of this lot to Lazarus, Noah, and Benjamin Rowe of Flintstown on May 29, 1794 (21/222 & 21/233). He was evidently unable to write, as his signature to these deeds was made with a mark.

Nothing has been found as to the dates of either Christopher Noble or his wife, Martha. A Christopher Noble of Flintstown sold to Josiah Milliken of Flintstown all his right, title, claim and interest in lot #5, second range west in Flintstown, excepting so much of said lot as he had sold to Lazarus and Benjamin Rowe, amounting to 70 acres, more or less, on June 28, 1798 (28/235). It is likely that it was Christopher Sr. rather than Christopher Jr. to whom reference is made in this deed. According to Standish records a Christopher Noble and Alice Lowell were married on Jan. 19, 1794. It is possible that this may refer to Christopher Noble Sr., which would have meant a second marriage for him. Christopher and Martha (Rowe) Noble were the parents of at least the following family:

i. MARTHA, bapt. at Dover, N.H., on May 22, 1746. She was probably the one who married June 6, 1765, in Scarboro James McKenney, born Mar. 11, 1742, in Scarboro son of John and Margaret (Wright) McKenney of Scarboro. They moved from Scarboro to Limington in 1791.

ii. CHRISTOPHER JR., said to be born at York, Maine, in 1760, bapt. in Pearsontown May 19, 1776. He came to Pearsontown with his parents about 1775 and moved with them to Flintstown about 1783. He, being of Flintstown, married in Dec. 1785 (John Dean, Esq. officiating) Joanna Rowe, born about 1762 daughter of Lazarus and Molly (Webber) Rowe of Flintstown. They lived in Baldwin (formerly Flintstown) where he was drowned in the Saco River on May 9, 1824. She died Nov. 20, 1859, age 96 yrs., 9 mos. They were parents of the following children:
   1. GEORGE, born in 1786, died in 1825, age 38. He married Sally Spencer, daughter of William and Elinor (Cooper) Spencer, who died in Oxford, Maine, Oct. 4. 1868, age 81. Both are buried in Baldwin.
   2. JAMES, lost at sea.

3. JOANNA, born about 1796, married Samuel Spencer of Gorham. She died in 1860, age 64, and he on Mar. 24, 1866, age 74. Both are buried in Baldwin.
4. MARTHA, born about 1792, married John Blanchard of Gorham, Maine.
5. MARY, born Feb. 21, 1794, married Jan. 26, 1818, Peter Cram of Baldwin and had nine children.
6. BELINDA, died young.
7. LYDIA, born about 1798, married Mar. 2, 1815, Charles Brown of Gorham.
8. ELEAZER, born in 1800, died Sept. 11, 1870, married Dec. 25, 1826, Rachel Burnell, daughter of Stephen and Polly (Sanborn) Burnell of Baldwin. She died Jan. 17, 1884, age 76.
9. MEHITABEL, born Dec. 14, 1804, a twin, married Elias Burnell of Baldwin.
10. FANNY, married Isaac Burnell of Baldwin.
11. ESTHER, a stepdaughter, married Joshua Larrabee and Luther Webber (Usher?).

iii. JOHN OR JONATHAN, (twin to Christopher) said to be born in York, Maine, in 1760, bapt. in Pearsontown May 19, 1776, married Dec. 26, 1791, Elizabeth Rowe, born in Portsmouth, N.H., Apr. 1, 1763, daughter of Lazarus and Molly (Webber) Rowe. Comparison of this birth date with data on death of Christopher Noble's wife indicates that they may have been twin sisters. John Noble was of Flintstown on Mar. 2, 1793, when he bought from Michael Philbrick of Flintstown the 100-acre lot #8 in the second range west there (20/300). He sold this land to Peter Kelly of Scarboro on July 6, 1798 (31/79), but was still living in Baldwin on Jan. 24, 1804, when he sold land there. On Feb. 24, 1813, John Noble and wife, Elizabeth, sold other land in Baldwin (66/566). They are said to have moved to Portland.

iv. MOSES, bapt. at Pearsontown Feb. 16, 1776.

v. LYDIA, bapt. at Pearsontown May 19, 1776, married (int. July 28, 1781, in Gorham) Charles Hall of Pearsontown. For particulars of family see Hall family.

ORDWAY

Jonathan Burbank Ordway was living in Pearsontown on Apr. 23, 1785, when his intentions of marriage to Mehitable Rackleff, born June 23, 1765, daughter of Benjamin and Sarah (Jordan) Rackleff, were filed in Gorham. At the time of the 1790 census he was living in Stark's Location, N.H., which was annexed to Conway, N.H., in 1796. However, his name is found on a school district list of Limington, Maine, in 1792, the name being spelled 'Ordway'. He bought land in Unity, Maine, as early as 1789, but it was not until 1798 that he moved his family there. He was born June 20, 1762, in Goffstown, N.H., son of Joseph and Mehitable (_____) Ordway. At the time of the 1800 census he was living in Unity with a family consisting of him and his wife, three sons under 10 years of age, and one between 10 and 16 years old. His wife, Mehitable, died May 17, 1838, age 73 years, in Newport, and he died in Orono, Maine, where he was living at the time of the 1850 census at the age of 88 years.

PAINE

Members of the Paine family moved to Pearsontown during the Revolutionary War. The names of Joseph and Thomas Paine are found on the 1788, 1789, 1790, 1795, 1796, 1799, and 1808 tax lists of Standish and in the 1790, 1800, and 1810 censuses of the town. They were brothers and sons of Richard[4] (Joseph,[3] Thomas,[2] Thomas[1]) and Phebe (Myrick) Paine of Eastham, Massachusetts.

Joseph[5] Paine, born Apr. 21, 1741, in Eastham, married Jan. 20, 1767, Phebe Rich, born Mar. 3, 1747, in Truro, Mass., and moved to Pearsontown in 1780 and settled in the southeastern part of town, near the Buxton line. At the time of the 1790 census his family was listed as 3-3-5; in 1800 of him and his wife, two males between 10 and 16, and two males and one female between 16 and 26; and in the 1810, of one male under 10, two males between between 16 and 26, one male between 26 and 45, one male over 45, one female between 10 and 16, one female between 16 and 26, and two females over 45 years old. They continued to live in Standish until their deaths, his occurring Oct. 7, 1827, age 86 years, 6 months, and hers on Oct. 5, 1828, age 81 years, 7 months. They were buried in the Old Cemetery on the Dow Road at Dow's Corner in Standish. Their children were as follows:

i. MYRICK, born July 22, 1768, in Eastham, Mass., came to Pearsontown with his parents. On May 12, 1791, he married Dorcas Myrick, born Sept. 12, 1769, daughter of William and Hannah (Paine) Myrick of Eastham, Mass., and were first cousins. She as his wife was admitted to the Standish Church in 1795. They lived in Standish in the Paine Neighborhood where she died on Nov. 4, 1838, age 76 yrs., 7 mos., and he on Apr. 4, 1858, age 89 yrs., 8 mos., and 12 days. Both are buried in the Paine Cemetery on Route 113 in Standish. They were parents of the following children:
   1. HANNAH, born Feb. 17, 1792, bapt. June 4, 1795, married May 27, 1817, William E. Butler, born Aug. 5, 1793, son of William and Abigail (Cross) Butler of Standish. They moved to Thomaston, Maine. She died Oct. 26, 1881, age 89 yrs. Buried in Hollis, Maine.
   2. NANCY, born Apr. 20, 1794, bapt. June 4, 1795. She died June 24, 1860, age 66 yrs., unmarried.
   3. WILLIAM, born Jan. 12, 1796, bapt. Sept. 25, 1796, married

Sept. 29, 1829, Louisa A. Otis, born Apr. 7, 1807, daughter of Capt. David and Anna S. (Libby) Otis of Limington. They lived in Standish where he was a music teacher. He died in Standish on Nov. 8, 1881, at the age of 85 yrs., 10 mos., and she on Mar. 12, 1898, age 90 yrs., 11 mos. and 5 days. They are buried in the Village Cemetery at Standish Corner. They were parents of the following children:
- (1) LUCINDA, born Apr. 1, 1833, was a music teacher at the time of the 1860 census of Standish. She married Capt. Gregory Croston. She died Jan. 17, 1904, Standish.
- (2) MARCIA ANNE, born Mar. 15, 1839, married John Dean Higgins, born Jan. 23, 1826, son of Enoch F. and Miriam (Dean) Higgins of Standish. He died Jan. 18, 1897, and she died in 1928. They are buried in the Village Cemetery at Standish Corner.
- (3) CLARA LOUISE, born June 1, 1845, died Dec. 14, 1865, age 20 yrs., 6 mos., and 14 days.
- (4) GEORGE PRESTON, born Jan. 30, 1847, died Sept. 21, 1865, age 18 yrs., 8 mos., and 22 days. He died in Philadelphia, Pa., and is buried with his sister Clara L. in same plot as their parents in the Village Cemetery at Standish Corner.

4. LUCY, born Jan. 13, 1798, bapt. June 10, 1798, probably died young.
5. JOSEPH W., born June 13, 1800, married on Sept. 4, 1822, Sarah Nudd, born Nov. 23, 1800, daughter of Joseph and Mary (Martin) Nudd of Standish. They lived in Standish and Bridgton, Maine, and were parents of the following children:
- (1) ANN MARIA, born June 23, 1823, in Standish.
- (2) JOHN F. A., born Mar. 1, 1825, in Standish, died there Mar. 4, 1825.
- (3) FRANCIS N., born May 21, 1826, in Standish.
- (4) BENJAMIN F., born Apr. 10, 1828, in Standish, and died there Nov. 19, 1832.
- (5) SARAH E., born Feb. 12, 1835, in Standish.
- (6) AMANDA C., born Oct. 31, 1842.

6. LUCY, born May 21, 1802, bapt. July 4, 1802, married July 15, 1827, Stephen G. Watson of Standish.
7. MIRIAM, born Jan. 18, 1804, bapt. July 29, 1804, died Aug. 23, 1824.
8. SAMUEL OSBORNE, born Oct. 31, 1807, bapt. Jan. 1, 1809, married (int. Oct. 30, 1830, in Standish) Nov. 24, 1830, Jane Mitchell, born Sept. 4, 1811, daughter of Robert and Lydia (Berry) Mitchell of Standish. She died Aug. 3, 1888, age 76, Standish. He died May 12, 1900, age 92 yrs., 6 mos., 12 days, Standish. Children were:
- (1) LUCY ANN, born May 1, 1831.
- (2) MARSHALL, born Sept. 7, 1833.
- (3) OLIVE, born May 19, 1836.
- (4) PARKER FRANCIS, born Nov. 7, 1851.

9. DORCAS, born Dec. 15, 1810, bapt. Sept. 8, 1811, married Marshall Thomas of Harrison, Maine.

ii. JOSEPH JR., born Aug. 6, 1771, in Eastham, Mass., married Aug. 7, 1794, Eleanor Martin, born in Eastham, Mass., June 13, 1770, daughter of Bryan and Elizabeth (Higgins) Martin of Eastham and Standish. They lived in Standish and are buried in the Paine Cemetery on Route 113. She died Aug. 28, 1848, age 78, and he died in Bridgton Apr. 28, 1859, age 87 yrs., 8 mos., and 22 days. They were parents of the following children:
1. JONATHAN GOULD, born July 2, 1795, bapt. July 30, 1797, married Mar. 24, 1819, Sarah S. Haven of Baldwin. He died Mar. 26, 1827, age 32 yrs., in Baldwin, and she married second (int. Sept. 26, 1835) Simon Plaisted of Limington. She died Jan. 1, 1870, age 73 yrs., 3 mos., in Limerick.
2. ELIZABETH OR ELIZA, born May 4, 1797, bapt. July 30, 1797, married June 2, 1822, Frederick Scammon of Bridgton. She died June 23, 1823, age 26 yrs., in Standish.
3. BRYAN, born Dec. 9, 1798, bapt. June 30, 1799, married Dec. 1, 1846, Mary M. Warren, born May 1, 1801, daughter of Samuel and Anna (Pinkerton) Warren of Standish. He was a cooper and lived in Standish. She died Jan. 22, 1870, age 68 yrs., 8 mos., and was buried in Maplewood Cemetery in Standish in the same burial plot as her parents and he died on Feb. 18, 1881, age 82 yrs., 2 mos., and was buried in the Paine Cemetery on Route 113 in Standish.
4. EBENEZER, born Oct. 5, 1800, married Dec. 11, 1825, in Portland, Harriet Short of Portland. They lived in Standish where he was a cooper. He died Mar. 28, 1875, and she on Sept. 6, 1875, age 69 yrs., in Standish.
5. PHEBE, born June 17, 1802, bapt. July 25, 1802, married Nov. 15, 1843, John Proctor of North Bridgton. She died Aug. 25, 1851, in Waterford, Maine.
6. ELEANOR, born June 17, 1804, bapt. June 2, 1805, married Feb. 15, 1824, James W. Haven, born Mar. 30, 1803, of Baldwin. She died May 24, 1825, in Baldwin and he on Feb. 17, 1870.
7. REBBECA, born Apr. 16, 1806, bapt. Aug. 24, 1806, married Nov. 28, 1832, Josiah Proctor. She died Jan. 23, 1868.
8. CHARLES COATESWORTH PINCKNEY, born July 3, 1808, bapt. Sept. 11, 1808, married Oct. 5, 1837, in North Yarmouth, Mary M. Haven. She died Apr. 2, 1846, and he married second June 17, 1847, Martha M. Paine, born Mar. 4, 1818, daughter of Freeman and Hannah R. (Clark) Paine of Standish. She died Aug. 1, 1874, age 56 yrs., 5 mos.
9. CHARLOTTE, born Sept. 1, 1811, bapt. Sept. 8, 1811, married Nov. 12, 1834, John G. Haven of Baldwin. She died Nov. 6, 1861, in Calif.
10. JOSEPH, born Apr. 5, 1813, bapt. Oct. 24, 1813, married Oct. 12, 1836, Elizabeth Ann Lowell, born in Sept. 1818 daughter of Daniel Jr. and Mercy (Higgins) Lowell of Standish, Buxton, and Bridgton. She died May 6, 1862, age 44, and he died Apr. 5, 1886, age 73. They were the parents of the following children:
(1) SIDNEY PAINE, born Nov. 24, 1837, died Sept. 27, 1858.

(2) JOSEPH HENRY, born May 16, 1840.
(3) GEORGE FRANKLIN, born Sept. 19, 1846.

iii. RICHARD, born Sept. 24, 1773, in Eastham, Mass., came to Pearsontown with his parents when he was 7 yrs. old. He married Nov. 20, 1794, Sarah Meserve, born Mar. 11, 1766, daughter of Clement Jr. and Mary (Wooster) Meserve. He lived all his life on his farm in the Paine Neighborhood on the shores of Watchic Pond. She died in Standish Oct. 14, 1831, age 65, and he on Oct. 1, 1848, age 75, as the result of a rupture. Both are buried in the Paine Cemetery on Route 113 in Standish. They were parents of the following children:

1. STEPHEN, born Sept. 24, 1795, bapt. Sept. 17, 1798, married Aug. 19, 1818, Patience Whitney of Standish. He died Sept. 14, 1859, at Lyndon, Wis. Children as follows:
    (1) RICHARD H., born Aug. 15, 1819, in Bridgton, Maine.
    (2) SARAH ANN, born May 25, 1821.
    (3) MARTHA M., born Apr. 3, 1823.
    (4) PATIENCE JULIA, born Aug. 31, 1826.
2. MARY, born July 5, 1797, bapt. Sept. 17, 1798, married first Sept. 22, 1834, John Kimball of Standish, who died Apr. 16, 1850, age 56 yrs., 8 mos., and second sometime after 1860 William Paine. She died Feb. 8, 1879, age 81 yrs., 6 mos., and 25 days, and was buried with her first husband in Paine Cemetery on Route 113 in Standish.
3. RICHARD JR., born May 22, 1799, bapt. July 7, 1799, married Nov. 13, 1833, Olive Shedd Poland, born Sept. 22, 1813, daughter of Capt. Benjamin and Sarah (Dinsdale) Poland of Standish. He died Sept. 3, 1868, age 69, and she on July 23, 1884, age 71 yrs., 10 mos. Both are buried in the Paine Cemetery on Route 113 in Standish. They were the parents of the following:
    (1) PHINEAS INGALLS, born July 31, 1834, in Standish, married Dec. 15, 1861, Ellen Frances Hobson, born July 8, 1834, in Buxton. He died Aug. 24, 1911, in Portland and she on Feb. 13, 1924, in Peabody, Mass.
    (2) JULIA ANN, born July 16, 1835, in Bridgton, died May 30, 1852, in Standish.
    (3) JOHN HENRY, born Mar. 25, 1837, in Sweden, Maine, died Jan. 8, 1862, in the hospital at Washington, D.C.
    (4) CARROLL SHEDD, born Feb. 23, 1839, in Lovell, died May 28, 1839, in Lovell.
    (5) FRANCIS OSMAN, born Oct. 18, 1840, in Lovell, married Elizabeth H. Chase. He died Feb. 5, 1921, in Standish.
    (6) CHLOE POWERS, born May 12, 1843, married Nov. 8, 1884, at Steep Falls, Richard D. Warren. She died Oct. 29, 1914, in Steep Falls.
4. SARAH, born Feb. 1, 1801, married Nathan Barnard of Bridgton, Maine. She died Nov. 12, 1863, age 62 yrs., 9 mos. and 11 days.
5. HENRY, born Aug. 20, 1802, bapt. Jan. 11, 1809, married Apr. 17, 1828, Eliza Elder Parker, born June 16, 1810, daughter of Eliphalet and Jane (Small) Parker of Standish. They lived in

Sweden, Maine, and on Jan. 10, 1838, moved to Milan, N.H., where he died on Nov. 20, 1862. She died July 17, 1899, in Berlin, N.H. They had eleven children.
6. JULIA, born Apr. 12, 1804, bapt. Jan. 11, 1809, was living in Standish with her sister Mary P. Kimball in 1850 and 1860. She died unmarried on Sept. 23, 1863, age 59, in Hiram, and was buried in the Paine Cemetery on Route 113 in Standish.
7. CHLOE, born Jan. 25, 1806, bapt. Jan. 11, 1809, married Oct. 8, 1833, Luther Farnum Powers of Sweden, Maine, who was born in Lovell, Maine, on Feb. 22, 1810, son of Calvin and Abigail (Nabby) Powers. In 1852 they moved to Pennsylvania and lived in Elk County.
8. JOHN, born Sept. 10, 1807, bapt. Jan. 11, 1809, married first Jan. 15, 1834, Sarah Davis of Standish and second Angeline Bradbury, bapt. July 20, 1817, daughter of Reuben and Eunice (Freeman) Bradbury of Standish. He died Feb. 16, 1869, age 61 yrs., 5 mos., and was buried in Evergreen Cemetery in Portland. She was born Apr. 27, 1817, died Oct. 29, 1899.

iv. PHEBE, born Sept. 24, 1773, in Eastham, Mass., twin to Richard, married Jan. 8, 1795, in Standish, William Higgins, perhaps son of William and Elizabeth (Young) Higgins of Eastham, Mass., and Standish. They were the parents of eleven children, for list of whom see Higgins family. She died Dec. 3, 1829, and he on Sept. 20, 1834.

v. URIAH, born Nov. 27, 1775, in Eastham, Mass., married Nov. 16, 1797, Ruth Adams of Standish. They continued to live in town until their deaths, his occurring on Oct. 8, 1835, at the age of 60 and hers on Nov. 18, 1838, age 59. Both were buried in the Paine Cemetery on Route 113 in Standish. They were members of the Standish Church in which all of their children were baptized. Children were as follows:
1. ZEBULON ADAMS, born Aug. 10, 1798, bapt. July 23, 1809, married Margaret Starbird.
2. DANIEL, born Dec. 9, 1800, bapt. July 23, 1809, married Jan. 21, 1824, Sarah Nudd, born Mar. 8, 1800, daughter of Joseph and Mary (Martin) Nudd of Standish. They lived in Waterville.
3. OLIVER, born Jan. 20, 1803, bapt. Mar. 21, 1809, died young, unmarried at Waterville, Maine.
4. NABBY (ABIGAIL) born Feb. 23, 1805, bapt. July 23, 1809, died Oct. 29, 1860, age 55 yrs., Standish.
5. HARRISON, born Sept. 26, 1808, bapt. July 23, 1809, died Jan. 14, 1836, age 27, unmarried.
6. OLIVER, born Dec. 12, 1810, bapt. Apr. 11, 1811.
7. JOSHUA, born Jan. 11, 1813, bapt. May 23, 1813.
8. LOUISA, born Aug. 31, 1815, bapt. Oct. 15, 1815, died Aug. 15, 1835, age 21 yrs., Standish.
9. ISABELLA, born Feb. 9, 1818, bapt. July 26, 1818, married Chesley Higgins.
10. AROLINE, born May 27, 1820, bapt. Jan. 21, 1821, died July 25, 1822.

vi. **THOMAS**, born Mar. 2, 1778, in Eastham, Mass., married Feb. 11, 1802, Achsah Jordan of Gorham, possibly daughter of Benjamin Allen and Sarah (Trudy) Jordan of Cape Elizabeth and Gorham, Maine. He was known as Thomas Paine Jr. and his wife was a member of the Standish Church in which their children were baptized. She died Oct. 24, 1838, age 59 yrs., and he in Feb. 1847 or 1848 in Boston, Mass.
1. MARTHA JORDAN, bapt. Apr. 2, 1813, born 1804.
2. MARY, bapt. Apr. 2, 1813.
3. ALLEN JORDAN, bapt. Apr. 2, 1813, born 1806.
4. THEOPHILUS PARSONS, bapt. Apr. 2, 1813, born 1809.
5. ACHSAH, bapt. Apr. 2, 1813, born 1814.
6. SAMUEL BRADBURY, bapt. Oct. 2, 1814, born 1813.
7. SARAH, bapt. May 9, 1817, born 1816.
8. ELIZABETH S., born 1819, married in 1856 Lewis F. Whitney.
9. JOSEPH, born 1822, married in 1866 Marietta Wendall.

vii. **HULDAH**, born Feb. 15, 1780 in Eastham, Mass., married July 27, 1807, Pierce Sanborn, born Sept. 17, 1783, son of John and Abigail (Jones) Sanborn of Standish. They lived in Baldwin where he died on May 5, 1834, and were the parents of seven children, for list of whom see Sanborn family.

viii. **FREEMAN**, born Aug. 8, 1782, in Pearsontown, bapt. Nov. 13, 1785, married Oct. 26, 1812, Hannah R. Clark. They lived in Standish where he died Dec. 29, 1831. She was born in Mass., at age 71 was living in Standish at the time of the 1860 census. Children were as follows:
1. GEORGE, born Aug. 13, 1813, died Nov. 30, 1831.
2. CAROLINE, born Oct. 1, 1815, died June 16, 1819.
3. MARTHA MARIA, born Nov. 18, 1818, married June 17, 1847, Charles C. P. Paine, born July 3, 1800, son of Joseph Jr. and Eleanor (Martin) Paine of Standish. She died Aug. 1874, age 56 yrs., 5 mos.
4. CAROLINE, born Nov. 18, 1819.
5. FREEMAN JR., born Mar. 15, 1822, was living with his mother at the time of the 1860 census and is given as being a blacksmith, age 36. He died Apr. 28, 1890, in Standish, and his body was found in the woods near Dow's Hill. He was crazy.
6. HANNAH CLARK, born Sept. 18, 1824.
7. SUSAN JANE, born Oct. 18, 1827, died Apr. 24, 1833.
8. HARRIET ELIZABETH, born Aug. 21, 1830, was living with her mother at the time of the 1860 census and was given as being a teacher, age 27. She married David Sturgis of West Gorham June 12, 1862. She died July 4, 1881 and he on Nov. 26, 1882.

ix. **JOSHUA**, born Apr. 25, 1785, in Pearsontown, bapt. Nov. 13, 1785, married Jan. 25, 1832, Phebe Davis, born Jan. 31, 1795, daughter of James and Thankful (Paine) Davis of Gorham and Standish. She died Dec. 7, 1839, age 44, and he married second Dec. 2, 1841, Lucy Hawkes, born Sept. 8, 1802, daughter of Joshua

and Lucy (Briant) Hawkes of Buxton. He died July 23, 1849, age 64 yrs., 3 mos., in Standish. Children by first marriage were as follows:
1. FRANCIS, born Dec. 2, 1832, died Oct. 22, 1864.
2. JAMES HENRY, born Aug. 8, 1834, died Jan. 5, 1885, Somerville, Maine.

x. JOHN KNOWLES, born Mar. 20, 1787, in Standish, married Feb. 22, 1810, Jane Small, born May 19, 1791, daughter of Maj. Daniel and Anna (Tyler) Small of Limington. He had a music shop near Watchic Pond where he manufactured church organs. He died Aug. 28, 1835, in Portland and she on Mar. 17, 1863. They were the parents of five children. John Knowles Paine, his grandson, born in Portland, Maine, Jan. 9, 1839, was the son of his son Jacob Small Paine, who was a noted organist and composer.

Thomas[5] Paine, born Dec. 19, 1745, in Eastham, Mass., son of Richard[4] and Phebe (Myrick) Paine, was probably the Thomas Paine who married in that town on Feb. 20, 1770, Reliance Rogers with the Reverend Mr. Cheever officiating. They had a son Thomas Jr. baptized May 5, 1782, in the First Church of Eastham, later Orleans. Thomas Paine evidently moved to Pearsontown about 1784, a few years after his brother Joseph. His name is found on the 1789, 1790, 1795, 1796, and 1799 tax lists of Standish and in the 1790 census with a family of 1-1-3. His first wife apparently died prior to Apr. 26, 1792, when he married Mary Cooking Whitney, born in York, Maine, Oct. 25, 1754, daughter of Amos and Sarah (Paine) Whitney of York and Gorham, Maine. He and his second wife were admitted into membership in the Standish Church on Feb. 24, 1799. Ay the time of the 1800 census his family consisted of himself, over 45 years of age, one female over 45 (probably his wife), one male and one female between 16 and 25, and one female between 26 and 45. The *Eastern Argus* issue of Apr. 21, 1804, gives the death of Mary Paine, wife of Thomas. In 1810 his family consisted of him and a female, both over 45 years of age. Nothing further about this family has been discovered.

Thomas[6] Paine, baptized May 5, 1782, son of Thomas[5] and Reliance (Rogers) Paine in the First Church of Eastham, Mass., came to Pearsontown with his father's family about 1784, married Mar. 10, 1808, Permelia E. Thompson of Standish. He was living in Standish at the time of the 1850 census at the age of 68 with his wife, Emily P., age 63, and a daughter Mary, age 16. He was known as Thomas 3rd to distinguish him from his cousin Thomas Jr. son of Joseph Paine, and from his father, Thomas. A Pamelia Paine died in Standish on Aug. 6, 1865. Thomas and Permelia (Thompson) Paine were parents of the following children:
1. ROSANNA, born Jan. 29, 1809.
2. LEONARD. born June 21, 1810.
3. SAMUEL, born Dec. 28, 1811.
4. SARAH MARIA, born July 25, 1813.
5. EXPERIENCE, born Mar. 15, 1815.
6. ALVAH, born Mar. 13, 1823.
7. HENRY HATCH, born Apr. 26, 1826.
8. MARTHA JANE, born Dec. 23, 1829.
9. ELLEN FRANCES, born Apr. 18, 1831, died Aug. 9, 1837.
10. MARY HARMON, born Sept. 13, 1833.

Two brothers of Joseph and Thomas Paine who settled in Standish, moved from Cape Cod to Gorham about 1770. They were Richard, born Aug. 14, 1736, and William, born Sept. 30, 1743. All were sons of Richard and Phebe (Myrick) Paine of Harwich, Mass. Richard Paine Jr. married as his first wife on Nov. 16, 1762, prior to moving to Gorham, Thankful Harding of Eastham. Their first child, although not listed in the *History of Gorham* was a daughter Rachel, born Jan. 20, 1764, who married Jan. 21, 1791, Simeon Murch, born Feb. 24, 1769, son of Walter and Jerusha (Brown) Murch of Gorham. They moved to Unity, Maine, and were the parents of six children. The second child of Richard and Thankful (Harding) Paine was a son of Josiah, born in Eastham July 24, 1767, who settled in the part of Buxton that was annexed to Standish in 1824, and an account of whose family is therefore included in these genealogies.

Josiah Paine married on Nov. 24, 1791, Elizabeth Ayer, born May 3, 1771, daughter of Peter and Rebecca (Wheeler) Ayer of Buxton. He died Sept. 22, 1832, at the age of 66 and she on Sept. 6, 1852, age 81. They with some of their descendants were buried in a small family burying ground in Standish located on the Dow Road between Cabbageyard (Elmwood) and Chicopee near the Buxton town line. They were parents of the following family:

i. THANKFUL, born Sept. 21, 1792, married Nov. 22, 1810, John McGill, born Feb. 18, 1787, son of John and Rebecca (York) McGill of Standish, and was the mother of a daughter Margaret, born June 5, 1812. Following the death of John McGill, his widow married second (int. Mar. 27, 1831) as his third wife Simeon G. Bradbury of Buxton and became the mother of a son Josiah Paine Bradbury, born Apr. 27, 1833.

ii. PETER, born Jan. 27, 1795, married first Jan. or June 3, 1817, Sally Leavitt of Buxton; second on Nov. 10, 1822, Mary G. Nash of Gorham, who died Oct. 30, 1856, age 55 yrs.; and third on Nov. 21, 1858, Mrs. Sarah J. Watts, who died Apr. 21, 1877, age 71 yrs., 7 mos. He died May 12, 1872, age 77 yrs. Peter and Mary (Nash) Paine were the parents of at least the following children:
1. SARAH, born about 1824, married as his first wife Ellis B. Usher, born Dec. 24, 1819, son of Col. Abijah and Susan (Nason) Usher of Bonney Eagle in Standish. She died Oct. 5, 1852, age 28.
2. JAMES I., born about 1831, married Emeline Hopkinson, who died July 19, 1911, age 80 yrs. He died Dec. 3, 1902, age 71 yrs., 6 mos., 5 days.
3. JOSIAH, born about 1835, died Dec. 30, 1860, age 25 yrs.

iii. ELIZA, born Apr. 8, 1797.
iv. REBECCA, born Sept. 12, 1799, died Sept. 6, 1802.
v. JOSEPH, born Sept. 28, 1801.
vi. ROBERT STRONG, born Apr. 23, 1804, died Apr. 30, 1805.
vii. RICHARD, born Mar. 19, 1806.
viii. REBECCA, born Sept. 15, 1808.
ix. JOSIAH, born Oct. 8, 1810.
x. SALLY, born Sept. 22, 1815.

PARKER

There were several men by the name of Parker who lived in Standish in the early days. The names of Aaron and Moses Parker are found on the 1789, 1790, 1795, and 1796 tax lists and in the 1790 census. They were brothers and sons of Thomas and Eunice (Hammond) Parker of Newton, Massachusetts.

Moses[5] Parker (Thomas,[4] Noah,[3] Nathaniel,[2] Samuel[1]) was born in Newton June 9, 1742, and died in Cornish Oct 27, 1809, age 69 years, by drowning in the Saco River. According to his obituary given in the Nov. 9, 1809, issue of the *Eastern Argus*, he was of Standish and in crossing Saco River he was suddenly thrown from his horse and drowned. On Feb. 18, 1773, he married Mary Mills of Needham, Mass., who died Feb. 24, 1851, in Scarboro at the age of 97 years and 8 months. Both she and her husband are buried at Gorham Village. He was living in Newton on Dec. 3, 1782, when he bought from Thomas Parker and Aaron Richardson of Newton the 30-acre lots Nos. 3 and 112 in the first division in Pearsontown (16/308) and also on May 1, 1783, when he sold to Philip Cannell the 30-acre lot #53 (15/91). However, he is given as a yeoman of Pearsontown on Oct. 4, 1783, when Thomas Parker, Samuel Richardson and Aaron Richardson, all of Newton, sold him the 100-acre lot #123 in third division in Pearsontown (16/307), half of which he sold to Ebenezer Shaw on Mar. 1, 1785 (16/320). Moses and his wife and two of their children are buried in Gorham. Known children of Moses and Mary (Mills) Parker were as follows:

i. MOSES, born about 1772, married Aug. 22, 1802, Mary Ingalls, born in Hiram, Maine, Nov. 25, 1779, daughter of Benjamin and Mary (White) Ingalls, the first white child born in that town. He died Nov. 30, 1848, age 70 yrs., and she on Oct. 29, 1850, in Baldwin.
ii. HADASSAH, married Feb. 16, 1797, William Larrabee of Scarboro, born July 28, 1769, son of William and Lydia (Mitchell) Larrabee.
iii. MARTHA, married Moses Hanson of Cornish on Sept. 6, 1797.
iv. MARY, born about 1785, married Feb. 9, 1815, Ebenezer Sawyer, born Dec. 14, 1789, son of Samuel and Abigail (Dyer) Sawyer of Baldwin. She died Mar. 11, 1840, age 55 yrs., and he on Oct. 10, 1877, in Baldwin.
v. SARAH L., married Nov. 24, 1814, Benjamin Larrabee of Baldwin, born in 1788 son of Zebulon and Susan (Goodwin) Larrabee.
vi. JOHN MILLS, born Aug. 15, 1799, married June 3, 1825, Louisa Worcester, born Nov. 20, 1804, daughter of Thomas and Susanna (Edwards) Worcester of Gorham. They lived in Scarboro, the part later annexed to Gorham, where they died, he on July 31, 1873, age 74, and she on Apr. 17, 1885, age 80.
vii. BETSEY, died Mar. 13, 1869, age 73 yrs., So. Gorham, unmarried.
viii. CLARISSA, married first Mar. 9, 1824, Gardner Merrill, born Apr. 21, 1798, son of Daniel and Priscilla (Crockett) Merrill of Gorham. He died Feb. 18, 1835, and she married second _____ Brown.

Aaron[5] (Thomas,[4] Noah,[3] Nathaniel,[2] Samuel[1]) Parker, born in Newton, Mass., Feb. 26, 1759, son of Thomas and Eunice (Hammond) Parker, married May 3 or 5, 1785, Hannah Robinson, born in Natick, Mass., July 14, 1763, daughter of John and Hannah (Carver) Robinson. She was a sister of the John Robinson who lived for a while in Pearsontown before finally settling in Baldwin. It is likely that they moved to Standish soon after their marriage, settling on the 100-acre lot #32 in the second division located on Standish Neck, which together with lot #31 he and his brother Benjamin had purchased from Thomas Parker, Samuel and Aaron Richardson on Sept. 23, 1783, at which time they were living in Newton (15/320). He sold the southwest half of the lot #32 to John Miller of Gorham on Oct. 15, 1798 (28/527), and quitclaimed his right and title to lot #31 to his brother Benjamin, then of Newton, on Nov. 9, 1798 (29/22). On Apr. 14, 1812, he sold to Benjamin Parker of Standish (probably his son) 30 acres of lot #32 with half of the buildings thereon (70/459). At the time of the 1790 census his family is recorded as 1-1-3, while in 1800 it consisted of three females under 10, one male and his wife, both between 26 and 45. He served in the Revolutionary War prior to coming to Standish, where he died July 5, 1844. He and his wife were probably the ones (he between 80 and 90 and she between 70 and 80) who were living in Benjamin's family in 1840. Since two blind persons are listed as living in the family, it is likely that both of them were blind. Place of burial is not definitely known but it was likely in the family graveyard known to have been located on their farm.

Aaron and Hannah (Robinson) Parker were the parents of at least six children, two boys and four girls, according to census records. Among them were probably the following:

i. BENJAMIN, born in 1789 (age 61 in 1850 census and 65 on Mar. 16, 1855), married (int. May 2, 1812) Lucy Walker, born about 1791 (59 in 1850 census) daughter of John and Elizabeth (Grant) Walker of Gorham. They lived on his father's homestead where he died on June 25, 1867. They were the parents of at least the following children:
   1. A SON, born between 1812 and 1820 (under 10 in 1820). Also listed in 1830 and 1840 censuses.
   2. A DAUGHTER, born between 1815 and 1820 (over 10 and under 15 in 1830). Not listed in 1840 census.
   3. A DAUGHTER, born between 1815 and 1820 (over 10 and under 15 in 1830). Not listed in 1840.
   4. A SON, born between 1815 and 1820 (over 10 and under 15 in 1840). Also listed in 1840.
   5. MARTHA, born between 1820 and 1825 (over 15 and under 20 in 1840 and age 26 in 1850).
   6. CHARLES F., born between 1830 and 1835 (over 5 and under 10 in 1840 and age 17 in 1850).
   7. A DAUGHTER, born between 1830 and 1835 (over 5 and under 10 in 1840). Not listed in 1850.
   8. A DAUGHTER, born between 1830 and 1835 (over 5 and under 10 in 1840). Not listed in 1850.

ii. HANNAH R., born Nov. 12, 1791, married (int. Dec. 1, 1816) Henry Milliken, born Aug. 4, 1791, son of Isaiah and Eunice (Nason) Milliken of Old Orchard, Maine. He was a brother of Hannah Milliken who

married David Sawyer and lived near the Parker homestead on Standish Neck. She died Aug. 29, 1862, age 71 yrs., in Scarboro. They were the parents of seven children.
iii. ELIZABETH, born Oct. 7, 1794, married Dec. 26, 1821, Gardner Newcomb, born Feb. 15, 1798, son of Enos and Abigail Myrick Libby Newcomb of Gorham. He died Dec. 3, 1871, and she on Dec. 21 or 22, 1864, or according to another account on Jan. 29, 1865.
iv. AARON, born 1801 (49 in 1850), married first on Oct. 23, 1823, Abigail Walker, sister of his brother Benjamin's wife, and lived near his brother on Standish Neck. She apparently died before 1850 and he probably married second (int. Oct. 20, 1850) Hannah Binford of Baldwin. He died Dec. 21, 1880. Children by first marriage were at least the following:
   1. CYNTHIA, born Jan. 27, 1828, Standish, married Apr. 15, 1847, John Isaiah Sawyer of Standish.
   2. ELIZABETH, who married a Kimball.
   3. MARTHA ANN, born 1830, married George Grey Young, born Aug. 30, 1830, or 1834, son of Joseph and Mary (Green) Young of Standish. He died Feb. 10, 1915, and she on Feb. 10, 1913, in Springfield, Mass.
   4. GEORGE W., born Mar. 12, 1832, died Aug. 12, 1865, married Lucinda B. _____ born June 13, 1831, died June 20, 1866.
   5. WILLIAM, born about 1833 (17 in 1850).
   6. JOHN W., born in 1839, died Oct. 2, 1908, age 69 yrs., 11 mos., 7 days, Standish, married Martha J. Bennett.

The name of Eliphalet Parker is found on the 1790, 1795, 1796, 1799, and 1808 tax lists of Standish and in the 1790 census of the town. At the time of the 1800 census his family consisted of him and his wife, both between 26 and 45 years of age; and three males and two females under 10 years old. In 1810 there were in his family besides him and his wife (both still between 26 and 45 years old) one male and two females under 10; and two males and one female between 10 and 16. He was born in Saco, Maine, on July 27, 1764, son of Chase and Rebecca (Chase) Parker, but was living in Buxton, Maine, when he married on Apr. 15, 1790, Jane Small, born Jan. 20, 1767, daughter of Joshua and Susanna (Kennard) Small of Scarboro and Limington, Maine. They evidently moved to Standish soon after their marriage, but belonged to the Baptist Church in Limington, which she joined on Sept. 15, 1802, and he in 1834.

On Apr. 10, 1801, Chase Parker of Buxton sold to Eliphalet Parker of Standish, yeoman, the 100-acre lot #119 in second division of lots in Standish bordering on the Saco River, and on Dec. 13, 1805, Eliphalet Parker of Standish sold Nathaniel Sawyer, Jacob Small and Abraham Parker, all of Limington, three-quarters of sawmill and privilege on his homestead farm in Standish. This was probably located at what are known as Parker's Rips a short distance above the present bridge over the Saco River between Standish and Limington on Route 25.

Eliphalet Parker died on Sept. 30, 1840, in Standish, and his wife, Jane, survived him until Oct. 5, 1849. They are buried in family lot in Eastern Cemetery in Gorham. They were parents of the following children:

i. REBECCA, born Feb. 6, 1791, married July 5, 1819, Francis Hamlin, born in Waterford, Maine, Nov. 2, 1791, son of Ebenezer and Sally (Bancroft) Hamlin. She died May 30, 1819, in Sweden, Maine, leaving her husband and a son Francis Hamlin Jr., who was born Nov. 21, 1818.
ii. SAMUEL, born Apr. 9, 1793, died Aug. 3, 1815.
iii. AMOS, born July 22, 1795, married Evaline Trull, born Sept. 12, 1803, in Sweden and died Jan. 2, 1874, in Wayne, Maine. As a young man he joined the Baptist Church at Limington but was excluded June 16, 1827. He was an inventor, living at various times in Standish, Sweden, Windham, Westbrook, and Portland. He died in 1864 in Wayne, Maine.
iv. SUSAN, born Dec. 22, 1798.
v. JOSHUA, born June 2, 1800, married (int. Sept. 13, 1823) Oct. 18, 1823, Mary Chase, born in 1803 daughter of Abner and Elizabeth (Hight) Chase of Limington. They moved to Sweden, Maine, where the births of their children are recorded. After remaining at Sweden for a while they moved to Milan, N.H., where she died Nov. 18, 1868, age 65 yrs., and he died on Apr. 25, 1878. Their children were:
 1. CHASE ELDER, born Mar. 29, 1824, Sweden, Maine, moved to Kansas where he settled near Mankato in that state.
 2. HARRIET ELIZABETH, born Aug. 23, 1828, died May 10, 1832, Sweden, Maine.
 3. JAMES MADISON CHASE, born Jan. 23, 1831, Sweden, died Apr. 20, 1864, Gilead, Maine, married Lucia Marilla Twitchell.
 4. SAMUEL, born Dec. 30, 1833, died July 15, 1834, Sweden, Maine.
 5. HARRIET ELIZABETH, born 1838, married Thomas Alexander McMaster and moved to Kansas in 1879.
 6. MARSHALL, born about 1847.
 7. SARAH JANE, married George R. Eaton and living At Lancester, N.H., in 1927.
vi. DOROTHY, born May 9, 1802, married Mar. 9, 1825, Stephen Thomes, born July 4, 1794, son of Amos and Mehitable (Burnell) Thomes of Standish.
vii. HANNAH, born Aug. 18, 1804, married Sept. 29, 1830, Farnum Stevens born Nov. 24, 1801. She died Aug. 7, 1877, and he Feb. 25, 1887, age 85 yrs., 3 mos.
viii. ANNIS, born Feb. 14, 1807, married July 25, 1830, Ebenezer McLellan of Limington. She died June 29, 1839, in Limington and he died May 20, 1865, age 59 yrs., 5 mos., Standish.
ix. ELIZA, born June 16, 1810, married Apr. 17, 1828, Henry Paine of Sweden, Maine, born Aug. 20, 1802, son of Richard and Sarah (Meserve) Paine of Standish. After their marriage they went to Sweden to reside and there remained for ten years. In 1838 they moved to Milan, N.H. She died July 17, 1899, in Berlin, N.H., and he died Nov. 23, 1861, in Milan, N.H.

The name of Ebenezer Parker is found in the 1800 census of Standish with a family consisting of him and his wife. They may have been living with his son Eleazer Higgins Parker. At the time of the 1790 census he was living in Cape Elizabeth with a family of 1-0-7. He married in Falmouth, Maine, on Sept. 26, 1761, Esther Higgins, born Sept. 27, 1741, daughter of Reuben and Hannah (Cole) Higgins of Truro, Mass., and Falmouth, Maine. She died in Cape Elizabeth Dec. 27, 1807.

Eleazer Higgins, their son, was born about 1770 and was living in Standish on Nov. 20, 1794, when he and Betsy Rand, daughter of Jeremiah and Lydia (Blake) Rand of Gorham, were married by John Dean Esq. of Standish. She was born in Gorham in Nov. 1774 and died there Apr. 4, 1858, at the age of 83 years, 6 months. His name is found on the 1795 and 1796 tax lists of Standish, where he lived on the Neck, and in the 1800 census with a family consisting of him and his wife and one man, and two daughters under 10 years of age. He died Jan. 29, 1814, age 43 years, in Standish, from the effects of a bite of a wildcat which broke into his home during the night and attacked his family. His daughter Esther also succumbed from a similar cause. His widow died Apr. 4, 1858, age 83 years, 6 months. Children of Higgins Parker (as he was known) and Betsy (Rand) Parker were as follows:

1. **ESTHER**, born in Sept. 1795. bapt. Oct. 14, 1800, died Mar. 30, 1813, age 17 yrs. and 6 mos., from the effects of a wildcat's bite.
2. **LYDIA**, born in 1797, bapt. Oct. 14, 1800, married (int. June 6, 1822) Josiah Moses, born in Aug. 1799 son of Josiah and Elizabeth (Harmon) Moses of Standish. He died Feb. 22, 1860, and she at the home of her son Marshall H. Moses in Gorham on June 30, 1879, age 81 yrs., 8 mos.
3. **ISAAC**, born in 1800, bapt. Oct. 14, 1800, married Anna Flood, born Oct. 7, 1804, daughter of Morris and Lydia (Roberts) Flood of Gorham (int. Sept. 13, 1823). They moved to Gorham about 1830 and lived at White Rock. He died Sept. 24, 1879, age 79 yrs. and 2 mos., and his wife, Ann, died Apr. 29, 1893, age 89 yrs., 6 mos. They were the parents of eight children.
4. **SUSAN**, born 1803, married Dec. 11, 1825, Ebenezer Hicks, born May 26, 1805, son of Ephraim and Rachel (Norton) Hicks. He died May 21, 1844, age 39, and she on Sept. 5, 1873.
5. **JEREMIAH**, born in 1807, married (int. Apr. 10, 1836) Sally Nason, born Apr. 7, 1818, daughter of James and Susanna (Proctor) Nason of Gorham. He moved from Standish to Gorham in 1821 and settled at Great Falls. Mrs. Sally Parker died Mar. 19, 1850, age 32, and he married second in 1851 Ellen A. Plummer of Raymond. He died Nov. 14, 1890. There were six children by the first marriage and ten by the second.
6. **EMILY**, born about 1810, married (int. Nov. 4, 1838) Silas Flood, born Nov. 10, 1812, son of Morris and Lydia (Roberts) Flood of Gorham. They lived at White Rock on the old Flood place. He died July 10, 1874, and she on June 23, 1882. No children.
7. **JOSEPH W.**, born in 1813, moved to Gorham with his brother Isaac about 1830. He lived at Great Falls. In 1846 he married Mary P. Lombard of Standish, who died June 23, 1891, age 65. He died Sept. 18, 1901. They were parents of eleven children.

PARTRIDGE

A man by the name of John Partridge lived in Pearsontown in the early days of it settlement. Nothing has been found as to his antecedents, but Thomas Shaw says in his notes that he was an Irishman, a term often applied to the Scotch-Irish in the early days. He came to Pearsontown from Hampton, N.H., and was deeded the 30-acre lot #108 in Pearsontown by Moses Pearson on May 30, 1769, in consideration of his having cleared five acres of land and built a house upon it, which would lead one to believe that he had been living here several years prior to that date (6/314). He was a brother-in-law of Jonathan Philbrick, having married his sister Abigail, who was born Sept. 4, 1737. It seems likely that Philbrick was instrumental in getting them to move here shortly after he had taken up settlement. On Sept. 12, 1762, Abigail, wife of John Partridge, was baptized in the Hampton Church together with three of their children. A son, Ebenezer Rogers, was baptized in the Pearsontown Church on Aug. 13, 1769. It was probably not long after this that they moved down east, as noted by Thomas Shaw.

Although not definitely established it appears that John Partridge moved to Bristol, Maine, at about the same time that Timothy Crocker and the Meserves settled there. A John Partridge with a family of 3-2-2 is found in the 1790 census of Bristol and Nobleboro. He was taxed for one house and 50 acres of Bristol in 1798. In the 1800 census a John Partridge was living in Bristol with a family consisting of him and his wife, two males between 16 and 26, and one female between 26 and 45 years of age. An Abigail Partridge who married as his second wife Appolos Cushman of Bremen on Oct. 15, 1815, may have been the widow of John Partridge. Following is a list of possible children of John and Abigail (Philbrick) Partridge, but aside from those whose dates of baptism are given, there is no definite proof of the relationship. However, the similarity of names leads one to suspect some connection. Children:

i. **DOLLY**, bapt. in Hampton, N.H., Sept. 12, 1762. A Dolly Partridge married Ezekiel Collamore of Bristol on Aug. 24, 1800.
ii. **JACOB**, bapt. in Hampton, N.H., Sept. 12, 1762. A Jacob Partridge married Betsy Brackett of Bristol on Nov. 9, 1801.
iii. **JOHN**, bapt. in Hampton, N.H., Sept. 12, 1762. A John Partridge married Margaret Brackett of Bristol on Dec. 12, 1793.
iv. **EBENEZER ROGERS**, bapt. in Standish Aug. 13, 1769.
v. **ICHABOD**, possibly a son, married Sarah Laballister of Bristol Dec. 31, 1795.
vi. **BETSY**, possibly a daughter, married John Arnold of Bristol on Oct. 9, 1800.

PEARSON

While there is no record of his ever having taken up permanent abode in the town, no account of the families of early settlers in Pearsontown would be complete without some mention of Moses Pearson. It was he from whom the town took its early name and it was through his efforts as an active Proprietor that the success of the early settlement of the town was assured. It was he who on June 11, 1772, "in consideration of my regard to the inhabitants of Pearsontown" deeded to the town one-half acre off the northerly corner of the 30-acre lot #36 as a place for the burying of their dead (4/464). This is the site of the Village Cemetery today.

Besides his interest in the development of Pearsontown, Moses Pearson was actively engaged as a Proprietor of both Falmouth and Gorham. He also became the first sheriff of Cumberland County when it was established from a part of York County in 1760. The following is a short account of his life as copied from the writings of Fabius M. Ray:

> Moses Pearson was born in Newbury, Mass. in 1697 and migrated to Falmouth Neck in 1728, which ever after remained his home. He was by trade a joiner [carpenter], but being a man of intelligence and great capacity for business, he was soon elected to positions of responsibility and trust in the young town, serving as town clerk, selectman and treasurer in the first years after settling there. In 1737, 1740 and 1749 he was representative in the General Court. In 1745, having raised a company in this vicinity, he joined the army in the memorable and important expedition against Louisburg. After the capture of that stronghold of the French King, he was made treasurer of the regiments which had been engaged in the siege and appointed to receive and distribute the spoils of victory. The principal part of what is now the town of Standish was granted to Pearson and others as a remuneration for their sufferings in the Louisburg expedition, and was called Pearsontown until its incorporation by its present name in 1785. In 1760 on the establishment of the Couty of Cumberland, Pearson was appointed the first sheriff and served until 1768, when he was succeeded by Col. William Tyng. Although not a lawyer, he was made Judge of the Court of Common Pleas and continued in office until the War of Independence. He died on June 5, 1778, age 81 years. He married Sarah Titcomb, daughter of William Titcomb of Newbury and sister of Col. Moses Titcomb, who was killed at Ticonderoga on Sept. 8, 1755. She was born in 1693 and her death on Nov. 2, 1766 is thus noticed by Rev. Dr. Dean, who was her son-in-law.

Moses and Sarah Pearson had six daughters, all of whom married. They were:

i. MARY, born Dec. 4, 1720, married Ephraim Jones in 1739 and died in 1775. Their daughter Elizabeth married Timothy Pike of Saccarappa.
ii. ELIZABETH, born Feb. 20, 1722, married first Joseph Birney in 1745 and second Joseph Wise.
iii. SARAH, born Nov. 27, 1723, married Daniel Dole and died in 1785 (?). Their descendants resided in Stroudwater. (She died in Falmouth July 11, 1784).

iv. EUNICE, born Jan. 25, 1727, married Rev. Samuel Deane, D.D., second pastor of the First Parish Church of Falmouth (now Portland) on Apr. 3, 1766, and died in Portland Oct. 14, 1812. No children.
v. ANNE, born Jan. 19, 1729, married in 1753 her cousin Benjamin Titcomb. She died in Portland July 8, 1800.
vi. LOIS, born Aug. 11, 1733, married Joshua Freeman Jr. in 1750 and died in Portland Mar. 21, 1813. He died Nov. 11, 1796, in his 66th year.

PHILBRICK

Michael[5] Philbrick (Zachariah,[4] Joseph,[3] James,[2] Thomas[1]) born Nov. 10, 1734, in Newbury, Mass., lived in Hampton, N.H., and about 1762 moved to Parsonsfield, Maine, where he stayed only a short while before settling in Pearsontown. About 1763 or 1764 he took up residence on 30-acre lot #115 here, this lot being deeded to him by Moses Pearson on May 30, 1769, in consideration of his having cleared five acres and built a house thereon (6/310). On Dec. 5, 1777, he bought the 30-acre lot #106 of Ephraim Jones of Pearsontown (12/202), and on Sept. 15, 1783, he purchased the 30-acre lot #79 from Thomas Parker et al. of Newton, Massachusetts. His name is found on the 1789, 1790, 1795, and 1796 tax lists of Standish and in the 1790 census with a family of 2-1-3. At the time of the 1800 census his family consisted of him and his wife, three males and one female under 10, one male between 10 and 16, and one male and two females between 26 and 45 years old. Since the records indicate that two families were included, it is likely that his son Gideon and his family were living with him at this time. About 1803 he and his family moved to Thorndike, Maine, where he died in 1813. The maiden name of his wife Mary (Mercy?) has not been discovered. She was admitted to membership in the Pearsontown Church on July 4, 1773, he being one of the seven original members of the church at the time of embodying in 1768. Michael and Mary (____) Philbrick were parents of the following children:

i. WILLIAM, born in Hampton, N.H., Dec. 10, 1759, married (int. May 31, 1783, in Gorham) Martha Nickerson. On Mar. 12, 1790, he and his brother Gideon bought the 30-acre lot #86 from Stephen Longfellow of Gorham. His name is found on the 1789, 1790, 1795, and 1796 tax lists of Standish and in the 1790 census with a family of 1-1-2. At the time of the 1800 census his family consisted of him and his wife, three males and one female under 10, and one male and one female between 10 and 16. About 1802 he and his family moved to Thorndike, Maine, where he died May 15, 1850, age 91 yrs., 5 mos., and his wife died Sept. 4, 1840. Known children were as follows: Joseph, born Mar. 12, 1785; Ruth, born Dec. 9, 1789; James, born June 6, 1794; Aphia born Nov. 15, 1799; Paul, born Dec. 18, 1802; Samuel, born July 25, 1807.

ii. **OLIVE**, born Jan. 6, 1762, at Hampton, N.H., died Nov. 28, 1840, age 79 yrs., in Thorndike. She never married but had a son named Edmund Mussey.

iii. **GIDEON**, born Apr. 21, 1764, at Pearsontown, married June 3, 1793, Eunice West of Raymond, born Apr. 24, 1772, daughter of Desper and Mary (Green) West. His name is found on the 1789, 1790, 1795, and 1796 tax lists of Standish and in the 1790 census with a family of 1-0-0. At the time of the 1800 census he and his family were probably living with his father. On Mar. 12, 1790, he purchased with his brother William the 30-acre lot #86. He moved to Thorndike, Maine, with his brother before 1804 and died there Aug. 15, 1848. His widow died Jan. 17, 1860, age 87 yrs., and was buried with her husband in Thorndike, Maine. He and his wife had eleven children, nine of whom lived to maturity.
  1. **MARY**, born Oct. 30, 1795, married Daniel Cates of Thorndike. She died Aug. 27, 1888, age 92 yrs., 11 mos., in Thorndike.
  2. **WILLIAM**, born Sept. 6, 1797, died Apr. 6, 1888, in Thorndike. He came to Thorndike with his parents at the age of six.
  3. **ELISHA**, born Jan. 25, 1800, died Sept. 5. 1879, age 79, Troy, Maine.
  4. **RHODA**, born Aug. 3, 1802, in Thorndike.
  5. **EUNICE**, born Nov. 21, 1806, in Thorndike, died Feb. 1, 1864, Thorndike, Maine, unmarried.
  6. **ELI**, born Mar. 3, 1800, in Thorndike, died Sept. 27, 1884, Thorndike, Maine.
  7. **LYDIA**, born Aug. 8, 1813, in Thorndike.
  8. **NATHAN**, born Aug. 15, 1804, in Thorndike, died Nov. 5, 1890, Thorndike, Maine.

iv. **MICHAEL JR.**, born June 19, 1766, married (int. Aug. 3, 1788) Sept. 4, 1788, Jane or Jennie Snow, daughter of Benjamin and Bathsheba (____) Snow of Gorham. His name is found on the 1789 and 1790 tax lists of Standish but not in the 1790 census. It is likely that he moved to Flintstown (Baldwin) for on Sept. 20, 1791, Zachariah Fitch of Groton, Mass., sold land in Flintstown to Michael Philbrick of the same town (20/278). They had a daughter Hannah, born Apr. 6, 1789.

v. **EUNICE**, born Mar. 18, 1768, married Mar. 18, 1790 (int. Jan. 25, 1790, in Standish) Aaron Snow of Gorham, son of Thomas and Jane (Magne) Snow. They settled in Livermore, Maine. She died Mar. 10, 1847, in Jackson, Maine.

vi. **STEPHEN**, born Feb. 27, 1770, bapt. Apr. 15, 1770, married (int. Mar. 14, 1793) Betsy Nowlen of Hallowell. Nothing further known.

vii. **RHODA**, born Apr. 22, 1772, bapt. May 31, 1772, married Dec. 25, 1792, Enoch Shaw, born June 8, 1772, son of Sargent and Sarah (Roberts) Shaw of Standish. He died Aug. 28, 1863, and she on Jan. 3, 1819. Eleven children.

viii. **MARY**, born ____, bapt. Apr. 17, 1774, nothing further known, but perhaps died young.

ix. **SAMUEL**, born Mar. 15, 1777, bapt. May 4, 1777, married Anna Simonton of Cape Elizabeth and died at sea about 1824 leaving children Samuel, Mary, and Ellen.

Jonathan[5] Philbrick (John,[4] Samuel,[3] Thomas,[2] Thomas[1]) born in Hampton, N.H., Oct. 2, 1739, son of John and Judith (Sanborn) Philbrick, was a nephew of the wife of Ebenezer Shaw. His name is found on all Standish tax lists consulted and in the 1790 census with a family of 2-1-4. At the time of the 1800 census his family consisted of him and his wife, one male under 10 years of age, and two males and one female between 10 and 16. He moved from Hampton, N.H., to Pearsontown in 1763. Benjamin Titcomb of Falmouth sold Jonathan Philbrick of Hampton, N.H., joiner (carpenter) the 30-acre lot #44 in Pearsontown with all of the lands that shall be laid out in the last division of right No. 44, supposed to be 65 acres or thereabouts, together with the buildings standing thereon on Apr. 16, 1763 (2/285). On Nov. 24, 1764, Jonathan Philbrick of Pearsontown, yeoman, bought of Cornelius Durant of Boston, Mass., the 30-acre lot #45 in Pearsontown (4/56). After his removal to Pearsontown he became a farmer, but also made spinning wheels, chairs, and other articles of furniture. He was the first deacon of the Pearsontown Church, being admitted to full communion on June 18, 1769, and baptized on the same date.

Jonathan Philbrick married first Dec. 14, 1762, probably shortly before his settlement in Pearsontown, Sarah Pike, who died Apr. 5, 1786, age 47. He married second on Dec. 11, 1786, Sarah Mussey, born Mar. 29, 1749, daughter of Benjamin and Abigail (Weeks) Mussey of Falmouth and Standish. She died Oct. 8, 1841, age 92 years, and he on May 4, 1821, age 82. Children by first wife were:

i. **JUDITH**, born Aug. 27, 1763, bapt. June 18, 1769, reputedly the first white child born in Pearsontown, married (int. Jan. 31, 1780 in Gorham) Ephraim Jones Jr., born May 27, 1749, son of Ephraim and Mary (Pearson) Jones of Falmouth and Pearsontown. He died Mar. 31, 1831, age 83 yrs., 10 mos., in Lewiston and his wife on July 1, 1833, age 71 yrs. For list of children see Jones family.

ii. **MARY**, born June 24, 1765, bapt. June 18, 1769, married Oct. 6, 1794, Benjamin Pike, a blacksmith of Saco, and had one child, a daughter.

iii. **CALEB PIKE**, born Nov. 4, 1770, bapt. Nov. 18, 1770, married Apr. 7, 1794, Betty or Elizabeth Blake of Gorham, born Dec. 15, 1772, daughter of Ithiel and Apphia (Higgins) Blake. He was a farmer in Standish. She died Feb. 5, 1844, age 72, and he on Mar. 30, 1855, age 84. They were the parents of the following children:
1. **JAMES**, born June 6, 1794, in Gorham, bapt. June 11, 1797, died in 1837.
2. **FANNY**, born Apr. 26, 1796, in Standish, bapt. June 11, 1797, married Nov. 25, 1825, James M. Stone, born July 30, 1798, son of Solomon and Hannah (Mains) Stone of Limington.
3. **APPHIA**, born Nov. 15, 1799, married May 14, 1821, Edward T. Boynton of Cornish. She died Jan. 14, 1852, in Cornish.
4. **ITHIEL**, born Feb. 16, 1802, bapt. June 20, 1802, married (int. Oct. 11, 1823) Miranda Blake of Bridgton. They had a family:

  (1) CALEB, born Oct. 25, 1824.
  (2) MARGARET M., born May 8, 1827.
  (3) NOWELL, born Sept. 29, 1831.
  (4) CAROLINE REBBECA, born Mar. 13, 1834.
  (5) CHARLES, born Mar. 29, 1836.
 5. MARTHA, born Sept. 5, 1804, bapt. June 2, 1805, married on Dec. 12, 1822, Ebenezer Moulton of Standish, born Oct. 20, 1806, son of Jonathan and Agnes (Foss) Moulton.
 6. JONATHAN, born July 2, 1809, married (int. June 16, 1833) July 7, 1833, Irene Mitchell, born Jan. 22, 1812, daughter of Samuel and Margaret (Berry) Mitchell of Standish.
 7. MARY ELIZAETH, born July 10, 1812, bapt. June 12, 1814, died Oct. 18, 1831.
iv. SARAH, born Aug. 20, 1772, at Portland, bapt. Aug. 23, 1772, died in Sept. 1776.
v. ELIZABETH, born Apr. 20, 1775, bapt. June 4, 1775, married Christopher How of South Berwick, Maine, on Jan. 18, 1796. They were the parents of two children who died young.

By second marriage:

vi. JOHN, born Dec. 19, 1787, bapt. May 18, 1788, died July 5, 1790.
vii. JOHN, born June 18, 1791, bapt. Oct. 9, 1791, married in 1815 Miriam Hasty, born Oct. 14, 1793, daughter of James and Rachel (Dean) Hasty of Standish. He died July 4, 1816, age 25 yrs., in Standish, and she a suicide on Oct. 8, 1841, age 48. They had a son John H., born Oct. 26, 1815, bapt. Oct. 6, 1816, who married Isabella G. Weston, daughter of Rev. James and Sarah (Chase) Weston of Standish. They were the parents of two daughters.

PHINNEY

 The name of Ebenezer Phinney is found on the 1795 and 1796 tax lists of Standish. He was a nephew of Stephen Phinney and was born in Gorham Dec. 14, 1759, son of John and Rebecca (Sawyer) Phinney and married (int. May 20, 1781, in Gorham) Sarah P. Stuart, born in Gorham Feb. 28, 1764, daughter of Wentworth and Susanna (Lombard) Stuart. He evidently settled in Standish about 1793, for he is given as a resident of the town on Nov. 15, 1793, when he bought from John Glover of New Gloucester 91 acres of the 100-acre lot #50 in the second division and the 100-acre lot #95 in the third division (20/505). He sold the 100-acre lot #95 to John Hobby of Portland on Apr. 6, 1794, (21/188) and 71 acres of lot #50 to Sarah Wilder of Lancaster, Mass., on Oct. 9, 1795. Dates of death of either Ebenezer or his wife, Sarah, have not been discovered although he is said to have died in Standish. They were the parents of the following children:
i. STATIRA, married Thomas Files, born in 1783 son of Samuel and Esther (Thomes) Files of Gorham on June 11, 1807. They lived in Raymond and were the parents of eight children.

ii. WENTWORTH S., married ____ Moore of N.Y.
iii. JOHN, lived in Stockton, Maine.
iv. PATIENCE, married Mar. 18, 1818, Robert Files, born about 1787 son of Samuel and Esther (Thomes) Files of Gorham. She died Sept. 16, 1850, and he on Mar. 7, 1860, age 72. They were parents of eight children.
v. ISAAC, married Edie Merrill.
vi. REBECCA, married Charles Jordan, born in Raymond Mar. 30, 1795, son of William Jordan and his second wife. They lived and died in Gorham and were the parents of seven children. He died Nov. 15, 1857, and she died on Oct. 5, 1848, age 53.

The name of Stephen Phinney is found in the 1790 census of Standish with a family of 1-0-1, but it is not likely that he lived long in the town. He was born in Barnstable, Mass., Dec. 16, 1725, son of John and Martha (Coleman) Phinney and came to Gorham, Maine, with his father who was the first settler in that town. He married Olive Early, who was probably the daughter of Anthony and Mehitable Early baptized in Berwick, Maine, on Jan. 23, 1734-5. They lived in Gorham until about 1784 when he was deeded land in Otisfield, Maine, by the Proprietors of that town. The first meetings of that plantation were held at his house in 1787, 1788, and 1789. Shortly afterwards he evidently returned to Gorham, for he is given as living in that town on Mar. 13, 1790, when he bought from David Kneeland of Standish the 30-acre lot #13 in the first division in Standish with buildings standing thereon. It seems likely that he was living on this lot at the time of the 1790 census. On May 9, 1792, he sold 30-acre lots #13 and #14 to Moses Whitney of Gorham and apparently returned to Gorham, where he died June 19, 1796, age 71.

Stephen and Olive (Early) Phinney were the parents of only one child, a daughter Mercy, who married Mar. 21, 1779, Ephraim Jones, born in Gorham Aug. 10, 1758, son of Henry and Lydia (____) Jones. They had three children. They lived with his wife's parents in Otisfield and it is likely that he was the Ephraim Jones Jr. listed with a family of 1-1-1 in the 1790 census of Standish.

PIERCE

John Pierce, another of the early settlers in Pearsontown, is said to have been born in Ipswich, Massachusetts. At any rate he married there (int. Jan. 26, 1744) Elizabeth Johnson, baptized Apr. 6, 1724, daughter of John and Sarah (Pain) Johnson. He moved to Hampton, N.H., and thence about 1762 to Pearsontown. On May 24, 1762, Moses Pearson of Falmouth deeded to John Pearce of Hampton, N.H., weaver, the 30-acre lot #41 in Pearsontown in consideration of his moving himself and his family into town and there making and performing a settlement according to the order of the general court granting the township (7/473). John Pierce, weaver, of Pearsontown, sold John Thompson of Pearsontown, clerk (clergyman), the 5-acre lot #15 here on Apr. 26, 1771 (8/464). On Feb. 10, 1773, John Pierce of Pearsontown, weaver, for and in consideration of of his maintenance during life and Christian burial after death and 20 shillings paid by John Pierce Jr., sold to the latter all his lands and rights, including personal estate and buildings in Pearsontown (9/174). This deed was signed by both John Pierce and his wife, Elizabeth.

John Pierce Sr. is said to have entered the Revolutionary army and to have died in Boston while in the service. His widow married on Sept. 27, 1785, John Sanborn Sr. of Standish. She died here July 30, 1812, age 87 years, some ten years after the death of her second husband. Children of John and Elizabeth (Johnson) Pierce were as follows:

i. JOHN JR., bapt. in Ipswich Nov. 17, 1745, moved from Hampton, N.H., to Pearsontown with his parents about 1762. He, being of Pearsontown, obtained from the Pearsontown Committee on July 12, 1768, the 30-acre lot #142 by agreeing that on or before the 12th of July 1770 he would have built a good dwelling house 18 feet square and 7 feet stud at the least and would have cleared 5 acres of land and brought it to English grass or fit for mowing (6/223). On Oct. 20, 1773, he sold James Moody, blacksmith, of Pearsontown, the 30-acre lot #41 which had been deeded to him by his father in February of that year (8/147).

His name is found on all the tax lists consulted and in the 1790 census with a family of 1-1-2 and in the 1800 census with a family consisting of only himself and his wife. He married on July 9, 1765, Mercy Thorn, born Apr. 14, 1736, daughter of Joseph and Hannah (Harvey) Thorn of Pearsontown. After her death he married second on June 25, 1800, Susannah (Sanborn) Linnell, born Aug. 13, 1753, daughter of John and Lucy (Sanborn) Sanborn, and widow of Enoch Linnell of Standish. He was admitted to the Standish Church on Mar. 15, 1795. He died Sept. 2, 1830, age 85 yrs., in Standish and his widow on Mar. 25, 1840. He and his brother-in-law John Sanborn contracted to build a new meeting house in 1804, which proved his financial ruin and nearly ruined his brother-in-law.

ii. ELIZABETH, bapt. in Ipswich Oct. 18, 1747, married _____ Graffam of Portland and lived to be old.

iii. SARAH, bapt. in Ipswich Feb. 3, 1749, married _____ York of Baldwin. He was perhaps Abraham York Jr. born about 1751 son of Abraham and Lydia (Jordan) York of Pearsontown, whose wife, Sarah, had children Stephen and Eliza baptized in the Standish Church on Oct. 8, 1778.

iv. SUSANNAH, bapt. in Ipswich Sept. 20, 1753, probably died young.

v. RICHARD, born in Ipswich in Sept. 1756, bapt. June 9, 1771, moved with his parents to Pearsontown about 1762. On Feb. 6, 1785, he and Zebulon Young bought the 100-acre lot #71 in second division in Standish from Richard Codman of Falmouth. His name is found on all the tax lists consulted, in the 1790 census with a family of 1-0-2, and in the 1800 census with a family consisting of him and his wife, two male children under ten, and one female between ten and sixteen. On Aug. 21, 1789, he married Sarah Dow, born Aug. 20, 1766, daughter of Jabez and Dorothy (Wood) Dow of Falmouth and Pearsontown. John Dean Esq. officiated at the ceremony. He was killed by the overturning of a cart on the Flaggy Meadow Road in Gorham on evening of July 17, 1810, while returning home from a trip to Portland. The incident was given in Aug.

12, 1810, issue of *Eastern Argus*. He was collector of taxes for the town at that time. His widow died Aug. 10, 1845, and is buried in the old cemetery at Dow's Corner in Standish. Children were as follows:
1. SUSAN, born Nov. 29, 1789, died in Standish 1813.
2. WILLIAM, born June 7, 1792, married Mehitable Charles, who died Jan. 9, 1842. He died June 23, 1831, age 44 yrs., in Standish, leaving his widow with a family of small children, as follows:
    (1) MARSHALL, born Aug. 16, 1823.
    (2) ANNA G., born Aug. 21, 1825.
    (3) HENRY, born Aug. 28, 1827.
    (4) WILLIAM, born Nov. 19, 1829.
    (5) LEWIS, born Mar. 16, 1832.
    (6) IRA, born Dec. 26, 1836.
3. SAMUEL, born Aug. 10, 1795, married Rachel Lowell. He died in Apr. 1842, age 47 yrs., in Standish.
4. DOLLY, born in Mar. 1799, died 1799.
5. DOLLY, born Dec. 31, 1800, married David Brown Jr. of Baldwin.
6. ANNIE P., born Apr. 19, 1803, married Reuben Brown of Baldwin and died there Jan. 15, 1885.

vi. MOLLY(MARY), born in Hampton, N.H., bapt. June 9, 1771, married July 18, 1779, Jonathan Lowell of Pearsontown. They were the parents of ten children, for list of whom see Lowell family.

vii. HANNAH, born about 1755, married Nov. 25, 1784, William Waterhouse, born in Falmouth, Maine, in 1765. He died June 3, 1820, age 55, and she on Apr. 13, 1828, age 72. Children:
1. ELIZA, born Apr. 28, 1785.
2. HANNAH, born Nov. 7, 1792.
3. JOHN PIERCE, born 1794.
4. MARY, born Apr. 1800.

viii. JOHNSON, born about 1766, bapt. June 9, 1771, married (int. Jan. 8, 1804) Frances Howe of Portland, he of Standish, and moved to Portland. They had one son, Johnson Pierce, who died in 1841, age 75. His name is found on the 1789, 1790, and 1795 tax lists of Standish.

ix. SUSANNAH, born about 1767, bapt. June 9, 1771 (age 83 in 1850 census), married Mar. 12, 1792, Moses Sanborn, born July 21, 1767, son of John and Lucy (Sanborn) Sanborn of Pearsontown. For children see Sanborn family.

PLAISTED

The name of John Plaisted appears on all tax lists of Standish consulted, in the 1790 census with a family of 1-0-1, and in the 1800 census as the head of a family consisting of him and his wife and one male child between 10 and 16 years old. He was born in Scarboro, Maine, on July 1, 1759, son of Samuel and Elizabeth (Libby) Plaisted of that town.

He served in the Revolutionary War and in his later years received a pension of his services. William Vaughan of Portland quitclaimed to him 60 acres of the 100-acre lot #46 in second division in Standish adjoining Sebago Pond and located on the Neck (16/115). It was about this time that he moved to Standish, for on Nov. 9, 1786, he and Lydia Moulton, born Dec. 27, 1767, daughter of Peter and Joanna (Shaw) Moulton of Standish, were married by John Dean Esq. They had no children and he died in Standish Jan. 16, 1834, age 75 years, his widow surviving him until Feb. 12, 1854 (July 5?).

RACKLIFF OR RACKLEY

There were two brothers, Benjamin and Joseph Chandler Rackliff, who settled in Standish before 1790. They were sons of John and Mehitabel (Chandler) (Davis) Rackliff of York who moved to Scarboro in 1736, she being the widow of Ichabod Bowdoin Davis. Their mother, Mehitabel, was born Feb. 26, 1699, daughter of Joseph and Sarah (Abbott) Chandler of Andover, Mass., and married second Aug. 6, 1730, John Rackliff Jr. of York, Maine. According to their son's Bible record, she died June 3, 1764, age 66 years, and John Rackliff died Mar. 3, 1773, in his eighty-first year, both in Scarboro. Mehitabel Rackliff is given as having married a third husband in Scarboro Jan. 1, 1746, Thomas Cummings of Cape Elizabeth, whose sons appeared in early Standish, but that is apparently in error, as Mehitabel (Chandler) (Davis) Rackliff died before her husband and would have been too old to bear the Cummings children. According to York records John and Mehitabel Rackliff were the parents of the following children born in that town:
i. BENJAMIN, born May 21, 1731.
ii. JOSEPH CHANDLER, born Feb. 26, 1732.
iii. MARY, born Oct. 5, 1734.
iv. JOANNA, born Oct. 5, 1734, a twin.

However, it appears that at least three of these children died, perhaps with the throat distemper so prevalent throughout New England from 1735 to 1740, for we find in Scarboro records three more children for this couple with the same names. John and Mehitabel (Chandler) (Davis) Rackliff were parents of three more children:
v. JOSEPH CHANDLER, born in Scarboro Mar. 26, 1737, bapt. there Apr. 10, 1737, married Dec. 3, 1767, in Cape Elizabeth (int. Nov. 9, 1767, in Cape Elizabeth) Mary Welch, born July 31, 1737, at the Great Island at Portsmouth, N.H., daughter of George Welch of Cape Elizabeth. He went by the name of Chandler Rackliff and his name appears thus in the records. His name is found on the 1789, 1790, 1795, and 1799 tax lists of Standish and in the 1790 census with a family of 2-0-3. At the time of the 1800 census he was living in Standish with a family consisting of him and his wife, one male and one female between 26 and 45, and one male and one female under 10 yrs. of age. These latter were probably his son George, wife, and daughter.

He was living in Scarboro on May 11, 1789, when he sold land there to Thomas Lancaster of that town (16/305) and also on Mar. 24, 1789, when he bought from Benjamin Boulter of Standish, 50 acres of land in Standish, it being the southeast half of the 100-acre lot #95 in second division (16/382). This land with half of lot #96 and 10 acres off the northwest end of lots Nos. 81 & 82 bought at later dates became the homestead farm of 110 acres which he sold to his son George on Dec. 16, 1817 (89/153).

Joseph C. or Chandler Rackliff served in the Revolutionary War and was granted a pension for his services. According to pension records he died Dec. 15, 1828, in Scarboro. His wife died Mar. 18, 1818, age 80 yrs. The children of Joseph Chandler and Mary (Welch) Rackliff, as given in his family Bible, were as follows:

1. SARAH, born Feb. 17, 1770, in Scarboro, married Nov. 23, 1790, Josiah Hopkins, born May 4, 1772, in Orleans, Mass., son of Theodore and Hannah (Hurd) Hopkins. About 1797 they moved to Unity, Maine, where they were living at the time of the 1800 census. He died July 7, 1856, and his wife, Sarah, died June 25, 1850, both in Dexter, Maine. For children see Hopkins family.
2. GEORGE, born Sept. 30, 1772, in Scarboro, married first on Dec. 27, 1798, Mary Higgins, born July 24, 1775, daughter of Ebenezer and Rebecca (Dyer) Higgins of Standish. She died Apr. 30, 1807, and on Jan. 16, 1808, he married as a second wife, Mary (Martin) Nudd, widow of Joseph Nudd of Standish, born Sept. 29, 1780, daughter of Bryan and Elizabeth (Higgins) Martin of Standish. He died May 30, 1849, age 75 yrs., 8 mos. and she on Jan. 14, 1870, age 89 yrs., 3 months and 13 days. Children of George Rackliff were as follows and given in his father's Bible:

By first wife:
(1) MARY, born Aug. 24, 1799, died July 14, 1808.
(2) KNOWLES H., born Sept. 30, 1801, bapt. Apr. 29, 1807, and died May 30, 1807.
(3) JOSEPH C., born Nov. 12, 1803, bapt. Apr. 29, 1807.
(4) STEPHEN, born Mar. 24, 1806, died Nov. 22, 1820.

By second wife:
(5) MARY, born Nov. 25, 1808, married Dec. 28, 1826, William Rackliff of Portland. He was born Mar. 18, 1795, died Aug. 5, 1876, Myrtle Point, Oreg. She died Nov. 28, 1880, Myrtle Point, Oreg.
(6) HANNAH, born Apr. 6, 1811, bapt. Mar. 19, 1818, married Isaac Boulter, born about 1803 son of Samuel F. and Charity (Merrow) Boulter of Standish. He died June 13, 1833, and she married second (int. Nov. 19, 1837) John Green Eaton, born Aug. 10, 1802, son of John and Keziah (Dearborn) Eaton of Buxton. They lived in New Gloucester, Maine, and were the parents of two children. She died Dec. 21, 1850.

(7) **LYDIA**, born Jan. 7, 1813, bapt. Dec. 2, 1814, married Nov. 4, 1834, James Norton, M.D., born Oct. 19, 1806, son of Joseph and Anna (Whitmore) Norton of Standish. She died Dec. 24, 1850, age 35 yrs., 1 mo., and he died Dec. 21, 1850.

(8) **MEHITABEL**, born July 24, 1816, bapt. Oct. 24, 1816, married Nov. 4, 1834, Aaron S. Nason, born 1811 son of Edward and Susannah (Small) Nason of Limington and Standish. He died in 1902 and she on Apr. 8, 1892, age 75 yrs., 8 mos., in Standish. Known children were: Elvira O., born about 1835; George H., born 1838, died 1865; Mary S., born about 1841; and Edward L., born 1849, died 1884. All are buried in Maplewood Cemetery at Bonney Eagle in South Standish.

(9) **GEORGE KNOWLES**, born Dec. 27, 1819, bapt. June 9, 1823, died Oct. 28, 1850, San Francisco, Calif.

(10) **JAMES B.**, born July 22, 1822, bapt. June 19, 1823, died June 12, 1892, age 71 yrs., 11 mos., in Danvers, Mass.

(11) **JOHN**, born June 20, 1825.

3. **MEHITABEL**, born Oct. 21, 1775, in Scarboro, married Dec. 24, 1801, Ezra Davis, born Sept. 3, 1771, in Saco son of Ezra and Susannah (Hanscom) Davis of Biddeford and Limington, Maine. They lived in Limington where he died Apr. 2, 1836, and she on Mar. 30, 1862. They were the parents of four children.

4. **LYDIA**, born Oct. 31, 1782, in Scarboro, married (int. July 4, 1797, in Standish) Joseph Woods Jr., born in 1778 son of Joseph and Susan (York) Woods of Standish. They settled in Unity, Maine, and lived together for 73 yrs. He was 93 yrs. old when he died and she was 89 at the time of her death.

vi. **BENJAMIN**, born in Scarboro Oct. 18, 1739, bapt. in the First Church of that town Nov. 3, 1749, married July 14, 1763, Sarah Jordan, daughter of Dominicus Jordan of Cape Elizabeth. They lived in Scarboro until about 1781 when they moved to Pearsontown. He is given as living in Scarboro on Sept. 17, 1781, when he sold land in that town to John Sawyer of Rowley, Mass. (12/147), but he was residing in Pearsontown on Feb. 7, 1782, when he bought from Joseph Ingraham of Falmouth the 100-acre lot #120 in the second division in Pearsontown bordering on the Saco River (19/158). This land Rackliff re-sold to Ingraham on Oct. 2, 1787 (19/519). In Dec. 1787 he purchased part of #6 on range C in Limington from David Richardson and was living in Little Ossipee Plantation (Limington) on Mar. 8, 1788, when he sold land in Cape Elizabeth to Abraham Tyler. He died in January 1789 in Limington.

Widow Sarah Rackliff is listed in the 1790 census of Limington with a family of 1-1-3. In 1794 she moved to Unity, Maine, in company with her sons and their families. About 1815 she married Ebenezer Pattee of that town, he being about 80 yrs. old at that time. He died in 1825, but she lived another 14 years, passing away in 1839, at the age of 97.

Benjamin and Sarah (Jordan) Rackliff were parents of the following children:

1. JOANNA, born Dec. 22, 1763, in Scarboro, bapt. May 6, 1764, was of Pearsontown when she married on Sept. 2, 1784, Joseph Stevens, born Mar. 14, 1764, son of Benjamin and Sarah (Pride) Stevens of Gorham. They lived for awhile in Gorham, but in 1794 moved to Unity, Maine, where they afterward resided. They had three children born in Gorham.
2. MEHITABEL, born June 23, 1765, in Scarboro, bapt. June 30, 1765, married (int. Apr. 23, 1785, in Gorham) Jonathan Burbank Ordway of Pearsontown. They were living in Limington in 1792. He bought land in Unity, Maine, as early as 1789, but it was not until 1798 that he moved his family there. At the time of the 1800 census he was credited with a family of four sons besides him and his wife. He died in Orono, Maine, where he was living at the time of the 1850 census at the age of 88 yrs.
3. PHEBE, twin to Mehitabel, born June 23, 1765, in Scarboro, bapt. June 23, 1765, married Dec. 2, 1788, Benjamin Libby, born June 23, 1765, son of Elisha and Abigail (Meserve) Libby of Scarboro. They lived in the north part of Gorham where they raised a family of nine children. She died Aug. 15, 1840, at the age of 75 and he on Apr. 8, 1843.
4. PAULINE, born Apr. 24, 1767, in Scarboro, bapt. June 22, 1767, married Nov. 27, 1792 Benjamin Frost, born Oct. 31, 1768, son of Benjamin and Susannah (Frost) Frost of Gorham. Nothing further known.
5. JOHN, born Jan. 23, 1769, in Scarboro, bapt. Apr. 2, 1769, married Mar. 14, 1803, Lucy Libby, born Aug. 13, 1772, daughter of Elisha and Abigail (Meserve) Libby of Scarboro and sister to Benjamin Libby who married his sister Phebe. They settled in Unity, Maine. After his death she married John McDaniel on Sept. 23, 1810.
6. BENJAMIN JORDAN, born Sept. 10, 1771, in Scarboro, married Mar. 28, 1793, Mary Small, born in 1774 daughter of Daniel and Joanna (Cobb) Small of Limington. In 1794 with his mother and brothers John, Clement, and Dominicus, he moved to Unity, Maine. At the time of the 1800 census his family consisted of three adult males and three adult females, three male children under 16, and one female child under 16. His wife died June June 30, 1816, at the age of 42 and he died May 25, 1849, age 77 yrs., 8 mos., in Knox, Maine. They are buried in Unity, Maine.
7. CLEMENT, born Apr. 8, 1774, in Scarboro, moved to Unity in 1794, married Hepsibah Chase, died Mar. 16, 1858, in Unity.
8. SOLOMON, born Apr. 23, 1777 in Scarboro, nothing further known, perhaps died young.
9. DOMINICUS, bapt. Sept. 19, 1779, in Scarboro, died June 5, 1852. He married Anna Small, sister of his brother Benjamin's wife. She died July 31, 1864, at the age of 86 yrs. He went to Unity in 1794 with his mother and brothers.

10. SARAH, bapt. May 22, 1783, in Pearsontown, married in Unity, James Mitchell, born in 1774 son of William and Elizabeth (Clark) Mitchell. She died in 1864 in Unity, Maine.
vii. JOANNA, born Dec. 10, 1741, in Scarboro, died Mar. 1759.

RAND

The name of Nathaniel Rand is found on the 1808 tax list of Standish, but for no poll; in the 1810 census between 26 and 45 years of age, one son under 10 years old, and two daughters under 10; and on an 1814 Cumberland County tax list of the town. He was born in Scarboro in 1774 son of Christopher and Hannah (Fogg) Rand, who had moved to Gorham about 1789, where he was living at the time of the 1790 census with a family of 1-3-4. Nathaniel Rand married Dorcas _____ and soon after 1800 moved to Standish where he lived on Oak Hill. He died Sept. 1, 1825, at the age of 51 years in Standish, and she on Aug. 7, 1843, age 65 years. They were buried in the Rand Cemetery on Oak Hill. They were parents of the following children:

i. HANNAH, born Aug. 2, 1802, married June 11, 1820, in Standish, Isaac Mayo, born Jan. 3, 1804, son of Robert and Sarah (Hamblen) Mayo of Gorham and Standish. She died on Sept. 27, 1879, age 76 yrs., 11 mos., and 25 days, and he on Aug. 24, 1881, age 77 yrs., 7 mos. and 21 days.

ii. LOVELL, born in July 1804, married (int. Dec. 22, 1825, in Standish) Jane Webster of Gorham and lived in Standish. He died May 28, 1886, age 81 yrs., 10 mos., and she on Feb. 26, 1885, age 78 yrs., 11 mos., and 9 days. They were buried in the Rand Cemetery. They were parents of the following children:
1. NATHANIEL.
2. SARGENT S., born Sept. 8, 1828, married Abby Thompson, who was born June 7, 1828, and died Nov. 28, 1910. He died Sept. 4, 1912. They are buried in the Rand Cemetery.
3. LORENZO D., born in Standish Feb. 17, 1830, married Oct. 8, 1859, Harriet S. Blake, born in Gorham on Oct. 28, 1831. He died on Mar. 23, 1901, and she on Mar. 14, 1901.
4. ALBION K. P., born Feb. 17, 1830, twin to Lorenzo D., died Sept. 22, 1897, age 67 yrs., 7 mos., and 5 days.
5. DORCAS, born Mar. 2, 1832, married David D. Thorn, born in June 1833 son of Stephen and Desire (Davis) Thorne of Standish. She died Sept. 30, 1875, age 43 yrs., 6 mos., 28 days.
6. LUCINDA, born about 1836, living in 1860 in Standish.
7. MARY, born in 1840, died in 1919, married Andrew R. Whitney.
8. CHARLES T., born about 1841, living in 1860 in Standish.
9. PRESTON W., born in Dec. 1843, died Jan. 16, 1875, age 31 yrs., 1 mo. Buried in Rand Cemetery.
10. LESTER, born about 1848.
11. LIZZIE, J., born about 1851, living in 1870 in Standish.

iii. SYLVESTER, born Dec. 17, 1811, married Aug. 25, 1833, Betsey Newcomb, born June 22, 1811. He died Sept. 13, 1884, age 72 yrs., 8 mos. and 26 days, in Standish, and she on Sept. 22, 1895, age 84 yrs., 3 mos., in Standish.
iv. LEWIS, born 1814, married (int. Nov. 29, 1840) Mary Jane Whitney of Westbrook. He died June 17, 1889, age 75, and she on Feb. 18, 1905, age 87 yrs., 8 mos., 3 days. Both are buried in Oak Hill Cemetery, both of Standish.
v. EDMUND, born about 1800, married Oct. 30, 1824, Ann Morton of Standish. They were living in 1850 in Standish.
vi. LYDIA, born about 1817, married (int. Nov. 1, 1840) in Westbrook, John W. Bixby. Both living in 1850 in Westbrook.
vii. LOUISA, born ____, married Nov. 21, 1831, Ebenezer C. Richardson, both of Standish.

RICH

The names of James and Lemuel Rich are found on the 1788, 1789, 1790, 1795, and 1796 tax lists of Standish and in the 1790 census, James with a family of 1-2-5 and Lemuel with one of 4-4-3. They were brothers and sons of Lemuel and Elizabeth (Harding) Rich of Gorham.

James Rich, born in Truro, Mass., Feb. 5, 1748-9, came to Gorham, Maine, with his parents, his father having a sawmill on Little River at the foot of Fort Hill. He married (int. May 3, 1775, in Gorham) Abigail Stevens, born in Gorham Apr. 27, 1753, daughter of Benjamin and Sarah (Pride) Stevens. They lived several years in Gorham after their marriage, but were living in the Plantation of Little Ossipee, now Limington on Jan. 24, 1783, when he bought from Ephraim Jones lot #16 in the third division in Pearsontown (12/550) and was also a resident of that place when he bought land in Gorham from his brother Zephaniah Rich on June 30, 1784 (12/546). He was living in Gorham, however, on Sept. 15, 1784, when he sold land and buildings there to his brother Amos Rich (14/16). It is likely that he moved to Pearsontown about this time. On Dec. 17, 1792, he, being of Standish, mortgaged to Mehitabel Preble of Portland the 100-acre lot #121 in the second division in Standish and is given as late of Standish when he lost this same lot by foreclosure on Oct. 25, 1804 (43/432). He is said to have settled in Thorndike, Maine, in 1795. Children of James and Abigail (Stevens) Rich as far as has been determined were as follows:
i. ROBERT, born Feb. 4, 1776, in Gorham.
ii. MARY, born Feb. 15, 1778, in Gorham.
iii. ABIGAIL, born Apr. 23, 1780, in Gorham.
iv. JOSEPH, born near mouth of Ossipee River in Limington June 7, 1782, married Lydia Farwell born Oct. 16, 1789, daughter of Henry and Anne (Pattee) Farwell of Unity, Maine.
v. MOSES, born near mouth of the Ossipee River.
vi. Probably others.

Lemuel Rich, born in Truro, Mass., Oct. 20, 1735, son of Lemuel and Elizabeth (Harding) Rich, came to Gorham with his parents about 1762. He married Molly Colley, whose daughter Ann Thompson by a previous marriage became the third wife of Sargent Shaw. They lived in Gorham for a number of years after their marriage but moved to Standish on Mar. 12, 1788, where he became the second settler in that part of town called Richville (John Robinson was the first). He and his son Lemuel Jr., mortgaged to Samuel Freeman of Portland the 100-acre lot #17 in the second division on Apr. 13, 1792, which they bought the same day (19/352). He died in Standish on July 8, 1804, age 68, and his wife died on Nov. 24, 1805. They were the parents of the following children:

  i. LEMUEL JR., born Jan. 3, 1770, married Jan. 23, 1794, Elizabeth or Betty Smith, daughter of John and Mary (Rounds) Smith of Buxton. They lived in Standish where he died Apr. 20, 1849, age 79, and she died Dec, 29, 1863, age 93 yrs., 4 mos. Children were:
1. LEMUEL, born Oct. 16, 1794, married Feb. 25, 1821, Sarah Phinney of Standish, died Dec. 5, 1862.
2. JOHN, born Oct. 12, 1796, was the John Rich who married on Dec. 26, 1827, Susan Phinney of Standish. He died Nov. 17, 1871, age 75; she died July 18, 1873, age 71, Standish.
3. MOLLY, born Mar. 15, 1802, died Oct. 27, 1805.
4. BOAZ, born Mar. 21, 1803, married Lydia G. Nason of Standish on Mar. 31, 1830 (int. Jan. 6, 1830), died Sept. 25, 1832, age 28; she died Dec. 17, 1834, age 29 yrs., in Standish.
5. DANIEL, born Nov. 23, 1807, perhaps married first (int. May 4, 1834) Lydia G. Rich, his brother Boaz's widow, and second in Dec. 1835 Nancy Hawkes, born Sept. 24, 1811, daughter of Joshua and Lucy (Briant) Hawkes of Buxton. He died Mar. 14, 1872, age 64 yrs., in Standish.
6. WILLIAM, born Oct. 15, 1809.
7. BETSEY, born Apr. 12, 1814, died Oct. 28, 1814.

  ii. BOAZ, born Feb. 23, 1772, married Dec. 15, 1796, Mary or Molly Richardson, born in Pearsontown June 20, 1775, daughter of Moses and Lydia (Hall) Richardson. On Oct. 5, 1818, Boaz Rich of Standish conveyed to John Freeman of Gorham "my homestead farm in said Standish" it being the southwest half of 100-acre lot #23 in second division (86/269). He left town and settled in Exeter, Maine. He died Sept. 25, 1832.

  iii. SAMUEL, born May 13, 1774, married July 12, 1798, Esther Richardson, born Aug. 4, 1779, in Pearsontown daughter of David and Hannah (Mills) Richardson. They lived in Portland and were the parents of fourteen children.

  iv. ISRAEL, born July 25, 1776, married Dec. 27, 1798, Rhoda Smith, born Feb. 5, 1779, daughter of Thomas and Rhoda (Rounds) Smith of Buxton. They lived in Standish where he died Apr. 13, 1851, age 74 yrs., 8 mos. She died Sept. 11, 1871, age 93 yrs., 7 mos., and 6 days. Children were as follows:
1. MARY, born in Oct. 1799, married Jan. 21, 1819, William Norton of Buxton.
2. RHODA, born in Oct. 1801, married Ezra Merrill of Buxton, died Aug. 1865.

3. LEMUEL, born Aug. 24, 1804, married (int. Nov. 20, 1831) Esther Bangs of Buxton. He died June 11, 1901, in Standish.
4. SARGENT, born Dec. 2, 1806, married Jan. 31, 1832 (int. Dec. 25, 1831) J. Lucetta Whitney, daughter of Levi and Happy (Higgins) Whitney of Standish. He died Dec. 26, 1872, age 66 yrs., 27 days. She died 1879 age 73 yrs., 6 mos., 25 days, Standish.
5. DANIEL, born Nov. 23, 1807, married Nov. 29, 1835, in Buxton, Nancy Hawkes. He died Mar. 14, 1872, in Standish.
6. ANN, born Dec. 6, 1809, married Joseph Higgins (int. June 28, 1832) Aug. 16, 1832.
7. SUSAN, born Feb. 5, 1812, married Mar. 8, 1837, Samuel Hawkes of Buxton. She died Oct. 20, 1885, in Standish.

v. MARY, born Jan. 30, 1779, married Jan. 28, 1806, William Merrill of Buxton.

vi. ZACHARIAH, born Apr. 15, 1781, married June 18, 1809, Lydia Dearborn, born Apr. 14, 1786, daughter of Jacob Dearborn of Buxton. He died in Dec. 1835, age 54 yrs., in Standish (*Yankee Farmer*, Dec. 21, 1835)

vii. JOHN, born Jan. 25, 1785, married June 17, 1811, Elizabeth Dearborn, who was born July 7, 1790, Buxton, sister of his brother Zachariah's wife. They moved to Exeter, Maine. They had born in Buxton Rachel on Dec. 2, 1811, Ira on Feb. 18, 1813, Eliza Ann on July 14, 1815.

viii. DELILAH, or DELIVERANCE, born Oct. 4, 1787, married May 18, 1787, married May 18, 1806, Joseph Thompson of Standish, born about 1781. Children as follows:
1. MILES, born Dec. 25, 1806.
2. IRA, born Mar. 22, 1809.
3. LEVI, born Mar. 28, 1811.
4. LEMUEL, born Jan. 23, 1814.
5. MARY, born June 9, 1817.
6. JOSEPH, born Jan. 25, 1820.

RICHARDSON

There were a number of men bearing the surname of Richardson who settled in Pearsontown just prior to or following the Revolutionary War. One of these David[4] Richardson (David,[3] Samuel,[2] Samuel[1]), born in Newton, Mass., Feb. 24, 1732, son of David and Remember (Ward) Richardson, married first on Feb. 13, 1755, Mary Hall, born Mar. 7, 1734, daughter of Edward and Mary (Miller) Hall of Newton. She died in 1775, age 43, and he, then of Pearsontown, married second (int. July 24, 1778, in Gorham) Hannah Mills of Needham, Massachusetts.

He was living in Newton on Apr. 12, 1773, when he bought from Reuben and Katherine (Thorn) Freeman of Pearsontown 70 acres of land here with house and barn standing thereon, this land consisting of the 30-acre lot #122, 5-acre lots Nos. 11 and 12 adjoining and the 30-acre lot #99 located across the road (7/258). On Feb. 13, 1778, he being of

Pearsontown bought of Rev. John Thompson 100 acres of land in Little Ossipee (Limington) (York deeds 56/34), it probably being the 100-acre lot #6 on letter C which he sold to his son David on Dec. 4, 1787.

His name is found on the 1789, 1790, 1795, and 1796 tax lists of Standish and in the 1790 census with a family of 1-2-6. At the time of the 1800 census he was living in Standish with a family consisting of him and his wife, both over 45 years of age, one male between 10 and 16, and two males and three females between 16 and 26. He moved to Monmouth, Maine, about 1806 or 1807, his name not being found on the 1808 tax list of Standish. He died in Monmouth May 27, 1825, age 93. He was the father of the following children:

By first marriage:
i. SARAH, born Aug. 25, 1755, died young.
ii. MARY, born Mar. 23, 1757, married in Nov. 1788 Isaac Small, born in Scarboro, Maine, May 4, 1752, son of Joshua and Susannah (Kennard) Small.
iii. THOMAS, born Nov. 2, 1758, died young.
iv. DAVID JR., born Mar. 20, 1761, in Newton, Mass., came to Pearsontown with his father about 1778. On July 1, 1784, he married Sarah Wiley, born Sept. 10, 1762, daughter of James and Bethia (Frye) Wiley of Andover, Mass.--Mr. Wiley is said to have been a veteran of the French and Indian and Revolutionary Wars. David Richardson settled in Little Ossipee Plantation (Limington) soon after his marriage, and all of his children were probably born there. His wife died Nov. 11, 1826, at the age of 64 yrs. and 2 mos., and he died on July 3, 1827, age 66 yrs. and 5 mos. They were parents of the following family:
   1. DAVID JR., born Sept. 13, 1785, married in 1805 Anna Tyler of Limington. They moved to Standish in 1812 and back to Limington in 1815. He was killed with his son Isaac, then 6 yrs. old, when his house burned on the night of Mar. 22, 1822. His widow married Theophilus Waterhouse. She died Feb. 13, 1861, age 72 yrs. 3 mos.
   2. JAMES, born Oct. 13, 1786, married Hannah Hibbert of Cornish in 1813, she born Apr. 28, 1795. He moved in Dec. 1822 to Verona Co., New York, but returned to Limington after the death of his wife on Sept. 16, 1825, and died in that town on Jan. 16, 1840, age 53.
   3. THOMAS, born Nov. 15, 1788, married Nancy Small on Aug. 18, 1811, she born Feb. 1, 1790. He lived in Limington except from 1817 to 1820 when resided in Standish. He died in Limington Dec. 12, 1873, age 85.
   4. CHARLOTTE, born Oct. 2, 1791, died unmarried Sept. 25, 1818.
   5. ISAAC, born Feb. 24, 1794, married July 11, 1819, Abigail Chick of Limington, born in Falmouth, Maine, Mar. 25, 1795. He bought the farm of Thomas Moulton in Standish, in 1818, but died in Gorham Oct. 4, 1872, age 78. His widow, Abigail, died there on Jan. 18, 1875, in her 80th year.
   6. ABNER, born Oct. 24, 1796, married Olive T. Lewis of Hiram, born Jan. 8, 1804, on Mar. 18, 1827. They lived in Limington where both of them died.

7. **EZRA**, born Nov. 12, 1799, drowned in Limington on July 18, 1822, unmarried.
8. **WILLIAM**, born July 13, 1802, married Rebecca Frink of Gorham. He died insane in July 1847.

v. **JOSEPH**, born July 3, 1763, in Newton, Mass., came to Pearsontown with his father about 1788. He married (int. Jan. 12, 1782, in Gorham) Molly or Mary Carpenter, both being given as residents of Pearsontown. She was born May 25, 1754, probably in the vicinity of Marblehead, Mass. About 1785 he moved to Flintstown (Baldwin) where he afterwards lived. He died there Feb. 21, 1836, age 72 yrs., and 7 mos., and his wife died there on Sept. 20, 1846, age 92. He served in the Revolutionary War, his widow being a pensioner, age 87, living in Baldwin at the time of the 1840 census. They were the parents of the following children:

1. **SAMUEL**, born in Standish May 26, 1782, died Mar. 14, 1785.
2. **ABIGAIL**, born Jan. 10, 1784, married Sept. 8, 1805, Benjamin McCorrison, born Jan. 10, 1783, son of James and Mary (Flood) McCorrison of Gorham. They lived in Standish where she died July 24, 1848. They were the parents of the following children:
   (1) **MARY**, second wife of Loammi Kimball.
   (2) **REBECCA**, wife of Loammi Kimball.
   (3) **DANIEL**, married Martha Cressey of Gorham and Harriet Clay of Buxton.
   (4) **BENJAMIN**, married _____, lived in eastern part of Maine.
   (5) **SAMUEL**, killed by falling tree when 14 yrs. old.
   (6) **JAMES**, a dentist, twice married.
   (7) **CATHERINE**, married _____, died a few months after marriage.
   (8) **LUCY**, died young.
   (9) **TWINS**, died young.
3. **JOSEPH**, born July 3, 1785, married May 26, 1808, Charlotte Thompson, born May 2, 1786, in Reading, Mass., daughter of Dr. Isaac S. and Charlotte (Hay) Thompson. Her father was the first physician in Standish. They lived in Baldwin where she died Feb. 26, 1843. He died Sept. 21, 1848, age 63.
4. **SARAH**, born June 22, 1787, in Baldwin, married Eleazar Marr on Oct. 10, 1810.
5. **SAMUEL**, born May 1, 1789, married Sarah Mansfield and Hannah Towle. He died in Missouri in 1864.
6. **HULDAH**, born July 10, 1791, married Oct. 19, 1815, Barnabas Sawyer of Buxton.
7. **EPHRAIM**, born June 11, 1793, twice married.
8. **MARY**, born May 22, 1795, married Dudley Moody.
9. **HANNAH**, born Dec. 22, 1798, died in 1799.

vi. **ELISHA**, born Mar. 21, 1766, in Newton, Mass., came to Pearsontown about 1778 with his father. His name is found on the 1789 tax list of Standish for poll tax only. He married Dorothy Frost of Little Ossipee (Limington) (int. Nov. 15, 1789, in Standish) and at the time of the 1790 census was living in Limington and credited with a family of 1-1-1. He lived in Limington for several years then moved to Falmouth, but later returned to Limington. She died on Apr. 13, 1837, age 67, and he died in Baldwin Feb. 7, 1852, age nearly 86.

vii. JONATHAN, born Sept. 10, 1768, in Newton, Mass., came with his father to Pearsontown about 1778. On Mar. 14, 1790, he married Mary Thomas, daughter of John Thomas of the Stroudwater section of Westbrook, Maine, now a part of Portland. He is listed in the 1790 census of Standish with a family of 1-0-1. About 1814 he moved to Monmouth, Maine, where he died Oct. 3, 1848, age 80. His wife died June 25, 1839, age 70. They were the parents of the following children, all born in Standish:
1. MARY, born Dec. 31, 1790.
2. JOHN THOMAS, born Oct. 27, 1792, married Mary Orcutt.
3. HENRY, born June 8, 1794, married Sally Withington.
4. THOMAS, born Jan. 11, 1800, married in Standish in May 1829 Bathsheba Stevens of Winthrop. They settled in Winthrop. He died in Brunswick July 8, 1869, and she died in Aug. 1870.
5. JONATHAN, born Apr. 23, 1802, married Ruth Lewis. He died in Jan. 1837.
6. BENJAMIN, born May 1, 1805, twice married, died Apr. 28, 1881.
7. LOUISA, born June 26, 1808, married in 1835 Moses Fogg of Wales, Maine.
8. LUCY, born June 8, 1812, married James B. Johnson of Monmouth and settled in that town.

viii. HULDAH, born May 13, 1771, married Sept. 1, 1791, Ephraim Brown of Baldwin. He died Nov. 26, 1840, age 75, and she died Aug. 3, 1828, age 57.
ix. EDWARD, born about 1773, died young.

By second wife, all born in Standish.

x. HANNAH, born Aug. 4, 1779, married Apr. 18, 1804, Jonathan Moor Jr., born Jan. 17, 1783, son of Hugh and Margaret (Nesmith) Moor of Buxton.
xi. ESTHER, born Aug. 4, 1779, twin to Hannah, married July 12, 1798, Samuel Rich, born May 13, 1774, son of Lemuel Jr., and Mary (Colley) Rich of Standish. They lived in Portland and were the parents of fourteen children.
xii. SARAH, born Apr. 27, 1781, died 1786.
xiii. THOMAS, born Apr. 27, 1781, twin to Sarah, married first (int. Mar. 2, 1805) Mary Ayer, born Feb. 2, 1788, daughter of Timothy and Elizabeth Ayer. She died Nov. 21, 1818, a few days after the birth of her last child, Mary, born Nov. 13, 1818. He married second Mary Dearborn, daughter of Benjamin and Anna (Freese) Dearborn of Monmouth. On Mar. 28, 1807, he moved with his father to Monmouth. He was the father of eleven children, only the first of whom, Lucy Ayer Richardson, born Mar. 28, 1806, was born in Standish.
xiv. NANCY, born Oct. 8, 1782, married Artemas Richardson, born Feb. 17, 1780, son of Israel and Elizabeth (Hutchinson) Richardson of Templeton, Mass.

xv. LUCY, born Oct. 8, 1782, twin to Nancy, married Jan. 27, 1803, Philip Ayer, born Nov. 11, 1778, son of Peter and Rebecca (Wheeler) Ayer of Buxton. She died Mar. 23, 1804, leaving a daughter and he married second Sept. 13, 1809, Mary Moody. He lived in Monmouth, Maine, and died Mar. 4, 1857.
xvi. WILLIAM, born Sept. 4, 1784, married (int. Dec. 19, 1806) Lydia Ayer, daughter of Benjamin and Rachel (Sanborn) Ayer of Standish. They lived in Monmouth, Maine, where he died Apr. 1844 age 59 yrs.

Moses^4 Richardson (David,^{3} Samuel,^{2} Samuel^1) born in Newton, Massachusetts, May 17, 1738, son of David and Remember (Ward) Richardson, married Apr. 26, 1763, Lydia Hall, perhaps a sister to the wives of his brothers David and Jeremiah. The record of his marriage describes him as of Brookline, Mass., later moved to Dorchester. In Apr. 1773 he was living in Pearsontown when he witnessed a deed for his brother David. On Sept. 17, 1773, he, a yeoman of Pearsontown, bought from Joseph McLellan of Falmouth the two 30-acre lots Nos. 101 and 102 in Pearsontown (8/45). He died in Standish in 1794 and his widow married May 13 (29?), 1808, Ephraim Batchelder of Baldwin. She died Nov. 12, 1823, age 80. His name is found on the 1788, 1789, and 1790 tax lists of Standish and in the 1790 census with a family of 2-2-5. He was the father of the following children:

i. LYDIA, born in Brookline June 20, 1763, married (int. Oct. 23, 1780, in Gorham) Peter Sanborn, born July 9, 1751, son of John and Lucy (Sanborn) Sanborn of Hampton Falls, N.H., and Standish. They moved to Baldwin about 1800. He died Aug. 4, 1827, and she died Nov. 6, 1827, of the same year.
ii. ANNA, born in Brookline June 5, 1765, married (int. Nov. 5, 1783) in Gorham) Samuel Batchelder, born Apr. 21, 1765, son of Ephraim and Apphia (Lowell) Batchelder, her stepbrother. They lived in Baldwin and Danville, Vt., but about 1810 with his son Levi and and his wife he migrated to New York State. He died there on Oct. 8, 1819, and she died Sept. 22, 1849.
iii. ELIZABETH, born in Brookline Aug. 23, 1767, married John Cummings Flint on Sept. 1, 1791.
iv. MOSES JR., born in Dorchester, Mass., Mar. 13, 1770, married Nov. 27, 1806, Jemima Eaton, daughter of Israel and Sarah (Mackintyre) Eaton of Standish. He was a one-legged man, a shoemaker, and lived on the 30-acre lot #33 in Standish. He was living in Standish, age 80, at the time of the 1850 census. Both he and his wife died in Baldwin. They had at least the following children:
1. AARON, married Martha Higgins. He died at Port Hudson in the Civil War. She died Sept. 3, 1897, age 85.
2. ISRAEL EATON, born about 1811, married Mary Higgins, daughter of Ephraim Higgins of Standish. He died in Baldwin Jan. 5, 1889, age 78, and she died Aug. 25, 1895, age 76 yrs. 5 mos.
v. MEHITABEL, born in Newton, Mass., May 22, 1772, married Nov. 6, 1792 (int. Oct. 17, 1792, in Gorham) Lemuel McCorrison of Baldwin, born in Gorham Aug. 28, 1769, son of James and Deliverance (Rich) McCorrison. They lived in Buxton and Baldwin.

She died Apr. 6, 1821, age 49 yrs., and he died Jan. 19, 1856, age 86 yrs. They were the parents of the following children, born in Buxton:
1. WILLIAM, born Nov. 13, 1792.
2. LEMUEL JR., born July 21, 1794.
3. LYDIA, born Aug. 17, 1796, died Aug. 23, 1796.
4. LYDIA, born Aug. 14, 1798.
5. JAMES, born Aug. 17, 1800.
6. MOSES, born Mar. 22, 1804.
7. AARON, born May 2, 1806, married Phebe J. Sanborn, died in Aug. 6, 1871, age 63 yrs., in Hiram.
8. SYLVANUS, born Nov. 19, 1808, died Aug. 6, 1871, age 63 Hiram.
9. DELLEN, born Sept. 30, 1810.

vi. MOLLY, born June 20, 1775, in Pearsontown, bapt. June 16, 1776, married Dec. 10, 1796, Boaz Rich, born Feb. 23, 1772, son of Lemuel and Mary (Colley) Rich of Standish. About 1818 they moved to Exeter, Maine. He died Sept. 25, 1832.
vii. SARAH, born Dec. 6, 1776, bapt. Dec. 8, 1776, married Oct. 11, 1798, Joseph Butterfield, born Dec. 7, 1775, son of Joseph and Mary (Harding) Butterfield of Standish. They were the parents of four children, three boys and a girl.
viii. AARON, born Sept. 1, 1779, bapt. Sept. 5, 1779, married Jan. 13, 1808, Mehitabel Cummings, probably daughter of Thomas and Rachel (Jackson) Cummings of Standish.
ix. ABIGAIL, born June 21, 1782, married Mar. 3, 1803, Sylvanus Batchelder of Baldwin, born Oct. 30, 1777, son of Ephraim and Apphia (Lowell) Batchelder and her stepbrother. She died May 11, 1849, age 67. He died Feb. 3, 1868, age 90. They were the parents of ten children.
x. EDWARD, born Mar. 14, 1788, settled in Lynn, Mass.

Thaddeus[4] Richardson (David,[3] Samuel,[2] Samuel[1]), born in Newton, Mass., May 29, 1750, son of David and Remember (Ward) Richardson was a blacksmith the same as his father. He moved to Pearsontown about 1775 and married (int. Jan. 6, 1776, in Gorham) Mary Sanborn, born Dec. 22, 1754, in Hampton Falls, N.H., daughter of Daniel and Jane (Moulton) Sanborn, later of Pearsontown. He moved to Little Ossipee Plantation (Limington) soon after his marriage, probably before July 1779 and was there at the time of the 1790 census. Before 1800 he returned to Standish to live, but later moved to Readfield, Maine, where he died Apr. 6, 1819, age 69. His wife, Mary, died there July 14, 1841, age 87 years. They were the parents of the following children:
i. DANIEL, bapt. at Standish May 4, 1777, died young.
ii. THADDEUS, JR., born in Limington Oct. 7, 1779, married Sarah Blethen and had twelve children. They lived in Unity, Readfield, and Philips, Maine. He died in Presque Isle, Maine, after 1832.
iii. DANIEL, born Oct. 22, 1781, drowned in 1806 in Twelve Mile Pond in Unity, Maine.
iv. EBENEZER, born Nov. 6, 1784, married Relief Eaton. He died in 1846; she was born in 1790, died in 1874.

v.   ASA, born Nov. 11, 1787, married Sarah Cottle of Augusta, Maine.
vi. MARY, born Aug. 9, 1790.
vii. STEPHEN, born July 5, 1792, died July 28, 1847, unmarried.
viii. JANE, born Feb. 14, 1795, married Jesse Eaton Jacobs.
ix. JOSEPH, born _____, was said to have been a Congregational minister.

ROBERTS

Joseph Roberts was one of the early inhabitants of Pearsontown whose stay was not of long duration. He was born probably in the vicinity of Dover, N.H., about 1727. He married Hannah Young and a few years later settled in Windham, Maine. On July 2, 1778, he, being a yeoman of Windham, purchased from Theophilus Bradbury Esq. of Falmouth the 100-acre lot #59 in second division of lots in Pearsontown in exchange for 100 acres of land in Windham (10/219). This lot was located on Standish Neck and bordered on Sebago Lake at the head of Presumpscot River.

On Aug. 29, 1787, while an inhabitant of Pearsontown, he sold the same land to Peter White of Bucktown (Buckfield), Maine, and went to Buckfield to live (14/368). He is listed as an inhabitant of Buckfield with a family of 2-0-3 in the 1790 census and was living there in 1800. However, in 1804 he was living in Washington Plantation, now Brooks, Maine. He is said to have died in Buckfield about 1805. His widow died at the home of her daughter, Elizabeth Irish, in 1816. He is said to have seen service in the Revolutionary War.

Joseph and Hannah (Young) Roberts were parents of the following children:

i.   JOSEPH JR., born Feb. 6, 1756, in Brentwood, N.H., married first on Nov. 28, 1777, Esther Hamlin of Gorham, Maine, born June 30, 1758, daughter of Joseph and Hannah (Whitney) Hamlin. He was one of the first settlers in Brooks, Maine, where he died Jan. 10, 1843. His first wife died in Buckfield Feb. 21, 1801, and he married second Mrs. Margaret Forbes, widow of Zadoc Forbes and daughter of Hatevil and Ruth (Winslow) Hall. He was the father of twenty-four children, twelve by each wife.
ii. HANNAH, born about 1762, married James Jordan Jr., son of James and Phebe (Philbrick) Jordan, in 1780. She lived to be 90 yrs. of age and he to be 96. They settled in Buckfield.
iii. SARAH, born in Windham in 1764, married Jotham Shaw and lived in Buckfield.
iv. JONATHAN 3RD, born about 1766, married Prudence Willard of Windham on Jan. 24, 1787. He was one of the early settlers of Buckfield and later moved to the eastern part of the state. He was the father of six children.
v.   ELIZABETH, born in 1769, married Thomas Irish and settled in Buckfield.
vi. MARY, born in 1773, married Richard Taylor. Settled in Buckfield.
vii. JOHN, born in 1777, married Miriam Irish. Moved to Ohio.

ROBINSON

The name of John Robinson is found on the 1788, 1789, 1790, 1795, and 1796 tax lists of Standish and in the 1790 census where he is listed with a family of 1-1-3. He was baptized in Natick, Mass., on June 19, 1763, at the age of two years and five months as the son of John and Hannah (Carver) Robinson of that place. John[5] Robinson (John Jr.,[4] John,[3] George,[2] George[1]) was born Jan. 21, 1760. He enlisted in the Revolutionary army at Watertown, Mass., but is given as being Natick on Mar. 23, 1785, when he bought from Thomas Parker of Newton, Mass., the southeast half of the 100-acre lot #23 in the second division in Pearsontown, lying on both sides of Sticky River (13/207). It is possible that he became interested in settling in Pearsontown by the fact that his sister, Hannah Robinson, had previously married Aaron Parker of Newton, son of the man from whom he purchased Pearsontown land and settled there.

John Robinson married (int. July 30, 1785, in Gorham) Phebe Sanborn, born in Pearsontown about 1767 daughter of David and Sarah (Hall) Sanborn. They lived in Standish until 1796 when on Apr. 13 of that year he sold his farm adjoining Sticky River to Thomas Cannell of Standish (24/277) and bought on the same day of Ephraim Rowe of Standish land in Flintstown (Baldwin) to which town they moved. He died in Sebago on Feb. 13, 1827, according to Revolutionary War Pension Records and his wife, Phebe, is listed as living there, age 72, on the 1840 pension list. His family in the 1800 census consisted of him and his wife, four females between 10 and 16 years old. Children of John and Phebe (Sanborn) Robinson as found in Standish and Baldwin records were as follows:

i. HANNAH, born Apr. 28, 1786, in Standish.
ii. SARAH, born Dec. 25, 1787, in Standish.
iii. JOSEPH, born Aug. 10, 1790, in Standish, married Nov. 30, 1815, Lucy Garey of Baldwin. He died Nov. 9, 1876, age 85 yrs., in Sebago. His wife was born 1795 and died in 1868.
iv. SAMUEL, born about 1793, living in 1820 age 27 yrs., in Sebago when his father filed his pension record. Samuel was a "fool," and living with his parents.
v. THOMAS, born May 13, 1797, in Baldwin.
vi. NATHANIEL, born Apr. 1, 1800, in Baldwin, married Apr. 26, 1827, Polly Scribner, born Apr. 15, 1807, daughter of Joseph and Polly (Knight) Ingalls Scribner. They lived in Otisfield, Maine, where he died Feb. 9, 1876, age 75 yrs., 10 mos., and she on Apr. 20, 1899. They were the parents of eight children.
vii. ANN, born July 11, 1803, married Simeon Lowell, son of Edward and Martha (Lamb) Lowell, and lived in Otisfield where a daughter Rosanna was born Apr. 16, 1837.
viii. JOHN JR., born Feb. 15, 1806.

ROBINSON

The name of Increase Robinson appears on a Cumberland County tax list of Standish in 1814 and had appeared as Capt. Roberson on a similar list the year before. Research discloses that this Capt. Robinson was the Increase Robinson who was born in Abington, Mass., on Apr. 26, 1756, son of Gain and Lydia (Dyer) Robinson and who had served from Pembroke, Mass., as a sergeant, ensign, and second lieutenant in the 3rd Plymouth County Regiment of Massachusetts Militia in 1775. On Mar. 11, 1781, he married Mary Josslyn Cox, born May 13, 1763, Pembroke, Mass., daughter of William and Mary (Josslyn) Cox and moved to what is known as Langdon's Location, now Chatham, N.H., with his father-in-law and is said to have been one of the first three settlers in 1781. He is listed as living there in 1790 and served as a selectman of that town from 1801 through 1804. His wife died in Chatham, N.H., on Feb. 4, 1812, age 48 years, 8 months, 22 days, and he may have moved to Standish soon after her death. On Sept. 7, 1814, Capt. Increase Robinson of Standish married Jane Libby, born Oct. 15, 1782, daughter of Jeremiah and Anna (Libby) Libby of Scarboro and Buxton who died Mar. 20, 1819. He died in Standish on Nov. 12, 1816, age 79 years. He is buried in a family plot on the banks of the Saco River, near Bonney Eagle. Originally his grave was enclosed by iron rods fastened to stone posts, now destroyed.

Details about the family of Capt. Increase Robinson have been hard to come by but the following were undoubtedly his children. There were five children according to Cox Family Genealogy.

i. INCREASE JR., born Oct. 12, 1781, married Nov. 17, 1808, Elizabeth Crocker, born June 10, 1784, died ____. He was in trade in Norway, Maine, with his mother's brother, William Cox, but sold out and in 1831 moved to Skowhegan, Maine, where he afterward lived and where he died Mar. 25, 1861. He was the father of eight children.

ii. POLLY, born Mar. 18, 1784, was the first white child born in Chatham, N.H., married a Bell.

iii. GAIN, born Sept. 2, 1792, died Oct. 22, 1812, Ohio.

iv. O'NEIL W., born Oct. 21, 1797, in Chatham, N.H., moved to Bethel, Maine, in the early 1820s, purchased large tracts of land, and built a house and store where he engaged in active trading for a number of years. He moved from Bethel to Portland and thence to Waterford, Maine. He served as a state senator and sheriff of the county from 1842 to 1850. He married May 15, 1823, Betsey Hilton Straw, born Feb. 28, 1797, in Newfield, and they were the parents of eight children. He died Nov. 18, 1867, in Waterford, and she died on May 14, 1878, in Malden, Mass.

v. JOSLYN C., born Apr. 20, 1806, Chatham, N.H., married Nov. 21, 1830 in Standish, Louisa Rich Moore, born Mar. 31, 1811, in Buxton daughter of Jonathan S. and Sally (Rich) Moore. They lived in Standish where he died Sept. 13, 1885, age 79 yrs., 4 mos. She died Apr. 2, 1881, age 70 yrs., in Standish.

ROWE

The names of Caleb, Ephraim, and Robert Rowe are found on the 1788, 1789, 1790, 1795, 1796, and 1799 tax lists of Standish. Caleb and Ephraim were brothers, while Robert was the son of Caleb.

Caleb Rowe was born at Hampton, N.H., Oct. 20, 1735, son of Robert and Apphia (Shaw) (Sanborn) Rowe, she being the widow of Peter Sanborn and the sister of Ebenezer Shaw Sr., an early settler in Pearsontown. On Jan. 9, 1759, he married Priscilla Perkins and set up housekeeping in Chester, N.H., where they lived until Nov. 17, 1765, at which time they moved to Falmouth, Maine. In the following February they moved to Pearsontown. His homestead was located on the 30-acre lot #118 in the first division, which he bought from Daniel Dole of Falmouth on Sept. 14, 1799. He sold this land to his son Robert on Nov. 1, 1783. He served as a second lieutenant in Capt. Wentworth Stuart's Company of the 31st Regiment of Foot commanded by Col. Edmund Phinney in 1775. On Apr. 8, 1770, he was admitted by letter to the Standish Church from the church at Kensington, N.H. At the time of the 1790 census he was living in Standish with a family of 3-0-4. He moved to Belgrade, Maine, where according to Revolutionary War pension records he died July 1, 1821, at the age of eighty-six. Children of Caleb and Priscilla (Perkins) Rowe were as follows:

i. CALEB JR., born in Chester, N.H., Nov. 15, 1759, served in Revolutionary War, lived in Providence, R.I.

ii. ROBERT, born in Chester, N.H., Jan. 26, 1761, came to Pearsontown in his father's family. In the 1790 census he is credited with a family of 1-2-1. His intentions of marriage to Dorcas Thompson of Pearsontown were published in Gorham on Dec. 27, 1783, but, if they were ever married, she must have died soon afterwards because on June 5, 1787, he married Hannah Fuller, with John Dean Esq. officiating. She was the mother of all his children. He moved to Belgrade, probably before 1800, where his wife died June 18, 1831. He died Nov. 14, 1813, while serving in the War of 1812. They were parents of the following children:
1. CALEB, born Oct. 26, 1788.
2. HANNAH, born Oct. 26, 1788, a twin.
3. ELISHA, born Feb. 27, 1790.
4. ASA, born July 20, 1793.
5. ESTHER, born Oct. 13, 1795.
6. AFFIA (APPHIA) born Aug. 17, 1799.

iii. SARAH, born in Chester, N.H., Aug. 26, 1762, married July 25, 1802, Joseph Rose of Limington. She died Mar. 3, 1845, age 83 yrs., Limington.

iv. APPHIA, born in Pearsontown, Nov. 6, 1766, married Aug. 8 or 18, 1801 (int. July 25, 1801, in Hollis), John Davis of that town. He died in Limington in 1818 and she on Aug. 26, 1836. They had four children recorded at Limington.

v. BENJAMIN, born in Pearsontown Apr. 23, 1770 (bapt. Aug. 5, 1770), married (int. Jan. 15, 1794) Mary Rowe of Shapleigh. A Benjamin Rowe settled in Unity, Maine, in 1801.

vi. EPHRAIM (called Jr. to distinguish him from his uncle Ephraim), born in Pearsontown Dec. 4, 1773, bapt. Oct. 9, 1774, married June 13, 1795, Martha (Patty) Twitchell, born May 6, 1774, daughter of Eleazer and Martha (Nason) Twitchell of Bethel, where they lived and raised a family. He died there in 1846 and she in 1861. They were parents of the following children:
1. LUCINDA, born Sept. 28, 1795, Bethel, Maine.
2. CALEB, born Aug. 17, 1797, married Abigail Plummer.
3. ELEAZER, born July 21, 1799, married Abigail Burbank of Gilead.
4. MARTHA (PATTY), born Apr. 28, 1801, married Isaac E. Cross.
5. MARY, born 1803.
6. EPHRAIM, born Mar. 15, 1805.
7. ASA, born Mar. 31, 1807.
8. LUCIA, born Oct. 7, 1809, died Oct. 31, 1811.
9. JOANNA, born Dec. 22, 1813, married Ira C. Kimball.
10. LUCIA, born Sept. 31, 1816.

vii. JOANNA, born in Pearsontown Apr. 4, 1777 (bapt. May 18, 1777), married on May 4, 1800, Peter Dorset of Standish. She died Apr. 10, 1807. For children see Dorsett family.

Ephraim Rowe, born in Hampton, N.H., about 1740, son of Robert and Apphia (Shaw) (Sanborn) Rowe, married Mary Philbrick. He was living in town on Apr. 16, 1771, when he bought from Moses Pearson the 30-acre lot #30 in the first division, on which he afterward lived and where he died Jan. 1, 1834, at the age of about 94 years. His wife died in Feb. 1829 and is said to have been about 90 years old at the time of her death. The *Christian Mirror*, issue of Feb. 12, 1829, gives her age at death as 85 years at Standish. In the 1790 census he is credited with a family of 2-2-2. At the time of the 1800 census his family consisted of him and his wife, and two males between 16 and 26 years of age. They were parents of the following family:

i. APPHIA, married (int. in Gorham Nov. 18, 1785) Benjamin Swett, son of Jonathan Swett of Standish. They lived in Baldwin and Standish. He is said to have left home, leaving her to bring up several small children, for list of whom see Swett family.
ii. ROBERT, never married, was an eccentric and very careless of his personal appearance.
iii. EPHRAIM (called 3rd to distinguish him from his cousin Ephraim), born Mar. 21, 1775, bapt. May 7, 1775, married Sept. 14, 1797, Sarah Moulton, born in Standish May 25, 1777, daughter of Peter and Joanna (Shaw) Moulton. They moved to Belfast, Maine, where she died Dec. 22, 1849, and he on Oct. 26, 1856. They were the parents of Enoch, Apphia, Peter, Robert, and Mary Rowe.
iv. PETER, bapt. May 4, 1777, married in Apr. 1809 Joanna Harmon, born about 1783 daughter of William and Abigail (Moulton) Harmon of Standish. They lived in Belfast, Maine, where he was a trader for 20 years, selectman, and a representative to the state legislature. He died there Aug. 21, 1847, and she died in Standish Aug. 11, 1857, age 75 yrs.

SANBORN

There were four men by the name of Sanborn who were early settlers in Pearsontown. They all were originally from New Hampshire and there were two sets of brothers.

Jonathan[5] Sanborn (Jonathan,[4] Stephen,[3] William[2]), born in Hampton, N.H., Apr. 20, 1738, bapt. May 14, 1738, son of Jonathan and Priscilla (Bryant) Sanborn, married there on Jan. 21, 1762, Rachel Fifield. In 1763 soon after the birth of their child they moved to Pearsontown at the time that so many families from New Hampshire settled in town. On May 30, 1769, Moses Pearson deeded to Jonathan Sanborn of Pearsontown, yeoman, the 30-acre lot #114 by right of settlement (6/313). Sanborn swapped this lot with Ebenezer Shaw for the 30-acre lot #123 on May 18, 1770 (6/472). On May 22, 1784, he was of Pearsontown when he sold Philip Cannell of Pearsontown this same lot (15/92), but he was living in Flintstown (Baldwin) on Oct. 25, 1785, when he sold land in that town to Charles Baker of Templeton, Massachusetts. He continued to live in Baldwin until his death on Dec. 24, 1809. His wife died there on Mar. 8, 1816. They were parents of the following children:

i. JONATHAN JR., born in Hampton, N.H., Aug. 12, 1762, served in the Revolutionary War, and moved to Baldwin with his father, where he married on Dec. 25, 1795 (Dec. 15, 1796?), Elizabeth (Betsey) Thorn, daughter of Bartholomew and Lydia (Couch) Thorn of that town and formerly of Pearsontown. They lived at East Baldwin where they raised a large family of children. She died May 16, 1846, and and he died Mar. 2, 1840. They were parents of the following children:
1. JOHN, born Apr. 6, 1797, died Nov. 12, 1849, age 52 yrs., 7 mos.
2. POLLY, born Aug. 15, 1798, died Oct. 1, 1879, age 81 yrs., 1 mo., 17 days. Married Oct. 10, 1847, Josiah Milliken of Sebago.
3. LEWIS, born Nov. 10, 1799, married Feb. 27, 1823, Hannah S. Gerry. He died Mar. 1826 and she married second July 1, 1827, William M. Cook of Sebago. Cook died Jan. 1, 1844, and his widow was living in 1855 age 51 yrs., in Hampden, Maine.
4. STEPHEN, born Nov. 17, 1803, died Nov. 28, 1857, Slaterville, R.I.
5. SALLY, born May 26, 1806, married Robert Martin of Sebago.
6. JAMES, born Apr. 19, 1808, died June 9, 1832, unmarried.
7. JANE, born Apr. 13, 1811, died Aug. 26, 1853, unmarried.
8. ELIZA, born Apr. 18, 1813, married May 17, 1829, Daniel McKenney of Sebago.

ii. DAVID, born in Pearsontown June 7, 1765, moved to Flintstown with his father and married Oct. 28, 1793 (1795?), Lucy Moulton Kelly, born in Scarboro Feb. 11, 1775 (1773?). They lived at East Baldwin where he died Mar. 22, 1829. They were the parents of a large number of children among whom were:
1. DAVID JR., born Feb. 15, 1796.
2. JONATHAN 3RD, born July 11, 1797.

3. FANNY, born Mar. 24, 1802.
4. JEREMIAH BURDITTE, born Mar. 31, 1804.
5. SEWALL LANCASTER, born Nov. 7, 1808.
6. PETER, born July 18, 1811.
7. MEHITABEL, born Nov. 25, 1814.
8. LUCINDA, born Feb. 25, 1818.

iii. DANIEL, born May 29, 1766, in Standish, married first on Nov. 8, 1793, Miriam Lowell of Bridgton, daughter of Moses and Miriam (Knowlton) Lowell, formerly of Standish, second on June 6 or 16, 1805, Mary Hardy of Cornish. He lived at East Baldwin where he died May 15, 1846. He was the father of a large number of children, among whom were:
By first wife:
1. RACHEL, born Jan. 28, 1795.
2. LUCY, born May 5, 1796.
3. MIRIAM, born July 12, 1797.
4. DAVID, born Apr. 15, 1798.
5. ABNER, born June 2, 1800.
6. DANIEL JR., born Jan. 3, 1802.
7. MOSES, born Oct. 29, 1804.
By second wife:
8. MIRIAM, born Oct. 13, 1806.
9. ANNA, born May 17, 1808.
10. DOLLY, born Mar. 3, 1810.
11. AMOS, born Nov. 20, 1812.
12. MARY, born Oct. 29, 1814.
13. JENNIE, born Oct. 4, 1815.

iv. RACHEL, born Apr. 28, 1768, married Mar. 18, 1787, Webber Rowe, born in 1765 son of Lazarus and Molly (Webber) Rowe of Flintstown. They lived in Baldwin and were the parents of eight children. Webber enlisted in the Revolution in 1782 and was one of 65 under Capt. Cherry in his scouting party for Indians and one of five who escaped alive. He died Feb. 5, 1851, age 86 yrs., Baldwin, leaving a widow and eight children. Children were as follows:(Rowe)
1. EDMUND, born July 2, 1788.
2. DANIEL, born Apr. 12, 1791, died Feb. 12, 1869, age 77yrs., 10 mos., Brownfield.
3. JOHN, born June 7, 1794, living in 1850 Baldwin.
4. PATTY, born Mar. 30, 1796, married Jan. 4, 1827, John Cole of Cornish. She died June 22, 1890, age 93, in Porter.
5. POLLY, born July 14, 1798, married Aug. 14, 1817, William Cole of Limington. She died May 14, 1840, in Limington.
6. ELIZA, born June 15, 1800, married Sept. 4, 1825, Francis Rowe of Baldwin. She living in 1850 in Brooks, Maine.
7. WINTHROP, born Jan. 15, 1803, died 1862 in Brooks.
8. WEBBER, born Mar. 9, 1807, died Mar. 7, 1892, Brooks.

v. JOSIAH, born June 22, 1770, married Dec. 22 or 26, 1791, Abigail McKenney, who died at West Baldwin Sept. 31, 1865, age 93 yrs., 6 mos., in Baldwin (*Portland Transcript*, Oct 21, 1865). They lived in East Baldwin where he died June 2, 1816. They were the parents of ten children.

vi. PRISCILLA, born June 24, 1775, married William Bickford (Binford?) of Baldwin, who moved in 1820 to New Orleans, La.
vii. MERCY, born May 12, 1777, married Nov. 19, 1795, James Lowell of Bridgton, born Sept. 8, 1771, son of Moses and Miriam (Knowlton) Lowell. They lived in Hiram, but she died in Baldwin Dec. 18, 1855. For children see Lowell family.
viii. MARY, born Aug. 11, 1779, married Nov. 28, 1799, Stephen Burnell of Baldwin, born Apr. 22, 1775, son of John and Elizabeth (Freeman) Burnell. They lived in Baldwin where she died July 23, 1847. For children see Burnell family.
ix. HANNAH, born June 18, 1782, married Dec. 1, 1803, Daniel McKenney, Sr., born June 2, 1781, son of James and Martha (Noble) McKenney of Limington. They first lived in Limington, but in 1803 moved to Baldwin and in 1830 settled on Peaked Mountain there. She died in Sebago Sept. 19, 1857, and he died there Sept. 14, 1855.

David[5] Sanborn (Jonathan,[4] Stephen,[3] William,[2] John[1]) brother of Jonathan, baptized in Hampton, N.H., May 23, 1742, son of Jonathan and Priscilla (Bryant) Sanborn, came as a single man with his brother to Pearsontown about 1763. On Dec. 9, 1765, he married Sarah Hall, daughter of Charles and Jemima (Dolliver) Hall of Pearsontown. They lived in Standish where at the time of the 1790 census he was credited with a family of 1-0-2. Children as follows:
i. JONATHAN, born about 1766, bapt. Apr. 28, 1771, probably died young.
ii. PHEBE, born about 1767, married (int. July 30, 1785, in Gorham) John Robinson of Pearsontown, born in 1761 in Natick, Mass., son of John and Hannah (Carver) Robinson of that place. They lived in Standish until about 1796 when they moved to Baldwin where they afterwards lived and died. For children see Robinson family.
iii. SOLOMON, born about 1768, bapt. Apr. 28, 1771, married Nov. 28, 1799, Rebecca Strout of Limington. He was living in Raymond next to John Strout by 1820 census. They had no children, but she begot a child by Israel Thorn Jr. according to Cumberland County records (Dec. 1789).
iv. PATIENCE, born about 1769, bapt. June 29, 1777, married Solomon Annis of Bethel, Maine.
v. NATHANIEL, born about 1770, bapt. May 8, 1774.
vi. JOSEPH, born Feb. 29, 1772, bapt. June 21, 1772, married first on Nov. 28, 1799, Lydia Kelly, born in Scarboro July 22, 1780, and died Jan. 3, 1832; second Sarah Graffam. They lived in Baldwin where he died Feb. 3, 1844. He was the father of nine children by his first wife.
vii. LYDIA, born about 1773, bapt. Sept. 27, 1778, married Jan. 11, 1798, Benjamin Thorn, son of Bartholomew and Lydia (Couch) Thorn of Baldwin. He died Sept. 22, 1843. For children see Thorn family.
viii. JAMES, born about 1775.
ix. SARAH, born about 1777, married Mar. 22, 1804, Isaac Kelley.

Daniel[5] Sanborn (Abner,[4] John,[3] John,[2] John[1]), born in Hampton, N.H. May 19, 1721, son of Abner and Rachel (Shaw) Sanborn, married Dec. 3, 1746, Jane Moulton. They moved to Pearsontown in 1763 at the time his Uncle Ebenezer Shaw came here. On Sept. 14, 1768, Moses Pearson deeded to him by right of settlement the 30-acre lot #19 (6/171). He is given as a joiner (carpenter) in this deed. He died in Pearsontown Jan. 14, 1786, age 65, and his widow, Jane, died here on Oct. 5, 1805, age 85 years, in Standish. Daniel Sanborn and his wife, Jane, were admitted to the Pearsontown Church by letter from the Hampton Falls Church on Dec. 8, 1771. They were parents of the following family:

i. DAVID, bapt. Dec. 13, 1747, married Mar. 1, 1792 (int. Dec. 23, 1791), Miriam Elder of Standish. They had a daughter Miriam who died Sept. 26, 1812, age 17 yrs. They lived in Standish where he died in 1822.
ii. STEPHEN, bapt. Mar. 26, 1749, married Molly Shaw, born Nov. 7, 1755, daughter of Ebenezer and Anna (Philbrick) Shaw of Pearsontown. He died in 1779 leaving his widow and two daughters: Jane, bapt. June 30, 1776, and Molly, bapt. Nov. 23, 1779. His widow married second John Mayall on Mar. 10, 1813, and died Oct. 29, 1840.
iii. JANE, bapt. May 26, 1751.
iv. JEREMIAH, bapt. Mar. 25, 1753, never married. He served in the Revolutionary War, lived in Standish and died Aug. 28, 1814, age 62 yrs., in Standish (*Eastern Argus*, Sept. 1, 1814).
v. MOLLY, bapt. Dec. 22, 1754, married (int. Jan. 16, 1776, in Gorham) Thaddeus Richardson, born May 29, 1750, son of David and Remember (Ward) Richardson. They lived in Standish, Limington and Readfield, Maine. He died Apr. 6, 1819, and she on July 14, 1841. For children see Richardson family.
vi. DOROTHY (DOLLY), born May 10, 1757, married July 7, 1791, Theodore Mussey, born Aug. 5, 1757, son of Benjamin and Abigail (Weeks) Mussey. They lived in Standish where he died Sept. 5, 1825, and she on Feb. 5, 1849, at North Bridgton. For children see Mussey family.
vii. SIMEON, born July 5, 1759, served in the Revolutionary War, married Jan. 9, 1783, Hannah Ward, born Oct. 13, 1763, and died June 20, 1850, age 87 yrs. They moved to Bethel about 1800 and later to Greenwood, where he was one of the early settlers. He died Oct. 28, 1832. They were the parents of nine children, the first eight of whom were born in Standish.
viii. EBENEZER born July 5, 1759 (twin to Simeon), probably died young.
ix. EUNICE(?), died unmarried.

John[5] Sanborn (Abner,[4] John,[3] John,[2] John[1]), brother of Daniel, born in Hampton, N.H., Jan. 9, 1723, son of Abner and Rachel (Shaw) Sanborn, married first on Jan. 28, 1748, Lucy Sanborn, born Jan. 16, 1725, daughter of Joseph and Susanna (James) Sanborn of Hampton Falls, and she died in September 1775; second (int. Sept. 27, 1785, in Gorham) Elizabeth (Johnson) Pierce, widow of John Pierce of Pearsontown. She died

July 6, 1812, age 87 years, in Standish (*Eastern Argus*, July 30, 1812) and he on Dec. 6, 1802. About 1763 he moved from Hampton to Falmouth, Maine, where he, a cordwainer (cobbler), was living on July 12, 1768, when the Proprietors of Pearsontown granted to him the 30-acre lot #139 on the condition that he fulfill the terms of settlement (8/299). He evidently moved into town about this time. He was a soldier in the Revolutionary War. He was father of the following children, all by his first wife:

- i. LYDIA, born Mar. 12, 1749, in Hampton Falls, bapt. Mar. 19, 1749/50, died unmarried in Sept. 1775.
- ii. PETER, born July 9, 1751, in Hampton Falls, bapt. July 14, 1751, served in the Revolutionary War and married (int. Oct. 23, 1781, in Gorham) Lydia Richardson, born June 20, 1763, in Brookline, Mass., daughter of Moses and Lydia (Hall) Richardson of Pearsontown. They moved to Baldwin where he died Aug. 4 or 6, 1827. She died Nov. 6, 1827, age 60 yrs., in Baldwin. They were parents of seven children.
- iii. SUSANNAH, born Aug. 13, 1753, married first Nov. 19, 1791, Enoch Linnell of Standish, second on June 25, 1800, John Pierce Jr. of Standish. She died Mar. 25, 1840.
- iv. LUCY, born Oct. 15, 1755, married in Feb. 1783 (int. Apr. 26, 1782, in Gorham) Joseph Dow of Pearsontown, born in Salisbury, Mass., Mar. 17, 1758, son of Jabez and Dorothy (Wood) Dow of Pearsontown. They lived in Standish where he died on Oct. 31, 1805, and she on Sept. 1, 1836. For children see Dow family.
- v. JOHN JR., born Oct. 15, 1757, served in the Revolutionary War, married Dec. 3, 1782, Abigail Jones, who died Oct. 19, 1836. He died Oct. 16, 1827. He was a soldier in the Revolutionary War. They lived in Standish and were the parents of the following children:
    1. PIERCE, born Sept. 17, 1783, bapt. Oct. 29, 1802, married July 27, 1807, Huldah Paine of Standish, born in Wellfleet, Mass., Feb. 15, 1780, daughter of Joseph and Phebe (Rich) Paine. He served in the War of 1812 and lived in Baldwin. He died May 5, 1854, age 70, in Standish and his wife died Dec. 23, 1853, age 63 yrs., 9 mos. Several children, all born in Standish:
        - (1) ALBERT, born May 21, 1808, bapt. Aug. 13, 1811, married Dec. 26, 1833, Louisa D. Sawyer of Baldwin.
        - (2) WILLIAM, born Feb. 21, 1810, bapt. Aug. 13, 1811, died July 23, 1853, age 42 yrs., 5 mos.
        - (3) DARIUS, born Nov. 28, 1811, bapt. July 5, 1812.
        - (4) LYMAN, born Nov. 20, 1813, bapt. July 10, 1814.
        - (5) PHEBE, born Feb. 7, 1816, bapt. Mar. 28, 1816.
        - (6) JOHN, born Oct. 14, 1818, bapt. Oct. 21, 1819.
        - (7) LORENZO, born Nov. 27, 1820, bapt. June 21, 1821.
    2. MERCY, born Feb. 11, 1785, died 1786.
    3. MERCY, born Feb. 28, 1787, bapt. Oct. 29, 1802, married Apr. 26, 1810, Weare Cram of Standish, born Sept. 14, 1783, son of Daniel Jr. and Chloe (Stevens) Cram. They lived on Oak Hill in Standish where he died Mar. 24, 1861, and she on May 22, 1855. For children see Cram family.

4. LUCY, born Sept. 1, 1789, bapt. Oct. 29, 1802, married Dec. 23, 1810, Jabez Dow of Standish, born Mar. 13, 1785, son of Joseph and Lucy (Sanborn) Dow, her cousin. They lived in Standish where she died on Oct. 4, 1854, and he on Oct. 31, 1868. For children see Dow family.
5. JOHN JR., born July 7, 1791, bapt. Oct. 29, 1802, a shoemaker by trade, moved west in 1815 and married at Marcellus, N.Y., Clarissa Smith, who died in 1835. He served in the War of 1812. He finally settled in Middleport, N.Y., and died there in 1854. Four children.
6. JOSEPH, born June 14, 1793, bapt. Oct. 29, 1802, moved west with his brother John and then to Michigan where he is said to have died in 1857.
7. ASA, born May 5, 1795, bapt. Oct. 29, 1802, married Jan. 18, 1825, Abigail Brown, daughter of David and Esther (Buttrick) Brown of Baldwin. They lived in Baldwin where he died Nov. 23, 1857, and his wife on June 6, 1865, age 62 yrs., 14 days. He was a farmer and the father of seven children.
8. ABIGAIL, born July 31, 1797, bapt. Oct. 29, 1802, married Apr. 13, 1826, Matthias Hutchinson, born in Buxton Apr. 1786 son of Joshua and Molly (Bradbury) Hutchinson. They lived in Standish near York's Corner and raised a large family of children. She died Dec. 28, 1875.
9. SUSAN, born July 23, 1799, bapt. Oct. 29, 1802, married Jan. 19, 1822, Thomas Cram of Standish born Aug. 3, 1797, son of Daniel Jr. and Chloe (Stevens) Cram.
10. WARREN, born May 5, 1802, bapt. Oct. 29, 1802, married Jan. 1, 1822, Jane W. Warren, born June 22, 1807, daughter of Samuel and Anna (Pinkerton) Warren of Standish. He was a farmer in Standish where he died on Mar. 20, 1844, and she Mar. 17, 1875. They had the following children:
    (1) ARAVESTA D., born Mar. 14, 1830, married (int. Sept. 11, 1859) Henry P. Waldron of Limington. She died in Limington Mar. 3, 1888.
    (2) MELINTHA S., born Apr. 28, 1832, married Apr. 15, 1858, John H. Davis, born Apr, 23, 1828, of Standish. She died in Standish on Jan. 6, 1917, and he on Jan. 2, 1867.
    (3) JOHN WARREN, born Mar. 21, 1835, married Ruth A. Libby of Standish., died Apr. 24, 1915.
    (4) BIGELOW THATCHER, born July 11, 1838, died Feb. 17, 1910, Augusta, Maine.
    (5) ORVILLE SCOTT, born May 31, 1841, died July 16, 1908, in Standish.

vi. RUFUS, born Feb. 5, 1760, died 1862.
vii. RACHEL, born July 19, 1762, married Apr. 25, 1785, Benjamin Ayer, born Nov. 23, 1763, son of Peter and Rebecca (Wheeler) Ayer of Buxton. He was a Methodist minister. They lived in Buxton, Standish, and Unity, Maine. She died in Freedom, Maine, on Mar. 2, 1832. For children see Ayer family.

viii. JOSEPH, born Oct. 8, 1764, in Falmouth, bapt. May 5, 1765, there, married Nov. 22, 1792, Deborah Yates of Standish, probably daughter of John and Thankful (King) Yates and sister to John Yates Jr. who settled in Standish. They lived and died in Standish, he on Oct. 16, 1831, age 67, and she on Feb. 12, 1854. They were parents of the following children:
1. SARAH, born Sept. 27, 1797, bapt. July 15, 1798, died unmarried Feb. 15, 1824, age 26 yrs., Standish.
2. JOSEPH, born 1800, died 1801.
3. JOSEPH, born Jan. 27, 1802, bapt. May 27, 1802, married Dec. 14, 1836 Catherine R. (Irish) Libby, born Jan. 27, 1813, daughter of Daniel and Abigail (Rounds) Irish of Gorham and widow of Ebenezer H. Libby. They lived and died in Standish, he on May 14, 1878, age 76 yrs., 3 mos., 17 days.
4. ABIGAIL, born Aug. 15, 1805, bapt. Nov. 21, 1805, died unmarried.
5. MARY, born Mar. 17, 1809, bapt. July 5, 1809, died unmarried Feb. 3, 1842.

ix. MOSES, born in Falmouth July 21, 1767, married Mar. 18, 1792, Susanna Pierce, born about 1767, daughter of John and Elizabeth (Johnson) Pierce, who settled in Standish. They lived in Standish, she dying Oct 9, 1852, age 85 yrs., 7 mos., and he on Aug. 25, 1857, age 90 yrs. They were parents of the following children:
1. INFANT, died Feb. 2, 1802, age 21 days.
2. MOSES JR., died Mar. 30, 1801, age 1 yr., 8 mos.
3. LYDIA, born Dec. 20, 1792, died Sept. 5, 1884, age 91 yrs., 8 mos., 16 days, unmarried, in Standish.
4. BETSEY, born Oct. 31, 1794, married Mar. 30, 1819 (int. Feb. 5, 1819, in Hollis), Magnus Ridlon of Hollis.
5. LUCY, born Jan. 12, 1797, married Dec. 31, 1823, John C. Flint of Baldwin.
6. MOSES, bapt. Aug. 29, 1799, died 1801.
7. MOSES, born Jan. 12, 1802, bapt. May 27, 1802, lived and died in Baldwin, married June 23, 1829, Susan Hopkinson of Hollis. She died Jan. 7, 1850. He died Sept. 14, 1879 (Old Dow's Corner Cem.)
8. TWIN brother to Moses, born and died 1802.
9. JOHNSON, born Sept. 13, 1804, bapt. June 6, 1805, died Oct. 22, 1865, in Standish, unmarried.
10. LEONARD, born June 20, 1807, bapt. Dec. 2, 1807, married Oct. 14, 1841, Caroline O. Cram, who died Aug. 20, 1852, age 80 yrs., 5 mos, and he died Apr. 26, 1866, age 58 yrs., 10 mos., in Standish. Three children.

SARGENT

Joseph Frye Sargent was an inhabitant of Standish for about ten years to the beginning of the nineteenth century. He was a grandson of General Joseph Frye of Fryeburg and his father was of Andover, Mass., or in the vicinity. He had a sister Hannah[1] Sargent who married (int.) Dec. 2, 1797, Uriah Ballard, both of Standish. The name of Joseph Sargent appears for one poll tax on a 1799 tax list of the town and in 1800 census with a family consisting of him and his wife, both between 16 and 26 years of age; and a son and a daughter, each less than 10 years old. According to deeds, he was a tailor and on Apr. 6, 1803, bought from Stephen Hinckley of Standish one-half acre of 30-acre lot #33 located on the Oak Hill Road a short distance beyond the Village Cemetery on the way to Oak Hill, where he evidently lived and had his tailor shop (52/353). This property he mortaged on Jan. 10, 1807, to Thomas Cram of Standish (54/449) and, having paid off the mortage on May 14, 1808, (56/70) sold or again mortaged it to Peter Rowe of Standish on the same day (56/71). This last deed was signed by him and his wife, Polly. She was Polly Pierce of Salem, Mass., when he, of Charleston, Mass., married her on Mar. 13, 1796, in Charleston. He continued to live in town and was listed in the 1810 census with a family consisting of him and his wife, both still between 26 and 45 years of age; two sons and three daughters. He left town soon after and moved to Fryeburg, where he and his wife, Polly, and their children were listed in that town's vital records, as follows: Joseph Fyre, born Oct. 9, 1796, Charleston; Mary, born Oct. 11, 1798, in Standish, married Apr. 6, 1822, Stephen P. Benton of Fryeburg; William, born Feb. 27, 1801, in Standish; Hannah, born Feb. 27, 1801, in Standish;, William, born Mar. 30, 1804, in Standish; Hannah, born July 25, 1804, in Standish; Lewis, born July 15, 1806, Daniel, born Nov. 18, 1808, in Standish; and Eliza, born June 17, 1811, in Fryeburg.

SAWYER

A young man by the name of John Sawyer was living in Pearsontown and had begun to clear and fence his land here prior to the burning of Falmouth in 1775. He was living in town on Apr. 18, 1782, when he bought from Benjamin Titcomb of Falmouth the 100-acre lot #82 in second division of lots (11/372). John and Lettice Sawyer of Standish sold 27 acres more or less of this lot to Nicholas Davis of Limington on Oct. 10, 1804 (45/53). This is good evidence that he was the John Sawyer who with wife Lettice owned the covenant in the First Parish Church of Falmouth (Portland) on Oct. 25, 1772, and whose daughter Jerusha was baptized there Nov. 1, 1772.

Parentage of this John Sawyer has not been definitely determined, but he may have been a son of Thomas[3] (Isaac,[2] James[1]) Sawyer, born in Gloucester, Mass., Oct. 12, 1711, but a resident of Falmouth on July 7, 1737, when he married at Hampton Falls, N.H., Mehitabel Blake of that town. Although we have been unable to find any record of the birth of a son John to this couple, Thomas and Mehitabel (Blake) Sawyer had the following children baptized in the First Parish Church of Falmouth:

i. MEHITABEL, bapt. 1738.
ii. ANNA, bapt. 1740.

iii. JERUSHA, bapt. 1745.
iv. ISAAC, bapt. 1749.

The similarity of these names with those of the children and grandchildren of John and Lettice (Whitney) Sawyer may indicate relatationship.

The name of John Sawyer is found on the 1789, 1790, 1795, and 1796 tax lists of Standish, in the 1790 census with a family of 2-2-5, and in the 1800 census as the head of a family consisting of him and his wife, both over 45 years of age, two females between 10 and 16 years old, and three females under 10 years of age. On Mar. 1, 1801, John Sawyer of Standish and his son Thomas then of Hampden, Maine, sold to Lemuel McCorrison of Buxton the 100-acre lot #112 in third division in Standish (59/445) which they had purchased from McCorrison on Dec. 16, 1796 (28/472). As indicated above, John Sawyer and his wife sold part of lot #82 in second division, probably the homestead farm, on Oct. 10, 1804. It seems likely that they left town about this time, but whence they went has not been determined. The John Sawyer whose name appears on the 1808 tax list of Standish probably was not the one concerning whom we are writing about, but a younger man from the Sawyer family of Buxton.

He married June 1, 1771, Lettice Whitney whose name is found in Falmouth and Standish Church records and in at least one deed. Widow Lettice (Whitney) Sawyer died Nov. 22, 1841, age 91 years, in Knox, formerly of Standish. No complete list of the children of John and Lettice (Whitney) Sawyer has been found, but has been compiled from numerous sources:

i. MOLLY, born about 1771, married Apr. 19, 1789, John Wood Jr., born in Exeter, N.H., Oct. 7, 1754, son of John and Sarah (Gorden) Wood of Exeter and Standish. He was living in Buxton with a family of 1-1-2 at the time of the 1790 census, but he died Oct. 11, 1791, and she married on Feb. 25, 1794, John Miller of Flintstown, later of Limington. She died Aug. 20, 1826, in Limington. For children by both marriages see Wood and Miller families.

ii. JERUSHA, born in Falmouth Sept. 15, 1772, bapt. in First Parish Church there on Nov. 1, 1772 as daughter of John Sawyer, married (int. June 11, 1791 in Gorham) Seth L. Hamblen, born in Barnstable, Mass., Jan 1, 1765, son of Samuel and Temperance (Lewis) Hamblen of Barnstable and Gorham. They lived in Standish, Limington, and Brownfield, in which latter town she died at the home of her son Seth on Apr. 18, 1851. For children see Hamblen family.

iii. JOHN JR., born Jan. 31, 1777, married Jan. 22, 1797, Susanna Hamblen, born Aug. 7, 1774, daughter of Ebenezer and Deborah (Lovell) Hamblen of Gorham. At the time of the 1800 census he, between 26 and 45 yrs. of age, was living in Standish with a family consisting of him and his wife and one male and one female child under 10 yrs. of age. His wife is said to have died in Knox, Maine, on June 1, 1825, so it appears likely that he is the John Sawyer listed as a settler in Knox Plantation in 1804. He died in Knox on Feb. 5, 1846, age 69.

iv. THOMAS, born ____, married Sept. 13, 1798, Hannah Simpson, bapt. in Buxton Nov. 23, 1779, daughter of Jonathan and Alice (Peach) Simpson. He, between 16 and 26 yrs. old, is listed as living in Hampden, Maine, at the time of the 1800 census with a family consisting of him and his wife and a son under 10 yrs. of age. Nothing further known.
v. JONATHAN LOWELL, bapt. in Standish Church on Feb. 28, 1779, as son of John and Lettice Sawyer. Nothing further known.
vi. SELINA, born about 1781, married July 17, 1800, William Chick, born about 1776 son of Nathan and Hannah (Small) Chick of Limington. They lived in that town where she died Jan. 27, 1826, age 44 yrs. and 4 mos. He married second on Aug. 10, 1826, Eliza Libby, and died Sept. 7, 1841, age 65 yrs., 9 mos.
vii. BARBARA, bapt. as daughter of John Sawyer in Standish Church Sept. 23, 1787. She married Charles Wiggin.
viii. LETTICE, bapt. as daughter of John Sawyer in Standish Church Oct. 9, 1791. She married Mar. 17, 1809, Thomas McLaughlin.
ix. POLLY, bapt. in Standish Church in Oct. 1793. She married Stephen Wiggin.

The names of John and David Sawyer are found on the 1808 tax list of Standish. They were brothers and sons of John[4] (Joseph,[3] John,[2] James[1]) and Isabella (Martin) Sawyer of Buxton.

John Sawyer was born in Buxton Oct. 4, 1775, and died in Standish May 6, 1849. He married June 2, 1799, Grace Jenkins, born Dec. 19, 1776, daughter of Dennis Jenkins. She died in Standish Feb. 16, 1853. Both are buried in a cemetery on Standish Neck where they lived on a farm adjoining that of his brother David. Children were as follows:

i. JOHN, born July 11, 1800, died Oct. 18, 1870, at Casco, Maine, married June 19, 1825, Rebecca Longley, born Aug. 28, 1802, at Waterford, Maine, daughter of Eli and Mary (Whitcomb) Longley, who died Feb. 24, 1879, at Casco. They were the parents of eight children.
ii. DENNIS, born about 1803, died Oct. 22, 1838.
iii. LEMUEL, born July 18, 1807, died Aug. 12, 1888, age 81 yrs., in Standish; married (int. Oct. 7, 1832, in Standish) Esther G. Purinton, born in Durham, Maine, Jan. 30, 1807, daughter of Meshach and Sarah (Gerrish) Purinton of Windham, who died Dec. 11, 1880, age 79 yrs., 10 mos. Both were buried in Harding Cemetery. He lived on his father's farm on Standish Neck. They were parents of the following children:
1. SARAH ANN, born July 8, 1833, died Dec. 21, 1859, married Mar. 15, 1857, George E. Mead of Bridgton, she of Standish.
2. DENNIS JENKINS, born Apr. 6, 1835, married first Sarah J. Varney, daughter of Hiram and Susan (Green) Varney of Windham, Maine, and had Eugene H. Sawyer (born Oct. 10, 1859, died Oct. 22, 1916), married second Charity Ann Smith of Windham. He died Aug. 12, 1912, age 77 yrs., 5 mos., Windham.
3. MARIA H., born Sept. 11, 1836, married Nov. 19, 1856, John B. Winslow of Casco. She was living in 1912 in Raymond.

4. ELLERY FOXCROFT, born Mar. 13, 1838, died Mar. 19, 1876, married June 10, 1864, Ellen Nichols, born in Vassalboro Sept. 23, 1840, and died Sept. 11, 1894.
5. JOHN PURINTON, born Oct. 30, 1839, married Louisa Bodge, born Aug. 11, 1838, daughter of Thomas and Abigail (Nason) Bodge of Windham. He was her second husband and she died June 13, 1910. They lived in Westbrook, Maine.
6. EMILY FREEMAN, born Apr. 21, 1842, died Mar. 13, 1888, married Charles A. Nichols, son of Charles and Esther (Owen) Nichols of Windam.
7. DR. ALFRED STANFORD, born Aug. 13, 1844, married Mar. 23, 1881, at Standish Hannah E. Rich, born July 25, 1857, daughter of William and Lucy (Freeman) Rich of Standish. He died Jan. 14, 1932, Portland.
8. HARRIET L., born July 1, 1847, died Dec. 29, 1850.
9. MARIETTA, born June 27, 1850, married Samuel C. Rich.

iv. THOMAS, born about 1810, married first (int. Aug. 14, 1831, in Standish) Esther Green, born about 1807 daughter of John and Esther (Shaw) Green of Standish. She died Jan. 29, 1834, age 27, and was buried in the Came Cemetery in Buxton. He married second Mar. 1, 1835, Mary Hutchinson, born in Mar. 1814 daughter of Matthias and Nancy (White) Hutchinson of Standish. He was a shoemaker and lived at Bonney Eagle in Standish near the bridge over the Saco River. He died in the prime of life on May 8, 1858, and was buried with his first wife in the Came Cemetery in Buxton. His widow continued to live in Standish for many years thereafter, passing away on Oct. 30, 1891, at the age of 77 yrs., 7 mos.

David Sawyer, brother of John, was born May 27, 1784, and baptized Oct. 3, 1784, son of John and Isabella (Martin) Sawyer of Buxton, married Hannah Milliken, born Nov. 7, 1787, daughter of Isaiah and Eunice (Nason) Milliken of Old Orchard. He settled on a farm adjoining that of his brother John on Standish Neck where he continued to live until his death on May 24, 1864, at the age of eighty. His widow died on July 12, 1879, age 93 years, 8 months. They were buried in Harding Cemetery. Probable children of David and Hannah (Milliken) Sawyer were as follows:

i. ISABEL, born Oct. 29, 1807, married Jan. 8, 1840, John S. Leighton and second to Hollis Foye, and died Apr. 30, 1888, age 80 yrs., 6 mos. Her gravestone is in the same burial plot as her parents in the Harding Cemetery.
ii. HENRY M., born Apr. 10, 1810, married June 24, 1839, Priscilla Jackson.
iii. DAVID, born Nov. 24, 1811, died Oct. 12, 1815.
iv. HANNAH L., born Sept. 5, 1813, married Sept. 14, 1838, Curtis B. Merrill. They were living with her parents in 1860 and are shown on an 1871 atlas map as living on the David Sawyer place in Standish. She died Nov. 21, 1871, age 58 yrs., and was buried in the Harding Cemetery in her family plot.
v. EUNICE M., born June 22, 1817, married Mar. 19, 1840, Hiram Ellis of Portland, and she died Nov. 23, 1855.

vi. DAVID, born Oct. 21, 1819, died Jan. 8, 1821, age 1 yr., 2 mos.
vii. JOHN ISAIAH, born May 3, 1822, married Apr. 15, 1847, Cynthia C. Parker.
viii. MARY M., born June 25, 1825, married Dec. 10, 1853, William F. Green, and died Mar. 15, 1898.
ix. ISAIAH, born Dec. 28, 1827, died Oct. 10, 1828.
x. ELIZA A., born July 22, 1830, married Nov. 18, 1850, Marshall Libby of Gorham.
xi. ELLEN J., born Apr. 2, 1833, married Feb. 3, 1852, William Webster and she died Mar. 16, 1892.

SEGAR

The name of Josiah Segar is found on the 1795 and 1796 tax lists of Standish and in the 1800 census with a family consisting of him and his wife, two boys and three girls under 10 years. Research discloses that he was born Oct. 11, 1745, son of Josiah and Thankful (Allen) Segar of Newton, Mass., and moved to Sudbury-Canada (Bethel) with his brother Nathaniel Segar, who was one of the early settlers of that town. He is given as a resident of Sudbury-Canada on Mar. 6, 1788, when he married Jane Meserve, daughter of John and Sarah (Strout) Meserve of Standish. Since he was living in New Penacook (Rumford) in 1792, it is likely that he was the Josiah Segar (1-0-3) who was living there at the time of the 1790 census. The Josiah Segar living in Bethel at the same time with a family of 1-0-2 was perhaps his father. Soon after 1792 he apparently left Rumford and moved to Standish, but it is likely that he did not remain in town very long for he moved to Unity, Maine, in 1804 where he is said to have raised a large family.

SHAW

The Shaw family has been represented among the inhabitants of Standish from the earliest days of its history. The names of Ebenezer, Joseph, Josiah, Sargent, and Thomas Shaw are found on the 1789, 1790, 1795, 1795, 1796 and later tax lists of the town and in the 1790 census. They were sons of Ebenezer[4] Shaw Sr. (Caleb,[3] Joseph,[2] Roger[1]), the first settler of the name in town. He was born in Hampton, N.H., Oct. 7, 1713, son of Caleb and Elizabeth (Hillard) Shaw and was left an orphan at an early age. Until his majority he was bought up in the family of Moses Pearson, who doubtless was instrumental in persuading him to settle in Pearsontown.

On Nov. 19, 1738, Ebenezer Shaw Sr. married Anna Philbrick, born Feb. 28, 1720, daughter of Thomas and Abiah (____) Philbrick of Hampton and aunt of Jonathan Philbrick, another of the early settlers in Pearsontown. They lived in Hampton and on Sargent's Island.

On Jan. 21, 1762, the Proprietors of Pearsontown chose a committee, of which Moses Pearson was the chairman "to look out a place for a sawmill and lay out 100 acres of land convenient for said mill for encouragement to such person for building said mill, to be completed on or before the first of October next." They also voted that "there shall be one hundred other acres drafted out of the second division and confirmed above said mill by the time above said." Under date of Mar. 16, 1763, the Proprietors confirmed "to Mr. Ebenezer Shaw and heirs the land and privilege on which he has built his mill." This mill stood where Shaw's Mill has since been located and is said to have been built in nine days.

Here then is evidence that Ebenezer Shaw was living in town as early as 1762, at least with some members of his family. His grandson gives 1762 as the date when Ebenezer came to town. Ebenezer was followed the next year by fifteen or more families from the vicinity of Hampton, N.H. On Apr. 5, 1763, he purchased the 30-acre lot #42 from Thomas Morton (2/332) and on Feb. 28, 1785, Moses Pearson deeded to him the 30-acre lot #123 by right of settlement (3/117). This lot abutted the mill site lot granted him and extented to the road leading from Standish Corner to Sebago Lake, it being the lot on which he established his homestead. Ebenezer Shaw was active in the Pearsontown Church to which he and his wife were admitted members on Aug. 18, 1769. He died in Pearsontown on Mar. 13, 1782, and his wife, Anna, survived him until Dec. 12, 1804, living with her son Thomas after the death of her husband. When she died there were thirty-four families of her descendants--she was survived by nine children, eighty-two grandchildren, one hundred and nine great-grandchildren.

Ebenezer and Anna (Philbrick) Shaw were the parents of ten children, all of whom were born in Hampton, N.H., and were as follows:

i. JOSIAH, born Jan. 31, 1740, married about 1760 Mary Lamprey of Hampton, N.H., and in 1763 moved to Pearsontown. He was living in town on Apr. 4, 1763, when he bought from Thomas Morton the 30-acre lot #43 (2/331) where he settled and kept the first tavern ever opened in town. His wife, Mary, was admitted into membership of the Pearsontown Church on May 14, 1769. He was elected first town treasurer in 1786. He is listed in the 1790 census with a family of 3-1-2 and in the 1800 census with a family consisting of him and his wife, one male between 10 and 16, and one male and one female between 16 and 26. By occupation he was a cooper and farmer. He died in Standish on Aug. 7, 1810, age 70 yrs., (*Eastern Argus*, Aug. 16, 1810, gives his death as Aug. 2) and his wife on Jan. 9, 1826, age 81 yrs. (*Christian Mirror*, Jan. 13, 1826). They were the parents of six children, as follows:

1. MARY, born in Hampton, N.H., Oct. 16, 1761, married Feb. 14, 1785 (int. Nov. 20, 1784 in Gorham), Jonathan Bartlett of Bethel, Maine, where they lived until his death on Apr. 14, 1798. She afterwards married Nathan Adams of Rumford, Maine. Four children by first marriage and one by second.
2. HANNAH, born in Pearsontown Dec. 22, 1763, married (int. Apr. 27, 1783, in Gorham) Asaph Brown of Waterford, Maine, where they lived. She died in Bethel, Maine, Feb. 11, 1841. He was a Revolutionary War veteran and came from Stowe,

Mass., to Waterford and settled in that town. He served in the Revolutionary War for four years. She died in Waterford on Dec. 15, 1830, and she on June 13, 1834. Nine children.
3. ANNA, born May 8, 1766, married Jan. 19, 1791, John Atherton of Waterford and settled in that town. She died in Waterford on Dec. 15, 1830, and he on June 13, 1834. Nine children.
4. JONATHAN, born Sept. 5, 1769, in Standish, bapt. Sept. 10, 1769, married (int. Jan. 1, 1800, in Gorham) Mary (Molly) Blake, born Feb. 14, 1778, daughter of Ithiel and Apphia (Higgins) Blake of Gorham. He died in West Gorham Oct. 19, 1855, age 87 yrs., 1 mo. (*Zion Advocate*, Nov. 2, 1855).
5. JOSIAH, born Oct. 3, 1773, bapt. Apr. 24, 1774, married in 1795 Sarah Poor of Brownfield and settled in Waterford, Maine. He was a preacher of the Methodist denomination. After the death of his first wife, he married second Betsey Haskell of Harvard, Mass. He died in Waterford Apr. 1, 1847. Eight children.
6. ELI, born Dec. 6, 1781, married May 7, 1820, Betsey Thomes of Buxton and lived on the homestead in Standish where he was a farmer and cooper. He died Sept. 21, 1852, and she in 1864. Four children as follows:
    (1) MARY LAMPER, born May 29, 1820, married Nov. 24, 1847, William H. Johnson of Gorham. She died Sept. 12, 1849.
    (2) ANNA, born June 27, 1822, married May 17, 1855, Rev. Edward E. Davies. She died in Scarboro Sept. 22, 1856.
    (3) CAROLINE MATILDA, born Nov. 15, 1824, died May 15, 1850, age 25 yrs., in Standish. Unmarried.
    (4) JOHN, born Feb. 15, 1828, married Sept. 22, 1855, Emily C. Shaw, born Mar. 29, 1837, daughter of Peter M. and Lydia (Morton) Shaw of Standish. They moved to Kansas in 1872 and he died there in Feb. 1898 leaving one son and two daughters.
ii. ABIAH, born Jan. 16, 1741, died Apr. 10, 1762, unmarried.
iii. JOANNA, born Apr. 4, 1743, married July 7, 1762, Peter Moulton, born in Hampton, N.H., in 1742 son of Worthington and Abigail (Garland) Moulton. They lived in Standish where he died June 3, 1812, and she on Jan. 16, 1834. For children see Moulton family.
iv. SARGENT, born Oct. 23, 1745, in Hampton, N.H., came to Pearsontown with his father. On Aug. 1, 1768, the Pearsontown Proprietors deeded to him the 30-acre lot #126 subject to his compliance with the terms of settlement within a period of two years (6/214). He was a cooper and farmer, an active member of the Congregational Church, a Revolutionary War veteran, and a town officer. He married first (int. Apr. 17, 1770, in Gorham) Sarah Knight of Windham, who died in 1776; second (int. July 12, 1777, in Gorham) Mrs. Salome (Lombard) Dorsett, born in 1764 daughter of Jedediah and Susan (Dorsett) Lombard of Gorham, who died June 2, 1786; and third on Sept. 17, 1786, Ann Thompson, daughter of Molly (Colley) Rich, wife of Lemuel Rich Jr., who died Feb. 16, 1834. His name is found on the 1790 census with a family of 2-1-7 and in the 1800 census with a family consisting of two males and two

females under 10, two females between 10 and 16, and four females between 16 and 26. He died Dec. 3, 1823. He was the father of sixteen children by his three wives, as follows:

By first wife:
1. ENOCH, born June 8, 1772, married Dec. 25, 1792, Rhoda Philbrick, born Apr. 22, 1772, bapt. July 20, 1777, daughter of Michael and Mary (____) Philbrick of Standish. She died Jan. 3, 1819, and he married second Sybil Titcomb, who died in Pownal, Maine, Apr. 13, 1875. He lived in Standish, Gorham, and Windham, Maine. He died in Windham Aug. 28, 1863. He was the father of eleven children by first wife and six by second.
2. SARAH, born June 5, 1775, bapt. July 20, 1777, married Joseph Smith Dec. 12, 1816, and died July 8, 1846.
3. A SON, born Apr. 10, 1776, died in infancy.

By second wife:
4. JOSEPH, born Oct. 3, 1778, married Mary Blethen of Thorndike, Maine, where he settled as a farmer. He was also a schoolteacher. He died in Thorndike Aug. 27, 1849, and his widow on May 18, 1860. They were parents of five children, all born in Thorndike.
5. ABIGAIL, born May 5, 1780, married May 8, 1803, William E. Files, born Apr. 3, 1781, son of Ebenezer and Molly (Elder) Files of West Gorham. She died Mar. 13, 1819, leaving eight children and he married second on Nov. 4, 1819, Elizabeth Moulton, born Oct. 7, 1794, daughter of Simon and Abigail (Plaisted) Moulton of Standish. He died Dec. 24, 1843, and she on Feb. 24, 1857. Six children by second marriage.
6. MARY, born Oct. 16, 1781, married Sept. 3, 1804, Simeon Coffin of Gorham, son of Simeon Coffin of Alfred, Maine. They moved to Thorndike where she died July 6, 1839, and he in 1871. Ten children.
7. ELIZABETH, born July 22, 1783, married June 17, 1802, Joseph Drew of Newfield. She died Jan. 30, 1861, age 71 yrs., in Limerick, and he died there Dec. 26, 1853, age 76 yrs., 17 days.

By third wife:
8. ANNA, born June 6, 1788, married July 17, 1808, Daniel Moulton, born Apr. 1, 1781, son of Peter and Abigail (Plaisted) Moulton of Standish. They settled in the northern part of Gorham where he was a farmer and a cooper. He died in June 1859 where he Jan. 8, 1861. For children see Moulton family.
9. HANNAH, born Nov. 12, 1789, married June 27, 1810, Edward Files, brother to her sister Abigail's husband, he born in Gorham Feb. 11, 1786. They lived in Otisfield, Standish, and Gorham, where he died Aug. 3, 1867, and she on Nov. 12, 1878. Eleven children.
10. REV. SARGENT, born Dec. 16, 1791, married first on Dec. 25, 1815, Susanna Swett, born Sept. 16, 1791, daughter of Joseph and Deborah (Linnell) Swett of Gorham. She died Nov. 18, 1838, age 47 yrs., 2 mos. 2 days, and he married second Cynthia Hanson, daughter of Joseph Hanson of Windham, who

died May 11, 1858, age 63 yrs., in Portland. In July 1860 he married third Abigail (Files) Libby of Gorham, widow of Luther Libby. She was born about 1789 daughter of Samuel and Esther (Thomes) Files of Gorham and died July 27, 1880, age 82. He was a Baptist minister and lived in Standish, Windham, Portland, Scarboro, and Gorham, where he died Mar. 4, 1866. One child by his first wife and two by his second.

11. PETER M., born Jan. 1, 1794, married Sept. 14, 1817, Lydia Morton, born Jan. 2, 1798, daughter of David and Sarah (Sanger) Morton of Gorham. He was a farmer and mill owner in Standish and died on the farm where he was born and always lived on July 2, 1866. His widow died Jan. 27, 1872, age 74, in Standish. Six children, as follows:
    (1) MARY ANN, born Nov. 9, 1821, married Oct. 25, 1852, Daniel Moulton of Gorham. They lived in Standish Village where she died July 26, 1888. He died at Little Falls in Gorham. No children.
    (2) WILLIAM M., born June 2, 1826, married Oct. 25, 1852, Lydia Rand, daughter of Edmund Rand of Standish. They lived in Portland where she died on May 3, 1886. He died in Gaylord, Mich., Sept. 2, 1901. One child, a son Frederick W. Shaw, who lived in Portland.
    (3) ALBION K. P., born May 26, 1828, married Sarah J. Strout. He died Apr. 21, 1891. He lived in Standish on homestead granted to his great-grandfather Ebenezer Shaw.
    (4) ANSEL, born Dec. 6, 1833, married Jennie McCluskey, and moved to New York. He died in Montgomery, Alabama, on way to Florida. Two daughters.
    (5) MILTON, born Mar. 29, 1837, married June 29, 1870, Nellie Horse of Gorham. He lived in Standish, Gorham, and New York. Three children.
    (6) EMILY C., born Mar. 29, 1837, married John Shaw born Feb. 15, 1828, son of Eli and Betsey (Thomes) Shaw. They moved to Hiawatha, Kansas.
12. SALOME, born Aug. 5, 1796, married Oct. 10, 1816, David Norton of Gorham, brother to her brother Peter's wife, born Jan. 9, 1792. They lived in Gorham and Standish, where she died Aug. 6, 1857, and he on Mar. 24, 1883, age 91 yrs. Ten children.
13. EUNICE, born Jan. 1, 1799, married George Gray of Buxton. They lived in Windham, Standish, and Buxton, where she died Oct. 25, 1854, age 55 yrs., 9 mos., in Buxton and he in 1866.
14. PHEBE, born Mar. 7, 1802, was a dwarf and died unmarried Mar. 20, 1880.
15. ACHSAH, born July 7, 1804, married Aug. 3, 1823, Josiah Swett, brother of her brother Sargent's wife, born in Gorham Sept. 13, 1802. They settled on Standish Neck, where she died Sept. 25, 1859, and he on May 15, 1884. Twelve children.
16. LYDIA, born May 26, 1807, died in childhood.

v. **EBENEZER JR.**, born Jan. 3, 1749, in Hampton, N.H., married first (int. Sept. 22, 1771, in Gorham) Sarah Wood, daughter of William and Hannah (____) Wood of Gorham; she died July 8, 1792. He married second on Mar. 4, 1793, Salome Green, born Feb. 3, 1771, daughter of John and Mary (Stuart) Green of Gorham, who lived in Aug. 1847. They lived in Standish where he followed the occupation of brick-making and was also a mason, cooper, and farmer. He is listed in the 1790 census with a family of 2-3-4 and at the time of the 1800 census his family was comprised of him and his wife, two males and five families under 10, two males and one female between 10 and 16, and one male and two females between 26 and 45, there being one of his sons and his family living with him. He died in Standish Aug. 11, 1836, age 87 yrs. His obituary was given in the *Christian Mirror*, issue of Aug. 25, 1836, in which it states that he had twenty-six children, of whom twenty were still living at the time. It further states that he was of a family of eleven who came to Standish about the year 1760 and who are all remarkable for having lived to a great age: none have lived under 65 years, and the average age is 79. He was the father of the following children:

By first wife:
1. **HANNAH**, born Oct. 4, 1772, bapt. Sept. 19, 1773, married first on Nov. 4, 1790, Wentworth Stuart Jr., born Aug. 17, 1770, son of Wentworth and Susanna (Lombard) Stuart of Gorham. They lived in Standish, where he died Jan. 23, 1807. She married second Lemuel McCorrison of Baldwin and died Mar. 2, 1848. Nine children by first marriage, for list of whom see Stuart family.
2. **CALEB**, born Jan. 9, 1774, bapt. May 8, 1774, married Abigail Whitney of Buckfield, Maine, and died in Gorham leaving no children.
3. **SAMUEL**, born Dec. 10, 1775, married Apr. 12, 1798 (int. Mar. 17, 1798, in Gorham) Mary Phinney, born Mar. 17, 1781, daughter of Joseph and Susan (Crockett) Phinney of Gorham. They lived on Standish Neck where he died Aug. 22, 1848, and she on Feb. 22, 1855. Ten children.
4. **BETSEY**, born Feb. 17, 1777, married Sept. 14, 1797, Elias Meserve of Scarboro, settled on Raymond Cape. He died Sept. 23, 1853, and she on Feb. 3, 1854. Eleven children.
5. **SARAH**, born Jan. 10, 1779, died in 1781.
6. **SARAH**, born Aug. 14, 1782, died Apr. 9, 1789.
7. **MOLLY**, born Nov. 21, 1784, bapt. July 18, 1807, married David Kneeland on May 22, 1816, and settled in Buckfield, Maine.
8. **EBENEZER JR.**, born July 21, 1787, bapt. July 18, 1807, married first Jan. 25, 1816, Rebecca Yates, born Mar. 17, 1794, daughter of John and Mercy (Hopkins) Yates of Standish. She died July 31, 1832, and he married her sister Mary on Oct. 20, 1833, who was born June 8, 1796, and died Sept. 5, 1865, age 68 yrs., 3 mos., in Standish. They lived on a farm on Standish Neck where he died Dec. 6, 1860. He had the following children as given in the family register:

(1) ELMIRA, born July 21, 1816.
       m. Mar. 1853 James Meserve.
   (2) ELIZABETH M., born June 20, 1819.
       m. Sept. 1842 Samuel L. Nason.
   (3) LEANDER, born Aug. 5, 1820.
       m. Jan. 1846 Mary Yates.
   (4) CURTIS, born July 23, 1822.
       m. May 6, 1849, Tryphena Crockett.
   (5) SARAH A., born Nov. 13, 1825, died Dec. 1826.
   (6) WILLIAM, born Nov. 19, 1827.
       m. Apr. 29, 1857, Catherine Rogers.
   (7) JOHN Y., born Feb. 20, 1830, died Apr. 1867, married June 1858 Ann E. Hodsdon.
   (8) INFANT, born Feb. 1836, died Feb. 1836.
   (9) THOMAS J., born Aug. 19, 1838, died Oct. 6, 1840.
9. WILLIAM, born Jan. 3, 1790, bapt. July 18, 1807, married Betsey Young of Farmington and settled in Mercer, Maine, where she died Oct. 6, 1846, and he on May 9, 1855. Eleven children.
10. ANNA, born July 8, 1792, bapt. July 18, 1807, married in 1815 John Marean Jr., born Dec. 17, 1787, son of John and Lois (Bean) Marean of Standish. They lived in Standish where he died June 6, 1853, and she on June 6, 1860. Ten children, for list of whom see Marean family.

By second wife:
11. SARAH, born Mar. 31, 1794, bapt. May 11, 1817, Ivory Butler, born Dec. 3, 1794, son of William and Abigail (Cross) Butler of Standish. They lived in Lebanon, N.H., Standish and other places until 1846, but moved to Lawn Ridge, Ill., where he died in 1870. Five children.
12. COL. JOHN, born Aug. 24, 1796, bapt. July 18, 1807, married Esther Higgins, born Sept. 18, 1806, daughter of Prince and Selina (Higgins) Higgins of Standish. They lived in Standish but in 1837 moved to Corinna, Maine, where he died July 3, 1875, and she on Mar. 21, 1872. Eight children.
13. JONATHAN PHILBRICK, born July 18, 1798, bapt. July 18, 1807, married first Nov. 24, 1825, Mary Higgins, sister of his brother John's wife. They lived in Standish where she died Apr. 15, 1854, age 54 yrs., 8 mos., and he married second Betsey Ross of Harrison, Maine, to which town he moved and where he died in Mar. 1868. His widow died in 1899. Three children.
14. SALOME, born Apr. 29, 1800, bapt. July 18, 1807, married Russell Lebanon of Harrison and lived there until her death in Mar. 1883.
15. REBECCA, born May 28, 1801, bapt. July 18, 1807, married Feb. 28, 1827, Seth Higgins, son of Seth and Experience (Higgins) Higgins. They lived in Standish where he was a blacksmith and where she died May 3, 1886, and he on Dec. 4, 1896. Two children.

16. LEWIS, born July 16, 1802, bapt. July 18, 1807, married Lucy A. Rollins and lived in Standish, Boston, Portland and finally settled in Gorham, where he died July 7, 1879. His widow married Samuel Gerry of Sebago, Maine. Six children.
17. JOANNA, born Oct. 3, 1803, bapt. July 18, 1807, married Nov. 10, 1824, Simeon Whitney of Harrison, Maine. She died Sept. 9, 1873, and he in 1885. Six children.
18. RHODA, born May 21, 1805, bapt. July 18, 1807, married first on Sept. 10, 1833, Enos L.W. Kilborn of Harrison where he died on Oct. 18, 1846. She married second Jonathan Peabody of Gilead, Maine, who died in Nov. 1853, and married third Melvin Farwell of West Bethel, who died there Aug. 20, 1866. She died at North Bridgton Aug. 20, 1886. Five children by first husband.
19. MARGARET, born Dec. 1, 1807, bapt. July 18, 1807, married Noah Trickey of Bangor and Saco, Maine. She died in Saco Feb. 12, 1886; he 4 days later, Feb. 16, 1886. Two children.
20. ALMIRA, born May 5, 1809, bapt. Sept. 6, 1810, died in 1814.
21. APPHIA, born June 11, 1810, bapt. Sept. 6, 1810, married David Purinton, born May 1, 1800, son of Daniel and Lois (Brown) Purinton of Gorham. They lived in Gorham and Harrison, but finally settled in Waterford, Maine, where he died Jan. 13, 1876, and she on Nov. 26, 1885. Eight children.
22. EUDOXIA, born July 29, 1811, married Thomas Trickey of Bangor, where she died about 1840. No children.
23. STEVEN, born June 10, 1812, died age 1 yr., 6 mos.
24. SOPHRONIA, born Aug. 6, 1813, married Charles Libby of Gorham and lived in Harrison, where he died June 28, 1884, and she on Jan. 29, 1899. One child.

vi. ELIZABETH, born Mar. 21, 1751, married (int. Sept. 2, 1769, in Gorham) James Moody, born about 1750 son of Samuel Moody. They lived in Standish where she died May 27, 1816, and he on Jan. 4, 1818. For children see Moody family.

vii. THOMAS, born Oct. 20, 1753, in Hampton, N.H., and was about nine years old when his father settled in Pearsontown. Here he continued to live until his death on Oct. 20, 1838. By occupation he was a cooper and farmer and built the first gristmill in town, which was operated by a windmill. He was noted for his rhyming and was the family historian, many of his records and originals of his works being in the keeping of the Maine Historical Society. His name is found in the 1790 census with a family of 2-2-2. He married first on Nov. 20, 1777, Anna Wood, born July 20, 1751, daughter of William and Hannah (____) Wood of Gorham and sister of the first wife of his brother Ebenezer. She died May 18, 1808, and he married second on Nov. 20, 1809, Mrs. Susannah (Smith) Thomes, widow of Daniel Thomes and daughter of Thomas and Rhoda (Rounds) Smith of Buxton, who died Feb. 11, 1825. He married third on Mar. 9, 1826, Mrs. Lydia (Prentiss) Partridge, widow of Jotham Partridge and daughter of Samuel and Dolly (Day) Prentiss. She died in Standish Apr. 3, 1858, age 83. Children of Thomas Shaw, all born in Standish, were as follows:
By first wife:

1. DANIEL, born Sept. 17, 1778, bapt. Jan. 3, 1779, died Jan. 2, 1781.
2. SUSANNAH, born Jan. 19, 1782, bapt. Nov. 13, 1785, died June 15, 1841, unmarried.
3. DANIEL, born May 10, 1784, bapt. Sept. 9, 1793, died in infancy.
4. DANIEL, born Aug. 26, 1787, married Mrs. Elizabeth (Clark) Hallowell, widow of David Hallowell and daughter of Deacon Joseph Clark, born in Eastport, Maine, Apr. 28, 1804, died Oct. 3, 1847. They lived in Standish on his father's homestead farm and he was a farmer and cooper. He died June 17, 1874, in the house in which he was born. They had five children:
   (1) THOMAS C., born Nov. 3, 1834.
   (2) ALONZO, born Feb. 11, 1836.
   (3) ALINDA, born Jan. 13, 1838.
   (4) DANIEL, born Feb. 29, 1840.
   (5) ELIZABETH, born Feb. 19, 1842.
5. HADASSAH, born May 18, 1793, bapt. Sept. 9, 1793, married Oct. 30, 1818, Isaac Davis of Standish, born Mar. 28, 1790, in Gorham son of Samuel Jr. and Mary (Skillings) Davis. They were parents of three children. She died May 26, 1824, age 31 yrs., in Standish, and he married second Mrs. Abigail (Whitney) Boucher. He died in 1867.
   By second wife:
6. COL. JOSEPH, born Aug. 30, 1810, married Nov. 23, 1839, Mary J. Higgins, daughter of Barnabas Higgins of Gorham. He was a farmer and cooper and died Oct. 8, 1849. His widow died Mar. 16, 1888. Three children. Children of Joseph and Mary Shaw were as follows:
   (1) DELMA, born Dec. 9, 1840.
   (2) JOSEPH C., born Sept. 17, 1843.
   (3) JULIA ANN, born July 26, 1845, married Joseph E. McDonald. She died Sept. 2, 1906, in Standish.

viii. MARY, born Nov. 7, 1755, married first (int. Feb. 17, 1774, in Gorham) Stephen Sanborn, born in Hampton, N.H., in 1749 son of Daniel and Jane (Moulton) Sanborn. They lived in Standish where he died in 1779. They were parents of a daughter Jane. His widow married second John Mayall and died Oct. 29, 1840.

ix. MARGARET, born Jan. 7, 1758, married (int. Dec. 30, 1780, in Gorham) Daniel Bean, born on Mar. 16, 1757, son of Jonathan and Abigail (Gordon) Bean. They lived in Bethel, Maine, where he died Mar. 16, 1833, and she in Aug. 1842. For children see Bean family.

x. JOSEPH, born May 10, 1760, in Hampton, N.H., married (int. May 12, 1780, in Gorham) Eunice Bean, born in 1763 daughter of Jonathan and Abigail (Gordon) Bean of Standish and Bethel. He was a Revolutionary soldier, cooper, and farmer, and lived on Standish Neck, where he died Aug. 24, 1830, and she on Aug. 17, 1832. Children, as follows:
   1. ENOCH, born Oct. 11, 1780, married Aug. 4, 1806, Delilah Morton, probably daughter of Ebenezer and Susan (Irish)

Morton of Standish. They lived for awhile on Standish Neck but later moved to Raymond Neck, then later moved to Raymond Cape where he was a farmer and chairmaker and where he died Apr. 22, 1860. Five children.

2. ESTHER, born in 1782, married Mar. 13, 1800, John Green, born June 12, 1777, son of John and Mary (Stuart) Green. They lived on Raymond Cape where she died about 1806. He married a second time and went down east. Four children by first marriage.

3. EBENEZER, born Feb. 12, 1784, married Feb. 27, 1814, Anna Morton, daughter of Ebenezer and Susan (Irish) Morton of Standish. After living on Standish Neck for awhile they moved to Chatham, N.H., where he died Sept. 17, 1857. His widow died Jan. 12, 1868, age 71 yrs., 5 mos., 23 days.

4. NANCY, born Sept. 15, 1785, married Apr. 14, 1808, Enoch Marean, born Jan. 29, 1785, son of John and Lois (Bean) Marean of Standish. She died in 1855. At least two children.

5. MOLLY, died in infancy, died Mar. 1785, age 2 yrs.

6. EDMUND, born in 1787, died Aug. 31, 1807, unmarried.

7. DOLLY, born in 1791 or 1792, married June 30, 1811, Joseph McDonald, born in 1788 son of John and Sarah (Towel) McDonald of Gorham. They moved to North Gorham where she died Mar. 31, 1845, and he married second Mrs. Agnes (Moulton) Harding, widow of William Harding, born Feb. 28, 1798, daughter of Jonathan and Agnes (Foss) Moulton of Standish. He died Nov. 1854 and she on Sept. 25, 1870. Nine children by first marriage.

8. MOLLY, born ____, married July 8, 1810, James Morton, son of Ebenezer and Susan (Irish) Morton of Standish. She died Apr. 10, 1875, in Standish.

9. MARGARET, died in childhood.

10. ZEBULON, died Oct. 27, 1820, unmarried.

11. REUBEN, born Feb. 25, 1799, married Sept. 21, 1823, Hannah Libby, born Jan. 18, 1800, daughter of Edward and Elizabeth (Libby) Libby of Gorham. They settled on Standish Neck where he was a farmer and wheelwright and where he died Dec. 15, 1851. His widow lived with her son Melvin and died in Otisfield, Maine, June 2, 1891, age 91 yrs. Five children.

12. EUNICE, born in 1800, married Abner McDonald, son of Peletiah and Dorcas (Stuart) McDonald of Standish. She died Mar. 9, 1851, age 50 yrs. and he married second on Nov. 17, 1853, Esther P. McDonald, born Mar. 10, 1814, daughter of Joseph and Dolly (Shaw) McDonald of Gorham and niece of his first wife. She died Mar. 9, 1851, age 50 yrs.

13. BENJAMIN, born in 1802, died June 27, 1859, age 56 yrs. Unmarried.

14. CAPT. JOSIAH B., born May 12, 1805, married Nov. 1, 1832, Polly Haskell, born in Standish Dec. 4, 1802, daughter of Benjamin and Sarah (Berry) Haskell. They lived in Standish until about 1848 when he settled on a farm near Great Falls in Gorham. He was a farmer, lumberman, and captain of militia.

He died suddenly at East Baldwin on Apr. 22, 1881, his widow surviving him until Aug. 26, 1895. Five children.

SIMPSON

A Jonathan Simpson lived in Standish a few years prior to 1800. His parentage has not been discovered, but his residence was given as Buxton at the time his intentions of marriage were filed in Gorham on Dec, 11, 1773, to Alice Peach of that town. It is possible that he was a brother of the Mary Simpson whose marriage to Daniel Murch of Buxton on Jan. 21, 1768, is found in the Gorham records. Jonathan Simpson served in the Revolutionary War from Gorham and with three other Gorham men, Lt. Cary McLellan, Jedediah Lombard, and William McLellan Jr., was a prisoner on the prison ship *Jersey*.

On Oct. 10, 1779, Jonathan Simpson and his wife, Alice, renewed the covenant in the Congregational Church of Buxton and over the years had a number of children baptized there. Sometime after 1785 he evidently moved to North Yarmouth for he is given as a resident of that town on Dec. 13, 1796, when he bought from Robert Higgins 50 acres of the 100-acre lot #73 in the second division in Standish (25/469). He was living in Standish on Mar. 13, 1798, when he secured by tax deed the 100-acre lot #55 in the third division (32/293) and on Oct. 3, 1800, when he sold to Isaac York of Standish the 100-acre lot #104 in second division (40/245). However, he is listed in the 1800 census of Hampden, Maine, with a family consisting of six males and two females as coming from Standish. He died in West Hampden Nov. 20, 1832, age 83, and his wife died Sept. 9, 1827, age 74. They were the parents of the following children as far as has been determined:

i. SARAH, bapt. in Buxton Nov. 23, 1779.
ii. JEREMIAH, bapt. in Buxton Nov. 23, 1779, was of Hampden on Dec. 12, 1800, when his intentions of marriage to Joanna Brooks of Orrington were filed. She was born Mar. 3, 1783, daughter of George and Mary (Atwood) Thompson Brooks. They were married June 1, 1801. He was a sea captain. His wife was a sister of Deborah Brooks who married Thomas Snow Jr. of Standish and Hampden.
iii. HANNAH, bapt. Nov. 23, 1779, married Sept. 13, 1798, in Standish Thomas Sawyer, son of John and Lettice (Whitney) Sawyer of Standish. He is listed in the 1800 census of Hampden with a family of two males and one female as coming from Standish. Nothing further known.
iv. JONATHAN JR., bapt. in Buxton Feb. 15, 1782, was living in Hampden, Maine, on Apr. 6, 1803, when his intentions of marriage to Abigail Knowles of that town were filed. They had a daughter Sophia born there Nov. 4, 1803. He was a sea captain and died in 1821 at the age of 40 at St. Pierres while master of the schooner *Triton* of Frankfort.
v. MERCY, bapt. in Buxton Dec. 16, 1784, was of Hampden on Dec. 24, 1803, when her intentions of marriage to Amasa Knowles of that town were filed.

SMALL

Isaac Small is given as a resident of Pearsontown when he served as a private in Capt. Samuel Whitmore's company of the Third Cumberland County Regiment of Militia on Dec. 25, 1777. He being of Little Ossipee (Limington) had married (int. Oct. 13, 1777, in Gorham) Mary Richardson, born Mar. 23, 1757, daughter of David and Mary (Hall) Richardson of Pearsontown. He was born May 4, 1752, in Scarboro son of Joshua and Susanna (Kennard) Small and probably moved to Little Ossipee with his father. It is interesting to note that two of his sisters were married and living in Pearsontown so that he likely visited them there. His sister Anna, born Aug. 1, 1744, had married Dominicus Mitchell of Cape Elizabeth on Aug. 1, 1765, and his sister Sarah, born Apr. 14, 1748, had married the Rev. John Tompson of Scarboro, who was the first settled minister of Pearsontown. Another sister, Jane, born Jan. 20, 1767, married Eliphalet Parker on Apr. 15, 1790, and lived in Standish.

He probably never resided very long in Pearsontown, but lived in Limington where he was a tanner, shoemaker, and farmer, and where he died Dec. 14, 1834.

SMITH

Ithiel[5] Smith (Ithiel,[4] Ithiel,[3] Jonathan,[2] Robert[1]) was baptized in Kington, N.H., on Mar. 22, 1740, son of Ithiel and Hannah (Gordon) Smith. About 1765 he married Bathsheba Foote and sometime later settled in Cape Elizabeth where he continued to live until about 1776 when he probably moved to Little Ossipee Plantation (Limington) in which town he had bought lot #83 on Winslow Plan on Mar. 3, 1772, from Daniel Small of Truro, Mass. He was a tailor and followed his trade in the various towns in which he lived.

Following the death of his first wife, he married second (int. July 17, 1779 in Gorham, he being of Little Ossipee Plantation) Anna Bean, born Mar. 19, 1753, daughter of Jonathan and Abigail (Gordon) Bean of Pearsontown. Soon after, they moved to what is now the town of Newry, where he was one of the first settlers, but after being plundered by marauding Indians in 1782 he moved his family along with those of other settlers to safer territory, perhaps to Bethel, where he is listed with a family of 1-5-2 at the time of the 1790 census. It is likely that not long afterward he returned to Newry, where he settled at the mouth of the Bear River and spent the rest of his days. He and his wife, Anna, of Newry, are mentioned among the heirs of Dolly Topping in a deed bearing the date of Mar. 12, 1820 (87/159). He died in Newry on June 18, 1821, age 80 years, 3 months, and his wife died Dec. 19, 1821. He was the father of the following children:

i. BETSEY, born Sept. 11, 1765, married John Lougee of Parsonsfield, died Nov. 10, 1849, age 84 yrs., Parsonsfield.
ii. ITHIEL JR., born Oct. 1767, married Lucy Littlehale, was living in Newry unmarried at the time of 1790 census. He died Dec. 26, 1838, age 70 yrs., 2 mos., Newry, Maine.

iii. POLLY, married May 4, 1794, Simeon Lougee of Parsonsfield.
iv. SALLY, born Aug. 20, 1775, married Jan. 29, 1793, in Bethel, Aaron Barton of Bethel. She died Jan. 1869.
v. JAMES YOUNG, born Mar. 3, 1776, married (int. June 3, 1797, in Standish) Elizabeth Mills of Parsonsfield, he of Standish at the time. He was a blacksmith of Yarmouth and later of Parsonsfield. He died Sept. 14, 1842, age 66 yrs., 5 mos., 21 days, in Parsonsfield.
vi. CATHERINE, married Stephen Bowers and moved to New York.
vii. JONATHAN, born about 1780, married Lydia Brown, died Aug. 1, 1859, age 79 yrs., in Bethel.
viii. JESSE, born about 1788, died June 15, 1871, age 83 yrs., 4 mos., in Grafton.
ix. DAVID, born about 1789, married Hannah Brown, died Feb. 18, 1856, age 67 yrs., 6 mos.
x. JOSIAH, born about 1791, died Jan. 19, 1880, age 88 yrs., 10 mos. Married (int. Nov. 3. 1812) Lucy Bean of Bethel, he of Newry.
xi. ANNA, married Sargent Bean of Bethel and resided at Grafton, N.H.
xii. PETER GILMAN, born Feb. 11, 1795, Newry, married Polly Brown, died Dec. 25, 1875, in Bethel.

SNOW

Thomas Snow was one of those who lived in and departed from Pearsontown prior to 1789. He was born in Eastham, Mass., Sept. 16, 1756, son of Elnathan and Phebe (____) Snow of that town. On Dec. 7, 1778, he married Abigail Higgins, born Sept. 20, 1758, daughter of William and Abigail (Mayo) Higgins of Orleans and Eastham, Massachusetts. William Higgins moved to Pearsontown in 1779 and Thomas Snow and his wife followed soon after. Record is found of the admittance to membership in the First Church of Orleans, Mass., on July 2, 1780, of Abigail, wife of Thomas Snow. It is likely that they moved to Maine soon after this date.

On Mar. 4, 1782, William Higgins of Pearsontown, yeoman, gave to his son-in-law Thomas Snow and Abigail, wife of Thomas, of Pearsontown two tracts of land there, one containing 15 acres of half of the 100-acre lot #73 in second division adjoining land of Bryan Martin and the other 100-acre lot #80 in second division (12/45). Thomas and Abigail Snow of Standish sold Robert Higgins (her brother) on Sept. 1, 1778, the 15 acres of lot #73 including a small house standing thereon adjoining the Buxton line (20/78). It is likely that about this time they left Standish and moved to Frankfort, Maine, where a Thomas Snow with a family of 1-14 is listed in the 1790 census. In 1800 a Thomas Snow with a family of five males and five females is listed in the census of Hampden, Maine, as coming from Cape Cod. Thomas Snow, son to Elnathan Snow, died Apr. 7, 1804, according to Hampden records. Children of Thomas and Abigail(Higgins) Snow were as follows:

i. ISAAC, born Oct. 6, 1779.
ii. EXPERIENCE, born Jan. 26, 1781, bapt. June 16, 1784, in Pearsontown, married in 1802 Richard Stubbs.
iii. WILLIAM, bapt. June 8, 1785.
iv. ABIGAIL, born Dec. 10, 1786, bapt. July 8, 1787, in Standish, married Jan. 19, 1809, John Cowan.
v. PHOEBE, born July 13, 1789, married Feb. 16, 1809, John Linsey.
vi. THOMAS, born Nov. 20, 1791, married first May 18, 1818, Deborah Atwood Brooks, born Apr. 10, 1787, daughter of George and Mary (Atwood) Thompson Brooks of Orrington, Maine; second June 11, 1827, Pamelia Hopkins.
vii. WILLIAM, born Apr. 6, 1794, married Feb. 26, 1818, Deliverance Swett.
viii. ASA, born Dec. 5, 1796, married Nov. 14, 1818, Sarah Rogers.
ix. ELIZABETH, born Aug. 13, 1799.
x. DORCAS, born Dec. 31, 1803, married Nov. 18, 1820, Yates Nickerson.

SPARROW

The name of Stephen Sparrow is found on the 1788, 1789, 1790, 1795, 1796, and 1799 tax lists of Standish and in the 1790 census with a family 3-0-3. He was living in town at the time of the 1800 census with a family consisting of him and his wife, both between 26 and 45 years of age, two males under 10, one female under 10, one female between 16 and 26, and one female over 45 years old. He was born Mar. 3, 1756, in Eastham, Mass., son of Jonathan Jr. and Elizabeth (Heard) Sparrow. His mother having died, his father married Mar. 12, 1766, Hannah (Knowles) Warren, widow of John Warren. Following the death of his father prior to Oct. 10, 1769, his stepmother married as her third husband Zacheus Higgins Jr. of Eastham. His stepmother and her third husband lived for a while in Pearsontown prior to 1790 and it may be through this connection he was influenced to come here to dwell.

On Mar. 8, 1788, Zacheus Higgins of Standish sold Stephen Sparrow, wheelwright, land in Standish comprised of one-third of lot #81 in the third division (24/76). Robert Higgins of Standish sold him Nov. 5, 1790, 23 acres more of lot #80 and 16.5 acres more of lot #81 (24/275). Stephen Sparrow and Sarah Yates, perhaps sister of John Yates of Standish, were married by John Dean Esq. on Mar. 16, 1790. He and his wife, Sarah, were admitted to the Standish Church on Feb, 1, 1795. She probably died soon after he married on Sept. 28, 1797, Rebecca Hopkins, daughter of Theodore Hopkins of Standish. He moved to Unity, Maine, and bought land in that town in 1795. The following children of Stephen and Sarah Sparrow were baptized in the Standish Church.

i. JONATHAN, bapt. June 4, 1795, may have been the Jonathan Sparrow whose marriage on Feb. 23, 1814, to Mary Rand of Gorham is found in the records of the Standish Church.
ii. ABIGAIL, bapt. June 4, 1795.
iii. ISAAC, bapt. Nov. 17, 1796.

While his name does not appear on any of the tax lists consulted, a Jonathan Sparrow was an inhabitant of Standish during the 1790s. He first appears in a school district list in Limington in 1792, but he was living in Standish on May 12, 1795, when Phineas Milliken of Limington sold him 30 acres of lot #9 in that town on that bought from Moses Whitney of Gorham, the 30-acre lots Nos. 13 and 14 in the first division in Standish with buildings standing thereon on Mar. 29,1796 (25/389). On Jan. 3, 1797, Jonathan Lowell of Standish sold to Sparrow the 30-acre lots Nos. 5 and 32, the farm on which he (Lowell) then dwelt (26/164) and on Jan. 23, 1797, Sparrow sold to Lowell the land and buildings he had bought from Whitney in 1796 (27/142).

Jonathan Sparrow was born in Eastham, Mass., Dec. 25, 1768, son of Jonathan Jr. and Hannah (Knowles) Warren and was a half-brother of Stephen Sparrow and Knowles Higgins, both of whom lived in Standish. He married Jan. 24, 1793, probably while living in Limington, Hannah (Jordan) Libby, born May 28, 1773, daughter of Aaron and Elizabeth (Weeman) Libby of Scarboro and Limington. She died Feb. 10, 1799, at Stroudwater, Maine, whence they had moved the year previous. He married second on June 27, 1802, Rev. Caleb Bradley officiating, Eleanor (Nellie) Porterfield, born Nov. 17, 1773, daughter of John Porterfield of Stroudwater. She died Aug. 5, 1865.

He was a very active businessman at Stroudwater from 1798 to his removal about 1820 to Portland. He was an innkeeper and storekeeper and when the town of Westbrook was created in 1814, the barroom in his inn was chosen as the office for the selectmen and headquarters of the other town officals. Because of his fine penmanship he was elected the first town clerk on Mar. 14, 1814, and also served as town treasurer. Following his removal to Portland he was a surveyor of lumber and ran a turning mill on Union Street, being a man of much mechanical ability. He died on Aug. 20, 1843, and was buried in the Stroudwater Cemetery, as were both his wives and several of his children.

Jonathan Sparrow was the father of ten children, four by his first marriage and six by his second, as follows:

i. MARY (POLLY), born about 1794, married Apr. 4, 1815, Francis Fontaine, the Rev. Caleb Bradley officiating.

ii. PHEBE, born in July 1796, died Dec. 5, 1798, age 2 yrs., and 5 mos.

iii. ISAAC, born about 1797, married (int. July 6, 1823) Aug. 3, 1823, Eunice Chesley, daughter of Joseph and Susanna (Bailey) Chesley. He was a shipjoiner (carpenter), erecting a one-story shop in Stroudwater in which he engaged in trade as a retail groceryman. He was the father of three daughters, the youngest being only 4 yrs. old at the time of his death on July 12, 1835, at the age of 38 yrs. His daughter Elizabeth E. Sparrow died Jan. 1, 1852, aged 25 yrs., and daughter Albr C. died Feb. 4, 1858, age 27 yrs., 3 mos.

iv. HANNAH, born about 1799(?), married (int. Apr. 22, 1818) Ting Smith, born Feb. 24, 1793, son of Thomas and Polly (Barker) Smith and grandson of the Rev. Peter Smith of Windham. They were the parents of two sons, Thomas and Tyng Jr. He died in Windham on Feb. 28, 1824, age 31 yrs.

v. MARIA, born June 1, 1803, died unmarried on July 29, 1885.

vi. THOMAS J., born Mar. 4, 1805, married (?), was for a time in business with John Knowles Paine in the manufacture of organs. He later became an architect and among other important structures designed the Cumberland County Jail and the Mechanics Building on the corner of Congress and Casco Streets. He died Dec. 22, 1870.

vii. ELEANOR, born about 1808, married (int. Dec. 14, 1834) Jan. 4, 1835, Charles Bartlett, who was born about 1793, died July 11, 1849, age 56 yrs. She died Dec. 7, 1846, age 38 yrs. He was a successful shipbuilder at Stroudwater and also ran a grocery business there. They were the parents of:
1. CHARLES R., died Nov. 7, 1839, age 1 yr., 9 mos.
2. FRANK M., died Nov. 7, 1839, age 7 mos., 10 days.
3. CHARLES, died May 20, 1843, age 9 mos., 16 days.

viii. ?

ix. WILLIAM, born about 1812, married Margaret _____, was a machinist. He ran a seed store for awhile in Portland and invented a machine for the splitting and cutting of slate. He moved to Woodfords Corner in Deering. In 1850 with his brother John he built a duplex residence at the corner of Winter and Pine Streets.

x. JOHN, born July 7, 1814, married Helen M. _____. For several years he was superintendent of the Portland Gas Works, but left that position to become superintendent of the Eagle Sugar Refinery. He wrote a book on the sugar manufacturing industry after a tour of investigation in Europe.

SPRING

Several members of the Spring family lived in Standish just prior to and following the year 1790. Jedediah[5] Spring (Henry,[4] Henry,[3] Henry,[2] John[1]), born Apr. 16, 1730, in Watertown, Mass., son of Henry and Keziah (Converse) Spring, married Mar. 8, 1753, Elizabeth Saltmarsh, a daughter of Thomas of Watertown. One of Jedediah's brothers was the Reverend Alpheus Spring, pastor of the church at Eliot, Maine. Jedediah served as an officer at Lake George, N.Y., in 1758 and continued to live in Watertown until about 1763 when he moved to Maine and settled in Fryeburg. About 1770 he moved across the Saco River to East Conway, N.H., at a location about two miles from Fryeburg. There he resided until after 1790 when he moved to Standish where he held an innholder's license in 1791. His name is found on the 1795 and 1796 tax lists and in the 1800 census when his family consisted of one female under 10, one male between 10 and 16, one male and two females between 16 and 26, one male between 26 and 45, and one male and one female over 45. He continued to live in Standish until his death, date of which has not been discovered. Children of Jedediah and Elizabeth (Saltmarsh) Spring were as follows:

i. SETH, born in Watertown, Mass., Sept. 29, 1754, served with New Hampshire State troops and in the Continental army during the Revolutionary War. He was living in Conway, N.H., on Sept. 25,

1782, when he purchased from John Ayer a 35-acre tract of land in Pearsontown on which Ayer then lived comprised of 5-acre lot #3 and 30-acre lot #71, as well as in addition 20 acres of lot #68 (12/232). He probably moved into town soon after, for the baptisms of two children are found in the Standish Church records. The name of Seth Spring of Pearsontown is found in the ledgers of Thomas Robison of Falmouth in 1785 and 1786. He was active in the incorporation of the town in 1786 and was granted an innholder's license on Feb. 22, 1786. However, he was living in Biddeford, Maine, on Sept. 23, 1789, when he filed suit against Ephraim Davenport of Bridgton according to the trial justice's records of Samuel Freeman of Falmouth. At the time of the 1790 census he was living in Biddeford with a family of 2-3-5-1 (slave). He did not dispose of his Standish property until Jan. 8, 1814, when he sold it to Seth Storer Jr. of Biddeford (70/63). It appears likely that his father lived on this property after Seth moved to Biddeford and that both of them had innholders' licenses.

Seth Spring became a wealthy merchant and owned Spring's or Factory Island in the Saco River between Biddeford and Saco where he built a mansion in which General Lafayette was entertained and spent a night during his visit to Maine in 1825. He was three times married, his first wife being Sarah McMillan, born July 29, 1762, daughter of Col. Andrew and Hannah (Osgood) McMillan of Concord and Conway, N.H. Her father came to this country from Ireland about 1754. Her father died Nov. 6, 1800, age 70 yrs., and her mother in 1827 at the age of 84. Sarah or Sally (McMillan) Spring died Aug. 18, 1803, age 41, and Seth Spring married June 3, 1804, Mrs. Anna Dearborn of Rochester, N.Y., who died Apr. 26, 1825, age 62. He married third in 1826 Lydia (Chase) Hight, widow of Elisha Hight, born in Saco, Maine, Aug. 26, 1771, daughter of Samuel and Hannah (Wingate) Chase. She died Oct. 19, 1834, age 63. Seth Spring died in Saco on Oct. 12, 1839, at the age of 85 yrs. He and his wives and many of his children and their families were buried in Laurel Hill Cemetery in Saco. Children of Seth Spring as far as has been determined were as follows:

1. ANDREW McMILLAN, born about 1780, died June 28, 1821, age 41 yrs.
2. JOHN, born May 6, 1782, married (int. July 28, 1804) Olive Storer born Dec. 19, 1784, daughter of Capt. Seth Storer of Saco. He was county sheriff and representative to the legislature. He died Aug. 17, 1858, and she on Feb. 28, 1860, both in Saco. Children as follows:
    (1) LEWIS M., born Dec. 5, 1805, married Feb. 4, 1829, Eliza Howe, his cousin once removed, born Sept. 24, 1802, daughter of Dr. Ebenezer and Catherine (Spring) Howe of Standish. They were the parents of two children.
    (2) SARAH ANN, born July 16, 1808, married Daniel Cole Jr. and died Aug. 10, 1863.
    (3) SETH STORER, born Apr. 19, 1811, died July 6, 1822.
    (4) CAROLINE A., born Aug. 28, 1813.
    (5) HANNAH K., born Jan. 26, 1817.
    (6) MARIA L., born May 2, 1821.

  (7) MARY SOPHIA, born June 13, 1831, died May 15, 1909, unmarried.
 3. HANNAH McMILLAN, bapt. in Standish Church June 8, 1785, married Dr. Hall Chase and had a son Marshall Spring Chase born in Waterville, Maine, Sept. 2, 1821. Marshall S. Chase was a lawyer in Boston, Mass., and San Francisco and Martinez, Calif. He died at the latter place on Jan. 24, 1869.
 4. MARSHALL, bapt. in Standish Church in June 17, 1787, married Dec. 18, 1815, Georgiana Seavey both of Hiram.
 5. HORACE BINNEY, born ca. 1794, died Apr. 11, 1822, age 28.
 6. SARAH, born in 1797, married Isaac Emery and died in 1876.
 7. A CHILD of Seth Spring died Oct. 14, 1826.

ii. THOMAS, born in Watertown Sept. 16, 1756, served in the expedition against Quebec under Montgomery and under Washington at White Plains, N.Y., during the Revolutionary War. On Dec. 17, 1780, he married Mary Osgood, born in Pembroke, N.H., Aug. 29, 1759, daughter of James and Jane (____) Osgood, and settled in Bartlett, N.H., but moved to Hiram about 1793. He was a magistrate, selectman, and captain of militia and kept the first public house in Hiram. He died July 27, 1842, age 86 yrs. She died July 7, 1832, age 73. Children were as follows: All born in Bartlett, N.H.

 1. JANE, born May 8, 1781, married Gen. James Steele, died Jan. 23, 1828, in Brownfield.
 2. JOHN, born May 4, 1784, married (int. Mar. 8, 1817) Joanna Hancock, and was a farmer in Hiram. He died June 26, 1859, age 75, and his wife died Sept. 21, 1866, age 80.
 3. COL. MARSHALL, born Feb. 4, 1786, married Dorcas W. Alexander on Dec. 22, 1842. He was a representative to the General Court of Massachusetts, member of the Constitutional Convention of Maine, and a representative to the Maine Legisature. He died Apr. 13, 1849, age 63 yrs., 2 mos., 7 days. His wife died Dec. 11, 1884, age 72 yrs., 8 mos., 20 days.
 4. SUSAN, born Dec. 17, 1789, died Sept. 5, 1876, age 86 yrs., 8 mos., 18 days.
 5. CAPT. ALPHEUS, born Feb. 24, 1791, married in Brownfield, Maine, July 10, 1815, Sally C. Goodenow, born in Henniker, N.H., Mar. 7, 1792, daughter of John and Rebecca Goodenow. He died Sept. 16, 1859, age 68 yrs., 7 mos., and his wife died Oct. 6, 1884, age 92 yrs., 7 mos. They were the parents of four children.

iii. JOSIAH, born in Watertown July 24, 1759, married in Fryeburg, Maine, May 22, 1788, Ann Evans, born there July 25, 1757, daughter of John and Elizabeth (Adams) Evans. He served in the Revolutionary War. They lived in Fryeburg, Standish, and Brownfield, where she died Aug. 3, 1838, and he on Sept. 10, 1836. They were parents of the following children:

 1. JOHN, born Mar. 12, 1789, died unmarried in Brownfield on Nov. 23, 1830, age 42. He was a sailor in early life.
 2. SETH, born June 16, 1791, a sailor, married Hannah ____, born May 21, 1795, and settled in Saco where five children were born. He died in Hiram Mar. 22, 1844.

251

3. ISAAC, born June 21, 1795, who died June 17, 1881. He died in Brownfield Apr. 15, 1880. They were parents of ten children.
4. THOMAS, born Oct. 8, 1795, died in Brownfield Oct. 26, 1824, unmarried.
5. SALLY McMILLAN, born Feb. 24, 1798, died Feb. 15, 1822, in Brownfield.
6. BETHIA, born July 8, 1800, married Peleg C. Wadsworth of Hiram. She died Oct. 10, 1836.
7. JACOB, born Aug. 21, 1802, died Oct. 22, 1803, in Brownfield.
8. ELIZABETH, born Aug. 31, 1804, married Samuel Tyler of Brownfield.
9. JACOB, born Oct. 7, 1806, died Oct. 28, 1824, in Stonington, Conn.
10. MARY ANN, born Dec. 3, 1809, married first William Cobb Bangs, born in Gorham May 29, 1797, son of Ebenezer and Mary (Cobb) Bangs. He died in Brownfield July 31, 1840, and she married second on Aug. 26, 1841 Andrew Tyler. She died Jan. 10, 1845.
11. SAMUEL EVANS, born May 15, 1812, married first Elizabeth Bean, second Zilpha Barker of Hiram. He died in Portland Aug. 8, 1884.

iv. ELIZABETH, born Feb. 27, 1764, at Fryeburg, Maine, married Jeremiah Lovejoy of North Conway, N.H.
v. MARY, born about 1768, married as his second wife Thomas Chase, son of Jack Chase.
vi. ISAAC SALTMARSH, born in 1774 at East Conway, N.H., married Sophia Hastings of Lexington, Mass., on June 9, 1809. They lived in Standish many years, his name first appearing on the 1808 tax list, but in 1836 moved to Charlestown. Mass. She was born Oct. 17, 1781, and died Nov. 1841 in Somerville, Mass. They were parents of the following children:
1. ANDREW CRAIGIE, born Nov. 18, 1811, married Charlotte W. Long or Lang who died July 18, 1849, age 34, leaving a son and daughter. He married second Eliza H., sister of his first wife. Eliza H. died Aug. 27, 1890, age 73.
2. SOPHIA AUGUSTA, born _____, married Dec. 19, 1831, Charles Thomas Mixer of Saco and died June 27, 1833, leaving a son Charles who was born Jan. 5, 1833. He married second on Sept. 18, 1859, Annie Elizabeth (Woods) Edgerley.
3. ISAAC HASTINGS, born Mar. 26, 1818, married Susan Phinney of Lexington, Mass., and had children: Sophia, Susan, and Alice.
4. FRANCES ABIGAIL, bapt. in Standish Church on Sept. 28, 1832, as adopted daughter of Isaac and Sophia Spring, married Windsor Leland of Somerville, Mass.
vii. CATHERINE, born in East Conway, N.H., on Feb. 5, 1780, married Feb. 15, 1800, Dr. Ebenezer Howe of Standish, born in Sturbridge, Mass., Apr. 2, 1773, son of Ebenezer and Sarah (Rice) Howe. For children see Howe family.

STARBIRD

The name of Henry Starbird is found on a 1799 tax list of the town for one poll but he may not have been a resident or may have been living in some household other than his own as he is not counted opposite his name in a town census taken at that time. His name does not appear in the 1800 census of the town so it appears that his stay in Standish was not of any great duration. He may have been the Henry Starbird of Raymond who on Sept. 24, 1799, married Joanna Wilson, also of Raymond, and who is listed in the 1800 census of that town with a family consisting of him and his wife, both between 26 and 45 years of age. If so, he was the son of Moses and Martha (Atwood) Starbird of Raymond.

A Moses Starbird and Lydia Whitney, both of Standish, were married on May 1, 1803, and, according to town records, had the following children born in Standish:

i. JOHN, born Jan. 12, 1804.
ii. NANCY, born Feb. 2, 1806.
iii. MOSES, born Feb. 29, 1809.

I have been able to find out a very little about this Moses Starbird. One might be led to believe that he may have been a brother of the Henry Starbird previously mentioned but, according to the Starbird Genealogy, while Henry did have a brother Moses, that Moses lived and died in Bowdoin, Maine, on July 19, 1845, at the age of 73 years, 10 months.

Lydia (Whitney) Starbird, wife of Moses of Standish, was born Apr. 30, 1782, daughter of Abel and Thankful (Morton) Whitney of Gorham and Standish. The name of Moses Starbird does not appear on the 1808 tax list of Standish, in the 1810 census, nor on the 1814 tax list of the town. The family may have been living with one of his wife's relatives in town and he may not have owned any property so that his name would not appear on tax lists, and members of the family could have been included in the census with those of the family in which they were living. At any rate, the Lydia Starbird admitted into membership in the Standish Church (First) on Jan. 12, 1817, was probably his wife and he may have been the Moses Starbird who died in Gorham on Oct. 26, 1835.

STEVENS

Another of the very early inhabitants of Pearsontown was a man by the name of Thomas Stevens. Nothing definite has been discovered as to his parentage but he may have been Thomas,[4] son of Josiah,[3] Nicholas,[2] Richard[1] Stevens, an orginal settler of Taunton, Massachusetts. His intentions of marriage to Elizabeth Knowles, sister of Samuel Knowles, another early inhabitant of Pearsontown, are found in the Falmouth, Maine, records under date of Dec. 27, 1754. It appears, however, that the marriage never took place because in the same records is found the intention of marriage of Elizabeth Knowles to Elijah Smith on Feb. 15. 1754-5, and also that of Thomas Stevens, then of Pearsontown on Apr. 20, 1757, to Anna Briant of Falmouth, who probably became his wife.

Under date of July 20, 1757, his name with those of Samuel Knowles and John Walker is found on a petition to the Massachusetts government from Pearsontown Plantation. He is listed among the men from Pearsontown who served from May to September 1759 in a company in His Majesty's Service under the command of Capt. William Gerrish of Brunswick. He was also one of the men from Pearsontown who served in Lt. Charles Lessner's party scouting eastward from Broad Bay (Waldoboro) during 1759-1760, and was also also among the Pearsontown men who worked on Gorham roads during the same year.

It seems likely that Thomas Stevens was the man by that name who, according to the *History of Thomaston, Maine*, being orginally from the vicinity of Providence, R.I., went to Falmouth, Maine, and moved from there in 1763 to Thomaston with his family. He was living in Thomaston with a family of 2-1-3 at the time of the 1790 census. In 1800 his family consisted of him and his wife, both over 45, one male between 26 and 45, and one female under 10 years of age. Dates of death of him and his wife have not been discovered. Children as compiled from the *History of Thomaston* and other sources were as follows:

i. NEHEMIAH, published to Nancy Blye on Aug. 20, 1789, lived in Thomaston. In 1790 his family consisted only of him and his wife, but in 1800 there were three sons and a daughter, all under 10 yrs. of age in his family. A son John married Eliza Tobey as his first wife, second Mrs. Mary Pease, and third Elsie Cummings. Children by his first wife were as follows:
   1. AMANDA, born Feb. 15, 1819.
   2. ELIZA JANE, born May 17, 1822.
   3. ANSON, born Oct. 25, 1824.
   4. EDWARD, born Nov. 18, 1826.
   5. HARRIET, born Sept. 4, 1830.
   6. JOHN SPENCER, born Oct. 9, 1832.
   7. MARY JANE, born July 28, 1846.

ii. THOMAS JR., born 1767, married (int. June 23, 1788) Hannah Spear, born in 1758 daughter of Capt. Jonathan Spear. They lived in Thomaston and in 1790 he had a family of 1-0-3, while in 1800 his family consisted of him and his wife and two males under 10 yrs. of age. He died on Mar. 22, 1830, and his wife on Sept. 12 of the same year. They had a son Samuel O. Stevens, born July 5, 1795, who married on Nov. 3, 1817, Katherine Hyler of Cushing and had a son Samuel born June 15, 1818.

iii. WILLIAM, died about 1810.

iv. HANNAH, born about 1777, married (int. Mar. 30, 1798) Nathan Blackington. Lived in Rockland, Maine, where he died Feb. 28, 1839.

v. EPHRAIM, born about 1781, resided in Rockland.

vi. SARAH, published to Ebenezer Thompson of Friendship, Maine, on Mar. 16, 1809.

vii. ELIZABETH, born ___, married (1) David Braley, (2) on Sept. 7, 1828, Charles Wight, born Mar. 9, 1809, son of John M. and Lavinia D. (Morse) Wight. Lived in Thomaston and were the parents of four children. He died Feb. 7, 1854, and she on Apr. 4, 1854.

viii. LUCY LEWIS, adopted granddaughter, married Samuel Kellock of Warren, Maine.

STROUT

A John Strout was living in Pearsontown before 1760. He probably was the John Strout, a whale fisherman of Provincetown, Mass., who with wife Ruth had children born there in 1736 and 1737 and who purchased thirty acres of land at Barren Hill, Cape Elizabeth, in 1743. He served with other Pearsontown men in Lt. Charles Lessner's party scouting eastward from Broad Bay about 1759-60, so it is likely that he was one of those men who lived in the Pearsontown Fort during the last of the French and Indian Wars.

The names of John Strout, John Strout Jr., and Jonathan Strout are found among those of Pearsontown men who worked on Gorham roads in 1760. It seems likely that the latter were his sons. He was granted the 5-acre lot #41, which he later sold to Reuben Freeman, another indication of his having lived in the fort during war times prior to 1760. The Proprietors also granted to him for fulfillment of terms of settlement the 30-acre lot #140 on Mar. 31, 1767 (9/318). This lot he sold to Peter Sanborn on Dec. 15, 1774 (8/296). He was living in Pearsontown as late as 1776 when his name is found on a petition to the general court by Pearsontown inhabitants dated Nov. 8, 1776. It is also possible that he was the John Strout who served with other men from Pearsontown in Capt. Joshua Jordan's company from Cape Elizabeth from the 7th of July to the 27th of September 1779 on the Penobscot expedition. John Strout's wife was Ruth Mayo who was born Apr. 17, 1719, in Eastham, Mass., and a great-granddaughter of Gov. Thomas Prince of the *Mayflower*. On Apr. 1, 1811, according to Cape Elizabeth town records, the overseers had the care of Ruth Strout for present year. She probably was the Mrs. Strout who by newspaper account died Feb. 1, 1810, age 92 years, in Cape Elizabeth. The date of death of John Strout has not been seen. Children of John and Ruth (Mayo) Strout were probably as follows:

i. RUTH, born in Provincetown, Mass., Feb. 19, 1736, married James Hayes, Nov. 19, 1767. She died before Jan. 18, 1771, when he married second Thankful Gent of Cape Elizabeth, who may have been a widow, as a Thankful Johnson married Jan. 26, 1754, George Gent of Falmouth.

ii. ELEAZAR, born in Provincetown Oct. 29, 1737. He was a Revolutionary soldier and reported missing at Valley Forge and when last heard from was very sick. His son Eleazer Strout Jr., was born about 1773 in Cape Elizabeth and was living in 1850 in Hiram. With the help of his pension agent Arthur McArthur of Limington, he applied unsuccessfully for his father's pension. Eleazer Jr. gives his mother as Joanna who after his father's death married William Chambers and moved to a place some thirty miles from Calais, Maine, on Magaquadavic River at St. George, Canada, where she died in Dec. 1839. Eleazar Strout may have married first

iii. Dec. 26, 1771, in Cape Elizabeth, Mary Lewis, both of Cape Elizabeth, Maine.
iii. JOHN JR., born ca. 1739 perhaps in Falmouth, Maine, was living in Pearsontown as early as 1760 and was an inhabitant of the town when his intentions of marriage to Jerusha Witham, also of Pearsontown were filed at Falmouth on Jan, 31, 1761. By 1790 John Strout had moved to Little Ossipee Plantation (Limington) where he was given in the census of that year with a count of 2-1-3. He married second by 1796 Lydia _____, when their grandson Moses Berry was baptized at the Congregational Church at Limington. This marriage has not been seen but there was a Jonathan Strout who married June 10, 1767, Lydia Cromwell both of Falmouth. John and John Strout Jr. are given in the 1798 direct tax list as living in Limington. After Sept. 1799 John Strout and his family with his brother Prince moved to Raymond, Maine.
iv. JONATHAN, born _____ perhaps in Falmouth, was living in 1760, but was perhaps the Jonathan Strout of Cape Elizabeth whose marriage intentions to Sarah Strout of that town were filed Dec. 29, 1768. He reportedly died while in service in Revolutionary War on Mar 1, 1778.
v. SARAH, born _____, was of Pearsontown when her intentions of marriage to John Meserve of this town were filed in Falmouth on Dec. 25, 1761. She was his second wife and the marriage took place on Jan. 28, 1762. For children see Meserve family.
vi. MOLLY, born _____, married Oct. 25, 1767, John Bozwell, both of Cape Elizabeth.
vii. RICHARD, born about 1752, married Mar. 24, 1775, Deborah Strout, both of Cape Elizabeth. He died Sept. 7, 1825, in Limington and his widow died Mar. 21, 1845, age 90 yrs., 3 mos., in Raymond, where she and the children moved soon after his death.
viii. PRINCE, born about 1754, married Dec. 11, 1775, Christina Dyer, both of Cape Elizabeth. He died July 3, 1834, age 81 in Raymond and his widow died in 1838, age 81 yrs.

An Elisha Strout settled in the area just south of what is now Steep Falls Village about 1818. He came into town from Limington where his father had settled in 1792. He was born Apr. 11, 1775, in Gorham, Maine, son of Elisha and Eunice (Freeman) Strout and on Oct. 12, 1795, had married Elizabeth (Betsey) Adams, who was born in Falmouth, Maine, Jan. 19, 1775. They continued to live in Standish until their deaths, his occurring on Apr. 13, 1851, at the age of 76 years and hers on Dec. 11, 1851, at the age of 77. They were buried in a small family graveyard now located on the Middle Road about one-quarter mile in from the Boundary Road. They were parents of the following children:
i. NATHANIEL, born June 11, 1797, died young.
ii. NATHANIEL, born July 10, 1798, married Jan. 1, 1826, Mercy Higgins, born Oct. 9, 1805, daughter of Robert and Sarah (Whitney) Higgins of Standish. Children as follows:
1. SARAH MARIA, born July 31, 1827, married Dec. 25, 1845, William Francis White, both of Steep Falls. She died Oct. 16, 1905, in Standish.
2. CAROLINE AMANDA, born Jan. 29, 1829, married Feb. 15,

1851, James H. White both of Steep Falls.
3. FEMALE CHILD, born Apr. 9, 1831, died Apr. 20, 1831, in Standish.
4. FEMALE CHILD, born July 27, 1832, died July 29, 1832, in Standish.
5. MARY JANE C., born Feb. 23, 1834, married Apr. 4, 1863, Albert Greenleaf Thorn, both of Standish.
6. FEMALE CHILD, born Aug. 14, 1836, died Sept. 8, 1836, in Standish.
7. CHARLES, born May 17, 1838, died Apr. 21, 1840, in Standish.

iii. SOLOMON, born May 19, 1799, died July 16, 1872, in Alexander, Maine, married May 19, 1824, in Baring, Maine, Lydia Bailey of Baileyville, Maine.

iv. MIRIAM, born July 27, 1800, married Nov. 8, 1821, Daniel Thorne, born Jan. 24, 1799, son of Israel Jr. and Hannah (Jones) Thorne of Standish. They lived in Standish where he died Apr. 18, 1842. She married second Sept. 9, 1860, Ebenezer Higgins, as his third wife. She and he were living in Standish in 1870 ceusus. See Thorne family for list of their children.

v. DAVID, born Apr. 21, 1802, married July 3, 1831, Sylvia Clark, both of Limington. He died July 26, 1876, age 71 yrs., 3 mos., Auburn.

vi. PATIENCE, born Sept. 24, 1803, died young.

vii. BETSEY, born Feb. 19, 1805, married May 8, 1825, Marrett Thorne, born Mar. 12, 1800, son of Israel Jr. and Hannah (Jones) Thorne of Standish. He died on Jan. 28, 1880, and she on Sept. 29, 1893. They were buried in Dow's Corner Cemetery in Standish. Eleven children, for list of whom see Thorne family.

viii. PATIENCE, born July 31, 1807, married Aug. 29, 1839, Sylvanous B. Dorset, both of Standish. She died May 29, 1882, age 75 yrs., 3 mos., 29 days, in Standish.

ix. SUSAN, born Sept. 11, 1808, married June 7, 1835, Ting Smith of Hollis. She died Jan. 18, 1849.

x. MERCY, born Mar. 1, 1810, married Oct. 12, 1836, William Swett both of Standish. She died Mar. 28, 1885, in Bartlett, N.H.

xi. BENJAMIN ADAMS, born Apr. 12, 1812, died Feb. 26, 1897, in Upper Mills, New Brunswick, Canada. He lived in Alexander, Maine.

xii. EUNICE, born Jan. 24, 1814, married Feb. 12, 1832, Alfred Swett, both of Standish. She died June 14, 1884, age 69 yrs., 4 mos., Conway, N.H.

xiii. ELISHA, born Mar. 18, 1816, married Oct. 16, 1834, Sarah Haskell, born in Limington Aug. 21, 1818, daughter of Levi Quimby and Abigail (Waterhouse) Haskell. He was a farmer in Standish and died there on Feb. 29, 1892, and she on Mar. 2, 1906. Their children were:
1. ABIGAIL WATERHOUSE, born Aug. 1, 1838, married Dec. 3, 1857 in Conway, N.H., Almon White Hanscom. Two children.
2. BENJAMIN MANSON, born June 13, 1844, married first Nov. 5, 1874, Emma Harding Wescott, born in 1853 daughter of Eliakim and Caroline (Harding) Wescott. She died in Standish

Nov. 2, 1886, and he married second Apr. 25, 1889, Emma Harding Spaulding, born in Gorham, Maine, Sept. 14, 1855, and died June 17, 1902. They had a daughter Elizabeth Mildred Strout, born in Standish May 29, 1892.
3. LOUISE MARIA, born in Standish Dec. 16, 1851, married Nov. 5, 1894, Joseph S. Tyler of Voluntown, Conn.

xiv. CLEMENT FICHETT, born Mar. 27, 1819, in Standish, married Oct. 16, 1834, Almira Hammons of Cornish and he living in Glenburn, Maine. He died soon after 1881 in Alton, Maine, and she died there Feb. 15, 1892, age 65 yrs.

xv. ANDREW J., born Nov. 25, 1825, was adopted by his grandparents, married (int. Dec. 30, 1851) Sarah B. Stone of Limington. He died Jan. 6, 1892, in Limington.

STUART

Wentworth Stuart Sr., was one of the men who were in the guard at the Pearsontown Fort in 1755. It is likely that all of the men of the guard were living in the fort with their families at this time. However, it does not appear that he ever took up land in the town or made a permanent settlement here.

Wentworth[4] Stuart (Joseph,[3] Samuel,[2] Duncan[1]) was born in Wells, Maine Oct. 20, 1731, son of Joseph and Mary (Lord) Stuart and came to Gorham from Berwick in 1753. On Sept. 4, 1753, he married Susanna Lombard, born in Truro, Mass., Aug. 14, 1734, daughter of Rev. Solomon and Sarah (Purrinton) Lombard. Her father was the first settled minister in Gorham. After the short time spent in the fort in Pearsontown he settled in Gorham, where they lived thereafter. Because of his good education he became a prominent citizen of Gorham, serving as town clerk, selectman, and representative to the General Court of Massachusetts. He served as a lieutenant of provincial troops in 1757 during the last of the French and Indian Wars and was commissioned a captain in the Revolutionary army. He died of smallpox on Apr. 17, 1776, at Sewall's Point near Boston while in the service. His widow married second on Mar. 4, 1779, William Wood of Gorham. Following his death about 1794 she went to live with her son Wentworth Jr. in Standish, at whose home she died on Aug. 7, 1803. Children of Wentworth and Susannah (Lombard) Stuart were as follows:

i. MARY, born Jan. 20, 1754, married July 3, 1770, John Green of Gorham and Standish. For list of children see Green family.

ii. SUSANNAH, born May 21, 1757, died Jan. 4, 1759.

iii. JOSEPH, born Apr. 3, 1759, married Hannah Smalley on Sept. 30, 1779. He was a fifer in his father's company in the Revolutionary War. He lived in Gorham and was lost at sea from the schooner *Martha* off Cape Ann on Feb. 5, 1802. His widow, Hannah, died on July 27, 1819, age 61. They were the parents of nine children:

iv. SOLOMON LOMBARD, born Feb. 13, 1762, died Dec. 29, 1763.

v. SARAH PURRINTON, born Feb. 28, 1764, married (int. May 20, 1781, in Gorham) Ebenezer Phinney, born Dec. 14, 1759, son of

John Jr. and Rebecca (Sawyer) Phinney of Gorham. They lived in Standish and were the parents of at least six children, for list of whom see Phinney family.

vi. DORCAS, born June 8, 1766, married Aug. 17, 1787, as his second wife Peletiah McDonald, born May 2, 1753 or 54, son of John and Susannah (____) McDonald of Gorham and Standish. For children see McDonald family.

vii. SUSANNA, born Apr. 1, 1768, married on Jan. 4, 1786, Francis Brooks of North Yarmouth. They were the parents of at least four children.

viii. WENTWORTH JR., born Aug. 17, 1770, married Nov. 4, 1790, Hannah Shaw, born Oct. 4, 1772, daughter of Ebenezer and Sarah (Wood) Shaw of Standish. She died in Standish where they lived on Jan. 23, 1807, and she married second Lemuel McCorrison of Baldwin and died there on Mar. 2, 1848. Wentworth and Hannah (Shaw) Stuart were parents of the following children:

1. WENTWORTH, born Feb. 6, 1791, bapt. July 21, 1806, married Mar. 21, 1815, Patience Thomes. He served in War of 1812 and died in Bridgton, Maine, at the home of his son E. T. Stuart. Both he and his wife are buried there. Five children.
2. HANNAH, born Jan. 1, 1793, bapt. July 21, 1806, died unmarried Oct. 5, 1848.
3. SOLOMON, born Apr. 7, 1794, bapt. July 21, 1806, married Lydia McCorrison and moved to Exeter, Maine, about 1829.
4. SARAH, born Feb. 3, 1796, bapt. July 21, 1806, married Dec. 1, 1814, Ebenezer Files of Gorham, born June 7, 1783, son of Ebenezer and Molly (Elder) Files. They lived at West Gorham where he died in May 1872 and she on Apr. 8, 1878. They were parents of six children.
5. ROSANNA F., born Sept. 27, 1797, bapt. July 21, 1806, married Apr. 7, 1820, James Moody, her cousin, son of James and Elizabeth (Shaw) Moody of Standish, who died Dec. 4, 1822. She married second on Dec. 30, 1823, Timothy Higgins of Standish, born June 20, 1791, son of Timothy and Reliance (Yates) Higgins. She died Dec. 14, 1858, and he on May 21, 1863.
6. CAROLINE, born Apr. 18, 1799, bapt. July 21, 1806, married June 24, 1821, Capt. Joseph Shaw of Waterford. They were the parents of four children.
7. MARY, born May 3, 1801, bapt. July 21, 1806, married Oct. 24, 1822 (int. Sept. 21, 1822), Horace Moulton, both of Standish. They lived in Brownfield, Maine.
8. JOSEPH, born Mar. 24, 1803, bapt. July 21, 1806, married Dec. 25, 1825, Joanna Whitney, born Aug. 1, 1801, daughter of Nathaniel and Zelpha (Martin) Whitney of Standish. He died in Standish in 1866.
9. JAMES G., born Apr. 20, 1805. bapt. July 21, 1806, married first on Nov. 20, 1828, Julia M. Bean, born Feb. 9, 1810, of Thomas and Elizabeth (Osgood) Bean, who died Feb. 14, 1862; second Mary A. Robertson, who was born in Nov. 1824. He lived in Brownfield and was the father of thirteen children. He died there on May 9, 1879.

ix. SOLOMON LOMBARD, born Feb. 24, 1773. No further record.
x. ANNA, born Oct. 31, 1775, married Nov. 17, 1791, Nathaniel Stevens Jr. born Jan. 17, 1772, son of Nathaniel and Elizabeth (Sinclair) Stevens of Gorham. They were the parents of at least three children and moved to Unity, Maine.

SWETT

The name of Jonathan Swett and Jonathan Swett Jr. are found on the 1789 and 1790 tax lists of Standish. Jonathan^5 Swett (Benjamin,^{4} Moses,^{3} Benjamin,^{2} John^1) was born in Dartmouth, Mass., May 16, 1720, son of Benjamin and Ann (Davol) Swett. He seems to have been living in Sanford, Maine, between 1754 and 1762 and signed a petition from that town in 1756. On Dec. 17, 1776, he being a yeoman of Fryeburg, Maine, bought from Thomas Thompson the 100-acre lot #90 in second division in Pearsontown (23/403). He being of Standish bought land in Flintstown from Josiah Milliken on Dec. 25, 1788. At the time of the 1790 census he was living in Standish with a family of 1-1-4. His name also appears on the 1795 and 1796 tax lists, but does not appear thereafter. Name of his wife has not been discovered. Possibly all of the following were his children:

i. JONATHAN, born about 1761, served in the Revolutionary army, where records indicate he was 17 years old on June 4, 1778. He was listed for poll tax only on the 1789 and 1790 tax lists of Standish and his name is found on the 1796 tax list also. Nothing further known.
ii. BENJAMIN, his name is found on the 1795 and 1796 tax lists of Standish and in the 1800 census with a family consisting of him and his wife, two males and two females under 10, two males and two females between 10 and 16 and one female over 45 years old. His intention of marriage to Apphia Rowe, daughter to Ephraim and Mary (Philbrick) Rowe of Pearsontown, was filed in Gorham Nov. 18, 1785. At the time of the 1790 census they were living in Flintstown with a family of 1-1-2. They later moved back to Standish and lived on the farm of his father-in-law Ephraim Rowe. He is said to have departed from home never to return, leaving his wife to bring up a family of small children, partial list of whom is as follows:
1. BENJAMIN JR., married Jan. 17, 1819, in Hiram, Dorothy Burbank of that town. She was born Aug. 12, 1794, and died in Portland Apr. 22, 1885. He died Mar. 11, 1837, in Standish. They were the parents of three sons.
2. JONATHAN, born in Standish about 1800, is said to have been the father of nine children, three boys and six girls, and to have died in 1845.
3. EPHRAIM, lived in Belfast, Maine. Two sons and a daughter.

      4. **GIDEON**, born in 1786, lived in Standish, married Oct. 8, 1810, Hannah Higgins, born Feb. 4, 1791, daughter of Robert and Sarah (Whitney) Higgins of Standish. Seven children, six boys and a girl, He died in 1839.
- iii. **MEHITABLE**, married (int. Oct. 9, 1784, in Gorham when both were listed as living in Pearsontown) Jedediah Witham. They lived in Flintstown (Baldwin) and at the time of the 1790 the family consisted of 1-3-1.
- iv. **JOHN**, his name is found on the 1796 tax list of Standish. In the Standish records are found the intentions of marriage of John Swett to Elizabeth Yates, both of Standish, on Oct. 24, 1790. However, the Swett Genealogy states that the following John Swett was a son of Jonathan Swett Jr. of Standish. This John Swett married Huldah Winslow, born Jan. 10, 1777, daughter of Oliver and Sarah (Hanson) who died in 1830. They lived in Falmouth where he died in 1822, in which year a guardian was appointed for his minor children who were heirs to his estate. *Falmouth Friend's Records* lists the births of the following children, all of which are said to have occurred in Falmouth:
    1. ANNA, born May 25, 1800.
    2. DORCAS, born Apr. 2, 1802.
    3. ELIZA, born Nov. 5, 1803.
    4. MARTHA, born May 7, 1806.
    5. SOPHIA W. born July 15, 1808.
    6. CATHERINE, born May 2, 1810.
    7. JOHN W., born May 28, 1811.
    8. HULDAH, born ____.

    I am not all at sure that this John Swett here referred to was the son of Jonathan of Standish.
- v. **MARY**, she of Standish filed intentions of marriage to Noah Linscott of Francisborough (Cornish) on Aug. 16, 1793, and was married to him on Nov. 7, 1793.

Israel[6] Swett (Stephen,[5] Joshua,[4] Stephen,[3] Benjamin,[2] John[1]); bapt. in Newbury, Mass., married Sept. 20, 1781, Mary Freeman Haskell, daughter of Benjamin and Lydia (Freeman) Haskell. He had previously served in the Revolutionary War and was pensioned for his services at the age of 76. They were living in Falmouth at the time of the 1790 census, but had moved to Standish by 1794. At the time of the 1800 census he was living in Standish with a family consisting of him and his wife, one male and two females under 10, two females between 10 and 16, and one male between 16 and 26. He lived on the northeast half of lot #53 in second division, which he sold on Mar. 31, 1801, to Eliakim Wescott. He was living at Stroudwater in 1817 and died in Paris, Maine, about Mar. 1840 at the age of 80. Children of Israel and Mary (Haskell) Swett were as follows:
- i. **WILLIAM**, married Sarah Milliken.
- ii. **SARAH**, married as his third wife Seth Carpenter, born Nov. 23, 1762, son of Elisha and Anna (Whitaker) Carpenter of Sutton, Mass. They lived in Paris, Maine. Three children.

iii. ELIZABETH, married ____ Elwell.
iv. HANNAH, bapt. in Standish Church June 19, 1798, joined Shakers and died unmarried.
v. ISRAEL JR., born in Standish Apr. 25, 1796, bapt. June 19, 1798, married Olivia (Goold) Libby, daughter of Capt. Moses Libby of Scarboro. They moved to Paris, Maine. Their children were:
  1. BETSEY, born 1824, died 1825.
  2. JOHN GOULD, born July 20, 1826, married Lydia Ann Fuller.
  3. MOSES, born Nov. 1, 1827, lost in 1821 gale on fishing banks.
  4. EDWARD, born Sept. 1, 1830, married Rebecca Coffin, lived in Kennebunk, Maine.
  5. HARRY, born June 1, 1834, married Harriet Bryant.
  6. OLIVIA, born Sept. 1836, died Aug. 1, 1837.
vi. BENJAMIN, died unmarrried.
vii. MARY HASKELL, bapt. in Standish July 8, 1800, died unmarried.
viii. HULDAH, born Mar. 12, 1805, married Jan. 27, 1832, Moses Gage, born Sept. 6, 1808, son of Moses and Joanna (Norton) Gage of Kittery. They settled in Paris, Maine, in 1834. Eight children.
ix. ABIGAIL, born in Albany, Maine, Apr. 28, 1808, married Amos Brown.

TENNEY OR TINNEY

George Tinney was an inhabitant of Pearsontown prior to 1760. He probably was the George Tinney bapt. July 7, 1728, son of John and Deborah (Ingersoll) Tinney or Tenney of Kittery and Falmouth, Maine. George Tinney, age 31, a resident then of Pearsontown, but previously from York, enlisted Mar. 3, 1760, in His Majesty's Service. Prior to this time he was of Gorham, when he served from May 2 to Nov. 14, 1757, in Capt. Joseph Woodman's company. His name is found on a list of Pearsontown men who worked on Gorham roads in 1761, but is found on a tax list of Gorham in 1763, although it is not listed on one for 1772.

George Tinney and Bethiah Elwell filed intentions of marriage in Falmouth on May 9, 1759, and presumably were married. She was probably a sister to the Sarah Elwell who married Samuel Knowles, another early settler in Pearsontown and his comrade in His Majesty's Service. Undoubtedly they lived with their families in the Pearsontown Fort during their tour of duty in the service. Like Samuel Knowles he moved his family to Washington County probably sometime before 1770. He is listed as an early settler in township No. 13 (Columbia) and noted as coming from the vicinity of York, Maine. His name along with that of Samuel Knowles is found on a petition of the inhabitants of the township No. 6 or Addison in 1770, and he is given as living there with a family of eleven persons on Apr. 27, 1778. Little has been discovered concerning the family of George Tinney but in the 1790 census are found recorded in Plantation No. 13 west of Machias (Columbia) the families of George Tinney (1-2-4) George Tinney Jr. (1-0-0). John Tinney(1-0-0). David Tinney (1-0-0) and Samuel Tinney (1-0-0). The latter four were probably sons of George Tinney Sr. and unmarried at that time.

TITCOMB

Benjamin[4] Titcomb Sr. (Joseph,[3] William,[2] William[1]) served under Moses Pearson at the siege of Louisburg when only 19 years old. He was born Jan. 14, 1727, in Newbury, Mass., son of Joseph and Ann (Smith) Titcomb, and settled in Falmouth, Maine, about 1746. In 1753 he married Ann Pearson, born Jan. 19, 1729, daughter of Moses and Sarah (Titcomb) Pearson, and the following year built a house on Plum Street.

He was blacksmith by trade, his shop being on the breastwork from which Central Wharf was extended. Because of his service at the siege of Louisburg he became one of the grantees of land in Pearsontown, drawing right number 107 as his share of the township. The 30-acre lot #107 which was a part of this right he sold on Mar. 14, 1781, to Joseph Butterfield (10/536). He was one of the guards of soldiers on duty during the building of the fort in 1755 and later on took an active part as one of the Proprietors of the town. Although he apparently did not become a permanent resident of the town, he maintained a large farm here which was comprised of 5-acre lots Nos. 5, 6, and 10, 30-acre lots Nos. 38 and 121, and one third of 30-acre lots Nos. 119 and 120. This farm he sold to Rev. Jonathan Gould, the second pastor of the Pearsontown Church, on May 25, 1795. Part of this land was sold by Mr. Gould's father to the Rev. Daniel Marrett, the third minister, and it became the Marrett Homestead. The name of Benjamin Titcomb is found on the 1789 and 1790 tax lists of Standish.

Benjamin Titcomb led an active life in Falmouth, or Portland as it later became, being a deacon of the church, a selectman of the town and representive to the general court. After the Revolutionary War he lived in a house opposite the custom house and died Oct. 15, 1798, at the age of 72. His widow died on July 8, 1800, at the same age. Children of Benjamin and Anna (Pearson) Titcomb were as follows:

i. ANDREW PHILIP, born Jan. 28, 1754, died Nov. 19, 1818.
ii. MOSES, born Sept. 5, 1755.
iii. JOSEPH, born Feb. 2, 1757, died Aug. 6, 1836.
iv. EUNICE, born Sept. 9, 1759, died Oct. 14, 1798.
v. BENJAMIN JR., born July 26, 1761, in Falmouth, Maine, married on Nov. 19, 1786, Mary Fairfield, daughter of the Rev. John Fairfield, pastor of the Pepperellborough (Saco) Church. He evidently lived in Standish for a short while, probably on his father's farm, for under date of Aug. 23, 1789, is found in the records of the First Church of Pepperellborough the baptism by Rev. John Fairfield of Benjamin, son of Benjamin and Mary Titcomb, with the note "at Standish, I being there." Benjamin Titcomb Jr. served on apprenticeship as a printer and on Jan. 1, 1785, published the first newspaper, the *Falmouth Gazette and Weekly Advertiser*, issued in the District of Maine. A few years later he began to preach at the newly established Baptist Society in Portland (though having no preliminary theological education in Brunswick as pastor of the Baptist Church there) and continued to live in that town until his

death on Sept. 30, 1848. His wife, Mary, born May 22, 1768, in Saco, died July 24, 1838. They were the parents of the following children:
1. BENJAMIN, born Dec. 4, 1787, bapt. Aug. 23, 1789, died May 29, 1829, unmarried.
2. MARY GOODWIN, bapt. Aug. 2, 1789.
3. WILLIAM, born May 8, 1791, died Mar. 17, 1850.
4. JOHN FAIRFIELD, bapt. Aug. 25, 1793.
5. HENRY, bapt. Dec. 6, 1795, died Nov. 16, 1798.
6. ELIZABETH HARRIS, born Mar. 1, 1798.
7. EUNICE, born Dec. 11, 1799, died Sept. 5, 1800.
8. MOSES, born Feb. 22, 1801, died June 26, 1881.
9. SARAH CLEAVES, born in Nov. 1803.
10. SOPHIA ANN, born Oct. 13, 18__.
11. HARRIET MARIA, born Apr. 25, 1809.
12. HARRIET HARTLEY, born Jan. 1, 1811.
13. HENRY, born Oct. 12, 1815, died Sept. 19, 1844.

vi. ANN, born Oct. 28, 1763, died Nov. 3, 1788.
vii. HENRY, born Mar. 11, 1766, died in 1829.
viii. WILLIAM, born Dec. 15, 1767, died Apr. 18, 1786.
ix. MARY, born Aug. 26, 1769, died Apr. 1, 1770.
x. ELIZABETH, born Aug. 26, 1769, died in Mar. 1834.
xi. JEREMIAH, born Aug. 18, 1771, died Aug. 9, 1777.
xii. JOSHUA, born Nov. 30, 1774, died Nov. 14, 1776.

THOMES OR THOMBS

Amos Thomes, whose name appears in the 1790 census of Standish with a family of 1-4-2, was born in Falmouth, Maine, about 1757 son of Thomas and Mary (Banfield) Thomes of that town. His name also appears on the 1788, 1789, 1790, 1795, 1796, 1799 and later tax lists of Standish. At the time of the 1800 census he was still living in town with a family consisting of him and his wife, both between 26 and 45 years of age, one male between 16 and 26, three males and one female between 10 and 16, and three males and one female under 10 years of age.

Sometime prior to 1763 his parents moved to Gorham, Maine, where he grew up and where his name first appears in a tax list of that town in 1777, the same year in which he served as a private in Capt. Whitmore's company of Gorham militia during the Revolutionary War. He was listed as being an inhabitant of Pearsontown at the time his intention of marriage to Mehitable Burnell of Falmouth was published in that town on Dec. 20, 1781. They were married on the same day by the Rev. Samuel Dean, associate pastor of the First Church in Falmouth.

On Apr. 5, 1781, Richard Codman of Falmouth sold to Amos Thomes of Gorham the westerly half of the 100-acre lot #72 in the second division in Pearsontown (11/336). On July 11, 1797, Amos Thomes of Standish, yeoman, bought from Greenfield Pote of Freeport a quarter part of 100-acre lot #83 in the first division of 100-acre lots in Standish

(26/226). This land was directly across the road from his homestead farm located on lot #72. He continued to live in Standish until his death on Dec. 21, 1840 at the age of 83, his wife having passed away on Sept. 11, 1836, at the age of 77 years. Both were buried in a family graveyard on their farm.

Amos and Mehitable (Burnell) Thomes were parents of the following children, all of whom were probably born in Standish:

i. THOMAS, born July 12, 1782, married Nov. 20, 1806 (int. Oct. 22, 1806) Mehitable Whitney, born Dec. 31, 1786, daughter of Jonathan and Mary (Blake) Whitney of Buxton. He lived in Standish on a farm located on the Saco Stage Road not far from its junction with the Deer Hill Road. At the time of the 1850 census they were living in Standish, he age 67 and she age 64. He died in Standish Jan. 14, 1871, age 88 yrs., 6 mos. and 2 days, his wife having passed away on Jan. 31, 1861, age 74 yrs., 1 mo. Both were buried in a family graveyard on the farm of his brother Charles on Deer Hill.

ii. ELIZABETH, born Sept. 26, 1784, married June 28, 1810 (int. Feb. 5, 1810), Isaac Skillings, born May 24, 1786, son of Thomas and Mary (Burnell) Skillings of Gorham. They lived in Standish on a farm adjoining that of her brother on the Deer Hill Road, where a single stone indicates the place of her burial and bears her date of death as being Nov. 9, 1861, at the age of 77 yrs., 1 mo., and 14 days. For children see Skillings family under Burnell family.

iii. SAMUEL, born Apr. 19, 1786, married Nov. 16, 1809 (int. Feb. 25, 1809) Olive Norton, born Oct. 1, 1787, daughter of James and Mary (____) Norton of Buxton. They lived in Buxton for awhile, but following her death he married second (int. at Limington Nov. 12, 1826) Salome (Marr) Staples, divorced wife of John McArthur Staples and born in 1791 in Durham, Maine, daughter of James and Lydia (Libby) Marr of Limington. At the time of his second marriage Samuel Thomes was living in Baldwin but at the time of the 1850 census he was living in Limington. He must have died not long afterwards for on May 30, 1853, the marriage intentions of Mrs. Salome M. Thomes of Baldwin and Nicholas Davis were filed in that town and they were married the same day.

iv. GEORGE, born Mar. 4, 1788, married July 10, 1810, Martha Rowe of Baldwin and had:
1. AMOS, born June 16, 1813.
2. GEORGE, born Aug. 11, 1815.

v. JOHN, born Nov. 16, 1790, married Dec. 19, 1813 (int. Oct. 30, 1813) Mehitable Skillings, born June 19, 1791, daughter of Thomas and Mary (Burnell) Skillings of Gorham and sister to his sister Elizabeth's husband. She died in Baldwin June 6, 1865, at the age of 74 and he passed away on Dec. 23, 1867, age 78. They were parents of at least the following children:
1. JOHN JR., born ca. 1817, married Eunice Rowe, daughter of Thomas and Betsy (Lowell) Rowe; died Mar. 3, 1883, age 66.
2. ISAAC, born in ____, died before 1873, married Elmira daughter of Thomas and Betsy (Lowell) Rowe. He served in the Civil War. She died Nov. 13, 1913, age 87.
3. SARAH F., born about 1821, married Calvin Pease of Baldwin, and died in 1857, age 36.

vi. AMOS JR., born Aug. 26, 1792, married Feb. 24, 1818 (int. Jan. 10, 1818), Jane Ayer, born Apr. 17, 1799, daughter of Ebenezer and Elizabeth (Moore) Ayer of Buxton. He married second (int. Aug. 10, 1835) Mary Small Sawyer of Limington, born Aug. 31, 1818, daughter of Peter and Sarah (Small) Sawyer of that town. She married second (int. Aug. 29, 1840) Ira L. Allen, both of Portland.

vii. STEPHEN, born July 4, 1794, married Mar. 9, 1825 (int. Feb. 9, 1825), Dolly Parker, born May 9, 1802, daughter of Eliphalet and Jane (Small) Parker of Standish. At the time of the 1870 census he, age 75, with wife Dorothy, age 68, were living in Standish. They lived on the old Thomes Place on the Cape Road where he died Oct. 7, 1878, age 84 yrs., 3 mos., 3 days, and she on Nov. 10, 1883, age 81 yrs., 6 mos. Both were buried in the family graveyard on their farm. Children of Stephen and Dorothy (Parker) Thomes were:
1. ELIHU BAXTER, married Anne Taylor, moved to Iowa.
2. ELIZABETH A., married Edward A. Stockman.
3. ALMIRA, born May 22, 1831, married July 5, 1854, Elisha Strout Thorne of Standish. They went west in Oct. 1854 but returned by time of the 1860 census. She died Aug. 2, 1919, age 88 yrs., 2 mos., 11 days, Brunswick.
4. ELIPHALET,P., born 1833, married Elvira Nason and married second ____ Waterman.
5. ORLANDO JASPER, born about 1845, married Hadassah Boulter.

viii. MEHITABLE, born Dec. 15, 1796.

ix. CHARLES, born June 6, 1799, married (int. Aug. 8, 1828) Susan Ingalls of Baldwin. They lived on the Deer Hill Road. He died Oct. 12, 1865, age 66 yrs., 4 mos., 6 days, in Standish, and she on Dec. 30, 1868, age 69 yrs., 2 mos., 2 days. They with the last four of the following children were buried on a family graveyard on their farm. Children:
1. SUSAN MARIA, born Jan. 3, 1829, died Dec. 19, 1860, age 32 yrs.
2. CHARLES WARREN, born Dec. 39, 1831, died Apr. 7, 1881, age 50 yrs., 2 mos., in Standish.
3. MEHITABLE JANE, born May 24, 1834, died Feb. 22, 1840.
4. SARAH ELLEN, born Nov. 24, 1836, died Mar. 25, 1840.
5. DAVID INGALLS, born Jan. 29, 1839, died Feb. 18, 1840.

THOMPSON

Dr. Isaac[6] Snow Thompson (Daniel,[5] Samuel,[4] Jonathan,[3] Jonathan,[2] James[1]) was the first physician in the town of Standish. He was born in Woburn, Mass., June 28, 1761, son of Daniel and Phebe (Snow) Thompson and was less than 15 years old when his father was killed on Apr. 19, 1775, at the battle of Lexington. Following his father's death he went to sea in an American privateer, but was captured by the British at Barbados, from whom he made his escape by swimming three miles to a

French vessel. Soon after safely reaching his home he began the study of medicine under Dr. John Hay of Woburn, who later moved to Reading, Massachusetts. Early in 1785 he married his mentor's daughter, Charlotte Hay, and soon after the birth of their first child in 1786 he settled in Standish where he continued to practice until his death on June 7, 1799. He was small in stature and made his rounds on horseback, carrying his medicines in saddlebags.

The name of Isaac S. Thompson is found on the 1789, 1790, 1795, and 1796 tax lists of Standish and in the 1790 census with a family of 1-2-2. Charlotte Thompson with a family consisting of herself, two females under 10 years of age, and one male over 10 was living in Standish at the time of the 1800 census. Following the death of Dr. Thompson, his widow married on Sept. 4, 1804, Eleazar Flint of Baldwin, by whom she had two sons and a daughter.

Children of Dr. Isaac S. and Charlotte (Hay) Thompson were as follows:

i. CHARLOTTE, born May 2, 1786, at Reading, Mass., bapt. Aug. 25, 1799, married May 26, 1808, Joseph Richardson, born July 3, 1785, son of Joseph and Mary (Carpenter) Richardson of Standish and Baldwin. They lived in Baldwin where she died Feb. 26, 1843. Eleven children.

ii. DANIEL, born Nov. 2, 1787, bapt. Sept. 8, 1799, at Standish, married Feb. 26, 1821, Deborah Fitch of Baldwin, who died there Apr. 1, 1827. He died less than a year later on Mar. 18, 1828, leaving an only child, Daniel Josiah Pierce Thompson, who was born June 21, 1824, at Westbrook where his parents lived for a short time. He moved to Illinois where he married and became the father of two children.

iii. PHEBE, born Oct. 4 or 14, 1789, bapt. Sept. 8, 1799, at Standish, married Mar. 20, 1806, Ephraim Flint of Baldwin. She died Nov. 30, 1865, in W. Baldwin.

iv. SARAH HAY, born June 9, 1792, at Standish, married on June 11, 1816, Wilder Bowers and lived in Baldwin, where she died July 26, 1886. Thirteen children.

v. FRANCES, born Mar. 17, 1795, bapt. Sept. 8, 1799, at Standish, married Apr. 6, 1811, Abner Dow, born Nov. 20, 1792, son of Joseph and Lucy (Sanborn) Dow of Standish. He died Dec. 7, 1850, and she died in Gorham on Sept. 29, 1873. For children see Dow family.

vi. JOHN HAY, born May 2, 1797, bapt. Sept. 8, 1799, at Standish, died Oct. 17, 1799.

There was a man by the name of Thomas Thompson living in Pearsontown before the Revolutionary War period. Nothing has been discovered concerning his parentage nor whence he came. He was living in town, a yeoman, on Aug. 5, 1771, when he bought from Clement Meserve the 100-acre lot #90 in second division (7/246) and on Dec. 17, 1776, when he sold the same land to Jonathan Swett of Fryeburg (23/403). He served in the Revolutionary War as a private in Capt. Samuel Whitmore's company of the Third Cumberland County Regiment of Militia on Dec. 25, 1777. He is also given as a resident of Pearsontown on Mar. 3, 1778, when his intentions of marriage to Rebecca Hall, daughter of Charles and Jemima (Dolliver) Hall, were filed in Gorham. He must have moved to Buxton soon after his marriage since all of his children are said to have been born there. He lived in that town annexed to Standish in 1824 and in a real estate inventory of Buxton taken about 1798 he is listed as owning lot H-5 in the third division of lots in that town. At the time of the 1790 census he was credited with a family of 1-3-4, while in 1800 his family consisted of him and his wife, both between 26 and 45 years of age, two males between 10 and 16, one female under 10, one between 10 and 16, and one between 10 and 26 years old. His name is also found on a York County tax list assessed in 1813 for support of the War of 1812. No complete list of the children of Thomas and Rebecca (Hall) Thompson has been found, but the following were doubtless of his family:

i. MARY, born Oct. 4, 1779, married on May 23, 1804, as his second wife Capt. Artemus Richardson of Baldwin, born in Templeton, Mass., on Feb. 17, 1780, son of Israel and Elizabeth (Hutchinson) Richardson. He was of Standish on July 13, 1802, when he bought from Eleazar Flint about 100 acres of land in Baldwin (38/63). They lived in Baldwin until about 1825 when they moved to Hiram where he died June 13, 1844, age 64, and she Oct. 12, 1865, age 85 yrs., in Cornish. Children as follows: (Richardson)
  1. ARTEMAS JR., born Feb. 6, 1805, married first Dorcas Hubbard, second Sarah F. Ingalls.
  2. NANCY RICHARDSON, born Feb. 4, 1807, married Benjamin Chadbourne.
  3. JOANNA HUTCHINSON, born Dec. 25, 1808, married Nov. 12, 1843, John L. Clemons of Hiram.
  4. GEORGE EATON, born July 7, 1811, married Ruth W. Clemmons.
  5. MARY MARRETT, born Sept. 6, 1813, married Peleg C. Wadsworth.
  6. THOMAS JOHNSON, born May 24, 1816, married his cousin Hannah Richardson.
  7. THOMPSON HALL, born Mar. 21, 1819.
  8. BETSEY FITCH, born June 18, 1821.
  9. SARAH B., born May 14, 1825, in Hiram, married Reuben Small.

ii. REBECCA, born in Buxton in 1785, married (int. Jan. 30, 1806, she of Parsonsfield) Jeremiah Binford of Baldwin, born in Pearsontown Jan. 28, 1782, son of William and Dorcas (Richardson) Binford. They lived in Baldwin and Brownfield, where she died Feb. 5, 1823. He married second on Sept. 14, 1823, Shuah Meserve. He died in Baldwin Jan. 10, 1827. Children as follows: (Binford)
  1. THOMAS, born in Baldwin Jan. 26, 1807.
  2. ABIGAIL, born in Brownfield Apr. 17, 1809, married Nov. 14, 1830, John Black.
  3. JEREMIAH JR., born in Brownfield May 14, 1811, was a farmer and went west.
  4. CYRUS, born in Brownfield June 22, 1813, married Olive Sawyer and lived in Chatham, N.H.
  5. REBECCA, born in Brownfield Sept. 29, 1816. Lived in Garland, Maine.

      6. SAMUEL, born in Brownfield Apr. 4, 1819, drowned in Saco River near West Baldwin.
     By second wife:
      7. EMILY, married her cousin George Binford.

iii. EPHRAIM, born in Buxton Oct. 8, 1790, married by Rev. John Buzzell on Dec. 26, 1816, to Sally Thurston, born Feb. 27, 1795, daughter of Daniel and Hannah (Dutch) Thurston of North Parsonsfield. He was a farmer and moved to Brownfield, Maine, about 1812 and about 1828 moved to Eaton and Conway, N.H. He died Dec. 13, 1863, and she on Dec. 15, 1866. Children: (Thompson)
1. MARY ANN, born Dec. 23, 1817, in Brownfield, married Ephraim Hatch of Conway, N.H. She died in Dec. 1881.
2. HANNAH SMITH, born Mar. 14, 1819, married July 15, 1860, Isaac Meader. She died Dec. 22, 1889.
3. DANIEL THURSTON, born Oct. 23, 1820, a farmer in Minnesota, unmarried. He died June 29, 1889.
4. LORENZO DOW, born July 5, 1822, a farmer of Eaton, N.H.
5. JANE DUTCH, born Feb. 10, 1824, married May 19, 1842, Jonathan Leavitt, a farmer of Chatham, N.H. She died in Jan. 1843.
6. STEPHEN THURSTON, born Jan. 25, 1826, married Mar. 8, 1860, ____; He was a farmer in Minnesota. He died in Watertown in that state.
7. ARTEMAS RICHARDSON, born Feb. 24, 1828, died June 1829.
8. REBECCA HALL, born Nov. 15, 1830, married Dec. 5, 1853, George N. Merrill, a farmer in Danvers, Mass. She died Apr. 30, 1903.
9. THADDEUS BROAD, born in Conway, N.H., Dec. 15, 1833, married Mar. 7, 1861, Susan M. Stuart of Eaton, N.H.
10. SAMUEL DUTCH, born Dec. 13 or 31, 1806, in Eaton, N.H., married Feb. 25, 1864, Mary Estill. He was a farmer in Minnesota.

iv. JANE, born in Buxton ____, married Jonathan Thurston, born Nov. 23, 1797, brother of her brother Ephraim's wife. He was a carpenter and lived in Great Falls and Somersworth, N.H. He died in 1842 and she in 1872. Two sons died in infancy.

THORNE

    Joseph Thorne was perhaps the first settler to take up permanent residence in Pearsontown, possibly even sometime before the erection of the fort there in 1754. As a member of Capt. Moses Pearson's company of Falmouth, Maine, men at the siege of Louisburg in 1745, he was a grantee of right No. 38 in the new township laid out to reward those men, among others, for service in that expedition and was one of the only two men among all of the grantees to actually settle on the land awarded them. The 30-acre lot #38 in the first division of lots on which he settled was located on the Southwest (Portland) Road a short distance below the junction of the roads at the center of the settlement where the fort and First Church were located. It later became a part of the farm of Benjamin Titcomb that eventually was to be the homestead of the Rev. Daniel Marrett, the third settled minister of the town, where the Marrett House is still in existence today.

Joseph Thorne was or had been a hired man for Pearson in Falmouth (now Portland) and perhaps had been in charge of Pearson's farm located on the upper reaches of an inlet of Back Cove where Pearson had a wharf located about where the bridge on Deering Avenue now crosses over the railroad tracks and highway No. 295. In a paper written by Moses Pearson and dated Sept. 17, 1745, at Louisburg in which he listed the condition of a number of men serving there from Falmouth at that time, he stated as follows: "J. Gilkey and Jas. Thorn-These two out of my family. J. Thorne, my servant. J. Gilkey by the year." It is therefore clear that Joseph Thorne and his children had been a part of Moses Pearson's family for a number of years.

It is clear that Joseph Thorne was living in Pearsontown as early as 1754 because at a meeting of the Proprietors of the township held on Sept. 23, 1755, they voted him forty pounds for his cow killed at the fort the previous winter. As Pearson's hired man he undoubtedly had Pearson's confidence and had been early sent to the scene to look after the interests of the Proprietors (of whom of course Thorne was one) in developing the new township. Although he was then in his early fifties, Thorne continued to live in the fort during all of the years of trials and tribulations of the last of the French and Indian Wars. It is likely that he raised crops for food on his 30-acre lot #38, which was close enough to the fort to afford him protection from the Indian marauders while he was working there. He probably was unmarried at this time but his son Israel was also living in town at the time as well as may be his daughter Mercy, who later was to marry John Pierce of the town. His name does not appear on many of the available documents of the time, but one of them does indicate that he was paid for work on Gorham Roads in 1760. On May 25, 1762, he sold to his son Bartholomew, who had probably just returned from Canada after a lengthy period of captivity there following his capture by St. Francis Indians in Gorham in 1754, his 30-acre lot #38 (2/107), and on the following Dec. 30 of the same year sold to Moses Pearson all the remaining part of his right No. 38 in the township, thus disposing of all of his real estate (2/264). No wife is mentioned in either deed so it appears likely that he had not remarried following the death of his wife, Hannah (Harvey) Thorne. He probably was unable to read or write because his signature to both of the deeds above was made by his mark. No further details about his life has been found, except that he and his wife lived with their son Bartholomew and had according to Cumberland County records "grown old" by Apr. 1768 when Bartholomew took Israel Thorne to court in order to get help to pay their expenses. Joseph probably lived with his son Bartholomew at least until he moved to Flintstown (Baldwin & Sebago) about 1776 and perhaps afterward with his son Israel Sr. in Standish. He is said to have lived until about 1800, which would made him nearly 100 years old at the time of his death, and to have been buried in the field of Israel's farm in Standish which consisted of 15 acres, being the southeast half of 30-acre lot #74, and located on the Southeast (Buxton) Road, a short distance from the center of the settlement. His grave was said to have been marked by a large fieldstone that many years later was pulled up and thrown away by a hired man who was plowing there, destroying all traces of the spot where he was laid to rest.

One often wonders what these early pioneers were like in character and appearance, something that of course is difficult, if not impossible to ascertain at this late date. In the case of Joseph Thorne, we are fortunate to have information about him furnished by Dr. Albion K.P. Meserve (1833-1904), a native of Limington, who gathered a lot of material about the early history of Standish. Hannah (Jones) Thorne, the widow of Israel Thorne Jr., grandson of Joseph Thorne, was still alive in 1850 at the age of 79 and living with her son Stephen in Standish when Meserve was attending Standish Academy in the Old Red Church there. Born in 1771 she was alive when Joseph Thorne was living and told Meserve many things about him during their conversations together about the old days of Standish. From these conversations Dr. Meserve wrote his impression of the kind of man Joseph Thorne may have been, as follows:

> I picture him as of medium height but firmly and strongly built, capable of enduring much physical exercise and exposure--one who in the wrestle was rarely thrown, somewhat fond of drink, perhaps, but never seen intoxicated, a man for his time and surroundings, bold, fearless--a great hunter and trapper--much more fond of hunting wolves and bears than of working on the soil.

This seems to me to be a fitting memorial to one of those hardy individuals who was prominently responsible for the early beginnings of what is today the town of Standish.

Now let us continue this discourse with information concerning the ancestry of this bold pioneer as well as with an account of his many descendants as far as it has been possible to compile them. Joseph Thorne of Pearsontown is thought to have been the man bearing that name who was born Sept. 15, 1701, in Hingham, Mass., son of Joseph and Joanna (Pierson) Thorne and grandson of William and Mary (____) of Boston. Information about his early life is sketchy. He is said to have been a mariner and to have married Hannah Harvey in Hingham on Mar. 7, 1722-3. They continued to live in Hingham for some time, where six of their children are said to have been born, but later appeared in North Yarmouth, Maine, where the births and baptisms of additional children are found in the records, a note being made that Hannah, Joseph's wife, died in Brunswick, a neighboring town. By 1740 or before they apparently moved to Falmouth, Maine, where the baptism of two of his children are found in the records of the First Church there in 1739. It is likely that Joseph Thorne went to work for Moses Pearson at about or soon after he moved to Falmouth. Because of the discrepances and variations in the names and dates of births of the children of this couple as found in the several accounts available, it is difficult, if not impossible, to compile an accurate list of them. The following is an attempt at a compromise of all of the information available:

i. HANNAH, born in 1724, nothing further known.

ii. ISRAEL, born May 27, 1726, died Oct. 28, 1728.
iii. JOSEPH, born Jan. 17, 1728-9, served as waiter for Capt. Moses Pearson at Louisburg when only 16 yrs. old. As a member of that expedition he drew share No. 24 of land in Pearsontown, but evidently did not satisfy the terms of settlement because the Proprietors sold that right to Ephraim Jones of Falmouth on Dec. 15, 1768 (7/444). No evidence of Joseph Jrs. ever having lived in Pearsontown has been found and nothing further about him has been discovered.
iv. SARAH, born Aug. 3, 1731, died after.
v.   ISRAEL, born Nov. 25, 1733, according to records published in *Old Times in North Yarmouth*. Yet in an affidavit signed by him on Oct. 30, 1807, and recorded at the Cumberland County Registry of Deeds on Dec. 30, 1807 (53/370), he stated that he was then 77 yrs. old and, if he lived, would reach the age of 78 on the second day of the following December, thus making him about four years older than he would have been according to his recorded birth date. There are other statements in this affidavit that are also of social interest. He stated that he had been living in Falmouth (now Portland) at the time Louisburg was taken in 1745 and had lived there from the time he was 13 mos. old and had continued to live there thereafter most of the time until he was 23 yrs. old. He further said that he had lived in Moses Pearson's family while in Falmouth and that his work involved working at logging in the woods, sometimes rafting up and down the river, as well as performing such other duties as his master (Pearson) ordered him to perform; and that he had driven a team most every day along Middle and Back (now Congress) Streets to and from the Pearson farm on Back Cove.

Records indicate that he was living in Pearsontown sometime before 1760 because he was a member of the guard crew at the fort there in 1755 and was indicated as being a resident of the township when he served from May to Sept. 1757 in Capt. William Gerrish's Company in His Majesty's Service during the last of the French and Indian Wars. Inasmuch as he was a grantee of five-acre lot #18, it is clear he must have been an inhabitant during the war. His name found on lists of Pearsontown men who worked on Gorham Roads in 1760 and 1761, when he also was paid for use of his oxen. On May 4, 1770, he sold to Ephraim Jones of Falmouth his 5-acre lot #18 (11/361) and on the same day Jones transferred to him the southwesterly half (15 acres) of 30-acre lot #74 (14/531) located nearby on the Southwest (Buxton) Road. It is likely that he lived on both of these lots during the time of his ownership of them.

His name is found on the 1788, 1789, and 1790 tax lists of Standish and in the 1790 census with a family of 2-2-2, as well as in the 1800 census when his family consisted of him and his wife and one male child between 10 and 16 yrs. old. He remained single until fairly late in life, marrying about 1772 Sarah, widow of John York who was drowned in "the basin" of Sebago Pond about 1771 and who had owned and lived on the 5-acre lot #17 adjoining Israel's lot #18 so that they had been neighbors. There were eight in John York's family at the time of his death, some of whom had married and left home, but probably at least half of them were not old enough to fend for themselves.

Israel and his wife continued to live in town until their deaths. He died in December 1825, age 95 yrs., in Standish, as reported in the *Christian Mirror*, issue of Jan. 13, 1826. He is said to have died in Standish at the age of 96 yrs. and to have been buried in the Village Cemetery with only a fieldstone to mark his grave. The date of death of his wife has not been found but it was undoubtedly after 1810 because she and her husband were probably the male and female over 45 yrs. of age listed in the family of Israel Thorne Jr. in the census of that year.

Israel and Sarah (Strout) (York) Thorne were the parents of only one child:
1. ISRAEL JR., born Dec. 3, 1776, according to town records although he is said to have been 52 yrs. old at the time of his death in June 1823. On July 19, 1791, he married Hannah Jones, born about 1771 daughter of John and Mary (Savage) Jones of Scarboro and sister of the wives of Job and Ebenezer York, his half brothers, and of William McGill, all of Standish. Richard Codman of Falmouth on Mar. 1, 1791, conveyed to Israel Thorne Jr. the 100-acre lot #58 in the second division of lots in Standish located on Standish Neck and bordering on "the basin" at the head of Presumpscot River (14/532). He lived in Standish and his father was still alive at the time of his death in 1823 (*Eastern Argus*, June 24, 1823, reports his death). His widow was still living at the age of 79 with her son Stephen in Standish at the time of the 1850 census and died in 1853, age 82 yrs.

   Israel Jr. and Hannah (Jones) Thorne were the parents of twelve children, all boys and eleven of whom grew to manhood, as follows:
   (1) JOHN, born Apr. 1, 1792, died July 29, 1859, in Brownfield, married in Nov. 16, 1816 (int. Oct. 19, 1816, in Saco), Jemima Nason of Saco, who was born in 1797 and died June 23, 1886. They lived in Standish and Brownfield. Children were as follows:
      A. OLIVE, born June 12, 1814 (?), died July 14, 1831, wife of Jacob Boynton.
      B. FREDERICK STORER, born in Standish Aug. 15, 1817, married Almira Dutch of Brownfield. He died Sept. 29, 1895, age 78 yrs., in Brownfield.
      C. LYDIA ANN, born in Standish Feb. 27, 1820, died Feb. 2, 1823.
      D. EDGECOMB N., born in Brownfield Apr. 20, 1822.
      E. LYDIA ANN, born in Brownfield Feb. 2, 1825.
      F. JOHN GREENLEAF, born in Brownfield Dec. 9, 1829.
      G. HANNAH, born in Brownfield July 2, 1830, married in 1851 Richard McNair and died in South Boston on Mar. 11, 1856.
      H. ANDREW J., born Jan. 7, 1833, in Brownfield.
      I. MARY, born Aug. 15, 1834, in Brownfield.

J. MARIA, born May 1, 1837, Brownfield, died July 21, 1879, married May 29, 1855, Lewis W. Brown, both of Brownfield.
K. MARTHA T., born Sept. 19, 1841, in Brownfield.

(2) JOSEPH, born Apr. 29, 1793, married in 1818 Martha M. Stevens, born Nov. 20, 1800, of Macadavy (Magaquiodavic), N.B. They settled in Sullivan, Maine, about 1830 where he died Sept. 16, 1874. She died Jan. 29, 1881, age 78 yrs., 1 mo., 10 days, East Sullivan and there buried in the Birch Tree Cemetery. They were parents of the following children:
A. ABIJAH, born about 1820, married July 11, 1844, Joan Moon.
B. HANNAH, married Nov. 8, 1842, Sands Moon.
C. SARAH, married Nov. 17, 1852, Solomon Merchant.
D. SUSAN, born about 1837, married Nov. 26, 1855, James White.
E. LUCY A., born about 1839, married July 26, 1856, William White of Three Rivers.
F. MARTHA A., born about 1835, married Andrew Jackson Clark of Franklin, Maine.
G. ELMIRA, born about 1827, Dady Lancester of Sullivan.
H. MARIA, married _____ Leighton of Millbridge, Maine.
I. MARY, born about 1843, married Joseph White of Sullivan in 1859.
J. JOSEPH, born Apr. 18, 1847.

(3) ISRAEL, born Feb. 4, 1795, married Sally Stevens, sister of his brother's wife, and second _____ by whom he had two sons who probably lived in St. Andrews, N.B. He died Nov. 11, 1864, age 70 yrs., in St. George, N.B. He enlisted in the War of 1812.

(4) SIMEON, born Feb. 4, 1797, went to New Brunswick with his brothers Joseph and Israel and died there unmarried on Oct. 11, 1822.

(5) DANIEL, born Jan. 24, 1799, married Nov. 8, 1821 (int. Oct. 19, 1821), Miriam Strout, born July 27, 1800, daughter of Elisha and Betsey (Adams) Strout of Limington and Standish. She married second Sept. 9, 1860, Ebenezer Higgins, both of Standish, as his third wife. She was living in 1870, age 70 yrs., in Standish. Daniel died on Apr. 1842. Children were as follows:
A. SIMEON, born Dec. 4, 1821.
B. SOLOMON STROUT, born Mar. 6, 1823, living in 1860 in Limington. He married Sept. 5, 1847, Margaret E. Jordan, both of Portland.
C. LYDIS JANE, born Nov. 17, 1824, living in 1850 in Limington.
D. ELISHA NAPOLEAN STROUT, born Feb. 26, 1826, married July 5, 1854, Almira Thomes. He died Dec. 31, 1881, age 55 yrs., 10 mos., 4 days, in Standish

and she died Aug. 2, 1919, age 88 yrs., 2 mos., 11 days.
E. HANNAH, born Aug. 11, 1827.
F. ISRAEL, born May 9, 1829.
G. DANIEL, born Apr. 30, 1831.
H. BENJAMIN STROUT, born Aug. 25, 1832, living in 1850 in Limington.
I. JOHN, born Nov. 6, 1834, living in 1850 in Limington.
J. DAVID STROUT, born July 9, 1836, married Dec. 9, 1860, Eliza Johnson of Limington. He died Aug. 19, 1865, age 29 yrs., 1 mo., 10 days, Limington.
K. BETSEY, born Feb. 2, 1838.

(6) MARRETT, born Mar. 12, 1800, married May 8, 1825 (int. Mar. 8, 1825), Betsey Strout, born Feb. 19, 1805, daughter of Elisha and Betsey (Adams) Strout of Limington and Standish and sister to his brother Daniel's wife. They lived in Standish where he died Jan. 28, 1880, age 79 yrs., 10 mos., 15 days, and she on Sept. 29, 1893. Both were buried in the Dow's Corner Cemetery in Standish. Children were as follows:

A. NATHANIEL STROUT, born July 22, 1824.
B. MARTHA ANN, born Jan. 28, 1826, married Dec. 6, 1848, Aaron Marean, born July 27, 1823, son of Amos and Elizabeth (Knight) Marean of Standish (now Raymond Cape.)
C. ALBERT GREENLEAF (Known as Green), born Jan. 14, 1828, married May 6, 1854, Mary Jane Strout, both of Standish. She died Mar. 28, 1861, age 27 yrs.; and he married second Apr. 4, 1863, Eliza G. Marean, born Dec. 31, 1831, died Aug. 3, 1896. Albert died Oct. 12, 188_, and is buried in the Thorne Cemetery, located on Thorne's Hill, Standish. Their children were: Helen M., died Apr. 10, 1871, age 16 yrs., 5 mos., 28 days; Frank A., born 1861; Ada F., died Oct. 21, 1864, age 7 yrs., 7 mos. 1 day; Charles, born 1860, died young; Flora E., born June 16, 1863.
D. EMILY MARIA, born Dec. 20, 1829, married (int. Sept. 17, 1852) James A. Hussey of Thomaston. She died Sept. 23, 1897, age 67 yrs., 9 mos., Standish.
E. LEANDER M., born Nov. 30, 1831, married May 5, 1852, Mary Elizabeth Thorne, both of Westbrook. They moved to Illinois in 1863.
F. ELIZABETH L., born July 7, 1834, married Feb. 24, 1855, William Marean Jr., both of Standish. She died Dec. 29, 1918, age 83 yrs., 6 mos., Standish.
G. WILLIAM STORER, born Apr. 2, 1837, died Apr. 6, 1907, in Standish, married Aug. 25, 1905, Mrs. Mary E. Burns, both of Standish. She born Apr. 15, 1865, died Mar. 31, 1932.

        H.   CAROLINE AUGUSTA, born July 9, 1839, married Mar. 16, 1856, Maretius Thorne of Westbrook, Maine.
        I.   ELLEN R., born about 1843, married Feb. 12, 1860, Wilbur T. Chase, both of Standish.
        J.   JANE, born about 1845 (age 5 in 1850).
        K.   ABBY F., born about 1847 (age 3 in 1850).

(7) STEPHEN, born May 5, 1802 (bapt. Nov. 14, 1817), married Nov. 30, 1828 (int. Nov. 1, 1828, in Standish), Desire Davis, born May 25, 1811, daughter of David and Martha (____) Davis of Buxton. They lived on his father's place on the Limington Road (Route 25) until 1853 when they moved to Belvidere, Boone County, Ill., where he was living in 1891. Children were as follows:
        A.   ANN, born about 1829 (21 in 1850).
        B.   DAVID D., born about 1832 (age 18 in 1850), married Dorcas (Rand?) who died Sept. 30, 1875, age 43 yrs., 6 mos., 28 days. He died Nov. 25, 1876, age 43 yrs., 5 mos. Both were buried in the Rand Cemetery on Oak Hill in Standish.
        C.   WILLIAM H., born about 1835 (age 15 in 1850).
        D.   WINFIELD SCOTT, born about 1839 (age 11 in 1850), married Oct. 2, 1864, his cousin Ruth Ann Maria Davis, born June 22, 1843 daughter of Thomas and Ruth (Elwell) Davis. He was of Belvidere, Ill., at the time of his marriage.
        E.   JOHN M., born about 1851, died Sept. 11, 1853, age 2 yrs., 3 mos.; buried in Dow's Corner Cemetery.

(8) JOB, born Sept. 15, 1803, bapt. Nov. 14, 1817, married (int. Jan. 27, 1828, in Westbrook) his second cousin Nancy Ann Thorne, daughter of Thomas Thorne of Baldwin. He lived in Westbrook until after his children were born when sometime after 1850 he moved to Illinois perhaps at the same time as his brother Stephen. However, before 1870 he had moved to Iowa where he afterwards lived and died, his death occurring in Glidden, Iowa, in Nov. 23, 1884, age 81 yrs., 2 mos., formerly of Merrill's Corner, Deering, Maine, his wife died on Jan. 27, 1890, age 84 yrs., in Glidden, Iowa. Children as follows:
        A.   MARY ELIZABETH, born Nov. 18, 1828, married her first cousin, May 5, 1852, in Westbrook, Leander M. Thorne, born Nov. 30, 1831, son of Marrett and Betsey (Strout) Thorne.
        B.   MENZIE (MARATIUS), born about 1832, married Mar. 16, 1856, his first cousin, Caroline Augusta Thorne, born in Standish, July 9, 1839, daughter of Marrett and Betsey (Strout) Thorne. She died Sept. 10, 1910. In 1898 they were of Glidden, Iowa.
        C.   SARAH F., born about 1835, married Mar. 6, 1853, John W. Anson, both of Portland.

- D. WILLIAM M., born Oct. 23, 1837, married in Minnesota, Mary Baldwin Hardy, born Feb. 13, 1843, daughter of Charles and Waitie (Johnson) Hardy. He died Aug. 3 or 9, 1913, in Sundance, Crook Co., Wyo., and she died there Oct. 24, 1904. They were the parents of nine children, the first two born in Red Rock, Mower Co., Minn.; the next four were born in Benton, Iowa; one in Yankton, S.Dak.; and one in Crook Co., Wyo.

  The fifth child, John Merritt Thorn, born Jan. 25, 1875, in Belle Plain, Benton Co., Iowa, married Apr. 29, 1912, in Sundance, Crook Co., Wyo., Anna T. Petersen, born Apr. 29, 1887, in Nesemarka, Sweden, daughter of William and Elvara E. (Sait) Petersen. He died Apr. 2, 1942, in Colorado and she on Oct. 21, 1967, in Powell, Park Co., Wyo.
- E. HARRIET M., born 1841, married first Richard or Robert Carr, second Thomas Shaw.

(9) GREENLEAF, born Feb. 15, 1806, bapt. Nov. 14, 1817, married Dec. 12, 1839, Rebecca Makepeace both of Saco. They lived in Capisic in Deering (now Portland) where in early life he was a manufacturer of horn combs. He died Jan. 2, 1890, at his home at Capisic. She died Aug. 2, 1905, age 87 yrs., in Portland. He and his wife are buried in the Evergreen Cemetery in Portland. Three children, as follows:
- A. ELLEN W., born Oct. 14, 1841, married George A. Whitney and was living in Chicago in 1890.
- B. EDWIN G., born June 3, 1843, married Oct. 7, 1875, Mary S. Knight. He was in the grocery business in Portland. He died Feb. 19, 1916, age 72.
- C. EMMA S.G., born Apr. 8, 1848, married E. J. Pattee and lived at Fort Fairfield, Maine. Living in Washington, D.C., in 1890. Four children.

(10) LEONARD, born July 22, 1808, was a storekeeper in Portland. He married Nancy Murch who died in New York Feb. 19, 1845. They lived in Brooklyn, N.Y., and had children. One Leonard Thorne married Nov. 7, 1829, Nancy Frost in Portland, both of Gorham.

(11) WILLIAMS JONES, born Aug. 15, 1811, had three wives and lived in Westbrook. His wife Jane Sewell died Dec. 6, 1852, age 32 yrs., in Westbrook, and then he married Sept 6, 1858, in Westbrook, Adeline W. Andrews.

(12) BENJAMIN, died in infancy.

vi. MERCY, born Apr. 14, 1736, according to North Yarmouth records, married July 9, 1768 (Gorham records), John Pierce Jr. of Pearsontown, born about 1745 son of John and Elizabeth (Johnson) Pierce of that town. She died before June 25, 1800, when he married second Susannah (Sanborn) Linnell, widow of Enoch Linnell of Standish, born Aug. 13, 1753, daughter of John and Lucy (Sanborn) Sanborn of Pearsontown. He died Sept. 2, 1830, age 85 yrs. No children by either marriage.

vii. **BARTHOLOMEW**, born Jan. 14, 1738, according to North Yarmouth records, evidently grew up in Falmouth, Maine, where his father worked for Moses Pearson. Apparently he was fond of the woods and streams, and is said in his early days to have spent months alone in the woods without seeing the face of another white man. He became a well-known hunter and trapper acquainted with every pond, stream, and hill throughout the area comprising the territory of Gorham, Buxton, and Standish. Known as Bart Thorne, he was in constant conflict with the native Indians with whom there grew up a mutual hatred. McLellan in his *History of Gorham* writes about his many exploits and narrow escapes from death or capture by the Indians. He relates that it was in 1750 that Bart was finally captured, while returning unarmed from a church meeting, by a raiding party from the Indian village at St. Francis in Canada, where he was taken by them as a captive. It was most fortunate for Thorne that his captors were not native Indians, who because of their great hatred for him would have shot him on the spot. Actually, Thorne's capture was in June 1754 when the real warfare of the last of the French and Indian Wars was just beginning.

According to family tradition he remained a captive of the Indians for about a year before sold to a French gentlemen in Montreal for whom he became a gardener. Whether he eventually escaped or was released after the fall of Quebec in 1759 is not known but by about 1760 he had returned to his father's family then living in Pearsontown because his name is found on a list of Pearsontown men who worked on Gorham roads in 1761.

Bartholomew Thorne of Pearsontown married Lydia Couch of Falmouth (int. Jan. 7, 1762, in Falmouth) and evidently settled down to live in Pearsontown. On May 25, 1762, his father, Joseph, deeded to him the 30-acre lot #38 in Pearsontown, which his father had been granted for service at the siege of Louisburg (2/107). There he continued to live until about 1776 when on Mar. 27 of that year he and his wife, Lydia, sold this same lot to Benjamin Titcomb of Falmouth (8/465). Apparently neither of them could write because their signatures were made by marks. They moved to the neighboring township of Flintstown (Baldwin), but not until after the last of April of 1776 when Bartholomew's name is found on a list of inhabitants of Pearsontown at that time.

He is said to have been one of the first white settlers in Flintstown and to have operated the first gristmill in the town. The Proprietors of Flintstown in consideration of certain rights and services done and performed by Bartholomew Thorne for them conveyed to him on Sept. 2, 1788, lot #4 in the second range west in that town (20/256). His son William, born in Flintstown in July 1777, is said to have been the first white child born in that township. Bartholomew and his wife continued to live in Baldwin until their deaths, his occurring in 1820 and hers at an unknown date.

Bartholomew and Lydia (Couch) Thorne were the parents of at least the following children:

1. **THOMAS**, born in Pearsontown, May 14, 1767, married in Limington June 30, 1796, Margaret Guilford of Limington, born Feb. 14, 1776, daughter of John and Elizabeth (McKenney) Guilford of Scarboro. They lived in Baldwin where he died Sept. 29, 1849, age 82, and she on Oct. 30, 1863, age 87. They and their children were listed in Margaret (McKenney) Gordan records on Limington. They were parents of the following children:
   (1) **LYDIA**, born Nov. 12, 1796, married Nov. 13, 1819, John Cram of Baldwin. They lived in Baldwin where she died Aug. 28, 1864, age 68, and he on Aug. 30, 1868, age 72.
   - A. **JOSEPH**, born July 1, 1820, married Aug. 31, 1865, Adeline Chick of Parsonsfield.
   - B. **BETHIAH**, born Mar. 21, 1822, married in 1840, John Kimball.
   - C. **JOHN GARDINER**, born Mar. 2, 1826, died May 6, 1892.
   - D. **ABIGAIL**, born Feb. 2, 1824, died Apr. 4, 1841.
   - E. **ELIZA**, born Aug. 4, 1828, died Oct. 10, 1832, age 4 yrs.
   - F. **EUNICE**, born Oct. 24, 1830, died June 10, 1849.
   (2) **ELIZABETH** or **ELIZA**, born May 20, 1798, at Danville, Vt., married Dec. 25, 1823, Daniel McKenney, born May 29, 1799, son of James and Jane (Thorne) McKenney of Limington, her cousin. He died Oct. 26, 1883, age 83, and she on July 3, 1874, age 76.
   (3) **MARY** or **POLLY F.**, born Apr. 26, 1800, married her cousin, Benjamin D. Thorne, born Mar. 16, 1794, son of Joseph and Deborah (Dyer) Thorne. She probably died before Mar. 21, 1819, when he married second Mary Woodman of Buxton. He died June 27, 1856, at the insane asylum in Augusta.
   (4) **JOHN G.**, born Mar. 1, 1802, married Nov. 4, 1824, Mary Cram, born June 15, 1799, in Cornish, daughter of Joseph and Abigail (Pugsley) Cram of Baldwin. She died June 10, 1859, in Baldwin. He married second Jan. 26, 1865, Nancy (Hodgdon) Rankins of Hiram, who died June 10, 1883, age 72. He died May 18, 1885, age 83 yrs., in Brockton, Mass., formerly of E. Hiram.
   Children were:
   - A. **WILLIAM HENRY**, born Nov. 25, 1825, died Apr. 1894. He married (int. June 30, 1849) Susan A. Rankins of Hiram. She was born July 7, 1820, died 1890. They are buried in Hiram with parents.
   - B. **JOHN OTIS**, born Apr. 1, 1827, died Sept. 6, 1917, age 90 yrs., in Auburn, Maine. He married July 4, 1852, Louisa Mariner of Sebago, he of Baldwin.
   - C. **WARREN I.**, born July 29, 1829, died Feb. 2, 1914, in Sebago, married Catherine F. McKenney of Limington. They were buried in Hiram.

- D. MARY LOUISA, born Feb. 14, 1832, died Jan. 27, 1913, in Hiram, married William Shaw of Sebago and married second Aug. 2, 1852, Samuel A. Brown, both of Baldwin.
- E. AUGUSTUS, born July 21, 1834, died 1839.
- F. VAN BUREN, born July 3, 1836, died 1838.
- G. HARRIET FRANCES, born July 19, 1839, died Aug. 20, 1843.
- H. JAMES CELOYN, born Dec. 16, 1842, died age 8.

(5) NANCY, born Mar. 20, 1805, married (int. Jan. 27, 1828, in Westbrook) Job Thorne, her second cousin. She died Jan. 27, 1890, age 84 yrs., Glidden, Iowa.

(6) MARGARET, born Jan. 3, 1808, married Aug. 31, 1834, Joseph D. Farnum, born Feb. 27, 1814, at Belgrade, Maine. He died July 27, 1854, at Portland, and she married second Hugh Barber, who died Nov. 9, 1868. She died Oct. 31, 1898, at the age of 90 yrs. in Portland. Children as follows: (Farnum)
- A. ABIGAIL O., born Nov. 4,, 1836, at Scarboro, married Oct. 20, 1880, Charles A. Donnell, and died Nov. 22, 1890.
- B. SAMUEL T., born June 25, 1838, at North Baldwin, died Oct. 8, 1838.
- C. SARAH H., born July 11, 1839, at Baldwin, died there Oct. 11, 1839.
- D. FRANCIS S., born Nov. 8, 1840, at Baldwin.
- E. PHEBE J., born Oct. 9, 1841, at Baldwin, married ____ Byrnes. She died Sept. 8, 1897, at Chicago, Ill.
- F. JOSEPH H., born Apr. 5, 1843, at Scarboro and died July 22, 1857, at Limington.
- G. JOHN P., born June 29, 1844, at Portland, died there Oct. 13, 1844.
- H. THOMAS T., born Sept. 25, 1845, at Portland, died there Feb. 14, 1846.
- I. GEORGE H., born Oct. 24, 1846, at Portland.
- J. JOHN L., born Jan. 4, 1848, at Portland, died there Jan. 16, 1849.
- K. LEMUEL P., born June 14, 1850, at Portland, died there July 29, 1854.

(7) PHEBE, born July 7, 1810, married ____ Hoyt and had at least two children, John Hoyt (1838-1909) and Annie M. (Hoyt) Jenness (1841-1907), buried with their mother in Laurel Hill Cemetery in Saco. She married second Dimon Taylor of Wells, as his second wife. He died Jan. 28, 1858, age 72 yrs., in Wells, and she died Jan. 11, 1867, age 68 yrs., in Saco.

(8) LOUISA, born July 7, 1812.

(9) SAMUEL G., born July 10, 1814.

(10) THOMAS JR., born Apr. 2, 1816, married (int. Nov. 28, 1839) Ann Pearl of Porter and lived there. He died Nov. 1848.

(11) BARTHOLOMEW, born May 28, 1818, married May 26, 1846, Mary Sanborn, born in July 15, 1826, daughter of Daniel and Abigail (Rowe) Sanborn and lived in Baldwin. He died Jan. 2, 1903, and she on Nov. 16, 1912. They had eleven children.
2. JOSEPH, born in 1768 in Pearsontown, died in Baldwin in 1835. He doubtless went to Flintstown (Baldwin) with his father in 1776 and probably was the Joseph Thorne of that town to whom John Fry sold 20 acres of land there adjoining land of Bartholomew Thorne on Nov. 29, 1786 (14/248). He is said to have built the first farm house at East Baldwin. He married (int. Apr. 10, 1789 in Standish) Deborah (Dyer) Royal, widow of Isaac Royal of North Yarmouth and daughter of Benjamin and Abigail (Higgins) Dyer of Cape Elizabeth. They lived in Baldwin and were parents of the following children:
(1) ELEAZER, born Jan. 10, 1791, died Mar. 15, 1845 in Baldwin (pension record). He married Sept. 8, 1811, Rachel Sanborn, born Jan. 25, 1795, daughter of Daniel and Miriam (Lowell) Sanborn of Baldwin. She died May 19, 1884. Children as follows:
A. DEBORAH, born Feb. 7, 1813, married first Apr. 7, 1831, John Small of Limington, who died July 12, 1837, age 27 yrs., 6 mos.; second on Apr. 5, 1839, Sylvanus Batchelder Jr., of Baldwin; third Jan. 12, 1846, Oliver P. Rowe, both of Baldwin.
B. DANIEL, born Aug. 25, 1814, married Nov. 18, 1840, Martha Ann Wentworth of Baldwin. They lived in Augusta and afterwards in Bridgton. She died Feb. 27, 1898, age 73 yrs., 6 mos., Bridgton. Their children were: Edwin, born Mar. 4, 1844, died Sept. 5, 1903, Baldwin; Lucinda F., born May 7, 1846, died in 1932, married May 16, 1863, Harding L. Nason of Limington; Miriam, born Apr. 1, 1848; Daniel, born June 15, 1850; John W., born Sept. 30, 1853, died Feb. 26, 1944, Augusta; Charles H., born Aug. 11, 1860; Annie E., born May 12, 1863.
C. MIRIAM, born Aug. 25, 1814, twin to Daniel, she married Sept. 3, 1837, John Lord of Lyman. She died Aug. 24, 1864, and he died Sept. 7, 1896, age 81 yrs., 3 mos. Both are buried in Laurel Hill Cemetery, Saco.
D. STEPHEN, born May 2, 1816, married Caroline ____ and lived in Augusta. Had children.
E. EDWARD, born July 18, 1818, lived in Augusta.
F. CAROLINE, born ____, married ____ Harmon and lived in Saco.
(2) ISAAC, born May 14, 1792, died June 2, 1801.
(3) BENJAMIN DYER, born Mar. 16, 1794, married first Mary Thorne, born Apr. 25, 1800, daughter of Thomas and Margaret (Guilford) Thorne and thence his cousin. She evidently died young because he married second Mar. 21, 1819, Mary Woodman, daughter of Joshua and Sally

(Wheeler) Woodman. She at the age of 60 of Buxton and as widow of Benjamin D. Dyer applied for land warrant on Aug. 29, 1856. He died at the insane hospital in Augusta on June 27, 1856. Children all by his second marriage were as follows:
- A. MARY, born about 1823 (27 in 1850), married Benjamin Hoyt in 1863.
- B. SILAS, born about 1827 (23 in 1850), died May 8, 1930, unmarried.
- C. HIRAM, born about 1829 (21 in 1850).
- D. SABY, born about 1831 (19 in 1850).
- E. MEHITABLE, born about 1835 (15 in 1850), married ____ Woodman and went west.

(4) BETSY, born Mar. 23, 1796, married July 14 or 19, 1818, James Morton Riley, born May 6, 1799, son of Ephraim Higgins and Abigail (Morton) Riley or Wriley of Baldwin. They lived near Pigeon Brook. She died in Baldwin Sept. 2, 1884, age 88. Children as follows: (Riley)
- A. ABIGAIL, born Feb. 2, 1819, married Joseph Burnell of Baldwin.
- B. STILLMAN, born Mar. 5, 1821, married Eliza Storer of Brownfield and lived at North Conway, N.H.
- C. REUBEN, born 1823, died 1825.
- D. ELIZABETH, born Dec. 3, 1824, married Samuel Guptill and lived in Baldwin.
- E. NATHAN APPLETON, born May 18, 1829, married first Mary Given; second Annette ____, widow, died at Lynn, Mass.
- F. JAMES OSGOOD, born Mar. 29, 1832, died Sept. 1832.
- G. JAMES OSBORNE, married Oct. 20, 1840, Sarah Bowie, died Dec. 2, 1906.

(5) MARTHA, born Feb. 20, 1798, died 1845, married in 1819 Abner Sanborn, born June 2, 1800, son of Daniel and Miram (Lowell) Sanborn of Baldwin. He died in 1888. Children as follows: (Sanborn)
- A. CATHERINE, born May 22, 1820, died June 23, 1840, at Saco unmarried.
- B. EPHRAIM, born July 1822, married Sarah Walker of Denmark.
- C. CLARINDA, born June 29, 1824, married first Albert Bailey on July 22, 1845.
- D. REUBEN, born about 1827, married first Mary Smith of Kennebunk; second Marantha Sanborn of Baldwin. He died Feb. 15, 1868, age 41 yrs.
- E. JESSE BUTTERFIELD, born Feb. 1830, died 1813 in Baldwin. Married in Canada.
- F. ISABELLA, born Jan. 27, 1823, died 1908 in Baldwin, married Heber Wilkins and lived in Cornish and Midwest.
- G. ROYAL, died Feb. 22, 1901, age 67, unmarried. Mill owner.

- H. MARTHA ANN, born Feb. 22, 1835, married Allen E. Rich of Hastings, Minn., June 2, 1854.
- I. NATHAN, married Augusta Tarbox. Died 1907, age 80 yrs. Three children.

Abner Sanborn married second Jan. 16, 1849, Abigail Cuptill, both of Baldwin and had children: (Sanborn)
- J. CAROLINE DYER, married Mr. Pattee and lived in Mass. and Florida.
- K. DANIEL WILSON, born May 22, 1850, married June Cross of Sebago and lived in Bridgton.
- L. KATHARINE, born Nov. 5, 1851, died at age of 52.
- M. ALBERT BAILEY, born Aug. 2, 1853, married Ellen Chadbourne.

(6) ISABELLA, born Apr. 7, 1800, died May 17, 1802.

(7) NATHAN, born Aug. 9, 1804, married first in 1833, Hannah Hallowell of Windsor, Maine. Married second Mary ____ and they in 1860 were living in Island Falls, Maine. Children were:
- A. AMELIA D., born Dec. 17, 1835, married Apr. 5, 1859, John Henry Small, born May 17, 1836, son of Deborah (Thorne) Small. He died Apr. 9, 1895, age 68 yrs., 11 mos., in Augusta.
- B. JOHN H., born 1838, died Apr. 9, 1895, age 68 yrs., 11 mos., 2 days, Augusta.
- C. MARY, born 1840, living in 1860 Island Falls, Maine.
- D. JOSEPH F., born 1846, died Aug. 15, 1865, in Company F., 31st Reg't., Maine Vols.
- E. LUCY E., born 1848, married Arthur Hallowell.
- F. NATHAN F., born about 1851.
- G. HANNAH E., born about 1853.

(8) ISABELLA, born Aug. 7, 1806, died Jan. 15, 1883, age 77, married Jesse Butterfield May 15, 1831. He died Aug. 30, 1886, age 84. Children as follows: (Butterfield)
- A. AUSTIN S., born Aug. 5, 1832, died June 12, 1910, married Laura A. Hatch of Hiram in 1853.
- B. JOHN C., born July 3, 1836, married Melissa E. Booker of Hallowell and had three daughters.
- C. SARAH BELLE, born May 16, 1839, died Mar. 8, 1883, of pneumonia, married Charles K. Evans and lived in N.H.

(9) ISAAC, born May 20, 1802, lived at West Baldwin, married Mar. 20, 1828, Elizabeth Graffam, born Feb. 23, 1810, died Aug. 23, 1894. He died in Baldwin Aug. 24, 1866, age 64 yrs. Children as follows:
- A. ELIZABETH, died young. (By first wife.)
- B. SARAH J., born about 1832, married May 24, 1854, Lorenzo Stackpole of Cornish, she of Baldwin. He died Nov. 29, 1886, age 62 yrs., in Cornish, and she died insane Aug. 16, 1899, age 67 yrs.

- C. ALMEDA, born 1838, married William Henry Dearborn and lived in Baldwin. She died Feb. 1, 1906, age 69 yrs., 1 mo., 13 days, in Baldwin.
- D. MELVINA, born ____, married first Orrin Davis; second George Littlefield; third Andrew Wentworth of Lebanon.
- E. DEBORAH, married Randall Sanborn.
- F. SUSAN, born Oct. 24, 1844, married Charles J. Weymouth, lived in Baldwin. She died July 17, 1924.

(10) THANKFUL DEBORAH, born June 24, 1808, married Veranus Foss Nov. 7, 1830. He was born in 1807 and died in 1892. She died in Baldwin Nov. 12, 1871. Children: (Foss)
- A. ALBERT M., a Civil War veteran, died in Baldwin June 26, 1868, age 25, of consumption.
- B. JOHN, died young.
- C. ALONZO, served in Civil War, a peddler and eventually a publisher of city directories. He died in Hopkinton, Mass., at the age of 93. He married and had no children.
- D. MARY S., born ____, married Lorenzo Sanborn, born Nov. 27, 1820, son of Pierce and Huldah (Paine) Sanborn of Standish.
- E. ELLEN, possibly.

3. JANE, born Nov. 19, 1771, in Pearsontown, married Mar. 22, 1798, James McKenney Jr., born May 20, 1775, son of James and Martha (Noble) McKenney of Scarboro and Limington. She died May 4, 1841, and he on Feb. 24, 1845, both in Limington.

4. BENJAMIN, born in Pearsonstown Sept. 11, 1772, served in War of 1812. He lived in that part of Baldwin that later became Sebago and on Jan. 11, 1798, married Lydia Sanborn, born about 1773 daughter of David and Sarah (Hall) Sanborn. He died in Sebago Sept. 22, 1843, age 70 yrs., 11 days. His widow died Sept. 8, 1861, age 84 yrs. Children as follows:

(1) HANNAH, born Mar. 14, 1803, married James Gray, who was born July 12, 1796, in Beverly, Mass., and died Sept. 21, 1864, in Sebago. She died Sept. 8, 1861, age 84 yrs., in Sebago.

(2) JAMES, born about 1813, died Jan. 7, 1899, age 85 yrs., 2 mos., 7 days, in Baldwin.

(3) FREEMAN, born Oct. 21, 1818, Baldwin, died Mar. 4, 1895, in Hollis. He married Sept. 28, 1840, in Sebago, Mary Martin, born Oct. 14, 1822, died Mar. 2, 1885, in Standish. Their children were Catherine V., born Nov. 30, 1841, married Sept. 19, 1858, William H. Ward, and died Sept. 16, 1887, in No. Conway, N.H.; Elbridge, born June 1, 1844, died Feb. 16, 1932, in Limington; Ovesteese, born Nov. 28, 1850; Clary Maria, born Oct. 12, 1854, died July 26, 1919; Millore, born Sept. 28, 1856, died Dec. 24, 1863; Manville F., born Aug. 24, 1861, Bridgton, died May 13, 1941 in Hollis.

        (4)   OLIVE JANE, born about 1825, married Nov. 23, 1845, Albion K.P. Sanborn, both of Baldwin. She died Apr. 11, 1880, age 58 yrs., 10 mos., 3 days.
        (5)   LAVINIA.
  5. ELIZABETH (BETSY), born Sept. 4, 1774, married Dec. 25, 1795, (Dec. 15, 1796?) Jonathan Sanborn Jr. a Revolutionary War veteran, born in Hampton, N.H., Aug. 12, 1762, son of Jonathan and Rachel (Fifield) Sanborn of Baldwin. They lived at East Baldwin where they raised a large family. She died May 16, 1846, and he died in Sebago Mar. 2, 1840.
  6. WILLIAM, born July 1777 in Flintstown, was the first white child born in that township. He died Mar. 28, 1856, age 78 yrs. and 8 mos. He married first June. 10, 1804 (int. Jan. 15, 1804), Rachel Gould; second Olive Stevens Oct. 13, 1810 (int. June 10, 1810), who died in 1851, age 73. Children as follows:
        (1)   JANE, born in Aug. 1806, died May 30, 1884, age 77 yrs., 9 mos., married James Lord of Baldwin.
        (2)   RACHEL, born in Nov. 1808, died May 20, 1852, age 43 yrs., 6 mos., married Andrew Ray.
        (3)   WILLIAM, born June 7, 1808, died Apr. 13, 1896, age 87 yrs., 10 mos., 6 days. He married Mar. 10, 1838, Eunice Miller, born Jan. 27, 1820, in Denmark, daughter of Daniel and Patience (Stevens) Miller, died Nov. 24, 1886, in Baldwin. Children as follows:
            A. MERRITT, born 1840, married Mary Ann Winn of Sebago. He died May 16, 1896, age 57 yrs., 6 mos., 6 days, in Sebago and she died Aug. 13, 1911, age 70 yrs., 10 mos., 8 days.
            B. CAROLINE, born May 17, 1843, No. Baldwin, married in 1867, John Alfred Winn of Hiram, born Jan. 20, 1843. She died Sept. 19, 1903, age 60 yrs., 3 mos., 26 days, in Bridgton.
            C. LORENZO, born 1848, died May 16, 1937, age 89. He married in 1871 Emma White of Standish, who died June 16, 1935, age 85.
            D. MELINDA, born 1850, died Nov. 27, 1882, age 32 yrs., 7 mos., 21 days, married Lorenzo Gammon.
viii. JANE, born Mar. 15, 1740, bapt. July 12, 1741, according to North Yarmouth records. Nothing further known.
ix. MARTHA, born about 1738, according to some sources, but probably not. She married George Freeman (int. Jan. 26, 1760, in Falmouth), both listed as residents of Falmouth; marriage, Feb. 14, 1760. She was said by Dr. Meserve and Ridlon in *Saco Valley Settlements* to have been a daughter of Joseph Thorne of Pearsontown. According to gravestone in Standish Village Cemetery, she died Sept. 11, 1807, which would make her date of birth about 1738.

    However, Bartholomew Thorne, son of Joseph, was born the same year on Jan. 14, 1738, according to North Yarmouth records, making it questionable if they could have been born the same year unless they were twins as some accounts of the Thorne family have stated. If that was true, why was the date of Martha's birth not recorded with that of Bartholomew.

George Freeman was a son of Capt. Joshua Freeman, a prosperous merchant and sea captain of Falmouth and an active proprietor of Falmouth. He was a member of the merchant class and a cut above the Thorne family whose members were poorly educated. At this time there was living in Topsham, Maine, another Thorne family, whose head was William Thorne, born Mar. 17, 1704/5, son of Thomas and Martha, Scotch-Irish immigrants from Ireland. William Thorne, a well-educated man and the first town clerk of Topsham, was the father of ten children. Since Katherine, born June 7, 1743, married Reuben Freeman, son of Capt. Joshua Freeman of Falmouth, on Sept. 26, 1764, and William Freeman Jr., born Aug. 18, 1749, married Lucy Freeman, a daughter of Capt. Joshua Freeman and sister to George, we know the two families were acquainted, and what would be more natural that George would have married another sister of the Topsham family of Freeman. As it happens, there was in the Topsham family a daughter named Martha who with a twin sister Sarah was born on Oct. 13, 1738. It was she I believe who married George Freeman and not Martha, the unrecorded daughter of Joseph Thorne of Standish, if she ever existed.

TOMPSON

The Rev. John Tompson, the first minister of the Pearsontown Church, was born Oct. 14, 1740, in Scarboro, Maine, son of Rev. William and Anna (Hubbard) Tompson. His father having died when he was only 19 years old, his mother being an enterprising woman with many able friends and determined that he should be educated for the ministry, placed him under the care of the famous preceptor Moody, who kept a grammar school at York, Maine.

Following the course of study under Mr. Moody, he matriculated at Harvard College in 1761 and graduated therefrom in 1765. He then studied theology with the Rev. Dr. Wigglesworth of Cambridge. After preaching in several places he was ordained pastor of the church in Pearsontown on Oct. 26, 1768. His ordination took place in the First Church of Falmouth, now Portland, because of the lack of facilities in Pearsontown and the more convenient location of Falmouth for convening the council.

The next month on Nov. 22, 1768, he was married to Sarah Small, born in Somersworth, N.H., Apr. 15, 1748, daughter of Joshua and Susannah (Kennard) Small of Scarboro and Limington, Maine. The ceremony was performed by his brother William Tompson Esq. of Scarboro. He remained as pastor of the Pearsontown Church until Apr. 7, 1783, when he was dismissed at his own request. The following month he was installed as pastor of the church at South Berwick, Maine. Here he served as the only minister for more than 40 years until, because of his great age and infirmities, a colleague, the Rev. George W. Campbell, was settled to relieve him of many of his duties and cares of the church and parish.

As was the custom in the case of those townships which were laid out and granted for service in the various colonial wars, one share or right was always set aside for the first minister of the township. Accordingly, when John Tompson became the first pastor of the Pearsontown Church, he became owner of right No. 1 consisting of the 30-acre lot #1 in first division, the 100-acre lot #6 in third division. However, at the time of the last of the French and Indian Wars the 30-acre lot #1 was one of those subdivided by the Proprietors into 5-acre lots and granted to those settlers who continued to live in the township with their families during those perilous times. Accordingly on Apr. 1, 1770, the Proprietors granted to him a new 30-acre lot #1 in lieu of the one originally given that designation (7/124).

As opportunity offered, John Tompson purchased from their owners a number of the 5-acre lots, all located directly at the Corner in close proximity to the fort. Lot #60 in the second division, which was granted to him at the time of the second drawing of lots, was sold by him to Peter White of Standish on Oct. 26, 1796 (25/472).

Soon after Rev. Tompson had moved his family to South Berwick, his wife, Sarah, died suddenly on Aug. 30, 1783, leaving him with eight children to care for among strangers. On Feb. 9, 1784, he married second Mrs. Sarah Morrill of Biddeford, widow of Capt. Jordan Morrill and daughter of Mr. Elisha Allen, both of that town. She was born in Salisbury, Mass., Feb. 14, 1743. He died Dec. 21, 1828, in his 89th year and the 64th year of his ministry. His second wife died in Aug. 1825. They are buried in South Berwick in "Old Fields" Cemetery. Children of the Rev. John Tompson, the first seven born in Pearsontown, the latter three in South Berwick, were as follows:

i. WILLIAM, born Oct. 17, 1769, bapt. Dec. 17, 1769, married Mar. 30, 1793, Hannah Goodwin, born in 1775 daughter of Dominicus and Betsy (Littlefield) (Perkins) Goodwin. They moved to Standish from South Berwick in Oct. 1793. He lived in Standish Village on the corner made by the junction of the roads leading to Portland and to Buxton. His father gave to him a 10-acre lot of land consisting of the two 5-acre lots Nos. 1 and 2, which were orginally a portion of the 30-acre lot #72, and on which a store was fitted out for country trade. He built a house in 1801 and continued to live in Standish most of the time until his death on Jan. 8, 1859, age 89 yrs. His wife died Oct. 19, 1831. Children of William and Hannah (Goodwin) Tompson were as follows:
1. WILLIAM, born July 22, 1796, bapt. Apr. 15, 1798.
2. JOHN GOODWIN, born Apr. 30, 1799, bapt. May 12, 1799.
3. CHARLES, born Oct. 30, 1801, bapt. July 15, 1804, died 1891 (June).
4. HETTA LORD, born Jan. 30, 1804, bapt. July 15, 1804, died June 2, 1823, in Standish.
5. DANIEL GOODWIN, born Dec. 12, 1805, bapt. July 6, 1806, died in Aug. 1888, No. Yarmouth.
6. ELIZABETH GOODWIN, born Dec. 2, 1810, married Elliot Bradley, died in 1907.
7. OLIVE, born Nov. 12, 1812, died Oct. 9, 1831.
8. HENRY GOODWIN, born Mar. 29, 1815, died in 1848.

ii. EDWARD, born Dec. 18, 1771, bapt. Dec. 22, 1771, married Sarah Sewall of York, Maine. He was a farmer and lived in Standish on a farm containing 30 acres, it being the original 30-acre lot #1 which was given to him by his father together with a house which his father had built for him. This lot was located at Standish Village at the junction of the roads leading to Sebago Lake and to Oak Hill and was diagonally across the square from the property of his brother William. He died Jan. 29, 1834, age 64 yrs., in Standish, and his wife survived him until Oct. 5, 1843. They were parents of the following children, all born in Standish:
1. SARAH, born Jan. 19, 1798, bapt. Feb. 18, 1798.
2. LUCY, born Apr. 10, 1800, bapt. May 18, 1800.
3. OLIVER, born May 17, 1802, bapt. June 13, 1802.
4. JOSEPH SEWALL, born Sept. 17, 1804, bapt. Mar. 24, 1805, married Oct. 25, 1845, Charlotte P. Weston of Standish.
5. MARY JEWETT, born Oct. 22, 1806, bapt. Dec. 1806, died in infancy.
6. MARY JEWETT, born Mar. 7, 1810, died in infancy.
7. HENRY, born Apr. 21, 1811, bapt. Nov. 3, 1811, died Dec. 9, 1841.
8. JOHN, born Aug. 4, 1813, bapt. May 30, 1819.
9. MARY JEWETT, born Nov. 26, 1818, bapt. June 29, 1826.
10. SAMUEL, bapt. June 29, 1826.

iii. SAMUEL, born Oct. 10, 1773, bapt. Oct. 17, 1773, went to live with his uncle William Tompson in Scarboro and afterwards continued to live there.
iv. SARAH, born July 14, 1775, bapt. July 16, 1775.
v. ANNA, born Mar. 15, 1777, bapt. Mar. 16, 1777, married Ichabod Goodwin Sr. of Berwick.
vi. JOSEPH, born July 21, 1778, bapt. July 26, 1778, married Betty Clements of Somersworth, N.H., in 1800. About that time he migrated with his wife and her parents to Frankfort, Waldo County, Maine. His first wife died May 4, 1819, and on Feb. 17, 1820, he married Mary Dunham of Belfast, Maine. He died suddenly in Mar. 1859, nearly 81 yrs. of age. His second wife died in Mar. 1864. Eight children.
vii. MARY, born Aug. 13, 1781, bapt. Aug. 13, 1781, died of tuberculosis Mar. 28, 1808.
viii. JOHN STORER, born at South Berwick Aug. 5, 1783, and died there Feb. 20, 1872.
By second wife:
ix. BETSEY, born May 19, 1785, died June 10, 1817.
x. WILLIAM ALLEN, born Apr. 18, 1787, died in Oct. 1835.

TOPPING

The name of Luther Topping is found on the 1789, 1790, 1795, and 1796 tax lists of Standish, in the 1790 census with a family of 1-1-2, and in the 1800 census with a family consisting of him and his wife, both over 45, and one male and one female between 10 and 16 years of age. It is likely that he was the Luther Topping whose name is found on the 1766 and 1772 tax lists of Falmouth and that Capt. Luther Topping whose death on Feb. 6, 1804, at the age of 58 is found on the Falmouth records. His death was reported in the *Gazette of Maine*, issue of Feb. 4, 1804. He died at Falmouth; he was of Standish. No trace of his ancestry has been discovered.

On Nov. 15, 1774, Joseph McLellan, mariner, of Falmouth sold Luther Topping of Falmouth, mariner, one whole right of land in Pearsontown, exclusive of the 30-acre lot #87 in first division, which had been sold to Dominicus Mitchell, but including the 100-acre lot #114 in second division located on the bank of the Saco River. This latter lot subsequently came into the hands of Lydia Woodman and was divided between her sons Isaac and Jacob York and her daughter Mary (York) Cookson. Luther Topping of Pearsontown, mariner, bought of Josiah Noyes of Falmouth, gentleman, the 30-acre lot #92 and 100-acre lot #1 in Pearsontown on May 11, 1778 (11/94). This same 30-acre lot he sold to Ephraim Jones, yeoman, of Gorham on Feb. 24, 1792 (22/459). He being of Pearsontown bought from Ephraim Jones of Falmouth, administrator of the estate of Abraham York, the 30-acre lot #9 on Aug. 25, 1783 (12/282).

Luther Topping married Dorothy or Dolly Bean, born before 1755 daughter of Jonathan and Abigail (Gorden) Bean of Pearsontown and Bethel, Maine. After his death, which occurred at Saccarappa while on the way home from Portland in 1804, she married second on Aug. 10, 1806, Samuel Mountfort of Falmouth. Although Thomas Shaw and Dr. Meserve state that Luther and Dolly (Bean) Topping were childless, the fact that both the 1790 and 1800 census indicated two children living in their family makes this questionable, especially since there was another Luther Topping of about the right age to be their son who lived in Standish later on. Dolly (Bean) Topping Mountfort died sometime after 1820.

Luther Topping, ancestry not determined, married May 10, 1807, Mercy Dow, born Mar. 5, 1785, daughter of Abner and Martha (Sawyer) Hinckley Dow of Falmouth and Standish. They lived in Standish and Baldwin. He died Aug. 14, 1831, at the age of 51 and she survived him until Oct. 1869. Children were as follows:

i. **MARY M.**, born Dec. 3, 1807, gravestone Dec. 5, 1808, changed her name to Tappan, and died unmarried Mar. 5, 1896. She was buried in the cemetery at West Gorham.
ii. **ELIAS**, born in Baldwin in Aug. 1809, died July 31, 1831, age 22.
iii. **DOLLY D.**, born about 1812, married George Clement of Gorham Mar. 27, 1842. She died Apr. 17, 1893, age 81. They lived at West Gorham and were the parents of six children.
iv. **MARTHA D.**, born about 1814, married John Higgins of Gorham, born in Sept. 1803. She died Mar. 26, 1880, age 66, three children.
v. **ELIZABETH**, born ____, died in infancy.
vi. **SAMUEL**, born about 1816, died Oct. 5, 1831, age 15.
vii. **ELIZABETH**.
viii. **LYDIA**, died in infancy.
ix. **LYDIA**.
x. **SYBIL**, born Mar. 2, 1824, died Feb. 6, 1899, unmarried.

xi. NANCY, born Feb. 1828, married in 1852 George Crockett. She died at West Gorham Apr. 11, 1910.
xii. CAROLINE M., born Dec. 31, 1831, married Charles E. Jordan of West Gorham. She died Nov. 8, 1895, age 63. Three children.

TUCKER

The name of James D. Tucker is found on the 1795, 1796, 1799, 1808, and 1814 tax lists of Standish, in the 1800 census with a family consisting of him and his wife, both between 26 and 45 years of age, two females under 10, one male between 10 and 16, three females between 26 and 45, and one female over 45, who may have been his wife's mother, Martha (Higgins) Linnell, who was admitted to the Standish Church in 1794. At the time of the 1810 census his family consisted of two males over 45 years of age, three females under 10, one female between 10 and 16, one female between 26 and 45, and three females over 45. By 1820 his family consisted of one male under 10, two males 26 to 45, two males over 45, two females under 10, two females between 16 and 26, and three females over 45. One of these older males was his aged father John Tucker who died Sept. 17, 1822, age 89 years, in Standish, and formerly of Saco.

He was born James Davenport Tucker on Sept. 1, 1765 (bapt. Oct. 6, 1765), son of John and Rebecca (Davenport) Tucker of Saco, and was a resident of Standish on Sept. 16, 1792, when he married, with John Deane Esq. officiating, Mary Linnell, born Jan. 30, 1770, daughter of Elisha and Martha (Higgins) Linnell of Eastham, Massachusetts. He and his wife were admitted to the Standish Church on Nov. 24, 1793. He lived near York's Corner at South Standish and besides being a schoolteacher and mail carrier, was a hatter, the old potash kettle that he used for a hat kettle having been sold to Thomas Cram and set in a chimney arch.

James D. Tucker was active in town affairs, serving as a selectman in 1793, 1795, 1796, 1798, 1799, 1800, and 1804, and as town clerk in 1796. Dates of death of him and his wife have not been found but his must have been after 1820 and hers after 1850. They were parents of the following children:

i. CATHERINE, born Apr. 28, 1793, bapt. July 7, 1793, married June 16, 1812 (int. May 16, 1812), George Smith, son of Capt. William Smith of Buxton. Their family consisted of: (Smith)
 1. MARK, born Apr. 13, 1813, died May 2, 1813.
 2. MARTHA ANN, born June 19, 1814.
 3. ENOCH COFFIN, born Apr. 26, 1816.
 4. REBECCA DAVENPORT, born Feb. 19, 1818.
 5. MEHITABLE, born Aug. 25, 1820.
 6. _____, born Sept. 25, 1824.
ii. REBECCA, born Apr. 3, 1795 (bapt. Apr. 5, 1795), married Jan. 27, 1820, Benjamin Harmon of Buxton. They both died in 1887 according to gravestones in Hillcrest Cemetery in Hollis at West Buxton.
iii. MARTHA, bapt. May 14, 1797, evidently died young.

iv. MARTHA, bapt. Mar. 4, 1799.
v. SALLY BRAGG, bapt. May 27, 1802.
vi. MARY, bapt. June 12, 1804, married Sept. 30, 1832, Oliver Strout of Bradford, Maine, who was born Nov. 14, 1804, in Limington, Maine, son of James and Sarah (Johnson) Strout. She married second Dec. 30, 1847, in Standish, Samuel Bradeen of Standish, born June 15, 1804, in Limington, son of Henry and Jemima (Nason) Bradeen of Limington. She was living in Standish in 1880, age 76 yrs.
vii. JAMES DAVENPORT JR., bapt. Aug. 18, 1807.
viii. ANN L., bapt. Sept. 10, 1809, married Sept. 12, 1835, James McDugal of Gorham.
ix. JOHN LINNELL, born Dec. 12, 1812 (bapt. Feb. 12, 1814) married Jan. 14, 1843, Martha M. Smith of Standish, born July 14, 1822, daughter of Hugh McLellan and Eunice (Bacon) Smith of Buxton. They lived in Standish where he was known as Col. John L. Tucker and was fatally injured by being crushed between heavy timbers while in charge of the demolition of a double sawmill at Steep Falls on July 27, 1849, passing away a day or two later. His wife died Jan. 29, 1854, age 32. They with an infant son are buried in Bonney Eagle Pond Cemetery on the west side of Route 22 in Buxton. They were parents of the following children:
1. FERNANDO CORTES OR CARTER, died May 11, 1844, age 10 mos.
2. REBECCA S., born Mar. 11, 1845, nothing further known.
3. CHARLES O., born Aug. 27, 1846, married in the Midwest. He served from Dec. 5, 1864, to Oct. 5, 1865, as a private in Co. G. of the Eighth Maine Volunteer Infantry Regiment during the Civil War. After the war he migrated to Ohio and then to California where he died on Oct. 2, 1901, in Sawtelle, Los Angeles County, and was buried in the Veteran's Cemetery there.
4. ROSETTA DEERING, born Mar. 21, 1848, never married. In her youth she lived for a while on Cape Cod, perhaps being brought up by some of her mother's relatives who lived there. She moved to California and after the accidental death of her brother's wife in 1914, cared for by her nephew Lester Brann. She died in California about 1931.
x. TABBA (TABITHA?), bapt. July 11, 1817, was living, age 32, and unmarried, in the family of Samuel Bradeen of Standish in 1850. Her mother, Mary (Linnell) Tucker, age 80, was living in the same family at that time.

WALKER

A John Walker lived in Pearsontown during its earliest days. He was one of the soldiers in the guard who lived in the fort with their families during the last of the French and Indian Wars. He with Thomas Stevens and Samuel Knowles on July 20, 1757, petitioned the governor and

General Court of Massachusetts for help for the sixteen families living in the fort at that time, who were trying to live on the pay allowed by the Province for only ten of the families. He is listed among men from Pearsontown who served in Lt. Charles Lessner's party scouting east from Broad Bay (Waldoboro) about 1759-60. His name is also found among those of Pearsontown men who worked on Gorham roads in 1760 and 1761. No record has been found of his having been in town at a later date than this. He was one of those who built barracks to live inside the fort, money to pay for the construction of which was voted him by the Proprietors in 1759 and 1763.

Record of the parentage of John Walker has not been discovered, but it is evident that he lived in Falmouth, Maine, and perhaps Gorham prior to his short sojourn in Pearsontown. Although early records of Falmouth show the marriage intentions of a John Walker and Mary Riggs of Falmouth (Portland) on Oct. 5, 1751, records of the First Parish Church indicate the marriage by Parson Smith of a Joseph Walker and Mary Riggs. Since a Joseph Walker and wife settled in Fryeburg, Maine, and had children whose names were similar to those in the Riggs family, it seems likely that it was not John Walker who married Mary Riggs.

It is said that John Walker, born in 1728, resided at Falmouth, at Standish in 1756, in Gorham, and for some years at Gouldsborough in Hancock County, Maine. A John Walker of Gouldsborough sold land there on Nov. 2, 1771 (Lincoln County deeds). The name of John Walker is found on a petition of inhabitants of Gouldborough in Mar. 1787. A John Walker with a family of 1-0-2 was living in Gouldborough at the time of the 1790 census. On Jan. 30, 1800, William Shaw of Quincy, Mass., deeded to David Cobb of Gouldsborough one hundred acres of land on west of Broad Bay taken up and improved by John Walker, late of Gouldborough deceased, as a settler in the town.

It is said that John Walker had a son Josiah, who served in the Revolutionary War, and another son, William, who settled at Freeman, Maine, and had a daughter Lounda, who married Warren Getchell of Emden. A William Walker, age 79, died in Philips, Maine, on Apr. 15, 1847.

The *Eastern Argus* issue of Nov. 29, 1810, gives the death of a James Walker who was killed by a wheel of his team.

WARD

The name of Jonathan Ward is found on the 1795 and 1796 tax lists of Standish. He was born in 1774 son of John (Joseph,[3] George[1]) and Hannah (Wiley) Ward of Eastham, Mass., and Gorham, Maine. He married on Feb. 3, 1794, Sarah, born Apr. 2, 1771, daughter of John and Naoma (York) Hall of Standish. They were parents of seven children, all of whom are said to have been born in Standish:

i.   **GEORGE,** born Sept. 27, 1794, died in Sebago Aug. 4, 1866.
ii.   **JONATHAN JR.,** born July 26, 1796, died Oct. 11, 1857, in Prospect.
iii. **SARAH,** born Mar. 17, 1798, married Nathan Wood of Portland.

iv. WILLIAM, born Dec. 18, 1799 (Reverend), lived in North Sebago, died Mar. 20, 1879.
v.   JACOB, born Apr. 6, 1802, died in 1885.
vi. ISAAC, born Feb. 3, 1804, died Sept. 15, 1870, Standish.
vii. DAVID, born Mar. 24, 1806.

The name of Jesse Ward is found in the 1800 census of Standish when his family consisted of him and his wife, both between 26 and 45 years of age, and three daughters, all under 10 years of age. He was living in Standish on Dec. 3, 1801, when he sold to William Elwell of Gorham his right and title to 53 acres and 154 rods of land in Standish, it being the S.E. end of lot #30 in second division (39/368). He was a brother of Jonathan and was born in 1771, Eastham, Massachusetts. He married (int. Nov. 17, 1796) Hannah Mitchell and settled in Gorham near Great Falls. He was a farmer and died May 23, 1845. His wife died Mar. 29, 1856, age 83. They are buried in the cemetery at No. Gorham. They were parents of thirteen children.

WARREN

The name of Samuel Warren is found in the 1800 census of Standish, at which time he was credited with a family consisting of him and his wife and a daughter under 10 years of age. Samuel[6] Warren (James,[5] Samuel,[4] James,[3] James,[2] James[1]) was born in Gorham, Maine, July 14, 1775, the oldest child of James and Martha (McLellan) Warren. On Nov. 28, 1798, his intentions of marriage to Anna Pinkerton of Londonderry, N.H., were filed in Gorham. It was about this time that he settled at Bonney Eagle in Standish. Here he cleared land on the Saco River above Josies Brook and built a house there, where he continued to live until his death on Oct. 10, 1863, his wife having passed away on Jan. 6, 1849, age 75.

Samuel and Anna (Pinkerton) Warren were parents of the following children:

i.   ANN McCARDY, born Nov. 3, 1799, bapt. May 27, 1802, married _____ Coolbroth and died in 1882.
ii. MARY McLELLAN, born May 1, 1801, bapt. May 27, 1802, married Dec. 1, 1846, Bryan Paine, born Dec. 9, 1798, son of Joseph Jr. and Elinor (Martin) Paine of Standish. She died Jan. 22, 1870, aged 69 yrs. and 8 mos. He died Feb. 18, 1881, age 82 yrs. and 2 mos.
iii. HUGH McLELLAN, born Jan. 18, 1803, bapt. Nov. 3, 1803, married Nov. 28, 1826, Sarah Nason, born Jan. 19, 1804, son of Nicholas and Molly (Elder) Nason of Buxton. He died Sept. 8, 1876, and she on Jan. 25, 1893.
iv. ELIZA PINKERTON, born Sept. 12, 1804, bapt. Feb. 4, 1806, married (int. May 1, 1831) Asa Mayo Jr. of Standish.
v.   JANE WILSON, born June 22, 1807, bapt. Dec. 2, 1807, married Jan. 1, 1827, Capt. Warren Sanborn. She died Mar. 7, 1875.

vi. MARTHA PINKERTON DAVIS, born May 4, 1809, bapt. Dec. 9, 1816, died Dec. 29, 1834.
vii. REBECCA WILSON, born Jan. 28, 1814, bapt. Jan. 9, 1817.

WATERHOUSE

The name of Joseph Waterhouse is found on the 1789, 1790, 1795, and 1796 tax lists of Standish and in the 1790 census with a family of 1-2-5. Joseph[4] Waterhouse (Joseph,[3] Timothy,[2] Richard[1]) was born in Scarboro Feb. 12, 1754, and was baptized there on March 17 of the same year son of Joseph and Mary (Libby) Waterhouse. He served in the Revolutionary War and during a short interval in his army life married on Apr. 4, 1776, Lydia Harmon, born in 1765 daughter of William and Elizabeth (Hoyt) Harmon of Scarboro. They lived on the paternal acres near Scottow's Hill in Scarboro until 1782 when they moved to Standish Neck where members of his wife's family had settled and where two of his half-sisters, Sarah (Waterhouse) Libby and Susannah (Waterhouse) Berry, later came to live. He was a farmer and continued to live in town until his death on Aug. 2, 1837, his wife having passed away on Mar. 28, 1836, age 81 years, in Standish.

Joseph and Lydia (Harmon) Waterhouse were the parents of ten children, as follows, the first three born in Scarboro and the remainder in Standish:

i. LYDIA, born Jan. 3, 1777, bapt. Aug. 3, 1777, married Nov. 23, 1797, Abraham Webb, son of Eli and Sarah (Cloudman) Webb of Gorham; lived in Gorham and Windham, Maine, and in Chatham, N.H., where she died Oct. 10, 1865.

ii. WILLIAM HARMON, born Oct. 14, 1779, married Jan. 31, 1802, Sarah B. Smith, born Aug. 13, 1780, daughter of Capt. Ephraim and Elizabeth (Harding) Smith of Gorham, who died Oct. 10, 1843; married second Sept. 21, 1846, Mrs. Sarah T. Donnell of Portland. He was a farmer in Standish and Gorham and died Nov. 4, 1867. They were parents of nine children, all born in Standish.

iii. ELIZABETH, born Nov. 20, 1781, married June 10, 1804, Joseph Nason born Jan. 30, 1783, son of Uriah and Abigail (Knight) Nason of Gorham. They were the parents of four children. He died Apr. 8, 1860, and she on Aug. 6, 1863.

iv. JOSIAH, born Sept. 23, 1784, in Standish, married July 26, 1807 (int. June 13, 1800), Rebecca Brown, daughter of Ezra and Sarah (Graffam) Brown of Windham. They were the parents of four children. He and his son Freeman left home together and were never heard from again.

v. OLIVE, born June 14, 1787, married Aug. 30, 1806, Edward Anderson, born May 2, 1786, son of Col. Edward and Mary (Mayberry) Anderson of Windham. She died Apr. 14, 1863, and he died Apr. 5, 1876. Ten children.

vi. **ABIGAIL,** born Aug. 16, 1790, married Aug. 29, 1811, Levi Quimby Haskell, born in Sept. 1788 son of Benjamin and Sally (Berry) Haskell of Standish. They lived in Limington and were the parents of six children. He died there on June 3, 1837, and she on Jan. 30, 1855.

vii. **JOSEPH,** born July 15, 1793, married first May 10, 1818, Elizabeth Chase, daughter of John and Elizabeth (Hooper) Chase, married second Rhoda Bancroft of Albany, Maine. He lived in Limington, Portland, Waterford and Albany, Maine, and had ten children, seven by his first wife who died in Albany Dec. 4, 1832, and three by his second, who died in June 1882. He died in Albany Apr. 2, 1869.

viii. **MARTHA,** born July 16, 1796, married June 1, 1817, George Anderson, son of Col. Edward and Mary (Mayberry) Anderson of Windham. She died in Windham May 11, 1862, and he died on Mar. 11, 1879.

ix. **MARY,** born Mar. 3, 1798 or 1800, married Nov. 4, 1819, William Davis, son of Major Nicholas and Charity (Haley) Davis of Limington; he died in Waterboro Sept. 17, 1864, and she in Portland May 29, 1871.

x. **MONTGOMERY,** born Sept. 9, 1801, died Oct. 9, 1825, unmarried.

WEEMAN

The names of John and Edward Weeman are found on the 1808 tax list of Standish with Edward being charged for no poll and John is listed on a Cumberland County tax list of Standish in 1814. In the 1810 census of the town John Weeman is indicated as having a family consisting of himself, over 45 years old; his wife, between 26 and 45; and three males and one female under 10 years old. At the time Edward Weeman's family consisted of him and his wife, both between 26 and 45, three males and two females under 10, and one female between 10 and 16 years old.

John Weeman was born about 1750 son of Valentine Weeman of Cape Elizabeth and married there on Sept. 12, 1772, Betsey Small. In 1777 he moved to Limington where he was one of the early settlers. His farm was located one mile east of Limington Village on Route 11 on the present Meserve place. On Aug. 16, 1802, John Weeman bought of Joseph Davis 50 acres of lot #120 in second division and settled on this farm just off what is now Route 25 not far from the bridge to East Limington. Here he afterwards lived and was living in 1819 and died at a date not discovered; he was probably buried in a small graveyard on his farm, one of the fieldstones there likely indicating his resting place. His wife died shortly before the 1800 census was taken, undoubtedly in Limington, and he married second on Feb. 20, 1804, Esther Davis, who died June 19, 1840. He was the father of at least the following family:

i. **EDWARD**, born ____, married (int. Aug. 7, 1802) Mrs. Marcy (Mann) Phinney of Gorham, widow of Eli Phinney. On Oct. 29, 1803, he bought from Obediah Irish of Standish 50 acres of lot #120 in the second division, which was the other half of the lot purchased by his father. He probably moved to Standish about the same time as his father. He was given of Limington in Oct. 1810, May 1812, and Aug. 1814. Nothing further known.

ii. **ABIGAIL**, born Feb. 7, 1779, married Mar. 21, 1798, Thomas Morrill, born May 7, 1763, in Berwick. She died Feb. 7, 1847, and he on Dec. 8, 1855, both in Newburgh, Maine.

iii. **ANNA**, born Mar. 7, 1784, married Mar. 4, 1807, at Raymond, Virgil Wright and died in Casco on May 3, 1871.

iv. **BENJAMIN**, born about 1787, married Mar. 4, 1810, Phebe Spencer of Limington, who died Sept. 16, 1836, age 46 yrs. He married second June 10, 1838 Phebe (Nason) Hussey, born in 1808 daughter of Simon and Esther (Merrifield) Nason of Limington and widow of Benjamin Hussey who died June 24, 1832, age 46 yrs., in Limington. He died Aug. 16, 1843, age 56, and she died May 25, 1877, age 68 yrs., 10 mos., in Bangor. They were buried in a family graveyard.

v. **MICAH**, bapt. Jan. 25, 1798, in Limington Church, died young.

vi. **EBENEZER**, bapt. Jan. 25, 1798, in Limington Church, died young.

By second wife, Esther Davis:

vii. **OBEDIAH**, born in Oct. 1804, married first on Mar. 29, 1830, Hannah H. Foster, born June 12, 1812, daughter of Dr. Thomas Foster of Limington, who died Dec. 17, 1841, age 29 yrs., in Standish; second on Mar. 26, 1843, Lydia S. Black of Standish, who died Nov. 21, 1848, age 35 yrs., 8 mos.; and third Apr. 25, 1849, Elizabeth Allen of Biddeford, who died Feb. 20, 1891, age 76. He died May 20, 1877, age 72 yrs., 7 mos., in Standish and was buried with his three wives in the family graveyard.

viii. **JOHN JR.**, born about Oct. 1804, was of Standish when he married on Mar. 2, 1831, Tryphena York, born about 1806 daughter of Abraham and Betsey (Boulter) York of Standish. He died in Oct. 31, 1886, in So. Bridgton and she July 30, 1892, age 85 yrs., 8 mos., in Sebago.

ix. **JOSEPH**, born Dec. 26, 1808, married (int. Nov. 13, 1831) Judith Wentworth born July 12, 1812, in Limington daughter of Benjamin and Sally (Bryant) Wentworth of Limington. He died July 10, 1899, age 90 yrs., 6 mos., and she died July 16, 1899, age 87 yrs., both in Standish. Their children born in Standish were:
1. **SARAH W.**, born Sept. 23, 1832, married Franklin J. Berry.
2. **ALBERT W.**, born Feb. 11, 1835, married Sarah Boothby of Limington.
3. **ELIZA**, born Jan. 8, 1837.
4. **CHARLES EDWIN**, born Feb. 28, 1839.
5. **MARTHA A.**, born Feb. 1, 1841.
6. **JOSEPH W.**, born Aug. 23, 1848.
7. **BENJAMIN R.**, born June 1, 1851, died July 8, 1855, in Standish.
8. **ANNA M.**, born July 8, 1853, died Aug. 31, 1854, in Standish,

x. HANNAH, born Apr. 28, 1810, married July 12, 1829, Stephen Fogg, born Jan. 12, 1807, son of Lemuel and Rebecca (Powers) Fogg of Limington. He died Feb. 2, 1841, age 34 yrs., 20 days, and she on Sept. 24, 1889, age 79 yrs., 4 mos., 26 das. They were buried in the Weeman graveyard.

xi. ORRIN, born 1811, married Sept. 14, 1830, Dorothy Fogg of Brownfield, born Feb. 29, 1804, in Limington daughter of Charles and Anna (Small) Fogg of Limington and Brownfield. He died Aug. 1879 in Hiram and she died Feb. 3, 1896, in Baldwin. Orrin may have been a son of Benjamin & Phebe (Spencer) Weeman, as given in the Fogg Genealogy.

WEEKS

Samuel Weeks, born about 1775 son of William and Dorcas (Dyer) Weeks of Cape Elizabeth and Gorham, Maine, married about 1809 Eleanor West, born Oct. 9, 1789, daughter of Desper and Mary (Green) West of Gorham and Raymond, Maine. After their marriage, they lived for a while in Newfield, Maine, where their child was born but soon thereafter settled in Standish in the vicinity of what is now Sebago Lake Village they afterwards lived and died. He died Dec. 20, 1869, age 94, and she died on Dec. 31, 1864. They were parents of the following children:

i. ALVAH, born Apr. 9, 1810, in Newfield, Maine, married (int. May 20, 1833, in Standish) Angelina Smith, born Dec. 12, 1813, daughter of Hugh and Eunice (Bacon) Smith of Buxton, Maine. She died in 1892 and he in Aug. 21, 1887, age 77 yrs., in Standish. They lived in Standish and were parents of the following children:
  1. GARDNER D., born Aug. 12, 1834, was an engineer and marble dealer in Gorham in 1884. He died in 1893.
  2. ALONZO, born Mar. 7, 1836, was living in Washington, D.C. in 1884. He died in 1907.
  3. ALBERT P., born July 6, 1840, was a medical doctor living in Chelsea, Mass., in 1884.
  4. ORLANDO P., born July 3, 1846, was a jeweler at Sebago Lake Village in 1884.

ii. JOHN W., born Dec. 25, 1814, in Standish, married Jan. 30, 1834, Clarissa W. Haines, born Oct. 20, 1809, daughter of Thomas and Polly (Hancock) Haines of Buxton, Maine, and had:
  1. JOHN WALTER APPLETON, born Nov. 21, 1834.
  2. ELLEN M., born Dec. 1836.

iii. CAROLINE, born July 2, 1822, married Apr. 21, 1839, Charles Howard of Westbrook. She died Apr. 6, 1886, age 65 yrs., 3 mos.

iv. HARRIET, born June 5, 1826, married Dec. 7, 1843, Richard M. Whitney, who died Dec. 3, 1887, age 66 yrs., 9 mos. She died Dec. 23, 1896, age 70 yrs., 6 mos.

v. ALBION, born Feb. 6, 1830.

vi. LUCY A., born 1831, married Frederick W. Poor, born 1832, who was a member of Co. K. of the 50th Reg't of Mass. Volunteers and died at Cairo, Ill., on Aug. 13, 1863, age 31 yrs., 5 mos. She died in Jan. 12, 1906, age 74 yrs., 1 mo., 8 days, Standish.

WESCOTT

The name of Eliakim Wescott is found on the 1795, 1796, 1799, 1808, and 1814 tax lists of Standish; in the 1800 census with a family consisting of one male between 10 and 16, two males between 16 and 26, one male 45 or over (himself) two females under 10, one female between 10 and 16, one female between 16 and 26, and two females 45 or over; and in the 1810 census with a family comprised of two males between 16 and 26, one male 45 or over, one female 45 or over. At the time of the 1790 census he was living in Falmouth with a family of 1-3-3. He was still a resident of Falmouth on Nov. 27, 1791, when he bought from Elizabeth Wise of Gorham the 100-acre lot #55 in the second division in Standish (18/443). This lot located on Standish Neck bordered on the Presumpscot River and Wescott Falls. The first falls on the river below its source were probably named because of his ownership of the area where they were located. He also bought on Mar. 31, 1801, from Israel Swett of Standish the northeast half of the 100-acre lot #53 in the second division located nearby (34/204). It seems likely that he moved from Falmouth to Standish soon after his purchase of Lot #55 in 1791, although one source says that he did not do so until 1795.

Eliakim Wescott was baptized in the First Church of Scarboro on Sept. 21, 1755, son of Richard and Mary (Wardwell) Wescott. He married in Falmouth on Nov. 18, 1780, Joanna Knight, born about 1757 daughter of William and Hannah (Babb) Knight of that town. He died in Standish on Nov. 3, 1816, age 61 yrs. (*Eastern Argus*, Nov. 25, 1816) and she on Feb. 11, 1835, age 77. He served in the Revolutionary War and was taken prisoner while serving in the crew of a prize brig captured by the schooner *General Putnam*, privateer. On Dec. 7, 1818, his son Daniel Wescott of Standish, as administrator of his estate, sold Abraham Nason land in Standish (93/113).

Children of Eliakim and Joanna (Knight) Wescott were as follows:

i. JOHN, born Sept. 10, 1782, married (int. Dec. 29, 1803, in Standish) Rebecca Haskell, born Apr. 6, 1785, daughter of Benjamin and Sally (Berry) Haskell of Falmouth and Standish. They lived in Standish where he died Oct. 23, 1866, age 84 yrs., 1 mo., and 13 days and she on July 27, 1870, age 85 yrs., 3 mos., and 21 days, in Standish. They were buried in Harding Cemetery on Standish Neck. They were the parents of four children.

ii. DANIEL, died at the age of 49. A Daniel Wescott, probably he, died in Standish May 22, 1835, which would make his date of birth about 1786. No evidence found that he was married.

iii. WILLIAM, born in Westbrook, then Falmouth, on Jan. 22, 1788, married Sept. 10, 1820, Abigail Haskell, born in Jan. 1793 daughter of Benjamin and Sally (Berry) Haskell. They lived in Standish where she died on June 17, 1865, age 72 yrs., 5 mos., in Standish, and he on Oct. 22, 1874, age 86 yrs., 9 mos. They were buried in Harding Cemetery. They were the parents of seven children.

iv. BETSEY, born Apr. 2, 1793, married (int. July 20, 1813, in Standish) Sept. 5, 1813, Ebenezer Proctor of Gorham, perhaps son of Ebenezer and Bethia (Mayberry) Proctor, of Windham. He died Aug. 1827 in Windham, a veteran and pensioner of the War of 1812. She was living 1855 in Windham.

v. POLLY, born Aug. 21, 1790, married Oct. 12, 1817, Abraham Nason Jr. of Standish, probably son of Abraham and Lydia (Lombard) Nason. She died in Jan. 1878. He died May 22, 1874, age 78 yrs.

vi. SALLY, born about 1797, married Mar. 30, 1823, Solomon Lombard, born Feb. 23, 1798, son of Ephraim and Polly (Perkins) Lombard of Gorham. They lived in Standish where he died on Nov. 11, 1875, age 77 yrs., 8 mos., and she on Feb. 15, 1880, age 83 yrs., and were buried in Harding Cemetery.

WEST

The name of Joseph West is found on the 1795, 1796, 1799, and 1808 tax lists of Standish and in the 1800 census with a family consisting of him and his wife, two sons and three daughters under 10 and one daughter between 10 and 16 years of age. He was born in Falmouth, Maine, on July 8, 1768, son of Desper and Mary (Green) West. His parents married in Falmouth Nov. 26, 1764, and lived in Gorham where their children were recorded. In April 1787 Desper was of Falmouth and living in Raymond at the time of the 1790 census. Joseph's mother was a daughter of Daniel and Mary (Bloom) Green (he alias Morgrage) and died in Windham, Maine, on July 24, 1807, age 65 years; and his father, a veteran of the Revolutionary War, died in Thorndike, Maine, on Feb. 15, 1820, at the age of 74 years.

Joseph West of Raymond and Nancy Cannell of Standish, born Oct. 16, 1766, daughter of Philip and Jane (____) Cannell, were married on Aug. 16, 1789, by John Dean Esq., justice of the peace of Standish. They lived near the shore of Sebago Lake and raised a family of eight children. He died about 1813 during the War of 1812 and his widow survived him until her death on Feb. 7, 1835, age 78 years, in Standish. Children of Joseph and Nancy (Cannell) West were as follows:

i. ELEANOR born Oct. 9, 1789, married Samuel Weeks, born about 1775 possibly son of William and Dorcas (Dyer) Weeks of Gorham. She died Dec. 31, 1864.

ii. JOHN, born Dec. 9, 1790, married first on Nov. 4, 1812, Abigail (Nabby) York, bapt. Sept. 7, 1797, in Standish Church, daughter of Ebenezer and Mehitable (Jones) York. She died sometime after 1830 and he married second on May 18, 1834, Sarah H. Whitney, born about 1800 daughter of William and Hannah (Bangs) Whitney of Standish. At the time of the 1830 census he was living in Seba-

go, Maine, with a family consisting of him and his wife, one male and one female under 5, two males between 5 and 10, one male and one female between 10 and 15 and one female between 15 and 20 yrs. of age. He later moved to Upton, Maine, where both he and his wife and seven children were living as late as 1860. He died in Greenwood, Maine, in 1877, age 87 yrs. Children by his first wife as follows:
1. JOSEPH, died in infancy.
2. MEHITABLE Y., born ____, married May 19, 1833, Benjamin Clark of Naples. She died and he married second Feb. 20, 1838, Emily J. Larrabee of Sebago. He died Oct. 26, 1854, age 42 yrs., in Naples, Maine. Children of Benjamin and Mehitable: Morris, born Dec. 30, 1833; Orrin, born Dec. 29, 1838; Susan E., born Aug. 14, 1840; John, born Mar. 2, 1844.
3. ELI, born about 1817 (age 33 in 1850), married Zilpha Dyer, age 35 in 1850, and lived in Naples and Upton.
4. MARY JANE, born about 1820 (age 30 in 1850), married (int. Mar. 3, 1838, in Naples) Benjamin Bailey of Sebago (age 22 in 1850, of Sebago). He was a brother of Cyrus's wife and lived in Naples and Sebago. They had children John Fairfield and Amanda Eliza.
5. DR. JOHN D., born May 22, 1822, in Standish, married Nov. 25, 1847, Sophia A. Tracy, daughter of Rev. Jonathan Tracy; second in 1853 Irena H. Mitchell and he died childless. He graduated from medical college in Philadelphia and was later a Free-Will Baptist minister. He died Sept. 13, 1865, in New York, and was buried at Parker's Head, Maine.
6. LYDIA ANN, born Jan. 3, 1823, married May 2, 1850, Horace Gerry of Naples, she of Sebago. She died Feb. 7, 1912, age 83 yrs., 1 mo., and 4 days, and he Aug. 28, 1902, age 85 yrs., 6 mos., 3 days, both in Greenwood. They lived in Sebago and had three or more children.
7. CYRUS H., born about 1824 (age 26 in 1850), married May 2, 1850, Abigail Bailey of Naples, he of Sebago. He died Dec. 12, 1905, age 81 yrs., 5 mos., Bethel, Maine.
8. WILLIAM AMBROSE, born about 1827 (age 23 in 1850), married Maria Nason. They lived in Sebago, but had no children.
9. EBENEZER, died in infancy.

Children by his second wife, Sarah Whitney, were as follows:
10. ABBY H., born Apr. 27, 1835.
11. JOSEPH H., born Nov. 1, 1839.
12. ABNER W., born Oct. 29, 1843.

iii. SUSANNA, born July 11, 1792, married Feb. 25, 1808, James Small Chick, born Nov. 24, 1782, son of Ephraim and Phebe (Cobb) Chick of Falmouth and Limington. They lived in Limington where he died on Jan. 7, 1855, and she on Jan. 5, 1859, age 66 yrs., 6 mos. Children were as follows: (Chick)
1. SOPHIA ANN, born Nov. 25, 1809, in Falmouth, married first ____ Morrell; married second Dec. 4, 1845, William Green of Westbrook, she of Portland. She died in Falmouth Aug. 22, 1879.

2. MARY JANE, born Mar. 14, 1812, in Limington, married Oct. 9, 1831, George D. Crawford of Falmouth. She died in Sebago on July 11, 1879.
3. LYDIA MARIA, born May 15, 1814, married (int. Oct. 18, 1839) Jesse S. Morrison of Limington. She died at Chelsea, Mass., on Mar. 25, 1880, age 66 yrs.
4. LAVINIA, born Aug. 20, 1816, married (int. Apr. 5, 1839) John Nason Jr. of Limington. She died in Denmark, Maine, July 7, 1891.
5. PHEBE COBB, born Mar. 6, 1819, married (int. Apr. 6, 1839) Joseph Green of Portland. She died in Portland Dec. 28, 1865. They are buried in Steep Falls Cemetery.
6. HENRY S., born June 18, 1822, died in Concord, N.H., Oct. 30, 1885, married Frances A. Sturgis of Standish.
7. JAMES MONROE, born Nov. 30, 1824, married first on July 6, 1848, Mary Jane Warren of Standish. She died Aug. 27, 1858, age 28 yrs., 8 mos., 2 days. He married second (int. Apr. 26, 1859) Rhoda Smith, daughter of John and Lydia (West) Smith of Standish. He died May 17, 1892, age 67, and she on Apr. 21, 1912, age 73. He is buried in Dow's Corner Cemetery in Standish.
8. NOAH BENNETT, born Sept. 15, 1826, a shoemaker, married (int. Apr. 20, 1851) Abigail Bean of Hollis. He died in Standish Sept. 8, 1904. This family claims an Indian line which comes by way of the West family, also claimed by other West descendants.
9. JOSEPH E., born July 14, 1829, married (int. Sept. 8, 1856) Sarah E. Mayo of Baldwin. He died in Limington Feb. 24, 1902.
10. SUSAN R., born June 3, 1832, married Oct. 11, 1854, Thomas Thombs of Boston, born in Waterford, Maine, in 1827 son of Edmund Thombs. He died at Chelsea, Mass., on Mar. 18, 1866, and she in Sebago, Maine, on Feb. 14, 1901. Both are buried in Chelsea.
11. SARAH ELIZA, born Dec. 27, 1836, married Edward Warren Knight. She lived in Chelsea and died in Melrose July 18, 1933, age 96.
12. SAMUEL BRADBURY, born Apr. 19, 1839, died Apr. 21, 1839.

iv. THOMAS, born Oct. 16, 1794, was living in Baldwin when his intentions of marriage were filed on Nov. 5, 1817, to Sarah McGill of Standish, born May 22, 1793, daughter of John and Rebecca (York) McGill of Standish. They lived in Standish near the Otter Pond. Dr. Meserve states that he was a traveling tinker of intemperate habits, but of good natural abilities. He, age 75, and a basket maker, was living alone in Standish at the time of the 1870 census. He died Mar. 13, 1874, age nearly 80 yrs. She died July 15, 1855. Children of Thomas and Sarah (McGill) West were as follows:
1. MARGARETTE, born Jan. 29, 1818, married Aug. 4, 1839, William Hall, both being of Naples at that time. She died Jan. 30, 1897, age 78 yrs., 11 mos., 29 days, Harrison.

2. **SILAS**, born July 29, 1820, married Hannah Parker of Cornish, born May 18, 1827, Cornish, who died Mar. 10, 1852. He married second Elmira Pike of Cornish, born Oct. 22, 1821. He died Jan. 29, 1904, and she died in July 24, 1879, both in Parsonsfield.
3. **JOSIAH**, born Mar. 24, 1823, died Oct. 29, 1871.
4. **AI**, born Apr. 12, 1825, died Apr. 1825.
5. **ABIGAIL MARRETT**, born Sept. 20, 1827, married Thomas Welch and died Oct. 6, 1904, in Standish.
6. **AI**, born June 29, 1830, married Fanny Clark and had three children born in Buxton. She was born in 1837, died Jan. 22, 1896, and he died Dec. 2, 1901, both in Hollis.
7. **IRA G.**, born Mar. 26, 1833, married Mary E. Miner, born Sept. 12, 1848.

v. JANE, born Aug. 6, 1796, married Nov. 2, 1817, Robert T. Berry of Baldwin, born Aug. 15, 1795, son of Walter F. and Polly (Dearborn) Berry of Standish. He died Dec. 30, 1845.

vi. EUNICE, born Mar. 12, 1800, married (int. July 28, 1817) Sargent Lombard, born in 1803 son of Jedediah and Lydia (Rand) Lombard of Gorham and Standish. They lived in Standish near Sebago Lake. He died on Nov. 11, 1876, and she in 1855. They were parents of the following children: (Lombard)
1. **SARAH**, born May 4, 1829, married first _____ Robinson; second Thomas Bragdon.
2. **ANDREW JACKSON**, born June 15, 1831.
3. **EMELINE**, born July 30, 1833, married Elisha Whitney.
4. **CHARLES BEANE**, born Apr. 15, 1835, died June 17, 1914, in Standish.
5. **MARY KNIGHT**, born Feb. 20, 1839, married on Nov. 12, 1865, Lewis Smith of Windham, Maine.
6. **JOHN WEST**, born Dec. 28, 1836.

vii. MARY, born Apr. 26, 1801, family register, owned by Mrs. Leona (Dyer) Green of Sebago, says she was born Apr. 25, 1802. She married Jan. 25, 1820 (int. Jan. 6, 1820), David Wiggin of Baldwin. He was born Jan. 1, 1798, and died Oct. 29, 1884, age 86 yrs., No. Baldwin. She was living in 1859 in Baldwin. A Mrs. Mary Wiggin died Oct. 16, 1872, age 70 yrs., 21 days, Sebago. Children were David Jr., born May 24, 1820, married July 4, 1842, Martha Ann Elliot both of Baldwin; Nancy, born June 23, 1821, married Aug. 6, 1841, Arthur Dyer, both of Baldwin; Joseph, born Oct. 4, 1822, married Aug. 6, 1843, Julia Ann Larrabee, both of Baldwin; Susan, born Aug. 6, 1824, died May 6, 1825; Susan, born Mar. 6, 1826, married Aug. 6, 1843, Robert L. Larrabee, both of Baldwin; a son, born Nov. 25, 1827, and died; Lovina, born Nov. 29, 1828, died Feb. 13, 1833; Mark, born Apr. 10, 1832, died Mar. 11, 1833; Mark, born Dec. 10, 1833; Lucinda, born Feb. 29, 1836; Lovina, born May 2, 1833; Mary Ellen, born Mar. 12, 1840, died Sept. 19, 1843; Clarissa, born Feb. 1, 1844, died July 5, 1861, married Nov. 24, 1859, Aaron W. McCorrison of Baldwin; Erastus, born Sept. 4, 1843, died Jan. 16, 1846; Erastus; and Samuel.

viii. LYDIA, born Aug. 13, 1805, married June 30, 1835 (int. May 29, 1835), John Smith Jr. of Standish.

WHETCOMB OR WHITCOMB

The name of Silas Whetcomb is found on the 1789, 1790, 1795, and 1796 tax lists of Standish, and in the 1790 census with a family of 1-2-4, and in the 1800 census when his family consisted of him and his wife, both between 26 and 45 years of age, one male and two female children under 10 years old, one male between 16 and 26 years of age. No record of his owning property in town has been found, but he was living here as early as 1788 since his name is found on a list of inhabitants of the town dated Feb. 4 of that year and testifying to the good character of Gideon Philbrick.

Silas Whitcomb (Simon,[4] David,[3] Josiah,[2] John[1]) born Mar. 26, 1757, son of Simon and Thankful (Houghton) Whitcomb of Lancaster, Mass., was probably the one who lived for a time in Standish. He married Oct. 12, 1780, Lydia Underwood of Lancaster, Mass., and was living in Sudbury, Mass., when their first child, Silas Jr., was born Feb. 3, 1781. He served in the Revolutionary War from Bolton, Massachusetts. Silas and Lydia Whitcomb resided in Standish until about 1802 when, according to Thomas Shaw, with five or six children they moved to Jackson, Maine, located in Waldo County and situated near Thorndike and Unity where so many families from Standish settled about this time.

Silas and Lydia (Underwood) Whitcomb were parents of at least the following family:
i. SILAS JR., born Feb. 3, 1781, in Sudbury, Mass., married Mary Varnum and was a farmer in Alton, Maine, where he died. His wife died in Thorndike, Maine. They were parents of six children.
ii. LYDIA, bapt. Aug. 15, 1794, in the Standish Church.
iii. SIMON, bapt. Aug. 15, 1794, in Standish, lived in Thorndike.
iv. MARY, bapt. Aug. 15, 1794, in Standish.
v. JOHN.
vi. ASA.

A recent Whitcomb Genealogy gives the Silas Whitcomb who settled in Maine and is credited with some of the above children as being a son of Nathaniel[4] Whitcomb (Jonathan,[3] Jonathan,[2] John[1]), but I think that is an error.

WHITE

The name of Peter White is found on the 1789, 1790, 1795, and 1796 tax lists and in the 1790 census with a family consisting of him and his wife, three males under 10 years of age, two males and one female between 10 and 16, and one male and one female between 16 and 26 years old. Both he and his wife are indicated as being over 45 years of age at this time.

Accounts differ as to his ancestry, one stating that he is thought to have been born in Dedham, Mass., while another states that he and his brother John, sons of Solomon White, came to this country from England when young men and were living in that part of Falmouth now Westbrook as early as 1769. John and Peter White bought 100 acres of land in Gorham from Rev. Solomon Lombard on Sept. 21, 1769, at which time they were living in Falmouth (8/215). Both Peter and his brother John served in the Revolutionary War. John White moved to Sebago and lived on Northwest River. He married Sarah Lamb, who lived to be over 80 years of age. He died at the age of 96.

They were the parents of ten children.

Peter White was living in Falmouth when he sold the land in Gorham which they had bought in 1769 on May 8, 1776, (8/454) but was of Gorham on Dec. 4, 1778, when he got a tax deed of land in Windham (10/270). He next appears in Buckfield, Maine, when he was granted land there on Feb. 10, 1790, for having settled and made improvements upon it prior to Jan. 5, 1784 (25/38). However, previous to the date of this deed he bought on Aug. 29, 1787, the 100-acre lot #59 in second division in Standish from Joseph Roberts (14/368) and moved here before the census was taken in 1790. On Oct. 26, 1796, he bought from the Rev. John Tompson of Berwick the 100-acre lot #60 adjoining his farm (25/472). This land was located on Standish Neck bordering Sebago Lake at the upper end of Sebago Lake Basin at the point where White's Bridge is located. On June 13, 1795, he sold his land in Buckfield to Jonathan Roberts, who was then living there (26/328). Peter White's service in the Revolution occurred in Capt. John Brackett's company at the time of the Lexington alarm and in Capt. Alexander McLellan's company of Col. Jonathan Mitchell's regiment in the Bagduce expedition in 1779.

Peter White married Alice Wescott of Westbrook on Apr. 21, 1774. He died June 2, 1804, age 56 years, and she on Oct. 7, 1812, age 60 years. Both are buried in the family burying ground on their farm at White's Bridge. They were the parents of the following children:

i. PETER, born about 1775, married Huldah Hanson, daughter of Ezekiel and Martha (____) Hanson of Windham on Feb. 25, 1811. He built a large house at Windham Hill, where he died Apr. 9, 1851, at the age of 75 yrs. His wife died in Aug. 11, 1865, at the age of 77, in Windham. They had sons, Hanson D. and Alexander.

ii. MARY, born Nov. 11, 1776, married Dec. 31, 1798, John Trickey. They lived at Great Falls, where he died Apr. 5, 1811, age 42 yrs. She died July 14, 1817, age 40 yrs. They had children, Zebulon Peter, Otis and Mark.

iii. REUBEN, Died in Canada in 1814 in War of 1812.

iv. MARK, born Oct. 19, 1781, married Jan. 1, 1815, in Raymond, Mary Dingley and lived on his father's farm at White's Bridge. He died Aug. 20, 1832, age 51 yrs., in Standish, and his wife on Aug. 4, 1856, age 65 yrs., 11 mos. Children were:
1. EDWIN, born Apr. 24, 1815, died Feb. 18, 1899, unmarried.
2. SOLOMON, born about 1817, died of consumption Feb. 13, 1841.

v. JOHN, born about 1784, married Nov. 21, 1819, Huldah Morrell, daughter of Elijah Morrell. He was a farmer and manufacturer at Great Falls, where he died Apr. 4, 1838, age 54. His widow died Jan. 15, 1879, age 88 yrs., in Windham. Children: John, Ann and Ellen.

vi. ANN, born about 1786, married Jan. 26, 1809, Abraham Mabry or Mayberry of Standish Neck, son of William and Rose (Walden) Mayberry. She died Aug. 10, 1820, age 34. He married second Miss Fanny Harmon, who died Apr. 2, 1824. He died Jan. 26, 1870. Children were Charlotte, Enoch, Jefferson, Sally, and Angeline.

vii. JOSEPH, born May 24, 1789, married first Catherine Leavitt, who died Dec. 11, 1822, age 24 yrs., and second in Apr. 23, 1824, Elizabeth Leavitt, her sister, who died May 26, 1863, age 67 yrs. He was ordained a Free-Will Baptist minister on Nov. 1, 1815, and died May 17, 1837, age 48 yrs., in Standish. His widow married Aug. 24, 1845, in Limerick, Levi Hall of Gorham and lived at Great Falls. He lived on Standish Neck and is buried in the cemetery there. Children were:
1. SAMUEL L., died June 13, 1860, age 35.
2. ALICE M., died Dec. 9, 1865, age 35.

viii. SOLOMON, born in Jan. 1792, never married and died Jan. 22, 1817, age 25.

ix. NATHANIEL, born in Mar. 1798, died unmarried Jan. 21, 1853, age 55 yrs.

x. ENOCH, born about 1803, married in 1834 Mary Ann Smith, who died Mar. 11, 1877, age 76 yrs. They lived at Great Falls, where he died May 2, 1866, age 63. They were the parents of two children.

WHITMORE

The name of William Whitmore and son appears in the 1808 tax list of Standish, but it is likely that he was an inhabitant of the town several years prior to that date. William[4] (John,[3] Samuel,[2] Francis[1]) Whitmore was born May 31, 1752 (baptized June 7, 1752 in Dudley, Mass.), son of John and Mary (Burnell) Whitmore. He came to Gorham, Maine, sometime before 1772 when his name appears on a tax list of that town. He married Nov. 18, 1775, Amy or Ruhama Knight, born Nov. 18, 1753, daughter of William and Hannah (Babb) Knight of Windham. Sometime before 1790, after service in the Revolutionary War, he moved to Little Ossipee Plantation (Limington), Maine, where in the census of that year his family consisted of him and his wife, two sons under 16 years of age, and three daughters.

He continued to live in Limington until at least as late as 1797 as indicated by deeds. He was a blacksmith, his house and shop, which he sold to his son William Whitmore Jr. on June 13, 1816, being located at South Standish near York's Corner, so called, on the road leading to Standish Corner. He died in Standish in 1827 and his widow died in July or August 1841 in Limington.

Children of William and Amy (Knight) Whitmore were as follows:
i. ANNA, born Nov. 5, 1775, married May 13, 1804, Joseph Norton of Gorham, who settled in Standish about this time. He died May 5, 1857, age 80 yrs., 2 mos., 5 days, in Standish. His wife was living

in 1850, age 75 yrs., in Standish. Joseph lived on the Cape Road and afterwards built a house on Norton Hill. Children as follows: (Norton)
1. LUCY, born Mar. 24, 1805, married Feb. 12, 1837, Zachariah Libby of Hollis.
2. JAMES, born Oct. 19, 1806, died Dec. 21, 1850, married Nov. 4, 1834, Lydia Rackliff of Standish.
3. MARY, born Aug. 22, 1808, married Johnson Hill of Sebago.
4. WILLIAM, born Aug. 1, 1812, married Catherine Heath.
5. RUHAMAH (AMY), born Aug. 4, 1810, married May 30, 1835, Jeremiah Libby of Hollis, she of Standish.
6. HANNAH, born Mar. 23, 1815, married Enoch Sawyer.
7. JOSEPH, born Mar. 22, 1817.
8. SIMON, born Mar. 22, 1820, married Dec. 29, 1845, Hannah R. McDonald. He died in 1892 and she died Jan. 27, 1878, in Standish, age 51 yrs., 6 mos.

ii. SIMON, born Jan. 12, 1777, settled in Hampden, Maine, where he married Nov. 11, 1798, Susanna Atwood of that town. They had births of children recorded as follows:
1. DORKIS (DORCAS), born June 4, 1799.
2. WILLIAM, born Jan. 19, 1801.
3. JOSEPH, born Jan. 19, 1803.

iii. JOSEPH, born Mar. 4, 1779, married May 7, 1809, Elizabeth Martin, bapt. Oct. 8, 1786, daughter of Bryan and Elizabeth (Fogg) Martin of Standish. A son Joseph Whitmore Jr. was born May 15, 1812, and recorded at Buxton.

iv. MARY, born June 17, 1781, died in 1799 at age of 18 yrs.

v. HANNAH, born Dec. 6, 1784, married Nov. 27, 1806, Samuel Hamblen, born May 4, 1783, son of Gershom and Deborah (Jenkins) Hamblen of Gorham. He was given as a resident of Brunswick when intentions of marriage were filed in Standish Oct. 6, 1806. They were parents of seven children.

vi. AMY RUHAMA, born June 4, 1786, married Mar. 29, 1807, first John Newbegin, second (int. Apr. 4, 1818) Henry Crockett, born May 13, 1793, son of Ephraim and Martha (Gray) Crockett of Standish. Her first husband died Jan. 21, 1816, age 33 yrs., 4 mos. She died Nov. 4, 1863, and her second husband died Dec. 17, 1872.

vii. SARAH, born Jan. 18, 1789, married Feb. 15, 1807, Abner Martin, born Nov. 19, 1782, son of Bryan and Elizabeth (Higgins) Martin of Standish. They lived in Standish where he died May 6, 1865, and she on Oct. 10, 1873. Children were as follows:
1. EBENEZER, born July 30, 1809.
2. JAMES, born Apr. 3, 1812.
3. ABNER, born Jan. 22, 1815.
4. WILLIAM W., born Sept. 26, 1825.

viii. WILLIAM JR., born Oct. 1791, married Apr. 26, 1812, Betsey Boulter Heath, born Jan. 29, 1794, daughter of Nicholas and Ruth (Boulter) Heath of Standish. He died in 1873 and she in 1877. They lived in Standish and Limington. Children were probably as follows:

1. SALLY MARTIN, born Dec. 12, 1812, married Feb. 11, 1830, (int. Dec. 12, 1829) Amos Burnham, born June 7, 1806, in Hollis, son of Anna (Foss) Burnham of Scarboro and Standish. She died in 1885 and he on May 10, 1872, in Taunton, Mass.
2. DANIEL HEATH, born Jan. 3, 1815, married Oct. 23, 1845, Sarah S. Sawyer, born July 31, 1820, daughter of Joshua and Mary P. (Sinclair) Sawyer of Limington. He died May 4, 1899, age 82 yrs., 4 mos., 1 day, in Standish and she on Feb. 19, 1902.
3. ELIZABETH, married June 16, 1832, (int. Mar. 18, 1832) John York of Standish.
4. MARY HIGGINS, born Sept. 17, 1819, married Apr. 25, 1847, Joshua W. Frost of Limington. She died Sept. 4, 1907, in Middleboro, Mass., and he died May 27, 1881.
5. JANE WHITNEY, born Nov. 13, 1824, married David Sumner Small, born Aug. 10, 1824, son of Nathaniel and Margaret (Phinney) Small of Limington. She died Nov. 23, 1863, in Myrickville, Mass., and he on Apr. 25, 1909, in New Bedford, Mass.

ix. JANE, born 1794, bapt. July 26, 1795, in Limington, died in 1797.
x. JANE, born in 1797, married Reuben Whitney, born July 2, 1794, son of Nathaniel and Zilpha (Martin) Whitney of Standish.

John Whitmore, born in Gorham, Maine, Feb. 21, 1773, son of Samuel[4] (John,[3] Samuel,[2] Francis[1]) and Mary (Whitney) Whitmore, married on Oct. 4, 1792, Jane Roberts, born Nov. 13, 1771, in Falmouth, daughter of Benjamin and Mary (Weeks) Roberts. They were living in Gorham at the time of the 1800 census with a family consisting of themselves, both between 26 and 45 years of age, three males and one female under 10 years old. About 1811 he bought land on Standish Neck from Ebenezer Gilman and Peter White and moved there soon after because he is listed in an 1813 tax list of the town. He was living in Standish in 1830 with a family consisting of him and his wife, both between 50 and 60 years of age, one male under 5, one female between 10 and 15, and one female between 20 and 30. His date of death has not been found, but she died Feb. 17, 1850, age 78 years, and was buried at Shirley Mills, Maine. Children, as far as has been determined, were as follows:

i. BENJAMIN, born about 1795 (of Casco, age 60 on Mar. 27, 1855, when he applied for bounty because of his service in 1812 War from Windham) married (int. May 1, 1816, in Standish) Sarah Cressey of Windham. They lived in Raymond and Casco. Nothing further known.
ii. MAJOR, born Feb. 1796, married (int. Jan. 27, 1818) in Standish, Lydia Plummer of Raymond. He applied for a bounty on Apr. 5, 1855, for his service in the War of 1812 from Standish. They were living in Standish in 1830. He died Sept. 15, 1863, age 67 yrs., 7 mos., in Raymond and his wife died Sept. 19, 1853, age 53 yrs., 6 mos., 19 days.
iii. JOHN JR., born in Nov. 1796, married Dec. 5, 1822 (Standish record) Frances (Fanny) Gilman, born about 1798 daughter of Ebenezer and Lydia (Bonney) Gilman of Standish. They lived in

Standish where he died Feb. 11, 1869, age 72 yrs., 3 mos., and she on Nov. 28, 1876, age 78 yrs., according to gravestones in Harding Cemetery on Standish Neck.

iv. IRENE, born July 2, 1800, married (int. Mar. 16, 1822, in Standish) David Gilman, born Sept. 19, 1800, son of Ebenezer and Lydia (Bonney) Gilman. They moved to Shirley, Maine, where they were living in 1860.

v. SAMUEL, born Aug. 11, 1803, died June 13, 1879, age 75 yrs., 6 mos., Shirley, Maine, formerly of Standish.

vi. BETSEY, born Aug. 27, 1810, married Jan. 1, 1835, Samuel Arnold of Shirley, born June 22, 1807, died Feb. 11, 1879. She died Mar. 11, 1892. They lived in Shirley, Maine, where they died and were buried.

WHITNEY

The name of William Whitney is found on the 1796, 1799, and 1808 tax lists of Standish and in the 1800 census with a family consisting of him and his wife, and one son and two daughters all under ten years of age. William^6 Whitney (Abner,^{5} John,^{4} Moses,^{3} Richard,^{2} John^1), born Sept. 15, 1765, according to gravestone, was baptized in Aug. 1769 in Shirley, Mass., son of Abner and Sarah (Hilton) Whitney. He was living in Limington, Maine, when he married on Oct. 11, 1792, Hannah Bangs, born Apr. 19, 1775, daughter of Herman and Molly (Wood) Bangs of Gorham. They were living in Limington in 1793 when his name was recorded among the inhabitants of school district #7 there. By 1796 they had apparently moved to Standish and on Apr. 10, 1801, he bought from John Marean 35 acres of 100-acre lot #113 in the same division with buildings then standing thereon. This property located on a range road running between the Saco Road and the River Road and once known as the Whitney Road but now called the Milt Brown Road became the homestead farm of the family. They continued to live in Standish until their deaths, his occurring on Mar. 22, 1836, at the of 70 yrs., 6 mos., and 7 days, and hers on Dec. 15, 1861, age 86 yrs., 7 mos., and 26 days. Both were buried in the Moses Cemetery on the River Road at South Standish.

William and Hannah (Bangs) Whitney as far as has been determined were parents of the following children:

i. WILLIAM JR., born on Jan. 3, 1795, perhaps in Limington, married Oct. 25, 1818, Anna Hancock, born Sept. 30, 1798, daughter of John L. and Hannah (Prescott) Hancock of Buxton. They lived for many years in Standish but about 1834 moved to the Convene section of Sebago where they continued to live until their deaths, hers occurring on Sept. 28, 1849, and his on May 4, 1859. They were parents of the following children:

1. HARRIET S., born Aug. 19, 1819, died Oct. 21, 1822.
2. WILLIAM H., born Apr. 3, 1822, married Hannah Douglass and lived in Sebago and Rangeley, Maine, died Dec. 12, 1912.

3. HARRIET S., born Sept. 2, 1824, married William S. Phinney and lived in Sebago and Somerville, Mass.
4. JOHN H., born Mar. 2, 1831, married Hannah ____ and lived in Sebago and Deer Lodge County, Mont.
5. MARSHALL S., born July 29, 1828, married Susan Libby, born June 25, 1841, daughter of Phineas and Susan (Hancock) Libby of Buxton. They moved from Sebago to Upton, Maine, where they lived until about 1890, when they moved to Byron, Maine, where he prospected for gold.
6. SARAH ANNA, born Apr. 7, 1833, married ____ French and at time lived in Limington. She was born about 1833.
7. BENJAMIN FRANKLIN, born Apr. 11 or 16, 1837, married Matilda Jewell of Sebago where they lived until about 1865 when they moved to Upton. He was a shoemaker by trade and canoeing teacher by avocation and played the violin. She died Mar. 16, 1905, and he on Aug. 26 of the same year.
8. HENRY HARRISON, born Dec. 21, 1840.
9. JANE S., born Feb. 9, 1840, died Mar. 28, 1846.

ii. MARY, born Apr. 27, 1798, married Nov. 28, 1816, John Boulter, born Sept. 16, 1794, son of Nathaniel Jr. and Martha (Higgins) Boulter. She died Jan. 22, 1835, age 36 yrs., 8 mos. and 25 days.

iii. SARAH H., born about 1800, married (int. May 18, 1834, in Standish) as his second wife John West, born Dec. 9, 1790, son of Joseph and Nancy (Cannell) West of Standish. They lived in Sebago, Bethel, and Upton, Maine.

iv. ABNER, born about 1802, Aug. 1, 1831 (int. June 5, 1831, in Standish) Annis M. Phinney, born Aug. 15, 1798, daughter of Coleman and Margaret (Moor) Phinney of Gorham and Standish. They lived in Sebago and Baldwin where he died Feb. 7, 1890, at the age of 87. She died there on Oct. 29, 1873. Children were as follows:
1. MARIA A., born about 1835.
2. MARGARET, born about 1837.
3. JOANNA S., born about 1839, married (int. May 16, 1857) Cyrus K. Ward of Baldwin, died Feb. 6, 1878, in Baldwin.
4. FRANCES E., born about 1841.

v. THANKFUL H., born Oct. 14, 1805, married (int. Nov. 1834) as his second wife, N. Stickney Burhham of Standish. She died July 6, 1841, age 35 yrs., 8 mos. and 22 days and was buried in the same grave with her infant son in Moses Cemetery at South Standish.

vi. HERMAN B., born Nov. 5, 1807, lived on the family homestead in Standish until his death on Feb. 24, 1874. He never married.

vii. HANNAH BANGS, born Oct. 31, 1810, married Dec. 31, 1834, at Standish Isaac L. Johnson, born in Limington Jan. 5, 1807, son of William Jr. and Betsey (Lord) Johnson. They lived in Limington and Standish, where he died Apr. 23, 1875, and she on Dec. 8, 1886. Children as follows: (Johnson)
1. HANNAH ELIZABETH, born Aug. 21, 1835, married Erastus W. Elwell, born Feb. 22, 1830, son of Levi and Diadema (Rand) Elwell of Buxton. They lived in Standish and in Boston, Mass., where she died on Apr. 21, 1870, age 34 yrs., 8 mos.

2. PHEBE A., born Mar. 7, 1839, married Dec. 22, 1835, Odell R. Berry, born Nov. 7, 1836, son of Simon and Lucy (Anderson) (Nason) Berry of Standish. They lived in Standish where he died Feb. 23, 1918. She died in Westbrook, Maine, Oct. 23, 1928.
3. HERMAN WHITNEY, born May 8, 1841, married Aug. 15, 1869, Mary Elizabth Loomer, born in Windsor, Nova Scotia, daughter of Gideon and Mehitable (Ells) Loomer. They lived in Standish where she died Feb. 16, 1894, age 51 yrs., 7 mos. and 1 day. He died in Portland Apr. 19, 1935.
4. NATHAN R., born Aug. 8, 1843, died Jan. 22, 1845.
5. LUCRETIA D. born Jan. 2, 1846, married William D. Libby. They lived at South Standish where she died in 1922 and he in 1929.
6. MARY THANKFUL, born Apr. 29, 1848, married Isaac L. Boulter, born Jan. 29, 1838, son of John and Martha (Smith) Boulter of Standish. They lived at South Standish where he died July 5, 1907, and she on Apr. 24, 1925.
7. ROYAL A., born Dec. 3, 1850, married Mary Ann Edgecomb, born Feb. 26, 1856, daughter of Isaac L. Edgecomb of Standish. They lived in Standish where she died June 7, 1897, and he in Apr. or May 1916.

WHITNEY

There were a number of Whitney families living in Standish from 1790 on. The name of David Whitney is found on the 1789 and 1790 tax lists of Standish and in the 1790 census with only himself in the family. His ancestry has not been definitely determined, but he may have been the David Whitney, born Apr. 8, 1732, in Biddeford son of Nathan and Lydia (Young) Whitney, who settled in Gorham. He disappears from the local scene after 1790.

Joshua Whitney, whose name is also found in the 1790 census with a family of 1-1-3, was probably son of David Whitney above by his second wife, Abigail Knight of Falmouth, and born in Gorham Aug. 17, 1761. He is said to have lived in Buxton, but may have been the Joshua Whitney of Bridgton who on Dec. 16, 1793, sold to Israel Swett of Standish the 100-acre lot #53 in second division in Standish located on the Neck (21/104). Nothing further known.

The name of Nathaniel Whitney appears on the 1795, 1796, and 1808 tax lists and in the 1800 census with a family consisting of two sons and one daughter under 10 years of age besides him and his wife, both of whom were between 26 and 45 years old. Undoubtedly he was the Nathaniel Whitney born in Gorham June 20, 1769, son of Abel and Thankful (Morton) Whitney. On Mar. 16, 1794, he married Zilpha Martin, baptized in Eastham, Mass., Feb. 28, 1779, daughter of Bryan and Elizabeth (Higgins) Martin of Eastham and Standish. His twin sister Sarah Whitney

married Robert Higgins of Standish. He died Apr. 21, 1844, age 75 years, in Standish. Children of Nathaniel and Zilpha (Martin) Whitney were as follows:
i. REUBEN, born July 2, 1794.
ii. HANNAH, born Oct. 14, 1796.
iii. SIMEON, born Apr. 12, 1799, living in 1860 in Harrison.
iv. JOANNA, born Aug. 1, 1801, married Dec. 25, 1825, Joseph Stuart.
v. NANCY, born Aug. 1, 1801, twin of Joanna.
vi. JAMES, born Feb. 19, 1807.

Simeon Whitney, whose name is found on the 1795 and 1796 tax lists was born in Gorham Feb. 9, 1774, son of Abel and Thankful (Morton) Whitney and hence brother of Nathaniel above. He did not live long in Standish and is said to have settled in eastern Maine.

The name of Abel Whitney, father of Nathaniel and Simeon, is found on the 1795 and 1796 tax lists and in the 1800 census with a family consisting of him and his wife, both over 45, and one male child under 10 years of age. He was born in Biddeford Aug. 20, 1734, son of Nathan and Lydia (Young) Whitney, and on Dec. 16, 1758, married Thankful Morton, born about 1739 daughter of Bryant and Thankful (Parker) Morton of Cape Elizabeth and Gorham. He served in Capt. Josiah Jenkins' Company, Col. Brewer's 12th. Mass. Regiment in the Revolutionary. His death and that of his wife have not been discovered, but his name does not appear on the 1808 tax list. Children of Abel and Thankful (Morton) Whitney were as follows:
i. JOSEPH, born May 1, 1760, died in Alfred with the Shakers Sept. 19, 1847.
ii. LYDIA, born July 28, 1763, died in July 1767.
iii. BETTY, born July 22, 1765, married Mar. 24, 1812, William Boynton Jr., born Dec. 18, 1766, son of William and Mary (McLucas) Boynton of Buxton (int. Nov. 10, 1792). They lived in Brownfield and had children Hannah, Thomas, William, Phineas, Sally, Mary, Jacob, and Happy Boynton.
iv. SARAH, born June 20, 1769, married (int. Sept. 19, 1789) Robert Higgins, born Jan. 17, 1769, son of William and Elizabeth (Young) Higgins of Standish. For children see Higgins family.
v. NATHANIEL, born June 20, 1769, twin of Sarah, for particulars see above. He died Apr. 21, 1844, age 75 yrs., in Standish.
vi. REUBEN, born July 21, 1771, married Mercy Baker, died in Litchfield Feb. 13, 1836.
vii. SIMEON, born Feb. 9, 1774, went to eastern Maine after living a short while in Standish.
viii. SUSANNA, born Apr. 2, 1776, married on Sept. 26, 1794, Benjamin Hale.
ix. LEVI, born May 18, 1779, married Nov. 11, 1802, Happy Higgins and moved to Standish where his name is found on the 1808 tax list.
x. LYDIA, born Apr. 30, 1782, married May 1, 1803, Moses Starbird.

WILEY

The names of David, James, and William Wiley are found on the 1789 and 1790 tax lists of Standish, but David and James were assessed for poll tax only. David Wiley (1-1-1) and William Wiley (2-1-2) are found in the 1790 census. While the name of James Wiley does not appear in this census, it seems likely that he was living in the family of William Wiley, for his name appears in the 1795 and 1796 tax lists and in the 1800 census, while those of David and William do not appear in the records after 1790. James Wiley's name first appears on the tax lists of Andover, Mass., in 1764 and disappear in 1789, when his name appears in Standish.

It appears that James Wiley was the owner of the 100-acre lot #87 in the second division, the westerly half of which he sold to Shubael and Asa Mayo on June 14, 1799 (37/474). He also bought from Ephraim Jones land in Standish on Jan. 1, 1803, (54/493) which he sold to John McDonald of Limerick on Mar. 9, 1808, at which time he is given as living in Limerick. At the time of the 1800 census he was living in Standish with a family consisting of himself and a woman, perhaps his wife, both over 45 years of age, on land adjoining that of Ephraim Jones.

James Wiley was baptized Oct. 29, 1738, in Andover, Mass., son of Robert and Jane Wiley of that town. His wife, Bethia Fyre, born June 13, 1727, daughter of Nathan and Sarah (Bridges) Frye of Andover, had before her marriage to him sometime after Apr. 26, 1758, been the wife of William Johnson or Johnston of Andover, who died Feb. 26, 1757. By him she had four children, three boys and a girl, all of whom died by the time they were five years of age. She is said to have been a cousin to Gen. Joseph Frye for whom the town of Fryeburg was named. James Wiley died Nov. 21, 1816, age 79 years, in Standish, reported in the *Eastern Argus* issue of Dec. 2, 1816.

James and Bethiah (Frye) (Johnston) Wiley were the parents of the following children:

i. **CHLOE**, born about 1761, married Oct. 3, 1782, James Davis of Andover. They settled in Standish sometime after 1785 and continued to live here until their deaths, hers occurring on May 18, 1829, at the age of 67 yrs. and his on Apr. 8, 1835, at the age of 73 yrs. They with their son Nathaniel are buried in a cemetery on Oak Hill in Standish. For children see Davis family.

ii. **SARAH**, born Sept. 10, 1762, married July 1, 1784, David Richardson, who was at that time a resident of Pearsontown (Standish). Soon after their marriage they moved to Little Ossipee Plantation (Limington) where all their children were probably born. She died Nov. 11, 1826, at the age of 64 yrs. and 2 mos. and he died on July 3, 1827, age 66 yrs. and 5 mos. For children see Richardson family.

iii. **DAVID**, born _____, married Apr. 20, 1789, in Andover, Mass., Chloe Holt, bapt. Sept. 21, 1766, daughter of Nathaniel and Elizabeth (Stevens) Holt of that town. They evidently lived a short while in Standish, but probably returned to Andover, where they had baptized in the church there James, on Feb. 28, 1790, and David on

Oct. 9, 1791. David Wiley died and his widow, Chloe Wiley, married second on Feb. 25, 1800, John Holt, who died Oct. 21, 1815. She married third John Frye, who died Mar. 26, 1824.

iv. WILLIAM, born _____, married Jan. 29, 1788, in Andover, Sarah Hadley. They apparently lived a short while in Standish but evidently returned to Andover to live. Following his death widow Sarah Wiley married on Dec. 1, 1808, Stephen Russell of Danvers, Mass., William and Sarah (Hadley) Wiley had children as follows:
1. LYDIA CALAHAN, born July 3, 1788.
2. JONATHAN, bapt. Aug. 14, 1791.
3. JOSEPH, bapt. June 21, 1795.

v. LYDIA, born Dec. 26, 1772, married Apr. 14, 1796, John McDonald, born Apr. 16, 1773, son of Robert and Mary (Kendrick) McDonald of Buxton, Limington, and Limerick, Maine. They lived in Limerick, where he died Mar. 16, 1826, and she on Apr. 4, 1826, age 53.

WOOD

Among the early settlers of Pearsontown was a man by the name of John Wood. He was born in Newbury, Mass., Mar. 1, 1730, but his parentage has not been determined. About 1753 he married Sarah Gorden, born in Exeter, N.H., Oct. 1, 1734, and lived in that town several years. Sometime after 1762 and before the birth of his son Isaiah on Oct. 30, 1764, he moved to Pearsontown. He was granted the 5-acre lot #4 by the Proprietors and sold it on May 11, 1771, to Benjamin Titcomb of Falmouth (7/181). It is likely that he lived on this lot until about Mar. 21, 1770, when Josiah Noyes of Falmouth sold to him the 30-acre lot #93, bordered on the south by Narragansett land, on the condition that he clear five acres and build a house upon the land. He also bought from Benjamin Mussey of Falmouth the 30-acre lot #93 on Dec. 26, 1770, (26/470) and sold to Jabez Dow, then of Falmouth, on the same day the 30-acre lot #93 which he had purchased on Mar. 21, 1770 (8/475).

The name of John Wood is found in the 1790 census with a family of 3-1-5, also on the 1789, 1790, 1795, and 1796 tax lists, and in the 1800 census with a family consisting of him and his wife, and a male child under 10 years of age. His wife, Sarah, was admitted to the Standish Church on May 11, 1777, and in the records of that church may be found the baptisms of many of their children. They lived in Standish until their deaths, his occurring on Aug. 1, 1809, age 82 years (*Eastern Argus*, Aug. 10, 1809) and his wife on Apr. 20, 1829, age 95 years, both in Standish. He is buried in the Village Cemetery at Standish Corner. John and Sarah (Gorden) Wood were parents of the following family:

i. JOHN JR., born in Exeter, N.H., Oct. 7, 1754, bapt. Nov. 4, 1770, served in the Revolutionary army from Pearsontown. He was living in Pearsontown on May 20, 1777, when his father sold to him 48 acres more or less in Buxton adjoining the town line next to land of Lydia York, it being part of lot #1 on Range H in third division of land in Buxton. He was living in Buxton at the time of the 1790 census with a family 1-1-2. He was married on Apr. 19, 1789, by

John Dean Esq. to Molly Sawyer, born about 1769 daughter of John and Lettice (Whitney) Sawyer of Pearsontown. She may have been his second wife. He died Oct. 11, 1791, in Buxton, and his widow married second on Feb. 25, 1794, John Miller of Limington. For further details see Miller family. Children were as follows:

By first wife:
1. BENONI, bapt. in Standish Church on June 18, 1780, as grandson of John and Sarah Wood, married Sept. 3, 1797, Eunice Decker, daughter of John and Catherine (Hall) Decker of Standish. She died before Apr. 4, 1807, when he married on May 3, 1807, Eleanor McDonald of Standish. Benoni Wood is said to have left home and was never heard from again. Benoni and Eunice (Decker) Wood were parents of at least the following children:
   (1) ESTHER, born in Standish Aug. 5, 1796, married in Brownfield, Maine, James Johnson, born in Sanford Nov. 8, 1795, son of Jonathan and Lydia (Nason) Johnson. He died in Brownfield Nov. 1, 1857, and she on Apr. 15, 1877.
   (2) ELI, born May 28, 1804, married Mary A. Dunn of Gorham and lived there. He died May 27, 1874. Their children were:
      A. WARREN, born Aug. 14, 1826, died Sept. 7, 1829.
      B. LYDIA A., born Mar. 9, 1828, died Oct. 3, 1832.
      C. WARREN H., born Mar. 20, 1831, married May 15, 1858, Margaret Wetherell, born Apr. 27, 1838, daughter of Samuel and Marjorie (Murch) Wetherell of Buxton.
      D. ZEBULON D., born Aug. 17, 1833, lived in Buxton.
      E. MARY, born Nov. 20, 1835, died Dec. 20, 1853.
      F. ALONZO, born Dec. 20, 1839, lived at Cape Elizabeth.
      G. ELIZA A., born Jan. 13, 1844, married John Berry.

By second wife:
2. DORCAS, born Aug. 26, 1789, bapt. May 21, 1797.
3. POLLY, born June 25, 1791, bapt. May 21, 1797.

ii. ANNA, born at Exeter, N.H., Oct. 17, 1756, bapt. Nov. 4, 1770, married June 19, 1788, as his second wife, Benjamin Rowe, son of Lazarus and Molly (Webber) Rowe of Flintstown (Baldwin). He married first June 10, 1777, Jane Spencer of Berwick and was a Revolutionary soldier. He moved to Jackson, Maine, in 1800 and later to Brooks, where he married third the widow Betsy Dodge. He died in Mar. 1832, age 78 yrs., in Brooks, Maine. Benjamin Rowe's children, as given in his pension records found in Arthur McArthur's Papers, Special Collections, Bowdoin College Library: The six children by his first wife were Benjamin, Susan, Thomas, Amos, Richard, and Jane; the five children by his second wife were Anna, James Matthew, Hannah, Hepsibah, and Francis; and the five children by his third wife were Learned, Caleb, Benjamin Jr., Mary, and James Rowe.

iii. ISAIAH, born Oct. 30, 1764, in Pearsontown, bapt. Nov. 4, 1770, married Aug. 24, 1786, Sarah Taylor, born in Poplin, N.H., Aug. 20, 1768. After the birth of their first children, they moved to Topsham, Maine. They both died in Kingfield, Maine, she on Nov. 17, 1826, and he on June 9, 1833. They were parents of the following children:
1. SAMUEL, born at Standish May 2, 1787, died there Feb. 2, 1788.
2. SAMUEL, born at Standish Aug. 18, 1788, died Jan. 4, 1848.
3. SALLY, born at Topsham Sept. 2, 1790, married Feb. 5, 1826, as his second wife Theophilus Libby of Scarboro and Danville, Maine.
4. ISAIAH JR., born Mar. 29, 1792.
5. LYDIA, born Oct. 18, 1794.
6. MERCY, born Sept. 12, 1796.
7. MARY, born June 10, 1798, died at Kingfield on July 25, 1824.
8. ANNA, born Aug. 18, 1800.
9. EDWARD T., born Sept. 9, 1804, married Patience Ellsworth, born June 3, 1808, in Strong, Maine. They were the parents of six children. She died in Portland June 15, 1844, and he married second Elizabeth J. Ham. Two children by second marriage.
10. REBECCA, born May 1, 1806.

iv. REBECCA, born Dec. 13, 1760, in Exeter, N.H., bapt. Nov. 4, 1770.
v. SARAH, born Sept. 8, 1762, in Exeter, N.H., bapt. Nov. 4, 1770.
vi. APPHIA, born at Pearsontown Mar. 17, 1766, bapt. Nov. 4, 1770.
vii. DEBORAH, born at Pearsontown July 20, 1768, bapt. Nov. 4, 1770.
viii. MOSES, twin, born at Pearsontown July 30, 1770, bapt. Nov. 4, 1770, married May 6, 1791, Jane Robinson of Portland. He was living in Buxton at the time of the 1800 census with a family consisting of him and his wife, and three male and two female children under 10 years of age. He died Jan. 31, 1843, age 72 yrs., 6 mos., and she on May 4, 1841, age 67 yrs., 7 mos. Both are buried in a cemetery on Oak Hill in Standish.
ix. HANNAH, twin, born at Pearsontown July 30, 1770, bapt. Nov. 4, 1770.
x. AARON, born Aug. 20, 1772, at Pearsontown, bapt. Nov. 1, 1772, married Sally ____ and lived in Standish and Saco. At the time of the 1800 census he was living in Pepperrelborough (Saco) with a family consisting of him and his wife, and two males and one female under 10 years of age. He died in Saco June 6, 1815. They were parents of the following children:
1. JEREMIAH, born in Standish Dec. 19, 1795, died Dec. 26, 1831.
2. PETER, born in Standish May 2, 1797.
3. ABIGAIL, born in Saco Apr. 13, 1799.
4. EUNICE, born in Saco July 11, 1801.
5. FOXWELL CUTTS, born in Saco Feb. 28, 1805, died of spotted fever Apr. 16, 1814.

6. **CHARLES**, born Jan. 25, 1807, a seaman, died in Buenos Aires in 1829.
7. **DEBORAH**, born June 4, 1809, died of spotted fever Apr. 14, 1816.
8. **JOHN**, born June 4, 1809 (twin) died Aug. 8, 1816.
9. **APPHIA**, born ____, died of spotted fever Apr. 16, 1814.
10. **REBECCA**, born Jan. 17, 1816.

xi. **CUTTING MOODY**, born May 2, 1774, bapt. Dec. 2, 1774, was of Hampden, Maine, on Mar. 13, 1804, when he married Mehitable Grant of that town.

xii. **EDWARD**, born Dec. 22, 1779, bapt. June 18, 1780, married (int. Dec. 27, 1807, in Portland) Abigail Wiswell, born about 1784 only child of Enoch and Jane (Hoyt) Wiswell of Portland. He was living in Portland age 81 in 1861. They were parents of the following children:
1. **CAROLINE**, born Dec. 17, 1808, married William Hartshorn Jr. of Portland on Aug. 21, 1837.
2. **JOHN**, born June 14, 1813, died Sept. 27, 1829, age 18, Standish.
3. **SARAH JANE**, born June 14, 1813, died Oct. 14, 1829, in Standish.
4. **GEORGE INGRAHAM**, born Mar. 9, 1820.

WOODMAN

The name of Nathan[4] (Benjamin,[3] Joshua,[2] Edward[1]) is found in the 1790 census of Standish with a family of 1-1-1 as well as on the 1795 and 1796 tax lists in the town. He was living in town at the time of the 1800 census with family consisting of him and his wife, and one female between 16 and 26. He was born in Newbury, Mass., June 26, 1726, son of Benjamin and Elizabeth (Longfellow) Woodman. About 1756 he settled in Narragansett No. 1 (Buxton), Maine, where his brothers, Joseph and Joshua, had previously settled. He had a tanyard at the location known as Pleasant Point.

He married first on Dec. 28, 1749, Olive Gray, born Feb. 6, 1730, daughter of Capt. John and Elizabeth (Tarbox) Gray of Biddeford. She and two of their children, Susan and Sewall, died of a bilious fever in the fall of 1774. He served a long term in the Revolutionary War, and later married (int. Aug. 5, 1784, in Gorham) Lydia (Jordan) York, widow of Abram York of Pearsontown. They lived in Standish until sometime after 1800 when they moved to Limington where she died. He died about 1812 at the home of his son Shubael in Hollis. All of his children were by his first marriage.

Children of Nathan and Olive (Gray) Woodman were as follows:
i. **JOHN**, born Oct. 4 or 5, 1750, in Newbury, Mass., married Jan. 30, 1772, Mary Bean, born Jan. 17, 1752, daughter of Jonathan and Mary (____) Bean of Buxton. She died June 1, 1800; he married second on Nov. 22, 1801, Dorcas (Foss) Elden, widow of John Elden. He died Nov. 18, 1828; she, Mar. 11, 1843. Eight children.

ii. ELIZABETH, bapt. Feb. 23, 1752, in Newbury, married on Oct. 12, 1780, Jonathan Gilman of Buxton. He died and she married second (int. May 17, 1794) Clement Meserve of Scarboro. One child, a daughter of first husband.
iii. BENJAMIN, bapt. in Newbury Feb. 17, 1754, married Sept. 27, 1781, Sally Bryant, who died Nov. 6, 1826, age 69 yrs. They lived in Saco near the Buxton line where he died Aug. 14, 1834, in the 82nd year of his age. Nine children.
iv. OLIVE, bapt. Feb. 1, 1756, in Newbury, married on Sept. 5, 1776, Joseph Chase, born Oct. 10, 1754, son of Deacon Amos Chase of Saco and Limington. He died Mar. 1, 1811, age 56 yrs., in Standish, and she married second Oct. 10, 1816, Josiah Black of Limington where she died Apr. 9, 1841. For children see Chase family.
v. SEWELL, bapt. Aug. 20, 1758, died in 1774 unmarried.
vi. SUSAN, died young in 1774.
vii. AMOS, lived to grow up, but died young and unmarried.
viii. MOSES, bapt. Mar. 2, 1766, married on Dec. 8, 1791, Abigail, daughter of Daniel Leavitt. She died between Dec. 1, 1804, and Apr. 29, 1809, the date on which he was published to Martha Tibbetts. His second wife died Apr. 20, 1823, and he on Jan. 19, 1838. They lived in Buxton. Ten children, seven by first wife and three by second.
ix. NATHAN, was a sailor and died in 1807 unmarried.
x. SHUBAEL, born on or about Sept. 1, 1772, married first on Feb. 28, 1799, Shuah Tarbox of Biddeford; second on May 5, 1805, Susanna Tarbox, sister of his first wife; and third (int. Dec. 8, 1810) widow Abigail (Burnham) Scamman of Scarboro. He lived on the west bank of the Saco River in Hollis. Six children, all born in Hollis.

WOODS

The name of Joseph Woods is found on 1788, 1789, 1790, 1795, 1796 and 1799 tax lists of Standish, in the 1790 census with a family of 1-3-2 and in the 1800 census with a family consisting of him and his wife, both over 45 years of age, four male children and one female child under 10 years of age, one male and one female between 10 and 16, and one female between 16 and 22 years of age.

Joseph[4] (John,[3] Samuel,[2] Samuel[1]) Woods was born on Apr. 5, 1731, in Lancaster, Mass., son of Joseph and Hannah (White) Woods. On Nov. 30, 1757, he married at Lancaster, Lucy Butler, born at Lunenburg, Mass., on June 25, 1738, daughter of William and Lucy (Story) Butler of Lunenburg. Sometime after 1772 he moved to Bridgton, Maine, where his wife died soon after. He married second (int. Aug. 19, 1776, in Gorham, Maine) Sarah (Susan?) York, born Apr. 11, 1756, daughter of Abram and Lydia (Jordan) York of Pearsontown. They lived in Bridgton for some time where two of his children are said to have been burned when his dwelling was destroyed by fire. Just when they returned to Pearsontown has not been determined but he was given as a resident of Standish on Mar. 27, 1788, when he sold land in Bridgton to John Cotton of Gilmanton, New Hampshire. Soon after 1800 they moved to Unity, Maine, where their son Joseph had previously settled. On May 2, 1802, he was of Sandy Stream (Unity) when Isaac York, his attorney and brother-in-law, sold to Nathaniel Boulter land in Standish, part of it at least being 50 acres of 100-acre lot #98 which Boulter had sold him in 1793 (65/69). He died in Unity on June 12, 1815, and she died there on Aug. 15, 1830. Complete records of his children are not available, but his family is said to have been a large one. Known children as follows:

By first wife, Lucy Butler:
i. SAMUEL, born Jan. 2, 1759, bapt. Apr. 29, 1759, in Lancaster. Mass.
ii. RACHEL, born Jan. 28, 1761, bapt. July 19, 1761, in Lancaster, married June 1, 1785, John Fletcher.
iii. URSULD, born Feb. 24, 1763, bapt. May 8, 1763, in Lancaster.
iv. LUCY, bapt. in May or June 1772 as daughter of Mr. Joseph Woods and wife.

By second wife Sarah (Susan?) York.
v. JOSEPH JR., born Sept. 22, 1778, bapt. in Standish Church on Nov. 27, 1779, married Aug. 27, 1797, in Standish, Lydia Rackliff, born in Scarboro, Maine, on Nov. 1, 1781, daughter of Joseph Chandler and Mary (Welch) Rackliff of that town, who moved to Standish about 1789. In 1798 not long after the birth of their first child in the fall of 1797, they moved across country on horseback to Unity, Maine, she holding her infant son in one arm while she guided the horse with her free hand. They cleared a farm in South Unity where they continued to live the rest of their days, having lived together for 73 years. She died Mar. 3, 1871, at the age of 89 and he on Jan. 3, 1872, at the age of 93. They were the parents of at least thirteen children, as follows: (Woods)
1. GEORGE, born Oct. 18, 1797, in Standish, died June 12, 1809, in Unity.
2. JOSEPH III, born Dec. 18, 1799, in Unity, married July 4, 1824, Arabella Rackliff Mitchell, born in Unity on Aug. 10, 1802, daughter of James and Sarah (Rackliff) Mitchell. She died in Unity on Sept. 6, 1878, and he on Jan. 10, 1878. They had at least the following children: (Woods)
    (1) ELVIRA A., age 20 in 1850.
    (2) HEPZIBAH, age 19 in 1850.
    (3) AMAZIAH S., born Oct. 16, 1834, married Olive Boynton.
    (4) ELLEN M., age 5 in 1850.
3. FANNY, born Feb. 18, 1802, married in Jan. 1825 Nathaniel Carll.
4. MEHITABLE, born Mar. 12, 1804, died Mar. 18, 1866.
5. CHANDLER, born Aug. 24, 1808, married Sept. 17, 1838, Sarah Meservey.
6. ANNIS C., born May 10, 1810, married (____) Rollins and died Oct. 5, 1875.
7. GEORGE, born Jan. 7, 1813, married Dec. 2, 1838, Sarah M. Ells.

8. **LYDIA,** born Dec. 18, 1815, married Dec. 12, 1839, Benjamin Small Plaisted born Mar. 6, 1814, son of Simon and Frances S. (Thompson) Plaisted of Limington. She died Dec. 22, 1872, and he in Mar. 12, 1888, both in Unity, Maine.
9. **BETSEY AYER,** born Jan. 17, 1819, died June 7, 1860.
10. **JOHN WESLEY,** born Aug. 10, 1821.
11. **GREENLEAF F.,** born June 30, 1823, died May 25, 1845.
12. **AMANDA,** born Feb. 3, 1825, married Feb. 18, 1845, Hiram Harding and died Mar. 21, 1898.
13. **BENJAMIN JONES,** born Jan. 24, 1828, died Dec. 3, 1895.

vi. **SARAH,** bapt. at Limington, Maine, on Sept. 23, 1781, by Rev. Chadwick of the Second Church of Scarboro.
vii. **LEVI,** moved from Standish to Unity about 1810.
viii. **MOSES W.,** born Nov. 30, 1798, in Standish, lived in Belfast, Maine.
ix. **HANNAH,** born July 2, 1788, married (____) Harding.

WOOSTER

James Wooster, born Sept. 15, 1712, in Bradford, Mass., son of Francis and Mary (Cheney) Wooster, moved to Falmouth, Maine, where on Mar. 9, 1739-40, his intentions of marriage to Patience (Mills) Low, widow of Daniel Low, were filed. He was shot and killed at Pearsontown on Mar. 13, 1757, by John Clark while assisting Deputy Sheriff Alexander Gray in an attempt to search Clark's house there for allegedly stolen goods. It is likely that he was living in town at the time, for his widow, Patience, and daughter Mary were both given as inhabitants of this town at this time of their marriages. Mary Wooster and Clement Meserve, both of Pearsontown, were married Sept. 19, 1757, according to Gorham records. Patience Wooster was of Pearsontown in May 1761 when she married as her third husband Dennis Lary of Gorham.

Patience Wooster was born Patience Mills at Lynn, Mass., on Jan. 26, 1716, daughter of James and Deborah (Larrabee) Mills, who later moved to Falmouth, Maine. She married (int. Oct. 26, 1735) Daniel Low of Kittery and Scarboro, Maine. His fate is not known, but as noted above she married again in 1740, this time to James Wooster. There is no record of her having children by Daniel Low, but it is possible that the James Low who was born in Scarboro and was an inhabitant of Pearsontown before 1760 was her son and that it was with him that she and her daughter Mary Wooster lived there after the death of James Wooster.

Patience Wooster owned the covenant in the church at Falmouth (Portland) in 1741 and had a son James Wooster baptized there on the same day. Sarah, daughter of James Wooster, was baptized there in 1745. It is possible that Hannah Wooster, born in Falmouth in 1751, who married Amos Thompson of Bowdoin, Maine, was a daughter of James and Patience Wooster.

Dennis and Patience (Wooster) Lary of Gorham had a son Stephen born there Feb. 14, 1763. Dennis Lary died in Gorham in Dec. 1796 at the age of 102 and she died there in 1809, age 94.

While it would seem that Mary Wooster, born June 10, 1733, who married Sept. 13, 1757, Clement Meserve, would have been a daughter of James and Patience Wooster, she in fact was a daughter of Timothy Wooster, born Dec. 6, 1693, died 1751 in Falmouth son of Frances and Mary (Cheney) Wooster.

YATES

The name of John Yates is found on all of the tax lists consulted and in the 1790 census with a family of 1-3-1. At the time of the 1800 census his family consisted of him and his wife, one male and two females under 10, and two males between 10 and 16 years old. He was born Jan. 7, 1755, son of John[4] (John,[3] John,[2] John,[1]) and Thankful (King) Yates of Harwick, Mass., and was brother of Reliance Yates who married Timothy Higgins and possibly of Deborah Yates who married Joseph Sanborn on Nov. 22, 1792, and of Sarah Yates who married Stephen Sparrow on Mar. 16, 1790. He came to Pearsontown at the same time as Timothy and Reliance (Yates) Higgins about 1781 or soon thereafter and settled on a lot adjoining theirs.

On Oct. 12, 1780, he married Mercy Hopkins, born Nov. 13, 1761, daughter of Joshua and Rebecca (Sparrow) Hopkins of Eastham, Massachusetts. He is given as being of Cape Cod on Sept. 9, 1781, when he bought from Levi Wilder of Lancaster, Mass., the 30-acre lot #51 in the first division in Pearsontown (14/182), and it was evidently on this lot that he settled. He was a veteran of the Revolutionary War and in his later years received a pension for his services.

John Yates died in Standish Apr. 4, 1834, age 79 years, and his wife died here June 6, 1826, at the age of 65 years. They were parents of the following children:

i. **JOSIAH**, born about 1782, bapt. in Standish Sept. 30, 1798, married Nov. 13, 1805, Thankful Higgins, born Dec, 28, 1779, daughter of Seth and Martha (Linnell) Higgins of Eastham, Mass., and Standish. They lived in Standish and Baldwin, but later moved to Monroe, Maine. She died in 1865 and he died on Jan 17, 1847, in Fairfield, and was buried in Shaw lot in Standish Neck Cemetery. They were parents of the following children:
1. **EBENEZER**.
2. **LUCY**, bapt. in Standish Dec. 5, 1816, lived in North Windham.
3. **NANCY**, born Sept. 16, 1808, bapt. Dec. 5, 1816, married John Hodgdon, born July 7, 1808, died June 26, 1883. She died Apr. 22, 1886.
4. **LUCINDA**, bapt. Dec. 5, 1816, married Ebenezer Shaw, born June 10, 1808, son of Samuel and Mary (Phinney) Shaw of Standish. They lived in Standish where he died Feb. 28, 1864, and she on Sept. 9, 1865. Three children.

5. MARY E., bapt. Aug. 20, 1818, married Jan. 14, 1846, her cousin Leander Shaw, born Aug. 5, 1820, son of Ebenezer and Rebecca (Yates) Shaw of Standish. They lived on Standish Neck where he died Feb. 18, 1879, and she sometime after 1894.

ii. JOHN JR., born Oct. 14, 1784, bapt. Sept. 30, 1798, married Dec. 11, 1815, Sally Binford, born June 19, 1788, daughter of William and Dorcas (Richardson) Binford of Baldwin. They lived in Baldwin where he died Dec. 2, 1871, and she on Mar. 31, 1876. They were parents of the following children:
1. SARAH MARIA, born in Baldwin Oct. 16, 1816, died Mar. 12, 1832.
2. JOHN, born June 30, 1819, died at New Orleans, La., Nov. 5, 1863, married Apr. 7, 1847, Abby T. Flood of Buxton, born July 3, 1820, daughter of Calvin and Mary (Binford) Flood. She died Mar. 22, 1872, age 47 yrs., 8 mos., Buxton.
3. SYLVANUS RICHARD, born Jan. 23, 1820, married June 6, 1851, Deborah Thompson, born Sept. 6, 1829, in Baldwin, daughter of Abner Dow. She died July 7, 1908, age 78 yrs., 10 mos., 1 day, and he died Jan. 29, 1916, in Baldwin.
4. LUCY ANN, born Aug. 2, 1824, died Nov. 12, 1831.
5. JOSIAH, born Aug. 4, 1826, died Aug. 7, 1827.
6. WILLIAM, born Feb. 22, 1829, died May 6, 1830.
7. JEREMIAH, born Aug. 21, 1833, married Feb. 1, 1859, Eliza Harding, died Aug. 10, 1885.
8. SARAH, born Feb. 22, 1836, died Dec. 17, 1839.

iii. JOSHUA, born about 1786, died young.

iv. CURTIS B., born Oct. 14, 1790, bapt. Sept. 30, 1798, married Huldah Lowell of Baldwin May 21, 1826. They lived in Baldwin where he died Mar. 18, 1848, and she married as her second husband Elisha Yates, brother of her first husband. Children of Curtis and Huldah (Lowell) Yates were as follows:
1. SALLY IRISH, born in Baldwin Feb. 23, 1827, married Isaac Gilman of Baldwin Nov. 23, 1847.
2. CURTIS JR., born July 30, 1829, died young.
3. SYBIL, died young.
4. ALBERT, born June 1840, lived in Paris, Maine, died in 1907.

v. JOSHUA, born about 1792, died young.

vi. REBECCA, born Mar. 17, 1794, bapt. Sept. 30, 1798, married Jan. 25, 1816, Ebenezer Shaw, born July 20, 1787, son of Ebenezer and Sarah (Wood) Shaw of Standish. She died July 31, 1832, and he married her sister Mary Yates. They lived on a farm on Standish Neck, where he died Dec. 6, 1863. There were nine children by his first wife.

vii. MARY H., born June 1797, bapt. Sept. 30, 1798, married as his second wife the widower of her sister Rebecca, Ebenezer Shaw Jr., on Oct. 20, 1833. She died Sept. 5, 1865.

viii. ELISHA, born Jan. 17, 1799, married first on Dec. 19, 1824, Abigail Meserve, born about 1802 daughter of Elias and Betsey (Shaw) Meserve. They lived in Standish where she died July 18, 1848, age 46 yrs., 3 mos. He married second Apr. 13, 1851, Mrs. Huldah

(Lowell) Yates, widow of his brother Curtis Yates. He lived in Oxford, Maine, in his later years and died June 1, 1873. Children by first wife were:
1. MERCY, born Mar. 2, 1829, married (int. May 17, 1857, in Baldwin) Eleazer Flint Jr.
2. CAROLINE, born Feb. 18, 1831.
3. MARSHALL, born Feb. 19, 1833.
4. CYRUS, born May 20, 1835, died in the army at the age of 29 yrs.
5. WILLIAM HENRY, died young.
6. SAMUEL.
ix. SARAH OR SALLY, born Mar. 8, 1801, bapt. May 17, 1801, married Apr. 3, 1825, Thomas Irish and lived in Standish. She died May 4, 1874.
x. MERCY, born July 8, 1804, bapt. July 8, 1804, died Aug. 22, 1831, age 27, unmarried.

YORK

Abram (Abraham) and John York were among the very early settlers in Pearsontown. There is little doubt that both of them were brothers. While there is considerable question as to their ancestry, family tradition has it that the original ancestor in this country came from England to settle on Cape Cod. They probably moved into town from that part of Falmouth, Maine, that later became Cape Elizabeth, and perhaps had come there from Boston, Mass., or its vicinity. Reason for believing this is due to the fact that in the Boston records is found information relating to the family of an Abraham and Amiable York in which the two oldest children are named Abraham and John and are of the right age to have been the settlers in Pearsontown.

Abraham York of Boston and Naomi (intentions read "Naomi") Blake of Rentham (Wrentham) Mass., were married in Boston by Samuel Checkley Esq., justice of the peace, on June 22, 1726. Record of the marriage of Abraham York and Noomi (Naomi) Blake on the same date is found in the Wrentham records, note being made that the marriage occurred in Boston. The genealogy of "John Blake of Wretham, Mass." contains the record of an Amiable Blake, who was born in that town on Oct. 25, 1706, daughter of John Jr., and Joanna (Whiting) Blake. It appears that Naomi may have been a nickname for Amiable and that the Naomi and Amiable (Blake) York referred to in the Boston records were one and the same person. Children of Abraham and Amiable (Blake) York as found in the Boston records were as follows:
1. Abraham, born Dec. 29, 1726.
2. John, born Dec. 8, 1728.
3. Joseph, born Feb. 5, 1730.
4. Ann Langdon, born July 9, 1733.
5. Mary, born Apr. 21, 1736.

Futher reason for assuming that Abraham and Amiable York were the parents of the Pearsontown settlers is the fact that one of John York's daughters was named Naoma (Naomi?).

Abraham York, the first of the brothers, was one of the original grantees of the town. He drew right No. 9 and was one of the very grantees who actually settled on the land given to them. He apparently was one of those living in the fort in the early days because he was the original owner of one of the 5-acre lots. He was one of a group of Pearsontown men in His Majesty's Service under the command of Capt. William Gerrish and also served with other men from the town in Lt. Charles Lessner's party scouting eastward from Broad Bay (Waldoboro).

His name is found in a list of Pearsontown men who worked on Gorham roads during 1760 and 1761.

The intentions of marriage of Abraham York and Lydia Jordan, both of Falmouth, were filed in that town on Apr. 3, 1749. He therefore must have had quite a few children in his family when he first moved to Pearsontown and it is likely that they were living in the fort with him. He died about 1770 when he is said to have drowned in Sebago Lake while fishing by going through a "breathing hole" in the ice. His brother John discovered the loss when he found his (Abraham's) dog lying by the hole. Ephraim Jones of Falmouth was appointed administrator of his estate, final administration being granted on Oct. 5, 1783.

The 30-acre lot #9 drawn by him in the first division of lots, on which he undoubtedly lived after it became safe to do so following the end of hostilities, was sold to Luther Topping on Aug. 27, 1783, by Ephraim Jones, the administrator of his estate (12/282). The second division 100-acre lot #115 drawn to right No. 9 was deeded by administrator Jones to his widow, Lydia (Jordan) York, on Aug. 23, 1783 (12/283). The 5-acre lot #16, which he cultivated and on which he possibly lived during his sojourn in the fort was confirmed by the Proprietors to his widow, Lydia, in 1771 and sold by her to Ephraim Jones on May 17, 1771 (9/183). Benjamin Thrasher of Cape Elizabeth in consideration of the fact that Lydia York, widow of Pearsontown, had cleared five acres of land and a house on 30-acre lot #77 deeded the lot to her on Sept. 19, 1777 (10/55). She sold the same lot to Jabez Dow on Sept. 24, 1777 (10/53).

Lydia (Jordan) York married second (int. Aug. 5, 1784, at Gorham) Nathan Woodman of Buxton. On Mar. 7, 1786, she and her husband sold to her sons Isaac and Jacob York the 100-acre lot #115 and 50 acres of 100-acre lot #114, both in the second division in Standish (16/132). They lived for a time in Standish and Nathan Woodman is listed with a family of 1-1-1 in the 1790 census of the town. While he is also listed in the 1795 and 1796 tax lists, he is not charged for a poll tax in either year, which may indicate he was living elsewhere. Sometime after 1790 they moved to Limington where she died, but date of her death has not been found. He died in 1812 at the home of his son Shubael in Hollis.

Abraham and Lydia (Jordan) York were the parents of at least the following children:
i. MARY, born about 1750 (over 45 in 1800 census), married Feb. 1, 1769, (Gorham records) Reuben Cookson of Pearsontown. They probably lived on 50-acres of the 100-acre lot #114 in the second division bordering on the Saco River, which they sold to their son-

in-law Daniel Smith of Standish on Jan. 8, 1802 (36/78). The other half of this lot was sold in 1786 by Nathan and Lydia (Jordan) (York) Woodman to Isaac and Jacob York, which leads to the assumption that Mary was the daughter of Abraham and Lydia (Jordan) York. About 1802 Reuben and Mary (York) Cookson moved to Unity, Maine, where they afterward lived and died. For list of their children by Cookson family.

ii. ABRAHAM JR., born about 1752 (he was of age in 1773), married Sarah (Pierce ?). He enlisted on May 16, 1775, in Capt. Wentworth Stuart's company of Col. Edmund Phinney's regiment, which took part in the siege of Boston. He later enlisted in the Continental army for three years and on July 7, 1771, was reported as being taken prisoner and as being missing on company returns after that date. Nothing has been found to indicate his return from the war, at least to Pearsontown, but he may later have lived in Baldwin. His name does not appear on any of the lists consulted. Abraham and Sarah York had the following children baptized in the Pearsontown Church:

1. STEPHEN, bapt. Oct. 18, 1778, married at Standish on Apr. 14, 1795, (int. Mar. 30, 1795) Sarah Strout of Limington. His name is found on the 1796 tax list. He was probably the Stephen York Jr. who was in Woodstock, Maine, in 1831, whence he is said to have come from Riley Plantation (then called Kitchum) and originally from Standish. Deeds show he was of Kitchum by 1818. Stephen York Jr. of Kitchum married (int. Sept. 25, 1823) Nancy Young of Newry, daughter of Joshua Young, and moved to Albany, Maine, where she died Feb. 18, 1860. One Stephen York Jr. died in Dec. 1854, age 76 yrs., in Norway, formerly of Bethel.

iii. JONATHAN, born ____, married Sarah. They had a daughter Hannah baptized in the Pearsontown Church on Mar. 3, 1776. Nothing further known.

iv. JOHN, died unmarried. Was he the John York of Pearsontown who enlisted in Capt. Wentworth Stuart's company on May 16, 1775, or was it his cousin John York Jr.?

v. SARAH (some records say Susan, but gravestone in Unity, Maine, gives Sarah), born Apr. 11, 1756, married (int. Aug. 19, 1776, in Gorham) as his second wife Joseph Woods of Bridgton, Maine, died Aug. 15, 1830, in Unity, Maine.

vi. ISAAC, born Aug. 15, 1758, in Pearsontown, married first (int. May 6, 1780, in Gorham) Betsy Meserve, born Apr. 14, 1760, daughter of John and Mary (Yeaton) Meserve of Pearsontown. She died June 29, 1804, and he married second on Oct. 20, 1805, Polly Merrow, born Nov. 1, 1776 probably in Biddeford or Saco daughter of William and Margaret (Haley) Merrow, later of Hollis and Standish. His homestead farm was on the bank of the Saco River at the bend in the River Road in the Boulter Neighborhood. He served in the Revolutionary War, where he is said to have learned to read, write, and figure, and in his later years received a pension for his services. His name is found on Standish valuation and tax lists and in the 1790 census with a family of 1-1-2. At the time of the 1800 census his family consisted of him and his wife, one male and three females under 10 years of age, two males and one female between 10 and 16, and one male and one female between 16 and 26. In 1810 there were still eleven persons in his family which included six males and three females besides him and his wife. He died on Nov. 25, 1846, age 89 yrs., and was the oldest inhabitant born in town (*Eastern Argus*, Dec. 16, 1846). His widow died on Nov. 22, 1861, age 85 yrs., in Standish. Both are buried in Standish in a family graveyard on his farm. Isaac and Betsy (Meserve) York were the parents of the following children:

1. SUSAN, born ____, married Dec. 30, 1802 (int. Dec. 4, 1802, in Hollis) John Nason of Hollis.
2. ABRAHAM or ABRAM, born about 1783 (in 1850 age 67 of Sebago) married Apr. 2, 1806, Betsy or Elizabeth Boulter of Standish, daughter of Nathaniel and Ruth (Sprague) Boulter. She was living in 1850 in Sebago, age 68, and in 1860 was age 78, living with her daughter Mrs. Henry Hatch in Sebago. They moved to Sebago about 1830 from Standish. They were the parents of the following children:
   (1) TRYPHENA, born 1806, married Mar. 2, 1831, John Weeman Jr., born in Oct. 1804, son of John and Esther (Davis) Weeman of Standish, where they were living in 1880. She died July 30, 1892, age 85 yrs., 8 mos., in Sebago, and he died Nov. 1, 1880, age 82 yrs., in Sebago.
   (2) HARRIET C., born about 1823, living in 1860, age 37 yrs., in Sebago. She married Henry C. Hatch.
   (3) DANIEL B., born about 1812 and maybe was the Daniel B. of Sheridan, Maine, in 1880. He married July 10, 1831, Betsey Martin of Bridgton. If he was the Daniel B. of Sheridan and Ashland, Maine, then he married second Serena Morrison.
   (4) SAMUEL H., born about 1817, living in 1860 in Harrison.
   (5) FREEMAN, born about 1818, living in 1850 in Sebago.
   (6) ABRAM.
3. SARAH, Dec. 2, 1808, Samuel Knight, born May 12, 1799, son of Samuel and Hannah Knight of Buxton.
4. JOHN, born about 1789 (he was in Feb. 1826, age 37), married Sept. 17, 1810, Mary Knight of Hollis. He was a trader and ran a tavern at South Standish and it was probably from him that York's Corner received its name. Children as follows:
   (1) ALBERT, born Mar. 11, 1811, living in 1850 age 37 yrs. in Monroe.
   (2) SUSAN, born Dec. 1, 1812, died unmarried in 1832.
   (3) JOHN JR., born June 20, 1816. Did he marry his cousin Mary M. York, born June 24, 1823, daughter of Samuel and Sarah (Meserve) York?
   (4) JOSEPH, died Aug. 18, 1903, age 72 yrs., 9 mos., Monroe.

5. MARTHA, born about 1794 (56 in 1850) married Nov. 19, 1815, John L. Edgecomb, then of Standish, born about 1791 son of Gibbins and Abigail (Lane) Edgecomb of Gardiner, Maine. She in 1870 was living in Standish with her son.
6. MARY, born 1798. She was living in 1824 with her sister, Martha (York) Edgecomb in South Limington.
7. JOSEPH, born Mar. 4, 1796, married (int. Oct. 18, 1817) Eunice Nason, born about 1798 daughter of David and Sarah (Smith) Nason of Limington. She died Nov. 6, 1874, age 76 yrs., and he on Sept. 22, 1876, age 80 yrs., 6 mos., 18 days, both in Biddeford. They had at least a son Isaac whose son Frank was living in Biddeford, Maine, in 1891 with daughters Sarah and Eliza.
8. FANNY, born about 1800, married on May 12, 1822, John Elden Chase, born Feb. 11, 1801, son of John Elden and Abigail (Hooper) Chase. He died July 26, 1885, in Bradford, Maine, and she died there Sept. 22, 1885, age 84 yrs.
9. SAMUEL, born July 4, 1802, married on Mar. 13, 1822, his first cousin Sarah Meserve, born Jan. 2, 1800, daughter of Charles and Mary (Cookson) Meserve of Standish. In 1821 they were living in North Belmont, Maine, and in 1830 in Sebago, Maine, but by 1850 had returned to Standish. He married second May 20, 1869, Hannah M. Judkins, born July 1, 1829, and both were living in Standish at the time of the 1870 census. He died June 14, 1883, in Porter at the home of his daughter Mrs. Charles French.

Children of Samuel and Sarah (Meserve) York as follows:

(1) MARY M., born June 24, 1823, married (int. May 15, 1848) John York Jr. of Frankfort, she of Standish. Was he her cousin by that name who was born June 20, 1816, son of John and Mary (Knight) York? She died Feb. 22, 1887.

(2) ELIZA ANN, born May 14, 1825, married Apr. 20, 1845, Levi Harmon of Gorham, son of Dominicus. She died Sept. 5, 1881.

(3) SARAH JANE, born Feb. 16, 1827, married in Standish on June 24, 1847, John Madison Brown, born Mar. 1, 1824, died May 3, 1900. She died on July 27, 1905. Both were buried in the Moses Cemetery at South Standish.

(4) AURELIA SEYMOUR, born Jan. 23, 1829, married Sept. 2, 1849, Thomas Boothby Jr., born Mar. 30, 1824, son of Thomas and Sally (Dyer) Boothby of Limington. She died Sept. 6, 1883, age 54, and he on Dec. 1, 1895, in Portland. Three children.

(5) CHARLES MESERVE, born Dec. 4, 1830, died Sept. 24, 1854, of smallpox in Portland.

(6) SUSAN NASON, born Oct. 14, 1834, married Charles A. Morton, who died Apr. 28, 1879, age 45, and she died June 30, 1892, age 58 yrs., 3 mos., 7 days, Biddeford, and he died Apr. 28, 1879, age 45 yrs.

- (7) **WILLIAM FRANKLIN**, born Feb. 28, 1836 in Sebago, a Civil War veteran, who married Jan. 13, 1866, Julia Libby, born Apr. 3, 1835, daughter of Levi and Eliza (Boothby) Libby of Porter. She died Aug. 26, 1912, age 77 and he died Mar. 29, 1925, age 89 yrs., in Porter.
- (8) **GEORGE W**, born June 23, 1838, married Mahala P. Libby on Oct. 25, 1861. He was a member of Co. K., 25th Maine Volunteers and died in Georgetown, Va., on Dec. 22, 1862.
- (9) **LUCY MARIA**, born Nov. 8, 1841, married Feb. 16, 1865, Charles French of Porter. She died Nov. 14, 1906, age 64 yrs., 6 days, in Porter.

Children of Isaac and Polly (Merrow) York were as follows:
- 10. **NANCY**, born 1806 in Standish, married Nov. 29, 1827, Nathaniel Davis, born in May 1787, son of James and Chloe (Wiley) Davis of Standish. He died Dec. 29, 1843, age 56 yrs., 7 mos., and was buried in the Oak Hill Cemetery in Standish. His widow moved to Biddeford and there died Nov. 17, 1885, age 79 yrs. They were the parents of two daughters (see Davis). She stated that her father was a boy of fourteen when he enlisted as a drummer boy in the Revolutionary War and was at Bunker Hill. His farm home was on the banks of the Saco River, where a large family was born and raised. Her parents grew and spun their own flax, and the nails that were used in building their home were made by hand.
- 11. **ISAAC JR.**, born Oct. 18, 1808, married Sept. 3, 1833, Mindwell Libby, born Oct. 26, 1811, daughter of Elias and Martha (Bradbury) Libby of Buxton. He lived on the family homestead in the Boulter Neighborhood at South Standish and died July 30, 1885, age 74 yrs., 10 mos., 25 days. Both were buried in the family graveyard on the York homestead. They were the parents of the following children: (York)
  - (1) **MARTHA J.**, born Feb. 23, 1833, died June 21, 1908, age 75 yrs., 3 mos., 28 days, in Standish.
  - (2) **WILLIAM**, born Apr. 11, 1834, died Mar. 10, 1835.
  - (3) **WILLIAM H.**, born Sept. 11, 1835, died in 1851 and was buried in the York family graveyard.
  - (4) **ELBRIDGE G.**, born Jan. 12, 1837, died 1914, married Lizzie E. Berry, born Mar. 13, 1839, died Sept. 26, 1921. Both were buried in Moses Cemetery.
  - (5) **FREDERICK**, born Oct. 22, 1841, died July 17, 1860, and was buried in the York family graveyard.
  - (6) **LUCY F.**, born Jan. 16, 1844, died Feb. 24, 1937, married Levi W. Libby, born Aug. 11, 1842, died June 28, 1920. Both are buried in Moses Cemetery.
  - (7) **BELA G.**, born June 13, 1846, died Mar. 16, 1923, in Parsonfield, married first Mary E. Hutcherson, daughter of Mark and Mary Hutcherson of Standish; she died Apr. 27, 1867, age 19 yrs., 2 mos., and third Isabel S. Lowell, born July 18, 1851, died June 16, 1933. All but has last wife, who was buried in Maplewood Cemetery, were buried in the family graveyard on the York homestead.

12. **WILLIAM**, born about 1811, died at sea, unmarried. His age was given as 9 yrs. old in June 1820, when his father filed for his pension.
13. **ELIZABETH** or **ELIZA**, born 1813, married June 28, 1841, David Wilson of Parsonsfield, she of Standish.
14. **CHARITY**, born about 1815, married July 31, 1837, Jacob Bradbury Libby of Buxton, born May 2, 1815, and brother of the wife of her brother, Isaac York Jr. She died Oct. 15, 1872, in Cape Elizabeth.

vii. **JACOB**, born about 1762, married (int. Oct. 24, 1782) Edie or Edith Moody, born in Scarboro on Mar. 9, 1750, daughter of Joshua and Elizabeth (____) Moody, she being of Cape Elizabeth at the time of her marriage. He probably lived on either lot #114 or #115 in the second division in Standish, which he purchased with his brother Isaac from their mother, Lydia, on Mar. 7, 1786 (16/132). He is listed on all tax lists consulted; in the 1790 census with a family of 1-1-3; and in the 1800 census with a family consisting of him and his wife, two males and one female between 10 and 16, and one female between 16 and 26 yrs. of age. About 1822 he moved to Baldwin where he died on Oct. 27, 1849, at the age of 87. Children of Jacob and Edie (Moody) York, as far as have been determined, were as follows:

1. **LYDIA**, born about 1783, married Jan. 27, 1803, Daniel Whitten of Buxton, who served in the War of 1812. They lived in Baldwin, where he died Apr. 5, 1833. She was still living on Mar. 19, 1855.
2. **JACOB JR.**, born in 1787, married May 13, 1810, Susanna Boulter, born about 1792 daughter of Benjamin and Sarah (Brown) Boulter of Standish. They lived in Baldwin, where she died Nov. 14, 1868, age 76, he surviving her until his death on May 1, 1869, at the age of 82. They were parents of at least the following children: (York)
    (1) **EUNICE MELINDA**, born 1811, who married Mar. 24, 1834, Josiah Webb Mayberry of Windham and died June 28, 1881, age 70 yrs., 4 mos., Windham.
    (2) **SUSAN**, born about 1819, married on Mar. 8, 1840, Ignes Windling of Baldwin and Turner, Maine. She died in Baldwin Oct. 19, 1854, age 35 yrs., 19 days.
    (3) **JACOB III**, born about 1824, married Oct. 17, 1846, Lydia Decker, born about 1826 perhaps daughter of Charles and Lydia (Hall) Decker. He died Oct. 17, 1903, age 78 yrs., 11 mos., 20 days, and she on Jan. 21, 1908, age 81.
    (4) **PHINEAS E.J.**, died Mar. 19, 1849, age 21 yrs., 9 days.
3. **JOSHUA**, born about 1788 (age 62 in 1850), married first on Nov. 3, 1809, Abigail Linnell, born Apr. 14, 1788, daughter of Samuel and Anna (York) Linnell of Standish, they being second cousins. She died about 1820 and he married second (int. Mar. 21, 1821) Martha Tibbetts of Buxton, born about 1788. At the time of the 1850 census they were living in Standish with children Daniel, age 27; Amos, age 21; and Abigail, age 18. Children by his first wife, Abigail Linnell, were as follows:

- (1) **MARY**, born Oct. 16, 1809, married Dec. 25, 1834, Joseph Johnson of Limington, born Sept. 23, 1807, son of Daniel and Eunice (Foss) Johnson of that town. They lived on the Johnson family homestead at South Limington, where he died on Feb. 10, 1877, and she on Jan. 14, 1888. They were the parents of four children.
- (2) **JANE**, born in Nov. 1812, married Nov. 21, 1832, at Standish, Simon Berry of Limington, born in Sept. 3, 1803, son of James and Mary (Haines) (Nason) Berry of that town (she being the widow of Samuel Nason). She died at Limington on Feb. 14, 1853, age 41 yrs., 3 mos., 7 days, and he died there Aug. 6, 1864. They were buried with her parents in Limington.
- (3) **LEANDER**, born in 1814, married Eliza Rumery, born Sept. 25, 1825, daughter of Joseph and Nancy (Gordan) Rumery of Hollis. He died Dec. 14, 1894, age 80, in Hollis, and she on June 8, 1904, age 78 yrs., 9 mos., 13 days.
- (4) **JOEL**, a twin.
- (5) **DESIRE**, twin of Joel, married a Mr. Pinkham.
- (6) **JOSHUA**, died in infancy.
- (7) **DANIEL**, age 27 yrs. in 1850.
- (8) **AMOS**, age 21 yrs. in 1850.
- (9) **ABIGAIL**, age 18 yrs. in 1850.

4. **BETSEY**, born about 1790, living in 1860, age 70 yrs., in Sebago with her daughter, Mrs. Levi Dyer. She married William Lord, son of Nason Lord, who died July 27, 1826, in Naples, a Revolutionary War soldier. They are reported as having lived in Harrison and were of Sebago, where in June 1832, William was sick. Had daughters, Sarah and Naomi. Naomi was born about 1815, married Levi Dyer and was living in Sebago in 1860 (census report).

John York, the other early settler in Pearsontown bearing the surname of York, was born Dec. 8, 1728, if the assumption is correct that he and Abraham his brother were the sons of Abraham and Amiable (Blake) York of Boston. No record of his marriage has been found, unlike his brother Abraham. The given first name of his wife was Sarah, and she was young enough to have had a son Israel Thorne, Jr., born on Dec. 13, 1773, by her second marriage. According to Dr. Meserve, a great-granddaughter of Isaac I. York by the name of Mrs. Files stated that Sarah (____) York, her great-grandmother, was married when she was only eleven years old and that her first child, Col. John York (John York Jr.), was born when she was twelve years of age, and that she lived to be over 80 years old. Since Isaac I. York was 95 years old at the time of his death on Aug. 5, 1844, making his date of birth about 1749, it appears that Col. John York, the first born, must have been born as early as 1748 or perhaps before. On this basis Sarah (____) York, wife of the Pearsontown settler would have been born about 1736. The identity of this Sarah is given in a bill found in Suffolk court records (case 63,990, vol. 398) of Sarah Strout for nursing John Yorke, 18 weeks, dated Apr. 21, 1748. The bill is headed: "Falmouth in Casco Bay, Oct. 1747, a true acompt per me,

Sarah Strout." On the reverse side is written that Sarah Strout received 38 pounds and the signature of Sarah York in a very awkward hand. This seems to show that Sarah Strout married John York, about the date of 1748. Sarah (Strout) York was perhaps one of the younger, if not the youngest, child of of Capt. George and Bridget (Cooley) Strout of Cape Elizabeth and thus a sister of John Strout an early settler of Pearsontown.

Although John York was not an original grantee of Pearsontown like his brother Abraham, the fact that he was given 5-acre lot #17 makes it evidence that he must have been living in the fort soon after its construction in 1754. In fact there is reason to believe that both he and his brother together with their families were among the thirty men, women, and children living in the fort in 1755 as stated by Moses Pearson in his petition to the general court. John and his brother Abraham were among the service in Capt. Charles Lessner's party scouting eastward from Broad Bay (Waldoboro) in 1759 and 1760. In 1760 and 1761 John was paid for several days' work on Gorham roads with his oxen. Besides the 5-acre lot #17 on which he lived and which he mortaged to Moses Pearson on Nov. 14, 1767, (3/327) John York owned the 30-acre lot #29 together with the 100-acre lot to be drawn later to right No. 29, which were conveyed to him by Moses Pearson on Mar. 31, 1761, in consideration of his having moved his family into the township and having brought forward a settlement according to the act of the general court (1/343). This 30-acre lot was located on the Oak Hill Road about opposite lot #9 belonging to his brother Abraham. On Mar. 29, 1769, John York sold to Ebenezer Mayo of Falmouth the 30-acre lot #29 together with the house, barn, and all other buildings thereon standing, and also the first 100-acre lot drawn to right No. 29 (6/260). This may have been a mortaged deed, for on Apr. 10, 1773, John York Jr. purchased from Mayo the 30-acre lot #29 which his father had sold to him (Mayo) four years earlier. On June 4, 1771, John York Sr. bought from Enoch Illesley of Falmouth the 30-acre lot #28 in Pearsontown adjoining his other. He is said to have drowned in "the basin" of Sebago Pond in 1771, leaving a widow and eight children. Following his death, his widow, Sarah, married about 1772 Israel Thorn who lived next to them on 5-acre lot #18 when they were living on #17 and by whom she had a son Israel Jr. born on Dec. 13, 1773. She probably did not die until after 1815. John and Sarah (Strout) York were parents of at least the following children:

i. JOHN JR., born about 1748, married about 1771 Abigail Bean, born about 1748 daughter of Jonathan and Abigail (Gorden) Bean of Pearsontown. It is likely that he made his home on 30-acre lot #29 which he bought from Ebenezer Mayo of Falmouth on Apr. 10, 1773. On Feb. 25, 1777, he bought from John Meserve of Bristol, Maine, formerly of Pearsontown, the 100-acre lot #118 drawn to right #4 in Pearsontown (8/558). John York Jr., still of Pearsontown, sold this same lot to Samuel Chase of Pepperrellborough (Saco) on Mar. 8, 1777 (8/561). Just when John York Jr. moved with his family to Sudbury-Canada (Bethel) is not known, but it must have been between Apr. 25, 1779, when his daughter Ruth was baptized at Pearsontown and 1781 because he is said to have been living in Bethel at the time of the Indian raid on the town in that year. This was about the same time that his wife's parents and

brothers with their families moved to Bethel. He died Apr. 7, 1838, and his wife died in 1827, age 78 yrs., their gravestones in Bethel. John and Abigail (Bean) York were parents of the following children:
1. ABIGAIL, bapt. in Pearsontown Church on Oct. 4, 1772, married Thomas Frost and became the mother of seven children. She died on Apr. 7, 1842.
2. ANNE, born Feb. 11, 1774, bapt. on Apr. 17, 1774, married on May 6, 1790, John Kilgore Jr. Thirteen children.
3. SARAH, bapt. Oct. 3, 1775, died young.
4. JONATHAN, born Aug. 13, 1777, bapt. Aug. 31, 1777.
5. RUTH, bapt. in Pearsontown Apr. 25, 1779, married first Ezekiel Duston, by whom she had eight children; and second Timothy Capen, by whom she had four more.
6. PETER, born Aug. 29, 1777, or Dec. 10, 1777?, married Abiah Russell, born 1779. She died July 15, 1830, and he on Dec. 17, (10?) 1862, age 85 yrs. Twelve children.
7. LOIS, born Feb. 20, 1781, died Feb. 14, 1786.

ii. ISAAC INSLEY (ILLESLEY?), born about 1749, served in the Revolutionary War. There appears to be some confusion as to his middle name, it appearing as Insley in many records, but as Illesley in the marriage record. The intentions of marriage of Isaac Illesley York of Sudbury-Canada and Margaret Shaw of Standish were filed in Standish on Aug. 5, 1786. This marriage evidently, however, never took place because on Sept. 17, 1786, John Dean Esq. of Standish married him to Elizabeth Thompson according to Cumberland County marriage records.

Isaac I. York moved to Sudbury-Canada (Bethel) sometime after his brother John, but undoubtedly in the early 1780s. There he lived until about 1825 when he moved to the Magalloway region, where he was the fourth settler and where he died on his homestead farm on Aug. 5, 1844, at the age of 95 yrs. Children of Isaac and Elizabeth (Thompson) York were as follows:
1. JOHN, born July 5, 1787, married Sally Kilgore, his cousin, born Mar. 19, 1796, daughter of John Jr. and Anne (York) Kilgore and settled in Newry, Maine.
2. HANNAH, born Dec. 16, 1788, married George Tucker of Bethel and had the following children: (Tucker)
    (1) ISAAC INSLEY, born at Lyndon, Vt., Aug. 3, 1818.
    (2) HANNAH, born Jan. 18, 1823.
    (3) FRANCINA, born Feb. 4, 1825.
    (4) MAROAH, born Dec. 23, 1828, married Ephraim Bryant.
3. LEVINA, born Aug. 30, 1789, married Ephraim Rowe Jr.
4. BETSEY, born Apr. 10, 1791, married son of Jonathan Jr. and Abigail (York) Bean. They were first cousins. They lived on her father's farm at Magalloway.
5. MERCY, born June 12, 1794, married Josiah Carter.
6. ISAAC, born Apr. 17, 1796, died the following November.
7. JOEL, born Oct. 17, 1797, went to New York.
8. JACOB, born June 13, 1799, married Apr. 3, 1821, Dolly Fogg, both of Bethel.

       9.   LYDIA, born Mar. 20, 1803, married Lorenzo Bumpas of Hebron, Maine.
      10. LEVI, born Feb. 17, 1805.
      11. ANNA, born Jan. 2, 1807, married ____ Bennett.
      12. DELINDA, born Oct. 21, 1809, married John Hubbard.

iii.   EMMA OR NAOMA (NAOMI?), born about 1751, married on Feb. 1, 1769, John Hall, born probably before 1750 son of Charles and Jemima (Dolliver) Hall of Pearsontown. They lived in Standish where he died on May 2, 1819, and she on Feb. 23, 1840, age 88. For children see Hall family.

iv.   ABIGAIL, born about 1753, married (int. Oct. 22, 1774) Jonathan Bean Jr., born about 1754 son of Jonathan and Abigail (Gorden) Bean of Pearsontown. About 1781 they moved to Bethel, Maine, where he died Nov. 19, 1826. She died there some years later on Mar. 6, 1833. For children see Bean family.

v.   REBECCA, born Feb. 20, 1754, married about 1771 John McGill, born Sept. 16, 1744, son of Arthur and Mary (____) McGill of Pearsontown. They lived in Standish where she died in 1814, she surviving him. For children see McGill family.

vi.   ANNA, born in Aug. 1764, married (int. June 15, 1782) Samuel Linnell, born Jan. 12, 1763, son of Elisha and Martha (Higgins) Linnell of Eastham, Mass. They lived in Standish where she died on May 13, 1821. He married second (int. Apr. 26, 1823) Susannah Newcomb of Portland. He died in Standish on May 12, 1837. For children see Linnell family.

vii.   EBENEZER, born May 31, 1766, married on Dec. 27, 1789, Mehitable Jones, born in June 26, 1767 (bapt. July 5, 1767, in the First Church of Scarboro), daughter of John and Mary (Savage) Jones of that town. She was a sister to the wives of his brother Job York, his half-brother Israel Thorne Jr. and nephew William McGill. He lived in Standish and on Oct. 11, 1790, bought from Nathaniel Dyer of Cape Elizabeth the 100-acre lot #102 in the second division in Standish, on which he cleared his homestead farm. He is listed in the 1790 census with a family of 1-0-1; in the year 1800 with a family consisting of him and his wife, two daughters under 10 yrs. old, and one daughter between 10 and 16 yrs. of age; and on the 1788, 1789, 1790, 1795, 1799, 1808, and 1814, tax lists of the town. At the time of the 1830 census he was still living in Standish with his wife, one male between 15 and 20, and one female between 10 and 15. He died Apr. 12, 1833. His wife, age 83, was living in Standish in the family of Randall Foss, her grandson, at the time of the 1850 census. She died Sept. 30, 1851, age 85 yrs., Standish (*Christian Mirror*, Dec. 13, 1853). Ebenezer and Mehitable (Jones) York were the parents of the following children:

    1. HANNAH, born Sept. 7, 1791, bapt. in Standish Church Sept. 7, 1797, married Nov. 21, 1811, Ebenezer Foss, born Jan. 18, 1785, son of Job and Eunice (Chick) Foss. After the death of his father by drowning at Stroudwater in 1801, his mother had married John Haskell and moved to Standish. Hannah (York) Foss died Dec. 28, 1825, and her husband died on Aug. 20, 1855.

2. MARY (POLLY), bapt. Sept. 7, 1797, married July 3, 1814, John Foss, brother to Ebenezer Foss, her sister's husband. They had one child.
3. ABIGAIL (NABBY), bapt. Sept. 7, 1797, married on Nov. 4, 1812, John West, born Dec. 9, 1790, son of Joseph and Nancy (Cannell) West of Standish. Sometime after 1830 she died and he married second on May 18, 1834, Sarah H. Whitney of Standish. He lived in Standish, Sebago, and Upton, Maine, and died in Greenwood, Maine, in 1877 at the age of 87. For children see West family.
4. SARAH, died in infancy.

viii. JOB, born about 1768 (82 in 1850) married Mar. 26, 1789, Sally or Sarah Jones, born about 1773 daughter of John and Mary (Savage) Jones of Scarboro. He was living in Standish with a family of 1-0-1 at the time of the 1790 census. Sometime after 1796 when his name appeared on a Standish tax list for that year, he moved to Bethel where he settled in the eastern part of the town on a hill back from the river. At the time of the 1850 census he was age 82; his wife, Sally, age 77; and their daughter Clarissa, age 39, was living in Bethel. He died Oct. 16, 1853, at the age of 83 (according to *Christian Mirror*, Dec. 13, 1853) and his wife dying two months later on Dec. 6, at the age of 81 yrs., 6 mos., in Bethel. They lived together 64 years. Children of Job and Sally (Jones) York were as follows:
1. DESIRE, born Apr. 7, 1791, in Standish, married Israel Linnell, born in Standish Dec. 2, 1782, son of Samuel and Anna (York) Linnell, her cousin. They lived at Magalloway and were the parents of five children.
2. SALLY, born May 18, 1793, in Standish, married Elihua Kilgore.
3. REBECCA, born Mar. 6, 1795, in Standish, married Joseph McGill, born Apr. 14, 1796, son of John and Rebecca (York) McGill, her cousin. She was killed in Bethel by lightning on July 11, 1819, leaving besides her husband a son, Emery McGill, born Feb. 6, 1819.
4. RANDALL, born in Bethel Apr. 7, 1798, died unmarried Nov. 8, 1849.
5. ESTHER, born Feb. 23, 1800, married Samuel Robertson.
6. MEHITABLE, born Mar. 5, 1802, married Aaron Barton Swan of Paris, Maine.
7. MARY, born Feb. 9, 1804, married James Estes.
8. HANNAH, born Aug. 4, 1806, married George Fessenden.
9. CLARISSA BARTLETT, born Apr. 7, 1810, died unmarried.
10. ABIAH, born Sept. 17, 1812, married Nathan W. Elbridge of Bethel.
11. LOIS, born Aug. 4, 1815, never married.

YOUNG

A Zebulon Young lived for a short while in Standish prior to 1789. He was apparently living here on Feb. 6, 1785, when he and Richard Pierce bought the 100-acre lot #71 in the second division of lots. He is given as living in town on Oct. 7, 1786, when he sold his half of the lot, it being the southwest portion thereof to John Sanborn of Standish (19/424). It is likely that he left town about this time or soon thereafter since his name does not appear in town records later on.

It seems likely that he may have been the Zebulon Young Jr., born Sept. 2, 1760, in Eastham, Mass., son of Zebulon and Elizabeth (Higgins) Young and the Zebulon Young listed as an inhabitant of Hampden, Maine, in the 1800 census as coming from Cape Cod. This Zebulon Young married first Phoebe _____ and second Martha (Brooks) Dillingham, daughter of George Brooks and widow of Henry Dillingham. A Zebulon Young, a veteran of the Revolutionary War, died in Bangor, Maine, on Oct. 6, 1832. Children were as follows:

By first wife:
i. ZEBULON, born Mar. 3, 1791.
ii. BANGS, born Mar. 3, 1793.
iii. ISAAC, born July 31, 1798.
iv. ROBERT, born Mar. 27, 1800.
v. ELIZABETH, born Dec. 2, 1801.
vi. ELNORA, born Mar. 3, 1804.

By second wife:
vii. MARY ANN, born Nov. 15, 1815, died unmarried.
viii. WILLIAM, born May 20, 1818, died unmarried.

The name of Joseph Young is found only on the 1796 tax list of Standish. It likely that he was the Joseph Young 3rd who lived in the Nason District in the northern part of Gorham and who married on Nov. 7, 1793, Lydia Snow, born in Feb. 1776 daughter of Thomas and Jane (Magne) Snow of Gorham. It seems evident that this stay in town was of short duration since his name does not appear in later tax lists nor in the 1800 census. He died in Gorham about 1810 and his wife died there July 9, 1850, at the age of 74. Children were:

i. SALLY, born Mar. 15, 1794, married Enos Humphrey and lived in Livermore, Maine.
ii. ENOS, born July 20, 1795.
iii. AFFIA, born July 17, 1797, married Cyrus Blanchard of Cumberland, Maine, May 12, 1816.
iv. ANNA, born Apr. 7, 1800, married William Clay Apr. 7, 1822.
v. JOSEPH, born Apr. 25, 1804, married Mary Green of Standish, May 21, 1824, died in Longmeadows, Mass., Mar. 25, 1889. She was born Aug. 7, 1802, in Standish and died Aug. 31, 1888, in Longmeadow, Mass.
vi. JANE, born about 1810, married Jonathan Clay Apr. 23, 1829. She married second John Hardy of Raymond. She died July 12, 1864, in Raymond.

INDEX

The Table of Contents lists the families discussed in this book. Names included in this index are only those of persons whose surname differs from the primary family name under discussion in the text.

----, Abiah 234 Bathsheba 199 Caroline 281 Dorcas 209 Edmund Mussey 199 Eleanor 102 Elizabeth 1 328 Fear 166 Frances 174 Hannah 10 239 241 251 309 Helen M 249 Jane 53 251 Jemima 77 Lucinda B 193 Lydia 202 256 Margaret 162 249 Martha 42 276 304 Martha T 39 Mary 198 237 265 271 283 316 332 Mehitable 182 183 Phebe 246 Phoebe 334 Rosilla 29 Sally 315 Sarah 78 162 324 329 Susannah 259

ABBOT, Hannah 121

ABBOTT, Albert 27 Elizabeth 121 Hannah 127 Isaac 121 Moses 121 Nancy 121 Rebecca Linnell 27 Sarah 205

ADAMS, Betsey 83 256 274 275 Elizabeth 251 256 Hezekiah 34 Maria 15 Mary 235 Nathan 235 Ruth 155 187 Tamar 34 Winborn 2

ALDEN, Austin 43 85

ALEXANDER, Dorcas W 251

ALLEN, Ebenezer 89 Elisha 287 Elizabeth 296 Ira L 266 Jane 21 John 19 Margaret 19 Sarah 287 Thankful 234

ANDERSON, 139 Edward 18 294 295 George 295 George Parker 106 Hannah 96 Lucy 18 310

ANDERSON (continued) Martha 295 Mary 139 294 295 Mrs William 57 Olive 18 294 Sarah 90 Solomon 90 Thomas 96 William 57

ANDREWS, Adeline W 277 Clarissa 42 Lydia 20 Samuel 35 Sophia 34 Sophronia 35

ANNIS, Patience 225 Solomon 225

ANSON, John W 276 Sarah F 276

APPLETON, Sarah 84

AREY, Thomas 157

ARNOLD, Benedict 1 Betsey 308 Betsy 196 John 196 Samuel 308

ASHTON, Jacob 89

ATHERTON, Anna 236 John 236

ATKINS, Joanna 108

ATKINSON, John 57 Mary 57

ATWICK, Martha 174

ATWOOD, Elisha 113 Martha 253 Mary 244 247 Mercy 113 Susanna 306

AVERY, Mary 68

AYER, Anna 47 Benjamin 47 135 216 228 Ebenezer 169 266 Elizabeth 145 169 190 215 266 Jane 266 John 10 20 59 250 Lucy 216 Lydia 216 Mary 215 Peter 134 169 190 216 228 Philip 216 Rachel 47 135 216 228 Rebecca 134 169 190 216 228 Sarah 134 135 Timothy 215

BABB, Hannah 298 305

BACON, Apphia 119 Elizabeth 124 Eunice 291 297 George D 98 Hannah 17 118 Josiah 118 119 Keziah 98 Lucy 118 119 Lucy Jenkins 5 Martha 119 Nathaniel 81 119 Richard Hopkins 5
BAGLEY, Susannah 99
BAILEY, Abigail 300 Albert 282 Amanda Eliza 300 Benjamin 300 Clarinda 282 John Fairfield 300 Lydia 257 Mary Jane 300 Susanna 248
BAKER, Charles 223 Mary 51 Mercy 311
BALLARD, Hannah 230 Uriah 230
BANCROFT, Rhoda 295 Sally 194
BANFIELD, Mary 91 264
BANGS, Ebenezer 252 Esther 212 Hannah 25 39 299 308 Herman 308 Mary 252 Mary Ann 252 Molly 308 William 42 William Cobb 252
BARBER, Hugh 280 Margaret 280
BARKER, Polly 248 Sally 8 Sarah 8 Susanna 66 Thomas 8 William 66 Zilpha 252
BARNARD, Nathan 186 Sarah 186
BARRON, Frances Winston 153
BARTLETT, Affia 48 Anne 95 Betsy 13 Charles 249 Charles R 249 Eleanor 249 Enoch 95 Frank M 249 Jonathan 235 Mary 235
BARTON, Aaron 246 Anna 150 Sally 246 William 79
BATCHELDER, Abigail 217 Anna 215 Apphia 216 217 Deborah 281 Ephraim 7 216 217 Harriet 33 Levi 216 Samuel 216 Sylvanus 217 Sylvanus Jr 281
BATES, Hannah 5
BEAKER, Mary 51 52
BEAL, Elizabeth 54 55 136 Thomas 54 55 136
BEAMAN, Janette P 57
BEAN, Abigail 59 145 148 242 245 289 301 330-332 Anna 145 245 246 Anne 145 Betsey 331 Daniel 242 Dolly 289 Dorothy 289 Elizabeth 252 259

BEAN (continued) Eunice 93 103 142 148 172 242 James G 259 John 145 Jonathan 59 148 242 245 289 316 330 332 Jonathan 3rd 145 Jonathan Jr 145 331 332 Joseph 7 Josiah 9 59 Julia M 259 Lois 93 148 240 243 Lucy 246 Margaret 242 Mary 59 316 Molly 59 Rebecca 144 Sargent 246 Thomas 259 Vier 144
BECK, Elizabeth H 31
BELL, Emeline H 25 John 25 Polly 220
BENNETT, Anna 332 Bethiah 43 Emeline 26 John 45 Margaret 45 Martha J 193
BENSON, Abigail 74 139 Abner 42 Arthur M 139 Catherine 42 Elizabeth 139 James 74 139 Nabby 74
BENTON, Mary 230 Stephen P 230
BERRY, Asa 170 Betsey A 30 Betty 27 Eleanor 83 Elias 35 Elisha 165 Eliza A 314 Franklin J 296 George 39 43 102 Hannah 39 170 James 27 60 329 Jane 165 302 329 Joanna 30 139 John 314 John Henry 82 John Lowell 30 Lizzie E 327 Lucy 310 Lydia 165 184 Margaret 165 201 Mary 27 82 108 329 Nancy Emery 35 Odell R 310 Olive 38 Phebe A 310 Polly 82 302 Richard 158 Robert T 302 Sally 102 295 298 Sarah 102 243 Sarah W 296 Silas 30 139 Simon 310 329 Susannah 127 294 Timothy 127 Walter 82 Walter F 302
BICKFORD, Priscilla 225 William 225
BIGFORD, Anna 146 Joshua 146
BINFORD, Abigail 268 Cyrus 268 Dorcas 64 268 321 Emily 269 George 269 Hannah 193 Jeremiah 268 Jeremiah Jr 268 Mary 321 Olive 268 Priscilla 225 Rebecca 268 Sally 64 66 321 Samuel 269 Sarah 64

BINFORD (continued)
　Thomas 268 William 225 268
　321 William Jr 64
BIRNEY, Elizabeth 197 Joseph
　197
BISHOP, Nancy 11
BITHER, Eunice 161 Harriet
　Ripley 35 Hiram Hall 35
　Stephen 161
BIXBY, John W 210 Lydia 210
BLABAN, Mary 161 Polly 161
BLACK, Abigail 268 Joab 7 97
　John 268 Josiah 47 54 317
　Lydia S 296 Mercy 54 Olive 47
　317
BLACKINGTON, Nathan 254
BLAKE, Amiable 322 323 329
　Ann 176 Apphia 26 28 108 200
　236 Benjamin 175 Betsey 175
　Betty 200 Desire Parker 108
　Elizabeth 200 Elizabeth D 175
　Ephraim 108 Eunice 180
　Hannah 118 Harriet S 209 Ithiel
　108 200 236 Joanna 322 John
　322 John Jr 322 Joseph 23 24
　118 Lydia 113 133 195 Mary
　108 236 265 Mehitabel 230
　Miranda 200 Molly 236 Naomi
　322 Nathaniel 108 Noomi 322
　Rebecca 108 Susanna 108
　Timothy 108
BLANCHARD, Affia 334 Cyrus
　334 John 182 Martha 182
BLETHEN, Mary 237 Sarah 217
BLISS, Theodore 157
BLOOM, Mary 299
BLYE, Grace 23 Nancy 254
BODGE, Abigail 233 Louisa 233
　Thomas 233
BOLTER, Daniel 158
BOLTON, Daniel 172 Mary 145
　Thankful 172
BONNEY, Joel 89 Lydia 89 90
　307 308
BOODY, Robert 50
BOOKER, Melissa E 283
BOOTHBY, Aurelia Seymour 326
　Brice 42 David 63 Eliza 327
　Elizabeth 5 Emeline H 25
　Hannah 5 Isaac 5 Israel 25
　James 63 Jonathan 6 Lydia 32

BOOTHBY (continued)
　Mary 6 Rachel 63 Sally 326
　Sarah 296 Susanna 42 Thomas
　326 Thomas Jr 326 Walter 5
BOUCHER, Abigail 66 106 242
BOULTER, A 17 Adeline 112
　Amos 17 Benjamin 22 206 328
　Betsey 296 Betsy 325 Charity
　158 206 Daniel 98 112 Eliza 84
　Elizabeth 22 109 132 325
　Hadassah 266 Hannah 206
　Isaac 206 Isaac L 310 J 17
　John 17 309 310 Lemuel 160
　Lettice 98 Lettis 98 Martha 84
　309 310 Mary 22 160 309 Mary
　Thankful 310 Nathaniel 318
　325 Nathaniel 3rd 84 Nathaniel
　Jr 84 109 132 309 Nathaniel Sr
　107 Ruth 106 107 158 160 306
　325 Samuel F 158 206 Samuel
　Fowler 158 Sarah 328 Susanna
　328
BOWEN, Margaret 88
BOWERS, Catherine 246 Sarah
　Hay 267 Stephen 246 Wilder
　267
BOWIE, Sarah 282
BOYLE, 51
BOYNTON, Apphia 200 Daniel
　169 Edward T 200 Hannah 311
　Happy 311 Jacob 273 311 Mary
　169 311 Olive 273 318
　Phebe 22 Phineas 311 Robert
　50 Sally 311 Samuel 22
　Thomas 311 William 169 311
　William Jr 311
BOZWELL, John 256 Molly 256
BRACKETT, Betsy 196 James
　100 Jane 34 John 304 Margaret
　196 Mary 34 Mehitable 100
BRADBURY, Andrew 179 Ange-
　line 187 Elizabeth 78 Eunice
　87 187 Hannah 85 88 Josiah
　Paine 145 190 Martha 327
　Mary 27 179 Molly 228
　Reuben 87 187 Sarah 122
　Simeon 145 Simeon G 190
　Thankful 145 190 Theophilus
　122 218 Thomas 88
BRADEEN, Henry 291 Jemima
　291 Mary 291 Samuel 291

BRADISH, David 73
BRADLEY, Caleb 82 111 248
    Elizabeth Goodwin 287 Elliot
    287
BRAGDON, Edmund 50 Jane 127
    Sarah 133 302 Thomas 133 302
BRALEY, David 254 Elizabeth
    254
BRANN, Lester 291
BREWER, Col 311
BRIANT, Anna 254 Lucy 189 211
    Polly 170
BRIDGES, Sarah 312
BRIGGS, Susan 135
BRIGHAM, Daniel 12 Hannah 47
    William 12
BROAD, Henry 139 Mary 139
BROOKS, Deborah 244 Deborah
    Atwood 247 Elizabeth 62
    Francis 259 George 244 247
    334 Joanna 244 John 62 Martha
    334 Mary 244 247 Susanna 259
BROWN, 191 Abiah 166 Abigail
    228 262 Abigail Libby 62
    Amos 262 Ann 116 Annie P
    204 Asaph 235 Betsey 101
    Charles 182 Clara E 83 Clarissa 191 David 10 228 David Jr
    204 Dolly 204 Elizabeth 80
    Ephraim 215 Esther 228 Ezra
    294 Fear 166 Hannah 24 235
    246 Henry 107 Henry Young
    106 Hezekiah 166 Huldah 215
    James 101 James Madison 83
    Jerusha 190 John 116 John K
    31 John Madison 326 Joseph Jr
    24 Lewis W 274 Lois 241
    Louisa 136 Lydia 182 246
    Maria 274 Martha J 31 Mary 56
    139 Mary Louisa 280 Melina
    132 Polly 246 Rebecca 294
    Reuben 204 Samuel A 280
    Sarah 24 126 294 328 Sarah J
    83 Sarah Jane 326 Stephen 139
    Sylvanus 166
BRYANT, Betsey 131 Bryant 171
    Charles 162 163 Harriet 262
    John 141 Jonathan 180 Mary
    141 Nancy 162 163 Patience 7
    Priscilla 94 223 225 Sally 296
    317 Thankful 171

BUFFUM, Joseph 137 Robert Jr
    137
BUMPAS, Jane 93 Lorenzo 332
    Lydia 332
BURBANK, Abigail 222 Dorothy
    260 Jane 82
BURGE, Keziah 97
BURGESS, Martha 24 108 109 153
BURKE, Susannah 14 William 14
BURNELL, Abigail 137 282 Elias
    182 Elizabeth 225 Fanny 182
    Isaac 182 John 56 225 Joseph
    282 Mary 225 265 305 Mehitabel 182 Mehitable 5 194 264
    265 Polly 182 Rachel 182
    Stephen 182 225
BURNHAM, Abigail 317 Amos
    307 Anna 307 Betsey 8 172
    Hannah 17 Hannah E 26 Mary
    18 N Stickney 309 Patience 3
    Sally Martin 307 Solomon 3
    Susannah 10 Thankful H 309
BURNS, Mary E 275
BUTLER, Abigail 183 240 Anne
    163 Annie 163 Hannah 183
    Ivory 240 Lucy 317 318 Sarah
    240 William 119 183 240 317
    William E 183
BUTTERFIELD, Anna 58 Austin
    S 283 Elizabeth 37 Isabella
    283 Jesse 283 John 37 Joseph
    58 80 178 217 263 Laura A 283
    Lydia 37 Mary 58 80 178 217
    Melissa E 283 Sarah 217 Sarah
    Belle 283 Thankful 178
BUTTERIELD, John C 283
BUTTRICK, Esther 228
BUXTON, Ebenezer 21 Eunice 21
BUZZELL, Joanna 67 John 67
    269
BYRNES, Phebe J 280
CAME, 233 Phebe 30
CAMPBELL, George W 286 Mary
    100
CANDAGE, James 166
CANNELL, Hannah 90 Jane 93
    299 Margaret 90 Nancy 16 133
    145 299 309 333 Philip 93 191
    223 299 Philip Jr 93 133
    Rebecca 93 Thomas 90 219
CANNON, Lyn 13

CAPEN, Charles D 40 Ruth 331
  Timothy 331
CARLE, Anna 154 Elias 154 Mary
  154
CARLL, Fanny 318 Nathaniel 318
CARLTON, Elizabeth 10 Hannah
  119 Phineas 10
CARPENTER, Anna 261 Elisha
  261 Laura E 150 Mary 214 267
  Molly 214 Oren F 150 Sarah
  261 Seth 261
CARR, Harriet M 277 Richard 277
  Robert 277
CARSELY, Ebenezer 168
CARSLEY, Betsey 6 Dorcas 36
  Ebenezer 36 Elizabeth 6 John
  168 Mark 6 Mary 168 Patience
  36
CARTER, Abigail 44 Bethiah 117
  Henry 44 Josiah 331 Lucy 44
  Lydia 44 Mercy 331 Thomas
  44
CARVER, Hannah 192 219 225
CATES, Daniel 199 James 128
  Margaret 128 Mary 199
CAVENDER, Abigail 51 52
CHADBOURNE, Benjamin 268
  Elizabeth 8 Ellen 283 Francis
  9 Joseph 8 Joshua 8 Nancy
  Richardson 268 Patience 9
  Rebecca 152 Susanna 8
CHADWICH, Rev 54
CHADWICK, Rev 319
CHAMBERS, Joanna 255 William
  255
CHANDLER, Almira 109 Mary
  152 Mehitabel 61 155 205
  Sarah 205
CHANEY, Mary 48
CHAPMAN, Edward 146 Eleanor
  146 Lydia 146 147 Mary 134
CHARLES, Mehitable 204
CHASE, Abigail 326 Abner 194
  Amos 317 Annis Moore 4
  Axina 101 Caty 163 Eda 140
  Elizabeth 194 295 Elizabeth
  H 186 Ellen R 276 Fanny 326
  Gowel 113 Hall 251 Hannah
  250 Hannah McMillan 251
  Hepsibah 208 Jack 252 Jerusha
  113 John 295 John Elden 326

CHASE (continued)
  Joseph 4 20 317 Katherine 163
  Lavinia 29 Lydia 250 Marshall
  Spring 251 Mary 194 252
  Nathan W 4 Nathaniel 4 Olive
  4 20 317 Oliver 163 Rebecca
  193 Samuel 250 330 Sarah 152
  201 Thomas 252 Wilbur T 276
CHECKLEY, Samuel 322
CHEEVER, Rev Mr 189
CHENEY, Mary 319 320
CHERRY, Capt 224
CHESLEY, Eunice 248 Joseph
  248 Susanna 248
CHICK, Abby B 79 Abigail 39 90
  213 301 Adeline 279 Betsey 39
  Elizabeth 39 Ephraim 82 300
  Eunice 26 39 81 82 332
  Frances A 301 Hannah 232
  Henry S 301 James Monroe 301
  James Small 300 James Stillman 79 Joseph E 301 Lavinia
  301 Levi 97 Lydia Maria 301
  Mary 90 Mary Jane 301
  Nathan 232 Noah Bennett 301
  Peter 39 82 90 Phebe 300
  Phebe Cobb 301 Rhoda 301
  Samuel Bradbury 301 Sarah E
  301 Sarah Eliza 301 Selina 97
  232 Sophia Ann 300 Susan R
  301 William 232
CHIPMAN, Mary 114
CHOATE, 76 George G 76 Widow
  76
CHRISTY, Lucy 161 Richard 161
CHURCH, Benjamin 55 Mary 55
CHUTE, Olive 109 Sarah 19
CLARK, Abigail 2 Abraham 2
  Andrew Jackson 274 Benjamin
  300 Elizabeth 2 242 Emily J
  300 Ephraim 35 62 Eunice 9
  Fanny 302 Hannah R 185 188
  James 9 John 161 300 319
  Joseph 242 Lydia 34 Martha A
  274 Mehitable Y 300 Morris
  300 Orrin 300 Sally 59 Sarah 59
  Susan E 300 Sylvia 257 Valentine 2 William 59
CLAY, Anna 334 Harriet 214 Jane
  334 Jonathan 334 William 334
CLEAVES, Elizabeth 7 Mary C 6

CLEAVES (continued)
  Patience 7 Robert 3 Robert Jr 7 Susannah 3
CLEMENT, Dolly D 289 George 289 Mary Ann 120 Simeon G 120
CLEMENTS, Betty 288
CLEMMONS, Ruth W 268
CLEMONS, Joanna Hutchinson 268 John L 268
CLOUDMAN, Sarah 294
COBB, David 292 Ebenezer 126 Elisha Jr 36 Joanna 208 Mary 36 50 126 252 Molly 36 Phebe 300
COCHRANE, James 169 Jane 169 Janet 169 Jennet 169
COCKS, Joshua 166 Tabitha 166
CODMAN, Richard 46 103 116 154 203 264 273
COFFIN, Benjamin 9 Enoch 24 Joanna 177 Mary 24 237 Rebecca 262 Simeon 237 Tristram 177
COLBURN, Catherine 42 Jerathnael Sr 42
COLBY, Frances 134 Hannah 13 Israel 13
COLE, Daniel Jr 250 Hannah 195 J 110 Jemima 83 109 John 224 Lydia 74 Martha 110 Patty 224 Polly 224 Sally 133 Sarah 47 132 Sarah Ann 250 William 224
COLEMAN, Martha 202
COLLAMORE, Dolly 196 Ezekiel 196 Rebecca P 31
COLLEY, Belinda T 24 Mary 215 217 Molly 211 236
CONANT, Hannah 92
CONVERSE, Keziah 249
COOK, Eunice 128 Hannah S 223 Joanna 93 154 Mercy 69 138 Peggy 59 William M 223
COOKSON, Elizabeth 136 Jemima 95 John 20 95 John Jr 136 Lucy 161 Marcy 19 Martha 19 161 Mary 19 95 161 289 323 324 326 Mercy 19 20 Reuben 95 161 323 324

COOLBROTH, Ann McCardy 293 Lydia 174
COOLEY, Bridget 330
COOLIDGE, Elizabeth 87 Silas 87
COOPER, Elinor 181
CORLISS, Lucinda 4 134 135
CORNER, Mary Ann 176
COSS, Mary 72 114
COTTLE, Sarah 218
COTTON, John 318 Lydia 173 Molly 106
COUCH, Lydia 223 225 278
COVELL, Hannah 155 156
COWAN, Abigail 247 John 247
COX, 220 Capt 85 Catherine 117 Joshua 166 Mary 170 Mary Josslyn 220 Mrs 85 Tabitha 166 William 220
CRAM, Abigail 135 279 Anna 42 Bethiah 279 Bradley 128 Caroline O 229 Chloe 135 227 228 Daniel 36 42 104 135 Daniel Jr 227 228 Eliza 279 Eunice 279 Greenleaf 135 John 279 John Gardiner 279 Joseph 279 Levi 42 Lydia 279 Marcella 156 Mary 182 279 Mercy 227 Nehemiah 40 Peter 182 Sarah 42 104 Susan 128 228 Thomas 104 143 228 230 290 Weare 227
CRANMORE, Hannah 101
CRAWFORD, George D 301 Mary Jane 301
CRESSEY, Ashley 108 Hannah 170 John 108 Joseph 108 118 158 Martha 108 214 Noah 170 Sarah 170 307
CROCKER, Abigail 148 149 Elizabeth 220 Hannah 13 162 Mary 13 Molly 13 Timothy 7 13 159 162 196
CROCKETT, Abigail 179 Amy Ruhama 306 Ephraim 306 Eunice 102 George 290 Henry 306 Hezekiah 102 John 179 Martha 306 Mary 179 Nancy 290 Peter 179 Polly 179 Priscilla 191 Rebecca 119 Susan 239 Tryphena 240
CROMWELL, Lydia 256

CROSBY, Mercy 113
CROSS, Aaron 136 Abigail 40 183 240 Elsie 54 Isaac E 222 June 283 Lois 54 Martha 222 Miriam 136 Patty 222 William W 54
CROSTON, Gregory 184 Lucinda 184
CUMMINGS, Anna 174 Elsie 254 John 103 Jonathan Jr 77 Lucy 172 Mehitabel 205 217 Nancy 103 Rachel 217 Sarah 174 Stephen 77 Susanna 91 Thomas 91 205 217 William 174
CUPTILL, Abigail 283
CURRIER, Anna 10
CUSHING, Loring 125
CUSHMAN, Abigail 196 Appolos 196 Mary 81
CUTTS, Caroline 139
DAM, Elizabeth 20
DANA, Frances A 153 William 153
DAVENPORT, Ephraim 250 Rebecca 290
DAVIES, Anna 236 Edward E 236
DAVIS, Aaron 99 Abigail 54 Apphia 221 Betsy 8 Charity 150 157 295 Charles 29 Chloe 312 327 Daniel 8 David 276 Desire 209 276 Eliphalet 87 Elisha 148 150 Esther 295 296 325 Ezra 23 207 Hannah 86 Ichabod Bowdoin 205 Isaac 242 James 50 188 312 327 John 163 221 John H 228 Joseph 166 295 Josiah 166 Lydia 99 Martha 87 276 Mary 23 29 150 160 242 295 Mehitabel 155 205 207 Mehitable 61 205 Melintha S 228 Melvina 284 Mercy 71 126 137 Nancy 327 Nathaniel 144 312 327 Nicholas 54 157 230 265 295 Noah 150 Orrin 284 Paulina 148 Phebe 188 Ruth 276 Ruth Ann Maria 276 Salome M 265 Samuel Jr 242 Sarah 23 42 46 150 166 187 Sarah Moor 163 Susan 148 150 Susannah 207 Thankful 166 188 Thomas 276 William 86 295

DAVOL, Ann 260
DAY, Betty 44 Dolly 241 James 44
DEAN, John 19 24 105 132 168 181 195 203 205 221 247 299 314 331 Miriam 105 184 Rachel 105 201 Rev Dr 197 Samuel 62 63 264
DEANE, Eunice 198 John 116 290 Samuel 85 87 198
DEARBORN, Almeda 284 Anna 215 250 Benjamin 215 Elizabeth 212 Jacob 177 212 Keziah 28 206 Lydia 212 Mary 7 107 215 Nancy 177 Polly 16 82 302 William Henry 284
DECKER, Catherine 95 140 314 Charles 96 328 Dorcas 95 140 Eunice 314 Harriet 109 John 95 140 314 Lydia 96 328 Martha 140 Moses 140 Sarah 58 159
DENNETT, Mary 120 139 Nicholas 139 Nicholas Jr 139 Olive 30 Phebe 139 Polly 139 Samuel 120 121 139 Sarah 139 170
DILLINGHAM, Henry 334 Martha 334
DIMOCK, Ebenezer 65 Marguerite 65 Melissa Ellen 65
DINGLEY, Abigail 128 Charles 128 Mary 304
DINSDALE, Abigail 9 Sarah 186
DINSDALL, Sally 71
DINSMOOR, Mary 169
DODGE, Betsy 314 Caleb 161 Eleanor 161 Mehitable 136 Sarah 161
DOLE, Daniel 104 137 197 221 Daniel 12 Mary W 104 Sarah 197
DOLEVER, Jemima 93
DOLLIVER, Jemima 69 93-95 225 268 332 John 93
DOLLOFF, Almon H 150 Gene A 150
DONNELL, Abigail O 280 Charles A 280 Mary 33 Sarah T 294
DORE, Mary 158
DORIFY, John 88 Lois 88 Susie 88

DORSET, Joanna 222 Patience 257 Peter 222 Sylvanous B 257
DORSETT, Lucy 78 Peter 78 Salome 236 Susan 133 236
DOUGHTY, Enoch M 21 Jane 21 John M 21
DOUGLAS, Elizabeth 120
DOUGLASS, Hannah 308
DOW, 142 Abigail 15 139 Abner 15 108 114 267 289 321 Catherine 104 Dorothy 114 203 227 Emeline 104 Jabez 114 203 227 228 313 323 Joseph 56 104 227 228 267 Lucy 104 227 228 267 Martha 15 114 289 Mercy 289 Sarah 203 Susannah 104 176
DRESSER, Angelina 30 Cassandra 58 Charity Ann 29 Daniel R 30 Jane 29 Joanna F 148 Jonathan 77 Joseph 30 Mark 29 Olive 30 Sally 29 Sarah 77 William A 29 William D 30 William H 58 Winthrop 148
DREW, Chesley 2 Elizabeth 237 Jane 2 Jenny 2 Joseph 237 Martha McLellan 2 Sally 2 Winborn Adams 2
DUDLEY, Mary Elizabeth 153 Myron S 153
DUNHAM, Elijah 84 Eliza 70 Mary 288
DUNN, Mary A 314
DURANT, Cornelius 200
DUREN, Abraham 152 Caroline Augusta 152 Mary 152 Mary Ann 152 Warren 152
DURGIN, Abigail 141 Jane 24 Naomi 142 Nathaniel 24
DURHAM, Elizabeth 80 John 80
DUSTIN, Polly 160
DUSTON, Ezekiel 331 Ruth 331
DUTCH, Almira 273 Betsey 136 Elizabeth 136 George 136 Hannah 269
DYER, Abigail 158 159 191 281 Arthur 302 Benjamin 281 Benjamin D 282 Christina 256 Daniel 79 Deborah 107 279 281 Dorcas 297 299 Isaac 158 John 107 Leona 302 Levi 329

DYER (continued) Lydia 220 Mary 107 158 173 282 Mercy 173 Mrs Levi 329 Nancy 302 Naomi 329 Nathaniel 332 Olive 159 Rebecca 108 206 Sally 326 Susan 154 171 Watson 158 White 159 Zilpha 300
DYMOND, Hannah 178
EAMES, Mary F 47 Thomas 47
EARLY, Anthony 202 Mehitable 202 Olive 202
EASTMAN, Benjamin 75 Job 75 Sarah 4 75
EASTON, Lucy 73
EATON, Electa Goodenough 106 George R 194 Hannah 28 Henry 27 Israel 72 216 Jemima 216 John 28 206 John G 28 John Green 28 206 Josiah G 28 Keziah 28 206 Lucy 72 Mary 28 Mary Elizabeth 27 Relief 217 Sarah 216 Sarah Jane 194 Tamson 28
EDGECOMB, Abigail 326 Gibbins 326 Isaac L 310 John L 326 Martha 326 Mary Ann 310 Rachel 157 Sarah 23
EDGERLEY, Annie Elizabeth 252
EDMONDS, Mehitable 36
EDWARDS, Diana 131 Eliza 131 John 131 Susanna 191
ELBRIDGE, Abiah 333 Nathan W 333
ELDEN, Dorcas 316 John 316
ELDER, Jane 46 Mary J 102 Miriam 226 Molly 131 175 237 259 293 Peter 102
ELLIOT, Martha Ann 302 Rhoda 47
ELLIS, Eunice M 233 Hiram 233
ELLS, Mehitable 310 Sarah M 318
ELLSWORTH, Patience 315
ELMORE, Phoebe 147
ELWELL, Abigail 41 Annie 149 Bethiah 124 262 Diadema 309 Elizabeth 262 Erastus W 309 George 148 Hannah Elizabeth 309 Isaac B 41 Joanna F 148 Jonathan 41 168 171 Levi 309 Mary 41 Nancy 148

ELWELL (continued)
  Rachel 135 171 Rhoda 78 Ruth
  276 Sarah 124 125 262 William
  93 293
EMERSON, 76 Joshua 76 Lucinda 148
EMERY, Isaac 251 Joshua 86
  Martha 86 Sarah 251
ESTES, James 333 Julia A 29
  Mary 333 Olive 18 Stephen 18
  Sylvanus Bean 29
ESTILL, Mary 269
EVANS, Ann 251 Charles K 283
  Elizabeth 251 John 251 Sarah
  Belle 283
FABYAN, Mehitable 100 Phebe
  71
FAIRBANKS, Caroline M 31
FAIRFIELD, John 263 Mary 263
FARNSWORTH, Betsy 179
  Nancy 179 Samuel 179 Samuel
  Jr 179
FARNUM, Abigail O 280 Francis
  S 280 George H 280 John L 280
  John P 280 Joseph D 280
  Joseph H 280 Lemuel P 280
  Margaret 280 Phebe J 280
  Samuel T 280 Sarah H 280
  Thomas T 280
FARRINGTON, Hannah 86 Henry
  27 Lois J 126 Martha Ann 27
  William 86
FARWELL, Anne 210 Henry 210
  Lydia 210 Melvin 241 Rhoda
  241
FELCH, Abijah 34 Harriet Ripley
  35 John 35 Lydia 34 Sarah 34
FENDERSON, John Jr 61 Keziah
  61
FERGUSON, Eliza H 135
FESSENDEN, George 333 Hannah
  333 Mary 121 William 121
FICKETT, Anna 150 Daniel 150
  Eliza C 150 Ezra 154 Sally 154
FIELD, Hannah 21 Rachel 21
  Tabitha 21 Zachariah 21
FIFIELD, Rachel 37 136 137 223
  285
FILES, Abigail 237 238 Ebenezer
  131 175 237 259 Edward 237
  Elizabeth 175

FILES (continued)
  Esther 201 202 238 Hannah 237
  Molly 131 175 237 259 Mrs 329
  Patience 202 Polly 131 Robert
  202 Samuel 201 202 238 Sarah
  259 Statira 201 Temperance G
  4 Thomas 201 William E 175
  237
FISHER, Jonathan 44
FITCH, Betsy 179 Deborah 267
  Elizabeth 105 Zachariah 199
FLATT, Margaret 87
FLETCHER, Abraham 59 John
  318 Margaret 59 Pendleton 51
  Rachel 318
FLINT, Eleazar 267 268 Eleazer
  Jr 322 Elizabeth 216 Ephraim
  267 John C 229 John Cummings 216 Lucy 229 Olive S
  105 Phebe 267 Richard T 105
FLOOD, Abby T 321 Ann 195
  Anna 195 Calvin 321 Lydia 195
  Mary 214 321 Morris 195
FOGG, Abigail 154 Anna 20 297
  Betsey 20 Charles 20 297
  David 20 Dolly 331 Dorcas 82
  Dorothy 297 Elizabeth 306
  Hannah 103 209 297 Joseph 14
  Leah 113 Lemuel 297 Louisa
  215 Lydia 60 Mary 108 Mercy
  14 Moses 215 Persis Mercy 14
  Rebecca 297 Reuben 164
  Stephen 297 Wilmot 61
FOLSOM, Abigail 89
FONTAINE, Francis 248 Mary
  248 Polly 248
FOOTE, Bathsheba 245
FORBES, Margaret 218 Zadoc
  218
FOSDICK, Abigail 123 Nathaniel
  F 123
FOSS, Abigail 98 Agnes 176 201
  243 Albert M 284 Alonzo 284
  Ann 38 Anna 307 Aralinda 149
  Benjamin 99 Dorcas 316
  Ebenezer 332 333 Eleanor 17
  Elizabeth 109 Ellen 284
  Eunice 39 329 332 George 99
  Greenville Monroe 149 Hannah
  5 17 109 Job 17 39 149 332
  John 109 284 333 Joseph 98

FOSS (continued)
  Lena Gove 149 Lucinda 149
  Martha 26 Mary 17 99 333
  Mary S 284 Mrs John 109
  Nancy 38 Pauline G 149 Polly
  333 Randall 332 Randall M 17
  Thankful Deborah 284 Veranus
  284
FOSTER, Asahel 64 Eben 59
  Hannah 38 Hannah H 296
  Isaiah 60 Lucy 136 Lydia 60
  75 Moody 139 Sarah 75 77
  Susan 59 Thomas 296 Wilmot
  60 61
FOWEL, Sarah 176
FOWLER, Mary 127
FOY, John 112 Ruth 112
FREEMAN, Elizabeth 35 36 225
  Eunice 187 256 George 33 80
  285 286 Hannah 33 34 John 211
  Jonathan 126 Joshua 33 134
  286 Joshua Jr 198 Katherine
  212 286 Lois 198 Lucy 233 286
  Lydia 261 Margaret 55 Martha
  80 285 Patience 33 Reuben 34
  94 212 255 286 Samuel 17 211
  250 Sarah 126 286 William 286
FREESE, Anna 215
FRENCH, Charles 327 Lucy
  Maria 327 Sarah Anna 309
FRENCY, Lucy Maria 327
FRINK, Rebecca 214
FROST, 50 66 Abigail 13 331
  Anna 68 165 Benjamin 173 208
  Betty 93 173 David 128 Dominicus 15 Dorothy 214 Elizabeth
  164 Eunice 68 Hannah Atkins
  108 James 67 79 164 Jeremiah
  108 Joshua W 307 Love 164
  Margaret 128 Mary 108 Mary
  Higgins 307 Nancy 67 277
  Nathaniel 108 Pauline 208
  Phineas 13 Polly 131 Sarah 66
  Susanna 15 173 Susannah 208
  Thomas 13 331 Wingate 50 67
  68 164 165
FRY, John 281
FRYE, Bethia 63 213 312 John
  313 Joseph 229 312 Nathan 312
  Sarah 312 Simon 160

FULLER, Betty 137 Hannah 221
  Lydia Ann 262
FURLONG, Mary 70
GAGE, Huldah 262 Joanna 262
  Moses 262
GAMMON, Joshua 40 Lorenzo
  285 Melinda 285 Ruth Wadsworth 40
GAREY, Lucy 219
GARLAND, Abigail 174 236
GARLING, James 70 Mary 70
GATES, Susan 120
GAY, Andrew R 128 Ann Rebecca
  128
GENT, George 255 Thankful 255
GERRISH, Sarah 232 William 35
  58 59 76 125 134 254 272 323
GERRY, Hannah S 223 Horace 300
  Lucy A 241 Lydia Ann 300
  Samuel 241
GETCHELL, Lounda 292 Warren
  292
GIBBS, Ezra 11
GIBSON, Hannah 124 161 Jacob
  124 161
GILES, Mary 124
GILKEY, J 270 Mary 42 178
GILMAN, David 308 Ebenezer 307
  308 Ebenezer Jr 45 Elizabeth
  317 Fanny 307 Frances 307
  Hannah 45 Irene 308 Isaac 321
  Jonathan 317 Lucy A 45 Lydia
  307 308 Sally Irish 321
GIVEN, Mary 282
GLOVER, John 201
GOAD, Edward 144 Mary 144
GODGDON, Caleb 101
GOODENOW, John 251 Rebecca
  251 Sally C 251
GOODRIDGE, Nancy 61
GOODWIN, Anna 288 Betsy 287
  Dominicus 287 Hannah 287
  Ichabod Sr 288 Susan 191
  Ursula Cushman 87 William C
  87
GOOKIN, Simon 94
GOOLD, Olivia 262
GORDAN, Abigail 148 Margaret
  279 Nancy 329
GORDEN, Abigail 289 330 332

GORDEN (continued)
  Sarah 231 313
GORDON, Abigail 12 59 242 245
  Ann 101 Betsey 101 Daniel 101
  Hannah 245 Lydia 101
GORE, Caroline Mussey 120
  Martin 120
GORHAM, David 159 Jason 151
  Mary 66 Sarah J 151 Thankful
  67 166
GOSSUM, Betsey 144 Elias 145
  Elijah 145 Hannah 145 Ira 145
  John Dean 145 Joshua 145
  Marbie 144 Mary 144 Rachel
  145 Rebecca 144 Sally 145
  Samuel 144
GOTT, Rachel 88
GOULD, Anna E 135 Clement 50
  Eunice 99 George 177 Jonathan
  24 125 132 263 Jonathan Jr 151
  Jonathan Sr 151 Moses 51
  Rachel 285 Sarah 177
GOVE, Eunice 32
GRAFFAM, Elizabeth 203 283
  Sarah 225 294
GRANT, Elizabeth 192 Lucy H
  127 Mehitable 316
GRAY, 48 Alexander 48 49 319
  Anna 92 Elizabeth 316 Eunice
  238 George 238 Hannah 129
  284 James 284 James M 60
  Jane 125 John 63 316 Martha
  59 60 306 Mary 72 Olive 20 47
  316 Patience 141 Sarah 172
  Susanna 63 Tabitha 59 Taylor
  59
GREEN, Daniel 299 Eliza 150
  Esther 233 243 John 45 150
  233 239 243 258 Joseph 150
  301 Leona 302 Mary 45 150
  193 199 239 243 258 297 299
  334 Mary M 234 Molly 154
  Phebe Cobb 301 Rebecca 45
  Ruhamah 172 Salome 40 239
  Sarah 42 56 104 Sophia Ann
  300 Susan 232 William 300
  William F 234 Wyer 172
GREENLAW, John 86 Lucy 86
  Mary 86 Richard 86
GREENLEAF, Joseph William 65
  Mary S 64

GREGG, Elizabeth 169
GROSS, Abigail 76 George 76
GROVER, Dolly 14 Elijah 14
  George W 14 Hadassah 14
GROW, Hannah 47
GUILFORD, Elizabeth 279 John
  279 Margaret 279 281
GUPTILL, Charles W 149 Elizabeth 282 Ellen Augusta 149
  James 121 Mehitable C 121
  Samuel 282
GUSTIN, Darius 83 Susan Melissa
  83
HADLEY, Sarah 313
HAGGETT, Joseph 102 Rebecca
  P 102
HAINES, Betsey L 82 Clarissa W
  297 Mary 329 Polly 297
  Thomas 297
HALE, Almira 34 Benjamin 311
  Joseph 34 Susanna 311
HALEY, Charity 157 295 Margaret
  28 157 158 160 324 Rachel 157
  Susannah 54 William 157
HALL, Abigail 70 Catherine 69 70
  140 305 314 Charles 69 71 181
  182 225 268 332 Daniel 100
  Dorcas 71 140 Edward 212
  Elizabeth 55 136 Emma 71 332
  Eunice 70 Hannah 100 Hatevil
  168 218 Jemima 53 69 225 268
  332 John 53 71 140 332 Levi
  100 305 Lydia 10 11 41 63 71
  182 211 216 227 328 Marbie
  144 Margaret 100 Margarette
  301 Mary 14 100 212 245
  Naoma 140 292 332 Naomi 332
  Nathan 144 Noami 53 Oliver 71
  140 Phebe 89 Rebecca 267 268
  Ruth 218 Sarah 219 225 284
  Sarah Jane 40 William 14 301
  William S 40 Winslow 100
HALLOWELL, Arthur 283 David
  242 Elizabeth 242 Hannah 283
  Lucy E 283
HAM, Elizabeth J 315
HAMBLEN, Anna 36 Deborah 20
  231 306 Ebenezer 231 Gershom
  20 306 Hanna 92 Hannah 20
  118 306 Jerusha 231 Samuel
  231 306 Sarah 209 Seth 231

HAMBLEN (continued)
　Seth L 231 Susanna 231
　Temperance 231 Timothy 36
　44
HAMBLIN, Abby 105 Cotton 105
HAMILTON, Sarah 164
HAMLEN, Elizabeth 170
HAMLIN, Charles 104 E Cotton
　104 Ebenezer 194 Esther 218
　Francis 194 Francis Jr 194
　Hannah 218 Joseph 218 Lucy
　104 Rebecca 194 Sally 194
HAMMOND, Eunice 191 192
HAMMONS, Almira 258
HANCOCK, Anna 308 Elizabeth
　78 83 109 Hannah 27 109 308
　Joanna 251 John L 308 John
　Lane 27 109 Polly 297 Ruth H
　27 Stephen 109 Susan 309
HANLEY, Col 3
HANSCOM, Abigail 154 Almon
　White 257 George 154 Hannah
　154 Sarah 158 Susannah 207
　William 158
HANSCOMB, Abigail Water
　HOUSE 257
HANSON, Almon 31 Augusta 31
　Cora 149 Cynthia 237 Ezekiel
　304 Huldah 304 Joseph 237
　Lucy A 177 Martha 191 304
　Moses 191 Sarah 261
HARDEN, Joseph 37 Sally 37
HARDING, Agnes 176 243
　Amanda 319 Amaziah 30 118
　Anna 36 Caroline 257 Eliza
　321 Elizabeth 210 211 294
　Elkanah 176 Hannah 30 176
　319 Hiram 319 John 41 Lettice
　30 Martha 176 Mary 41 58 80
　178 217 Phebe 118 Seth L 94
　Thankful 5 41 190 Thomas 118
　William 176 243
HARDY, Charles 277 Jane 334
　John 334 Mary 224 Mary
　Baldwin 277 Samuel 11 Sarah
　11 Waitie 277
HARMON, Abigail 175 222 Anna
　175 Benjamin 290 Caroline 281
　Dominicus 326 Ebenezer 47
　Edward 172 Eliza Ann 326
　Elizabeth 62 174 195 294

HARMON (continued)
　Elliot 19 Eunice 112 Fanny
　305 Jane 47 Joanna 222 John
　175 Josiah 175 Levi 326 Lucy
　112 Lydia 103 294 Mary 164
　Mary Ann 165 Rachel 172
　Rebecca 290 Rufus 112 Rufus
　Jr 112 Sarah 45 Sarah A 45
　Thomas 164 Wealthy S 167
　William 175 222 294 Zebulon
　K 147
HARTSHORN, Caroline 316
　William 316
HARVEY, Hannah 203 270 271
　John 160
HASELTON, Sally 40
HASKELL, 25 28 Abigail 39 90
　168 257 295 298 Anne 102
　Benjamin 243 261 295 298
　Betsey 236 Daniel 145 Eleanor
　E 79 Eliza 23 26 Ephraim 82
　Ephraim Chick 26 Eugene M
　27 Eunice 26 39 82 Francis 82
　83 Hannah 17 39 332 James
　Edwin 27 Jemima 83 John 26
　27 39 82 332 John Franklin 27
　Jonathan 83 Levi Quimby 257
　295 Lydia 261 Mark 76 Martha
　Ann 27 Mary 102 145 261 Mary
　Elizabeth 27 Mary Freeman
　261 Mehitable 82 Mehitable B
　27 Mehitable York 83 Nancy 63
　Nathaniel Boulter 27 Polly 243
　Rebecca 298 Rebecca Linnell
　27 Rhoda 131 Sally 295 298
　Sarah 243 257 Solomon 17 39
　82 William 23 145 William
　Gould 27
HASTINGS, Dorcas 151 152 Lydia
　151 Samuel 151 Sophia 252
　Timothy 13
HASTY, Anna Clark 127 Daniel 56
　74 98 116 159 175 Daniel Jr 74
　176 Hiram 175 James 69 201
　Martha 56 74 175 176 Mary 98
　175 Miriam 201 Rachel 69 201
　Sarah 56 Sukey 74 Susannah 74
　176 William 161
HATCH, Ephraim 269 Harriet C
　325 Henry C 325 Laura A 283
　Mary Ann 269 Mrs Henry 325

HAVEN, Charlotte 185 Eleanor 185 James W 185 John G 185 Mary M 185 Sarah S 185
HAWKES, Briant 189 Joseph 21 Joshua 188 189 211 Lucy 188 189 211 Nancy 211 212 Olive 21 Samuel 212 Susan 212
HAWLEY, Eunice 79 80
HAY, Charlotte 75 214 267 John 267
HAYES, James 255 Ruth 255
HEARD, Elizabeth 247
HEATH, Ann 170 Ann M 33 Asa 33 170 Bartholomew 170 Betsey 39 Betsey Boulter 306 Catherine 306 Nicholas 28 306 Ruth 28 306 Sarah 33 170
HERICK, Rachel 88
HERRICK, Humphrey 88 Nancy 88 Samuel 88
HIBBERT, Hannah 213
HICKS, Ebenezer 195 Ephraim 172 195 Rachel 172 195 Susan 195
HIGGINS, Abigail 149 246 281 Adeline 31 Ann 212 Apphia 200 236 Barnabas 242 Chesley 149 187 Ebenezer 24 74 83 153 206 257 274 Ebenezer Jr 24 Edmund 155 Elisha 25 135 Eliza 150 166 Elizabeth 24 83 153 154 185 187 206 306 310 311 334 Elkanah 24 83 153 Elvira 150 Enoch 69 Enoch F 69 184 Ephraim 18 83 216 Esther 155 195 240 Experience 17 18 138 240 Hannah 83 98 155 156 195 247 261 Happy 212 311 Huldah 166 Isabella 187 Ivory Page 150 Jemima 83 John 289 John Dean 184 Joseph 69 138 212 Knowles 98 150 248 Lucy 101 Marcia Anne 184 Martha 24 25 129 130 140 153 216 290 309 320 332 Martha D 289 Mary 83 206 216 240 Mary B 149 150 Mary J 242 Mercy 69 138 185 256 Miriam 69 83 184 257 274 Phebe 166 187 Prince 149 240 Rebecca 18 135 206 240

HIGGINS (continued) Reliance 138 259 320 Reuben 195 Robert 31 244 246 247 256 261 311 Rosanna F 259 Samuel 140 Sarah 31 256 260 310 311 Selina 149 240 Seth 24 130 138 240 320 Thankful 156 157 320 Timothy 110 138 259 320 William 140 153 166 187 246 311 Zacheus 98 140 Zacheus Jr 247
HIGHT, Elisha 250 Elizabeth 194 Lydia 250
HILL, Charles 86 Charlotte 86 Daniel 43 143 Johnson 306 Mary 306
HILLARD, Elizabeth 234
HILLMAN, Cyrus Stebbins 33 Mary M 33 Samuel 33
HILTON, Abigail 41 Hannah 9 Nathan 9 Sarah 308
HINCKLEY, Martha 15 74 289 Mary 59 72 Stephen 72 74 230
HOBBY, Hensley 55 John 201 Rachel 55
HOBSON, Ellen Frances 186
HOCKEY, Joseph 31 Mary 31
HODGDON, Abigail 101 Israel 101 John 320 Lucy 101 Nancy 279 320
HODGES, Miriam 68 105
HODSDON, Ann E 240 Eliza Ann 158 Israel 158 Zillah 158
HOLBROOK, Elizabeth 120 Jane 36 Sally 29 Samuel 120
HOLLINGSWORTH, Elizabeth 114
HOLT, Chloe 312 313 Elizabeth 312 John 313 Mary 14 103 Nathaniel 32
HOOK, Mary 7
HOOPER, Abigail 326 Elizabeth 295
HOPKINS, Desier 130 Desire 130 Hannah 22 206 Joshua 320 Josiah 98 206 Mark B 167 Mercy 110 239 320 Nancy 167 Nathaniel 130 Pamelia 247 Rebecca 247 320 Sarah 206 Theodore 22 206 247 Theodoreus 140 Theodorus 111 113

HOPKINS (continued)
  Thomas 64 123 William 113
HOPKINSON, Emeline 190 Susan 229
HORN, Martha 50 William 50
HORR, Abraham 95 Mary 95
HORSE, Nellie 238
HORTON, Abigail 80
HOUGHTON, Thankful 303
HOW, Abigail 179 Christopher 201 Daniel 179 Elizabeth 201
HOWARD, Caroline 297 Charles 297 Mary 136
HOWE, Abigail 90 Catherine 72 250 252 Dorothy 121 Ebenezer 72 77 121 157 250 252 Eliza 250 Eliza R 72 Frances 204 Greenleaf 72 Lydia 11 Mary 72 Sarah 252
HOXIE, Rose A 109
HOYT, Abigail 99 Annie M 280 Benjamin 282 Elizabeth 294 Jane 316 John 280 Mary 282 Phebe 280
HUBBARD, Anna 286 Delinda 332 Dorcas 268 John 332
HUMPHREY, Enos 334 Sally 334
HUNT, Abigail Whitney 138 Rebecca 59
HUNTRESS, Sally 97
HURD, Amy 114 Hannah 118 206
HUSSEY, Benjamin 296 Emily Maria 275 James A 275 Mary 100 Phebe 296
HUTCHERSON, Mark 327 Mary 327 Mary E 327
HUTCHINS, Eunice 34 Huldah S 31 Isaac 24 Sarah 24
HUTCHINSON, Abigail 228 Elizabeth 215 268 Gov 125 Hannah 39 Joshua 228 Joshua Jr 147 Mary 233 Matthias 39 228 233 Molly 228 Nancy 39 233 Sally 147 Sophronia B 39
HYLER, Katherine 254
ILLESLEY, Betty 122 Daniel 122 Elizabeth 122 Enoch 330 Isaac 56 161 Isaac Jr 36 87 Mary 122
INDIAN, Chief Sackett 115 Lois Smith 46

INGALLS, Benjamin 51 191 Elizabeth J 136 Mary 191 Nancy 66 Polly 219 Sarah F 268 Susan 66 266
INGERSOLL, Deborah 262 Elizabeth 125 William 125
INGRAHAM, Edward 114 Joseph 57 207 Joseph Holt 121
IRISH, Abigail 229 Adeline 152 Amy 37 Benjamin 36 180 Catherine R 229 Daniel 229 Deliverance 37 172 Elizabeth 218 Esther 36 James 152 Jenny 36 Miriam 218 Obediah 296 Phebe 101 Rebecca 152 Sally 322 Sarah 322 Susan 242 243 Susanna 92 172 Susannah 62 128 172 Thomas 37 172 218 322
JACK, Ira 27 Mehitable B 27
JACKSON, Affia 48 Ann 61 62 Daniel 77 Emily Jane 156 Francis 61 Hannah 179 Jane G 77 Joseph 77 Lydia 180 Mary 70 Priscilla 233 Rachel 62 217
JACOBS, Anne E 126 Charles 126 Charles R 126 Eleanor F R 126 Fannie P 126 Jane 218 Jesse Eaton 218 Lucretia Ann 126 Lucy Lowell 126 Nancy 126 Nathaniel 126 William S 126
JAMES, Betsey 140 Elizabeth 14K0 Samuel 140 Susanna 226 William 140
JELLISON, Patience 3
JENKINS, Abiah 114 Deborah 20 306 Dennis 232 Grace 232 Josiah 311 Mary 114 Paul 3 Samuel 114 Sarah 3
JENNESS, Annie M 280
JEWELL, Charlotte 135 Elizabeth 11 12 Jacob 130 Mary Jane 130 Matilda 309
JEWETT, Daniel 101 James 68 Joseph 68 Lydia 101 Mary 68
JOHNSON, Bethia 312 Betsey 119 309 Daniel 329 Desire 82 Elisha 32 Eliza 54 275 Elizabeth 140 202 203 226 229 277 Esther 32 314 Eunice 329 Fletcher 32 Hannah 28

JOHNSON (continued)
Hannah B 79 Hannah Bangs 309 Hannah Elizabeth 309 Henry 119 Herman Whitney 310 Isaac 28 Isaac L 79 309 James 314 James B 215 Jeremiah 149 John 202 Jonathan 314 Joseph 329 Lucretia D 310 Lucy 215 Lydia 314 Mary 149 329 Mary A 78 Mary Ann 79 Mary Lamper 236 Mary T 28 Mary Thankful 310 Nathan R 310 Phebe A 310 Portius 61 Royal A 78 79 310 Ruth 32 255 Sarah 202 291 Susannah 6 Thankful 255 Thesis 61 Thia 61 Waitie 277 William 312 William H 236 William Jr 309

JOHNSTON, Bethia 63 312 William 312

JONES, Abigail 57 188 227 Elizabeth 159 Ephraim 51 71 73 80 81 85 99 125 197 198 200 202 210 272 289 312 323 Ephraim Jr 200 202 Hannah 144 257 271 273 Henry 202 John 65 144 273 332 333 Judith 200 Lydia 63 65 202 Mary 85 144 197 200 273 332 333 Mary F 32 Mary Jane 65 Mehitable 82 83 144 299 332 Mercy 144 Mrs 137 Sally 144 145 333 Sarah 130 144 333

JORDAN, Abigail 128 Achsah 188 Benjamin Allen 188 Caroline M 290 Catherine 108 Charles 202 Charles E 290 Dominicus 207 Elizabeth 95 Hannah 118 218 248 Isaac 128 James 95 218 Joshua 255 Lydia 158 160 203 316 317 323 324 Margaret E 274 Mary 140 Miriam 164 Phebe 218 Polly 140 Rebecca 202 Rishworth 3 Samuel 51 Sarah 3 182 188 207 208 William 202

JORDON, Lydia 52

JOSSLYN, Mary 220

JUDKINS, Hannah M 326

KEENE, Daniel 87 Lucy 87

KELLEY, Elizabeth 25 Isaac 225 Sarah 225

KELLOCK, Lucy Lewis 255 Samuel 255

KELLY, Isaac 2 Lucy Moulton 223 Lydia 225 Nancy 2 Peter 182

KENDALL, Anna 14 Bezaleel 14 Eunice 14

KENDRICK, Mary 141 313

KENNARD, Susanna 193 245 Susannah 164 213 286

KENNERSON, Benjamin 39 Eliza Anne 40 Isaac 40 Lydia 39 40 Nathaniel 39 40 Olive 39

KENNISON, Lucinda 97

KEYES, Dolly 13 Francis 13

KILBORN, Enos L W 241 Rhoda 241

KILGORE, Alice 9 Anne 331 Elihua 333 John 9 John Jr 331 Sally 321 331 333

KIMBALL, Almira 170 Asa 13 Benjamin Jr 33 Bethiah 279 Caroline 67 Daniel 139 170 Eliza 33 Elizabeth 193 Elmyra 170 Emma 13 Francis 67 Hannah 13 Huldah 13 Ira C 222 Joanna 222 John 186 279 Loammi 214 Lydia 13 Mary 13 186 214 Mary P 187 Molly 13 Moses F 13 Polly 170 Rebecca 214 Samuel 13 Sarah 139 Susannah 1

KING, Mary 99 of France 197 Thankful 110 229 320

KINNEY, Lydia 89

KNEELAND, 161 David 160 202 239 Dorcas 160 Molly 239 Sarah 160

KNIGHT, Abigail 37 45 294 310 Amy 155 305 Chloe W 65 Chloe Wiley 65 Edward Warren 301 Elizabeth 150 275 Hannah 298 305 325 James 65 Joanna 298 Martha 176 Mary 325 326 Mary S 277 Nathan 22 Nathaniel 60 150 Polly 133 219 Reliance 109 Ruhama 107 305 Samuel 325 Sarah 114 236 325

KNIGHT (continued)
  Sarah Eliza 301 Stephen B 109
  Susanna 150 William 133 298
  305 Zebulon 108
KNOWLES, Abigail 244 Amasa
  244 Betsey 101 Elizabeth 253
  Hannah 98 113 247 248 Mercy
  244 Paul 113 Samuel 84 113
  151 253 254 262 291 Sarah 262
KNOWLTON, Mary Elizabeth 28
  107 Miriam 55 134 173 224 225
LABALLISTER, Sarah 196
LABAN, Mary 161 Polly 161
LADD, Mary 24
LAFAYETTE, Gen 250
LAGBEN, Jenny 52
LAMB, Arthur 53 Charlotte 86
  Edmund 86 Elizabeth 86
  Eunice 86 Hannah 53 Martha
  86 219 Mary 86 Nancy 86
  Phebe 86 Richard 86 Samuel
  86 86 Sarah 304
LAMPREY, Mary 235
LAMPSON, Eunice 32
LAMSON, Marcy 138 Mercy 138
  William 40 138
LANCASTER, Thomas 206
LANCESTER, Dady 274 Elmira
  274
LANDERS, Lucy J 139
LANE, 109 Abigail 78 326 Elizabeth 78 Jabez 28 107 157 John
  3 78 Mary 107 177 Mary Elizabeth 28 107 Rebecca M 28
LANG, Charlotte W 252 Eliza H
  252 Theodate 138
LARRABEE, Benjamin 191
  Deborah 319 Emily J 300
  Esther 182 Hadassah 191
  Joshua 182 Julia Ann 302
  Lydia 191 Robert L 302 Sarah
  150 Sarah L 191 Susan 148 191
  302 William 191 Zebulon 191
LARY, Dennis 48 134 319 Patience 48 134 319 Stephen 319
LEADBETTER, Eunice Clark 40
  Nelson 40
LEAVITT, Abigail 317 Catherine
  305 Daniel 317 Elizabeth 305
  Jane Dutch 269 Jonathan 269
  Sally 190

LEBANON, Russell 240 Salome
  240
LEIGHTON, Isabel 233 John S
  233 Maria 274 Paul 89 Phebe
  89
LELAND, Frances Abigail 252
  Windsor 252
LESSNER, Charles 43 59 94 254
  255 292 323 330
LEWIS, Betsey 101 Henry S 15
  Martha 15 Mary 256 Mary W
  72 Olive T 213 Phebe 101 Ruth
  215 Samuel 101 Temperance
  231 William J 101
LIBBY, Aaron 248 Abigail 102
  103 173 208 238 Abner 47
  Alvah 102 Amos 20 Amy 306
  Ann 102 174 Anna 62 146 174
  220 Anna S 184 Benjamin 208
  Betsey 119 Catherine R 229
  Charity 328 Charles 241 Daniel
  62 174 Dorothy 152 Ebenezer H
  229 Edward 23 Elias 327
  Elisha 208 Eliza 232 327 Eliza
  A 234 Elizabeth 62 174 175
  176 204 243 248 Freeman M
  135 Gardner 175 Hannah 175
  243 248 Isaac 119 Jacob
  Bradbury 328 James 2 Jane 45
  165 220 Jenny 36 Jeremiah 220
  306 Jonathan 174 Joseph 174
  Josiah S 99 Julia 327 Levi 327
  Levi W 327 Lucretia D 310
  Lucy 208 306 Lucy F 327
  Luther 238 Lydia 20 63 99 265
  Mahala P 327 Mariam Knowlton 135 Marshall 234 Martha
  165 327 Mary 172 294 Mary
  Eliza 149 Mary Ingerson 20
  Mehitable 174 Mercy 20
  Mindwell 327 Molly 56 Moses
  262 Olive Gray 47 Olivia 262
  Phebe 208 Philemon 165
  Phineas 309 Polly 2 Rebecca
  119 Richard 3 Ruhamah 306
  Ruth A 228 Sally 315 Sarah 3
  100 294 Sarah C 48 Sarah M 40
  Sophronia 241 Stephen 48
  Susan 309 Theodore 100
  Theophilus 315 William 45
  174 William D 310

LIBBY (continued)
Zachariah 306 Zebulon 20
LINNELL, Abigail 328 Anna 132
328 332 333 Deborah 237
Desire 132 333 Elisha 25 109
132 290 332 Eliza 25 84 Elizabeth 109 Enoch 203 227 277
Hannah 109 132 132 Israel 333
John 109 157 Joshua 328
Luther 132 Martha 25 109-111
132 290 320 332 Mary 109 290
291 Samuel 109 132 157 328
332 333 Susannah 203 227 277
LINSCOTT, Mary 261 Noah 261
LINSEY, John 247 Phoebe 247
LINSKET, Esther 134
LITTLEFIELD, Betsy 287 Ellen
31 George 31 284 Melvina 284
LITTLEHALE, Lucy 245
LLEWELLYN, Cordelia 141
LOBDELL, Isaac 91
LOCKE, Eliza Ann 153 Frances
153 Frances A 153
LOMBARD, Andrew Jackson 302
Bathsheba 173 Charles Beane
302 Desire 131 Emeline 302
Ephraim 299 Eunice 302
Hannah 109 131 132 Jedediah
236 244 302 John West 302
Lydia 299 302 Mary Knight 302
Mary P 195 Polly 299 Sally
299 Salome 46 236 Sarah 258
302 Sargent 302 Solomon 258
299 304 Susan 236 Susanna 92
142 201 239 258 Susannah 128
129 258 Thomas 109 131 132
LONG, Charlotte W 252 Eliza H
252 Prudence 64
LONGFELLOW, Elizabeth 316
Stephen 171 198
LONGLEY, Eli 232 Mary 232
Rebecca 232
LOOMER, Gideon 310 Mary
Elizabeth 310 Mehitable 310
LORD, Betsey 309 329 Elizabeth
37 42 Hosea 2 James 285 Jane
2 285 Jenny 2 John 281 Mary
258 Miriam 281 Naomi 329
Nason 329 Polly E 88 Rhoda
135 139 Sarah 329 William 329
Zillah 158

LORING, Friend 167 Lucy Ann 35
Rhoda 167
LOUGEE, Betsey 245 John 245
Polly 246 Simeon 246
LOVEJOY, Elizabeth 252 Jeremiah 252 Mary 76
LOVELL, Deborah 231
LOW, Betsey 138 Caleb L 3
Daniel 319 James 84 319
Patience 48 162 319
LOWELL, Abigail 37 57 Alice
181 Ann 219 Apphia 10 11 216
217 Betsy 265 Daniel 71 80
111 126 Daniel Jr 110 185
David 37 Dorcas 70 95 Edward
219 Elizabeth 11 15 55 Elizabeth Ann 185 Experience 110
111 Gideon 55 Huldah 321 322
Isabel S 327 James 225 Joanna
30 Jonathan 13 57 70 204 248
Jonathan Jr 95 Jonathan K 173
Lendall B 104 Lucinda 4 104
Marcy 26 Martha 219 Mary 70
71 120 204 Mercy 71 126 185
225 Miram 282 Miriam 55 173
224 225 281 Molly 204 Moses
55 173 224 225 Nabby 37 Polly
71 Rachel 57 173 204 Rosanna
219 Salome 147 Samuel 2
Sarah 2 4 Simeon 219 Stephen
15 Sylvanous 10 Thomas 4
Wealthy 15 William 147
LUFLIN, Sarah Woods 26
LUNT, Capt 3 Eda 140 James 159
173 Tabitha 21
LURVEY, Betsey 42 Elvecy 42
Job 42
MABRY, Abraham 305 Angeline
305 Ann 305 Charlotte 305
Enoch 305 Jefferson 305 Sally
305
MACK, Mrs 109
MACKINTYRE, Sarah 216
MAGNE, Jane 199 334
MAINS, Elizabeth 150 Hannah 200
MAKEPEACE, Rebecca 277
MALAN, Mary 99
MANCHESTER, Lorana 45
MANN, Marcy 296
MANSFIELD, Nancy 138 Sarah
214 Simeon 138

MARCH, Abigail 151 James 147
151 Joanna 123 124 Mary 147
Susannah 130
MAREAN, Aaron 275 Amos 275
Anna 240 Eliza 93 Eliza G 275
Elizabeth 275 Elizabeth L 275
Enoch 243 John 15 19 20 34 93
240 243 308 John Jr 240 Lois
15 93 240 243 Martha Ann 275
Mrs John 34 Nancy 243 William Jr 275
MARINER, Louisa 279 Rachel 81
MARR, Eleazar 214 Elizabeth 79
Isaac Jr 79 James 265 Libby
265 Lydia 265 Salome 265
Sarah 214
MARRETT, Daniel 91 263 270
Frances 153 Samuel H 153
MARSTON, David 9 Mary 9 Nancy 9
MARTIN, Abigail 59 Abner 306
306 Betsey 325 Bryan 24 93
185 206 246 306 310 Ebenezer
306 Eleanor 185 188 Elinor 293
Elizabeth 24 185 206 306 310
Hannah 67 113 126 Isabella
232 233 James 306 Joanna C
93 John 162 Jonathan 113
Joseph 67 Leah 113 Letty 162
Margaret 162 Mary 28 162 184
187 206 284 Nabby 59 Rebecca
162 Robert 126 223 Sally 127
223 Sarah 306 William 59
William W 306 Zelpha 259
Zilpha 307 310 311
MARWICK, Jane 128
MASON, Eunice 9 Moses Jr 9
Thirza 9
MATHER, Cotton 51
MAYALL, John 226 242 Mary 242
Molly 226 Robert 23 Ruth 23
MAYBERRY, Abraham 100 305
Almira 124 Angeline 305 Ann
305 Bethia 299 Charlotte 305
Enoch 305 Eunice Melinda 328
Fanny 100 Jefferson 305
Josiah Webb 328 Mary 294 295
Richard 163 Rose 100 305
Sally 305 William 100 305
MAYO, Abigail 111 246 Arza 57
Asa 144 312 Asa Jr 293

MAYO (continued)
Ebenezer 81 143 330 Eliza
Pinkerton 293 Eunice 149
Hannah 209 Isaac 209 Marcella
57 Robert 209 Ruth 160 255
Sarah 20 67 209 Sarah E 301
Shubael 312 William D 149
MCARTHUR, Arthur 25 255
MCCASLIN, John 125 Sarah 125
MCCLUSKEY, Jennie 238
MCCORRISON, Aaron 302 Abigail
214 Benjamin 214 Clarissa 302
Deliverance 216 Hannah 239
259 James 214 216 Lemuel
141 216 231 239 259 Lydia 259
Mary 214 Mehitabel 216
Mehitable 141 Sally 141 Sarah
141 William 141
MCDANIEL, Abigail 128 Anna
128 John 128 208 Lucy 208
Lucy Libby 128 Polly 54
MCDONALD, Abner 243 Agnes
176 Dolly 243 Dorcas 243 259
Eleanor 70 314 Esther P 243
Eunice 243 Hannah R 306 John
243 259 312 313 Joseph 176
243 Joseph E 242 Julia Ann
242 Lydia 313 Mary 313 Olive
72 Peletiah 70 243 259 Robert
313 Sarah 176 243 Susannah
259 William 72
MCDUGAL, Ann L 291 James 291
MCGILL, Anne 13 Arthur 332
Emery 333 Hannah 14 John 13
14 56 190 301 332 333 Joseph
333 Mary 332 Rebecca 13 14
190 301 332 333 Sarah 301
Thankful 190 William 273 332
MCINTIRE, Dorothy 81
MCKENNEY, Abigail 74 224
Catherine F 279 Daniel 223
279 Daniel Sr 225 David 17
Eliza 223 279 Elizabeth 279
Hannah 225 James 181 225
279 284 James Jr 284 Jane
279 284 John 181 John 3rd 17
Joseph W 25 Lucinda B 17
Margaret 181 279 Martha 181
225 284 Mary Ann 25 Susan 17
Susan T 17
MCKUSICK, Francis 8

MCLAIN, Betsey 163 Elizabeth 163 Fergus 163 Martha 162
MCLAUGHIN, Martha 56
MCLAUGHLIN, Agnes 105 Charles 105 Lettice 232 Martha 74 103-105 175 Robert 105 Ruth 105 Thomas 232 William 105
MCLELLAN, 278 Alexander 304 Annis 194 Brice 146 Cary 244 Ebenezer 194 Hugh 94 James 1 Joseph 134 143 216 289 Martha 293 Mary 1 146 Samuel 35 Susanna 35 William 94 William Jr 244
MCLUCAS, Elizabeth 6 133 Jeremiah 133 Marcy 133 Mary 33 169 311
MCLUCUS, Abigail 70
MCMASTER, Harriet Elizabet H 194 Thomas Alexander 194
MCMILLAN, Andrew 250 Hannah 250 Sally 250 Sarah 250
MCNAIR, Hannah 273 Richard 273
MEAD, George E 232 Sarah Ann 232
MEADER, Hannah Smith 269 Isaac 269
MEANS, Dorcas 127
MEEDS, Artemas 82 Desire 82 Lucinda 82 149
MERCHANT, Sarah 274 Solomon 274
MERILL, Mial Jordan 35 Priscilla 191
MERRIFIELD, Esther 296
MERRILL, Abel 6 20 Abigail 27 Clarissa 191 Curtis B 233 Daniel 191 Edie 202 Elizabeth 6 Elizabeth McLucas 6 Eunice 26 Ezra 211 Gardner 191 George N 269 Hannah 6 21 Hannah L 233 Humphrey 6 Isaac 21 John 104 John E 147 Levi 178 Lydia 20 21 147 Lydia C 35 Mary 178 212 Rebecca Hall 269 Rhoda 211 Ruth 6 Sarah 104 Sarah S 26 William 212
MERROW, Charity 25 28 206 Margaret 28 160 324

MERROW (continued) Polly 64 160 324 327 William 28 160 324
MESERVE, 196 295 Abigail 128 208 321 Albion K P 271 Benjamin 73 Betsey 32 78 133 239 321 Betsy 324 325 Charles 53 326 Clement 103 267 317 319 320 Clement Jr 43 59 186 Clement Sr 58 Dorcas 124 138 Dr 72 85 164 171 285 289 301 329 Ebenezer 133 Elias 239 321 Elizabeth 317 Elmira 240 Hannah 13 58 59 James 240 Jane 234 John 23 53 60 103 124 234 256 324 330 John Jr 98 Mary 23 53 186 320 324 326 Sarah 53 58 124 186 194 234 256 325 326 Shuah 268 William 23
MESERVEY, Clement 151 Sarah 318
MESSENGER, Anne 55
MESSER, Mary 10
METCALF, Lois 149 William 149
MILK, James 94 180 Lucy 180
MILLARD, Ann 170
MILLER, Daniel 285 Eunice 285 John 231 314 Mary 212 Molly 231 314 Patience 285
MILLETT, Bethiah 43 117 Elizabeth 43 John 43 117
MILLIKEN, Eunice 192 233 Hannah 192 233 Hannah R 192 Henry 192 Isaiah 192 233 Josiah 181 223 260 Phineas 248 Polly 223 Samuel 87 Sarah 261
MILLS, Abiah 14 Cyrus 14 Deborah 319 Elizabeth 246 Hannah 5-7 170 211 212 James 48 319 Mary 191 Patience 134 162 319
MINER, Mary E 302
MITCHELL, Anna 67 68 245 Arabella Rackliff 318 Clark 209 Dominicus 6-8 67 245 289 Dorcas 34 Hannah 293 Irena H 300 Irene 201 James 318 Jane 184 Jonathan 304

MITCHELL (continued)
Lydia 184 191 Margaret 201
Mary 78 Reuben 78 Robert 184
Samuel 201 Sarah 67 209 318
Sarah J 128 Susanna 78 Zachariah 78
MIXER, Charles 252 Charles Thomas 252 Sophia Augusta 252
MOODLY, Eliza 112
MOODY, Abigal 103 Amos S 83
Betsey 175 Daniel 64 112
Daniel Jr 112 Dorcas 82
Dudley 214 Ebenezer 103 Edie 24 328 Edith 131 328 Elizabeth 5 22 101 241 259 328 Esther 81
Gilman 5 Hannah 64 111
Huldah 112 Isaac 101 James 7 43 111 203 241 259 259 Joseph 112 Joshua 328 Mary 5 112 214 216 Mary Ellen 83 Mr 286
Rebecca 22 Rosanna 111
Rosanna F 259 Samuel 241
Wealthy S 101 William 101
William Pepperell 5
MOON, Joan 274 Sands 274
MOOR, Hannah 215 Hugh 33 215 Jonathan Jr 215 Margaret 33 38 47 215 309 Mary 33 Sarah 33
MOORE, 202 Elizabeth 4 266
Hannah 71 Hugh 4 Jane 2
Jonathan 71 Jonathan S 71 220
Louisa Rich 220 Margaret 4 5
Sally 220 Sally Gray 71 Samuel 5 Sarah 122
MOORS, Rhoda 131
MORAN, Jennie Martha 27
MOREY, Polly 76
MORGRAGE, Daniel 299
MORILL, Thomas 296
MORRELL, Elijah 304 Huldah 304 John 104 Sarah 104 Sophia Ann 300
MORRILL, Abigail 296 Anne 9
David 9 Harriet 122 Jordan 287
Josiah G 122 Moses 157 Sarah 287 Susan 9 Thaddeus 9 Thomas 296
MORRISON, Jesse S 301 Lydia Maria 301 Serena 325

MORSE, Abiah 132 Isaac E 31
Jonathan Jr 87 Joseph 132
Lavinia D 254 Letice Meline 31 Rachel 10
MORTON, Abigail 282 Ann 210
Anna 154 243 Benjamin 93
Betty 93 Bryant 100 311 Caleb 92 Charles A 326 David 43 100 238 Delilah 90 242 Ebenezer 62 92 121 128 242 243 Esther 179 Fanny 132 Hannah 154
Jacob 128 James 154 243
Joseph 132 Lucy 62 Lydia 236 238 Martha 92 121 Mary 43 100 128 Molly 243 Patty 121 Polly 43 Rachel 57 135 Ruhamah 92
Sarah 92 93 121 238 Susan 154 242 243 Susan Nason 326
Susanna 92 Susannah 62 128
Thankful 112 135 154 253 310 311 Thomas 62 93 100 135 235
MOSES, Alonzo 26 39 Cyrus 39
Elizabeth 62 195 Eunice 39
Frances 3 Hannah E 26 Hannah Elizabeth 39 Josiah 62 195
Lydia 195 Marshall H 195
Orianna 26 Ruth 25 Ruth Sprague 25 Sarah 62 174
Thomas Gannett 25
MOSHER, Susanna 74
MOULTON, Abigail 100 104 222 236 237 Agnes 201 243 Anna 100 101 237 Daniel 237 238
Ebenezer 201 Elizabeth 237
Hannah 34 Horace 259 Jane 179 217 226 242 Joanna 100 205 222 236 Jonathan 13 201 243 Josiah 104 Lydia 205
Martha 104 210 Mary 104 259
Mary Ann 238 Peter 10 100 205 222 236 Sarah 222 Simon 104 237 Susan 16 Thomas 213
William 34 Worthington 236
MOUNTFORT, Dolly 15 289
Dorothy 289 Samuel 15 168 289
MOWATT, 143 180
MOWATTIN, 114
MUCKINTIRE, Sarah 77
MURCH, Daniel 244 Jerusha 190
Joanna 123 124 Johanna 123

MURCH (continued)
Marjorie 314 Molly 36 Nancy 277 Rachel 190 Simeon 190 Tabitha 59 91 Walter 190
MURRAY, Benjamin 158 Mary 158
MUSSEY, Abigail 119 120 200 226 Benjamin 64 119 200 226 313 Daniel 42 Dolly 226 Dorothy 226 Mary 42 Sarah 105 200 Thankful 42 Theodore 226 William 42
MUSSY, William 151
MUTCHERSON, Mary 327
MUZZY, Lydia 151 Mary 151
MYRICK, Abigail 173 Dorcas 40 183 Eunice 161 Hannah 164 183 Phebe 183 189 190 William 183
NASH, Abigail 125 Joseph 125 Lydia 55 Mary 190 Mary G 190 Susanna 125
NASON, Aaron S 207 Abigail 37 45 179 233 294 Abraham 298 299 Abraham Jr 299 Catherine 142 Daniel 45 David 50 326 Edward 156 207 Edward L 207 Eleanor 179 Elizabeth 37 294 Elizabeth M 240 Elvira 266 Elvira O 207 Enoch 21 Ephraim 179 Esther 296 Eunice 192 233 326 George H 207 Harding L 281 Harriet Frances 83 James 195 Jane 45 Jemima 83 273 291 John 325 John Henry 83 John Jr 301 Jonathan 17 Joseph 294 Keziah 40 Lavinia 301 Lucinda F 281 Lucy 18 310 Lydia 21 39 40 90 299 314 Lydia G 211 Marcy 18 Margaret 45 90 Maria 300 Martha 50 222 Mary 156 329 Mary S 207 Mehitabel 207 Molly 293 Moses 18 Nicholas 293 Phebe 296 Polly 49 50 299 Robert 142 Sally 195 Samuel 329 Samuel L 240 Sarah 293 326 Simon 296 Solomon 90 Susan 29 190 325 Susanna 195 Susannah 156 207 Uriah 37 45 294 William 37

NELSON, Lydia 151 Mary Louisa 151 Samuel 151
NESMITH, James 169 Margaret 4 33 169 215 Mary 169
NEVENS, Abigail 124 William 124
NEWBEGIN, Amy Ruhama 306 John 60 306 Ruhama 60
NEWCOMB, Abigail Myrick LIBBY 193 Betsey 210 Elizabeth 193 Enos 135 173 193 Gardner 193 Joshua 130 Rachel 135 Samuel 173 Susannah 130 332 Thankful 135 173
NEWTON, Clarissa 14
NICHOLS, Charles A 233 Ellen 233 Esther 233
NICHOLSON, Zube 168
NICKERSON, Dorcas 247 Elizabeth 15 Martha 198 Yates 247 Zube 168
NOBLE, Christopher 96 Lydia 71 96 Martha 96 225 284
NORCROSS, Eunice 163 Nathaniel 163
NORMAN, Rachel 19 127
NORTON, Amy 306 Anna 207 305 David 238 Hannah 306 James 207 265 306 Joanna 262 Joseph 207 305 306 Lucy 306 Lydia 207 Mary 211 265 306 Olive 265 Rachel 195 Ruhamah 306 Salome 238 Simon 306 William 211 306
NOWLEN, Betsy 199
NOYES, Joshua 140 Josiah 13 140 289 313 Lois 54 Louise 54
NUDD, Elizabeth 155 Joseph 155 184 187 206 Martin N 155 Mary 28 155 184 187 206 Sarah 155 184 187
NUTTING, Samuel 116
OBER, Martha 88 Samuel 88
ORCUTT, Mary 215
ORDWAY, Jonathan Burbank 208 Mehitabel 208
OSBORNE, Susannah 55
OSGOOD, Betsey 141 Elizabeth 259 Hannah 250 James 141 251 Jane 251 Mary 251

OTIS, Anna S 184 David 184 Louisa A 184
OWEN, Elijah 24 Esther 233 Ruth 24
PAGE, Eliza 113 150 Elizabeth 6 Mary 9
PAIN, Sarah 202
PAINE, Bryan 293 Charles 138 Daniel 155 David 86 Dorcas 40 Eleanor 154 Elinor 293 Eliza 135 194 Elizabeth 5 86 145 Eunice 22 180 Hannah 40 Hannah Sewall 138 Henry 194 Huldah 227 284 Jane 165 John Knowles 249 Joseph 112 139 154 162 227 Joseph Jr 293 Joshua 139 Josiah 5 145 Lydia 22 Martha 180 Mary Mclellan 293 Mercy 139 Mrs Myrick 164 Myrick 40 165 Paine 102 Phebe 112 154 162 166 227 Richard 5 22 86 162 180 194 Ruth 155 Samuel Osborne 165 Sarah 67 155 162 194 Thankful 5 67 145 Thomas 22 Uriah 155 William 67
PALMER, Betsey 142 Charles 73 Tirzah 73
PARKER, Aaron 219 Abraham 164 Cynthia C 234 Dolly 266 Dorothy 266 Eliphalet 186 245 266 Elisha 94 Eliza Elder 186 Hannah 302 Jane 186 245 266 Lydia 174 Mary 164 Moses 44 Rebecca 41 Sarah 88 126 Thankful 32 171 311 Thomas 219
PARSONS, Samuel 180
PARTRIDGE, Jotham 241 Lydia 241
PATRICK, Elizabeth 86
PATTEE, Anne 210 Caroline Dyer 283 E J 277 Ebenezer 207 Emma S G 277 Mr 283
PATTEN, Actor 114
PATTERSON, Col 157 Mary 1 32 Sarah 128
PAUL, Betsey 172
PEABODY, Aaron 116 Jonathan 241 Priscilla 14 Rhoda 241 Susannah 116

PEACH, Alice 232 244
PEARL, Ann 280
PEARSON, Ann 263 Anna 263 Elizabeth 85 Lois 84 Mary 85 122 200 Moses 13 52 68 84 85 94 115 116 121 122 137 143 159 161 164 167 175 196 198 202 222 223 226 235 263 269-272 278 330 Sarah 84 122 263
PEASE, Calvin 265 Mary 254 Prince 163 Sally 2 Sarah 2 163 Sarah F 265 Zedediah 163
PENFIELD, Benjamin 93 154 Joanna 93 154 Joanna C 93 Mary 93 Molly 93 154 Nathan 93 Nathan C 93 Nathan Cook 154 Sally 154
PENNELL, Sarah 122 Thomas 122
PERKINS, Betsy 287 James B 136 Joanna F 136 Polly 299 Priscilla 72 221
PERLEY, Enoch 11 Mary M 56 Sarah A 56
PERRY, Harriet 56 William 56
PETERSEN, Anna T 277 Elvara E 277 William 277
PETTINGILL, Mary 34
PHEBE, Taylor 280
PHILBRICK, Abiah 234 Abigail 17 196 Anna 14 92 166 174 226 234 235 Elizabeth 120 Gideon 303 John 105 Jonathan 19 105 120 122 178 196 234 Judith 122 Martha 176 Mary 177 222 237 260 Michael 179 182 237 Michael Jr 116 Miriam 105 Olive 179 Phebe 218 Rhoda 237 Sarah 101 105 120 122 178 Thomas 234
PHILBROOK, Abigail 16
PHILIPS, Betsey 144 Joshua 144 Marguerite 65
PHILLIPS, Eliza J 35
PHINNEY, Abner 309 Annis M 309 Coleman 38 47 169 309 Decker 92 Ebenezer 258 Edmund 161 221 324 Eli 296 Elizabeth 161 Hannah 92 Hannah Moor 47 Harriet S 309 Jane 169 Janet 169

PHINNEY (continued)
   John 161 168 John Jr 103 259
   Joseph 239 Lucy 22 Marcy 296
   Margaret 38 47 169 307 309
   Martha 103 161 Mary 87 121
   239 320 Miriam 165 Nathaniel
   Jr 22 Patience 36 92 Peggy
   169 Rebecca 103 168 259
   Samuel 87 Sarah 38 161 211
   Sarah Purrinton 258 Stephen
   123 Susan 211 239 252 William S 309
PICKERING, Samuel 76
PIERCE, Elizabeth 140 203 226
   229 277 John 107 129 140 202
   203 226 229 270 277 John Jr
   203 227 277 John Sr 203 Mary
   70 140 Mercy 270 277 Molly
   140 Polly 230 Richard 75 334
   Sally Brown 107 Sarah 75 324
   Susan 93 Susanna 229 Susannah 129 227
PIERSON, Joanna 271
PIKE, Benjamin 200 Elizabeth 7
   8 120 122 197 Elmira 302 John
   7 Mary 7 200 Sarah 120 122
   200 Timothy 122 197
PINGREE, Parsons 66 Sarah 66
PINKERTON, Anna 156 185 228
   293
PINKHAM, Desire 329 James E
   39 Martha M 39 Martha T 39
   Mr 329
PIPER, Lydia 124
PLACE, Eunice 69
PLAISTED, Abigail 104 175 177
   237 Andrew 56 Ann 45 Benjamin Small 319 Betsey 56
   Dorcas M 45 Elizabeth 175 176
   Frances S 319 Francis 45
   Hannah 1 John 19 176 Lydia
   176 319 Mary 176 Molly 56
   Polly 176 Samuel 175 176
   Sarah S 185 Simon 185 319
PLUMMER, Abigail 222 Ellen A
   195 Isaac 101 Joseph 34 Lydia
   307 Mary 34 Phebe 164 Polly
   117 Rebecca 66 Rhoda 34
   Sarah 101
POLAND, Benjamin 71 186
   Hannah 71 Lucy 71

POLAND (continued)
   Olive Shedd 186 Sally 71 Sarah
   186
POLLARD, Elizabeth 142
POOR, Frederick W 298 Lucy A
   298 Sarah 236
PORTERFIELD, Eleanor 248
   John 248 Nellie 248
POTE, Greenfield 264
POTTER, Christopher 147 Mary
   123 Phoebe 147 Susan 147
POWERS, Abigail 187 Amos 13
   Calvin 187 Chloe 187 Luther
   Farnum 187 Nabby 187 Rebecca 297
PREBLE, Mehitabel 210
PRENTISS, Dolly 241 Lydia 241
   Samuel 241
PRESCOTT, Daniel 33 Gen 79
   Hannah 27 109 308 Mary 33
PRIDE, Mary 36 Nancy B 102
   Rebecca 19 Sarah 208 210
PRINCE, Thomas 255
PROCTOR, Bethia 299 Betsey
   299 Ebenezer 299 John 185
   Josiah 185 Phebe 185 Rachel
   51 Rebecca 185 Rhoda 63
   Susanna 195 William Jr 63
PUGSLEY, Abigail 279
PULFREY, Hannah 24
PULSIFER, Allen 131 Anna 131
PURINTON, Apphia 241 Daniel
   241 David 241 Esther G 232
   Lois 241 Meshach 232 Sarah
   232
PURRINTON, Sarah 258
PUTNEY, Ruth 79
QUINBY, John 80
RACKLEFF, Benjamin 61 182
   George 28 Hannah 28 John 61
   Joseph C 24 Joseph Chandler
   61 118 Mary 28 Mehitabel 61
   Mehitable 182 183 Sarah 182
RACKLIFF, George 155 Joseph C
   155 158 Joseph Chandler 119
   318 Lydia 306 318 Mary 119
   155 318 Mehitabel 155 Phebe
   128 Sarah 119 318
RAMSEY, Catherine 139
RAN, Susan A 279
RAND, Anna 167 Benjamin 167

RAND (continued)
  Betsy 195 Diadema 309 Dorcas 276 Edmund 238 Hannah 177 Jeremiah 113 195 Lydia 113 133 195 238 302 Mary 113 247 Samuel M 177
RANDALL, Jacob 81 James 77 Mary 81
RANKINS, Nancy 279 Susan A 279
RAWLINS, Polly 53
RAY, Andrew 285 Fabius M 152 197 Mary Muzzy 152 Rachel 285
RAYNES, Eliza 131
REED, Isaac 88 Lydia 151 Sarah 88
RHODES, Esther 45 John 45
RICE, Sarah 120 252
RICH, Allen E 283 Amos 170 Ann Thompson 236 Boaz 217 Deliverance 216 Esther 215 Eunice 170 Hannah E 233 Huldah 7 Lemuel 217 Lemuel Jr 215 236 Lucy 87 233 Lydia 118 Martha Ann 283 Mary 215 217 Molly 217 236 Phebe 112 154 162 183 227 Rebecca 110 Sally 170 220 Samuel 215 Samuel C 233 Thankful 41 William 87 233
RICHARDS, Hannah 59 William 59
RICHARDSON, Aaron 12-14 63 191 192 Abigail 10 11 Anna 10 11 Artemas Jr 268 Artemus 268 Betsey Fitch 268 Charlotte 267 David 5-7 87 170 207 211 226 245 312 David Jr 143 Dorcas 64 268 321 Ebenezer C 210 Eliza 37 Elizabeth 268 Esther 211 George Eaton 268 Hannah 5-7 71 170 211 268 Israel 268 James 88 Jemima 78 Joanna Hutchinson 268 Joseph 267 Louisa 210 Lucy 5 Lydia 10 11 41 63 211 227 Lydia Sanborn 4 Mary 6 7 211 245 267 268 Mary Marrett 268 Mehitable 63 141 Molly 211 226 Moses 10 11 41 63 78 211 227 Nancy Richardson 268

RICHARDSON (continued)
  Rachel 88 Remember 226 Rhoda 88 Samuel 191 192 Sarah 41 312 Sarah B 268 Tamson 88 Thaddeus 99 226 Thomas 6 Thomas Johnson 268 Thompson Hall 268 William 4
RICKER, Ebenezer 41 Susan G 41
RIDLON, 285 Betsey 229 Daniel 46 Eleanor 46 Ellen 46 Magnus 229 Mary 66
RIDON, Ellen 46
RIGGS, Eliza 99 John 32 Mary 292 Susanna 32
RILEY, Abigail 173 282 Annette 282 Betsy 282 Eliza 282 Elizabeth 282 Ephraim Higgins 173 282 James Morton 282 James Osborne 282 James Osgood 282 Mary 282 Nathan Appleton 282 Reuben 282 Sarah 282 Stillman 282
RINGE, Sarah 174
ROBBINS, Alonzo 124 Eliza 124
ROBERTS, Benjamin 307 Eleanor 99 Eunice Haskell 82 Jane 90 307 Jonathan 304 Joseph 304 Jotham B 144 Jotham Welch 82 Lydia 195 Mary 307 Mehitable H 82 Moses 99 Robert 82 Sarah 199 Susanna 150 Susannah 99
ROBERTSON, Mary A 259 Samuel 333
ROBINSON, Caleb 2 Deborah 62 George 62 Hannah 58 117 192 225 Increase 170 Jane 117 315 John 62 99 192 211 225 Joslyn C 170 Mary 2 99 170 Mehitable L 62 Nancy 2 Phebe 225 Roscoe C 170 Roscoe G 170 Samuel 99 Sarah 99 133 302 Tamson 165
ROBISON, Thomas 250
ROGERS, 116 Catherine 240 Daniel 84 Edward 142 Isaiah 92 Lydia 92 Martha 142 Patience 33 84 Reliance 189 Sarah 84 166 247
ROLLINS, Annis C 318

ROLLINS (continued)
  Elizabeth 120 Jacob S 71 John
  120 Lucy 71 Lucy A 241
ROSE, Joseph 221 Sarah 221
ROSS, Betsey 240
ROUNDS, Abigail 177 229 Albion
  177 Catherine 74 104 Joseph
  74 Mary 211 Rhoda 25 211 241
  Susanna]74
ROUNDY, Charity 44 Hannah 44
ROWE, Abigail 281 Amos 314
  Anna 314 Apphia 112 260
  Benjamin 181 314 Benjamin Jr
  314 Betsey 137 Betsy 265 314
  Caleb 72 137 314 Daniel 224
  Deborah 281 Edmund 224 Eliza
  70 224 Elizabeth 182 Elmira
  265 Ephraim 177 219 260
  Ephraim 3rd 177 Ephraim Jr
  331 Esther 45 Eunice 265
  Francis 224 314 Hannah 314
  Hepsibah 314 James 314
  James Matthew 314 Jane 314
  Joanna 72 100 181 John 45 224
  Lazarus 181 182 224 314
  Learned 314 Levina 331
  Martha 96 180 181 265 Mary
  177 260 314 Molly 181 182 224
  314 Noah 181 Oliver P 281
  Patty 224 Peter 71 100 230
  Polly 224 Priscilla 72 Rachel
  224 Richard 314 Sarah 177
  Susan 314 Thomas 137 265 314
  Webber 224 Winthrop 224
ROYAL, Deborah 281 Isaac 281
RUGGLES, Daniel 72 Emeline 72
RUMERY, Eliza 329 Joseph 329
  Nancy 329
RUMNEY, Sally 14
RUSSELL, Abiah 331 Mary 152
  Peter 331 Sarah 313 Stephen
  313
SAHW, Rachel 226
SAIT, Elvara E 277
SALTMARSH, Elizabeth 120 249
  Thomas 249
SANBORN, Abigail 57 74 188 281
  283 Abner 282 283 Albert
  Bailey 283 Albion K P 285
  Apphia 221 222 Augusta 283
  Caroline Dyer 283

SANBORN (continued)
  Catherine 282 Clarinda 282
  Daniel 137 179 217 242 281
  282 Daniel Wilson 283 David
  94 219 284 Deborah 284 320
  Dolly 179 Elizabeth 203 Ellen
  283 Ephraim 282 Harriet 74
  Huldah 188 284 Isabella 282
  Jane 179 217 242 Jane Wilson
  293 Jesse Butterfield 282 John
  3 74 129 188 203 204 216 219
  334 John Jr 57 John Sr 203
  Jonathan 37 44 94 136 137 285
  Jonathan Jr 285 Joseph 320
  Judith 200 June 283 Lorenzo
  284 Lucy 3 71 74 104 129 203
  204 216 267 277 Lydia 216 284
  Marantha 282 Martha 74 109
  282 Martha Ann 283 Mary 136
  217 242 281 282 Mary S 284
  Mercy 57 136 Miriam 137 281
  282 Moses 145 204 Nathan 283
  Olive Jane 285 Peter 216 221
  255 Phebe 219 Phebe J 217
  Pierce 188 284 Polly 37 182
  Priscilla 94 Rachel 3 4 37 47
  135-137 216 281 285 Randall
  284 Reuben 282 Royal 282
  Sarah 94 219 282 284 Stephen
  242 Susan 58 Susanna 129
  Susannah 129 203 204 277
  Warren 293
SANDS, 48 Abigail 6 Ephraim 3rd
  6
SANGER, Mary 43 100 173 Sarah
  238
SAVAGE, Faith 55 Mary 144 273
  332 333
SAWYER, Abigail 191 Abraham
  73 Alma J 26 Annis C 30
  Barnabas 132 214 Chestina
  Emma 26 Cynthia 193 David
  19 193 Dorcas 167 Ebenezer
  191 Elizabeth 101 132 139 166
  167 Enoch 306 Eunice 101 112
  Gilbert A 30 Hannah 193 244
  306 Huldah 214 Jerusha 96 97
  Joel 101 139 166 167 John 97
  129 207 244 314 John Isaiah
  193 Joshua 307 Lettice 97 244
  314 Lorenzo Mellon 26

SAWYER (continued)
  Louisa D 227 Margaret 150
  Martha 15 74 114 289 Mary 112
  163 166 191 Mary A 26 Mary
  Ann 26 Mary P 307 Mary Small
  266 Molly 163 314 Nathaniel
  193 Olive 268 Peter 266 Polly
  163 Rebecca 103 168 201 259
  Samuel 191 Sarah 19 266 Sarah
  S 307 Selina 97 Thankful 32
  Thomas 244 Wealthy 15 139
SCAMMAN, Abigail 317
SCAMMON, Eliza 185 Elizabeth 5
  185 Frederick 185 Hannah 1
  James 1 Mary 80
SCOTT, Clara 26
SCRIBNER, Joseph 219 Mary 6
  Polly 219 Samuel G 6
SEARS, Nancy 126
SEAVEY, Eunice 88 Georgiana
  251
SEDGLEY, Sarah Phips 35
  Timothy 35
SEGAR, Jane 160 Josiah 160
SELLEA, Caleb 18 Elizabeth D
  18
SEWALL, Abigail M 138 Sarah
  288
SEWELL, Jane 277
SHAW, 320 Almira 90 Ann 92 177
  211 Anna 14 66 92 144 149 166
  172 174 176 177 226 Anne 146
  Apphia 221 222 Betsey 321
  Caleb 172 Caroline 259 Delilah
  90 172 Deliverance 172 Dolly
  142 Ebenezer 12 14 35 41 85
  92 149 166 171 172 174 191
  200 226 259 320 321 Ebenezer
  Jr 40 92 321 Ebenezer Sr 221
  Elizabeth 166 259 Elmira 90
  Enoch 90 172 199 Esther 93
  233 Eunice 15 92 93 103 142
  148 172 Hadassah 66 Hannah
  111 167 259 Harriet M 277
  Joanna 100 174 175 205 222
  Joseph 15 93 142 148 172 259
  Josiah 103 171 Jotham 218
  Leander 321 Leonard 60
  Lucinda 320 Margaret 14 331
  Mary 148 320 Mary A 177 Mary
  Ann 147 Mary E 321

SHAW (continued)
  Mary H 321 Mary Louisa 280
  Molly 172 226 Nehemiah 144
  146 Polly 103 Rachel 145 226
  Rebecca 321 Salome 40 92
  Samuel 320 Sarah 40 149 199
  218 259 Sargent 92 151 177 199
  211 Thomas 52 64 66 80 85 94
  95 196 277 289 303 Truman
  147 William 280 292
SHEPARD, Samuel 73 Sarah 73
SHIRLEY, Gov 116 143 William
  143
SHORT, Harriet 185
SHUTE, Anna 109
SIMONTON, Anna 200
SIMPSON, Alice 232 Hannah 232
  Jonathan 232 Mary 177
SINCLAIR, Eliz 260 Mary P 307
SKILLINGS, Amos T 36 Anna 36
  Benjamin 35 36 Besey 36
  Caleb C 36 Daniel 36 Deliver-
  ance 37 172 Edward 21 Eliza-
  beth 36 265 Emily Jane 156
  Esther 36 Eunice T 36 Isaac
  36 66 265 James P 156 Joanna
  99 John H 36 Martha 36 Mary
  35 36 66 242 265 Mary M 36
  Mehitable 265 Olive 21 Polly
  36 Susannah 66 Thomas 36 265
SMALL, Abigail 20 Amelia D 283
  Anna 20 67 164 189 208 297
  Benjamin 164 Benjamin Jr 47
  Betsey 295 Daniel 189 208 245
  Davis Sumner 307 Deborah 281
  283 Dorothy 152 Eleanor 146
  Elizabeth 20 26 Elizabeth D 18
  Francis 152 Hannah 232 Henry
  20 Isaac 213 Issacher 68 Jacob
  20 193 James 18 Jane 147 186
  189 193 266 Jane Whitney 307
  Jemima 89 Joanna 208 John 43
  50 281 John Henry 283 Joshua
  43 164 193 213 286 Louisa 152
  Lydia 74 Margaret 307 Martha
  165 Martha Jones 68 Mary 20
  47 147 208 213 Mimar 89
  Nancy 213 Nathaniel 307
  Phebe 164 Polly 20 Reuben
  268 Sarah 20 266 286 Sarah B
  268

SMALL (continued)
Susanna 193 Susannah 156 164
207 213 286 Susannah K 29
William 147 Zachariah 89
SMALLEY, Hannah 258 Lydia 118
SMITH, Abigail 54 Angelina 297
Ann 263 Anna 14 Anne 13
Beriah 124 Betsey 167 Betsy
14 Betty 211 Catherine 290
Charity Ann 232 Clarissa 228
Constable 51 Daniel 52 54 161
167 324 Edward 54 Elbridge
G 25 Elijah 253 Eliza 24
Elizabeth 37 38 124 211 294
Elizabeth L 25 Emeline H 25
Enoch Coffin 290 Ephraim 294
Eunice 70 291 297 George 24
290 Hannah 25 248 Hugh 297
Hugh McLellan 291 Ira 70
Ithiel 13 14 Jackson 9 James 4
Jane 24 Jatson 9 John 24 211
301 John Jr 302 Joseph 237
Josiah 14 Lewis 133 302 Lois
46 54 Lucy 14 54 161 Lydia 9
301 302 Margaret 55 101 Mark
290 Mark Marquis 25 Martha
24 25 310 Martha Ann 290
Martha H 28 Martha M 291
Mary 24 28 136 178 211 282
Mary A 136 Mary Ann 25 305
Mary Knight 133 302 Mehitable
290 Mollie 24 Molly 113 Mrs T
85 Nancy 148 Nathaniel 24
Parson 48 292 Peter 89 248
Polly 248 Rebecca Davenport
290 Rhoda 25 211 241 301
Rhoda E 25 Royal 25 Ruth 24
Ruth Sprague 25 Samuel 24 51
Sarah 123 124 160 237 326
Sarah B 294 Sarah V 161 Susan
257 Susannah 54 241 Theophi-
lus 136 Thomas 25 51 55 211
241 248 248 Ting 248 257 Tyng
Jr 248 William 24 28 290
SNOW, Aaron 199 Abigail 112
Bathsheba 116 199 Benjamin
116 199 Jabez 118 Jane 199
334 Jennie 199 Lucy 101 Lydia
334 Mary 116 Phebe 266
Thomas 112 199 334 Thomas
Jr 244

SOUTHARD, Asenath 8 Milton 8
Steneth 8
SPARROW, Betty 118 Hannah 98
113 Jonathan 80 98 Jonathan Jr
98 113 Lucy 118 Rebecca 118
320 Sarah 320 Stephen 98 113
118 320
SPAULDING, Emma Harding 258
SPEAR, Hannah 254 Jonathan 254
Rebecca 4 William 4
SPENCER, Elinor 181 Jane 314
Joanna 182 Phebe 296 297
Sally 181 Samuel 182 William
181
SPINNEY, Susanna 8
SPRAGUE, Ruth 23 158 325
SPRING, Catherine 72 120 Eliza
120 Elizabeth 120 Jedediah
120 John 120 Lewis 120 Olive
120 Seth 7
STACKPOLE, Lorenzo 283 Sarah
J 283
STANLEY, Sophronia 61
STAPLES, 76 James 128 Jane
128 John Mcarthur 265 Lorenzo
Dow 29 Lydia 67 Mary M 29
Salome 265 Samuel 76 Susan-
nah K 29 William S 29
STARBIRD, Lydia 311 Margaret
187 Moses 311
STEARNS, Lydia 124
STEELE, James 251 Jane 251
STETSON, Almira 34 James P 34
STEVENS, Abigail 128 210 Agnes
89 Bathsheba 215 Benjamin
134 143 161 208 210 Calvin
176 Catherine 35 Chloe 57 135
227 228 Elizabeth 312 Farnum
194 Hannah 89 194 Joanna 208
John 89 Joseph 128 208 Lydia
176 Martha M 274 Mary 128
143 Olive 285 Patience 285
Sally 274 Sarah 161 208 210
Thomas 125 291
STEWART, Hannah 70 Jane 98
John 98
STICKNEY, Sarah 102
STOCKMAN, Edward A 266
Elizabeth A 266
STONE, Abigail 167 Archeleus 93
Betsey A 126

STONE (continued)
　Elizabeth 101 139 166 167
　Fanny 200 Hannah 104 200
　James M 200 Joshua 123
　Margery W 136 Mary 118 Sarah
　159 162 Sarah B 258 Solomon
　200 William 126 136
STORER, Eliza 282 John 48 Olive
　120 250 Rachel 136 Seth 250
　Seth Jr 250 William 136
STORY, Lucy 317
STOWELL, Susan 34
STRAW, Betsey Hilton 220
STROTHERS, Mary S 152
STROUT, Albion Peter 72 Betsey
　83 274 275 276 Bridget 330
　Christopher 19 94 Daniel 19
　Elisha 83 274 275 Elizabeth
　149 George 330 James 291
　John 93 94 160 225 330 Margaret 19 Mary 72 291 Mary Jane
　275 Mercy 112 Miriam 83 109
　274 Nathaniel 112 Oliver 291
　Patience 73 Rebecca 19 225
　Ruth 160 Sally 72 Sarah 13 53
　95 124 130 143 160 234 273
　291 324 329 330 Sarah J 238
STUART, Dorcas 142 243 Hannah
　111 167 239 Joanna 311 Joseph
　311 Mary 45 92 150 176 239
　243 Rosanna 111 Rosannah F
　167 Sarah P 201 Susan M 269
　Susanna 92 142 201 239
　Wentworth 10 92 111 134 142
　167 201 221 239 324 Wentworth Jr 92 23J9
STUBBS, Experience 247 Richard
　247
STUBMAN, Sarah 65
STURGIS, Betsey Ayer 170 David
　188 Frances A 301 Hannah 22
　Harriet Elizabeth 188 Joanna
　142 Joseph 22 Nathaniel
　Gorham 170 Temperance 45
　William R 142
SWAN, Aaron Barton 333 Mehitable 333
SWETT, Achsah 238 Alfred 257
　Apphia 112 222 Benjamin 71
　112 222 Deborah 237 Deliverance 247 Eunice 257

SWETT (continued)
　Gideon 112 Hannah 112 154
　Israel 298 310 Jonathan 222
　267 Joseph 237 Josiah 154 238
　Mercy 257 Susanna 237 William 257
SYMONDS, Anna 114 116
TAPPAN, Mary M 289
TARBOX, Augusta 283 Elizabeth
　316 Shuah 317 Susanna 317
　Susannah 45
TAYLOR, Anne 266 Dimon 280
　Mary 218 Richard 218 Sarah
　315
TEAL, Abigail 117 Nabby 117
TEMPLE, Mary 14
THACHER, Peter 24
THOMAS, Dorcas 184 John 215
　Marshall 184 Mary 215
THOMBS, Edmund 301 Susan R
　301 Thomas 301
THOMES, Alfred 28 Alice 26
　Almira 274 Amos 5 36 91 194
　Amos C 29 Amos Jr 5 Anna 92
　Annis C 29 Apphia 26 28
　Betsey 101 236 238 Charity M
　28 Charles 92 Daniel 4 241
　Dorothy 194 Edmund 26 Eli 28
　Elizabeth 36 132 Esther 201
　202 238 Grace 28 Jane 5 John
　36 Mary 91 Mary Elizabeth 28
　Mehitable 5 36 194 Patience
　259 Samuel 101 Stephen 194
　Susanna 63 91 92 Susannah 241
　Thomas 26 28 91
THOMPSON, Abby 209 Amos 319
　Ann 92 177 211 236 Charlotte
　75 214 Deborah 321 Delilah
　212 Deliverance 212 Dorcas
　221 Ebenezer 254 Elizabeth 14
　331 Esther 156 Frances S 319
　Francis 75 Hannah 319 Isaac
　Snow 75 John 202 213 Joseph
　212 Lydia 74 Mary 83 109 244
　247 Permelia 189 Permelia E
　189 Sarah 254 Thomas 96 260
THORN, 159 Albert Greenleaf 257
　Angelia 57 Bartholomew 85
　223 225 Benjamin 225 Betsey
　223 Charles H 57 David D 209
　Dorcas 209 Eliza G 149

THORN (continued)
Elizabeth 149 223 Hannah 203
Israel 330 Israel Jr 225 330
Jane 85 Joseph 85 203 Katherine 212 Lydia 223 225 Marrett 149 Martha 80 85 Mary 85 Mary Ann 150 Mary Jane C 257 Mercy 85 203 Sarah 330 Thomas 85

THORNE, Almira 266 Bartholomew 151 Betsey 257 Daniel 83 109 257 Desire 209 Elisha Strout 266 Hannah 144 257 Israel Jr 144 257 329 332 Katherine 85 87 Lucy 88 Marrett 257 Martha 85 87 Miriam 83 109 257 Sarah 85 329 Stephen 209 William 85 87 William Jr 85 88 William Sr 85

THORPE, Angelia 57 Charles H 57

THRASHER, Benjamin 43 323 Eliza 120

THURSTON, Daniel 269 Hannah 269 Jane 269 Jonathan 269 Sally 269

TIBBETTS, Abigail 98 175 Abraham 70 Hannah 70 Martha 131 317 328 Rachel 21

TIDD, Abigail 151

TILTON, Margaret 10

TINNEY, Bethiah 124 George 124

TINNY, George 84

TITCOMB, Andrew 59 Anne 123 198 Benjamin 41 85 89 91 96 125 151 161 172 180 198 200 230 270 278 313 Enoch 123 Eunice 123 Joseph 123 Mary 59 Moses 197 Priscilla 20 Sarah 84 122 197 Sybil 237 William 197

TITOCMB, Joseph 123

TOBEY, Betsey 42 Eliza 254

TOMPSON, Edward 154 John 68 91 119 159 160 164 245 304 Sarah 245

TOPPING, Dolly 15 245 Luther 15 74 323 Marcy 74 Mercy 74

TOPSHAM, 286 Martha 286 Sarah 286

TOWEL, Sarah 243

TOWLE, Amos 16 Betsey 135 Hannah 1 214 Josiah 1 Lucinda 17 Lucinda B 16 Susan 16

TOWNSEND, 27 Elinor 28 Grace 23 32 Hannah 15 Mary 27 Nathaniel 32 Nathaniel Jr 23 William T 27

TRACY, Jonathan 300 Sophia A 300

TRICKEY, Eudoxia 241 John 304 Margaret 241 Mark 304 Mary 304 Noah 241 Otis 304 Peter 304 Thomas 241 Zebulon 304

TRUDY, Sarah 188

TRUE, Desire 131 Israel 103 John 73 Mary 99 Moses 131 Sally 103

TRULL, Evaline 194

TUCKER, Francina 331 George 331 Hannah 331 Isaac Insley 331 James D 109 129 James Davenport 132 Maroah 331 Mary 109 132

TUKEY, Sarah 178

TUPPER, Col 163

TUTTLE, Elizabeth 1

TWINING, Hannah 113 Ruth 111 113

TWITCHELL, Eleazer 222 Lucia Marilla 194 Martha 222 Patty 222

TWOMBLEY, Daniel 82 Eunice Haskell 82

TYLER, Abraham 207 Andrew 252 Anna 189 213 Elizabeth 252 Joseph S 258 Louise Maria 258 Mary 2 Mary Ann 252 Mary L 16 Mary Libby 16 Samuel 252

TYNG, William 197

UNDERWOOD, Eunice 39 Lydia 303

USEHR, Luther 182

USHER, Abijah 29 190 Ellis B 190 Emily C 29 Esther 182 Lucinda 141 Sarah 190 Susan 29 190

VARNEY, Hannah 141 Hiram 93 232 Sarah J 232 Susan 93 232

VARNUM, Mary 303

VAUGHAN, William 23 205

VITTUM, Grace B 41
WADSWORTH, Bethia 252
   Charles 7 Mary Marrett 268
   Peleg C 252 268
WALDEN, Rose 100 305
WALDO, Cornelius 55 Faith 55
WALDRON, Aravesta D 228
   Henry P 228
WALKER, Abigail 193 Elizabeth
   175 192 Hannah 2 John 125 192
   254 Lucy 192 Luther 2 Rebec-
   ca 70 Sarah 282
WARD, Cyrus K 309 Freeman 284
   Hannah 226 Hannah E 140
   Joanna S 309 Jonathan 12 95
   Mary 95 Remember 212 216
   217 226 Sarah 95 William H
   284
WARDWELL, Mary 298
WAREN, Mary Jane 301
WARREN, Anna 156 185 228
   Chloe Powers 186 David 3
   Eliza P 156 Hannah 30 98 99
   113 247 248 Harriet 33 James
   17 Jane W 228 John 98 113
   247 Louisa 18 Louisa B 150
   Mary M 185 Polly 179 Richard
   D 186 Rufus 99 Ruth A 228
   Samuel 17 156 185 228 Sarah 3
   81 William 18 Winslow 99 105
WASHINGTON, 251
WATERHOUSE, Abigail 103 257
   Anna 213 G A 131 Hannah 6
   204 Joseph 19 103 127 Joseph
   Jr 19 Lydia 103 Mary 2 131
   Moses 33 Olive 18 Rachel 19
   127 Sarah 127 Susannah 6 19
   127 Theophilus 6 213 William
   204
WATERMAN, 266 Betsey 107
   Eliza 107 William 107
WATSON, John 177 Lucy 184
   Mary 158 Miriam 177 Phebe 84
   Stephen G 184 Susannah 66
   Tabitha 177
WATTS, Betsey 107 Hannah 170
   Sarah J 190
WEBB, Abraham 294 Eli 294
   John 104 Lucy Ann 104 Lydia
   294 Margaret 55 Samuel 55
   Sarah 294

WEBBER, Esther 182 Luther 182
   Molly 181 182 224 314
WEBSTER, Adeline Loantha 31
   Ellen J 234 Jane 209 John E
   31 William 234
WEEKS, Abigail 119 178 200 226
   Dorcas 299 Eleanor 299 Mary
   307 Samuel 140 299 Sarah 178
   William 178 299
WEEMAN, Almira F 27 Elizabeth
   248 Esther 325 John 325 John
   Jr 325 Samuel H 27 Tryphena
   325
WELCH, Abigail Marrett 302
   Gabriel 129 George 205 Hannah
   129 Mary 119 205 206 318
   Sally 133 Thomas 302
WELLS, Nathaniel 7
WENDALL, Marietta 188
WENTWORTH, Abigail 21
   Andrew 284 Benjamin 296
   Esther 96 John 96 Judith 296
   Martha Ann 281 Melvina 284
   Sally 296 Timothy 21
WESCOTT, Abigail 103 Alice 304
   Caroline 257 Eliakim 102 103
   257 261 Emma Harding 257
   John 102 Lydia 65 Margaret
   162 Rebecca 102 William 103
   162
WEST, Abigail 333 Desper 199
   297 Eleanor 297 Eunice 133
   199 Jane 16 John 309 333
   Joseph 16 44 133 145 309 333
   Mary 199 297 Nabby 333 Nancy
   16 44 133 145 309 333 Sarah
   145 Sarah H 309 Thomas 145
WESTCOTT, Sarah 100 William
   100
WESTON, Charlotte P 288 Eliza-
   beth Bancroft 152 Isabella G
   201 James 152 201 Patience
   67 Sarah 152 201
WETHERELL, Margaret 314
   Marjorie 314 Samuel 314
WEYMOUTH, Charles J 284
   Susan 285
WHARF, Rachel 81 Thomas 81
WHEELER, Benjamin 3 Pamela
   21 Rebecca 3 134 169 190 216
   228 Sabra L 48 Sally 281 282

WHITAKER, Anna 261
WHITCOMB, Mary 232
WHITE, Caroline Amanda 256 257 Elizabeth 5 Emma 285 Hannah 5 317 James 274 James H 257 Joseph 274 Lucy A 274 Mary 191 274 Nancy 233 Nicholas 5 Peter 218 287 307 Sarah Maria 256 Susan 274 William 274 William Francis 256
WHITING, Abiel Frye 121 Joanna 322 Martha 121
WHITMORE, Amy 107 155 Anna 207 Betsey 39 Capt 10 66 264 Elizabeth 155 Elizabeth Boulter 107 Eunice 178 Fanny 90 Irene 90 Jane 90 John 90 Joseph 155 Joseph Jr 155 Ruhama 107 Sally M 39 Samuel 164 171 245 267 Sarah 155 Sarah M 39 Stuart 171 William 107 155 158 William Jr 39 107
WHITNEY, Abel 112 154 168 253 Abigail 66 67 167 239 24 Amos 189 Andrew R 209 Apphia 164 Asa 67 Damaris 162 Damaris S 167 Daniel 167 Elisha 133 302 Elizabeth S 188 Ellen W 277 Emeline 133 302 Eunice 166 George A 277 Hannah 24 25 28 39 218 299 Hannah B 79 Happy 212 Harriet 297 Isaac 179 J Lucetta 212 Jane 100 307 Joanna 53 241 259 Jonathan 265 Joshua 41 Lettice 97 231 244 314 Levi 212 Lewis F 188 Lucy 86 Lydia 253 Mary 25 70 167 179 209 265 307 Mary Cooking 189 Mary Jane 210 Mehitable 265 Moses 202 248 Nathaniel 154 159 168 259 307 Patience 67 186 Reuben 307 Richard M 297 Sarah 31 112 121 173 179 180 189 256 261 300 Sarah H 299 333 Simeon 241 Susan 111 Tabitha 177 Thankful 112 154 253 Thankful H 39 William 19 25 39 299 Zelpha 259 Zilpha 154 307

WHITTEN, Albert 130 Anna 141 Daniel 328 Elizabeth 130 Lydia 328 Nancy 67
WHITTLEMORE, Sarah 30
WHTMORE, Joseph Jr 155
WIGENT, Nancy 147
WIGGIN, Barbara 232 Charles 232 Clarissa 302 David 302 David Jr 302 Erastus 302 Joseph 302 Julia Ann 302 Lovina 302 Lucinda 302 Mark 302 Martha Ann 302 Mary 302 Mary Ellen 302 Nancy 302 Polly 232 Samuel 302 Stephen 232 Susan 302
WIGGINS, David 302
WIGGLESWORTH, Rev Dr 286
WIGHT, Charles 254 Elizabeth 254 John M 254 Lavinia D 254
WILDER, Levi 320 Sarah 201
WILEY, Bethia 213 Chloe 64 327 Hannah 292 James 155 213 Sarah 213
WILKINS, Augustus 136 Heber 282 Isabella 282 Sarah S 136
WILLARD, Jonathan 3rd 218 Josiah 177 Mary 177 Prudence 218
WILLARY, Polly 177
WILSON, Betsey 136 Charles 136 David 328 Eliza 328 Elizabeth 136 328 Eunice 14 Joanna 253 Samuel 14
WINCH, Abigail 21
WINDLING, Ignes 328 Susan 328
WINGATE, Hannah 250 Love 164
WINN, Caroline 285 John Alfred 285 Mary Ann 285
WINSLOW, 116 Huldah 261 John B 232 Maria H 232 Mary Ann 111 Nathan 89 Oliver 261 Ruth 162 218 Sarah 261
WINSOR, Eliza Anthony 152
WISE, Elizabeth 85 298
WISWELL, Abigail 117 316 Enoch 117 316 Jane 117 316 Nabby 117
WITHAM, Jedediah 261 Jerusha 256 Joanna 53 Mehitable 261 Mrs 133 Peter 53 Sally 133 Sybil 53

WITHINGTON, Sally 215
WOOD, Abigail 117 Anna 66 241
  Benoni 142 Charles 42 Dorothy
  73 114 203 227 Edward 117
  Elinor 142 Eliza Ann 42 Elsie
  45 Hannah 239 241 Jane 117
  John 73 151 231 John Jr 163
  231 Mary 42 163 Molly 163 231
  308 Moses 117 Nabby 117
  Nathan 292 Polly 163 Sarah 42
  149 231 239 259 292 321
  Susannah 258 William 239 241
  258
WOODING, Elizabeth 123
WOODMAN, Elizabeth 4 6 Eunice
  170 Hannah 5 Isaiah 5 John 5 6
  Joseph 58 262 Joshua 281 281
  Lydia 289 323 324 Mary 100
  279 281 Mary Boynton 5
  Mehitable 282 Nathan 20 47
  323 Olive 4 20 47 Ruth 6 Sally
  281 282 Shubael 323 Stephen
  171 Tamson 28 True 4 169
WOODS, Annie Elizabeth 252
  Benoni 70 Eunice 70 Joseph
  207 324 Joseph Jr 207 Lydia
  207 Sarah 324 Susan 207
  Susanna 258
WOODSUM, Abigail 131 Benjamin F 131
WOODWARD, Davis 86
WOOSTER, Francis 48 James 48
  49 134 162 Mary 48 162 186
  Patience 48 134 162
WORCESTER, Louisa 191 Susanna 191 Thomas 191
WORKS, Abel 127 Hannah 127
WORTON, Emery 31 Mary A 31
WRIGHT, Anna 296 Margaret 181
  Virgil 296
WRILEY, Abigail 282 282 Annette 282 Eliza 282 Elizabeth
  282 Ephraim Higgins 282
  James Osborne 282 James
  Osgood 282 Mary 282

WRILEY (continued)
  Nathan Appleton 282 Reuben
  282 Sarah 282 Stillman 282
YATES, Deborah 229 Elizabeth
  261 Hannah 109 John 110 229
  239 247 John Jr 229 Josiah 110
  Mary 239 240 Mercy 239
  Rebecca 239 Reliance 110 138
  259 Sarah 247 Thankful 110
  229
YEATON, Mary 23 160 324
YETTY, Mary 160
YORK, Abigail 12 13 131 145 299
  Abraham 32 158 203 289 296
  Abraham Jr 203 Abram 52 65
  160 316 317 Anna 130 132
  Betsey 32 78 160 161 296
  Betsy 14 David 40 Desire 130
  Ebenezer 82 83 144 273 299
  Edie 24 Edith 131 Eliza 40 203
  Elizabeth 14 160 307 Emma 71
  Hannah 17 81 82 141 Isaac 16
  32 64 78 97 158 160 161 244
  289 318 Isaac L 14 Jacob 24
  97 131 289 Joanna 99 Job 130
  144 145 273 John 12 13 95 130
  143 272 307 Joshua 131 Lydia
  52 158 160 160 203 289 313
  316 317 Martha 78 Mary 52 83
  95 158 161 289 Mehitable 82
  83 144 299 Nabby 299 Nancy
  64 65 Naoma 95 140 292
  Noami 53 Polly 64 83 158
  Rebecca 13 14 143-145 190
  Sally 40 144 145 Samuel 53 99
  161 Sarah 13 95 99 130 143 144
  161 203 272 273 317 318 Sarah
  J 83 Stephen 203 Susan 24 207
  317 318 Tryphena 296
YOUNG, Albert 26 Alice 26
  Betsey 240 David 26 Elizabeth
  26 111 187 311 George Grey
  193 Hannah 218 James 26
  Joseph 193 Joshua 324 Lydia
  310 311 Martha 26 Martha Ann
  193 Mary 193 Nancy 324
  Thomas 26 Zebulon 203

www.ingramcontent.com/pod-product-compliance
Lightning Source LLC
Chambersburg PA
CBHW071951220426
43662CB00009B/1088